MILLER'S
UNDERSTANDING
ANTIQUES

New Hall & Its Imitators
Creamware
English Delftware
ROYAL CROWN DERBY
CARRIAGE CLOCKS
ANTIQUE MEDICAL INSTRUMENTS
PAINTERS
FLIGHT AND BARR
WORCESTER PORCELAIN
THE HAN CIVILIZATION OF CHINA

MILLER'S UNDERSTANDING ANTIQUES

General Editors
Judith and Martin Miller

MITCHELL BEAZLEY

MILLER'S UNDERSTANDING ANTIQUES
General Editors
Judith and Martin Miller

Edited and designed by Mitchell Beazley an imprint of
Reed Consumer Books Limited
Michelin House
81 Fulham Road
London SW3 6RB
and Auckland, Singapore and Toronto

Editor	**Frances Gertler**
Art Editor	**Nigel O'Gorman**
Assistant Editors	**Sarah Polden, Paul Schlesinger**
Designer	**Christopher Howson**
Design Assistants	**Paul Tilby, Jonathan Stone**
Editorial Assistant	**Jaspal Bhangra**
Artwork	**Karen Cochrane, John Hutchinson**
Map Editor	**David Haslam**
Photo Re-touching	**Roy Flooks**
Production	**Ted Timberlake, Katy Sawyer**

First published in 1989 by Mitchell Beazley
This paperback edition published in 1992
Reprinted 1994

A CIP catalogue record for this book is available from
the British Library
ISBN 1-85732-001-8

Maps by Lovell Johns Ltd, Oxford, England
Typeset by Bookworm Typesetting, Manchester
Colour reproduction by Scan Trans Pte Ltd, Singapore
Produced by Mandarin Offset in Hong Kong

The italic initials that follow the captions indicate picture source.
See key on page 272.

Front cover picture credits: left, top *CNY*; left, centre *S*; left, bottom S; centre *S*; right, top *CHK*; right, centre *CNY*; right, bottom *S*

Produced by Mandarin Offset
Printed and bound in Hong Kong

CONTENTS

INTRODUCTION

Understanding Antiques grew out of a conviction that there is a tremendous groundswell of popular interest in antiques, perhaps reinforced by recent publicity of ordinary-looking objects that are in fact worth a fortune. However, for newcomers to the world of collecting it is not always easy to convert an interest in antiques to real, useful knowledge. *Understanding Antiques* will set you on the path to becoming more than just another enthusiastic amateur.

How do you find out about antiques? You may have seen dealers performing some sort of ritual with a chest of drawers or a porcelain vase, but what are they looking for? How can *you* tell if something is genuine 17th-century or a 19th-century copy?

Understanding Antiques is where you begin. A detailed analysis of twelve major collecting areas in terms of style, age and value, the book provides a unique general background to antiques and may help you to discover an area of special interest. As you become more informed, you will develop the kind of visual literacy that allows you to make confident and shrewd judgments about a piece. Above all, you will find that an apparently daunting and complex subject may turn out to be the most tremendous amount of fun!

Each chapter, divided according to the categories of object or material, examines in depth exemplary items, which are used to introduce some of the major collecting points. Also covered in detail are such important questions as fakes and likely areas of damage. Artwork is used to show the range of styles or their chronological development. Many affordable items are illustrated, as well as some pieces of exceptional quality and rarity. Helpful information is also provided about the care and maintenance of antiques. A time chart or map at the beginning of each chapter places the range of collectable items in their historical context. Each major collecting area (furniture, pottery and porcelain, glass, clocks, rugs and silver) also has a helpful "Basics" section that provides a background of general or technical information. All the chapters conclude with a reference section, containing a glossary of terms, a list of books for further reading and, where appropriate, information on major makers.

Even the best introduction to antiques cannot replace leg work as an essential part of the learning process. Get a feeling for your chosen subject by visiting museums and stately homes, finding specialist dealers and attending auctions. In museums you may not touch the exhibits but you can usually find a specialist who will answer a serious question. We still find searching out collections one of the great joys of travelling: most cities have at least one excellent museum or house furnished in the correct period style – ideal places to begin to observe the genuine article.

Make the most of the educational opportunities afforded by auctions. Buy the catalogue and attend the viewing. Go to the sale itself, make a note of the bids as the hammer goes down, as a start to getting a feeling for prices. You must learn how to really look at antiques: don't be afraid to hold and touch, to look underneath and inside. In addition to examining details, it is also very important to stand back from a piece and view it as an entirety: something that may seem perfect when viewed close up may seem slightly odd when viewed as a whole, indicating that it could be a fake, or have been tampered with in some way. Most important of all – you must learn to ask questions.

Do cultivate that bastion of the antique trade, – the friendly dealer. Not all dealers are friendly, but if you find a certain arrogance or rudeness, don't give up. Simply find another one. Most of the knowledge we have has been gleaned from a kindly dealer on a quiet day. The wonderful thing about antiques is that most people who deal in them tend to be collectors or enthusiasts themselves – and they respond to sensitive questioning.

Above all, don't be inhibited by the aura of superior learning that antique experts often have. They all had to learn once, as you will, with the help of *Understanding Antiques*.

Judith H. Miller

Periods and Styles

DATES	BRITISH MONARCH	BRITISH PERIOD	FRENCH PERIOD
1558–1603	ELIZABETH I	ELIZABETHAN	RENAISSANCE
1603–1625	JAMES I	JACOBEAN	
1625–1649	CHARLES I	CAROLEAN	LOUIS XIII *(1610-43)*
1649–1660	COMMONWEALTH	CROMWELLIAN	LOUIS XIV *(1643-1715)*
1660–1685	CHARLES II	RESTORATION	
1685–1688	JAMES II	RESTORATION	
1688–1694	WILLIAM & MARY	WILLIAM & MARY	
1694–1702	WILLIAM III	WILLIAM III	
1702–1714	ANNE	QUEEN ANNE	
1714–1727	GEORGE I	EARLY GEORGIAN	RÉGENCE *(1715-23)*
1727–1760	GEORGE II	EARLY GEORGIAN	LOUIS XV *(1723-74)*
1760–1811	GEORGE III	LATE GEORGIAN	LOUIS XVI *(1774-93)* DIRECTOIRE *(1793-99)* EMPIRE *(1799-1815)*
1811–1820	GEORGE III	REGENCY	RESTAURATION *(1815-30)*
1820–1830	GEORGE IV	REGENCY	
1830–1837	WILLIAM IV	WILLIAM IV	LOUIS PHILIPPE *(1830-48)*
1837–1901	VICTORIA	VICTORIAN	2nd EMPIRE *(1848-70)* 3rd REPUBLIC *(1871-1940)*
1901–1910	EDWARD VII	EDWARDIAN	

<table>
<tr><th>GERMAN PERIOD</th><th>UNITED STATES PERIOD</th><th>STYLE</th><th>DATES</th></tr>
<tr><td rowspan="3">RENAISSANCE
(to c. 1650)</td><td rowspan="2"></td><td rowspan="2">GOTHIC</td><td>1558–1603</td></tr>
<tr><td>1603–1625</td></tr>
<tr><td rowspan="4">EARLY COLONIAL</td><td rowspan="5">BAROQUE
(c. 1620-1700)</td><td>1625–1649</td></tr>
<tr><td rowspan="5">RENAISSANCE/BAROQUE
(c. 1650-1700)</td><td>1649–1660</td></tr>
<tr><td>1660–1685</td></tr>
<tr><td>1685–1688</td></tr>
<tr><td>WILLIAM & MARY</td><td>1688–1694</td></tr>
<tr><td>DUTCH COLONIAL</td><td rowspan="4">ROCOCO
(c. 1695-1760)</td><td>1694–1702</td></tr>
<tr><td rowspan="2">BAROQUE
(c. 1700-30)</td><td>QUEEN ANNE</td><td>1702–1714</td></tr>
<tr><td>CHIPPENDALE
(FROM 1750)</td><td>1714–1727</td></tr>
<tr><td>ROCOCO
(c. 1730-60)</td><td></td><td>1727–1760</td></tr>
<tr><td>NEO-CLASSICISM
(c. 1760-1800)

EMPIRE
(c. 1800-15)</td><td>EARLY FEDERAL
(1790-1810)
AMERICAN DIRECTOIRE
(1798-1804)
AMERICAN EMPIRE
(1804-15)</td><td>NEO-CLASSICAL
(c. 1755-1805)

EMPIRE
(c. 1799-1815)</td><td>1760–1811</td></tr>
<tr><td rowspan="2">BIEDERMEIER
(c. 1815-48)</td><td rowspan="3">LATER FEDERAL
(1810-30)</td><td rowspan="2">REGENCY
(c. 1812-30)</td><td>1811–1820</td></tr>
<tr><td>1820–1830</td></tr>
<tr><td rowspan="3">REVIVALE
(c. 1830-80)

JUGENDSTIL
(c. 1880-1920)</td><td>ECLECTIC
(c. 1830-80)</td><td>1830–1837</td></tr>
<tr><td>VICTORIAN</td><td>ARTS & CRAFTS
(c. 1880-1900)</td><td>1837–1901</td></tr>
<tr><td></td><td>ART NOUVEAU
(c. 1900-20)</td><td>1901–1910</td></tr>
</table>

FURNITURE

Knowledgeable collecting demands an awareness of the three main aspects of the subject – styles, materials and construction methods – and some understanding of historical context.

Collectors tend to specialize, as furniture of different materials, from different periods, can clash when juxtaposed – most collectors of oak will not look at a satinwood piece, however fine. The quality of wood can be as important as style and decoration. The type of house the collector lives in may also be a factor.

The best way to learn about furniture is to handle it, by turning pieces over, opening drawers, examining methods of construction and observing signs of wear and tear, colour and patina. Dating may be approximately determined from details, which changed with fashion, and from signs of technological development, such as the use of machine-cut, rather than hand-cut screws.

Reproductions and forgeries abound and details can, of course, be changed or faked. Copiers interpreted past styles freely, often incorporating incongruous features that will strike a loud wrong note if you are sufficiently familiar with the genuine article. These can often be detected by simply standing back from the piece and gaining an overall impression of style and proportions. The introduction of machine-cut veneering started a decline in quality in much 19th-century furniture. However, the best Victorian and Edwardian furniture is increasingly collectable.

As objects of utility, pieces of furniture were not always discarded when they became unfashionable. Instead, many pieces were "updated" – for example, by a change of handles, or by substituting bracket feet for bun feet. Changes that have been sensitively made, especially those that are non-structural or reversible, need not be detrimental to value. Some restoration is also acceptable, provided that it has been carried out skilfully and not "botched".

Furniture needs taking care of, and protecting from the potentially damaging effects of the weather: damp floors can eat into wood and direct sunlight can cause pigments and inlays to fade. Never stand antique furniture directly in front of a radiator – dramatic changes in temperature can cause shrinkage and warping. Regular wax polishing is essential, not only to maintain the natural sheen of the wood, but also to seal it for added protection. A good dealer or auctioneer will be happy to give advice about buying furniture wisely and about its maintenance.

The chart shows in general terms the main styles of furniture design by period, and the three woods that dominated furniture making in the last three centuries. The dates for the "introduction" of oak, walnut and mahogany are necessarily only approximate.

Oak

Walnut

Mahogany

	ENGLAND	FRANCE

1600-1650	JACOBEAN STUART	**Louis XIII** *(1610-43)*
1650-1700	CAROLEAN **Charles II** *(1660-85)* **William and Mary** *(1689-1702)* *Daniel Marot*	**Louis XIV** *(1643-1715)* *Jean Bérain* *Adam Weisweiler* *André-Charles Boulle*
1700-1730	**Queen Anne** *(1702-14)* **George I** *(1714-27)*	REGENCE *(1710-30)* *Charles Cressent*
1730-1770	BAROQUE **George II** *(1727-60)* *William Kent* ROCOCO	ROCOCO **Louis XV** *(1715-74)* *Bernard van Risenburgh* *Jean-François Oeben* TRANSITIONAL *(1755-17*
1770-1800	ROCOCO **George III** *(1760-1820)* *Thomas Chippendale* NEO-CLASSICISM *Robert Adam* *Thomas Sheraton* *George Hepplewhite*	NEO-CLASSICISM **Louis XVI** *(1774-93)* *J.H. Riesener* *Georges Jacob* *David Roentgen* DIRECTOIRE *(1790s)*
1800-1830	REGENCY *Henry Holland* *Thomas Hope*	EMPIRE *(1804-14)* *Jacob-Desmalter*
1830-1880	**William IV** *(1830-37)* **Victoria** *(1837-1901)* ECLECTICISM	ECLECTICISM REVIVALS
1880-1900	ARTS AND CRAFTS *William Morris* ART NOUVEAU	ART NOUVEAU
1900-1920	EDWARDIAN	MODERN MOVEMENT

LOW COUNTRIES	ITALY	GERMANY & AUSTRIA	UNITED STATES	

RENAISSANCE	BAROQUE	RENAISSANCE		*1600-1650*
BAROQUE *Daniel Marot*	BAROQUE *Andrea Brustolon*	RENAISSANCE/BAROQUE	EARLY COLONIAL "WILLIAM AND MARY" *(1689-1720)*	*1650-1700*
LATE BAROQUE	LATE BAROQUE	BAROQUE	"QUEEN ANNE" *(1720-70)*	*1700-1730*
ROCOCO	ROCOCO *Guiseppe Maggiolini* *Pietro Piffetti*	ROCOCO *Abraham Roentgen* *J.A. Nahl* *J.F. & H.W. Spindler* *François Cuvilliés*	QUEEN ANNE *Townsend Goddard* CHIPPENDALE *(from 1750s)*	*1730-1770*
NEO-CLASSICISM	NEO-CLASSICISM	NEO-CLASSICISM *David Roentgen*	CHIPPENDALE *(to 1790)* *Thomas Affleck* *William Savery* NEO-CLASSICISM EARLY FEDERAL *(from 1785)*	*1770-1800*
EMPIRE	EMPIRE	EMPIRE BIEDERMEIER *Josef Danhauser*	EARLY FEDERAL *(to 1810)* *John Seymour* LATER FEDERAL *(1810-20)* *Duncan Phyfe* EMPIRE	*1800-1830*
LATE EMPIRE/BIEDERMEIER ECLECTICISM	ECLECTICISM	REVIVALS *Michael Thonet*	EMPIRE ECLECTICISM *Shaker furniture*	*1830-1880*
ART NOUVEAU *Victor Horta* *Henri Van de Velde*	ECLECTICISM	JUGENDSTIL	ECLECTICISM ARTS AND CRAFTS	*1880-1900*
MODERN MOVEMENT DE STIJL/BAUHAUS	ART NOUVEAU FUTURISM	MODERN MOVEMENT BAUHAUS	ART NOUVEAU MODERN MOVEMENT *Frank Lloyd Wright*	*1900-1920*

Basics I

With any piece of furniture there are certain basic factors that have to be considered, such as the wood used and the construction, the proportions and style, the legs and feet, and, where appropriate, the handles. Of course, the quality and style of any carving or decoration can also be crucial. The following six pages show how to assess these factors, and cover the special considerations that apply to drawered pieces, items made in two parts and legged furniture.

Examining a chest of drawers is a useful way to start learning about furniture, as it includes most of the elements essential to an understanding of many different pieces. The first step is to obtain a general idea of the period by looking at the wood and the style of construction.

The late 17thC English chest illustrated (*right*) is made of walnut.

A late 17thC English solid walnut chest of drawers on bun feet and with original handles. MB

WOODS

There is no easy way to learn to distinguish between the many types of wood – there is no substitute for first-hand experience. However, some historical background is also essential: you need to know not only the principal woods but also the main periods when they were in use. The main woods you are likely to encounter are listed below (and, of course, shown in many pieces over the following pages).

Amboyna
A pale wood similar to burr walnut, used from the 18thC onward.

Beech
A brownish-white wood used from the 17thC for the frames of upholstered furniture as it does not split when tacked. It was also a base for much painted and gilded furniture.

Chestnut
This ranges in tone from light to dark brown. Used extensively for French provincial furniture in the 18thC.

Elm
A light brown hardwood used in the production of Windsor chairs and other English provincial furniture.

Mahogany
There are several types of mahogany of which San Domingan, Cuban, Honduras and Spanish are the most important. Mahogany was imported into England from the Americas from c.1730 when it became very popular with cabinet makers, and has been used ever since. Quality varies considerably: at best this wood has a beautiful rich golden colour; but it can look rather bland if of poor quality. Victorians tended to polish mahogany to a red colour. The natural finish is preferred today.

Maple
Pale wood used extensively in the solid and as a veneer in much American furniture. It was fashionable in Europe during the early 19thC.

Oak
Hard and coarse-grained, oak was the predominant wood in Britain from the Middle Ages until the late 17thC.

Olive
A hard green-yellow wood used principally in England in the late 17thC in veneer form in parquetry and oyster work (see page 21), and for applied mouldings.

Pine
Soft, pale wood used as a secondary timber for drawer linings, backboards and so on, and in the production of cheap furniture during the 19thC, when it was often painted.

Rosewood
Highly figured wood with almost black streaks, used predominantly during the Regency period in England.

Satinwood
The West Indian variety is a beautiful yellow colour and was much favoured by cabinet makers in England during the late 18thC. Poor-quality satinwood can have a greenish tinge.

Walnut
A highly figured wood used in the solid on fashionable furniture from 1660 until c.1690. From c.1690 until c.1735 walnut veneered furniture was predominant in England. From c.1730 American or Virginia walnut was imported and, along with mahogany, became very fashionable.

Yew
A red-brown hardwood that is found in either veneer or solid form on much of the very best English provincial furniture of the 17th and 18thC.

PATINA

Patina is the natural build-up of wax polish and dirt that gives antique furniture a rich mellow look. This takes many years to develop and is not easily faked. Don't expect an antique piece of furniture to be a uniform colour: the sides, mouldings and top may vary where dirt has built up on the mouldings. The tops are often considerably lighter as a result of natural fading.

PROPORTIONS

The proportions of any piece are important, both in determining its aesthetic value and in assessing authenticity. Quite often, when everything else appears right, a fake may be detected simply by its uncharacteristic proportions – for example, bookcases are often reduced in depth to the point where they are no longer useful.

CONSTRUCTION

The chest, *above*, has been made with the joined style of construction, using mortice-and-tenon joints, held by pegs or dowels rather than glue or screws. This method was common on most furniture until the late 17thC. Furniture of the 17thC is mostly quite coarsely constructed, as here, using hand-made pegs. From the Queen Anne period (1702-14) cabinet makers used more sophisticated forms of construction, with greater use of dovetailing and glued joints.

Typically for the 17thC, the boards have been laid so that the grain runs from front to back. Grain running from side to side usually indicates a later period – from c.1780.

TOPS

Tops of early pieces are made with two or more planks of wood. These often show gaps that are the result of *shrinkage*, a process that may be exacerbated by central heating. Large gaps or splits are sometimes infilled.

To prevent further shrinkage and warping, pieces of wood can be glued to the underside – a crude and amateurish preventative measure. While this is not the way that a skilled restorer would deal with the problem, it would not devalue the piece as, say, a replaced part would.

* On the tops of later pieces made from one piece of timber, the veneers (the thin pieces of decorative wood applied to the solid surface) can split if the boards onto which they are veneered move because of shrinkage or warping.

Pegs
The planks of the top of early chests are held in place and fixed to the carcass with *pegs*. Hand-made pegs, used throughout Europe from the Middle Ages until the late 17thC (and in the 18thC for provincial furniture), are irregular in shape. Original pegs are usually more patinated than the rest of the piece as, being tapered, they stand slightly proud of it. Later replacements, using machine-made dowelling, are perfectly circular and either flush with the surface or slightly recessed. A combination of original hand-made and newer, machine-made pegs is not uncommon in early chests.

Detail of drawer from the walnut chest above left, *showing the chamfered runner and irregular hand-made pegs.* MB

DRAWERS

Dealers usually look at the inside and outside of any drawers to check the points detailed below. They also want to see that each drawer matches the other; some may have replacement parts. The more replacements, the lower the value of the piece.

Drawer linings
Drawer linings are usually oak or pine. The linings used for the sides of 17thC drawers are chunky, as much as ¾inch (2cm) thick. Throughout the 18th and 19thC drawer linings became finer: the standard width for 18thC and later linings is ¼in (0.5cm).

Dovetails
The dovetails are the joints at the corners of the drawers where the pieces have been slotted together. Somewhat coarse and large in the 17thC, they became progressively finer throughout the 18th. The drawers of this 17thC chest have

three dovetails. A later piece may have as many as five or six. The dovetailing should correspond on each drawer.

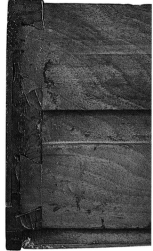

Detail of drawer from the walnut chest left, *showing three thick dovetails.* MB

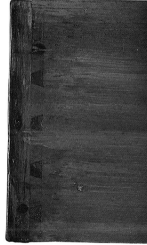

Detail of a drawer from an 18thC chest showing five dovetails. MB

Drawer bottoms

Many drawer bottoms have a gap between the boards. This is the result of shrinkage, but is not serious. A sliver of wood can be inserted, or the underside of the drawer can be taped with a strip of fine hessian soaked in glue.

* Taping to prevent or correct shrinkage is also used on the backs of chests and other case furniture.

Finish

The insides of most drawers are not finely finished and have a dry untouched look; there is no polish on the underside. On some 19thC and Edwardian furniture the insides of drawers are lightly polished.

Runners

Until the 18thC, drawers had thick linings which enabled channels to be cut into the sides; these slotted into runnners in the carcass.

* Some 17thC drawers don't have runners but simply run on the dust boards between the drawers. The bottom drawer runs on the base of the carcass.

From the Queen Anne period (1702-14) drawer runners were placed underneath the drawer, at the sides, and ran on bearers placed along the inside of the carcass.

* Drawer runners may need replacing every so often as they wear out; this is perfectly acceptable. In fact, if runners are left in a worn state this may cause damage to the bottom of the drawers and to the drawer dividers (the mouldings between the drawers).

Drawer fronts

On 17thC furniture, drawer fronts are moulded, or have a simple, raised decoration, often of geometric form.

The edges of 17thC drawers are plain, although the drawer dividers – the strips of wood attached to the carcass between the drawers – have applied decorative mouldings.

From the 18thC drawer fronts are flat, relying more on handles for decorative impact. However, they are neatly finished off with overlapping ovolo (quarter-round) moulding; or, usually from c.1725, a beaded moulding known as cock beading. Drawer dividers are plain.

Handles

Having assessed the drawer itself, look at the handles to check that they are stylistically right for the piece (see page 21). If they are, the next step is to establish whether they are original – handles were often replaced as fashions changed. Early handles are held in place with the split-pin method: a pommel, a kind of brass rivet, is pushed through the drawer, then split open to secure the handle. From the late 17thC handles are usually held by nuts and bolts. From the front, those that have been on a piece for a long time will have built up a layer of dirt and grease, causing dark shading around the edges and in the crevices. The moving parts of the handles may have marked the front of the drawer where the handles have swung and knocked against the wood over the years.

Detail of drawer from walnut chest above left, *showing dark shading and indentations caused by handle.* MB

There may be marks on the front of a drawer where other handles have been, or scars where the wood has been damaged in changing the handles. If handles have been replaced there will probably be plugged holes in the handle area – some pieces have had as many as four or five sets of handles, and the inside of the drawer in the handle area will be peppered with holes. Collectors try to find pieces that retain their original handles. However, these are becoming increasingly scarce, and provided that there are no bad scars on the drawer fronts replacements are acceptable to most buyers.

* The nuts used to secure handles in the 18thC are circular, whereas modern nuts are hexagonal.

Escutcheons

The inset brass keyhole escutcheon – the metal plate that surrounds the keyhole – is an aid to dating: in the 18thC the bottoms are rounded; from the latter half of the 19thC keyhole escutcheons are slightly skimpier and flat-bottomed.

Locks on 17thC furniture are held in place with hand-made iron nails. In the 18thC steel screws were used, the heads of brass screws being too soft. It is not serious if a lock has been replaced, although it is preferable to have the original one. Filled-in spaces around the present lock indicate that there was originally a larger lock.

THE CARCASS

Having examined all the drawers, take them out and look inside the carcass, which will be relatively crude in construction and is likely to be dusty. The inside should look dry and untouched with no new pieces of wood.

* "Dry and untouched" is a dealer's term for wood that looks and feels dry and has not been tampered with.

Underside

The underside of a piece of furniture will always be dry and roughly hewn, and may well have splits, caused by natural defects in the wood. Unless these are very bad, there is no need to worry about them. However, any active woodworm must be treated.

Backs

The backs of furniture designed to stand against a wall, rather than in the middle of the room, are not polished or finely finished. They are constructed of three or four backboards, sometimes chamfered off at the edges and roughly nailed onto the back. From the second half of the 18thC more attention was paid to finishing off the back, using a panelled construction, but it was still not polished. The backs of later pieces of high quality will be held in place with countersunk screws.

* At least some, if not all, of the nails should be uneven in shape and stand proud of the piece.

FEET

Styles of feet are one of the most useful guides to dating. However, feet do come in for a lot of rough treatment, and many worn feet have been replaced. Feet were also replaced as fashions changed. Close inspection should determine whether they are original or not: unaccountable marks or new wood on the underside of a chest are good indications that a replacement has occurred.

The two most common types of feet are bun feet and bracket feet.

Bun feet

Bun feet, like those of the chest, *left*, are the most common type of feet on furniture of the late 17th or early 18thC. They are very rarely original – it is estimated that as many as 95 percent have been replaced. This is not a problem provided that original bun feet have been replaced by other bun feet and the work has been carried out neatly. If the piece has had another style of feet at some time – for example, bracket feet – these will have left marks on the outside moulding to which the feet would have been mounted.

Distressing

Replacement bun feet may be detected by artificial distressing, which is regular and unnatural-looking. If the feet are contemporary with the piece, or at least fairly old, they will probably be heavily pitted with signs of age and rotting especially on the vulnerable front surfaces.

Bracket feet

Bracket feet were common from the beginning of the 18thC until the early 19thC. Approximately 50 percent of the bracket feet found today are original. The bracket foot *below*, although a replacement, is stylistically correct and has been sensitively fitted. The timber is relatively new but has been stained to look old, although it still doesn't have the signs of ageing that are apparent elsewhere on the underside. All the blocks on which the feet are mounted should have a similar appearance.

* Replaced handles and feet are acceptable – much more so than a replaced bureau fall or reveneering would be. Of course, replacements are valid only where they have been sensitively done.

Detail of an 18thC chest, showing a replacement bracket foot. MB

Basics II

TWO-PART PIECES AND MARRIAGES

Large furniture was often made in two or three pieces, which have subsequently become separated and used individually. Bureau bookcases, chests on chests, cabinets on stands have all been treated in this way. The crucial factor in assessing any two-part piece is to consider whether the parts have always been together. Pieces of furniture made up of elements taken from different pieces are known as "marriages". The parts may be of the same period, or one part may be later, even relatively modern, and coloured and polished to resemble the older part.

The following examination of the married cabinet-on-chest shown *right* is relevant to an assessment of most two- and three-part pieces.

STYLE and PROPORTIONS

The first thing to do with any furniture, is to stand back and gain an overall impression of the general *style* and *proportions*. With careful observation and a little experience it is generally possible to tell, for example, where a top looks too heavy for a base. Tops should be slightly narrower than bases: if the parts are of the same width or if the width difference is very marked, the piece as a whole will have an awkward, ill-designed appearance.

COLOUR and VENEER

External details should be examined next, and a careful comparison made between the two parts, for quality of wood, finish, style of construction, handles, and so on.

It can be difficult to make a direct comparison between the fronts of two-part pieces where the construction may legitimately differ – for example, the top of this piece has doors, while the base has drawers, which is not in itself indicative of a married piece. However, the sides of most pieces of composite furniture are the same, and an examination of these, top and bottom, may be a great help in determining the authenticity of a piece. The veneers should match, as on a genuine piece they will have been cut from the same piece of timber. However, the quality of veneer on the top part here, with its figuring and swirls, is better than on the lower part. The timber on the lower half lacks the patination of a really old piece and there are signs of artificial distressing, all indicative of recent veneer.

* 18thC veneer is hand-cut and varies in thickness. Modern veneer is machine-cut and therefore thin and of a uniform thickness.

QUARTER VENEERING

Quarter-veneered tops are associated with veneered pieces from the early 18thC and were added for both decorative and practical reasons. Walnut could not be cut into very large pieces, so tops were quarter-veneered, or laid in four sections of matching veneers. The mirrored or bookmatched effect of panels veneered in this way is apparent. Quarter-veneered tops are subject to a certain amount of shrinkage and seams may open up slightly.

Quarter-veneering was discontinued with the introduction of one-piece mahogany tops.

A late 17thC walnut veneered "married" cabinet-on-chest. MB

DECORATION

Many 18thC pieces of furniture have decorative veneers known as banding, used around the edges of drawer fronts, panels and on table tops to complement the principal veneer. There are three main types of banding:

* cross banding
* straight banding
* feather or herringbone banding

Cross banding

This is laid in short sections at right angles to the veneered surface.

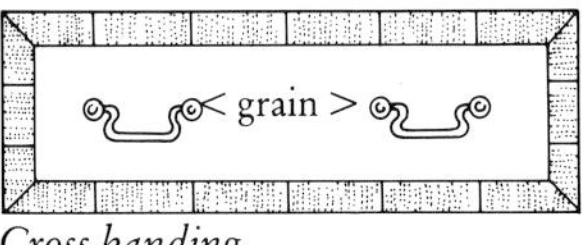

Cross banding

Straight banding

Straight banding is applied in one long strip along, say, a drawer front and is simpler to apply than cross banding as it follows the grain of the main veneer.

< grain >

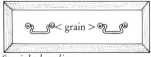

Straight banding

Feather or herringbone banding

This consists of two narrow strips of diagonally banded veneers placed together to give a feather-like appearance. It was popular during the early 18thC, especially on bureaux and bureau bookcases, when it was usually placed in widths of approximately ¼inch (0.5cm) between the cross banding and the main veneer.

< grain >

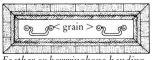

Feather or herrringbone banding

The dimensions, grain and angle of any decorative veneers should correspond on both parts.

Feather banding has been used on both halves of this cabinet-on-chest. On the top part the feathering on the left-hand door points to the left and that on the right-hand door points to the right. This nice attention to detail is not reflected in the bottom section, as it would have been if the two pieces had been made at the same time. In addition, the feather banding on the base is later than the date of the piece – there are places where the knife has cut into the veneer and torn the edges. This is a crucial way to identify later inlay: it is always difficult when inlaying a piece at a later date to cut into veneer that has already been glued down onto the ground wood.

* With genuine early walnut there is usually a fine dark seam around the stringing and at the joints of veneer where the sticky sap has seeped out of the wood from the seams and attracted dirt over the years. On veneer of a later date the join is often *too* perfect – generally speaking this is not the case with a genuine old piece.

MOULDINGS

After looking at the colour and veneer, examine the mouldings (the lengths of wood applied around the edges of a piece). The "waist" moulding between the top and bottom sections on this piece is flush with the base on the front but overhangs on the sides. A good cabinet maker would never design a piece in this way: the overhang of the moulding should be uniform on the front and two sides. Here, the moulding has been designed like this to allow for the fact that the top is slightly too shallow for the base. (If the moulding at the front were brought forward so that it overhung in order to match the sides, the top would also have to be brought forward, and would then not be flush at the back.)

* Mouldings are often replaced. This does not adversely affect value provided that the replacement is only partial.

DRAWERS

The checks for verifying date and authenticity, described on pages 12-13, should be applied. In addition, the construction of the drawers of the two sections should be compared. The drawers need not be the same size but should be constructed in the same way and are likely to have matching decorative details and similarly styled handles. In this example, the top drawers (inside the doors) are smaller than the lower drawers, which is not a problem, but they are differently constructed:

* The dovetailing does not match in style and has clearly been made by a different hand.
* The sides of the drawers in the upper section have squared-off tops; whereas those in the base have rounded-off tops.

* The drawer fronts of the cabinet are veneered onto oak; those on the chest are veneered onto pine.

These are typical discrepancies.

HANDLES

Again, the usual checks should be made for age and authenticity. The handles of the top section here are clearly original: there are no marks on the front or the back to indicate that other handles have been there.

FITTED INTERIORS

Top sections often have fitted interiors with cupboards or drawers, as in this example. These interiors have often been altered later – for example, many cabinets-on-chests with blind doors (mirrored or wood panels as opposed to glazing) have had their interior fittings removed and their wooden doors replaced with glazed doors so that they may be used as cocktail cabinets.

THE CARCASS

The *backboards* of any two-piece sections should be compared for colour match and method of construction. Even if both parts have the typical pine backboards, these should be compared in their thickness and density of grain.

The method of fitting the backboards should also correspond: on the top of this cabinet-on-chest the boards are recessed, whereas on the bottom they are not.

ASSEMBLY

The way in which the individual pieces of a composite piece fit together should also be examined. In this example there are marks on the top of the base, but no corresponding marks on the bottom of the top section. Moreover, if the parts had been designed together, the top would have sat on bearers running along the side and front edges of the base. This would have resulted in lighter patches where the air would not have reached the carcass. However, this piece shows no indication of having had bearers.

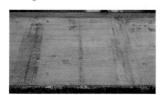

The top of the lower section of the cabinet-on-chest left, *showing the marks where another piece of furniture has stood on it.* MB

FAKES

Apart from marriages, which may or may not have been intended to deceive, the other main problem area is that of fakes – furniture made at a later date than the style suggests, with the specific intention of deceiving the buyer.

The furniture that is probably most faked (as distinct from reproduced) is that of the Queen Anne period: the walnut veneered and lacquered furniture of this era has for a long time been very expensive. Most fakers will try to find a genuinely old piece, such as an oak bureau bookcase, in poor but repairable condition to serve as the carcass for the fake. The piece will then be lacquered or veneered in walnut, possibly with old veneer taken from a large, unsaleable piece. The result is a piece of furniture with an old carcass veneered with old timber, but not an original. The experienced buyer may well sense that the piece is a fake without having to look too hard, but the inexperienced buyer should make a few precautionary inspections:

* The old oak piece may now be veneered in old walnut veneer but the oak mouldings will have had to be replaced by new mouldings in walnut – close inspection should be made for artificial colouring and distressing and any visible signs of new timber.
* The old veneer may well have had handle or escutcheon marks on its surface. The surface of the veneer should be inspected for patches where such marks may have been cut out.

The interior may reveal more than the exterior:

* There may be signs of damage that has been repaired. For example, if the back of a door panel has suffered a break or split, evidence of this should be visible on the outside. If there is a split inside, but the outer surface reveals a perfect unblemished lacquered surface, then the lacquering will have been done at a later date, probably to deceive.
* The drawers of an old oak piece will have had one or more sets of handles in its time. If there are plugged or unplugged handle holes inside the drawer, which are not reflected on the outside, the piece will have been veneered at a later date.

Another category of furniture that may confront the prospective purchaser is the piece that has been reduced in size, either for practical reasons or to increase its value (small furniture is generally more highly prized than large, unwieldy pieces). If a piece has been *reduced in depth* there will be:

* fresh surfaces at the back where it has been cut
* re-made and re-jointed drawer backs.

If a piece has been *reduced in width*:

* The central locks of the drawers will have been re-located and their original location will have been patched.
* The handles of any large drawer will have been re-positioned. The old holes may still be visible on what will now be the edge of the new narrower drawer.
* One side of the drawer will have had to be re-constructed. Compare both sides of the drawer for any variation.

If a piece has been *reduced in height* (usually bookcases):

* The doors will have had to be re-constructed and the astragals (glazing bars) may have needed adjustment.

DECORATION

An examination of the decoration is a useful guide to dating a piece and to assessing its quality: good decoration is indicative of fine quality throughout.

Inlays

This is the process of letting into the surface of a piece of furniture other woods, usually of contrasting colours. The practice is commonly associated with veneered furniture, but early pieces in the solid are occasionally inlaid. Inlaying was popular on English and Continental furniture of the 17th, 18th and 19thC. In America its appeal was more limited before the 19thC. The three main types of inlay are:

* line inlay
* marquetry
* parquetry.

Line inlay

This is the letting in of narrow lines of one or more woods, usually at the edge of a surface or slightly inset. It is also known as *stringing*. It was especially popular from the end of the Chippendale period onward.

Marquetry

The method is the same as for inlays but the result is more elaborate, with floral patterns and a wide range of other decorative motifs, including birds, urns, shells and scrollwork. This box is typical of late 18thC marquetry decoration. (The oval shape was also very popular in the late 18thC.) The top comprises a fan-shaped oval medallion made up of individual pieces of wood. The thin lines of chequered stringing are also typical.

* Some marquetry is of indifferent quality: leaves and other motifs should be well-drawn, with fine detail.

A Sheraton period marquetry box, c.1785. MB

* The *condition* in which any marquetry decoration has survived is crucial. A certain amount of restoration or replacement is acceptable, such as replaced bits of stringing around the edges and one or two bits of replaced outer banding, but a totally replaced central motif will dramatically reduce the value. This marquetry has survived in fine, untouched condition.

Parquetry

Parquetry is a decorative form of veneer often confused with marquetry. It is the process of building up a design of small pieces of veneer of contrasting colours, usually in a geometric design. It was popular in England during the second half of the 17thC, and there was a brief resurgence of interest during the early 19thC on smaller items. It enjoyed a longer period of popularity in Continental Europe.

Gilding

This is the process of covering or partially gilding (parcel-gilding) a piece with gold leaf. The surface to be gilded is first prepared with gesso – a plaster-like substance applied to the surface – and then dampened with water or oil. The gold leaf is laid while the gesso is still sticky. The highlights may then be burnished to create a contrasting effect.

Metal mounts

Much sophisticated Continental furniture (and some English furniture) has applied ormolu (gilt-metal) mounts. On fine pieces the mounts are cast in bronze and then gilded. On lesser pieces the mounts are cast in spelter (a base metal).

Lacquering and japanning

During the late 17thC the Continental fashion for lacquered and japanned furniture came to England and remained in fashion for 20-30 years. In France, cabinet makers had long been insetting lacquered panels imported from the Orient into their furniture. Lacquering involves laying gum from trees onto the surface of the wood and then applying colour. The most common colours are a combination of black and scarlet: green and blue are rare and expensive. Gilt highlights are added, invariably with chinoiserie scenes. Japanning involves building up layers of polish, mixed with various other substances and decorated in the same way as lacquer.

Painting

The practice of painting furniture goes back to medieval times when much oak furniture was painted. Paint was used again on furniture during the late 18thC. Satinwood in particular was highlighted with delicate paintwork in the Neo-classical style, and this technique enjoyed a big revival in Edwardian times when much previously undecorated 18thC furniture was decorated. Edwardian painting can be distinguished from Neo-classical painting by its relative lack of restraint and its sentimental subject matter. Some late 18thC and Regency furniture is painted all over.

Basics III

Most furniture can be dated by the shape and style of the legs, and by the style and quality of carving, if any, and decoration. Once again, keen observation is the key to assessing quality and authenticity. The collector should not be afraid to turn chairs and tables upside down in order to examine the details. Look carefully at the carving and the inlay; observe details such as the build-up of patina over the years; and see whether there are the knocks and scratches associated with age. If possible, compare the piece with another one that is known to be genuine.

The games table shown *right* is a typical, high-quality legged piece. The examination of it that follows applies to any legged piece and to most carved furniture. It has a cabriole leg, traditionally associated with the first half of the 18thC. The overall style, which is refined and sophisticated, accords with that date. The wood is Virginia walnut, which came to England c.1730 and was much used until c.1760. Thus the leg, the wood and the style all indicate that this games table dates from the George II period.

A high-quality George II Virginia walnut carved games table with carbriole legs and claw-and-ball feet. MB

CARVING

The carving of this table is *from the solid* – that is, the whole leg and the decoration are carved from the same solid piece of wood. Cabrioles are always carved from the solid. Straighter legs, such as the Chinese-Chippendale-style leg, have applied carved fretwork. Applied carving is also an inexpensive method employed by some 19th and 20thC reproduction firms. Most 17th and 18thC furniture is carved from the solid.

On 18thC pieces the carving is crisp, but, unlike on later carving, the edges will be of attained patination, and there will be a natural build-up of dirt and wax in the crevices. Any old carving will also be darker around the edges and the feet. The quality of carving is indicative of the quality of the piece as a whole. For example, in the case of this games table the cabriole (S-shaped) leg is a good, well-drawn shape, neither too heavy nor too exaggerated in its curve.

* While good carving is often associated with the 18thC and the Chippendale period in particular, it must be borne in mind that even then quality varied. This is why it is so important to closely inspect the quality of the very best, so that it can stand as a yardstick against which to measure other work.
* Victorian carving, although competent, lacks the crisp detail of 18thC carving – perhaps because furniture was made commercially and in relatively large quantities. The cabriole leg was a great favourite with the Victorians and in many cases the shape is too exaggerated.
* The carving of chair backs suffered a similar deterioration in quality during the Victorian period.

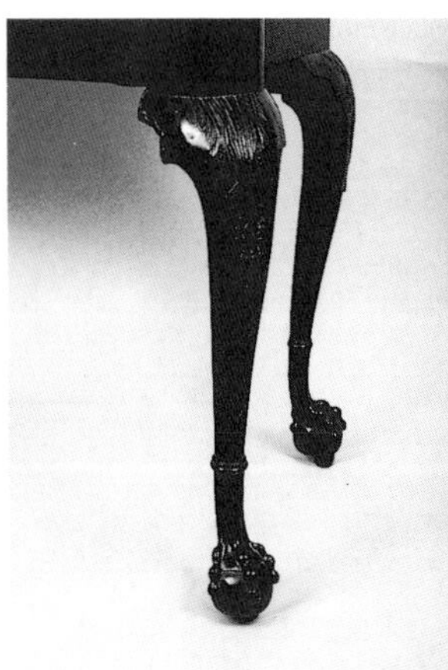

Detail of games table above, *showing the carved cabriole leg and the ear pieces at the top of the leg.* MB

LEGS

The legs and feet of a piece of furniture can provide a strong indication of the date, or at least the period, when the piece was made. Even though some styles were revived there were usually subtle differences between the original and the reproduction that will help to distinguish one from the other. With chairs in particular many popular 18thC styles were reproduced by the Victorians. For the main styles of legs and their dates see page 36.

* The mahogany used on furniture, especially chairs, during the Chippendale period varied in quality but is usually a warm mellow colour enhanced by the natural patina it will have developed. The timber of 19thC copies tends to be darker, and this effect is exaggerated by the coloured polish used by the Victorians. In the 1920s chairs were mostly mass-produced and the wood used is usually of relatively poor quality.

Ear pieces

The ear piece, the shaped piece at the top of a cabriole leg, is made separately from the leg in order to economize on wood. Thus, there will always be a visible seam or join where the ear piece meets the leg. As they are glued onto the leg, ear pieces tend to get knocked from the piece and are often replaced. It is virtually impossible to disguise a replaced ear piece against close inspection. Replacements can usually be detected by comparing the colour of the timbers and the patination, and by the quality of the carving – inspection at close quarters should reveal whether the carving is by the same hand.

FEET

The claw-and-ball foot of the table, *left*, is usually associated with the first half of the 18thC. It was also very popular in 19thC reproductions. However, in the best 18thC examples, the claw appears to grip the ball tightly, whereas in later versions, the claw usually merely sits limply on the ball.

Detail of games table above, *showing the claw-and-ball foot. The claws grip the ball tightly.* MB

FLUTING AND REEDING

Fluting and reeding are forms of carved decorative detailing dating from the late 18thC and used mainly on the slender legs of tables and chairs, but also on the main body of some furniture. Fluting consists of narrow parallel vertical grooves. Reeding consists of parallel convex strips. Delicate in the late 18thC, fluting and reeding became much heavier from c.1820, and by the Victorian period were of comparatively massive proportions.

FRETTING

This is the intricate pierced decoration, cut and shaped with a fret saw, found on some table friezes. Fretting was introduced c.1740 and used extensively by Chippendale and other makers of the time; it was popular in America from a slightly later date. It is a particularly desirable feature, always indicative of quality.

UNDERSIDES OF TABLE TOPS

With any legged piece it is necessary to establish that the top has always been associated with the base and legs. On the underside of the hinged top of the table shown *left*, there is shadowing in those areas where the top overhangs the base and has been exposed to the air and the natural oils of the hand. This is a good indication that the top has always been with that bottom. Similarly, there should be marks on the base where the top has rested; in this case, the marks should follow the arc of the gateleg action (the hinged wooden mechanism that allows the legs to swing open).

Brass hinges

Cabinet makers of the 18thC did not use brass screws as these were not strong enough. Steel screws were used; these were hand-made with the thread running right up to the head, unlike modern screws.

TILT-TOP TABLES

Some table tops can be tilted so that the table can be stored when not in use without taking up too much space. The top rests on a block which is supported by a pedestal. If the top has always rested on the block, there will be signs of this, often quite subtle, on the underside of the top, in between the bearers. The pedestal is usually tenoned into the block – the tenons extended right through the block for maximum strength. Owing to a degree of inevitable shrinkage of the block, these tenons often stand slightly proud of the block and this will cause corresponding marks on the underside of the top.

Detail from the tilt-top table right, *showing the pedestal base which supports the table-top.* MB

To establish whether the top has always been associated with its bearers, examine the underside carefully for marks of other bearers or plugged holes, which would indicate that the top has been on another table and has perhaps been cut down.

Detail from the tilt-top table right, *showing the bearers and catch on the top of the block.* MB

Next, examine the base to see whether it belongs with the block. There should be no suspicious signs underneath the block indicating that an alteration may have taken place – for example, where the top may have been cut down from a larger table to fit the base.

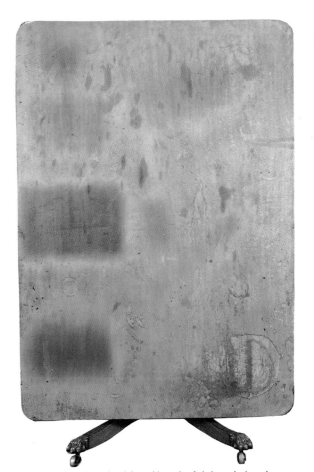

Regency mahogany tilt-top breakfast table with a faded, marked top, but otherwise in good condition. MB

CHAIRS

After examining the wood, legs and carving of a chair, the next step is to look at the seat. Early chairs have wooden seats and, like other furniture of the period, are joined and pegged (see page 24). Upholstery on English chairs generally dates from the post-Restoration period, when there was also a fashion for caned seats with small (squab) cushions: these returned during the Regency period.

Upholstery

The two main forms of upholstery for chairs of the 18th and 19thC are:

* stuff-over seats, which extend over the seat rail
* drop-in seats, which employ a separate beech frame which is dropped into the polished frame of the chair.

The older the chair, the more times it is likely to have been upholstered. The more it has been upholstered, the more holes there will be in the beech framework. Any re-upholstery should be carried out using traditional materials, such as horse-hair padding and tacks. Foam rubber and stapleguns should not be used. Take expert advice before attempting to change upholstery.

CONDITION

Antique furniture in good condition can be prohibitively expensive. However, there are many less expensive good, old pieces not in perfect condition, which, with proper treatment by a professional restorer or polisher, could be restored to their original condition. As a general rule, the finer the quality of the timber, the easier an article is to restore. Having said that, some pieces may need very complex or specialist restoration that can be very expensive – for example, badly warped card tables or brass inlaid items that are missing a large amount of brasswork. Other pieces are beyond repair and are suitable only for breaking up so that the parts may be used for restoration work on other furniture.

Repolishing

The mahogany breakfast table, c.1800, shown *above*, has clearly stood in one sunny spot for a long time with fairly solid items on it, preventing the light from getting to some parts of the table top. The original colour can be seen where the items have been undisturbed for years. The sun has caused the polish to fade in some parts and to perish completely in others. The top is covered in watermarks and stains.

At first glance, most people would reject this table, but it is still quite retrievable, as the wood itself is in good condition and there are no gouges or splits. Only the polish is in a bad state. Stripping and repolishing by an expert could completely transform the piece and make it a highly desirable item.

Other restorable faults often found with tables and other legged furniture are:

* an open join on a top made from two matched pieces of wood
* breaks in the legs
* casters that need re-bushing.

A warped top may be very difficult to rectify.

Chairs

The most likely areas of damage are:

* the tops of legs
* the back uprights, or vertical supports
* the area where the horizontal top rail meets the uprights.

Chairs will probably show most signs of wear around the feet where they have received kicks, and bumps from feet and vacuum cleaners, over the years. The undersides of the feet will have developed a well-worn look. The edges of square legs may well be quite rounded, especially low down on the front surfaces. Chairs with stretchers (the rails that connect the legs of some chairs and tables) will show most signs of wear on the front stretcher.

CARE

Antique furniture needs to be treated with respect. A piece that is well cared-for will appreciate in value more than an ill-treated item. There are a few simple ways to avoid unnecessary damage:

* Never place a piece against, or too near to a radiator, or in a very dry or very damp atmosphere: this will cause warpage or splitting. Dryness can be regulated by a humidifier.
* Never use aerosol sprays on wood.
* Never let people lean on the backs of chairs.
* Never allow an amateur restorer to repair a piece.

There are also a few simple guidelines to prevent deterioration:

* Polish at regular intervals with a wax polish.
* Check regularly for signs of deterioration. Have any necessary work done before further deterioration occurs.

Chests, Cabinets and Cupboards I

The chest or coffer is unquestionably the earliest form of furniture. From it evolved a variety of objects – settles (from which chairs derive), cabinets and chests of drawers.

The earliest surviving English chests date from the 13th century. The method of construction is very basic: planks nailed together, sometimes reinforced with iron bandings.

It was not until the 17th century that coffers, now joined and panelled, were made in large numbers. In spite of the increase in the number of cupboards, linen and clothing were still most often stored in these pieces of furniture.

The main problem with coffers was gaining access to items placed at the bottom, and from about the middle of the 17th century a very significant innovation occurred – the inclusion of a drawer in the base of the coffer. From this period there was a rapid development from the coffer, made by a joiner, to the fine chest of drawers of the later 17th century with a fixed top, the work of a cabinet maker. Drawers are now dovetailed, with runners on the bottom edges (see page 13). Chests on stands and chests on chests (known in America as highboys and tallboys respectively) followed in the reigns of William and Mary and Queen Anne.

From about the middle of the 18th century the influence of elegant French design is clearly perceptible with the introduction to superior English furniture of the French *commode*, subtly curvaceous, with carved and applied ornament, in contrast to the traditional, rectilinear style.

The commode was a prominent entry in trade catalogues of the period and no fashionable English drawing room was complete without one. Great attention was bestowed upon commodes by the leading designers and cabinet makers of the time – among them Thomas Chippendale, Ince & Mayhew, William Vile, John Cobb and Robert Adam.

An English court cupboard or buffet, c.1600-20 (ht 44in/111cm), made in oak as these items almost always were. This, the earliest type of cupboard, was constructed as a tiered table to display plate. Early examples are becoming increasingly rare. The many Victorian imitations tend to be stained very dark, lacking the originals' glowing patina. *S*

A mid-17thC inlaid joined press cupboard (wdth 58in/148cm) – effectively, an enclosed buffet. The carved columns of the upper part are a hangover from the previous form. Such cupboards were nearly always made in oak, usually in two parts. The style survived in the provinces until c.1800. These cupboards are still plentiful and relatively inexpensive. *S*

The ends of this very early (c.1640) chest of drawers (wdth 36in/91.5cm) show clearly the legacy of coffer construction, even though the carcass is fitted entirely with drawers. *S*

A typical mid-17thC carved oak coffer (wdth 53in/134cm). Huge numbers were made, so the supply remains plentiful and fakes largely non-existent. Prices reflect quality, which is variable. *S*

The coffer in transitional stage, with a drawer added. This American carved oak and pine "sunflower" chest was made in Wethersfield, Connecticut, 1685-1700 (wdth 41in/104cm). These hybrid coffer-chests are known in England as mule chests. *S*

Late 17thC and 18thC cabinets on stands were often opulent display pieces exhibiting the finest skills of cabinet making and decoration. This William and Mary olivewood example (ht 68in/173cm) is elaborately decorated with oyster veneers on the interior, as well as on the outer surfaces. The barley-sugar twist legs and flat, shaped stretchers are entirely typical of the period. *S*

* As they are not the most practical of pieces, cabinets have sometimes had their fitted interiors removed to turn them into drinks cabinets.
* Legs, being of fragile construction, are quite often replaced. Look for colour differences and signs of artificial distressing on the vulnerable surfaces, and for appropriate wear to the bun feet.

Inlaid circles in boxwood combined with oyster veneer is a style peculiar to the William and Mary period in England. This walnut chest (ht 37in/94cm) dates from c.1700. It would originally have had bun feet. *S*

* Many chests of this period were subsequently fitted with bracket feet, either because of damage or to update them to 18thC style. The holes where the bun feet were dowelled in should still be visible in the baseboard when the bottom drawer is removed.
* These chests are rare, expensive and very much sought after.

OYSTER VENEERING

To make oyster veneer, the smaller branches (2-3in/5-8cm diameter) of certain trees were cut transversely into veneers and pieced together as a parquetry, or mosaic. Oyster-pieces were generally cut from walnut and laburnum saplings, but other woods such as lignum-vitae, kingwood and olive were also used.

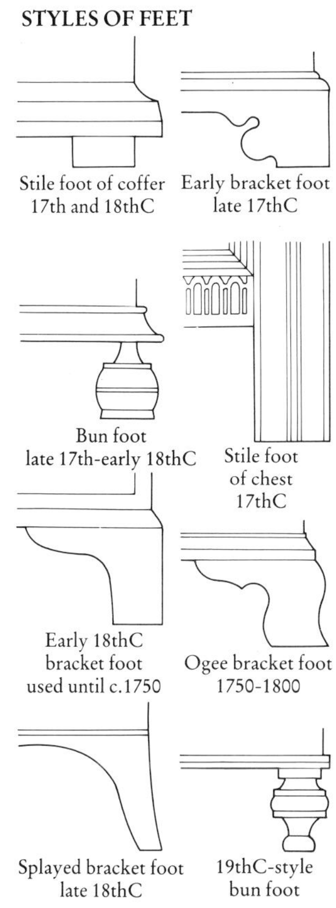

Good lacquered furniture always commands a high price because of its decorative quality. This fine example of a lacquered cabinet on chest (wdth 37in/94cm) dates from the end of the 17thC or the early 18thC. By c.1720 lacquered furniture had declined in popularity in England though the technique was much used in the rest of Europe for decades after. *S*

A Queen Anne figured walnut bachelor's chest, c.1710 (wdth 29in/75cm), in unrestored condition. *S*

* Original examples are rare but very popular because of their small size, and very expensive. As a result, many bachelor's chests are in fact large chests of the period cut down. To check authenticity, remove the drawers and look at the wear caused by the runners. If the piece is genuine, wear will stop about ½in/1.25cm short of the backboard. If wear continues right up to the backboard you may be sure that the chest has been reduced in depth.

A George I figured walnut cabinet on chest, c.1720 (ht 83in/210cm), with mirrored doors. Mirrored cabinet doors were popular during the first half of the 18thC. *S*

* Original mirror plates should show hand bevelling (shallower than 19thC machine bevelling) following the shaping of the doors.

The sophisticated, slender outline of the cabriole legs on this Queen Anne burr walnut veneered highboy marks it out as Massachusetts work. It was made in Boston, 1740-60, and stands 77in/195cm high. Note the matching flamed veneers and the turned pendants – features associated in England with the William and Mary period. *S*

Chests, Cabinets and Cupboards II

New York and Massachusetts pieces, like this block-front mahogany chest, c.1766-80 (ht 32in/81.5cm), have blocking extending uninterrupted all the way up. The block fronts of furniture made in Connecticut and Rhode Island usually terminate in one or more large shells below the top. *CNY*

A mid-18thC Neapolitan *bombé* commode in walnut, inlaid with ebony and other contrasting woods (ht 39in/100cm). *CR*
* The *bombé* shape was very popular throughout the Continent during the second half of the 18thC.
* Many Italian commodes of this period are much more lavishly embellished, with a profusion of gilding and all-over painting often disguising the presence of the drawers.

The commode became popular in England from the mid-18thC (along with other French styles). This Chippendale-period mahogany serpentine commode (wdth 45in/115cm) is enhanced by fine carving to the apron. *S*
* In the Hepplewhite and Sheraton periods commodes were veneered in lighter woods such as satinwood and tulipwood, and inlaid with marquetry decoration.

A handsome George I burr walnut chest on chest c.1725 (wdth 43in/109cm). The colour and figuring of the veneers are good, and there are three other particularly good features:
* a fitted secretaire drawer in the top of the base part
* fluted canted corners on both top and bottom sections – this softens the outline
* the bottom drawer is inlaid with a concave sunburst.

The ogee bracket feet are fairly obvious later replacements. As well as being stylistically out of period (see page 19), they are made of mahogany. *S*

After c.1735 most chests on chests were made in mahogany in a wide range of qualities. However, provincial examples in oak are not uncommon – as in most periods, traditional styles, construction methods and materials survive alongside more recent metropolitan fashions.
* Some chests on chests have a single long drawer at the top which can give the whole piece a rather box-like appearance. Two short drawers or even three, as in this piece, have the effect of breaking up the otherwise uniform lines of the piece.
* Walnut chests on chests, especially those in burr walnut, are by far the most expensive type, followed by mahogany and then oak.

This Queen Anne figured maple chest of drawers, made in Pennsylvania, 1750-70 (ht 40in/101.5cm), is a good example of a transitional piece – it is of the Chippendale period but retains earlier features. Note:
* the fluted quarter columns
* the trifid, that is, three-lobed feet. *CNY*

A Chippendale-period mahogany serpentine chest of drawers c.1760 (wdth 42in/107cm). Quality features include:
* the original brass swan-neck handles
* blind-fret carved angles
* chunky ogee bracket feet. *C*

This small chest of drawers, c.1760-65 (wdth 32in/81cm), makes an instructive comparison with the one above: they are of similar date, both made of mahogany, both with swan-neck handles and both very collectable. However, this example is quite plain and unpretentious. A desirable feature is the pull-out dressing slide below the top. *S*

HANDLE STYLES

Late 17th/early 18thC

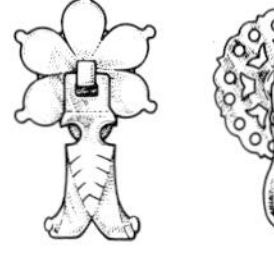
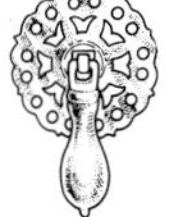
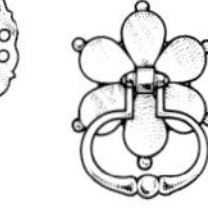

Early 18thC

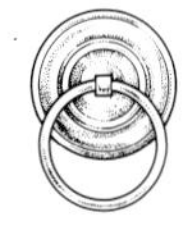
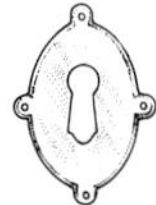

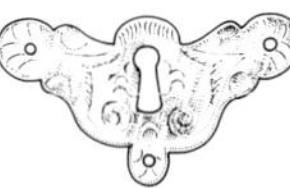
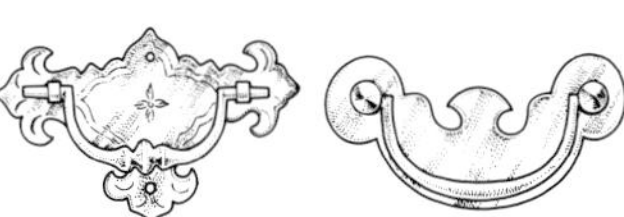

2nd quarter 18thC

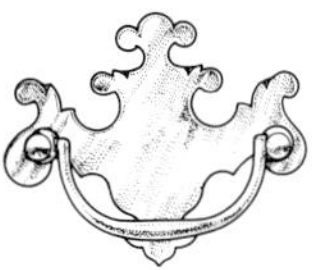

2nd half 18th C

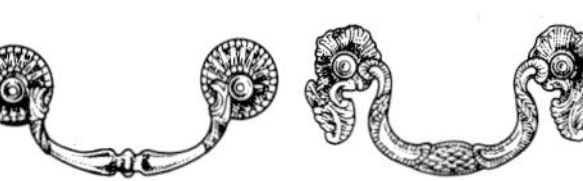

Late 18th-early 19thC

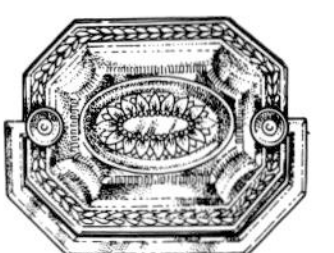

A piece of furniture in the grand manner, this superb Chippendale-period carved mahogany chest on chest, or highboy, was made in Philadelphia, 1765-80 (ht 92in/234cm). It is perfectly proportioned with delicate graduation of the drawers and a nice low waistline. The Chippendale pediment in Philadelphia case furniture is unsurpassed in America, and the carved Rococo decoration in this example is of the highest order. The pierced cabochon finial suggests the work of a London-trained carver, while the tall, twisted flame finials are characteristic of the region. *CNY*

AUTHENTICATING CHESTS ON CHESTS

While many chests on chests have been divided, some are the result of a "marriage". A few simple checks are:

* the dovetails in the drawers should match in both parts
* the backboards of both parts should be of similar timber and quality
* signs of handle changes (redundant holes inside the drawer fronts, marks on the drawer fronts themselves) should be the same on both parts
* the top part alone may have canted corners or both parts may have them, but not the bottom alone
* decorative detail, such as crossbanding, should be similar top and bottom
* the wood on both parts should match exactly.

This mid-18thC French chestnut commode (ht 32in/81.5cm) was provincially made, but the care taken with the serpentine front, the moulded raised panels and the good-quality cast ormolu handles and escutcheons all indicate that this piece of furniture was designed for use in a prosperous country home, rather than a cottage. *S*

Contrasting light and dark woods are typical of New England Federal-period furniture. This mahogany bow-front chest of drawers, made in Portsmouth, New Hampshire, 1800-10 (ht 39in/98cm), emphasizes the contrast with vertical and horizontal banding. English chests of this shape and period tend to have shorter splay feet and to be less ornate. *SNY*

Chests, Cabinets and Cupboards III

A mid-18thC French commode (wdth 50in/127.5cm) in walnut with moulded raised panels and with good-quality cast ormolu mounts. Although of provincial origin, this piece of furniture was obviously designed for use in a substantial country house rather than a modest dwelling. *C*

Contrasting light and dark woods are typical of Federal-period furniture. This mahogany bow-front chest of drawers, made in North Shore, Massachusetts, c.1800-20 (ht 47½in/107cm), has vertical and horizontal banding that emphasizes the contrast between the woods. English chests of this shape and period tend to have shorter feet and to be less ornate. *CNY*

Bow-fronted chests were made in large numbers during the first half of the 19thC. Many are large and of indifferent quality, and still relatively inexpensive. The fine features of this Regency chest, c.1810, that distinguish it from many other 19thC examples are:

* its compact size (wdth 33in/84cm)
* the reeded top edge and pilasters
* the shaped boxwood banding. *C*

A mahogany linen press of fine quality, c.1780 (ht 86in/218cm), showing several newly fashionable features: inlaid oval panels (rather than the plain rectangular panels of the Chippendale period), oval backplate handles, splay bracket feet and shaped apron. The piece also retains its sliding tray shelves. *S*

An English-style break-front rosewood commode in the French taste, c.1775 (ht 35in/89cm), representative of the lighter style that followed the Chippendale period. It is inlaid with marquetry decoration in the Neo-classical manner – the Classical urn, the Vitruvian scrolls to the frieze and the fan paterae to the sides are all typical. *S*

A French Empire burr maplewood commode of the early 19thC (ht 36in/91cm). It has a Belgian granite top. Neither this very severe style nor the use of pale woods was as popular in England as it was throughout the rest of Europe during the early 19thC. *S*

This very French-looking serpentine commode or chest (ht 35in/89cm) was made c.1780. Instead of bracket feet and canted corners it has a shaped apron and splay feet. The use of flame mahogany veneer figuring is unbroken across the entire front. *S*

Tall, narrow chests known as Wellington chests were introduced c.1840 as components of bedroom suites. This example (ht 53in/135cm), by Holland & Sons, is in ash; rosewood and walnut are more common. *S*

APPRENTICE PIECES
Many workshops were family concerns, and most boys (and occasionally girls) followed in their father's footsteps and entered the trade. Once they had served their apprenticeship, their capabilities were examined and, if successful, only then were they entitled to set up their own workshop. Many miniature pieces of furniture, such as chests of drawers, chests on chests, bureaux, bureau bookcases, and occasionally chairs, are the products of apprentices who made small-scale pieces to demonstrate their skill. These are highly collectable today.

The Victorians valued highly the decorative effects of gilt and inlay on ebonized grounds, whether in conventional cabinet making, as here, or in papier mâché work. This mid-19thC gilt metal-mounted side cabinet (wdth 56in/140cm) shows a profusion of ornament, most prominently the *pietra dura* panels in the door. *S*

* The design of this cabinet may not be to everybody's taste but there is no denying the quality of craftsmanship that went into its execution, as is the case with so much furniture of this period.

This splendid mid-18thC Dutch walnut cabinet (ht 97in/246cm) displays several signs of quality which include:

* the exuberant applied carving on the doors, cornice and apron
* the massive lion's paw feet
* the plateaux on the cornice where precious delftware or Oriental porcelain could be displayed
* floral marquetry inlay on the drawers of the bombé lower part
* the lavish nature of the Rococo mounts. *S*

Many plainer examples of this kind of cabinet were made in Holland in the period. The top sections of these cabinets were held together by removable pegs, allowing them to be dismantled for moving. This is also true of much larger Dutch case furniture.

A Regency brass-inlaid rosewood side cabinet, c.1825 (wdth 32in/81cm). Surprisingly, fakes of these items seem to be unknown. *CNY*

* This cabinet is typical of the smaller pieces produced in the first quarter of the 19thC to furnish smaller London townhouses. Being very practical in the modern drawing room, such pieces are highly sought after.
* Cabinets with a drawer at the top will fetch more than cabinets without.

BRASS INLAY
From c.1810 brass inlay and marquetry work, usually on cabinets and tables with flat surfaces, became very fashionable. The inlay and marquetry method is known as "Buhl" or "Boulle" work, after André Charles Boulle, cabinet maker to Louis XIV, who perfected the technique. To a great extent brass inlay supplanted the use of wood inlay, although dark woods such as ebony continued to be used to provide a contrast against light grounds. In French work, stained tortoiseshell was used as the ground; in England rosewood and mahogany were more usual.

A Regency black lacquer side cabinet with gilt chinoiserie decoration, c.1815 (ht 38in/96.5cm). This type of long shallow cabinet became popular during the Regency period, when there was a return to the taste for Chinese-inspired decoration. *B*

* These cabinets are often found in mahogany and rosewood.

The quality of this mid-Victorian amboyna, purpleheart and marquetry breakfront side cabinet (wdth 72in/183cm) is typical of the best Victorian craftsmanship: only good-quality materials were used in the construction of fine pieces. *C*

Chairs I

Early seat furniture, in oak, is limited to joint stools, and chairs and settles with panelled backs – all much copied in the 19th century.

After the 16th century, English chairs show a clear line of development, which may be simplified as follows – elaborate turning and carving (walnut) in the 17th century; solid back-splats (also walnut) in the Queen Anne period; carved and pierced splats in the age of mahogany; an elegant simplification of design in the late 18th and early 19th centuries; and, in the 19th century, bulging upholstery alongside ornate carving in various exaggerated interpretations of earlier styles. American chairs followed distinctive variations: for example, Hepplewhite- and Sheraton-style chairs were often hand-painted by their owners.

The first woven cane chairs date from the late 17th century. Initially cane was used on the backs, later on the seats as well. By c.1685 the canework had become finer, the holes more precise. Cane enjoyed a revival in the later 18th century.

Side chairs, particularly associated with the 18th century, are quality pieces intended for display against the walls of libraries, halls, salons and so on. They normally have wider seats and higher backs than dining chairs.

Armchairs in England enjoyed a heyday in the Queen Anne and George I periods. French influence became apparent in the latter half of the 18th century, and can be seen in the basic form of the bergère – an armchair with upholstered sides. An 18th-century overstuffed (thick upholstered) armchair can be difficult to distinguish from a 19th-century reproduction without lifting the overcanvas and examining the construction. The wing chair came in surprisingly early, in the Queen Anne period, and subsequently showed little change.

The Victorians reproduced many classic designs for the boudoir and the drawing room, and for use in hotels and boardrooms, as well as introducing their own distinctive forms – for example, the balloon-back chair and massively upholstered chairs for deep slumber.

Most Victorian reproductions pose no problems for the experienced collector: there are usually tell-tale signs. The proportions are often inauthentic – for example, the cabriole legs might be too meagre, or the rake of the chair back might be inelegant. In reproduction splat-back chairs the shoe-piece housing the base of the splat was an integral part of the seat rail; whereas in genuine 18th-century examples the shoe-piece was made separately. Edwardian chairs in the late 18th-century style, while very attractive, are often too finely drawn, to the point where they appear spindly and are structurally weak.

The most popular and recognizable type of English provincial chair is the Windsor chair, which was made continuously from the late 18th century. Key features are a saddle-shaped elm seat and a back of straight "sticks"; some have arms.

EARLY CHAIRS

In Europe until the end of the Middle Ages the only types of seating were settles and benches. The early chest, or coffer, doubled up as a seat and was the basis of the first true chair. The early enclosed settles, used for storage as well as seating, are basically coffers with a back and arms at each end.

The solid "close" or "joyned" chair of box- or coffer-like form with enclosed panelled sides was made from the end of the medieval period until the end of the 16thC.

By the middle of the 16thC joiners began to construct a lighter type of chair, known as the wainscot chair, which had no panelling at the base. This continued to be made – predominantly in oak with carved and sometimes inlaid decoration – until 1660.

In England, Charles II introduced a type of chair already popular on the Continent, in walnut with barley twist uprights, ornate carving and caned back-panels with upholstered seats. For the first time the chair was an object of comfort and fashion.

The wing chair, introduced toward the end of the 17thC, exhibited the first signs in England of the cabriole leg.

This James I panel-back joined armchair, c.1620 (ht 44in/112cm), with a fan-shaped cresting, is reminiscent of the carving over important doorways of the period. The detailed carving is of exceptional quality. Typically for an authentic chair of this type, only the front stretcher is worn where the feet rested on it. *S*

* Excessive wear on the back stretcher and sides may indicate a later copy, artificially distressed.

* Chair seats of the 17thC were high – as much as 28½-29in (72-4cm) from the ground. However, heights may vary as feet are sometimes trimmed to remove rot.

* Joined construction, where the joints were connected by mortice-and-tenon, and pegged in place, was used in the 16th and 17thC.

Early chairs show regional characteristics. The dragon-carved crest and the scrolling at the tip of the arms of this Charles I Gloucestershire joined armchair, c.1640 (ht 45in/114cm), are consistent features of chairs from this region. *S*

* Victorian copies exist. These are stained dark and have a blackish look. Carving is freer and more flowing on 17thC chairs than on the reproductions.

Triangular-seated "turners" armchairs, so called because they demonstrate the art of the turner, were made throughout Europe from medieval times. This mid-17thC example in yew wood, c.1650 (ht 40in/101cm), has a ringed frame filled with small turned bobbins in the back and front stretcher, and bulbous supports. *S*

A Charles II oak joint stool, c.1660, with a nulled, or carved and moulded, frieze on reel-turned legs with square stretchers (ht 20in/51cm). *C*
* Stools were made in sets, but it is rare to find them even in pairs: damp floors, woodworm and ill usage have taken their toll.

CONVERSIONS
Joint stools often have tops that have been replaced or re-made at a later date. The underside of an authentic top, inside the frieze, will have a dry, untouched appearance; the outer edge will appear darker and slightly patinated from absorbing the natural oils of the hand.

METHODS OF PEGGING

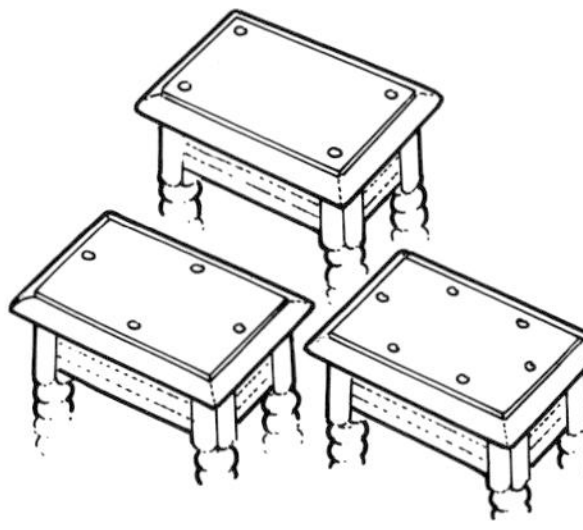

The tops of joint stools are pegged in any of the ways shown above: there should not be any unused or plugged holes. Pegs are hand-made, slightly tapered, and stand proud of the surface.

This type of Charles II walnut armchair, c.1680, with needlework upholstery, was made c.1600-80. Examples are scarce as the frames were often discarded when the upholstery wore out. *SM*

The Dutch influence of the late 17thC, when chairs tended to be long and thin, had all but disappeared by the time of this comfortable and beautifully proportioned Queen Anne walnut wing armchair, made c.1710. Its scrolled arms are covered in contemporary *gros*-and *petit-point*. The cabriole front legs have shaped lappets and unusual octagonal pad feet – both are indications of quality. *S*
* Circular pad feet are more common on 18thC armchairs.

The influence in the design of this walnut armchair, c.1690 (ht 47.5in/120cm), is strongly Continental. The shaped and carved arms give the chair a graceful appearance. The legs are forerunners of the cabriole. *S*
* Flamboyant stretchers are highly characteristic of 17thC chairs, including those from France and Holland.

A Philadelphia Chippendale mahogany easy chair, c.1760-90, with a shaped crest, "S"-shaped wings and carved cabriole legs. The finely sculptured claw-and-ball foot is typically Philadelphian. *CNY*
* The scrolled arm terminating in a horizontal roll was popular in Philadelphia throughout the American Chippendale period (1750-90).

A fine painted and carved maple bannister-back side chair, New England, c.1740-60. The turned stiles have mushroom-form finials with a bevelled and stylized fan-carved crest over split balusters. *SNY*
* This type of chair was common in England 50 years earlier at the turn of the century, but constructed in oak and polished, rather than in maple and painted.

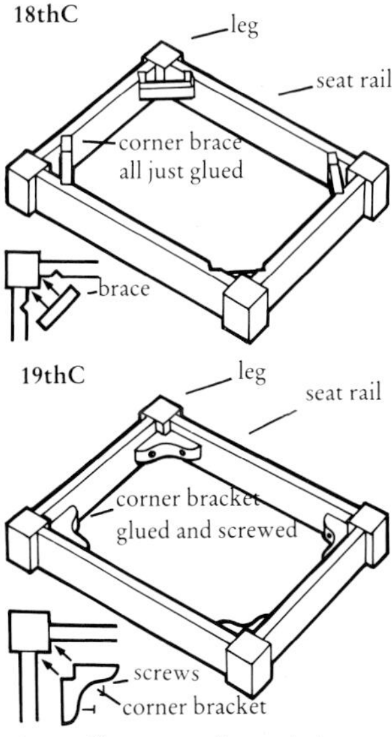

Seat rails are usually made in beech and are tenoned into the legs of the chair. Until c.1840-50 corner braces were added for extra strength (*above, top*). These fitted into slots in the seat rails and were simply glued. After c.1840-50 corner brackets were used (*above, bottom*). These were glued and screwed into the angle of the rails.

Chairs II

18thC CHAIRS

The cabriole leg remained a feature of English and American furniture for much of the 18thC. In the second half of the century, chairs tended to become lighter and simpler and initially were less expensive, to satisfy the demand from a burgeoning middle class. Chippendale-style chairs were in Rococo, Chinese, or Gothick styles. Adam chairs had straight tapered legs, and were lighter in appearance. Hepplewhite, although best-known for his shield-back chairs, also designed ovals, hearts and lyres. Sheraton chairs had rectangular backs, upright rather than curved.

English provincial chairs and chairs made in America show deviations from these classic styles. For example, a basic Chippendale form might be combined with a Queen Anne splat or kidney-shaped seat. In America cabriole legs tended to be more curvaceous than in England. The famous English provincial chair is the Windsor chair, made with cabriole legs after c.1740; the wheel splat appeared c.1790.

A distinctly American type was the Martha Washington or lolling chair – tall, upholstered, with scrolled, open arms. The most famous New York cabinet-maker was Duncan Phyfe, who began working in 1795, reflecting Sheraton's influence initially.

A George II walnut "parcel-gilt" (partially gilt) stool with square-section cabriole legs and "hairy" paw feet (wdth 24½in/62.5cm). The knees are carved with acanthus leaves, a feature commonly seen in the Chippendale period. *C*

* Most stools were made in pairs as part of a suite of drawing room furniture, although now they are usually found singly.

This Queen Anne walnut armchair, c.1710 (ht 41½in/105cm), has all the features of an early 18thC chair:

* vase-shaped splat
* figured walnut veneer to the splat, upright and seat rail
* improved construction, which obviated the need for stretchers
* well-pronounced bowed outline to the uprights
* carved ornament. This often depicts shells and foliage. On some chairs the carving is applied.
* typical rounded cabriole legs. Some sophisticated chairs have square section cabriole legs.
* standard height for 18thC: seat 18-19in (46-48cm) from the floor
* claw and ball foot. Pad and club feet are also common. *S*

ENGLISH CHAIR BACKS

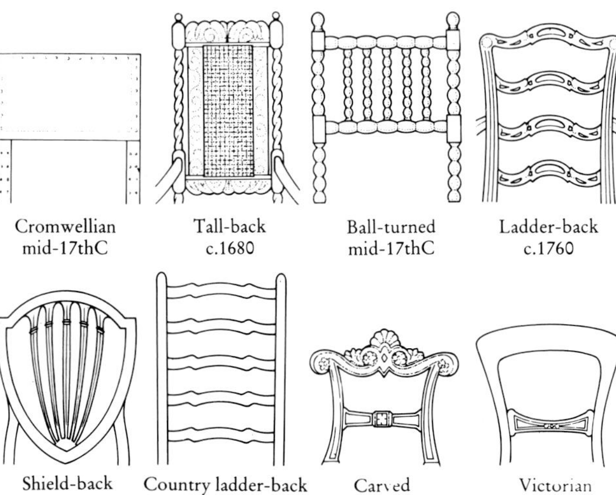

Corner chairs were an English fashion that developed during the first half of the 18thC. They may have been designed as gentlemen's writing chairs. This elegant George II walnut chair, c.1730 (ht 34in/87cm), has a shaped top rail terminating in carved eagles' heads. *S*

* Corner chairs are usually found singly rather than in pairs or sets. Quality varies considerably: good examples like this one are rare. More basic ones are made from oak, and are plain with straight legs and no carving.

A Philadelphia Queen Anne walnut side chair, c.1745-65, which represents the Queen Anne style at a high point of development in America, where Georgian influence had not yet made itself felt. Typical Philadelphia details are: the voluted crest enclosing a shell, the scrolled splat, and the moulding on the outer edge of the uprights. *SNY*

Carved mahogany Gainsborough chairs were very popular in the Chippendale period. This example, c.1770 (ht 39in/99cm), is relatively plain, with outscrolled padded arms and straight chamfered legs joined with pierced stretchers in the "Chinese Chippendale" manner. Others have cabriole legs with carved decoration, often with neat French-style scrolled feet. *S*
* Re-upholstery is common and does not reduce the value, as the original fabric rarely survives in good condition. However, old upholstery, such as needlework, is desirable. A chair may also be re-upholstered in such a way that the upholstery covers the seat rail, which on a genuine chair will exhibit signs of wear. If the rail is covered, the fabric should be lifted away so that the seat rail may be examined.

A classic Chippendale mahogany dining chair, c.1760 (ht 37½in/ 95cm), with a waved toprail edged with foliage above a baluster pierced Gothic-pattern splat. *C*
* Similar chairs were made during the American Chippendale period (1755-90), but with more evidence of Queen Anne details.
* In England this type of chair was reproduced by the Victorians in sets that are now valuable in their own right. These are often of good quality but are characterized by their efforts to crowd all the best Chippendale elements into a single chair.

CHIPPENDALE DESIGNS

Chippendale's *Gentleman and Cabinet Maker's Director* of 1762 was used by most English furniture makers as the basis of their designs. Unless the chair comes with its original receipt or is documented, it can be hard to prove that a particular piece came from Chippendale's own workshops as his work was unsigned. Six popular designs from the *Director* are shown above, including some with Gothic and Chinese motifs. There were hundreds of others, some of which were highly fantastical and were seldom, if ever, made into chairs.

A Louis XV beechwood fauteuil (armchair), from the third quarter of the 18thC, with a moulded voluted frame, upholstered in contemporary tapestry with scenes from Aesop's fables. It may have been gilded and subsequently stripped, for a more informal look. This model has been continuously reproduced. *SNY*

This Neo-classical elbow chair, or carver, of Adam design, c.1795 (ht 32in/82cm), is painted with a classical urn, swags and formal leaves. The light, square back with the emphasis on vertical and horizontal lines is associated with Sheraton. *C*

The shield-shaped back is associated with Hepplewhite and was one of the most popular shapes for chair backs in the late 18thC. This example dates from c.1780 (ht 37in/94cm). *S*

In the Sheraton period rectilinear lines replaced the earlier oval and shield backs. This example is one of a set of six dining chairs from c.1790, with stuff-over (extensively upholstered) seats on spare tapering legs with spade feet. *SNY*
* Spade feet are also found on tables and sideboards of the same period.

Chairs III

The stylish designs of the Regency period have long been popular and prices for good examples are high. In England the Trafalgar chair with sabre legs and a rope-twist back rail was the most popular form. Turned legs were also common: in the early Regency these were slender and reeded; by the late Regency they had become heavier, and were either ring-turned or reeded.

Mahogany and rosewood were the most popular woods of the period.

Upholstery took three forms: stuff-over upholstered seats, drop-in seats, or caned seats with squab (loose, flat) cushions.

The robust fluted legs on this George IV caned rosewood bergère, c.1820 (ht 35½in/85cm), were fashionable between c.1820 and c.1840. The fluted cup of the caster is an indication of quality. *S*

* Chairs with caned seats, backs and sides are usually referred to as bergère chairs. Bergères are found with "spoon backs", as in this example, or with rectangular backs and straight sides.

X frame stools, such as this example, c.1810 (ht 28in/71cm), reflect the Regency interest in ancient Greece and Egypt, and were very popular during the early 19thC. The finely carved rams' heads and hairy cloven feet are typical of the work of Thomas Hope; other Hope stools feature lions' heads. *CNY*

* This type of stool is rare and much sought-after today because of its distinctive design and decorative appeal.

The slender turned and tapering style of leg on these Regency painted elbow chairs, c.1800 (ht 33in/84cm), was first seen during the late 18thC and continued to be used on fashionable furniture until c.1815, when outlines became bolder. *C*

* Painted or japanned furniture was popular throughout the Regency period and varied in quality; many pieces were made in inexpensive woods such as pine and beech and then painted, most commonly in black picked out with gilding.

SETS

Sets come in fours, sixes, eights, or more. A set of six chairs will usually fetch double the price of a set of four, while a set of eight may be three or four times the price of a set of four. A set that includes a pair of elbow chairs is particularly desirable.

The collector should beware of "scrambling", whereby sets are completed by taking some chairs apart and replacing one or two parts of each chair with new members, using the replaced parts to make up an extra chair. Each chair should be examined for discrepancies in the colour of the wood, or signs of artificial distressing (see page 13).

The curved top rail, the sabre legs and the scroll arms supported by the side rails on these Regency chairs, c.1810 (ht 32in/81.5cm), are all typical features of the style of chair referred to as Trafalgar. This style of chair is often found with a caned seat and squab cushion as an alternative to the drop-in upholstered frame of some examples. *C*

* 20thC copies of Trafalgar chairs abound. They are made in inferior wood for the mass market and do not have the signs of wear and age that original examples have developed. The Regency originals are made mostly in mahogany or rosewood. However, *faux* rosewood and *faux* satinwood, which use paint to simulate these expensive woods, are often found on chairs of this period; good painted examples are currently much in demand.

The use of mahogany and the restrained design of this *fauteuil* (open-sided, upholstered armchair often with padded elbows), c.1820 (ht 37in/94cm), is typical of French chairs during this period. The dolphin motif, carved where the arm joins the leg, was used throughout Europe during the early 19thC and is often found on French chairs. *S*

* This piece is stamped "Ratte". In the 18th and 19thC French makers often stamped their products with their name or initials. In England, with the exception of a few prominent firms, this practice is rarely found before the early 1800s.

The pale wood and veneer on the back of this Russian side chair, c.1820 (ht 32½in/82.5cm), and its severe, Classical outline and ebony inlay, was a popular combination on the Continent of Europe during this period, and in Germany was one of the most distinctive features of the Biedermeier style. The quality is variable. *S*

VICTORIAN CHAIRS

Although chairs from the William IV and Victorian periods may lack the style and elegance of earlier chairs, they are often very well made. Prices are still relatively low and are bound to rise sharply over the next few years. The balloon-back chair was the most common type. The best examples, with elegant "French"-style cabrioles, are classics of English design. The Victorians produced many sets of dining chairs in the Chippendale manner. The best examples are keenly sought after by British and American buyers.

These Victorian chairs (ht of tallest 46in/117cm), demonstrate the extensive use of papier mâché in the second half of the 19thC. This form of decoration had previously been confined to small items such as trays. The main ground colour is black, but red, dark green and blue are also found. *S*

* Papier mâché is pulped and compacted paper that is easily chipped and damaged if not treated with care. Some pieces have been extensively restored and items should be examined closely for signs of overpainting and re-gilding. Minor restoration is acceptable, but items that have been heavily restored should be avoided. Prices are still relatively low.

JENNENS & BETTRIDGE

The firm of Jennens & Bettridge, founded in 1816, became one of the most important English producers of papier mâché furniture. Based in Birmingham, the centre of papier mâché production, they acquired an international reputation for high quality. Most of their work is signed.

Replaced leather coverings do not reduce the value if they are in the appropriate style for the period, as in the deep-buttoned upholstery of this William IV early Victorian walnut armchair, c.1835 (ht 37in/94cm). *SNY*

Stretchers are not usually found on Regency chairs, and chairs of this period with stretchers are usually considered to be of Scottish origin, like this mahogany dining chair, c.1820 (ht 33½in/85cm). The legs are characteristic of the late Regency period, being more solid than earlier Regency chair legs. *C*

The taste for Gothic was revived during the first decade of the 19thC and during the 1830s. This pair of chairs, c.1860 (ht 41in/104cm), dates from the Victorian "Gothick" period, when oak was one of the favoured timbers and early oak furniture provided the design influence. There are several features that help differentiate Victorian "Gothick" chairs from their early counterparts:

* The wood on Victorian pieces is inferior, being gingery in colour when polished and lacking in figuring.
* The backs and undersides of early Gothic furniture are roughly hewn; in the Victorian "Gothick" period they are well finished.
* Screws are used instead of pegs in the construction of Victorian "Gothick" pieces. *SNY*

From the early Victorian period there was a return to the cabriole leg. This mahogany side chair, c.1840 (ht 36½in/92.5cm), so-called because when not in use it would be placed along a side wall of the room, shows how the 19thC cabriole leg flows from the front rail, unlike the cabriole legs of the early 18thC which abut the rail. The legs terminate in a French-style foot, a feature of English chairs with cabriole legs and balloon backs. *SNY*

Settees and Sofas

The settle, an elongated form of the wainscot chair, was the earliest form of seat furniture to accommodate two or more people. In England settles were made principally in oak and date back to c.1500. Most extant examples date from the 17th and 18th centuries and are of joined and pegged construction. Settles were popular from c.1700 in America, where pine and walnut were used as alternatives to oak.

The more comfortable chair-back settee evolved from the settle in the first half of the 18th century. Found principally in walnut before c.1735 and in mahogany through the Chippendale period, these were generally made in double or triple chair-back form, and in most cases their design corresponds exactly with that of chairs. The other main 18th-century development from the settle was the fully upholstered, long seat or settee with a carved frame, where the wood was exposed (show-wood).

Sofas are similar in construction and style to settees, but larger and more comfortable. However, in 18th- and 19th-century catalogues the terms are often interchangeable.

The influence of contemporary chair design continued through the Hepplewhite and Sheraton periods, with the emphasis on lightness and elegance. American examples follow the English style but on a simpler, less adventurous scale.

The Regency period saw the introduction of the chaise longue, a fully upholstered chair with an elongated seat and inclined back and arms. Exotic decoration, such as crocodile feet on sofas, was incorporated within Classical forms.

Sofas and settees of the Victorian period, in both England and America, were characterized by ornate carving and bold curvaceous designs with deep buttoned upholstery, often using rich velvets and patterned fabrics. This period also saw the development of the chesterfield, one of the first settees or sofas to be entirely upholstered.

The stylized carving centred on a series of fan-shaped flower-heads on this late 17thC Lancashire oak settle (lgth 74in/188cm) is characteristic of South Lancashire and North Cheshire. *C*
* Settles were made principally in country districts, and remained popular into the 19thC, when there was a revival of interest in their design led by William Morris. They have never been in great demand.

The way in which early 18thC settees reflect the design of contemporary chairs is clear from this George I mahogany settee of double chair back form, c.1720 (lgth 50in/127cm). *C*
* Mahogany was eminently suitable for carving, and its use heralded a period of more elaborate furniture design.

This mahogany settee, c.1770 (lgth 61in/155cm), is typical of Chippendale in its moulded and chamfered straight legs. The stretchers, as with chairs of this period, are plain. The seat rails will be roughly constructed in beech. Some Chippendale settees are more ornately carved and gilded. *SNY*

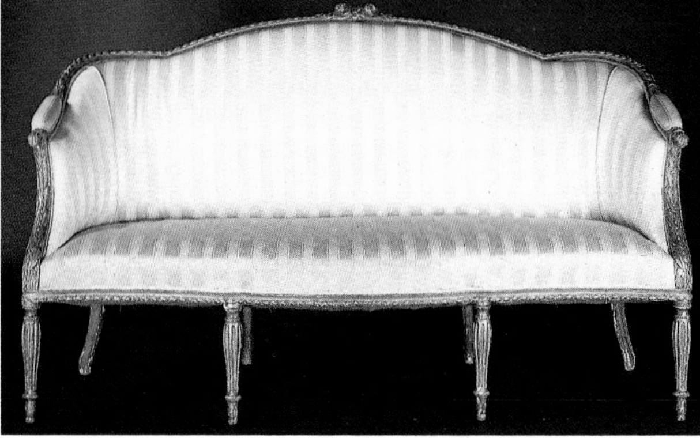

A Hepplewhite-period carved giltwood settee, c.1780 (lgth 73in/185cm), with fluted inverted baluster legs and the typical flowing shape of settee-backs of this period. The show-wood gilt frame, carved with foliage, together with the sweeping curves shows a strong French influence. *C*

During the last two decades of the 18thC the window seat, a backless bench designed to fit a window bay, became one of the most popular items of furniture. Although most window seats had outscrolled arms on both ends and often a taper from back to front, the decorative details varied greatly. This mahogany example, c.1780 (lgth 40in/101.5cm), has a fluted, slightly serpentine front seat rail, typical of other seat furniture by Hepplewhite. *C*

This fine George III yew and elm wood Gothic triple chairback Windsor settee, c.1770 (lgth 62in/160cm), like most of the two-, three- or four-back pieces of the period, was designed to be used *en suite* with a single chair of identical design. The arched top rails and Neo-Gothic splats reflect the revival in Gothic taste which became fashionable between c.1765 and 1800. *C*

* Chair-backed settees, being relatively uncomfortable, are not in as much demand with general collectors as settees with upholstered backs.

The sabre legs and brass inlay of this rosewood chaise-longue or day bed (lgth 76in/183cm) indicate its early 19thC origins: brass inlay, first used under Louis XIV, was revived in England c.1810. *C*

The boat design of this mahogany chaise longue, or day bed (lgth 87in/221cm), was popular in the Regency period. The caned back is also a feature of bergère chairs in this style, which originated in France and became popular in the early 19thC. *C*

A Federal carved mahogany settee, New York, c.1800-10 (lgth 63in/160cm). Decorative features such as the hairy paw feet and the cornucopiae of the central reserve of the crest rail, together with the scrolled arm rests, were popular in America during the first half of the 19thC. After 1820 styles became increasingly heavy. *CNY*

This early Victorian walnut sofa (lgth 75in/190cm) has many features that remained popular throughout the period: the deep buttoned back, boldly carved arm-terminals, sturdy cabriole legs and the use of walnut all identify the piece as unmistakably Victorian. *C*

Dining Furniture I

In the Middle Ages dining tables were to be found only in the dining halls or refectories of large houses, where the whole household, including servants, dined communally. These oak trestle tables were also employed as serving tables.

The trestle table gradually evolved into the refectory table (see below), and this remained the only form of dining table until about the middle of the 17th century, when the gateleg table was introduced for use in the now smaller dining room. At this period most dining rooms would also have a dresser for serving and storage.

The gateleg and the drop leaf table were popular 18th-century forms in both England and America. The first type of dining table to have central legs was introduced in England c.1780 and in America at a slightly later date. By this period the dining room was furnished with a sideboard and a host of convenient accessories, many of which are illustrated over the following 6 pages.

This 17thC Italian walnut trestle table (lgth 106in/269cm) is the earliest type of dining table in England and on the Continent; earliest examples date from the 15thC. Accurate dating is difficult as this type of trestle table was made over such a wide period using the same basic techniques. *C*

* The crude chamfered legs compare unfavourably with other more sophisticated examples.

REFECTORY TABLES

Most refectory and farmhouse tables available today date from the 17th and 18thC. Victorian and early 20thC copies are also common. The term "refectory" dates from the Victorian period. Refectory tables are of joined construction, being held together by pegged tenons, although later examples often use screws that are countersunk and camouflaged by false pegs. Most refectory tables are made of oak, and stand on four legs. Very long tables require two extra legs in the middle. All the legs are joined by stretchers. Farmhouse tables usually have square legs without stretchers. Most have tops made of two or three planks with cleated, or wedge-shaped, ends. It is only the style of the legs that changes significantly, and these therefore provide an essential guide to dating (see page 36).

This James I six-legged oak refectory table (lgth 165in/419cm) stands on cup and cover legs in use between 1560 and 1680, although they are not often seen after 1640. The tenoned and pegged method of construction can clearly be seen where the stretchers join the block feet. *C*

* The scrolled angles at the top of the legs first appeared on this type of table from the late 16thC, and add to its desirability.

FAKE REFECTORY TABLES

Floor boards and other old timber are often used to make up a new table top or to replace damaged parts. Replacement planks can be difficult for the inexperienced eye to detect, but certain signs may expose them:

* Circular saw marks indicate that the timber has been sawn since the early 20thC; hand saws leave straight marks.
* Refectory table tops sit on the base and are rarely fixed. If the top is lifted there should be marks where the heavy top has rested on the blocks of the legs and the frieze bearers.
* Pegs should be hand-made and stand slightly proud.

An early 17thC refectory or joined table (lgth 78in/198cm) with fluted baluster legs and Ionic capitals – features popular between 1560 and 1640. The use of pegs to hold the top together is characteristic of early refectory tables. *C*

* Most 17th and 18thC examples were made with stretchers down both sides. To make the table more comfortable to sit at, these were sometimes converted later to a single stretcher running down the middle, which was tenoned into the two short stretchers.
* Some examples can be found with an extending draw-leaf action, which pulls out from beneath the main top.

The width (38in/97cm) of this James I-style oak drawer-leaf table, c.1900, gives it away as a Victorian reproduction. Although it has the bulbous cup and cover legs typical of the early 17thC, Jacobean examples are rarely more than 34in/86cm wide. *S*

* Other indications that this is a later copy are the machine-made pegs and the pale colour of the straight-grained oak, which has been artificially stained.

GATELEG TABLES
English gateleg tables are nearly always oval in shape (Dutch versions are more usually square or rectangular) and were made in all sizes – from small tables with flaps supported by single "gates" to very large examples needing two gates to support each flap. Although early examples date from the middle of the 17thC, most gatelegs found today are from the late 17th and 18thC. The changing style of leg constitutes the best guide to dating (see page 36).

Most English gatelegs are made from oak. Occasionally walnut and other more unusual timbers, such as yew wood and fruitwood, were used. Victorian reproductions were made in Virginia walnut, which will have darkened over the years and despite polishing will often appear dull. Gatelegs were also popular in America, where they were made in oak, pine, walnut and maple.

Small gateleg tables, such as this William and Mary oval example, c.1690 (wdth 63in/160cm), can be awkward to sit at, especially if the "bed" or central section is narrow and incorporates a drawer or deep frieze. Consequently, many small gatelegs are used as centre tables. The baluster legs are turned with vase-shaped motifs, which enhance the table's value. However, the stretchers are square, with a moulded top, and are not as desirable as turned stretchers. *S.*
* Highest prices are usually paid for larger versions. These have become scarce as many large gatelegs had their tops reduced in the early 20thC, when small gatelegs were fashionable.

This William and Mary walnut gateleg table (wdth 62in/157cm), made in Massachusetts, c.1710, is unusual in having turned stretchers as well as turned legs; the stretchers on most examples are plain and simply moulded. The drawers on each side retain the original engraved handles. *PC*
* Legs on gatelegs were simple until the introduction of lathe turning, c.1640-60, made possible new forms, such as twist-turned, reel and bobbin legs, which quickly became popular. Victorian reproductions have over-ornate legs, and have a regularity that suggests they have been cut and turned by machine.

DRESSERS
Dressers were used as serving tables and for storage, and were made in various forms throughout Britain. They are found with and without racks for providing extra storage and display space. Oak was the timber most commonly used, although examples exist in yew wood and fruitwood. In France dressers were made in the provinces, usually in chestnut. The earliest dressers available today date from the mid-17thC, although the vast majority are from the late 17th and 18thC. Early dressers take the form of cupboard dressers and those raised on turned legs. From c.1730 a popular style of dresser incorporated the cabriole leg and a shaped apron below the three frieze drawers. The racks occasionally incorporate tall shallow side cupboards. Dressers became unfashionable by the early 19thC and are rarely found after this date, except for the obvious reproductions of the late 19th and 20thC.

The applied geometric mouldings, the drop handles and shaped escutcheons with cast decoration on this oak dresser, c.1680 (lgth 72in/184cm), are typical features of the late 17thC. *C*
* Most late 17thC dressers have three drawers; examples with two have almost certainly been converted. The linings of original drawers should have crude dovetailing or hand-made nails.
* Owing to changes in fashion and general wear, it is rare to find pieces of this period retaining their original handles.

Pot-board dressers such as this oak example, c.1750 (ht 82in/208cm), often have no back and are not as practical as cupboard dressers; they are therefore not as sought-after. However, the spice drawers and the open fretwork below the frieze drawers on this example are not often found and are good features that will bring the value up again. *S*

Cupboard dressers such as this oak example, c.1730 (ht 84in/213cm), were produced over a long period: they were still being made in the early 19thC. *S*
* Replacement baseboards and backboards are common, but do not detract from the value nearly as much as replacement doors, drawers or top boards.
* Oak cupboard dressers made in the 18thC tend to be paler than 17thC examples.

Dining Furniture II

SERVING TABLES

Side tables, used as serving tables, became fashionable from c.1730 and remained popular until the Regency period. Early examples, frequently with marble tops, were of imposing proportions and heavily carved. Some were gilded. Thomas Chippendale developed a lighter style which continued to the end of the 18thC. While the emphasis of the late 18thC was on restrained elegance, a grander style returned during the Regency period, exemplified by the designs of Thomas Hope and George Smith.

DROP-LEAF TABLES

In the 18thC the gateleg table was superseded by the more refined drop-leaf dining table. Most of these were constructed in either Virginia walnut or mahogany. They are more comfortable to sit at than gatelegs, as they have fewer legs and no stretchers; also, the overhang of the table is greater.

During the Chippendale period the D-ended dining table was introduced. This consists of two D-shaped ends which fit into a rectangular drop-leaf table. They are supported on square chamfered legs, usually 12, which can make the table awkward to sit at. This problem was resolved c.1780 with the introduction of the pedestal dining table comprising two, three or four pedestals with leaves that clipped in between.

A smaller variation of this table was the "breakfast table" on a single pedestal. Most breakfast tables are rectangular with rounded corners but they were also made in round and oval shapes. The best examples incorporate crossbanded decoration.

The Victorians introduced dining tables that extended by means of a cranking action and a mechanism of interlocking bearers that did away with the need for excessive numbers of legs. Most have only four legs.

The carved angle brackets on this fine late George II mahogany serving table, c.1755 (lgth 65in/165cm), are features frequently used on quality pieces during the Chippendale period. The frieze is carved with low-relief Gothic arches which were popular on tables from the mid-18thC. *S*

* Serving tables were a few inches taller than other side tables and generally had no drawers. Robert Adam introduced the fashion for *en suite* pedestal tables in c.1775; these were sometimes surmounted by urns to provide space for cutlery, china and bottles.

This American version of a drop-leaf table, made in the Goddard Townsend workshops, Newport, Rhode Island, c.1765 (wdth 54in/137cm), has claw-and-ball feet as opposed to the more common pad feet. These tables are characterized by the almost invariably high quality of the timber, which is usually a rich dark colour. *CNY*

* The most common type of repair is to the ear-pieces (which are joined to the top of the leg). These are sometimes replaced: the quality of the timber and the carving should reveal this.

This mid-18thC mahogany side or serving table (lgth 59in/150cm) has the fine carving characteristic of many high-quality Irish pieces of this period. The hairy paw feet are typical of the period. They first appeared on tables during the early 18thC. *CSc*

* Other examples of this type of table have gilding and marble tops.

The timber on this mid-18thC Virginia walnut oval drop-leaf table (wdth 54in/137cm) has faded to a warm golden colour that indicates the table is authentic. The legs are carved with beads and acanthus leaves and terminate in claw-and-ball feet – features popular on this type of table from the early 18thC. *CNY*

* As a general rule, carving to the legs will add to the value, as do the carved feet in this example.

The short "gun-barrel" supports on this Sheraton-period mahogany dining table, c.1790 (lgth 140in/360cm), allow an elegant and generous splay to the reeded legs. The feet incorporate the plain square-capped casters favoured during the late 18thC. *CNY*

* This type of table can also be found supported by pedestals with only three legs as opposed to the more usual four.
* Pedestal dining tables were almost always made in mahogany.

D-ended dining tables, such as this example from the Chippendale era (lgth 114in/290cm), were made from c.1760 until the beginning of the Regency period. Most were made in mahogany and incorporated a central drop-leaf section and square chamfered legs. *S*

The elegant lines and restrained decoration on this mahogany breakfast table, c.1795 (dia. 46in/116cm), are typical of Sheraton-period furniture. The edge, crossbanded in satinwood, indicates high quality. *C*

* Late 18thC round and oval breakfast tables are less common and more sought after than rectangular examples. Consequently, many plain rectangular-topped tables have been enhanced by having their tops reshaped. Tell-tale signs include: an irregular oval outline; little signs of wear on the "new" edges of the top; and bearers that have been reduced to accommodate the smaller top.

The shallow apron below the table top on this Regency calamander wood breakfast table (lgth 57in/144cm) was introduced to this type of table at the beginning of the 19thC and gives it a sturdier appearance. This example dates from c.1805. *S*

* The pedestal shown here is typical of the Regency period, when sabre legs were fixed to the sides of the column, rather than appearing to flow from the pedestal, as in earlier examples.
* Other Regency features include the brass lion's paw casters and the use of brass inlay on the edges of the top.
* Calamander, a very hard, light brown wood with black stripes, was used in Regency furniture principally for veneers and bandings.

The gadrooned decoration on the base and the boldly carved paw feet of this brass-inlaid rosewood breakfast table (lgth 60in/152cm) are characteristic Regency features. *C*

* The platform base was a feature of pedestal tables toward the end of the Regency period.

This early Victorian mahogany two-pedestal dining table, c.1840 (lgth 85in/215cm), has heavier stems and legs than the 18thC pedestal tables, although the design is essentially the same. *S*

* Many Victorian dining tables of this type divide to form two breakfast tables.
* The spare leaves of tables are often later replacements from other tables, and the figuring and the thickness of each leaf should be carefully compared to check that they correspond with each other and with the table itself. However, spare leaves kept in storage are often not as faded as the main table top, which is in regular use. A good restorer should be able to balance the colours.

The central legs on this Victorian D-ended extending dining table, c.1860 (lgth 120in/305cm), are recessed out of the way of the sitter. *CM*

* These Victorian tables are distinguished from 18thC examples by their interlocking bearers and winding mechanism, which enables the table to be extended without the need for extra legs – the leaves sit on the extended bearers.
* The robust turned and reeded legs are also characteristic of Victorian dining tables.

Dining Furniture III

SIDEBOARDS

The sideboard was developed by cabinet makers in the last quarter of the 18thC. It could be serpentine, bow- or straight-fronted. Most stand on six legs – two at the back and four at the front. A central drawer for cutlery is flanked by deeper drawers or cupboards, one of which is usually lead-lined and sectioned to hold wine bottles. This style was superseded during the Regency period by the pedestal sideboard, in which the cupboard space either side of the central drawer was extended to the ground. This development was taken a step further during the Victorian period when the open space beneath the central drawer was enclosed to provide further storage space. Edwardian and later reproductions are common today and many were made with cheaper veneers, such as birch, in imitation of the satinwood used in the original late 18th and early 19thC examples. However, some Edwardian copies made by firms such as Edwards & Roberts incorporate fine-quality inlaid marquetry.

The square tapering legs of this mahogany sideboard, c.1800 (wdth 50in/127cm), were a feature of late 18thC sideboards. They are considered more desirable than ring-turned legs, which were used on sideboards during the first 20 years of the 19thC. *C*

* Many of these later sideboards have had their original legs replaced by square legs. To detect whether a substitution has taken place, the legs should be examined along their length and the drawers should be removed so that the backs of the legs can be inspected. If the leg is original it will extend to the top of the sideboard and be constructed from one piece of wood. In making the alteration it will have been necessary to cut off the turned section at the base of the drawer. Careful inspection will reveal the join (which may be partially covered by inlay), and there will inevitably be a slight difference in colour between the two sections.

This mahogany sideboard, c.1780 (wdth 74in/189cm), has a serpentine-shaped front. The carved fan spandrels and the sunflower paterae above the legs indicate that the piece was made after c.1775.
* This type of sideboard, developed from the serving table, was first made c.1775 and continued to be produced for about 40 years. The degree of elegance varied, but the serpentine form is usually considered the most desirable. *CNY*

Serpentine sideboards with a recessed section under the central drawer, square ends and concave side cupboards were popular in New England toward the end of the 18thC. The inner legs set diagonally on this Federal example, c.1780 (wdth 74in/189cm), are also characteristic of the period. *CNY*
* The legs are inlaid with bell flowers, tulip heads and cuffs, which help identify this as American and post-1780, when high-quality sideboards were often inlaid with exotic woods.

The fluted legs terminating in bold carved lion's paws on this early 19thC sideboard, c.1820 (lgth 75in/190cm), help to identify it as late Regency. The capitals surmounting the legs are also typical of the imposing designs favoured in this period. *S*

LEGS AND FEET

Cup and cover 1560-1680 | Doric column 1570-1800 | Ringed baluster 1580-1740

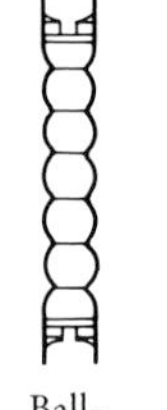

Parallel baluster 1620-1740 | Ball-turned 1650-1700 | Barley-twist 1660-1710

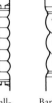

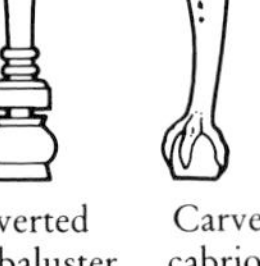

Slender baluster 1660-1800 | Inverted cup baluster 1675-1700 | Carved cabriole 1700-50

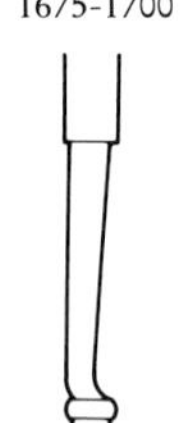
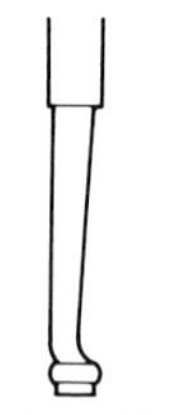
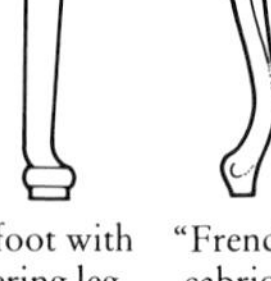

Cabriole leg 1700-1800 | Pad foot with tapering leg 1720-1800 | "French" cabriole 1750-1800

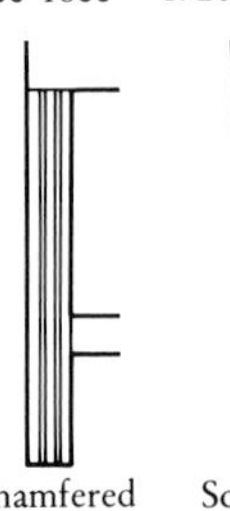
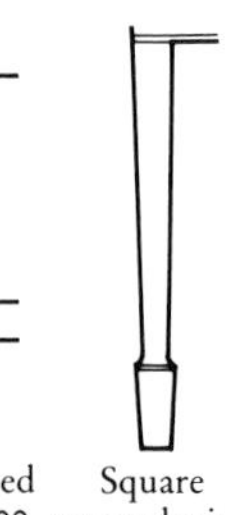
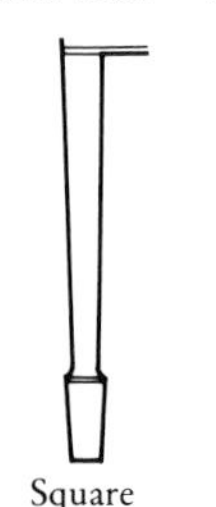

Chamfered 1750-1800 | Square tapered with spade foot 1750-1800 | Slender reeded 1780-1810

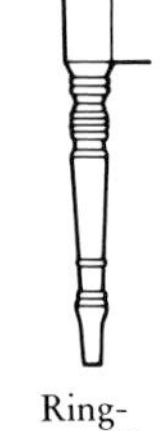
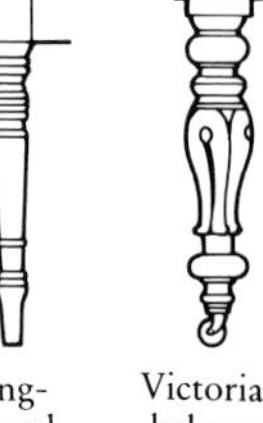

Sabre leg 1812-30 | Ring-turned 1812-30 | Victorian baluster 1835-80

MISCELLANEOUS

During the 18thC a number of smaller items were designed for use in the dining room.

Cellarets, lined with lead, were used in the dining room to store bottles of wine that were intended for immediate consumption. Most were made between c.1760 and 1830. This Chippendale-period example (28in/72.5cm), is typical in:

* its use of mahogany
* hexagonal shape
* wide brass banding with carrying handles.

Many cellarets of the period also have separate stands with moulded and chamfered square legs. *SNY*

Most cellarets made in the Sheraton period were veneered and decorated with inlay, as in this example, c.1790 (ht 28in/73cm). Brass banding was used less often than in the earlier Chippendale period. The West Indian satinwood veneer is well figured – an indication of the high quality of this piece.

* Less expensive 18thC cellarets were veneered in figured mahogany.

Urns which incorporated spouts in the base, as in this mahogany Georgian pair, c.1775 (25in/65cm), were used to serve iced water or to hold water for rinsing cutlery in the dining room. Other urns were made as knife boxes and had lift-up tops and compartmentalized interiors. *S*

* Urns were usually placed on top of matching sideboard pedestals, which were introduced by Robert Adam c.1775 to give storage space for cutlery, plates and bottles of wine.
* Georgian urns are usually extremely decorative and therefore much sought after. Pairs command a premium.
* Knife boxes were made in rectangular form, with a hinged sloping lid, silver escutcheons and small ring handles. Many of these were converted to stationery boxes in the 19th and early 20thC. Pairs are pricey; however, single boxes are inexpensive and similar, if not identical pairs, can sometimes be made up.

Most wine coolers were made between c.1760 and c.1830. This Regency example, c.1815 (dia. 29in/73.5cm), has the oval shape that superseded hexagonal and octagonal forms and was popular in the late 18thC and first half of the 19thC. The ebonized paw feet and lion's head handles are typical Regency features. *C*

* Wine coolers differ from cellarets in that they rarely have lids.
* Most wine coolers have a lead lining which enables them to be filled with crushed ice to chill the wine. A tap or plug can often be found in the base which allowed the melted ice to be drained.

This wine cooler in the manner of Gillows, c.1825 (ht 24in/61cm), is sarcophagus-shaped, a style that predominated in the late Regency period. The lion's paw feet and the architectural base also identify this as Regency.

* Sarcophagus-shaped cellarets are only now beginning to be as desirable as their hexagonal and oval counterparts. *C*
* Very few cellarets or wine coolers have been faked or reproduced. However, legs and stands have been replaced on some examples. On genuine pieces the stand will be marked where the cooler has rested on it.
* Lead linings have often been replaced. Provided that the work has been done skilfully, a replaced lining should not detract from a cooler's value.

The dumb waiter dates from the mid-18thC and continued to be produced until the Regency period. It was an English invention, consisting of two or three revolving tiers on a stand which was placed at the corner of a dining table and used to hold sauce boats, condiments and other dining accessories when servants were not present. This Chippendale-period example, c.1750 (45in/114cm), is typically made from mahogany. The tripod base reflects the style of pedestal tables of the period. *S*

Plate buckets, such as this Georgian example, c.1760 (dia. 14in/37cm), were made from c.1750 and were used for carrying and distributing dining plates. They are distinguished from other types of bucket by the slots in the body, which allow plates to be easily removed. *C*

Tables I

The improvement of joinery techniques during the 15th century made possible the development of "table boards" with permanent sub-frames. Prior to that "tables" had consisted of boards placed on trestles.

The standing low cupboard, which evolved from the coffer, was raised on extended legs known as stiles and was the first joiner-made piece of furniture to act as a table. It was used for serving food and also afforded good storage space.

Gradually, the cupboard space below the table top was reduced to a shallow frieze, with or without a drawer. In England after the Restoration small oak and walnut tables were made in large numbers. From this time on there was a greater emphasis on the decorative aspects of the table. The 18th century saw the introduction of many tables that had a specific purpose rather than being for general use – for example, card tables, library tables, and so on.

During the 17th and 18th centuries American table design was very closely influenced by English designs, but with localized characteristics. These regional traits became less pronounced toward the end of the 18th century. Many American tables of the early 19th century show the influence of French Empire furniture.

A walnut side table, c.1685 (ht 30in/76cm), oyster-veneered in kingwood and olivewood, inset with marquetry panels in various woods, including harewood, and ivory. It stands on barley-twist legs with the characteristic flat, shaped stretchers of the William and Mary period. *S*

* The inclusion of ivory in marquetry decoration is invariably an indication of quality.

* It is worth checking that the legs and the stretchers of these tables show the same signs of age and wear as the top. In the past some chests of drawers had their top sections cut off and were converted to side tables. It is most unlikely that this practice would occur today, owing to the high value of chests.

SIDE TABLES

These are tables intended to stand against the walls of a room. The backs are not meant to be visible and are therefore left relatively unfinished and undecorated, with roughly sawn backboards, usually in pine or oak. Side tables have been made virtually throughout the whole history of furniture-making and examples exist in nearly every style and wood.

Console tables, a term first used c.1730 in England, are a form of side table based on Continental designs.

The fine proportions and pierced shaped frieze of this William and Mary oak side table, c.1690 (ht 26½in/67cm; wdth 30in/76cm), make it especially desirable. It has typical brass drop handles and ball-turned legs. *S*

* The small bun feet appear on many oak tables of this period.

This type of side table, c.1715/20 (ht 28in/71cm; wdth 33in/84cm), more commonly known by its American name, lowboy, was popular in various forms throughout the first half of the 18thC for both writing and dressing. Country versions were made in oak, but this elegant example is of walnut, with a quartered top and feathered stringing. The corners of the moulded edge have subtle re-entrant corners (sometimes referred to as "baby's bottom" corners!) The tapered legs have lappets carved at the top and terminate in pad feet. *S*

* This type of leg is also found on other furniture such as pad foot drop-leaf tables and card tables.

This Philadelphia Chippendale dressing table, or lowboy, has the large and ornate handles that are commonly found on American furniture of the 18thC. The central drawer is carved with an intaglio shell and acanthus scrolls, c.1770-75 (ht 31in/79cm; wdth 33in/84cm). Tables such as these were often accompanied by matching highboys. *S*

* The carving of the drawer front is a feature not found in English cabinet work.

* Although the lowboy acted as a base for the high chest, it was also made as a separate piece of furniture in its own right and remained fashionable throughout the 18thC in America. It was originally intended for the bedroom as a dressing table.

A Swedish Empire parcel-gilt console, or pier, table with rectangular porphyry top and beaded imbricated frieze. The base is painted (wdth 30in/76cm). The table has the dolphin motif that was popular with furniture makers throughout Europe during the early 19thC. Such a table would originally have been accompanied by a matching pier glass. *C*

* Painted decoration was much used in Swedish furniture, with cream and green being the most commonly employed colours.

* Console and pier tables were made throughout Europe in the 18th and 19thC, often with marble tops and ornate gilt bases. They were not popular in America until the early 19thC, when Parisian Empire designs were followed by many New York cabinet makers.

CARD TABLES

The earliest type of table specifically designed for card-playing was introduced at the end of the 17thC. These early tables are veneered with walnut and usually have half-round folding tops with baluster-turned tapering legs united by flat stretchers. One or both of the back legs swing out to support the top. Early in the 18thC turned legs gave way to cabriole legs and the stretchers were abolished. Except for the pedestal versions made during the Regency and Victorian periods, the basic design of the card table has remained the same ever since. The interior surfaces are lined with baize. Similar tables with polished inner surfaces were used as tea tables.

This American Chippendale mahogany card or gaming table, c.1770, has five legs, one of which swings to support the top – a typical feature of card and tea tables made in New York. The pronounced serpentine form is also characteristic (ht 28in/71cm). *CNY*

* Other examples may be found with carving to the knees and to the moulded edge of the frieze.

This Philadelphia mahogany card table, c.1765-85 (ht 28in/71cm), is typical of late 18thC American furniture in its blending of styles adopted from England with contemporary American features: the blind fret carving of the frieze rails, and the pierced brackets are in the so-called "Chinese Chippendale" style that originated in England, but the ribbon carving to the edge of the top, and the beading to the moulded chamfered legs, are peculiarly American features. *CNY*

A classic Queen Anne walnut card table, c.1710 (ht 29in/74cm; wdth 34in/86cm), with a well-figured lobed burr-walnut top framed by herringbone lines. It has a baize-lined interior with counter-wells and candle-stands – regular features from the early 18thC. The knees of the cabriole legs are carved with a shell, a motif popular during the early 18thC. *S*

* The tops of most card tables are supported by the gateleg action of one or both of the back legs (see page 33). However, this table has the very desirable concertina action: both back legs pull out on a hinged mechanism so that when the top is unfolded all four legs stand neatly at the corners of the table.

By the last quarter of the 18thC, card tables, like other furniture, were often made and veneered in satinwood. The half-round, or demi-lune, shape had by now become popular. Inlaid legs with shaped paterae, or disks, replaced the carved legs of earlier examples – a development shown in this fine George III painted West Indian satinwood demi-lune card table, c.1785 (wdth 36in/91cm). The edges of the legs are strung with ebony to give a precise appearance, and neatly finished by spade feet. *S*

* Other card tables of the period were made in a "D" shape, which is fuller than the demi-lune style and has straighter edges.

This oak joined folding or "Credence" table, c.1640, is not strictly speaking a card table but it illustrates the first attempts to make a table that could easily be enlarged when required and took up little room when not in use (ht 31½in/80cm). The folding top is supported on a gateleg underframe; the frieze is carved with trellis work, concealing a drawer. *S*

* The term "Credence" is a misnomer which came about in the 19thC when these tables were used in English churches for preparing the sacrament. The word credence is also thought to refer to the buffet, cupboard or sideboard on which meat was tasted by the servants before being offered to guests.

Card tables on central pedestals were made and survive in quantity. The top of the table swivels at right angles to the frieze which supports it, and reveals a small recess that may have held counters or cards. This George IV rosewood card table, c.1825 (ht 28in/70cm), stands on a platform base. The carving to the feet is fairly basic. *C*

* In the Regency period, pedestal support card tables veneered in rosewood and inlaid with cut brass were particularly popular. Pedestal card tables on a platform base, like that exemplified above, were introduced c.1820. These are frequently supported on lion's paw feet, which are sometimes gilded.

* During the Victorian period pedestal card tables were the most popular type. They were most commonly veneered in walnut, although examples are also found in mahogany. The pedestals were always elaborately carved.

Tables II

TRIPOD AND TEA TABLES

The forerunners of the tripod table were the small, round-topped tables designed to support a lantern or candlesticks – a type popular in England during the second half of the 17thC. The tripod table was introduced in the 1730s and made in varying sizes, usually with a round top, although square and oval examples exist. Except in the smallest tripods, the tops are made so that they can tilt to a vertical position and fit neatly into the corner of a room. The heyday of the tripod table was the Chippendale period, when they were most often made in mahogany, with carved decoration. Tripods were largely an English phenomenon and were far less popular on the Continent. Small circular tables were of course made, but usually with different forms of support. In America the tripod table attained wide popularity, especially the type with a pie-crust top. In England in the mid-18thC small tripod tables were made as stands for silver tea kettles and their heaters; but they were undoubtedly used in the drawing room next to armchairs for other purposes, as they still are today.

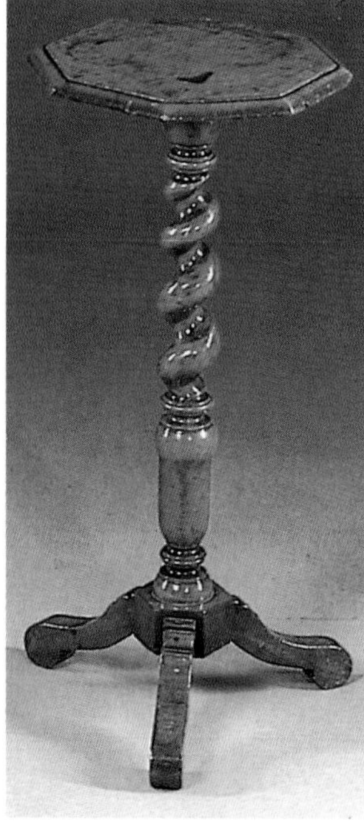

Most candle-stands of the late 17thC are in oak, walnut or gilt. Unusually, this William and Mary tripod candle-stand, c.1690 (ht 30in/76cm), is in yew wood, with an octagonal top and barley-twist support. It shows a distinct Dutch influence and may well have been made by one of the many immigrant Dutch craftsmen who were working in England during the late 17thC. *S*

An early 18thC oak tripod table, c.1700, the circular 3-boarded top on a "bird-cage" support (ht 28½in/67cm). The bird-cage is fixed to the underside of the tabletop and the whole mechanism slots into the top of the pedestal. The top can rotate or be held in place by means of a peg through the stem. *S*

* The legs of tripod tables are attached to the base of the pedestal by means of a dovetailed tenon. "Silhouette" legs, simply shaped from flat-sided boards, are sometimes found on provincial tripod tables.

Most gateleg tables were large enough to dine at. This William and Mary walnut gateleg table, made in Massachusetts, c.1710-30 (ht 28in/70cm), is a small version, which would have been used as an occasional table in the country home. It is of unusually fine quality: most gateleg tables have plain, simply moulded stretchers. *CNY*

* Walnut gatelegs were more common in America than in England.

A large mid-18thC mahogany tripod table with a plain top and carved baluster stem (ht 27in/70cm). Compared with the earlier oak tripod, left, the legs are more rounded and curvaceous. *S*

* Uncarved tripod tables are more common than carved ones.
* Country examples in oak continued to be made through the 18thC.

A small late George II Cuban mahogany tripod table with a dished, or hollowed-out, pie-crust top, c.1755 (ht 23in/58cm). The tops of these smaller tripod tables were not designed to tilt although the finest ones can sometimes be unscrewed. *S*

DISHED TOPS

Dished tops, with plain or pie-crust edges (see above) have often been "dished", or hollowed-out, from a plain top at a later date to make the table more desirable. It is generally quite easy to tell whether this has been done. A plain top will have bearers underneath that are attached by screws. As these tops are relatively shallow the screws will be just below the top surface of the table top. When the top is "dished" out, the screw-holes will appear and need to be plugged. It is virtually impossible, even for the most skilled restorer, to disguise these holes against close inspection.

The lighter, elegant feel of late 18thC English furniture is exemplified by this Sheraton-period small tripod table in satinwood, c.1790 (ht 29in/73cm). *S*

* Tripod tables of this period were usually made in veneered mahogany or satinwood but other exotic woods such as coromandel were also used.

The traditional tripod shape gradually diminished in popularity throughout the 19thC and by mid-century had virtually ceased to be produced. It was replaced by other forms of circular occasional table, such as this early Victorian black and gilt japanned papier mâché pedestal table (ht 28in/70cm). The top tilts to enable display of the painted top, copied from a well-known painting of the period. The table is stamped JENNENS & BETTRIDGE, who are probably the best-known makers of papier mâché in 19thC England. *C*

A Dutch late 18thC satinwood and lacquer tripod table, c.1800 (ht 27in/69cm). The combined use of satinwood with inset lacquered panels is characteristic of late 18thC Dutch furniture, although it is usually associated with cabinets, cupboards and escritoires. The decoration is invariably of Oriental design. *S*

* This type of elegant occasional table was also made in France, Holland, Scandinavia and Russia. There are many examples with marble tops on ormolu (gilded cast metal) legs. In France such tables were also made incorporating porcelain plaques from Sèvres and the Paris porcelain factories. These designs appear not to have been made in number in England and America.

Toward the mid-18thC the many tea gardens in and around London came to be regarded as vulgar and disreputable and it became customary for fashionable people to invite their friends to drink tea in each other's homes. It was at this time that cabinet makers turned their attention to designing suitably ornamental tables for the occasion. This mahogany tea or china table, c.1755 (ht 29in/73.5cm), with its profusion of open fretwork, is a particularly fine example. These tables are also referred to as "silver" tables. *S*

* American galleried-top tables are plainer, without the delicate open fretwork: the gallery is solid and wavy. They often stand on cabriole legs with claw and ball feet.

Teapoys were essentially 19thC items. The top of this early 19thC burr maple and ebony teapoy (wdth 16in/44.5cm) opens to reveal two tea caddies and a cut-glass blending bowl. *C*

* Teapoys were made in a wide range of woods as well as papier mâché. Quality varied enormously.

* Ebony or ebonized mouldings and inlays were used to a great extent on all types of furniture during the early 19thC.

A mid-19thC Roman black marble and micro-mosaic table (wdth 22in/56cm), inlaid with doves and vistas of the Colisseum, the temple of Vesta and other well-known buildings of Ancient Rome. It stands on an ormolu base. *C*

* This type of table would have been made in very large numbers, perhaps intended to seduce tourists.

A Chippendale-period mahogany urn table, c.1760-65 (wdth 12in/35cm), with a square tray top and cabriole legs with foliate carving terminating in pad feet. *C*

* The slide, which pulls out to accommodate a teabowl and saucer, was a usual feature of 18thC urn tables. After 1800 they seem to have gone out of fashion.

* These tables are particularly sought after today and are used as occasional tables, perhaps to stand next to a wing chair.

A late 18thC urn or kettle stand, c.1780 (wdth 14½in/36cm), with a galleried serpentine top, the frieze with a slide. The tapering legs are edged with boxwood stringing. *C*

* Urn tables were made singly rather than in pairs.

Italian subjects became popular during the second half of the 19thC as a result of people going on the "Grand Tour". The top of this mid-Victorian black, gilt and mother-of-pearl japanned papier mâché pedestal teapoy is painted with an Italianate scene entitled "Isola Bella, Lago Maggiore", c.1870 (ht 30½in/77.5cm). *C*

* Pedestal teapoys are not in great demand, being fairly impracticable. Some are adapted for use as jardinières or sewing boxes.

Tables III

PEMBROKE AND SOFA TABLES
Pembroke tables are small occasional tables, usually veneered, and made in a variety of woods, with a shallow drawer or drawers beneath the top, and round, oval or square hinged flaps on each side. The flaps are supported on hinged wooden brackets and usually have four square or turned tapering legs. According to Sheraton they derive their name from the Countess of Pembroke (1737-1831), who was the first to order such an item.

The sofa table was developed from the pembroke table toward the end of the 18thC. It is longer and usually narrower than the pembroke, and has flaps at each end. The best examples were made during the last quarter of the 18thC and in the Regency period, although production continued on a smaller scale until the mid-19thC. After this, most were copies or interpretations of the styles of an earlier period.

In America the pembroke table was more popular than the sofa table. Many date from the American Chippendale period; the commonest type has a rectangular or serpentine-shaped top with square chamfered legs and shaped flat cross-stretchers, frequently enchanced by pierced decoration.

Sofa tables from the Sheraton period are the most sought after, especially those that are not deeper than 24in (61cm). This pale mahogany example, c.1795 (wdth 58in/174.5cm open; dpth 24in/61cm), is of particularly fine quality, with crossbanding and inlaid satinwood panels. Its appealing simplicity is enhanced by the graceful sweep of the legs, and the high curved stretcher. *C*

* Other good-quality sofa tables are found in rosewood and mahogany, as well as a variety of exotic woods, with oak- or mahogany-lined drawers. Rosewood veneer with brass inlay was used from c.1800.
* The end-support with a high stretcher is more sought after than a low-positioned stretcher or a central pedestal. Later tables often have a lower, sometimes rather heavy stretcher to stabilize the table; this can interrupt its elegant lines.

This George III mahogany oval pembroke table on brass casters, c.1790 (wdth 2ft 6in/76cm), has many of the most desirable features:
* oval top (preferable to square)
* broad satinwood banded top and crossbanded frieze drawer (marquetry and inlay are also desirable)
* tapered square legs with stringing, better than the heavily turned and reeded legs common on later tables
* bowed drawer front following the shape of the top, as opposed to a flat-fronted drawer.

The piece also has many typical features:
* one real drawer, and one dummy drawer at the other end
* flaps supported by hinged wooden brackets
* made in mahogany (satinwood is less usual). *SS*

The end-supports on a platform base, and the carved lion's paw feet, of this figured rosewood sofa table, c.1820-25, are typical of the late Regency. Although not as sought-after as the earlier Sheraton type, this table (ht 28½in/72.5cm) has its value enhanced by the original carved rosewood handles, which were fashionable during the early 19thC, but were often subsequently replaced by brass handles in a similar style. *C*

"IMPROVEMENTS"
The less elegant sofa tables of the 1820s and 30s are sometimes "improved" and made to look earlier by using the end-supports of cheval mirrors as more desirable replacement legs. Any spare screw holes, or unaccountable patches where the original legs might have been, should be viewed with suspicion.

This satinwood oval pembroke table is in the Sheraton style (wdth 36in/91.5cm open), but is identifiable as Edwardian by:
* the sentimental nature of the painted medallions
* machine-made screws
* lock stamped with the lockmaker's company name – 18thC locks are unmarked
* thinner veneers than the 18thC hand-cut veneers. *RD*

The scalloped, or "butterfly wing", leaves of this Federal mahogany inlaid pembroke table (ht 27½in/70cm) are reminiscent of the Chippendale style, but the slender tapering legs and delicate proportions indicate a later period – c.1780-1800. *CNY*

This figured mahogany sofa table is characteristic of its period, c.1820/5, in that it stands on a pedestal base (lgth with flaps raised 60in/152cm). Typically, the frieze contains two real and two false drawers. *CNY*

REPAIRS
Damaged table tops are sometimes replaced. Observe the direction of the grain: on an original top the grain runs across the width of the table rather than along its length. Badly warped flaps should be avoided.

WORK TABLES AND "NESTS" OF TABLES
Special tables for embroidery and needlework were introduced in the second half of the 18thC. These are usually compact and are fitted with a silk bag and compartments for reels, bobbins and so on. "Nests" of tables were an ingenious and space-saving late 18thC invention consisting of sets of three or four tables. Edwardian nest tables are about two thirds the height of Regency ones and considerably less expensive. During the early 19thC there was a fashion for combination work-and-games tables.

Work tables are characterized by their combined regard for elegance and practicality. This late 18thC table (ht 27in/67cm) has a cubed marquetry top; the bag pulls out on a slide. *C*
* Work tables are rarely found with their original bags; replacements, often in pleated silk, are generally acceptable.

This set of Regency mahogany quartetto tables, c.1810, is simple but elegant, with a raised ebony bead rim on ring-turned twin column supports (wdth of longest 18½in/47cm). *C*
* Rosewood and mahogany are the most common woods.

Lyre-shaped supports were very fashionable in the early 19thC and are much sought after today. The lyre-shaped supports of this work table (ht 28in/71.5cm) are embellished with ebony line inlay, applied ormolu mounts and brass rods. *CNY*
* Price depends on fine workmanship: high-quality interiors and marquetry or inlaid decoration contribute to value.

Early nests of tables are light and elegantly simple in design, becoming more ornate during the 19thC, before returning to the Georgian style in Edwardian times. These amboyna and rosewood quartetto tables, c.1820 (ht of largest 29in/73cm), illustrate the more ornate style. *S*
* The largest table top is frequently paler than the small tables, being more often exposed to sunlight.

Combination work-and-games tables were usually of high quality, like this Regency rosewood example, c.1810 (ht 27in/68.5cm). The hinged top rises for reading and slides out to reveal a backgammon board; below is a chequerboard slide and a slide for a work bag (not fitted in this example). The sides are half-round compartments with hinged tops for work implements and games pieces. *S*

Not all work tables had bags: some tops lift up to reveal a fitted interior with lidded compartments, as in this mid-19thC Chinese black and gold lacquer work table (ht 28in/71.5cm), with intricate chinoiserie decoration. Alternatively, some work tables from the mid-19thC of conical shape, usually on a tripod base, have tops that rise to reveal an unfitted interior for holding wools and materials. This is an example of a table made in China for the European market. These are characterized by highly intricate gilt decoration. Quality is variable. Examples in very good condition are becoming scarce. Those that are badly worn fetch relatively small sums due to the problems of restoring intricate work. *C*

This rather unusually shaped early Victorian black, gilt and mother-of-pearl japanned papier mâché pedestal sewing box, c.1850/60 (ht 32½in/82.5cm), has a hinged top painted with a panel of Haddon Hall, in Derbyshire, England. *C*
* The most common type of Victorian work table is either in walnut or papier mâché, with an octagonal lift-up lid and a deep compartment below the top.

Tables IV

CENTRE AND DRUM TABLES

Centre and drum tables are used predominantly as decorative pieces in halls or large drawing rooms, although drum tables were initially used as writing tables.

The earliest drum tables date from c.1760. They were made in various forms until the middle of the 19thC. The top, supported on a pedestal base, is usually round and contains a series of drawers, which are sometimes lettered alphabetically for filing papers. The top also rotates to give the user access to all the drawers without having to stand up.

The "rent" table, a variation on the drum table, has a similar top but stands on a square cabinet base, used for storing papers.

The boldly shaped legs, finials and heavy, ornate stretcher on this mid-Victorian mahogany and marquetry centre table, c.1870 (lgth 4ft 10in/147cm), are all typical features of the period. *C*

* The inlay of summer flowers on the table-top reflects the move away from the architecturally based designs of the 18thC. Floral designs begin to appear during the mid-1820s.
* Quality tables such as this are veneered onto a mahogany ground rather than a secondary wood.

A George IV carved rosewood and specimen marble centre table, c.1825 (dia. 29in/73.5cm). The specimen-marble top would have been imported from Italy. *C*

* Rosewood was very expensive and the bulbous carved stems of tables of this period were often made in beech and stained dark to simulate the wood.

The grey mottled marble top on this German mahogany centre table, c.1820 (dia. 40in/101cm), is typical of Biedermeier furniture, as are the gilt-bronze mounts. *S*

* Marble tops were frequently used in early 19thC centre tables. Victorian examples are often of grand proportions, ornately decorated and often embellished with ormolu mounts in the "French" taste.

This William IV drum table in burr elm and oak, c.1840 (dia. 6ft 2in/188cm), is unlikely to have been used as a writing table, as the top is veneered – writing tables usually have leather tops. *SNY*

* Early 19thC oak furniture is polished paler than the oak of 17th and 18thC furniture. Oak also began to be used frequently in veneer form at this time.
* Oak furniture of the mid-19thC has for a long time been unfashionable and prices have been low. It has recently been receiving more attention and prices are steadily increasing.

This rosewood-veneered table, c.1815 (dia. 6ft 2in/188cm), incorporates many of the features of the best Regency drum tables: rotating top covered in leather, lion's mask and ring handles, and lion's paw feet. *S*

* The elegant legs on this table soon gave way to platform bases and gadrooned feet, which remained popular until c.1840.
* The pedestal support of this table is typical of the early 19thC in that the sabre legs are stepped from the column, whereas the legs of 18thC tables appear to flow from the column in a simple outline.

DRESSING TABLES
The earliest dressing or toilet tables, with complicated fitted interiors, appeared in the second half of the 18thC. Dressing tables were particularly popular with the Victorians, who reproduced many of Sheraton's finest designs.

The twin hinged flaps on this late 18thC Sheraton satinwood dressing table, c.1785 (ht 34in/86cm), open to reveal an interior fitted with compartments and toilet fittings, with a lift-up mirror on an adjustable ratchet device. This design was popular during the 18thC, but by the turn of the 19thC these pieces were superseded by dressing tables and separate toilet mirrors, and in the Victorian period by dressing tables with swing mirrors. *CNY*

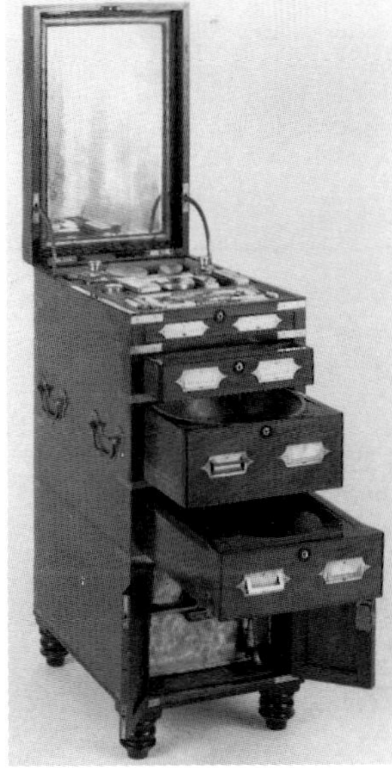

This early Victorian mahogany officers' campaign dressing cabinet, c.1850 (ht 39½in/100cm), incorporates the recessed handles and corner brackets typical of campaign furniture. It is also characteristically compact, containing a writing surface, a metal wash basin, a tap and water supply in its 16 × 23in (41 × 60cm) dimensions. *SNY*
* The ivory-handled articles and silver-topped cologne bottles contained in the top drawer of this cabinet are all original and increase the value.

This satinwood dressing table from the late 19thC (ht 75in/191cm) is an example of the Victorian preoccupation with reproduction furniture. The finishing helps to differentiate the piece from the Sheraton original. The backs and base, as with many of the best late 19thC pieces, are finished with quality timber and lightly polished – an 18thC example would most probably have a backing in a secondary timber and be left dry. Other indications of quality in this piece are the mirror-lined doors – another feature unlikely to be found in an 18thC Sheraton example – and the silver-plated handles. The mirror plate is quite white and without impurities whereas 18thC mirror plates are greyish. *S*

CAMPAIGN FURNITURE
Campaign furniture was used by army officers on the move to furnish their quarters. Most pieces date from the 19thC, when many ingenious and patented designs, including collapsible chairs and beds, were conceived by specialist firms of the day.

Furniture taken on campaign had to be compact, portable and strong. Pieces were therefore made predominantly from teak or mahogany and often incorporated handles for carrying. These were recessed into the wood to facilitate packaging and transportation. Brass corner brackets were inset into many pieces to provide protection from the rough handling such pieces suffered.

FAKE BEDSIDE TABLES
Genuine old bedside tables are sometimes "paired" with later copies – a pair may fetch as much as 10 times the price of a single table. When looking at tables that appear to be a pair the following precautionary inspections should be made:
* The quality and figuring of the timber of both tables, should correspond.
* The construction and signs of ageing, especially on the insides and undersides of the tables, should correspond.
* Signs of natural distressing should be comparable on both tables.
*Any brass fittings, such as locks, hinges and handles, should match.

BEDSIDE TABLES
Bedside tables were made from c.1750 and most conform to a uniform design. The cupboard area usually has two small doors, or a tambour sliding door (made of strips of wood stuck onto a canvas backing). Below this is a pull-out commode drawer. Most bedside tables have a tray top with a shaped rim which incorporates handles. Fakes do not occur as the originals have never been valuable enough to warrant the effort. However, pairs are much sought after, and very expensive compared to the price of a single table. They are also rare; however, it is possible to find individual pieces that offer an acceptable match.

Small night tables designed to contain a chamber pot were made in the second half of the 18thC. This mahogany example, c.1765/70 (wdth 20in/51cm), is fitted with leathered caster wheels, a feature introduced c.1750. *C*

This George III mahogany bedside cupboard or commode, c.1765 (wdth 21in/53.5cm), is typical of the period not only in its form, but also in its dimensions and choice of wood: approximately 95% of these pieces were made in mahogany. *C*

Writing Furniture I

Until the middle of the 17th century items of furniture used for writing were often extremely primitive. The first writing furniture specifically designed as such was derived from French and Italian furniture of the 16th century, and took the form of a cabinet (with a fall front) on a chest or stand, with drawers, known today as an escritoire. The front of the cabinet could be let down to serve as a writing surface, hence the term "fall-front escritoire".

The escritoire was popular on the Continent of Europe, although not in America, throughout the 18th and well into the 19th century. In England its popularity was fairly short-lived.

The bureau, basically a desk with a hinged flap that folds up when not in use, was widely manufactured in England from the early 18th century and remained in fashion until the end of the first quarter of the 19th century. Styles and quality varied from simple country pieces to much more sophisticated pieces made for fashionable townhouses. Bureaux were made in a number of woods, but most are in oak, walnut or mahogany; some were decorated with lacquer or marquetry. A bureau could be converted into a dual-purpose item by adding a bookcase or display cabinet.

The bureau and bureau bookcase were common in America, based on English designs but with influences from the Continent such as the block front and the bombé form, features rarely found in English cabinet making.

After the bureau the two main forms of writing furniture are the secretaire bookcase (or cabinet), a variant of the bureau bookcase, and the pedestal desk, both of which were common in the second half of the 18th century. From the last quarter of the 18th century other forms were introduced – for example, the writing table, the small ladies' writing desk known as the bonheur-du-jour, and the davenport.

All writing furniture is highly sought-after. Items of a small size and good quality command a premium.

TYPES OF WRITING FURNITURE

BUREAU AND SECRETAIRE CABINETS AND BOOKCASES

All the major styles of bureaux were also made in bureau-bookcase form from c.1690, in styles that matched other furniture of the period. Bureau bookcases were invariably made in two pieces, the top resting within the moulding on the top of the lower section, which is left unfinished, and held in place by screws. The secretaire bookcase was first seen c.1750 and fulfils the same function as the bureau bookcase. In place of the slant front of the bureau, it has a chest base: the deep top drawer pulls out to reveal a fitted interior, and the drawer front lowers to form the writing surface.

Some 18th and 19thC bureau bookcases are so large that they are not practicable for today's smaller rooms, and therefore not as collectable. The compact size of this Queen Anne burr walnut bureau cabinet, c.1710 (ht 88in/224cm), makes it a highly sought-after article. The doors retain their original hand-bevelled mirror plates. The fall front and drawers of the bureau section are feather-banded (see page 14). *C*

* Similar pieces were made in mulberry and elm or lacquered in black, scarlet or green with gilt decoration.

* The top section, which has a double dome surmounted by gilt flamed finials, is the rarest and most sought-after type of pediment and was the most highly prized in its day.

* Until c.1730 most bureau bookcases have applied moulding at the join or "waist" of the bureau (see page 48).

* Another type of double dome top is shown on page 45.

The ornamentation of this Rhode Island Chippendale maple desk and bookcase, c.1750–80 (ht 82in/205cm), is exceptionally rich. Typically, it has a shaped and stepped interior of drawers and pigeon holes. The bonnet top is carved with fans, pinwheels and finials. *CNY*

* By the mid-18thC in England overlapping drawer fronts had generally been superseded by those with cock beading (small, semi-circular mouldings).

Many of the more modest English bureaux were made in the provincial cities. Although this mahogany example, c.1770 (ht 7ft 3in/221cm), has a plain top and little decoration, it is desirable for its attractive colour and pleasing proportions. *C*

* The 13-pane glazing is the most common design to be found in provincial pieces of the second half of the 18thC.

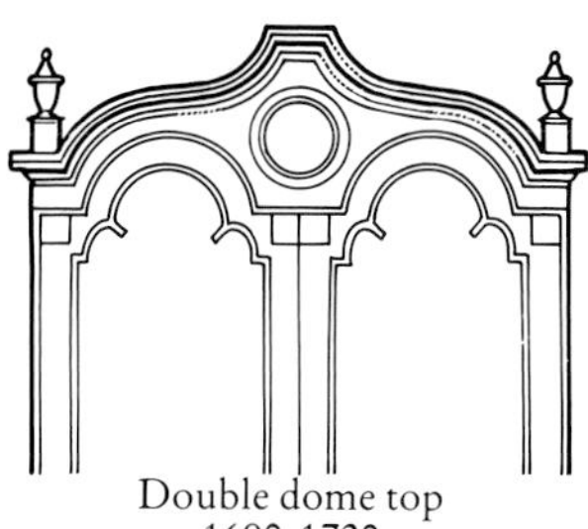

Double dome top
1690-1720

American bonnet top
1730–1760

Regency top
1800-1830

Broken pediment
1730–1800

Swan neck pediment
1760–1810

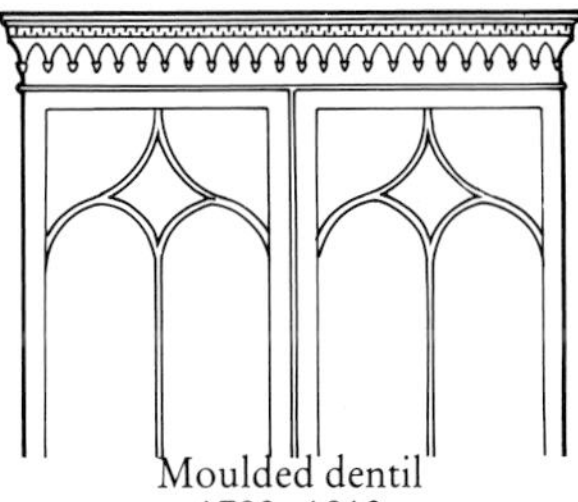

Moulded dentil
1780–1810

On the Continent, bureau bookcases were regarded as status symbols and, as such, tend to be more ornate than English ones. This Dutch late 18thC figured mahogany Neo-classical bureau bookcase (wdth 56in/ 143cm), with elaborately carved decoration and cast ormolu handles, is representative of cabinet making in Holland at its peak and of the general style of Dutch furniture of the period. Typically, it is constructed in three sections with a shaped base. The carving is crisp and the lay of the highly figured veneers gives a "flamed" effect. *S*

The fine colour and quality of wood in this George III mahogany secretaire bookcase/ cabinet, c.1770 (ht 8ft 6in/ 259cm), make this a rare piece, but stylistically it is typical of its period. *S*

* The applied mouldings around the drawer and panelled doors, and the ogee bracket feet, are typical of the period.
* As many secretaire cabinets were made with cupboards as were made with drawers.

MIRRORED DOORS AND CANDLE SLIDES

Until c.1730 bureau bookcases had mirrored or blind (wooden) doors, frequently with elaborate interiors, and with slides that pulled out to accommodate candles, from which light reflected off the mirror. By the mid-18thC mirrored doors, and with them candle slides, had ceased to be made, and glazed doors with astragal, or glazing, bars were used instead.

CARRYING HANDLES

These are sometimes found on bureau bookcases (and chests of drawers) of the late 17th and early 18thC. They may, but need not, match the handles on the front of the piece.

FEATHER AND CROSS BANDING

Feather banding should match on both the top and bottom sections of the piece. Any cross banding on the sides of the top section should correspond with that on the base sections (see page 14).

MARRIAGES

Tops or bottoms that have split are sometimes "married up" with other parts. Discrepancies in the colour of wood, and in the style of drawers, handles or decoration, may reveal that this has happened. The thickness of the sides of the fitted interior drawers in the top section, and the dovetails, should be the same as in any drawers in the lower section.

Many Scottish secretaire cabinets had a hollow area between the lower section and the cabinet, as in this, probably Scottish, early 19thC rosewood secretaire cabinet, inlaid with satinwood stringing backed by silk (ht 5ft 9in/176cm; wdth 2ft 6in/76cm).

* Rosewood is one of the most difficult woods to re-polish and can go a very dark colour, almost black, if mistreated by an incompetent restorer. *C*

Writing Furniture II

BUREAUX
Early bureaux were made in two parts – a bureau top and chest base, each with carrying handles and a "waist" moulding to cover the join. This moulding was retained even after bureaux began to be made in one piece, but was finally dropped c.1720. Bureaux either had a fall-front (a flap that was lowered and supported on lopers) or, from the late 18thC, a tambour front (which rolled up and allowed the writing flap to be pulled out on a slide). The basic design varied little throughout the period of production but the choice of wood, handles and the decoration will provide a clue for dating. As bureaux were intended to stand against a wall, the backs were made of a secondary wood and invariably quite coarse and unpolished. Early bureaux were made in oak. Walnut, walnut veneer and, additionally in America, Baltic pine and maple were more common from the early 18thC, and mahogany from mid-century.

The earliest type of bureau was relatively unsophisticated and resembled a bible box on a stand. This well-proportioned late 17thC oak bureau (ht 2ft 8in/81cm) shows the typical construction. *C*

DRAWERS AND WRITING FLAPS
The top drawer of an 18thC bureau was sometimes divided into two smaller drawers. This formation is considered more desirable than long drawers. Some early 19thC bureaux have three rows of deep drawers. These are not highly saleable. Interior fittings varied from simple divisions to those with a central cupboard, pull-out pilasters and ornate cappings, usually found in larger examples.

From the early 18thC most walnut bureaux had a protruding band of ovolo moulding to cover the join around the flap. Prior to this the flap was flush with the sides and top. When open, the flap usually provides a writing surface 29-30in (75cm) from the floor.

A fine American Chippendale mahogany bureau, or slope-front desk, c.1780 (ht 44in/112cm), with reverse-serpentine front, in which the central curve is inverted, and characteristic original brasses. It is attributed to Nathan Bowen of Massachusetts and bears his label in the top drawer. One of the interior drawers is inscribed with his name. *CNY*
* Reverse serpentine fronts are peculiar to America.
* The bulbous joints of the claws on the feet are typical of Bowen's work.

FAKES
Fakes of walnut bureaux do occur, whereas those of bureaux in other woods do not, because until recently they have been relatively inexpensive. The most convincing walnut fakes are those that have used an old, much less expensive oak bureau as the carcass to which veneers (sometimes old ones) have been added.

A good example of a rare walnut bureau chest on bun feet, c.1685 (ht 2ft 7in/79cm). It shows the transitional stage between the bible box type and the later bureau. The flap lifts up in the manner of a writing box, rather than pulling forward. The fine geometric mouldings and split turned decoration on the cupboard doors are typical of the period. This type of decoration had ceased to be fashionable in England by c.1700. It is also seen on American furniture from the end of the 17th until the early 18thC. *S*

The sides of this small, fine Queen Anne bureau (ht 3ft 4in/101cm) are veneered in a straight-grained walnut; figured veneers were reserved for the more visible surfaces. *C*
* A development of the period is the overlapping moulding of the drawer fronts. Previously, the edges of the drawers were plain, perhaps crossbanded, and a "D"- or double "D"-shaped moulding was applied to the drawer divisions. In later bureaux the divisions are plain and flat; any moulding or cockbeading is applied to the drawers.

Lacquering was at its peak of popularity during the late 17th and early 18thC, the period of this small lacquer William and Mary bureau, on a stand, with gilt chinoiserie decoration (ht 38in/95cm). *C*
* The turned legs with bun feet are united by typical flat and shaped cross stretchers.

FEET
The bun feet of early bureaux were generally made of walnut. Probably 90 percent of them have been replaced, not only because of the effects of wear and tear and dampness of floors on the soft walnut, but also in keeping with changes of fashion in the 18thC, when bracket feet came to be preferred. Many were changed at an early stage in their life; and many have since been converted back again to bun feet. These changes should not unduly deter a purchaser, provided they have been done neatly. Holes in the corners at the front of the base of a bureau with bracket feet, visible by removing the bottom drawer, are a sign that the original bun feet have been replaced.

Dutch and many other Continental bureaux are usually larger than English ones and are invariably made in two sections, even after this practice had ceased in England. This mid-18thC walnut and marquetry bureau, c.1750 (ht 44in/112cm), has several unmistakably Dutch features:
* bombé outline
* floral marquetry
* massive carved paw feet (these are often ebonized)
* carving along the apron (the frieze along the lower rail). *S*

OTHER TYPES OF WRITING FURNITURE

Writing furniture became increasingly popular with the spread of literacy in the 17th and 18thC, and many new types appeared. Some, such as the Spanish *vargueño*, were strongly regional. The escritoire, with a hinged pull-down front, was widely popular on the Continent, but less so in England and America.

This early 17thC Spanish walnut *vargueño*, or fall-front cabinet (ht 57in/145cm), has typical barley twist legs. Such pieces have a limited appeal, although they are popular in southern Europe and on the west coast of America. This type of cabinet was also made on a chest base, although turned open stands, like the one above, are more common. The escutcheon, hinges, locks and handles, all in pierced iron, as here, are the most common exterior decoration. *S*

Exotic veneers were popular in England in the second half of the 18thC. With its marquetry of sycamore, tulipwood, rosewood, harewood, mahogany, box and fruitwoods, this sophisticated George III lady's writing cabinet on stand, c.1775 (wdth 27in/68.5cm), would have been the height of fashion in its day. *CNY*

* The slender square tapering leg is a feature most closely associated with the late 18thC. These legs have applied anklets near the bottom.

The Gothic glazed doors and inlaid ivory escutcheons of this fine-quality late 18thC West Indian satinwood secretaire bookcase, with inlaid decoration, are typical of the late 18th-early 19thC. On both sections the veneers and the restrained style of inlay correspond. *C*

This South German walnut writing cabinet on stand, c.1740 (ht 50in/125cm), is typically elaborate and imposing, with decorative inlay and wide crossbanding. *C*

* The interiors of much German and north Italian writing furniture are often as elaborate as the exteriors.

Escritoires provided a perfect vehicle for elaborate veneers, as in this Empire-period escritoire, or *secretaire à abattant*, with a mottled black marble top (wdth 32in/81cm). The Neo-classical pillars are typical of French furniture of the Empire period. *S*

An early 19thC Austrian burr-veneered Austrian escritoire (wdth 45in/140cm). *S*

* Escritoires were popular in England only between c.1690 and c.1715, when they were usually veneered in walnut. *S*

Secretaries, on tall legs with open bases, were popular in America, especially in New England. The severe simplicity of this Federal inlaid mahogany lady's secretary made in Boston, c.1790-1810 (ht 85in/213cm), is counterbalanced by the use of decorative inlays. *SNY*

* Finials – much used by American cabinet makers – were popular throughout the 18thC.

Writing Furniture III

DESKS

Kneehole desks, introduced c.1710, were originally designed as dressing tables to stand against a wall and as such have backs in a secondary wood that is left unfinished. They have a recessed central cupboard in the kneehole, and are constructed in one piece with a single long drawer below the desk top and a set of three drawers on either side of the kneehole.

The grand freestanding pedestal desk, specifically designed for writing, first appeared in the mid-18thC and remained popular throughout the 19th and well into the 20thC. The flat top is usually leathered, with some form of gilt-tooled decoration, and has an upper central drawer flanked by banks of drawers to the ground.

From the last quarter of the 18thC other forms of writing furniture were introduced, such as the writing table and the small ladies' writing desk known as the bonheur du jour.

Most early kneehole desks are in walnut, which gave way to mahogany toward the mid-18thC. Only the later reproductions were made in less substantial woods such as pine. This example from the first quarter of the 18thC (wdth 36in/91.5cm) is in burr walnut. *C*

* The bracket feet in this example, although not original, have been well restored and will not significantly reduce the value. Replacement feet may be detected by non-matching veneers and signs of reworking.

KNEEHOLE DESK CONVERSIONS

It is not uncommon for a chest of drawers to be converted into a kneehole desk. Certain checks can be made for authenticity:

* The construction of the inner sides of the small drawers should correspond with the outer sides; the dovetails should match each other and look as if they were made by the same hand.
* The runners should have caused even wear to the carcass.
* The veneers used for the sides of the kneehole and for the recessed cupboard door should match the rest of the piece.

MARRIAGES AND "IMPROVEMENTS"

Pedestal desks are made in three parts: the top and two sides. Parts from different pieces are sometimes "married". Look for inconsistency in colour and veneer and for signs of wear. Some desks have been reduced in size: saw marks or patches on the inside, visible when the drawers are removed, should be viewed with suspicion. Carving was sometimes added later.

This mahogany kneehole desk, c.1755 (ht 33½in/85cm), can be identified as a quality piece by the following features:

* original cast swan-neck handles
* rich colour
* pull-out sliding shelf, or "brushing slide", for writing or for brushes when used as a dressing table
* double bracket feet (four feet at the front and two at the back). Single (four feet only) and double bracket feet were used throughout the period of production. Ogee feet were used from the mid-18thC.
* moulded canted corners, which were first used on English furniture in the early 18thC. *S*

This mahogany pedestal desk, c.1805 (wdth 54in/145cm), is in the manner of Gillows of Lancaster, whose furniture is always finely constructed. Its desirable features include carved legs and moulding around drawers and edges. *S*

* Short legs and casters are more unusual than flat plinth bases.
* The backs of pedestal desks should be veneered, but the underneath of the central drawer is usually unfinished.
* The handles of the top drawer or drawers should align with those of the drawers below.
* Original leather tops are rare. Replacements do not reduce value.
* Handles are unlikely to be original. Signs of replacements include spare fixing holes or scars on the drawer fronts. Many wooden knobs, fashionable in the 19thC, have been replaced, leaving tell-tale plugged dowel holes, usually ½in (1.3cm) in diameter.

One of the lightest and most elegant types of writing furniture is the Carlton House writing table, which appeared toward the end of the 18thC, so-called because a desk of this type is said to have been designed for the Prince Regent's bedroom at Carlton House, in London. The painted oval panels of this example, c.1900 (ht 40in/100cm), are an obvious sign that this is actually an Edwardian copy: a genuine Regency model would be more restrained, relying perhaps on floral swags only and oval panels of highly figured or "flamed" veneer. *S*

Early writing tables fetch far higher prices than later, chunky ones – still quite readily available and relatively inexpensive. Late 18thC writing tables are raised either on slender square tapering legs or on slender turned legs of simple outline. Both types terminate in casters. In the early 19thC a heavier leg turned with rings became more popular; it became steadily more robust as the century progressed. An early 19thC development was the writing table with end supports, as in this William IV example, c.1835 (wdth 4ft 3in/130cm), which shows several other typical 19thC features:
* handle-less drawers that pull out from below, rather than interrupting the lines of the piece
* applied paterae on the end supports
* short sabre feet inset with nulling (carved, reeded decoration)
* use of bird's eye maple, popular in the early 19thC. *S*

ALTERATIONS
Some writing tables have had their legs replaced by slender square tapering legs to give an earlier and more expensive appearance. The original legs had to be cut off and completely replaced. As timber is very difficult to match, there may be a discrepancy between the old and new timbers.

CASTERS
Casters can be useful dating aids – for example, lion's paw feet are probably post-c.1800. Modern casters are less finely cast, the wheels frequently being solid rather than hollow, as antique casters were.

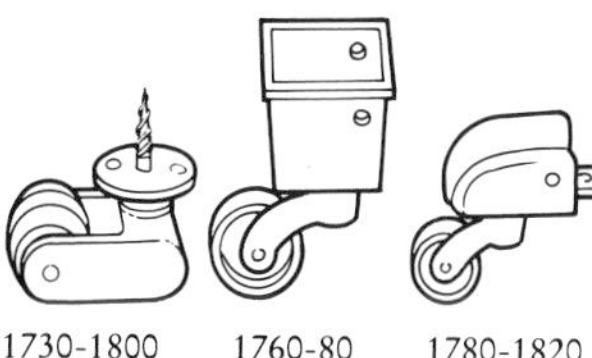

1730-1800 1760-80 1780-1820

1780-1810 1785-1810 1790-1830

1790-1830 1790-1820 1820-1830

This ormolu-mounted rosewood writing table (wdth 44in/112cm) shows the more ornate feel of Regency furniture as opposed to the restrained lines of the 18thC. Improved techniques in working metal are evident in the applied ormolu banding around the top, together with the other applied and inlaid metalwork. The stiff-leaf toe caps are invariable signs of quality that would not be found on a lesser desk. *C*
* The lyre shape is virtually unique to Regency design.
* These writing tables were made in mahogany as well as rosewood.

DAVENPORTS
Introduced in the late 18thC, these are compact writing tables with sloping tops, usually leathered, and a case of drawers below. The early ones were often quite plain, almost box-like in shape; the upper section pulled forward to provide a writing surface with knee space beneath. By c.1840 they had acquired fixed writing surfaces with curved and scrolled supports in front of a recessed case. The best examples have special features, such as hidden drawers, or lift-up tops with fitted stationery compartments.

An early 19thC mahogany davenport (wdth 20in/51cm), which retains the early box shape. The solid impression is lightened by:
* the brass-work gallery
* the tooled leather surface
* figured veneers
* a panelled front
* ornate brass drawer knobs.
Above the drawers is a pull-out slide and a small pen drawer. *C*

This mid-Victorian black papier mâché davenport with gilt and mother-of-pearl decoration (wdth 25in/63.5cm) is typically elaborate and shows the preference for moulded supports characteristic of the period. *S*
* Examples of this style are more commonly found veneered in walnut with inlaid decoration.

Bookcases and Display Cabinets I

The difference between bookcases and display cabinets is often very subtle. Some pieces have glazed sides and are more obviously intended for display purposes, but in most cases the terminology scarcely matters – the same item can be used for books, china or both.

Domestic bookcases are not found in England before Charles II's reign. Books were luxury items: most households owned few, if any, and a chest or wall cupboard was sufficient to hold them. It was in the 18th and 19th centuries, with the increasing availability of books, that the bookcase flourished.

The production of display cabinets parallels that of bookcases. Porcelain from China and Delftware from Holland were being imported in the 17th century, but it was only when porcelain services and decorative figures began to be produced widely in Europe, in the 18th century, that the demand for display cabinets became widespread.

Bookcases are to be found in a wide variety of sizes, from the very large breakfront bookcases made for the libraries of substantial houses to dwarf open items for smaller town houses. They are also to be found placed on bureaux and secretaire cabinets – this type is dealt with under Writing Furniture on pages 46-51. Many of the large breakfront bookcases designed by the likes of William Kent and Thomas Chippendale (see page 63) are of architectural design, surmounted by a broken pediment. Because of their size, these items have a limited market.

It was during the last quarter of the 18th century and through the Regency that attention was turned to designing smaller items such as chiffoniers, dwarf open bookcases, revolving bookcases and low breakfront cabinet/bookcases. These remain eminently collectable.

Such items were produced throughout the 19th century both in England and America. Strong French influence in both countries shows in the often sinuous forms of display cabinets, indebted to developments in glassmaking techniques that facilitated curving and sweeping panes.

Substantial Georgian bookcases were usually made in pine when they were going to be gessoed and painted to complement the décor in the room or library they were made for. This fine George II example (ht 99in/253cm) would have been gessoed and painted when it was first installed. The break in the pediment was commonly used to display a bust or prize piece of chinaware. *SNY*

ALTERATIONS
These items have sometimes been cut down to make them more saleable:
* Pediments may be removed to reduce height, in which case marks will be left where the pediment once sat.
* The cabinet may be reduced in depth by cutting through the sides and shelves and refixing the back: this is usually traceable by the obvious distressing of the newly cut surfaces.
* If the main carcass has been reduced in height, the slots for the adjustable shelves may appear too close to the top or bottom; there should be at least 8in/20cm clear to accommodate books.

This Federal-period standing corner cupboard, made in Baltimore c.1790 (ht 90in/225cm), shows the essential sobriety of the Hepplewhite style. The piece is solid, yet light, and the details of the veneering and stringing are refined. *PC*
* A pale-coloured paint on the interior enhances the lightness of such pieces. Unless the paint is original, there is no harm in repainting.
* Corner cupboards were popular on both sides of the Atlantic. As well as the two-section freestanding type, shown above, there is a smaller variety that hangs on the wall. Both types come in straight- or bow-fronted forms, with glazed or blind doors.

A good early George III mahogany display cabinet, c.1770 (ht 87in/221cm). Very much of its period, this piece could only exist in mahogany. Dating features include:
* the applied mouldings at the corners of the doors; in this case they are rams' heads, instead of the usual circular leaf paterae
* the discreet dentil cornice
* the shapely bracket feet.
Cabinets in this style were made with and without broken pediments: provided that there are no marks showing where a pediment once sat, the lack of one is no cause for concern.

The upper part of this example is unnecessarily deep for books, suggesting that it was made as a display cabinet rather than as a dual-purpose item. *SNY*

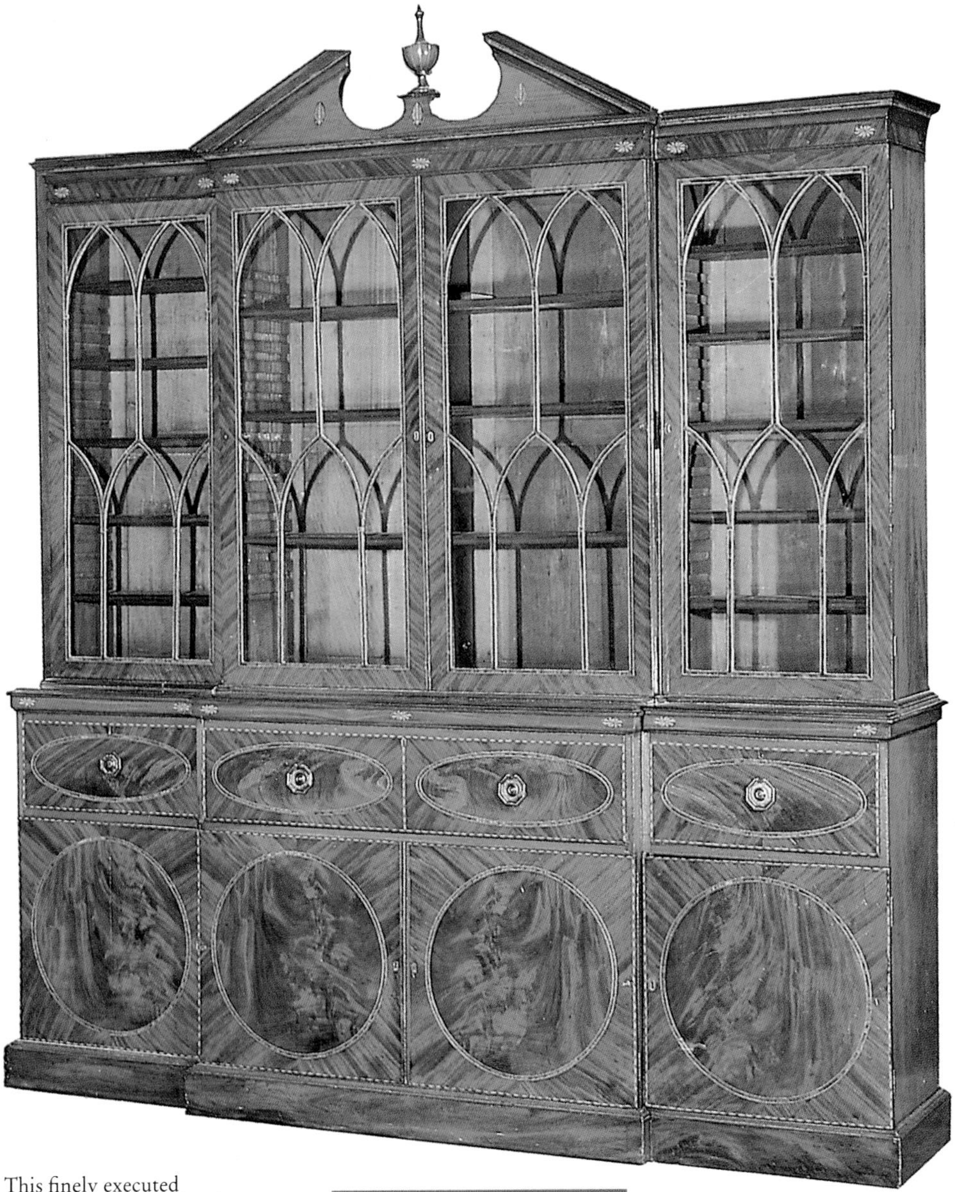

This finely executed Hepplewhite-period mahogany breakfront bookcase (ht 110in/ 280cm) dates from c.1785. All its main features are familiar:
* the Classical form with broken pediment and urn
* the Gothic arched glazed doors
* the use of contrasting veneers to create decorative circles and ovals
* the central secretaire drawer.

The strong chequered line inlay to the lower part and the excessive use of applied paterae above the drawers and glazed doors suggest that this is provincially made: on a London-made piece the decoration would probably have been more subtle. *C*
* Most large 18thC bookcases are constructed in mahogany or, occasionally, pine. A few fine examples from the end of the century are veneered in West Indian satinwood.

PATTERNS OF GLAZING

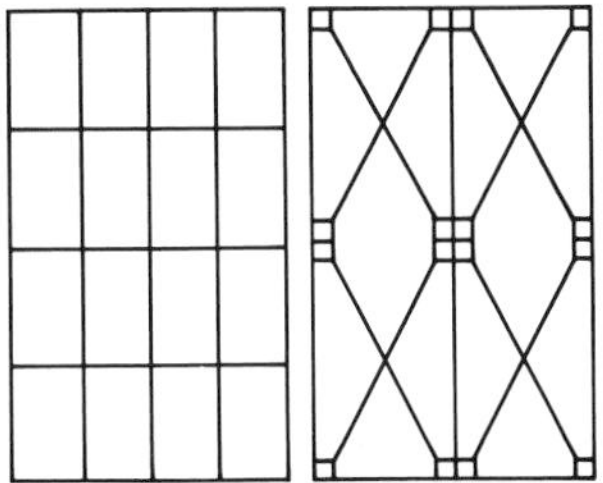
1690-1730 1750-1800

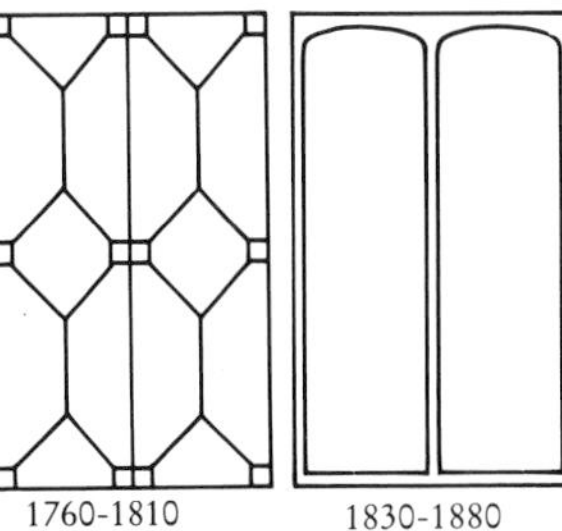
1760-1810 1830-1880

Until about the mid-18thC display cabinets and bookcases were glazed with rectangular panes of modest size retained by fairly solid glazing bars or astragals. Later, more intricate patterns called for lighter glazing bars. Small panes persisted well after glass factories had become able to produce large sheets of glass.

This Sheraton-period mahogany chiffonier, c.1800 (ht 47in/ 120cm), is refined and elegant, but to be fully authentic it should show pleated silk in the glazed panels. *S*

A marble-topped Regency chiffonier, c.1820-25 (wdth 46in/ 116cm), displaying features typical of its period:
* generous use of brass inlay and mounts
* rosewood, probably the most popular wood of the time
* quite hefty pilasters and feet, indicating the later Regency period. *C*

This early 19thC revolving bookstand (ht 55in/140cm) uses a mechanism patented in 1808. Each of the four tiers revolves independently. Books are supported by dummy book spines backed by wedge-shaped dividers. *S*

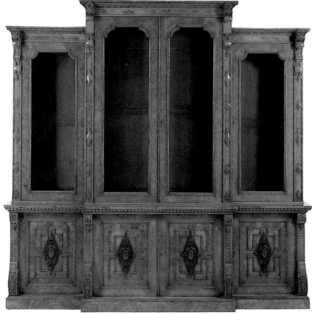

Bookcases and Display Cabinets II

The demand for display cabinets in the Edwardian period continued to run high. Many are still around, the best of them of high quality and priced accordingly. Designs were usually eclectic adaptations from the later 18thC and, under the influence of Adam, Hepplewhite and Sheraton, of lighter appearance. This fine example (ht 73in/185cm) is typical in that:
* the style is loosely Sheraton
* it is made of satinwood
* it is lavishly parcel-gilt
* the painted panels are sentimentally Watteauesque
* the legs are Louis XVI style. *S*

Credenzas (the Italian term for sideboards) were made in huge numbers in the last century and in a wide range of qualities. Although many have not lasted, good credenzas can still be found without much difficulty. This example (wdth 74in/187cm), veneered in burr walnut, displays many typical signs of quality:
* floral inlay

* a profusion of Rococo ormolu mounts
* curved glazed doors at either end.

The typical form of the 19thC credenza owes much to the serpentine shapes of French and Italian Rococo furniture of the 18thC. The main variations to be found are:
* solid doors, decorated with inlay or applied porcelain plaques
* mirrored doors
* fretwork doors
* open shelves at either side
* marble rather than wooden tops
* mirrored backs
* ebonized wood. *C*

Edwards & Roberts were one of the principal 19thC English firms of furniture makers and retailers. Their stamp is usually to be found on the top surface of drawer fronts, but can be misleading as they applied it to earlier items that they altered, as well as to their original products. This breakfront bookcase (ht 100in/255cm) was made in their workshops c.1840. Typical features of the period include:
* the applied Elizabethan-style ornament
* glazed doors without astragals and with shaped tops. *S*

An early Victorian figured rosewood breakfront side cabinet, c.1840 (wdth 54in/137cm). A good-quality piece that one might expect to find more commonly in burr walnut. The bold carving is typically Victorian but the basic outline retains the restraint of the late Regency and William IV periods. *S*
* An original marble top will display tell-tale signs of dirt and wear on the exposed and unpolished underside. The marble merely sits on top, so it can be easily lifted for checking.

SIDE CABINET CONVERSIONS

Many side cabinets started life with wooden panels to the doors that have subsequently been replaced either with glass, brass grilles or pleated silk to give a less solid appearance. The cabinet above may well have started life with blind doors. Provided the conversion has been skilfully carried out it should not adversely affect the piece and may well enhance it.

Mahogany bookshelves with trellis sides, as in this example, c.1810 (ht 37in/94cm), are rare, especially in their original pairs. The bun feet are original, with inset cup casters. Points to check:

* Feet should be less scuffed on the inside edges.
* Corners will be darker where dirt has built up.
* The trellis's inner surfaces will probably be darker than the outer. *S*

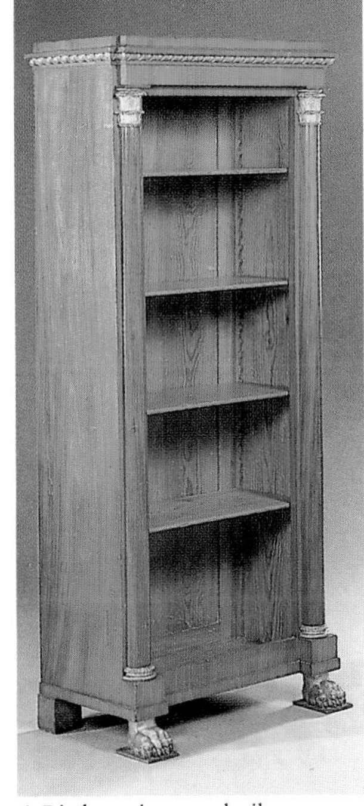

A Biedermeier parcel-gilt open mahogany bookcase, German, early 19thC (ht 75in/190cm), of a style that was popular throughout France, Germany, Russia and the Scandinavian countries and caught on with New York cabinet makers, although it was not nearly as popular in Regency England. The severe lines and lion's paw feet are characteristic. On this example the mahogany is veneered onto a pine carcass but not finished off inside, presumably for economy. *S*

This 19thC display cabinet, c.1880 (ht 88in/224cm; wdth 51in/130cm), one of a pair, is a copy of an original Chippendale design. Accurate 19thC copies of earlier designs, if well used and cared for, can be deceptive, as they will have built up an agreeable patina and show authentic signs of wear. This piece is well made and should appreciate in value, but the following factors identify it as a copy:

* The astragals are applied as one piece of fretwork to a single pane of glass – an original would have had individual panes puttied in.
* The mahogany is inferior, dark red in colour with virtually no figuring.
* The piece was French-polished and therefore lacks the softness of a wax-finished 18thC item.
* The carving is somewhat stiff and laboured, as is usually the case with copies of this period. *CSc*

KEYHOLE ESCUTCHEONS

The shape of the inset keyhole escutcheons can help to distinguish an English piece from a Continental one: Continental keyhole escutcheons are larger and more angular than those of English and American furniture. Keyhole escutcheons can also help to date a piece – for example, the escutcheon on the right was first found on English furniture from c.1870, when many copies of earlier styles were being made.

Continental

English

English, from c.1870

It follows that a cabinet in, say, the Chippendale style, fitted with this later type of escutcheon will be post-1870, rather than mid-18thC as the style might suggest.

The 1830s harked back to the mid-18thC tradition of well-figured timber ornamented only with carving. There was also a revival of Gothic taste in English furniture of the period, exemplified by this characteristic William IV mahogany bookcase cabinet, c.1835 (ht 116½in/296cm). The wood is markedly reddish (typical of the 19thC), but agreeably figured. *S*

* Tall as this piece is, it would be uneconomic to cut it down. The Gothic leaf-carved astragals at the tops of the doors could not be partially removed but would have to be eliminated altogether. The sturdy base would then appear too broad in proportion. To reduce the cabinet's width would require a total remake.

A French Empire mahogany, painted and parcel-gilt open bookcase, c.1810 (ht 74in/187cm). The crossed spears play on the military glory of Napoleonic France (compare Thomas Hope's contemporary "Trafalgar" chairs in England, page 28). *S*

* The Neo-classical ormolu mounts are typical of French furniture of the period. This style of decoration is not often found on English furniture but was a strong influence on early 19thC New York cabinet makers.

Mirrors

Before the invention of mirror plate, mirrors for the wealthy classes were made from burnished plates of gold or silver; the poorer classes used pewter and other base metals. The process of making mirrors from glass was established in the early 16th century at Murano, near Venice, and was adopted in England in the early 17th century. Frames inspired by European designs were made in America from the early 18th century, but the mirror plates for them were imported from Europe until c.1800.

Until the late 18th century, mirror plates were made from blown cylinders of glass that were slit open, flattened, and silvered on the back with mercury. The plates were small because of the limitations of the manufacturing process, so mirrors were made initially using two or more plates. Larger plates, three or four feet (90cm or 120cm) in length, were produced from the late 18th century.

In the 17th century, the only mirrors made were designed to be hung on walls. In Queen Anne's reign small toilet-mirrors mounted on miniature bureaux were introduced from the Low Countries. Overmantel mirrors and pier mirrors (designed to hang between sash windows) became an integral part of a room's design. The tall cheval mirror on a stand did not appear until c.1770 when it became possible to produce large enough mirror plates. Before c.1660 most mirrors were made for the bedroom; thereafter they became essential elements in the interior decoration of reception rooms.

Techniques for decorating frames varied considerably: from japanned work, through borders of bevelled silver plate, to "cushion" frames veneered with walnut, ebony or oyster laburnum. Fretted cresting and floral marquetry were also popular. High-relief naturalistic carving often overpowered small mirror plates.

During the 18th century the carved gessoed and giltwood mirror underwent several changes: the architectural style, popular early in the century, made way for Chinese Chippendale, Rococo and Neo-classical.

After the Regency, designs followed the general trend of Victorian furniture but, in addition, there were many copies of earlier styles. Stucco began to be used more frequently in the frames at this period.

Good mirrors, particularly those of the 18th century and the Regency, can be very expensive. Victorian and Edwardian reproductions can be acquired for relatively modest sums.

Pier glasses were particularly fashionable at the turn of the 18thC. This example, c.1700 (ht 58in/147cm), is typical of the period in its use of walnut, the fretted cresting and the shallow "cushion" frame. *S*

* The join between the plates indicates that the glass was produced before c.1770.

From the beginning of the 18thC, dressing, or toilet, mirrors were commonly mounted on miniature bureaux which followed the style of the period. These mirrors are usually veneered in walnut, or lacquered, as in this example, c.1705 (wdth 18½in/47cm). The shape of the frame, with its arched top surmounted by cresting, identifies this as a Queen Anne period mirror. *C*

* Toilet mirrors were popular throughout the Georgian era. They were superseded in the Victorian period by dressing tables with swing mirrors.

An early Georgian walnut mirror (ht 30in/76cm) which anticipates the lighter designs favoured by Chippendale and Adam. This modest style of mirror, the profile of which is cut by a fret saw, was popular c.1720-60. It is found veneered in walnut (sometimes Virginia or American) and from c.1735 in mahogany, usually onto a pine base. The back of the frame and the backboards are roughly finished. *C*

* This style is also found from the American Chippendale period.

* The plate is original and, although it shows considerable signs of deterioration, replacement would be ill-advised.

This carved giltwood mirror in the Chinese Chippendale style, c.1750 (ht 6ft 7in/201cm), is typical of the 1750s, when the symmetric designs of the previous decades gave way to a lighter style influenced by French Rococo. *S*

* The gesso has been re-gilded. Mirrors that retain their original gilding are more desirable, but finding original gilding in acceptable condition is becoming increasingly difficult.

* Many 19thC mirrors are covered with moulded composition or "compo", a putty-like substance which, when gilded, resembles carved wood, for which it is a cheap substitute.

This plate from Hepplewhite's *The Cabinet-makers and Upholsterers Guide*, published two years after his death in 1786, shows a design for a serpentine-fronted toilet mirror inlaid with fans, crossbanded and with an oval plate. This would have been made either in mahogany or satinwood.
* Toilet mirrors with a shield- or oval-shaped frame were especially popular in the late 18thC and are more desirable than mirrors fitted with a straightforward rectangular frame.
* Small ivory turned knobs on the drawers were common in the late 18thC; original ones in good condition will add to a mirror's value.

Circular convex mirrors, such as this carved giltwood example, c.1810 (ht 52in/132cm), were introduced in France in 1756 and became the most characteristic style of the Regency period in England and America. Some particularly grand examples may be adorned with candle arms or cut-glass sconces and hanging prisms; these fetch very high prices. *CNY*
* The eagle was a popular cresting motif throughout much of the 18th and the early 19thC.

The architectural design of this walnut and parcel-gilt mirror, c.1735 (ht 51in/130cm), is typical of a period in which mirrors, more than any other piece of furniture, were heavily influenced by architecture, echoing the treatment given to doorways, fireplaces and the panelling against which they hung. The plate of this mirror is a later replacement, which adversely affects its value. *CNY*
* Many 18thC mirror frames are completely gilt. Alternatively, gilded carved mouldings were combined with walnut or mahogany veneers.
* In the 17thC and 18thC bevels were hand-cut and are therefore shallower and less regular than the straight lines and even depth of 19thC machine bevelling.

PLATE CONDITION
The condition and thickness of the plate provide useful guidelines for distinguishing a genuine period mirror from a fake or later copy: the plates of old mirrors usually show signs of deterioration, being pitted with rust and dampness and having been subjected to the effects of coal fires. In extreme cases the silvering will show signs of flaking from the glass to the point where the mirror will need re-silvering. The colour of old plate is greyer than colourless modern glass, and the impurities that have accumulated give a much softer reflection. Early glass is also thinner and of variable thickness compared to modern mirror plate.

The intricate carving on this late 19thC Dieppe ivory mirror (ht 33in/84cm) reflects the stylistic revivals that occurred throughout Europe and America in the second half of the 19thC. This type of mirror is usually associated with the Dieppe region and is a revival of 17thC work. *C*

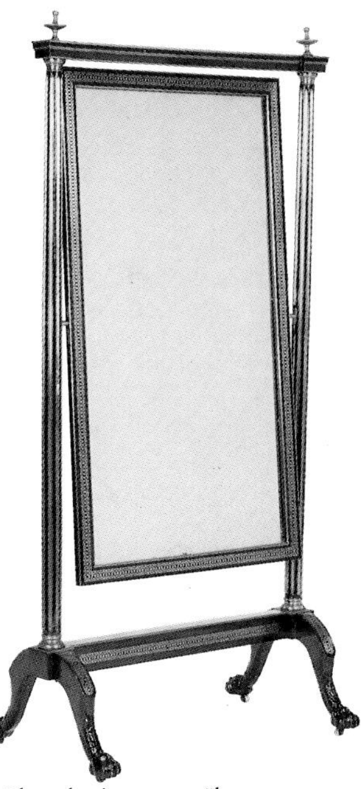

Cheval mirrors, or "horse dressing glasses", so called because of their four-legged frame, were introduced during the last decade of the 18thC, when it became possible to cast single mirror plates more than 10 feet (3m) in height. Most examples date from 1790-1830, but they were still being made as late as 1910. This Russian brass inlaid mahogany example (ht 75½in/192cm) is early 19thC. *S*
* Some cheval mirrors have adjustable candleholders, which is usually a sign of quality and increases the value.

Miscellaneous I

TEA CADDIES

Caddies are small lidded boxes for storing tea. Most incorporate a lock and key just below the lid: tea was very expensive in the 8thC, when caddies were introduced. Large examples are sometimes divided into sections for black and green tea. In the 19thC, cut-glass bowls were often fitted for blending the different teas. Caddies were made in a range of woods which were carved, veneered, inlaid or painted, as well as in other materials such as ivory, tortoiseshell and paper filigree.

The apple shape of this applewood caddy, c.1780 (ht 6in/15cm), helps to identify it as late 18thC. The ebonized stalk and original escutcheon indicate the caddy's authenticity. Fakes of these expensive small pieces abound, and it is important to examine the following areas to ensure that there are authentic signs of wear:

* the hinge, lock and screws
* the underside and the polished surface may have fake distressing
* the inner rim of the base on which the top sits. *C*

This satinwood caddy with inlaid marquetry decoration, c.1785 (wdth 7in/19cm), incorporates many characteristic features of the period:

* West Indian satinwood
* delicate marquetry
* crossbanded decoration in tulipwood
* diamond-shaped ivory inset escutcheon.

The base is typically lined with baize. Morocco leather (goatskin) was sometimes used as an alternative. *C*

The use of ivory with silver fittings on this decagonal caddy, c.1790 (5in/13cm), is typical of high-quality pieces of the late 18thC. The tortoiseshell stringing accentuates the angular shape. *C*

* The multi-angle design is found in many miscellaneous items of the period. Hexagonal and octagonal caddies are also found.

The use of rosewood and the brass inlay on this rectangular caddy, c.1815 (ht 6in/15cm), are typical Regency features. The pressed and embossed handles (see page 21) and the bronze feet are also typical. The coffer top that surmounts this piece first appeared at about this date. *C*

TRAYS

Trays made before the Chippendale period are rare. 18thC trays incorporate the spindle-turned galleries and marquetry decoration applied to furniture of the period. In the 19thC, papier mâché was the main material used in tray manufacture. Trays have rarely been faked, although copies of Chippendale and Sheraton examples were produced in the Victorian and Edwardian periods: these tend to be darker and heavier than the originals. Larger trays tend to fetch more money than smaller examples of the same period and quality because they are more suitable for conversion to coffee tables. A tray-table may come in for extensive use and care should be taken to promptly wipe clean any spillages. A good way to protect the top is to cover it with a plate-glass top cut to shape.

The finely turned spindles on this early 19thC mahogany tray (wdth 12in/30.5cm) are also found on other small furniture of the period. *C*

The rounded rectangular shape of this Victorian papier mâché tray, c.1840 (lgth 29in/73cm), is found from the early 19thC. The mother-of-pearl inlay around the border is a feature seen on trays from c.1825 and is not popular today; consequently such trays are relatively inexpensive. *C*

Papier mâché was especially popular in the Victorian period as it lends itself well to all-over decoration. The "Chippendale" shape of this papier mâché tray, c.1850 (wdth 34in/88cm), remained popular throughout the 19thC. *C*

Some papier mâché firms stamped or printed their wares with their name; in the case of trays, any mark will be on the back. Indistinct marks should be carefully examined.

* Chinoiserie designs are often used in the early 19thC. European subjects were predominant during the Victorian era.
* The price of papier mâché trays has risen considerably in recent years, largely owing to their potential for conversion to highly decorative coffee tables. These conversions are particularly popular in America.

LIBRARY STEPS
Library steps, used to reach books on the upper shelves of large bookcases, were introduced in the middle of the 18thC and continued to be made throughout the 19thC. Most are small, the standard height being 36in (92cm), but a few large sets were made for the important libraries of the major country houses such as the mobile spiral staircase made for Earl Spencer's house in Althorpe, England, in 1790; it stands 9 feet high (274cm) and has a seat and bookrest at the top.

During the second half of the 18thC and the early 19thC, much ingenuity was expended on designing furniture such as chairs, tables and stools that doubled up as library steps. The design for this "metamorphic library chair" was patented by Morgan & Saunders in 1811. Made in mahogany, c.1815 (ht 36in/92cm), with a rectangular padded back, it has scrolled arms and sabre legs. *SNY*

This folding mahogany library ladder, c.1840 (ht 38in/97cm), is of a design that was used throughout the 19thC. Many later examples have steps inset with turkeywork panels – sections of hand-knotted wool often found on 17th and 18thC seat furniture. *SNY*

GLOBES
During the 18th and 19thC the discovery of many new areas of the world led to an interest in cartography. Globes were usually made in pairs – terrestrial and celestial – and mounted on wooden stands. The wooden spheres were covered with printed paper maps and could be brought up to date with new prints as discoveries were made. Consequently, globes are sometimes found matched with stands of an earlier date.

This early Victorian mahogany globe (ht 13½in/34cm) was designed to stand on a table. The stands are typically made from mahogany. *C*
* Regency stands are distinguished by the gentle curves of the tripod bases, which are often joined by compass stretchers.
* Pairs of globes are very collectable but examples in good condition are rare.

SCREENS
Screens were made in England from the 17thC and were designed to keep out draughts as well as to decorate a room. They consist of a series of hinged boards, made in a variety of materials from lacquered or polished wood to wood frames covered in leather, canvas, decorated paper or needlework. Those made of delicate materials have often suffered from ill-treatment and have needed extensive restoration. The extent to which this detracts from the value will depend on the degree of damage and the calibre of restoration. Close inspection should be made of the front surface of the screen and also on the back, which is invariably quite plain. Some screens are very large, especially those from the 18thC, which can be as many as eight folds wide. Over the years some of these have been divided to make smaller screens. These may be missing a border at one end, alternatively, the design may stop abruptly or appear incomplete.

BEDS
Tester beds – four-poster beds surmounted by a wooden canopy – were made from the 16thC but most of those available today date from the second half of the 17thC. The heavily carved oak tester beds of the 16th and 17thC gave way to the more elegant mahogany beds of the 18thC. A heavier style of post re-emerged in the reign of George IV.

The half-tester bed, which incorporated a half-canopy, became very fashionable in the Victorian period. It had only two posts and was sometimes given additional support from the ceiling. Most Victorian half-tester beds dispensed with the need for additional support, but some had brackets concealed underneath the drapery.

Early American beds, made from oak, walnut and pine, are very simple. In the 18thC designs were based on those from England, and during the early 19thC the influence of the French Empire is evident.

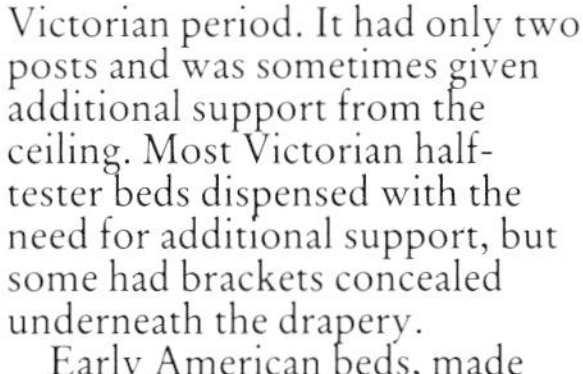

The carving on the headboard of this Charles I oak tester bed (ht 76in/193cm) is similar to that found on coffers of the same period. *SNY*
* When oak tester beds became unfashionable during the 18thC, many were dismantled and put into storage, where they fell into disrepair. Many were rebuilt later to suit Victorian tastes. Intact 17thC originals are rare.

This late 18thC mahogany and painted four-poster bed (ht 91in/231cm) is typical of the period in its light style and use of drapes. *C*
* The fluted footposts of 18th and early 19thC beds were sometimes converted to torchères (stands for candles) in the early part of this century.

The panels on this 19thC four-fold screen, c.1850 (ht 83in/211cm), are made from English painted wallpaper. The *faux* marble border at the bottom was a popular decorative feature on screens from the early 19thC. *PC*
* Hunting and pastoral scenes were popular subjects for screen designs, as were chinoiserie and floral motifs.

Miscellaneous II

CANTERBURIES AND DUET STANDS

There are types of furniture designed to hold sheet music: canterburies, for storing music books, and duet stands for supporting sheet music during performance. Both types first appeared in England in the late 18thC. Canterburies are eminently suitable today for holding magazines and newspapers.

The classic proportions, simple lines and use of brass inlay on this rosewood canterbury, c.1810 (ht 19in/48cm), help to identify it as high-quality Regency. The turned legs terminate in relatively large casters. *S*

* Most canterburies from this period were made in mahogany.
* Canterburies with three divisions often incorporate a handle in the central division.

The bold, simple carving and the bulbous turning to the legs on this rosewood canterbury, c.1835 (ht 18in/46cm), are typical of the early Victorian period. The more ornate lines provide a strong contrast to the simple rectilinear lines of early canterburies. Small turned wood handles were frequently used on small items of furniture as early as the Regency period. These are original. *SNY*

* Later Victorian canterburies were made in walnut; burr walnut was used in the more desirable examples.

This duet music stand, c.1790 (ht 43in/109cm), is made in oak, which is unusual for the Sheraton period. However, the elegant lines are typical, as are the delicate brass bun feet. The lattice stands and the height are both adjustable. *S*

This George IV mahogany duet stand, c.1825 (ht 48in/122cm), has several features characteristic of the period:

* tricorn platform base
* scroll feet
* heavy spiralled fluted shaft, or pedestal.

Lyre-shaped supports were popular during the Regency period. *S*

* Duet stands were also made in rosewood.

WHATNOTS

Whatnots, first made c.1800, were used to display a variety of books and objects. They are usually rectangular with tiered shelves supported by turned columns at the corners; and are sometimes fitted with a drawer.

The brass supports, finials and pierced gallery that surround the top tier of this brass and rosewood whatnot, c.1810 (ht 39in/99.5cm), enhance its value. *C*

* A demand for low, tiered tables for the ends of sofas has resulted in some four-tiered whatnots being cut in half, to make a pair.

This type of plain mahogany whatnot, c.1820 (ht 57in/145cm), was made in fairly large quantities and is inexpensive compared with more elaborate Regency examples. *C*

* Because of the relatively low value of such pieces, they are seldom faked.

This Victorian mahogany whatnot, c.1860 (ht 30in/76.5cm), has the turned bone spindle galleries and bulbous turned legs typical of the period. Its low rectangular shape makes it easier to position in a room. This aspect, together with the decorative galleries, make this whatnot particularly desirable. *SNY*

* With the introduction of machine-carved wood in the 1840s, elaborate, pierced galleries became more common.

WASHSTANDS

Washstands were made from c.1750 and stood on tripod or 4-legged bases. Although they appear in various forms – some are rectangular, others were designed in the form of a cabinet – all washstands have a hole in the top in which to place a basin, and a dished lower platform designed to hold a jug of water.

This early mahogany washstand from the George II period, c.1750 (ht 29in/73cm), is an unusual triangular shape and has a small wedge-shaped drawer and a dome-covered box for soap – desirable features. *C*

FIRE SCREENS
Because wax was used in the production of many cosmetics in the 18thC, polescreens were designed as a way of protecting complexions from the heat of the fire. Consisting of an adjustable screen attached to a wood or metal pole supported on a tripod base, they were developed during the first half of the 18thC. The screen itself, usually oval, rectangular or shield-shaped, was attached to the pole by a ring and screw. Polescreens became more decorative than functional by the 19thC.

Many polescreens have been converted to pairs of occasional tables; the pole is cut, a block is placed at the top of the pedestal and the screen is fixed horizontally to form a table top. Conversions are obvious from an examination of the underside of the table top, which will be of unusual construction.

American polescreens lack the Rococo-style carving of mid-18thC English examples.

This George II mahogany polescreen, c.1750 (ht 55in/140cm), has a number of features that help to identify it as mid-18thC and attest to its fine quality:
* a spirally fluted vase-shaped column
* carved acanthus on the knees of the legs
* hairy lion's paw feet.

The petit-point needlework panel is contemporary with the screen. Numerous floral designs were published and copied from the 1740s. The colours on this example have not faded, and this adds to its value. *C*

Many Victorian ebonized and gilt japanned polescreens, such as these papier mâché examples (ht 56in/143cm), have been converted to occasional tables. The hunting scenes in the manner of Landseer help to date them to c.1850. *C*
* The screen of 18thC polescreens was often covered in attractive needlework, which ensures their enduring collectability. The appeal of 19thC polescreens was more limited, and many have been converted.
* The edges of some screens, especially those with a crenellated border, are vulnerable to damage and should be examined before purchase. The gilding on papier mâché screens has often been rubbed away in parts.

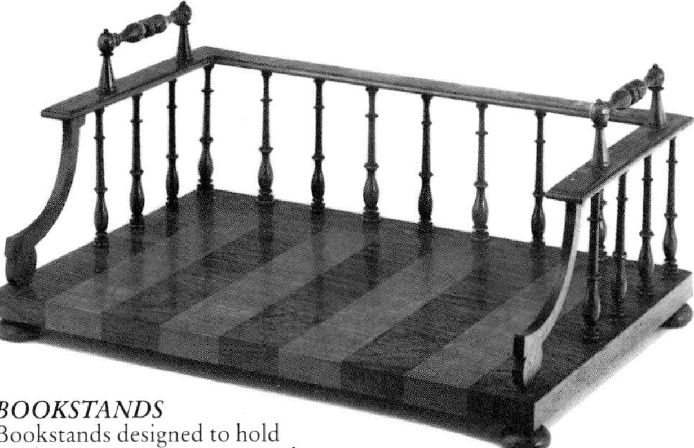

BOOKSTANDS
Bookstands designed to hold books in current use were made from the mid-18thC. The very fine baluster turnings of the balustrading and the handles on this example, c.1810 (wdth 15in/38cm), are typical Regency features, as is the combined use of rosewood and satinwood. *C*

The carved base, the embroidered design and the use of walnut on this Victorian firescreen, c.1870 (ht 45in/115cm), are typical of the period. *C*

HANGING SHELVES
Hanging shelves were popular from the mid-18thC to the Edwardian period, and provide an excellent way to display porcelain and other decorative objects.

The pierced ends of these mahogany shelves, c.1760 (ht 47in/119cm), are typical of the Chippendale period. *C*
* Shelves appear in a variety of woods, from the 17thC oak examples with carved decoration, to those made in the 18thC in mahogany and satinwood. Walnut was popular for shelves in the Victorian period. Some shelves are quite ornate, and may be painted, lacquered or decorated with marquetry work. Pairs are particularly desirable.

Reference

GLOSSARY

Acanthus A leaf motif used in carved and inlaid decoration.
Apron The decorative shaped skirt of wood that runs beneath the drawers and between the legs of a table or feet of a chest.
Armoire The Continental term for a large tall cupboard originally used for storing armour.
Astragal The half-round reeded **moulding** applied to the edges of door frames on bookcases and cupboards, intended to conceal the join. Astragals are often brass.
Backboard The unpolished back of wall furniture.
Balloon-back chair A chair with a rounded back, the best-known type of Victorian dining or salon chair.
Baluster The shaped **turning**, or slender pillar with a bulbous base, used on the legs and pedestals of tables.
Banding Decorative **veneer** used around the edges of tables and drawers. See page 14.
Barley twist The spiral shape much favoured for **turned** legs during the second half of the 17thC.
Bergère The term for a French armchair, applied in England to chairs with caned backs and sides.
Bevel The decorative angled edge of a mirror.
Bird-cage support The mechanism, located at the top of the pedestal, that enables some 18thC **tripod tables** to swivel.
Blind fret carving A solid background with **fretwork** carving in front.
Bobbin A type of **turning** found on the legs of 17thC furniture.
Bombé The double-curved or swollen shape found in **commodes** and **bureaux** in Continental Europe and occasionally in 18thC English furniture.
Bonheur-du-jour A small ladies' **writing table** of the late 18thC.
Boulle or **buhl work** A form of **marquetry** work using brass and tortoiseshell, developed in the 18thC.
Bow front The outward curved front found on chests of drawers from the late 18thC.
Bracket foot A squared foot, the most commonly found foot on 18thC cabinet furniture.
Breakfront The term for a piece of furniture with a protruding central section.
Broken pediment A symmetric break in the centre of a **pediment**, often infilled with an urn or eagle motif.
Brushing slide The pull-out slide found above the top drawer of some small 18thC chests.
Bun foot A flattened version of the ball foot, often found on **case furniture** of the second half of the 17thC.
Bureau A writing desk with a **fall front** that encloses a fitted interior, with drawers below.
Bureau bookcase A bureau with a bookcase above.
Burr (or **burl** in the USA) The tightly knotted grain from the base of a tree, used to decorative effect in **veneers.**
Cabriole leg A gently curving S-shaped leg found on tables and chairs of the late 17th and 18thC.
Canted corner A decorative angled corner, found on **case furniture** of the 18thC.
Canterbury A container for sheet music from the 19thC.
Carcass The main body of a piece of furniture.
"Carved up" A term describing furniture that has been carved at a date later than construction, usually in the Victorian period.
Carver or **elbow chair** A dining or salon chair with open arms.
Case furniture Furniture intended primarily as a receptacle, such as chests of drawers and cupboards.
Cavetto moulding A hollow concave **moulding** found on **pediments**, especially in the early 18thC.
Chaise longue An elongated 18thC upholstered chair or daybed, popular in England during the Regency period.
Chamfer An angled corner.
Chesterfield A deep-buttoned upholstered settee with no wood showing, popular in the late 19thC.
Chest on stand The English term for a highboy.
Cheval mirror A tall dressing mirror supported by two uprights.
Chiffonnier A side cabinet with or without a drawer and with one or more shelves above.
Chinoiserie Oriental-style decoration, on **lacquered** or painted furniture.
Claw-and-ball foot A foot modelled as a ball gripped by a claw, used with a **cabriole leg.**
Cockbeading A bead **moulding** applied to the edges of drawers.
Coffer A joined and panelled low chest, usually of oak, with a lid.
Commode A highly decorated chest of drawers or cabinet, often of *bombé* shape, with applied mounts.
Composition or **compo** A putty-like material that can be **moulded,** applied to mirrors and fire surrounds and gilded or painted.
Console or **pier table** A table intended to stand against a wall, between windows. It usually has a matching mirror above it.
Corner chair A chair with back splats on two sides and a bowed top rail, intended for the corner of a room.
Cornice The projecting **moulding** at the top of tall furniture.
Counter-well or **guinea-well** The small **dished** oval found in early Georgian card tables.
Country/provincial furniture The functional furniture made away from the major cities and the main centres of production.
Credence table Late 17thC oak or walnut half-round table with a folding top.
Credenza A long side cabinet with glazed or blind (solid) doors.
Crinoline stretcher A crescent-shaped **stretcher** that unites the legs of some **Windsor chairs.**
Cross banding A **veneered** edge to table tops and drawer fronts, at right angles to the main **veneer.**
Cup and cover A bulbous **turning** with a differentiated top, commonly found on legs until the late 17thC.
Cushion drawer A convex drawer found below a **cornice** that runs the full width of a piece.
Davenport A compact writing desk with a sloped top above a case of drawers.
Dentils Small rectangular blocks applied at regular intervals to the **cornices** of much 18thC furniture.
Dished table top A hollowed-out solid top, associated with **tripod tables** with **pie-crust** edges.
Distressed A term for a piece that has been artificially aged.
Dovetails A series of interlocking joints, used in drawers.
Dowel See **Pegged furniture.**
Drop-in seat An upholstered seat frame that sits in the main framework of a chair.
Drop-leaf Any table with a fixed central section and hinged flaps.
Drum table A circular writing table supported by a central pedestal.
Dummy drawer A decorative false drawer, complete with handle.
Ebonized Wood stained and polished black to simulate ebony.
End support A central support at the sides of a writing or **sofa table.**
Escritoire A cabinet with a hinged front, which provides a writing surface, and a fitted interior.
Fall front The flap of a **bureau** or ***secretaire*** that pulls forward to provide a writing surface.
Fauteuil An upholstered armchair.
Feather or **herringbone banding** Two narrow bands of **veneer** laid in opposite diagonals.
Fielded panel A raised panel with a bevelled or **chamfered** edge that fits into a framework.
Figuring The natural grain of wood seen in **veneers.**
Finial A decorative **turned** knob applied to the top of fine **bureau bookcases** and the like.
Flamed veneer A **veneer** cut at an angle to enhance the **figuring.**
Fluting Decorative concave, parallel grooves running down the legs of tables and chairs.
Foliate carving Carved flower and leaf motifs.
Fretwork Fine pierced decoration.
Frieze The framework immediately below a table top.
Frieze drawer A drawer in the **frieze.**
Gadroon A decorative border, carved or **moulded,** comprising a series of short **flutes** or **reeds.**
Gainsborough chair A deep armchair with an upholstered seat and back, padded open arms and, usually, carved decoration.
Galleried table A table with a deep wood or metal border around the top edge.
Gateleg A leg that pivots to support a **drop leaf** on a table.
Gesso A plaster-like substance applied to carved furniture before gilding; also used as a substitute for carving when **moulded** and applied.
Gilt-tooled decoration Impressed gold leaf on the edges of leather desk tops.
Greek key A **fretwork** design based on ancient Greek decoration.
Hairy-paw foot A paw foot, carved to give a furred appearance, first seen in the 18thC.
Harlequin A term used to describe a set of chairs that are similar but do not match.
Herringbone banding See **Feather banding.**
Highboy The American term for a chest on a stand, usually with **cabriole** legs.
Husk A decorative motif of formalized leaves.
Inlay Brass, mother-of-pearl or **veneer** set into the surface of solid or veneered furniture for decorative effect.
Intaglio An incised design, as opposed to a design in relief.
Japanned An item painted and varnished in imitation of Oriental lacquer work, popular in the early 18thC.
Joint stool A stool, usually in oak, of joined construction.
Kneehole desk A desk with a recessed central cupboard below the **frieze drawer.**
Lacquer A gum-like substance, coloured and used as a ground for **chinoiserie** and gilding.
Ladder-back A chair with a series of horizontal back-rails.
Lappet A carved flap at the top of a leg with a **pad foot.**
Lion's paw foot A foot carved as a lion's paw, popular in the 18thC and the Regency period; also found as brass casters, early 19thC.
Loo table A large card table, usually circular.
Loper A pull-out arm used to support the hinged fall of a **bureau.**
Lowboy A small side table on **cabriole** legs, from the first half of the 18thC.
Marquetry A highly decorative form of **inlay** using **veneers.**
Married The term used for an item that has been made up from two or more pieces of furniture, usually of the same period.
Mortice See **Pegged furniture.**
Moulding A shaped piece of wood applied to a piece of furniture, comprising a long strip or a small decorative motif.
Mule chest A **coffer** with a single row of drawers in the base.
Nest of tables A set of three or four occasional tables that slot into each other when not in use.
Ogee A double curve of slender S shape.
Ormolu A mount or article that is gilded or gold-coloured.
Overmantel mirror A mirror designed to hang over a mantlepiece.
Ovolo A **moulding** comprising a quarter-segment of a sphere.

Oyster veneer A **veneer** formed by cutting branches of trees, such as laburnum, at right angles to the grain, producing small circles.
Pad or **club foot** A rounded foot that sits on a circular base, used in conjunction with **cabriole** legs.
Papier mâché Pulped paper that is **moulded** or lacquered to make trays and small pieces of furniture.
Parcel gilding Partial gilding.
Parquetry A geometrical pattern made up of small pieces of **veneer**, sometimes of different woods.
Patera A small circular ornament made of wood, metal or **composition**.
Patina The build-up of wax and dirt that gives old furniture a soft mellow look.
Pedestal desk A flat desk, usually with a leathered top, that stands on two banks of drawers.
Pediment The gabled structure that surmounts a **cornice.**
Pegged furniture Early joined furniture constructed by a system of mortices (slots) and tenons (tongues), held together by dowels (pegs).
Pembroke table A small two-flap table that stands on four legs.
Pie-crust top The carved decorative edge of a **dished-top tripod table.**
Pier glass A tall, narrow mirror intended to hang against a pillar between the windows of a drawing room.
Pietra dura A composition of semi-precious stones applied to the panels of furniture.
Plinth base A solid base, not raised on feet.
Pole-screen An adjustable fire screen.
Provincial furniture See **country furniture**.
Quartered top A flat surface covered with four pieces of matched **veneer.**
Quartetto tables A **nest** of four tables.
Rail The horizontal **splats** of a chair back.
Reeding Parallel strips of convex flutes found on the legs of chairs and tables.
Re-entrant corner A shaped indentation at each corner of a table.
Runners The strips of wood on which drawers slide.
Sabre leg A curved chair leg in the shape of a sabre.
Scagliola A composite material that resembles marble.
Scalloped or **butterfly-wing leaf** The serpentine flap of some **Pembroke tables.**
Sconce A cup-shaped candle holder.
Seat rail The horizontal framework immediately below the chair seat that unites the tops of chair legs.
Secretaire A writing cabinet with a mock drawer front that lets down to provide a writing surface, revealing recessed pigeon holes.
***Secretaire* bookcase** A *secretaire* with a bookcase fitted above.
Settle The earliest form of chair to seat two or more people.
Side chair A chair without arms, designed to stand against a wall.
Side table Any table designed to stand against a wall.
Silhouette leg A two-dimensional leg shaped from a flat piece of timber.
Sofa table A rectangular table with two hinged flaps at the ends, designed to stand behind a sofa.
Spade or **therm foot** A tapering foot of square section.
Spandrel A decorative corner bracket, usually pierced and found at the tops of legs.
Splat The central upright in a chair back; loosely applied to all members in a chair back.
Squab The loose flat cushion on the seat of a chair.
Stiff-leaf toe cap A caster moulded with formalized leaves.
Stiles The vertical parts of a framework, a term usually associated with early furniture.
Stretchers The horizontal bars that unite and strengthen the legs of chairs and other furniture.
Stringing Fine inlaid lines around a piece of furniture.
Stuff-over seat A chair that is upholstered over the seat rails.
Swan-neck cresting A type of broken **pediment** with two S-shaped curves, one reversed.
Swan-neck handle A curved handle, popular in the 18thC.
Teapoy A small piece of furniture designed for holding tea leaves.
Toilet mirror A small dressing mirror with a box base, usually fitted with two or three drawers.
Trefoil Shaped like a clover, with three lobes.
Tripod base A small table with a round top supported by a three-legged pillar.
Turned A solid member made and modelled by turning on a lathe.
Uprights The vertical sides of the back of a chair.
Urn table A small 18thC table designed to hold a silver kettle or water urn.
Veneer A thin slice of timber cut from the solid.
Wainscot chair An early joined chair with a panelled back, open arms and a wooden seat.
Whatnot A mobile stand with open shelves.
Wheel-back chair A chair with a circular back with radiating spokes, made in the late 18thC.
Wing chair A fully upholstered chair with wings at the sides to keep out draughts.
Windsor chair A type of wooden chair with a spindle back.

SELECTED MAKERS

Adam, Robert (1728-92) Scottish architect and designer of household furnishings in the Neo-classical style. Highly influential in the late 18thC. His furniture designs for Harewood and Kenwood Houses were executed by Chippendale.
Boulle, André-Charles (1642-1732) Chief cabinet maker to Louis XIV. Famous for his tortoiseshell and brass marquetry, a technique that bears his name.
Boulton, Matthew (b. 1728) Birmingham (England) manufacturer of ormolu, silver plate and metal mounts.
Chippendale, Thomas (1718-79) The most famous and skilled of England's master cabinet makers. Published *The Gentleman and Cabinet-Makers Director*, 1754, the first catalogue of its kind.
Cobb, John (d. 1778) One of the foremost English makers of the period 1755-65. Partner in the firm of **Vile** & Cobb, cabinet makers and upholsterers to George III.
Eastlake, Charles Locke (1836-1906) Responsible for the revival of the "Early English" style through his book *Hints on Household Taste*, 1868, widely read in England and America.
Elfe, Thomas (1719-75) English-born cabinet maker, settled in Charleston, South Carolina. Known for his Chippendale-style furniture with fretwork.
Gillows Family firm of manufacturers, founded in Lancaster, England, in 1695. Opened showrooms in London's Oxford Street in 1769. Renowned for the quality of their work and materials. Amalgamated with Warings in 1900.
Hepplewhite, George (d. 1786) English designer and cabinet maker; his name has been coupled with one of the most influential styles of English furniture. His *Cabinet-Maker and Upholsterer's Guide* was published posthumously in 1788.
Hope, Thomas (1770-1831) English designer. Well known for his Classical designs of the early 19thC. Frequently used rams' and lions' heads.
Ince & Mayhew English partnership of high repute. Their *Universal System of Household Furniture*, 1759-63, rivalled **Chippendale's** *Director.*
Jacob, Georges (1739-1814). The leading *ébeniste* (cabinet maker) of the years leading up to the French First Republic, 1793.
Jennens & Bettridge Best-known English makers in the 19thC of papier mâché furniture and small articles. Wares are stamped.
Kent, William (1685-1748) English designer, architect and landscape gardener. Famous for his sumptuous furniture designs in the grand manner of the pre-Chippendale period.
Lock, Matthias A carver and designer, largely responsible for the introduction of the Rococo style to England.
Marot, Daniel Dutch furniture and interior designer. Influential in England; he worked for William III.
Phyfe, Duncan (1768-1854) One of the most famous American cabinet makers; Scottish-born, he settled in New York. Best known for his work in the Classical style, with influences of the French Empire style.
Pugin, Augustus Welby (1812-52) The leading influence on the 19thC English Gothic Revival.
Riesenburgh, Bernard Van Produced some of the finest Rococo furniture of the Louis XV period.
Riesener, Jean-Henri (1734-1806) Master *ébeniste* to Louis XVI.
Schuntel, Karl Friedrich (1727-1801) Influential German furniture and interior designer.
Seddon & Co. Company founded by George Seddon (1727-1801); it flourished in the 19thC.
Sheraton, Thomas (1751-1806) One of the best-known English designers of the late 18thC. His publications included the *Cabinet Maker and Upholsterers Drawing Book*, 1791-4, and the *Cabinet Dictionary*, 1803. Best known for his designs for elegant furniture with restrained inlay.
Smith, George One of the most prominent English cabinet makers and designers of the early 19thC.
Townsend-Goddard Highly successful partnership of American cabinet makers during the American Chippendale period.
Vile, William (d. 1767) Senior partner in the firm of Vile & Cobb.

BIBLIOGRAPHY

Agius, Pauline and Stephen Jones, *Ackermann's Regency Furniture and Interiors* (1984)
Cescinsky, Herbert, *The Gentle Art of Faking Furniture* (1931)
Chinnery, Victor, *Oak Furniture – The British Tradition* (1979)
Coleridge, A., *Chippendale Furniture* (1968)
Collard, Frances, *Regency Furniture* (1983)
Comstock, Helen, *American Furniture: 17th, 18th and 19th century styles* (1962)
Victorian furniture and Windsor Chairs (1958)
Edwards, Ralph, *Shorter Dictionary of English Furniture* (1964)
Fastnedge, Ralph, *Sheraton Furniture* (1983)
Gilbert, C., *Furniture at Temple Newsam House and Lotherton Hall* 2 volumes (1978)
The Life and Work of Thomas Chippendale 2 volumes (1978)
Goodison, N., *Ormolu: The Work of Mathew Boulton* (1974)
Jourdain, Margaret, *Regency Furniture* (1965)
Jourdain, Margaret, and J. Rose, *English Furniture and the Georgian Period* (1953)
Stevens-Claxton, Christopher, and Stewart Whittington, *18th century English Furniture: The Norman Adams Collection* (1983)
Symonds, W.R., and B.B. Whinneray, *Victorian Furniture* (1987)
Ward-Jackson, Peter, *English Furniture Designs of the 18th century* (1984)

POTTERY AND PORCELAIN

Ceramics is a field that often explodes the beginner's preconceptions. There are categories of pottery – such as French *faïence* – that can show the artistic subtelty commonly associated with porcelain, warranting the adjective "exquisite". And porcelain, conversely, can be decorated with a humble, naive charm, as illustrated by many English blue and white wares.

Chinese porcelain has exerted a magnetic pull over the West since the 17th century, when the European nobility began to compete hotly for the finest pieces, sometimes crediting them with a near-mystical significance. Vast quantities of Chinese porcelain were made, both for export and for home consumption. Although prices for wares with fine or rare decoration are escalating rapidly, you can still acquire slightly damaged wares – even those of the Ming dynasty – for a relatively small outlay.

Interest in Japanese porcelain centres mainly on Imari wares, whose distinctive colouring of underglaze blue was enhanced by iron-red and gilding. Quality varies greatly (as with the heavily potted Satsuma earthenware); value is closely related to size.

Western pottery was generally made for domestic use rather than for show, but there are some exceptions to this – for example, the superb painted chargers of Renaissance Europe. Even useful wares, such as drug jars, can have rich decoration.

The golden age of European porcelain is the 18th century – the era of Meissen in Germany, Sèvres in France, Capodimonte in Italy. Among English factories, Chelsea is pre-eminent for quality. Interest in the minor English factories is currently blossoming. Collectors of early English porcelain need to be able to identify the different types of porcelain used, and must familiarize themselves with the complex and often frustratingly inconsistent ways in which factories tended to mark their products. What is more, they need a generous budget.

Everyday domestic pottery of the 18th century has dramatically risen in value since it became collectable three decades ago. Saltglaze stoneware, in particular, can fetch extraordinary prices. However, there are still relatively neglected fields, such as creamware.

The 19th century offers immense scope to the collector. At one extreme there are the superb Empire-style cabinet wares – vases, urns and the like – with fine painting and gilding, made by Worcester and other factories. At the other are Staffordshire figures, presenting a fascinating tableau of the social and political history of the Victorian era.

This chart shows some of the principal types of pottery and porcelain, indicating the main periods of production. For hard-paste and soft-paste porcelain and bone china some of the main factories are shown.

Period of main production

Period of secondary production

Factory produced porcelain of a different paste

	1450-1500	*1500-155*
EARTHENWARE		
	LEAD-GLAZED EARTHENWA MAIOLICA	FAÏENCE
STONEWARE		
	RHENISH	
HARD-PASTE		
	CHINESE MING	
SOFT-PASTE		

BONE CHINA		

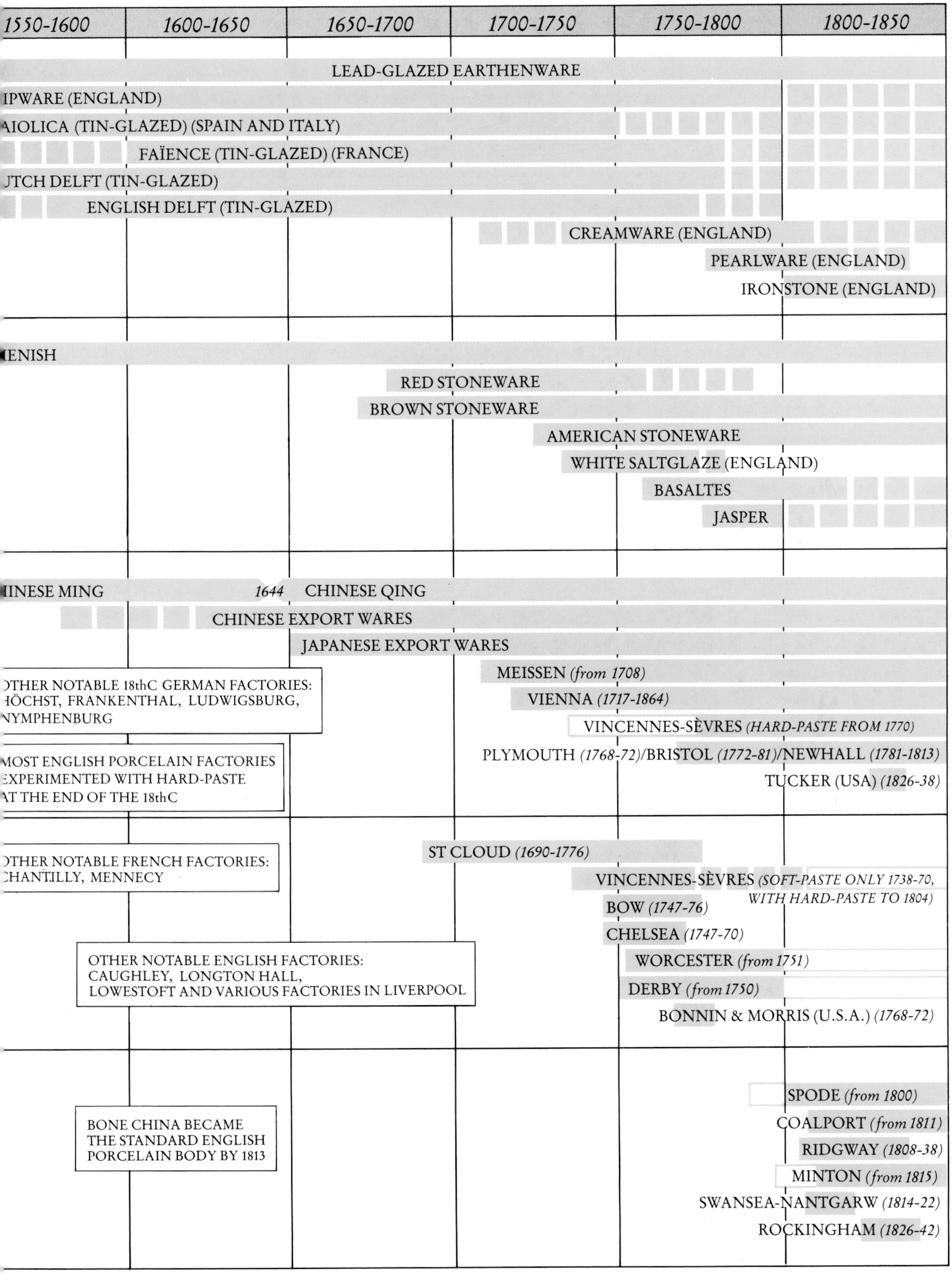

1550-1600	1600-1650	1650-1700	1700-1750	1750-1800	1800-1850

LEAD-GLAZED EARTHENWARE

IPWARE (ENGLAND)

AIOLICA (TIN-GLAZED) (SPAIN AND ITALY)

FAÏENCE (TIN-GLAZED) (FRANCE)

JTCH DELFT (TIN-GLAZED)

ENGLISH DELFT (TIN-GLAZED)

CREAMWARE (ENGLAND)

PEARLWARE (ENGLAND)

IRONSTONE (ENGLAND)

ENISH

RED STONEWARE

BROWN STONEWARE

AMERICAN STONEWARE

WHITE SALTGLAZE (ENGLAND)

BASALTES

JASPER

IINESE MING *1644* CHINESE QING

CHINESE EXPORT WARES

JAPANESE EXPORT WARES

)THER NOTABLE 18thC GERMAN FACTORIES:
HÖCHST, FRANKENTHAL, LUDWIGSBURG,
NYMPHENBURG

MEISSEN *(from 1708)*

VIENNA *(1717-1864)*

VINCENNES-SÈVRES *(HARD-PASTE FROM 1770)*

MOST ENGLISH PORCELAIN FACTORIES
EXPERIMENTED WITH HARD-PASTE
AT THE END OF THE 18thC

PLYMOUTH *(1768-72)*/BRISTOL *(1772-81)*/NEWHALL *(1781-1813)*

TUCKER (USA) *(1826-38)*

)THER NOTABLE FRENCH FACTORIES:
CHANTILLY, MENNECY

ST CLOUD *(1690-1776)*

VINCENNES-SÈVRES *(SOFT-PASTE ONLY 1738-70, WITH HARD-PASTE TO 1804)*

BOW *(1747-76)*

CHELSEA *(1747-70)*

OTHER NOTABLE ENGLISH FACTORIES:
CAUGHLEY, LONGTON HALL,
LOWESTOFT AND VARIOUS FACTORIES IN LIVERPOOL

WORCESTER *(from 1751)*

DERBY *(from 1750)*

BONNIN & MORRIS (U.S.A.) *(1768-72)*

BONE CHINA BECAME
THE STANDARD ENGLISH
PORCELAIN BODY BY 1813

SPODE *(from 1800)*

COALPORT *(from 1811)*

RIDGWAY *(1808-38)*

MINTON *(from 1815)*

SWANSEA-NANTGARW *(1814-22)*

ROCKINGHAM *(1826-42)*

Basics I

The following aspects of a piece are essential factors in the assessment of origin, date and value:

* body
* glaze
* shape
* decoration
* marks
* rarity
* condition
* authenticity

BODY

Collectors of ceramics need to be able to distinguish between the different "bodies" – that is, the materials in which a piece is made. Although some guidelines are offered here, there is no substitute for gaining experience by actually handling pieces, and every opportunity should be taken to do so.

Pottery or porcelain?
Porcelain is a fine variety of ceramics that was first made in China in the 9thC AD and widely imitated in the West in the 18thC.

Pottery is of much coarser texture. The two main types of pottery are porous *earthenware* and non-porous *stoneware*. The distinctions between these types of ceramics stem from the use of different materials, the temperature at which the piece is fired in the kiln, and the proportion of vitreous (glassy) ingredients in the body.

The most important test is to hold the article up to a strong light. If light shows through the body of the piece, it is either porcelain or thinly potted stoneware. If the body does not transmit light, it is earthenware. This is a reliable rule of thumb. Once a few known examples have been handled there will be little difficulty in differentiating between translucent stoneware and porcelain, particularly as stoneware is generally unglazed, or glazed with vaporized salt which creates a characteristically rippled surface not unlike orange peel.

China or porcelain?
Many people are confused about the difference between porcelain and "china". Strictly, "china" is porcelain made in China or in the Chinese manner. However, the term has also been applied to various kinds of pottery. Its use today is best confined to the phrase "bone china" (see below).

Hard-paste or soft-paste?
The formula for Chinese porcelain, sometimes called *hard-paste* porcelain, contains two essential elements – kaolin (china clay) and petuntse (china stone). Both are forms of decomposed granite. They are fused together by firing in a kiln. First the object is fired to about 1650°F (900°C), then dipped in glaze, then refired at about 2400°F (1300°C). The china stone bonds the clay particles together and gives translucency; the high temperature gives the object the consistency of glass (vitrifies it).

During the 17thC, the import of porcelain from China stimulated Europeans to attempt to discover the secret of its manufacture.

Augustus, Elector of Saxony, employed an alchemist J. F. Böttger, to assist in the quest to make hard-paste. A source of kaolin was found and porcelain manufacture was attempted at Meissen, near Dresden. By 1718 petuntse had been located, and so began the production of the extremely hard white porcelain for which Meissen became famed. Before long there was a rapid growth of factories producing hard-paste throughout Europe.

In England hard-paste porcelain was made by a formula which passed in succession from Plymouth to Bristol to New Hall. Production lasted only into the first decade of the 19thC. The paste was prone to twisting during turning and firing; moreover, underglaze blue colours were overly darkened by the high firing temperature.

Hard-paste: a Nymphenburg figure of Harlequin, c.1760. S

Meanwhile, another type of porcelain, known as *soft-paste*, had evolved. It was first made in Florence, Italy, in c.1575 under the patronage of the de Medici family. Later factories include those in France at Rouen (c.1673), St Cloud, Chantilly, Mennecy, Vincennes and Sèvres; and in Italy at Capodimonte.

Several varieties of soft-paste were made in England from the mid-18thC, beginning with Chelsea, London, c. 1745.

As its name suggests, soft-paste is more easily scratched than hard-paste. The glaze sits on the surface of the ware, feels warmer and softer to the touch, and is less glittering in appearance. Chips in soft-paste have a floury appearance like fine-grained pastry; whereas in true porcelain, chips appear smooth and glassy.

Overglaze decoration on hard-paste stands out distinctly: on soft-paste the decoration tends to sink into the glaze.

Soft-paste: a Bow figure group of the Fortune Teller, c.1752. S

The distinction between the two pastes is especially obvious on figures. The close-fitting glaze on hard-paste enables crisper, more detailed modelling, whereas soft-paste figures have blunter outlines, often with glaze pooling in the crevices.

Which kind of soft-paste?
Several soft-paste formulae were discovered, each using fine clay but adding different ingredients to provide the all-important translucency:

* *Frit porcelain*, using powdered glass made from a combination of substances including white sand and gypsum. At best, this body has a beautiful creamy or ivory appearance. (Chelsea, Longton Hall)
* *Soapstone porcelain*, using powdered soapstone (steatite). This yielded a white, more plastic body. (Lund's Bristol, Chaffer's factory at Liverpool, Worcester, Caughley)
* *Bone-ash porcelain*, using powdered calcined ox-bones. This body was denser, generally more thickly potted, and heavier. (Bow, Lowestoft, Chelsea, Chelsea-Derby, Pennington's factory at Liverpool)

Bone china
This characteristically English porcelain, invented c.1794, is nearer to hard-paste than soft-paste. It made use of a large proportion of bone-ash added to hard-paste ingredients. The resulting body was white, translucent and plastic. (Spode, Flight & Barr, Derby, Rockingham, Coalport, Minton)

Feldspar china
This was a type of English porcelain in which feldspar replaced china stone in the bone-china formula. It was less expensive even than bone china, as well as being harder and more robust. Spode experimented with it around 1815, followed by Coalport.

Biscuit
"Biscuit" is a term applied to a stage in the production of pottery or porcelain after it has been fired once and not glazed. It is specifically applied to porcelain figures sold in an unglazed state, characterized by their matt, porous surface. They were made from the mid-18thC by Continental factories and in England by Derby from 1773. The absence of glaze made it possible for the modelling to be very precise.

Earthenware or stoneware?
There are two temperature ranges for firing pottery. Below 2200°F (1200 °C) is the "low" temperature range: wares fired within this range are categorized as *earthenwares*. Most common clays are suitable for earthenwares, and the resultant body may be white, buff, brown, red or grey depending not only on the natural colour of the clay but also on its iron content.

Stoneware is made from clays that allow shapes to retain their form at temperatures up to 2250°F (1400°C). In this "high" temperature range the clay "melts" and fuses into a non-porous vitrified body of great strength. These vitrified bodies can be slightly translucent, are impervious to liquids and are extremely hard and durable. As with earthenwares, the resultant bodies can vary in colour.

Some stoneware bodies – the so-called "dry" bodies – could be left unglazed as they were imporous. Many such wares were made by Wedgwood – for example, basaltes and jasper wares. However, most stonewares were salt-glazed (see below).

Stoneware bodies were made in Europe, predominantly in Germany, from at least as early as the 15thC. They were also made in China, in England from the late 17thC and in America throughout the 19thC and into the 20thC.

Stoneware: a redware mug, English, by the Elers Bros., c.1695. P

Stone china is a heavy earthenware that resembles porcelain in appearance. It was first developed in Staffordshire c.1800.

GLAZES

The purpose of a glaze applied to a piece of pottery or porcelain is to make it waterproof, or enhance the brilliance of the colour. Glazes can be translucent, opaque or coloured.

Hard-paste porcelain was given a feldspar glaze similar in composition to the body itself. When fired, the body and glaze fused together.

The principal pottery glazes are:

* *Lead glaze*: a transparent, glassy, tight-fitting glaze used on most English and Continental soft-paste porcelain, and on earthenwares such as creamware. The lead in early lead glazes tended to absorb into acidic liquids, such as vinegar, making them poisonous. Stonewares were therefore used for storing pickles and the like.
* *Tin glaze*: a glaze to which tin oxide has been added, giving an opaque white finish. This is a very important and broad group of wares, divided into different categories according to country:
  maiolica (Renaissance Italy)
  faïence (17thC France and Germany)
  Delft (17th and 18thC Netherlands)
  delftware (17th and 18thC England)

Maiolica should not be confused with *majolica* – a type of 19thC earthenware decorated with coloured glazes.

Delft: an English (Bristol) puzzle jug, c.1730. S

* *Salt glaze*: a glaze formed by throwing common salt into the kiln at about 1800°F (1000°C) during the firing of stoneware. The sodium in the salt combined with silicates in the body to form a thin, glassy glaze. Adding red lead to the salt made the glaze thicker and more glass-like. Early Rhineland "saltglaze" appears in both grey and brown forms. In England brown stoneware continued to be made into the 19thC. By 1720 Staffordshire potters were making a white saltglaze resembling porcelain. The English saltglaze of the 1750s is light buff in colour, with a thin glaze pitted like orange peel.

Saltglaze stoneware: an English crinoline figure, c.1740. S

* *Coloured glazes*: used on earthenware in mid-18thC England by Thomas Whieldon and Ralph Wood. Coloured glazes are also found on Chinese pottery and porcelain: these are mainly derived from oxides of iron.

Crazing and firecracks

* *Crazing* is a network pattern that appears when a lead glaze "warps". It is a feature that occurs in pottery and some early soft-paste. It is not found on hard-paste, nor on early Worcester porcelain. Although crazing is a sign of age, it can be simulated by the faker.
* *Firecracks* are sometimes formed in soft-paste during firing in the kiln. Collectors will accept even quite large ones more readily than they will accept subsequent damage.
* *"Pinholes"* are minute air bubbles that cause patches of extra translucency. Larger patches thus caused are called *"moons"*. Similar flaws can be caused by variations in the glaze thickness.

SHAPES

A familiarity with the basic shapes of pottery and porcelain is essential to the collector. The shape reflected usage, which in turn often reflected the social background.

Chinese shapes were commonly imitated in the West, and should therefore not be taken as conclusive evidence of Chinese manufacture. Conversely, Western forms such as tureens were made in China for export. Chinese tureens in the shape of birds, for example, tend to look European to the inexperienced eye.

Tea and coffee wares

The tea drinking habit in Europe had begun to catch on by c.1600, and the first pottery teawares were made in the late 17thC. The first porcelain teawares were made c. 1685 in France, in the 1720s in Germany and c.1748-50 in England. Tea time was after dinner, rather than late afternoon, until the end of the 18thC.

* *Teapots* in the 18thC were globe-shaped, barrel-shaped or sometimes (in England) octagonal. By the late 1780s pots with a fluted, oval plan were standard. By the 1820s the pots had returned to circular plan but with a curved profile; many were mounted on feet.

The spout of a teapot is usually positioned low on the body, near the base, so that the tea can be poured out of the pot without causing undue disturbance to floating tea-leaves.

A globular teapot, Chinese, made for Europe, 18thC. CNY

A teapot with fluted oval plan, New Hall, c.1800. S

* Teapots became larger as tea became less of a luxury.
* Teapots with matching stands are very desirable.
* *Coffee pots* are taller than teapots. They are usually pear-shaped, with a long spout.
* Small *tea canisters*, with covers, were used on the tea table. They are now rare.
* *Cream jugs* include the familiar "sparrow-beak" form. The long, low form is generally identified as a *cream ewer*, although the terminology is not precise.

A cream jug with sparrow-beak mask spout, Liverpool, c.1770. S

* *Sugar bowls* (or sucriers, as they are also known) mostly had a cover. They usually corresponded to teapot shapes.

A teabowl and saucer, Meissen, c.1740. CG

* *Teabowls*, without handles, were inspired by Oriental practice. Initially, handled cups were exceptions. The handled teacup was universal by c.1810.
* Teacups and teabowls are the most commonly found porcelain teawares. The tea was poured into the saucer, and sipped from that. In the early 1800s a cup plate was supplied to put the cup on.
* *Coffee cups* are tall and narrow in comparison to teacups or teabowls.
* *Chocolate cups* tended to be bigger; they sometimes had two handles and a cover.
* *A coffee can* is a cylindrical, straight-sided coffee cup, made c.1750-1830; the handle shape often helps in attribution.
* Ornate *cabinet cups and saucers*, for display only, were made until c.1820.
* *Slop bowls* are small open bowls that were used at the tea table to receive the dregs of teacups.
* *Spoon trays* or spoon boats are narrow trays used to hold wet teaspoons. Few were made after c.1800. Today they are rare.

Services

* *Dinner services* were imported from China initially. The standard 18thC set included a highly elaborate *tureen* (perhaps shaped as a vegetable, or a hen, or a partridge) with cover, stand and ladle. *Sauce boats* occur in many attractive forms. Some have a lip at each end and two side-handles.
* *Dessert services* included leaf-shaped dishes, openwork baskets, as well as plates, comports (fruit dishes on pedestals), ice pails and other items. Vases, figures and candlestick figures were also intended for the table.

Basics II

* *Cabaret services* were a form of teaset or breakfast set, made in the later 18th and early 19thC. They included a plateau (flat serving tray with a low vertical rim) and jam pot, as well as a tea, coffee or chocolate pot, sugar basin, milk or cream jug, and cups and saucers.
* The *tête-à-tête* was a service for two people. The *solitaire* was a service for one.

MANUFACTURING

* Hollow wares (bowls, mugs and so on) were turned on a potter's wheel against an outline. Handles were made separately and applied to the ware before the clay dried, using slip (diluted clay) as an adhesive.
* By the early 18thC, small teapots were being made by moulding and casting.
* *Press moulding* involved pressing clay or a porcelain body into a mould. Two components made in this way would often be joined together to form the finished object. The seam mark would be disguised by trimming away the excess.
* *Slip casting* involved pouring slip into a finely carved cast, made in earthenware or, later, in plaster of Paris. The mould absorbed water from the slip, building up a layer of clay on the inside of the mould. On slip-cast pieces, any flutes, indentations or relief features on the outside surface show up prominently on the inside surface.

DECORATIVE TECHNIQUES

A thorough understanding of the techniques used to decorate pottery and porcelain will equip the collector with the means to identify a piece and assess its value.

Underglaze blue

Decorative designs can be added before or after glazing.

In underglaze decoration the colours are added before glazing. Thus, they have to withstand high temperatures in the kiln.

Chinese blue and white porcelain, an important example of underglaze decoration, made use of a pigment known as cobalt blue – a form of cobalt oxide, termed zaffre, which turned from black to blue when fired. The resulting effect ranges from a greyish or blackish blue to a sapphire, depending on the impurities present in the ore.

In Europe, underglaze blue decoration was first used to decorate delftware by copying chinoiserie designs onto the white tin-glazed surface, to create an imitation of Chinese porcelain. Its use continued on both Dutch and English delftware and on the soft-paste porcelain produced by French and English factories in the late 17th and 18thC.

Underglaze blue: a Bow saucer, c.1756. MB

Pearlware of the 18thC also made extensive use of underglaze blue designs, as did 19thC blue-printed earthenware (that is, earthenware with printed designs in blue, rather than painted designs).

Underglaze colours

Other "high-temperature" colours, so-called because of their ability to withstand kiln temperatures of 2200-2400°F (1200-1300 °C), were used on European *faïence* (tin-glazed earthenware) in the 15thC – but not on English delft until the late 16th and early 17thC. These colours were obtained from antimony (yellow), iron (brown), manganese (purple) and copper (green).

Overglaze enamels

Although Chinese potters had developed a palette of soft enamel colours as early as the mid-15thC, it was not until the early 18thC that the range of colours and shades was significantly extended.

Overglaze enamels: a Staffordshire saltglaze teapot, c.1757. S

Enamel colours were prepared from metallic oxides by adding the oxide to molten glass and reducing the cooled mixture to a fine powder which, when mixed with an oily medium, could be painted over the glaze and fused to it by firing. The oil burned out in the process. The range of colours obtainable by this method was greater than the range of underglaze colours, as they could be fired at lower temperatures – in the 1300-1750°F (700-950°C) range. These colours are known as the *petit feu* ("little fire") colours, as opposed to the higher-temperature *grand feu* ("large fire") colours.

Overglaze colours mature at *varying* temperatures, so that multi-coloured decoration might require a number of firings. This meant that the production of coloured wares could be costly.

In England, overglaze colours were first used to decorate white salt glazed wares in the mid-1740s and soft-paste porcelain from c.1747.

Coloured glazes

Most authorities credit Ralph Wood with the invention of coloured glazes in England in the 18thC (although his work had precedents in 17thC France). By the 1750s he had perfected the technique of applying the glazes without the colours intermixing.

Coloured glazes: a French figure (La Nourrice), c.1630. PC

Transfer printing

In the early 1750s the English soft-paste porcelain factories at Bow and Worcester began experimenting with a method of mass-produced overglaze decoration known as transfer printing. The process used a metal plate on which the design was etched. The plate was "inked" with a metallic oxide bound in an oil-based fluid and was used to impress the design onto paper, which was then applied to the ware. During firing, the design from the paper sank into the glaze. Thousands of prints could be taken from one plate. As early as 1754 Bow and Worcester were producing wares decorated with prints in purple, puce, red or black. By 1760, the technique had spread to other factories, and creamware was also being printed.

In the early 19thC, two techniques were in use – line engraving; and stippling with dots to produce light and shade effects. The engraved design was then transferred, not to paper, but to "bats" of glue which were then pressed to the wares in order to transfer the image.

In the late 1750s the porcelain factories tried to print in cobalt blue *under* the glaze. At first success was limited, as biscuit porcelain is not very absorbent and the print tended to lift into the glaze during firing, producing a blurred pattern. This difficulty was overcome during the 1760s, and underglaze blue printing replaced painting in the mass production of blue and white wares.

During the 19thC, multi-colour transfer printing under the glaze was perfected on the more absorbent pottery bodies. The availability of artificial colour pigments, in conjunction with lithography, enabled multi-coloured printed wares to be produced at low cost from 1839.

Transfer printing: a Worcester blue and white saucer, c.1770. MB

To distinguish printing from painting, note the following key points:

* A painted pattern is made by brushstrokes, which show greater fluidity than can be achieved by printing.
* The use of a brush is most obvious where there is shading of colour.
* Hatching is used to achieve a tonal effect in a print.

Gilding

The attractiveness of porcelain could be enhanced by gold decoration.

The particular method of gilding employed can be of help in dating a piece:

* *Japanned gilding* This process was used on English soft-paste porcelain from c.1740. Gold leaf was applied to the glaze using gum arabic and, after firing, was burnished, forming a thin, bright layer of gold.
* *Oil gilding* Oil gilding was used on some early soft-paste porcelain and on cheaper mid-18thC pottery bodies such as Jackfield ware. Patterns were first

outlined in a mixture of oil and gum arabic. The pattern was allowed to dry; then gold leaf was added and fired at a low temperature. Oil gilding is not durable and could not be burnished; few examples survive in good condition.
* *Honey gilding* Continental factories of the 18thC mixed gold leaf powder with oil of lavender and honey and applied the mixture to the porcelain with a brush. In this way layers could be built up and subsequently chased (worked with a tool to create a pattern). The method was brought to England in the early 1750s. Honey gilding is less bright than japanned gilding, but is extremely durable.
* *Mercury gilding* In the late 18thC, a technique was evolved whereby gold leaf powder was mixed with mercury and applied to the porcelain with a brush. The mercury vaporized in firing, leaving a film of gold which could then be burnished to a brassy, bright finish. This technique allowed rapid decoration and was suitable for use with stencils, making it popular for services.
* *19thC gilding* Attempts to develop less expensive methods of gilding were made during the 19thC. Three important methods were (a) the use of gold leaf transfer prints (b) painting with liquid gold (used on earthenwares) (c) the application of a paste after firing; this was then burnished.

Some early pottery techniques
* *Sgraffito* A technique of decoration in which a sharp pointed tool was used to cut through a coating of slip (diluted clay) to the underlying body. This decoration is particularly effective when a pale slip overlays a dark clay body. The technique was used throughout Europe on domestic earthenware and stoneware from at least as early as the 15thC. It was also used from an early date in America.
* *Slip combing* A technique of applying two colours of slip and combing one over the other to produce a feathered surface.
* *Slip trailing* A technique of decorating earthenware by trailing the body with contrasting coloured clay which has been watered down to a creamy consistency and applied through a nozzle – like icing squeezed on to a cake.

Sgraffito: a "scratch-blue" cider jug, English, c.1760. The sgraffito pattern is highlighted by an infilling of cobalt blue. S

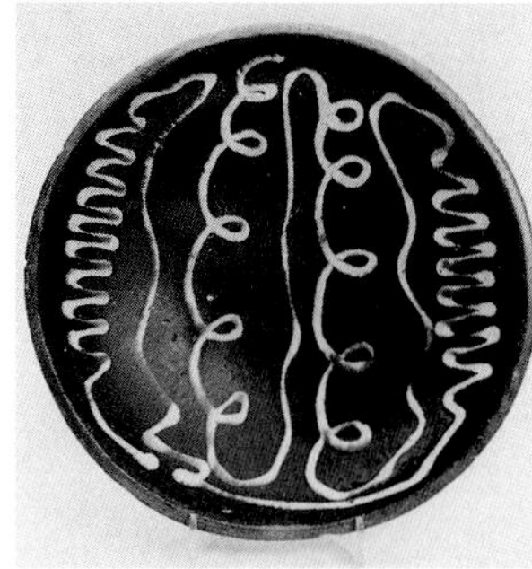

Slip trailing: a baking dish, English, late 18thC. S

Some 18thC techniques
* *Sprigging* This decorative technique involves the application of separately moulded reliefs to an object, using slip, prior to firing.
* *Stamping* This is a less expensive alternative to sprigging. A pad of contrasting clay was applied to the body and the design stamped into it. When dry, the excess was removed.
* *Piercing* In this technique, the unfired body is marked with an intricate design which is then cut out with a knife. In some cases a vessel intended to hold liquids was given a double-walled body, the outer one being pierced. Piercing was used widely on 18thC creamware and was reintroduced by Owen at the Royal Worcester factory in the 1880s.

Some 19thC techniques
* *Metallic lustres* In late 18thC England, Wedgwood experimented with lustres – the shiny metallic decoration found in European *maiolica* and Isnik wares of the 15thC. Lustres give the appearance of silver or copper – although copper lustre becomes pink or purple when applied to a light-bodied earthenware.

Early 19thC lustre decoration, c.1805, is found in distinct bands across the body of the ware. However, a variety of techniques was soon developed, including wax resist and splashed effects.
* *Sponging* A naive method of pottery decoration reintroduced by Staffordshire factories in the 1820s and extensively exported. Known as "spatterware" in America, sponged wares were popular in the period 1825-50.
* *Pâte-sur-pâte* This was a method of decoration developed at Minton in the late 1860s. Layers of slip were built up on the unfired ground colour, then tooled to the required design, then fired. The process produced a strongly three-dimensional effect with fine detailing.

Seven influential forms of decoration
* *Chinoiseries* Chinese motifs, or chinoiseries, are a major strand running through Western pottery and porcelain decoration. Direct imitation of Chinese designs appeared on European delft at the end of the 17thC. Similar designs appeared on English porcelain from c.1750. Temples, lakes, fishermen, bridges and pierced rocks are all in the standard repertoire of European decoration. However, the Chinese elements are often interpreted in a peculiarly Western way.

Chinoiseries: a Chaffer's Liverpool mug, 18thC. WW

* *Famille rose* A palette (colour range) of enamel painting that developed as a form of decoration on Chinese porcelain. The name derived from the use of a distinctive rose-pink colour, originating in the reign of Qianlong. The colours of *famille rose* were used on Chinese export wares after 1720, and influenced the palette of European porcelain decoration throughout the 18thC.

Famille rose: a Chinese plate, 18thC. CNY

* *Famille verte* A palette of enamels in which a strong green predominates, originating in the Kangxi period. Although ousted as the favoured palette by *famille rose* colours, it nevertheless influenced the decoration of English soft-paste porcelain in the mid-18thC.

Famille verte: a hexagonal puzzle jug, Chinese, c.1700. C

* *Kakiemon* This was a Japanese form of decoration featuring asymmetrical but well-balanced compositions of flowering branches (notably prunus) with added elements such as rocks,

Kakiemon: a Chelsea vase, c.1750-52. S

Basics III

quails (partridges) and banded hedges, all on a white surface. Porcelain in this style was copied at Meissen and other European factories in the 18thC.

* *Imari* This type of Japanese porcelain, made from the beginning of the 17thC, featured decoration based on native textiles and brocades. The motifs, and the palette dominated by a strong blue and rich red, were copied in Europe. In the late 18th and 19thC they inspired the "Japan" patterns used by some English porcelain factories.

Imari: a Japanese jar and cover, c.1700. SM

* *Ground colours* The use of a painted plain surface as a surround for painted decoration set into "reserves" (panels left blank for the purpose) was initiated in Europe at Meissen soon after 1720. The idea was borrowed from China. Soon this became an established method of decoration, used by almost all porcelain factories.

Ground colour: a Sèvres tureen stand with blue-green ground, c.1773. S

* *Blanc de Chine* This was a white or near-white porcelain with a thick, rich glaze, made (particularly in the form of small figures) in China during the Ming dynasty. On dishes and other vessels a common decoration was the prunus blossom in relief. *Blanc de Chine* was copied by Bow, Chelsea, Longton Hall, Mennecy and St Cloud in the 18thC.

Blanc de Chine: a Chinese figure of a cock, 16thC. SM

MAJOR STYLES

* The *Baroque* style of the 17thC, which developed in Catholic southern Europe, is characterized by grandness, rich symmetrical ornament and strong colours. These features are found on *maiolica* and on French *faïence* in the preSèvres age – the period of Louis XIV (1643-1715). A highpoint of the Baroque in ceramics is the porcelain figures made at Meissen by Kändler before c.1740.
* The *Rococo* style which followed on from Baroque is instantly recognizable. Asymmetric curvaceous shapes and soft, feminine colours (such as rose pink and pale yellow) are characteristic. Scrolls are a key feature – for example, on the bases of figures – and shells were also favoured. Rococo is especially associated with the France of Louis XV (1715-74) and with the Sèvres porcelain factory. The style came to England (by way of Meissen) in the mid-18thC, coinciding with the establishment of the first porcelain factories there.
* The *Neo-Classical* style arose from a new interest, from the 1750s, in the remains of Greek and Roman antiquity. Classical shapes were used for vases, and porcelain decoration included swags, husk borders, ram's heads and similar motifs. There was a return to symmetry.
* The *Empire* style of France (c. 1800-20) is a heavier form of Classicism, with Egyptian and exotic ingredients inspired by Napoleon's campaigns. For added grandeur, porcelain vases and the like were often mounted in gilt-bronze. The English Regency style (1790-1830) and American Empire styles (from 1815) were strongly influenced by the French Empire.
* *Rococo Revival* styles were favoured by numerous porcelain factories in the 19thC.

MARKS

Relatively few examples of English pottery or porcelain made before the 19thC bear a mark to indicate the factory of origin. Continental potters, however, tended to apply marks to some of their products as early as the 17thC.

Factory marks

Factory marks are usually found on the base of an object. Variations in the precise form of a mark can provide a basis for dating. The marks may take the form of the maker's initials, the maker's full name, a symbol or coat of arms, or a combination of these elements.

* A mark including the word "Limited" or "Ltd" will not be earlier than 1861.
* A mark including the words "Trade-Mark" will not be earlier than 1862 (when the Trade-Mark Act was passed in the UK).
* "Made in England" indicates 20thC manufacture. A mark giving the country of origin (without "made in") usually (but not always) indicates a date of manufacture after 1891.

Types of mark

* *Painted marks* Most are applied after glazing and fired with the overglaze decoration.
* *Printed marks* These are the most common form of 19thC marks, and are found both under and over the glaze. The mark is applied by means of a transfer either on paper or on rubber.
* *Incised marks* These are signed into the body prior to firing. Much 19thC art pottery is marked in this way.

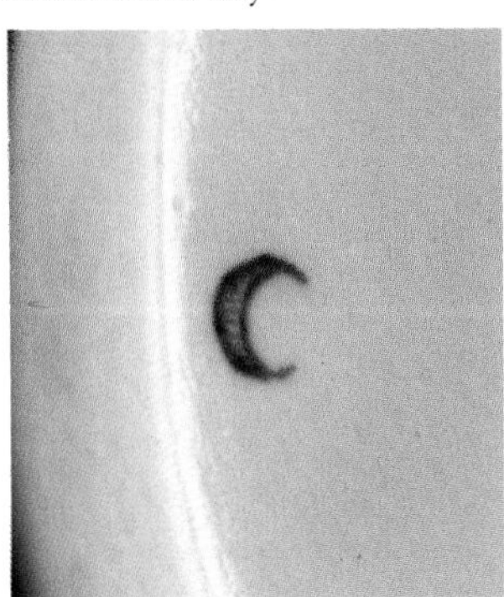

Printed mark: factory mark on Worcester sauceboat, 18thC. MB

* *Impressed marks* These are stamped into the clay prior to firing, using a metal die.

Impressed mark: excise mark on side of English stoneware mug. JH

* *Cast marks* These are found on moulded wares where the factory mark forms part of the mould.
* *Applied moulded marks* These can look similar to cast marks, but are moulded separately and applied to the ware before firing. The Chelsea raised anchor mark was applied in this way. Occasionally pieces are found with an unglazed patch where the mark has become detached.
* *Applied pad marks* These look similar to applied moulded marks but are stamped onto an applied pad of clay.

Painters' marks

Some 18thC wares bear a small mark usually in the form of a numeral or symbol to indicate to the foreman of the factory which decorator completed the design. The marks probably relate to piece-work payment. For example, Lowestoft wares prior to 1770 bear numerals on the base or inside the footrim. Worcester painters, prior to the introduction of the crescent mark, used various symbols.

Similar decorator's marks appear on some 19thC wares. Doulton, for example, often bears incised initials of the potter, artist responsible for incised decoration, artist responsible for painted decoration, and so on.

A gilder's marks also occur on some pieces.

Pattern names and numbers

* Pattern names are often found on mid-late 19thC and 20thC wares. Painted names identifying flowers or views usually indicate good-quality, collectable 19thC porcelain.
* Pattern numbers were used to identify patterns. They are mainly found on English 19thC porcelain and, in the absence of a factory mark, can be of help in indentifying makers.
* Diamond-shaped registration marks identify, by code letter, the year of a piece made between 1842 and 1883.

COPIES AND FAKES

Copies, reproductions and fakes have caused numerous problems of identification for modern collectors. Some experience is necessary before one can separate out the fakes even within a single specialized area of collecting.

Definitions vary to some extent, but a fake may be defined as a modern reproduction of an earlier ware made with the intention of tricking intending purchasers. It may bear spurious marks or be left unmarked.

A copy, on the other hand, is produced in imitation of earlier wares but is given the mark of the copyist. For example, some 20thC Spanish dishes look much earlier than they are; most have a flat back rather than a turned footring and bear the potter's initials on the underside of the rim. Sometimes the marks on honest reproductions have been removed by unscrupulous hands – in which case the piece becomes a species of fake.

Derivative pieces, imitating the style or shape of earlier wares, cannot be described as fakes but they are copies of a sort. For example, the Japanese Kakiemon wares were closely copied by Meissen and subsequently by the Chelsea factory in England.

Contemporary copies of popular types of ware were made by many factories. For example, Wedgwood's various bodies were much copied, and occasionally similar marks were used to confuse buyers – "Wedgwood and Co." and "Wedgwood and Wedgwood" are not related to the famous Wedgwood factory.

Some fakes were manufactured by factories now collectable in their own right. For example, there are pieces of Lowestoft and Coalport porcelain that bear the Meissen crossed-swords mark.

New fakes tend to appear on the market when a particular category of wares begins to fetch dramatically high prices. For example, few fakes of English white saltglazed stoneware exist at the moment, but as the value rises it seems likely that more deceptions will come to light.

Checklist of authenticity

Factors to consider when assessing the authenticity of a piece include the following:

* Is the date suggested by the mark consistent with the date suggested by the shape and style?
* Is the piece formed by the appropriate method for the factory (or region) and period. (For example, Staffordshire figures originally made by press moulding have often been copied by slip casting.)
* Is the mark consistent with the type of body? (The French forger Samson made hard-paste copies of wares that would originally have been in soft-paste; and some soft-paste wares have been copied in earthenware.)
* Is the mark correctly sized and positioned? (The Chelsea red anchor mark, for example, is often too big on fakes.)
* Are the colours of the decoration consistent with original practice? (Sometimes fakers use a palette that would not have been available at the time.)
* Are the weight and size of the piece correct? (Some copies are too heavy or too light, or wrongly proportioned.)
* Does the glaze look right? (Sometimes the glaze is made to look evenly crazed, as a sign of age, whereas on the original the crazing would perhaps be irregular.)
* Is the decoration too self-conscious? (The faker, in trying to obtain the correct degree of naivety on some types of early pottery, often betrays himself by producing decoration that looks contrived.)
* Is the piece appropriately irregular in appearance? (For example, unmarked copies of Sieburg, Westerwald and Cologne stonewares can usually be identified by their regular machine-made appearance, combined with unconvincing distressing.)
* Does the piece measure up to the aesthetic standards of the factory to which it is attributed? (Poor-quality painting, in particular, is a feature of many fakes.)

"Improvements" and "skimming"

Some wares have been "improved" by the addition of low-temperature colours fired in a "muffle kiln" at a later date. These additions are usually not in keeping with the style of the original.

Skimming is the practice of removing the original enamelled decoration from a piece and replacing it with fake decoration of a rarer or more desirable kind. Both Chinese and Western pieces have been treated in this way.

Some Chinese porcelain pitfalls

* Most Chinese porcelain bears marks of reigns earlier than the period of manufacture. These marks were added as an act of reverence, and not intended to deceive.
* European factories have used pseudo-Chinese marks. These are meaningless squiggles, with a vague resemblance to reign marks.

Some pottery pitfalls

* Some original pieces have had *faked dates and inscriptions* added to make them appear more valuable – for example, this is true of Dutch and English delftware, French *faïence* and Italian and Spanish *maiolica*. Such fakes can often be indentified by a lack of fluidity in the calligraphy, and by the presence of grey specks in unglazed areas, caused by moisture bursting from the body during refiring. Refiring can also cause damage to the glaze.
* *French faïence* produced in the 19thC is sometimes passed off as 18thC. The later wares are usually of a greyer body and the colours are "muddy". Most commonly copied are the wares of the Veuve Perrin factory.
* Many copies of Italian Renaissance *maiolica* were produced in the 19thC. Colours are very close to the originals but the decoration tends to be romanticized. As these were intended to be reproductions, most are marked: examples include those by Doccia, Molaroni (V. M. or M/Pesaro), Maiolica Artistica Pesarese (M.A.P.) and signed work by Bruno Buratti.
* In the late 19thC the *Cantagalli* factory reproduced Renaissance wares, Hispano-Moresque lustre wares and Isnik pottery. Sometimes the factory mark on the base, a singing cockerel, has been obliterated, leaving an area of gouged-out glaze, and the wares have been passed off as genuine.
* English *slipwares* and German *stonewares* have been honestly copied, as well as faked. Copies of Raeren brown stoneware are often very close to the style of the originals but are marked by the maker – for example, H. S. for Hubert Schiffer. Country potters worked with slipware until the mid-19thC.

Problems with Sèvres and Meissen

* Collectors should be aware that *Sèvres* porcelain has been extensively faked. Many minor French factories used the interlaced Ls mark on their own wares. Such pieces can usually be identified through their inferior quality and through the use of an early mark on a hard-paste copy of a piece that would have been made originally in soft-paste.
* After the French Revolution many undecorated Sèvres pieces were sold off by the factory to Paris decorators. The wares were then painted in the early Sèvres style. These pieces are still posing problems for collectors today.
* *Meissen* porcelain has been extensively copied and faked. Many factories – for example, the English factories of Bow and Chelsea – copied Meissen shapes and styles of decoration. Many also copied the crossed-swords mark or used a similar mark in the hope of confusing intending buyers.
* The Meissen conjoined AR monogram (Augustus Rex) has been extensively copied, particularly by a former Meissen decorator, Helena Wolfsohn, who faked early Meissen pieces at her own Dresden factory in the 1880s.

Samson

Edmé Samson, who worked in France from 1845, is the most famous of all copiers. The Samson factory copied Bow, Lowestoft and Worcester coloured porcelain, but in hard-paste instead of soft-paste.

Samson also copied Chinese and Japanese wares, sometimes very convincingly. Sometimes the factory used a smooth, well-controlled, slightly blue glaze, but this is not always easy to spot unless placed alongside a genuine piece. A meaningless mock-Oriental mark appears on these wares.

Samson copies of Meissen also occur.

Samson's work was often marked with an S, sometimes in addition to the factory mark of the original. Often this S mark has been removed from the base by unscrupulous hands. Samson wares are now collectable in their own right.

Restoration

Restoration often reduces the value of an object, because it creates doubt as to the degree of damage the restoration hides.

Even worse is the kind of restoration that destroys some of the characteristics of the piece. For example, a restorer camouflaging a crack may file away the glaze alongside the crack so that the masking material will adhere to the body.

To hide a restoration and avoid the difficulty of making the treated area tone in with the rest of the piece, the restorer may spray the whole of the piece with paint – thus obliterating the glaze and necessitating overpainting of the decoration.

Sometimes such exaggerated restoration can work to the advantage of the collector. Heavy restoration may sometimes be reversed to reveal a relatively small defect, such as a crack or small chip.

When a piece is damaged, the current orthodoxy is to leave the damage showing. Cracked or broken pieces may be carefully stuck together with a suitable glue, but they should not be overpainted. Chips may be filled and coloured to almost match, but again should not be overpainted. However, there are some collectors who prefer restoration that recreates the illusion of a pristine piece.

Early Chinese Pottery

Most types of early Chinese pottery are readily available to the collector. Worries about the ethics of archaeological digs and about the pervasiveness of fakes have had a stabilizing effect on prices in recent years. Condition and quality are more critical than sheer antiquity. The most desirable pieces tend to be figures.

Until the end of the Song dynasty in 1280, most Chinese ceramics were earthenware or stoneware. The Han dynasty (206BC-AD220) is especially associated with red earthenwares. Pottery objects were placed in tombs to furnish the dead on their journey into the afterlife.

The Tang dynasty (618-906) was a golden age of lead-glazed earthenware, tinted green, blue or amber by the addition of copper, cobalt or iron pigments, the bottom parts of vases usually being left unglazed. Tang tomb figures have been often faked.

Fine stoneware was made in the Song dynasty (960-1280), including the famous proto-porcelain Ding wares of north China, typified by their rich ivory glaze with incised or moulded decoration. Also from the north came Jun stonewares, with thick blue glazes. The celadon stonewares, with a greyish or olive-green glaze, were once thought by Westerners to change colour or fracture if touched by poison: these were first made in the Song dynasty, but pieces of such an early date are extremely rare.

The tomb figures of the Tang dynasty, often superbly modelled, are very much sought-after. This horse (ht 24in/61cm) is of a type that has been widely copied. Typically, the body is a buff pale earthenware, which is very soft. Some copies are more highly fired, and thus harder. The streaked effect is known as *sancai* ("three-coloured"). *S*

* Earthenware figures of Bactrian (two-humped) camels are also very desirable. Other Tang tomb figures include tomb guardians, ladies of the court and musicians, captured in vigorous movement.

CHINESE DYNASTIES

Shang Yin c.1532-1027BC
Western Zhou (Chou) 1027-770BC
Spring and Autumn Annals 770-480BC
Warring States 484-221BC
Qin (Ch'in) 221-206BC
Western Han 206BC-AD24
Eastern Han 25-220
Three Kingdoms 221-265
Six Dynasties 265-589
Wei 386-557
Sui 589-617
Tang (T'ang) 618-906
Five Dynasties 907-960
Liao 907-1125
Sung 960-1280
Chin 1115-1260
Yüan 1280-1368
Ming 1368-1644
Qing (Ch'ing) 1644-1916

A Jun Yao bowl (Yao means "ware"; dia. 7½in/19cm). Red or purple splashes are characteristic of Jun wares. The glaze is thick and contains a mass of tiny air bubbles. Interiors of bowls and dishes sometimes have small Y- or W-shaped grooves, known as "earthworm" tracks. In addition to bowls, wares include flower pots, bulb-pots and dishes. *S*

This pottery barking dog and model stove of the Han dynasty (ht of dog 11in/27.5cm; stove 8½in/21.5cm) were made to be placed in a tomb – a custom that continued until Tang times. Both these objects are amber-glazed, although a green glaze, imitating patinated bronze, was more common. Other tomb objects from this period include figures of servants and farm buildings. *S*

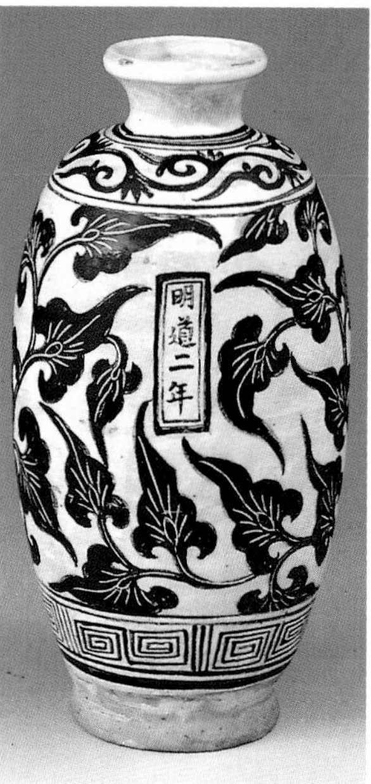

This early Ming brown and white inscribed vase (ht 9½in/23.5cm) belongs to a very varied group of domestic stonewares known as Cizhou wares, made in north China from late Tang times. The glaze, usually transparent, was applied over a layer of slip decorated by incising, slip-painting or other techniques. *S*

Celadon stonewares have a thick, green-coloured glaze, fogged by minute air bubbles. As in this 17thC Buddha (8¼in/21cm), areas are sometimes left unglazed, revealing a reddish-brown base. *S*

* Dark olive-green is typical of northern celadons, which often have fine carved or moulded floral decoration. Yueh wares may also be olive-green.
* Celadons from Longquan in S. Chekiang have a glaze ranging from leaf-green to blue-green.

Early Chinese Porcelain

Some porcelain was produced in the Yüan dynasty (1280-1368), decorated in underglaze blue. It took some time, however, for the fashionable celadon wares to be superseded by the crisply decorated porcelains, which were initially seen as vulgar in some quarters.

In 1368 the Mongol Yuan dynasty was overcome and the Ming dynasty was established: it was to last until 1644. During the early years of the first Ming Emperor's reign, porcelain in underglaze blue or red developed further. By the end of the 14th century, porcelain had gained fashionable status.

It is a misconception that all wares from the Ming dynasty are worth vast sums of money. The output was prodigious, many pieces were made for export to the West and the survival rate has been high. Many of the wares that can be found today were made not in the Imperial kilns but in the provinces, and were rather crudely potted and decorated. Such pieces, particularly if damaged, can be purchased for relatively modest sums.

The reign of Xuande (1426-35) is notable for superb blue and white wares in a blackish blue, but underglaze red was also employed. Xuande wares were convincingly copied in the 18th century.

Later Ming highlights include the coloured enamels of the Chenghua reign (1465-87). Blue and white was revived in the reign of Jiajing (1522-66), when overglaze iron red was added to the palette.

Eighty per cent of reign marks on Chinese porcelain are retrospective, intended as a tribute to Imperial ancestors. Square seal marks sometimes replace the more usual character marks. Reading from the top right down, a six-character mark includes: character for "great", dynasty, emperor's first name, emperor's second name, two characters meaning "in the reign of". Pieces that bear the correct mark for their period (catalogued "mark and period") are more valuable than those with anachronistic marks.

MING REIGN MARKS

洪武年製	**Hongwu** (Hung Wu)	1368-1398
永樂年製	**Yongle** (Yung Lo)	1403-1424
大明宣德年製	**Xuande** (Hsüan Té)	1426-1435
大明成化年製	**Chenghua** (Ch'éng Hua)	1465-1487
大明弘治年製	**Hongzhi** (Hung Chih)	1488-1505
大明正德年製	**Zhengde** (Chéng Té)	1506-1521
大明嘉靖年製	**Jiajing** (Chia Ching)	1522-1566
大明隆慶年製	**Longqing** (Lung Ching)	1567-1572
大明萬曆年製	**Wanli** (Wan Li)	1573-1620
大明天啟年製	**Tianqi** (Tien Chi)	1621-1627
崇禎年製	**Chongzhen** (Ch'ung Chéng)	1628-1644

This bowl with reign marks below the outer rim shows the characteristic features of the early Ming period:
* "heaping and piling" of the underglaze cobalt blue decoration: that is, areas where the blue is so thick it appears almost black
* vigorous, bold decoration, applied with apparent speed
* a milky, ivory-white glaze, clouded with myriad bubbles. On most Qing wares the glaze is thinner and more even
* a thin orange line (caused by an iron impurity) where glazed and unglazed sections meet, usually on the footrim
* knife-cut facets on the footrim. *CHK*

A late Ming blue and white dish, reserved on a blue wash ground (dia. 6in/15.4cm). The piece bears a Jiajing reign mark. Cloud scrolls (accompanied here by cranes) are a typical late Jiajing decoration. *C*

An early Ming (Yongle) imperial white stem cup (dia. 6in/15cm). The interior is decorated with a dragon in *anhua* – "secret" decoration lightly incised into the body with a needlepoint before glazing, and visible when the piece is held to the light. White was the predominant official ware of the Yongle period. *C*
* A very rare and desirable form of early Ming stem cup, copied in the early 18thC, is that painted with a trio of fishes or fruit in underglaze copper-red.

A fine Ming *wucai* cylindrical box (dia. 4½in/11cm). *Wucai* ("five-colour") decoration (underglaze blue combined with enamels) was especially popular in the Wanli reign. The similar *ducai* technique is more crisply executed. *CHK*

A yellow and green leys jar with a decoration of five-clawed dragons, from the Zhengde reign (dia. 5¾in/14.5cm). Green dragon designs on a yellow ground are a Zhengde innovation. Such wares are extremely valuable. *C*

Later Chinese Porcelain

After the death of Emperor Wanli in 1620, the Ming dynasty began to disintegrate. During this turbulent Transitional period very little was produced in the Imperial kilns. However, attractive porcelain was made in the provinces in private kilns, many of which employed potters who had defected from Imperial service. Freed from Imperial constraints, these makers developed new designs based on Chinese folklore. Pieces seldom bear reign marks.

In the Qing dynasty, the Kangxi period (1662-1722) is one of fine underglaze blue painting, the purplish blue of the Transitional period giving way to a clear sapphire blue. Major advances were made in technique; for example, a powder blue blown onto the body to produce a speckled background. Great care was also taken in the potting: it is said that each piece was carefully brushed with a feather before decoration to ensure a completely smooth surface. After 1710 *famille verte* enamelled wares, characterized by their brilliant green, were being produced in large quantities.

The Qianlong period (1736-95) is famous for new glazes – for example, *flambé* glazes with turquoise splashes – and for the first *famille rose* wares.

A sleeve vase of the Transitional period (1620-44), showing the interest in legendary subjects and the typical purplish-blue tone of underglaze decoration (ht 18in/46cm). *C*

* Transitional wares often feature scholars and sages with attendants in cloudy landscapes.

The delicate "peachbloom" (mushroom pink mottled) glaze is highly prized. It was used on small objects, such as this beehive-shaped water pot of the Kangxi period (dia. 5in/12.5cm). *C*

A large blue and white baluster vase of the Kangxi period, showing the typical sapphire blue (ht 18in/46cm). The glaze is thin with just a hint of bluish white: this feature helps to distinguish Kangxi wares from close copies made in the 19thC, which have a colourless glaze. Kangxi designs are very lightly outlined. *C*

This magnificent Kangxi dish, picturing warriors on horseback bearing down on a demon, shows the distinctive colours of the *famille verte* ("green family") palette (dia. 22in/53cm). This style of decoration, dominated by brilliant green, developed from *wucai* (see page 73) in the late 17thC – with the difference that overglaze blue was used instead of underglaze blue. Such wares were made in large numbers after c.1710. *Famille verte* was copied on early European porcelain and sometimes on faïence. *C*

* A sub-category of *famille verte* is the *famille noire* palette, which has a black ground washed over with transparent green enamel, and *famille verte* decoration on top. In the 19thC many genuine Kangxi pieces were stripped of their glaze and decorated with *famille noire* colours.

REIGN MARKS

Much Kangxi porcelain bears the retrospective six-character mark of the Chenghua period (1465-87). The Kangxi mark often appears on late 19th and early 20thC export wares – especially ginger jars.

QING REIGN MARKS, TO 1874

Buddhist lions were made in the 18th and 19thC: few exist from earlier periods. This is a 19thC example (ht 20in/50cm). The lions (also called "Dogs of Fo") were made in pairs, originally as tomb guardians. Females hold a cup, males a large ball. The many 20thC copies are of decorative value only. *C*

An interest in Chinese porcelain is greatly enhanced by a knowledge of the many decorative symbols used.

A dragon symbolized authority, strength, wisdom, goodness – and, by association, the Emperor.

Ducks in pairs symbolize a long and happy marriage.

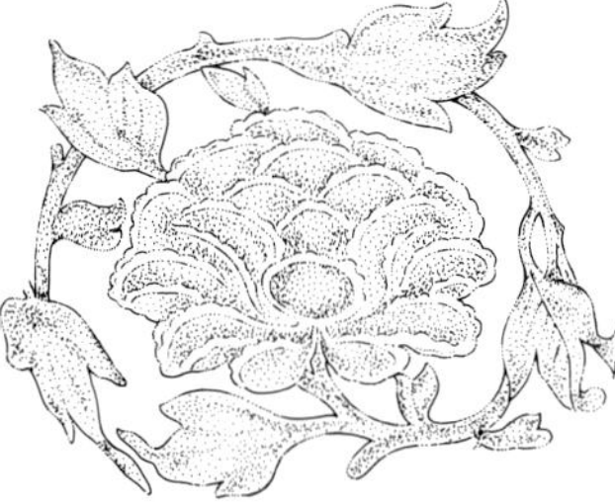

The peony denotes love, beauty, harmony, happiness and honour.

The Three Friends of Winter (pine, prunus and bamboo) symbolize spiritual harmony.

Cranes are emblems of longevity – and transport for Immortals.

An oblong octagonal soup tureen and cover made for the American export market, c.1840 (wdth 13in/34cm). The decoration shows The Surrender of Burgoygne, with American eagles. From the late 1780s on, America was as energetic as Europe in carrying across the seas Chinese porcelain made to special order. *CNY*

* In the Kangxi and Yongzheng periods, Western shapes made in China were largely confined to candlesticks, dishes and helmet jugs. In the Qianlong period the output was enlarged to cover massive tureens (sometimes in the shape of boar's heads), smaller crab-shaped tureens, fruit stands and other items.

Chinese Imari wares, like this bowl of c.1750 (dia. 24in/60cm), were produced to compete with the original Imari wares of Japan, which were based on brocade patterns. (The name is derived from the Japanese port of Imari, from which the wares, made at nearby Arita, were shipped.) Chinese Imari was made from c.1700 to c.1730. The decoration is typically in underglaze blue enriched with brick red, green and gilding. *C*

* The stilt marks found on Japanese porcelain (inside the foot-ring, showing where pieces rested on stilts in the kiln) are not present in the Chinese versions.

COPIES

Chinese *famille verte* and *famille rose* porcelain was copied in France in the 19thC by Samson. Later pieces never capture the luminosity of, say, a genuine Kangxi piece. Genuine enamelling is invariably crackled. Look at the blue especially: on an authentic piece there will be a narrow matt area around the colour, which is absent on copies.

JESUIT WARES

Jesuit missionaries had a strong presence in China in the 16th, 17th and 18thC, and in the first half of the 18thC influenced the decoration of some Chinese export porcelain. The Nativity, the Baptism and the Crucifixion are the most common Jesuit-inspired subjects, executed in *grisaille*. Some Jesuit porcelain was also in underglaze blue.

CHINESE EXPORT WARES

During the reign of the Emperor Qianlong (1736-95) vast quantities of porcelain were shipped to Europe and America. For the most part these wares were painted not with traditional Chinese designs but with motifs requested by the shippers and their clients – biblical scenes, coats of arms, commemorative images with inscriptions, and so on. Most pieces were underglaze blue, but a substantial quantity were decorated in coloured enamels dominated by a distinctive rose-pink – the *famille rose* palette, or in *grisaille* (monochrome). Increasingly, European shapes were copied.

Shipping bowls, like this one of c.1770 (dia. 10in/26cm), are very collectable. They were traded privately by the captains and crew of East India Company vessels. *WW*

A Chinese export lotus plate of c.1760, decorated in a bright *famille rose* palette, with a bouquet including peonies and asters (dia. 9in/23cm). *S*

This *famille rose* flower vase (ht 8in/20.5cm) is typical of a colourful class of 18th and early 19thC export porcelain called "Canton" in England and "Rose Medallion" in America. *SM*

Spanish and Italian Earthenware

The term *maiolica*, meaning tin-glazed earthenware, is derived from Majorca, whose traders first brought the method to Italy from Spain. In both countries the best examples of early tin-glaze decoration are found on large chargers and on storage jars. In Spain such wares were often decorated with lustres, giving a shiny metallic effect – a technique of Moorish origin that reached its peak in the 15th century. The most exciting developments in Italy took place during the Renaissance. (Earlier wares are scarce, as the belief that the Black Death could be transmitted via pottery vessels led to their mass destruction.) Florence was a major centre for manufacture of pharmacy wares, many examples of which survive from hospitals and monasteries. Another key centre was Faenza.

Precise attribution is often difficult, as migrant workers would move from one factory to another. This confusion continued into the 16th century when the production of *maiolica* expanded and potteries were set up in Casteldurante, Deruta, Gubbio, Siena, Urbino and elsewhere. Major artists, however, began to sign their work. It was during this period that the *istoriato* style developed, using the whole surface of the piece as a "canvas" for a painting. Urbino was the main centre of production. Copies of *istoriato* dishes are plentiful.

Renaissance *maiolica* turns up in the major auction rooms but one would be extremely fortunate to find anything of interest in a country sale or non-specialist antique shop. Copies abound, often very skilful ones, made in Sicily in the 17th, 18th and 19th centuries and in mainland Italy in the 19th century.

A Spanish blue and copper lustre dish decorated with a complex lace-like pattern of flower heads and leaves around the sacred initials, IHS – a Greek abbreviation of "Jesus" (dia. 19½in/48cm). This example, from Valencia, is typical of mid to late 15thC "Hispano-Moresque" decoration. Sometimes the backs of such dishes are also painted in lustre with heraldic animals. *C*

A late 15thC Tuscan albarello (waisted drug jar). Most albarelli are without handles: the waisted shape enabled one jar to be removed from a closely spaced row. Many have Latin inscriptions. *PC*
* The palette of cobalt blue, manganese purple and turquoise green was extended in the late 15thC to include yellow and orange.

A 17thC Venetian drug jar (ht 15in/38cm). In Venice drug jars tended to be cylindrical, with yellow scroll decoration on a blue ground, as here. Typically, there was an inscription on one side and, on the other, a portrait head or full figure of a saint. *SM*
* Wet-drug jars (syrup jars) took a different form, with a handle and spout on a bulbous body.

Istoriato ("storied") dishes feature polychrome scriptural or mythological scenes. This Urbino example (dia. 10½in/26.5cm) shows Salome receiving the head of John the Baptist. *S*

A Deruta blue and gold lustre dish, c.1520 (dia. 16½in/42cm). Note the brushstrokes which show that the ground was added after the design had been completed: copies do not have the same spontaneity. In auction catalogues the decorative styles used on such pieces are described by their Italian names. *C*
* *a candelieri*: a symmetrical arrangement of caryatids (head and torso figures) and trophies reserved on a blue ground.
* *a quartieri*: a style in which four or more compartments radiate from the centre.
* *a zaffera*: blue (cobalt oxide) decoration raised slightly above the surface.

A Casteldurante *coppia amatoria* dish, painted by Nicola da Urbino, c.1520 (dia. 8½in/22cm). Such dishes, with a portrait of a young woman and her name (with some term of praise, such as *bella*, or "beautiful") are a Casteldurante speciality. They were given by a man to his beloved. *C*

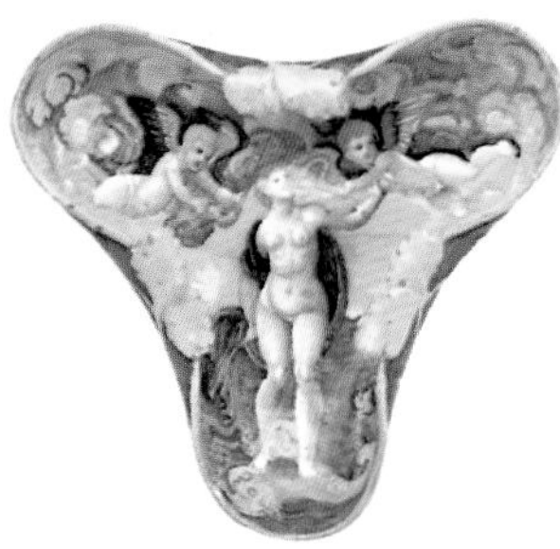

A lobed dish painted with a design showing the birth of Venus, made in Urbino, mid 16thC (lgth 6¾in/17cm). Such brightly coloured tablewares were used at banquets. *SM*

French Faïence

Tin-glaze techniques were imported to France in the 16th century by migrant Italian potters passing north through Lyons, Nîmes and Nevers. From these centres the knowledge spread west to Rouen, Moustiers and Marseilles, the Italian influence diminishing with distance. The term given to these wares is *faïence*, from the Italian town Faenza.

It is difficult to identify Lyons *faïence* with certainty, as Italian workers used their native language when inscribing pieces. At first the factories in Nevers and Nîmes followed styles of Italian wares some decades earlier. Nevers became the most important centre. Urbino-inspired pottery was made there until c.1650, but later influences came from Baroque silver and Chinese porcelain.

Edmé Poterat's factory at Rouen (founded 1647) was notable for the introduction of the blue and white wares in the *style rayonnant*, with rich borders. This style lasted until c.1735.

At Moustiers, c.1710-40, pieces were decorated in fantastically elaborate designs by Jean Bérain. Joseph Olerys, at another factory in this town, developed a style characterized by figures or animals scattered among flowers and foliage. Marseilles emulated Moustiers or Nevers but also produced original styles, notably flower painting on a yellow ground, and fine work in low-temperature (*petit feu*) enamels.

By the mid-18th century, French factories felt the influence of Meissen. This is shown most strongly at Strasbourg, where elaborate Rococo shapes prevail. Sceaux, a Parisian factory of the late 18th century, moved from Rococo to Neo-classical idioms.

A very rare Rouen *faïence* ochre-ground dish painted with cherubs, two bacchanalian figures and a satyr, c.1725 (dia. 15½in/30cm). A style of decoration based on textile patterns is characteristic of Rouen by the mid-17thC. *CG*
* A strong Chinese influence was another Rouen feature, dominating the output of its factories in the early 18thC. *CG*

A Rouen blue and white baluster sugar caster, c.1720 (ht 8¼in/21cm), with a typical design of lambrequins (drape-like motifs). Characteristically, the piece takes its inspiration from Delft. *CG*

The best-known style from Nevers is *bleu persan*, inspired by Persian sources – a solid blue ground decorated with a delicate tracery of white or sometimes white, orange and yellow. This vase in the style is part of a *garniture de cheminée* (set of vases for a mantelshelf), 17thC (ht 14in/36cm). *Bleu persan* was copied on English delft and on Dutch delft. *C*

After c.1740 the Moustiers factories, like those in Marseilles, moved away from blue and white toward polychrome enamelling in blue, green, orange-yellow and purple. Here the distinctive palette is shown on an Olerys plaque c.1740 (dia. 8in/21cm). *CG*
* Mythological figures in medallions with borders of garland and floral festoons were a typical Moustiers decoration. After the mid-18thC there was a trend for small grotesque figures among fantastic vegetation, often painted in monochrome green or yellow. Distinctive Moustiers products are écuelles (shallow bowls with two handles), plaques and powder boxes.

Figures were produced in tin-glazed earthenware, but it was not a good medium for detailed modelling. This fine Strasbourg huntsman, c.1750 (ht 8in/20.5cm), is typical. *C*

A Marseilles plate in *petit feu* enamels, from the Veuve (Widow) Perrin factory, second half of 18thC (dia. 9½in/24cm). The wavy rim and garlanded border are typical. *SM*

The factory at Sceaux (1750-93), being close to the French court, was sensitive to the fashions of the aristocracy. Sèvres porcelain was an influence. This pot pourri vase, c.1755 (ht 13in/33.5cm), shows a Rococo exuberance rivalled only at Strasbourg. *SM*

PETIT FEU ENAMELLING

The introduction of *petit feu* (low-temperature) enamels increased the decorative scope of *faïence* in the second half of the 18thC. Marseilles was the outstanding centre for fine decoration. Best-known are the naturalistic flowers and fish of Veuve Perrin, which were much copied (together with her mark, "VP"). There were two main styles of flower painting at Strasbourg: realistic *fleurs fines* and more stylized *fleurs des Indes*.

Dutch Delft

Tin-glazed pottery came to the Netherlands via either Spain or Italy. A pottery set up in Antwerp in 1512 produced wares strongly affected by Italian styles. Subsequently, potteries were founded in Rotterdam, Haarlem, The Hague and elsewhere. By the early 17th century, wares were also being made at Delft, which soon became a key centre and today lends its name to both Dutch and English tin-glazed earthenware generally. (See pages 80-81.)

In 1654 Delft was all but destroyed by a massive gunpowder explosion; after this a number of sites formerly used by breweries became free for development by delftware potteries, which retained the old brewery names – The Three Bells, The Metal Pot, The Young Moor's Head and so on.

From the early 17th century, Delft pottery emulated Chinese blue and white porcelain – both Wanli wares and the more elaborate Kangxi wares. Gradually the Chinese influence was absorbed into a Dutch-Chinese hybrid style.

Today many people rightly associate Delft with the vast output of tiles, used for wall panels, house and shop signs and composite tile pictures.

In the 18th century Delft began to be influenced by European porcelain. In particular, Meissen shapes and decoration were copied, and *petit feu* polychrome enamelling techniques were adopted. The Japanese-inspired *Delft doré* palette – red, blue and gold – was used from the 1720s.

The Delft industry was hit hard by the introduction of creamware in the late 18th century, when output was greatly reduced.

Delft is commonly forged. Samson made convincing copies. The many reproductions sold today in the Netherlands tend to be lead-glazed, not tin-glazed.

A polychrome Dutch Delft parrot, c.1700 (ht 7in/18cm), one of a pair based on Kangxi originals. The colours are very brilliant: often the yellow is burnt.

* Many pieces of Dutch Delft were given a coat of *kwaart* (a kind of lead glaze) after painting. This was fired and fused with the tin oxide. Its effect was to heighten the gloss.
* The palette includes blue, green and iron red. Yellow, pink and aubergine are rarer.

MARKS

Many pieces of Dutch Delft, even of superb quality, bear no mark. Sometimes the initials of the workshop or factory owner appear.

Lidded spice bowls like this, c.1730 (dia. 14½in/37cm), were used from the 17thC to store spices or bags containing different flavours of tea. Often the interior was divided into compartments. The knob on the lid is always elaborate, and may be naturalistic, as here. Surviving 17thC examples are rare. *SSA*

* A typical feature of Dutch Delft is the use of outlines (*trek*) of dark blue, purple or black, filled in with a wash of colour.
* Dutch Delft tends to be greyer in colour than English delft.
* Other distinctive Dutch shapes include tobacco jars with brass covers (these are not found in polychrome).
* Blue and white wares suffered a gradual decline in quality in the 18thC: the potting became thicker, the decoration coarser.
* Blue and white plates depicting months and whaling subjects are highly collectable.

Plaques made in Delft are often of high artistic merit. They are seldom signed. This example, decorated with ships within an elaborate polychrome border, dates from c.1730 (ht 13in/33cm). The soft pastel colours indicate 18thC manufacture. *SSA*

* A touch of red on the flags of the blue and white ships, as in this example, is a particularly desirable feature.
* Other subjects on Dutch Delft plaques include landscapes and biblical themes.

An early cushion-shaped tulip vase, signed AK (Adriaen Kocks), c.1690 (ht 5½in/14cm). Tulips were a Dutch obsession. This simple cushion form of vase, with five holes for the flowers, was popular in the later 17thC, but by 1690 larger and more elaborate shapes are also found: compare the architectural vase, above right. *SSA*

This piece of Delft blue and white, one of a pair fashioned as a city gate-arch, shows the complexity that tulip vases had acquired by the end of the 17thC (ht 12in/29.5cm). The decorative inspiration is 16thC European Grotesque, but the "tulip" motifs on the flower holders themselves derive from Chinese Transitional porcelain. Shown here is the plainer side of the arch, facing inwards, into the city: note the realistic cracks in the brickwork. *SSA*

* From c.1685, tulip vases could also take the form of tall, ornate pagodas, with up to 11 tiers of spouts supported by a plinth.

English Slipware

Slipware is a type of pottery that particularly flourished in England in the 17th century and the early years of the 18th. Essentially, it is red or buff earthenware decorated with white or coloured slip (diluted clay) that contrasts with the body. A yellowish lead glaze is characteristic.

Decoration took the form of slip-trailing, applied mouldings or sgraffito. In some areas combed (zig-zag), feathered and marbled patterns were favoured from the early 18th century.

The finest slipwares include large dishes made in Staffordshire, with naive slip-trailed decoration, often showing royal or legendary figures. Tulips became a popular motif after William of Orange came to the throne in 1689.

In Wrotham, Kent, where slipware was made from c.1610 to c.1710, a reddish clay was used for elaborate mugs (known as "tygs"), posset pots and other wares, now rare. There were also centres of production in Devon – notably Bideford and Barnstaple – where sgraffito decoration was favoured. Slipware was also made in Wales (Glamorgan), Wiltshire, the north of England and Sussex.

Many of the smaller slipware centres were still operating late in the 19th century. Slipware of the later 18th century is poised to rise dramatically in value over the coming years.

A Staffordshire bird feeder, c.1730, decorated with stylized fleurs de lys in cream slip on a dark brown ground (dia. 7in/18cm). The interior has a central dish. This type of robust, humble object, produced in many potteries, is difficult to ascribe and date unless associated with a particular kiln site. The simple slip-trailed decoration is typical of such pieces, although feathered or marbled decoration is also common. *S*

* Narrow-necked harvest jugs are another rustic object made in slipware (as well as stoneware). They were taken out to refresh field workers at the harvest or haymaking season.
* Marriage cradles, given as presents to newly wed couples, were made until well into the 19thC.

A small slipware puzzle jug, c.1730, with cream dots on a dark brown band below the pierced upper section (ht 4½in/10.5cm). The decoration has an appealing vigour. *S*

REPRODUCTIONS

Copies of slipware often have well-turned footrims, and flat rims instead of curved.

* Early slipwares tend to be large. Small objects such as egg cups suggest a later date.
* Some 19thC slipwares ("Welsh wares") are not reproductions but show the continuity of the tradition in rural areas. Pie plates in particular fall into this category.

Slipware baking dishes often featured a central bird motif, as in this example of c.1720-30 (dia. 16½in/42cm). The trailed criss-cross border and piecrust rim are typical features. *S*

THOMAS TOFT AND FAMILY

The acknowledged master of slipware is Thomas Toft, to whom about forty pieces are attributed. Some dishes by Toft (c.1670-85) have his name in large slip-trailed letters on the rim. His brother Ralph and his sons Thomas Toft II and James Toft worked in a similar style.

* Designs on dishes by Toft and family (and some other potters such as Ralph Simpson and William and George Taylor) include Charles II hiding in the "Boscobel Oak" (with accompanying lion and unicorn), pelicans "in their piety" (that is, feeding their young from their own breast), mermaids, and Adam and Eve.

An early slipware dish, c.1680 (dia. 16½in/41.5cm). The cream ground has been trailed in brown and washed in bluish-green with a pattern of cross-hatched fruit and foliage. The incorporation of green slip into the decoration is uncommon, and seems to be confined to Staffordshire. *S*

* Named, dated dishes are particularly sought after. The name is positioned on the rim or just inside it. The date may be large and prominent, off-centre, or sometimes it appears on the rim in style with the maker's name.
* Staffordshire dishes and chargers measure up to 20in (50cm).
* Press-moulded slipwares, including octagonal dishes, were made from the beginning of the 18thC, notably by Samuel Malkin, John Simpson and others.

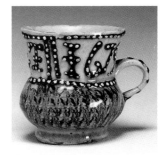

A north Staffordshire slipware thistle-form mug, dated 1679 (ht 3¼in/8.3cm). The body is "feathered" – a typical form of slipware decoration used throughout the 18thC and into the 19th. The "beaded" borders – blobs of slip dotted on – are also characteristic. *S*

* This is a very early date for a slipware mug of this type. The style was popular into the early 18thC, although the widely flared neck and bulbous body later became less pronounced.

Other forms of hollow ware

Tyg

Posset pot

Both these forms were made at Wrotham, which specialized in hollow ware. A "sprigged" form of decoration was favoured.

English Delft

Tin-glazed earthenware was made in England from c.1550. Only in Georgian times did it come to be known as delftware: the small initial is often used to distinguish English from Dutch examples.

Early wares showed the impact of Italian and French pottery, then (from c.1600) of Chinese blue and white porcelain, although many wares are highly individual. As links with Holland increased in the late 17th century, Dutch Delft affected English styles.

Chargers and some other associated shapes are decorated with a range of subjects including animals, domestic scenes, landscapes, and patterns of leaves, fruit and geometrical designs. Particularly collectable, even when damaged, are depictions of folk heroes, monarchs or The Temptation of Adam and Eve.

Typical examples of 17th-century London delft, made at Southwark, are posset pots and white-glazed wine bottles. Some London delft followed the Italian tradition of all-over decoration, in various shades of blue combined with small amounts of other colours. The Southwark potteries set the seeds of later factories at Lambeth (south London), Bristol and Liverpool. Bristol had the broadest palette and the brightest colours, painted on a pinkish buff body (distinct from the beige of Liverpool). Decoration in manganese as well as blue was used in Bristol, Brislington (near Bristol) and Wincanton. At Liverpool some transfer printing on delft was done. Production of delftware had all but ceased by c.1800.

Delftware in flawless condition is a great rarity, and small signs of damage are acceptable. Rims have seldom escaped chipping. Large decorative pieces such as chargers and bowls have considerable value even if broken and re-stuck.

A Southwark armorial salt, 2nd quarter of 17thC (wdth 5½in/13cm). The ends are moulded with the arms of the City of London. Very few salts of this type have been recorded, and the piece fetched a high price at auction. The quality is excellent in view of the date. Small glaze chips are acceptable even in pieces of the 18thC. The browning of the white enamel is typical of London delft of this early date. *C*

Malling jugs, of which this is a fine example, are the earliest tin-glazed wares known in England, dating from the mid-16thC. The name is borrowed from a village in Kent where a group was found. The round-bellied shape, with silver mounts, is typical. These jugs, in brown, blue or turquoise, or sometimes mottled, are very rare. *S*

A Lambeth wine bottle with inscription in blue, c.1650 (ht 7¾in/19.5cm). Most bottles are dated between 1640 and 1650, but production continued until c.1670. The inscription often announces the contents – "whit" (white wine), "sack", "claret", and so on. This example is especially valuable because of its historical associations: John Tomes sheltered the future Charles II on his flight from the Battle of Worcester in 1651. *CS*

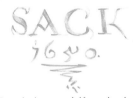

Barrel-shaped mugs are a typical Southwark product. This one dates from c.1635 (ht 5½in/14cm). Later mugs had a globular body with cylindrical neck. After mid-century there were so many London factories that attribution is very difficult. *CS*

Inscriptions on delft tend to have a spontaneous, extrovert flourish, as seen in the detail above. This freshness is hard to recapture in a copy. Many forgeries give themselves away by fiddly brushwork. Other signs of deception are an excessively white body and an even glaze with a regular crackle: in the genuine article, the glaze will be thick and undulating.

A blue and white Bristol delft bowl, c.1735 (dia. 14in/35cm). Inside the bowl is a landscape surrounded by an inscription. The Chinese influence in this, as in much other delft of this date, is filtered through contact with Dutch Delft, rather than absorbed directly. *C*

* Dutch forms copied in England include flower vases, tea caddies and puzzle jugs.

The cobalt-blue brushstrokes around the rim of this charger, c.1730, put it into the highly collectable category of "blue-dash" chargers, made at Bristol and London in the 17th and early 18thC. This is from Bristol. *S*

* The vigorous, unconsciously cartoon-like design, is typical of English delft.
* Such chargers were sometimes intended to be hung on the wall.
* The Bristol artists painted more loosely than London decorators.

* A decorative technique introduced at Bristol was *bianco sopra bianco* – opaque white over a glaze tinted pale blue, lavender or green. A typical design is a border of repeated leaf sprays, flowers and pine cones.

A polychrome portrait charger of Charles II, c.1666 (dia. 12¾in/32.5cm). The tradition of royal portraits on chargers started posthumously with Charles I and continued until George II (represented on only a few known examples). Charles II is usually, as in this example, portrayed with a moustache but without a beard. *CS*

* Royal or military figures on horseback also appear on chargers.

The rich palette of this dish of c.1740 (dia. 13in/33cm), and especially the strong red, indicates its Bristol origin. However, the value of such pieces depends more on the quality and individuality of decoration, and on the condition, than on a precise attribution of origin. *C*

A Liverpool ship's punch bowl, c.1760, the interior painted with a ship above an inscription (dia. 10½in/26.5cm). Delft was first made in Liverpool c.1710. Both Bristol and Liverpool made nautical punch bowls, in keeping with their function as ports. *S*

* A distinctive feature on some Liverpool delftware was a design of "Fazackerly" flowers painted in red, blue, yellow and green, with outlines in black.

TYPICAL WARES

Certain wares made in delft have a function that may not be immediately apparent from the shape. For example:

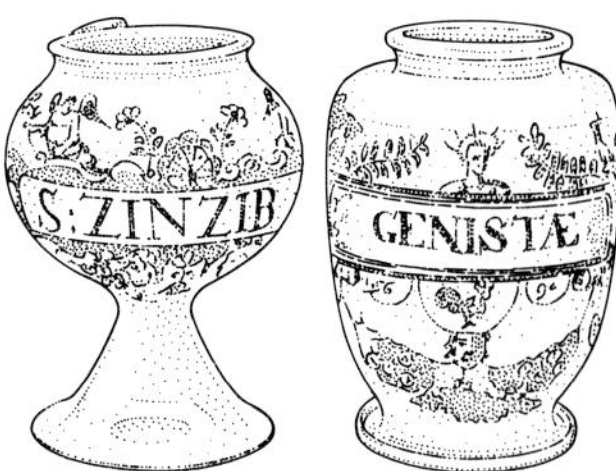

Apothecaries' jars: for dry or powdered drugs. There are two principal shapes (*above*).

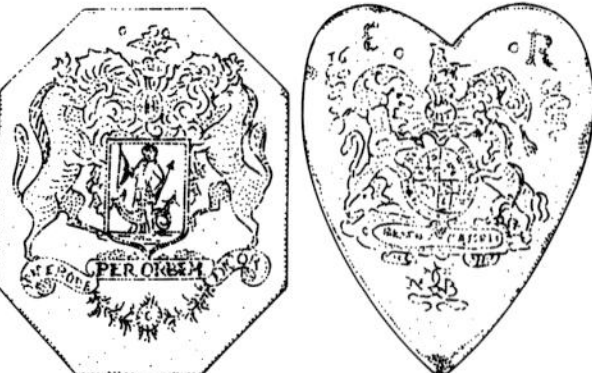

Pill slabs: used (despite the name) as pharmacy window displays. Usually decorated in blue with a coat of arms.

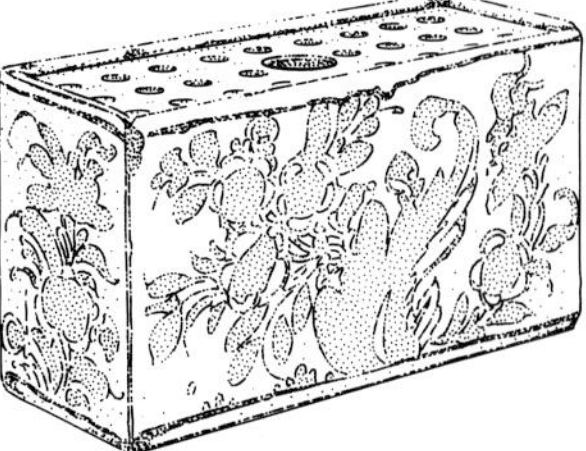

Flower brick: a small brick-like holder with holes in the top for cut flowers.

Barber's bowl (*above left*): the crescent curve fits under the chin. *Porringer* (*above right*): a shallow bowl with a flat horizontal handle, based on silverware.

Posset pot: a two-handled lidded pot for hot drinks. Made at Bristol.

Early German and English Stoneware

By the end of the 14th century, German potters had discovered a method of glazing stoneware by throwing salt into the hottest part of the kiln. Although there were many saltglaze centres along the Rhine valley, the major sources are Cologne, Frechen, Raeren (from c.1530), Sieburg and Westerwald.

German stonewares are often of typically Germanic shape – for example, tapered, cone-like tankards (*Schnellen*), cylindrical mugs (*Humpen*) and tall, narrow-necked jugs (*Enghalskrüge*). Sieburg is famous for the sharp detail of its applied moulding, seen at its best in relief medallions (12th-16th centuries), and for its white body. Equally distinctive are the grey-bodied wares decorated with relief moulding against a blue ground, made at Westerwald from the early 17th century onward.

The earliest identified English stonewares were made at Fulham, London, by John Dwight in the 1670s. By the end of the century he was making a variety of types, including grey-bodied saltglazed wares similar to those made in Cologne and red unglazed wares based on Chinese teapots brought over to England in tea chests.

At the end of the 17th century other potters followed Dwight's lead. David and John Elers, who came to England from Holland c.1688 and worked in London and Staffordshire, made attractive redwares until c.1700. Staffordshire potters soon began to produce red stoneware, continuing until the 1760s, and white saltglaze.

Brown stoneware teapots, mugs and the like (including the distinctive bear jugs) were made in Nottingham, Staffordshire and elsewhere.

A small Elers stoneware tea jar, unglazed, with silver top and Chinese-style relief decoration, late 17thC (ht 4½in/11.5cm). The countersunk decoration is unusual: applied reliefs are more common. Many red stoneware pieces by Elers have a pseudo-Chinese mark impressed on the base. Teapots are a characteristic form. *JH*

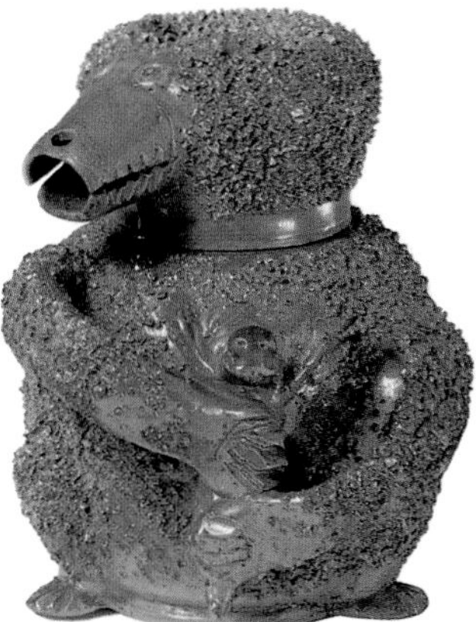

A large English saltglazed bear jug, 1745-50 (ht 8½in/21.5cm). The detachable head was probably used as a cup. The "fur" of clay chippings is typical. Sometimes the bear has a dog in its grip. *JH*

This is a Bellarmine – an ale flagon with a bearded mask at the neck representing Cardinal Bellarmine. The earliest were made at Cologne or Frechen. This example, 1594 (ht 15in/-37.5cm), bears the arms of Elizabeth I of England. Dwight of Fulham made cruder versions. Fakes tend to be too regular. *S*

A Staffordshire brownware pint mug, c.1700 (ht 5½in/13.5cm), stamped with an excise mark, WR. From 1700 it was illegal to sell ale in a vessel without such a mark. WR beneath a crown remained the official mark until 1825, but when Queen Anne came to the throne in 1702 most potters illicitly changed their mark to AR (for "Anna Regina"). *JH*

* Some attractive brown stoneware was made in Derbyshire in the later 18thC – for example, mugs, loving cups and ale jugs, finely incised.

Stonewares were produced at Meissen prior to the production of porcelain there. The best examples are finely potted and polished, with tooled decoration that shows the influence of silverware. This teapot, c.1708-15 (ht 4¼in/10.5cm), is cut with facets – a technique based on glass engraving. Such wares were produced in quantity until c.1715, but today are rare. *PC*

* The first red stoneware teapots made at Meissen included some cast directly from Chinese originals.
* Red and brown stoneware teapots were only around 4in (10cm) high. A larger size indicates a later date.
* Spouts on early teapots have a silver sleeve and lid to guard against chipping. The teapot lids were often held by a silver chain.

A rare English saltglaze puzzle jug, c.1741 (ht 8in/20.5cm). Drink can be sucked through one of the spouts if the others are stopped. *JH*

White Saltglazed Stoneware

From c.1740, English stoneware underwent a vigorous phase of development in response to competition from Chinese porcelain, the Staffordshire potters leading the way in evolving a whiter body for inexpensive utility wares such as bottles, jars and preserve pots. The basic improvement was to add white Devonshire clay and powdered flint to the ingredients. These additions, combined with a new method of slip cast moulding, allowed the production of a lightweight, durable, white body capable of being cast in delicate, detailed shapes, and of withstanding the impact of boiling water. As with brown saltglaze, a pitted "orange peel" surface is characteristic.

These wares were often put to daily use. Moreover, cast saltglaze, unlike delft or porcelain, tends to shatter rather than crack when knocked hard. Hence, although made in large numbers, these items are scarce and collectable today.

Products included loving cups, mugs, plates, jugs in the form of owls, and teapots in whimsical shapes – camels, houses and so on. Typically, stamped reliefs decorate early wares. Sgraffito decoration was also used, the incisions being filled in with blue pigment – a technique known as "scratch-blue". Some pieces were left undecorated.

Enamel colours became popular after c.1745, reproducing the fashionable *famille rose* and *famille verte* palettes of Chinese porcelain. The colours on enamelled saltglaze stand out bright and clear.

White saltglaze is an increasingly popular collecting area. Moulded wares and figure groups now fetch high prices.

A Staffordshire saltglaze four-sided teapot, cast and dipped, c.1740s (ht 6in/15cm). An unusual feature is the decoration: a portrait, Royal Arms and (turned to the back) a scene showing the capture of Portobello in the West Indies, 1739. The panelled design is typical. *JH*

* Relief designs on saltglaze tablewares include stag hunting, grotesque figures, birds and animals and armorial devices. The raised borders surrounding the panels hide lines left by joins in the mould.

* After c.1745 the moulds used for such wares were made from plaster of Paris, instead of clay: this made for crisper detail, often following silver designs.

Staffordshire saltglaze "pew groups" like this, c.1740 (wdth 7½in/19cm), are very rare. Made c.1730-40, they feature pop-eyed figures sitting upright on a high-backed bench, often flirting or playing music. The details are picked out in dark brown. *C*

* Similar in style are lovers under a tree, equestrian figures and bells in female form. All fetch high prices. Fakes sometimes appear.

The fashion for enamelling white saltglaze, from the late 1740s, was influenced by the London porcelain factories. This teapot dates from c.1750-55 (ht 4in/10cm). The skilful but childish painting has great appeal. *JH*

A saltglaze plate, c.1755 (dia. 8½in/21.5cm), with "scratch-blue" decoration – that is, a pattern incised and filled in with cobalt blue pigment. Usually, this technique is found on mugs, jugs, teapots and coffee pots. *JH*

This bowl, c.1760 (dia. 8½in/21.5cm), is enamelled with European figures in a landscape. By the 1760s potteries tended to have their own decorating workshops. *JH*

* A palette not restricted to pinks, mauves, yellows, greens and turquoise indicates a later date.

The Whieldon/Wedgwood Era

From the later 1740s pottery manufacturers increased their market share with a series of "new improved" bodies. By the 1770s pottery was as fashionable as porcelain, even in the most elevated circles.

The Staffordshire potter Thomas Whieldon, working at Little Fenton, rediscovered the technique of decorating with coloured lead glazes. Whieldon teawares, dinner wares and decorative wares, manufactured in the 1750s, used a palette limited initially to olive-green, grey, brown and slate blue; later colours include yellow and orange. The term "Whieldon" is often applied to pieces by various Staffordshire imitators as well as those by Whieldon himself. Coloured glazes were also used by the Wood family.

Josiah Wedgwood joined Whieldon as a partner in 1754 and became a dominant force in the industry. He developed various mottled glazes (agate, marbled and tortoiseshell) and perfected green and yellow glazes used on tureens and other wares based on fruit and vegetable shapes.

In 1758 Wedgwood established his own business and experimented with new bodies. It is often unclear whether a particular piece was made by Wedgwood during the Whieldon years or later, at the Wedgwood factory. However, Wedgwood fruit and vegetable wares tend to be more thinly potted, with crisper detail, than similar pieces by Whieldon.

Wedgwood's first major success was a lightweight, easily worked, lead-glazed, cream-coloured earthenware, which he termed "creamware" (see page 86). This was widely copied, and became the staple earthenware body of the late 18th century, superseding delftware and saltglaze.

"Astbury-Whieldon" wares
This is a term that can cause confusion. Whieldon is associated with coloured glazes, on figures and tablewares. John Astbury and his son Thomas are associated with (a) redware tablewares with applied reliefs (b) figures (musicians, horsemen, soldiers) using clays of two colours (white, and red or brown). "Astbury-Whieldon" figures are those in the Astbury style, but with coloured glazes.

The deep green glaze of this Whieldon-style creamware teapot, c.1760 (ht 4¾in/12cm), is particularly associated with tablewares moulded in the shape of a cauliflower, melon or pineapple. Wedgwood's work in this style is known as "cauliflower" ware. The "pineapple-moulded" spout is unusual. *C*

A Staffordshire "Astbury-Whieldon" figure of a violinist, mid-18thC (ht 5½in/14cm). Similar seated figures are recorded, but this musician is unusual in having a "blackamoor" style of head. *S*

A superb Whieldon-type figure of a pug, mid-18thC (ht 5in/12.5cm). The creamware body is splashed in translucent green, dark grey and manganese. *S*
* "Whieldon-type" lead-glazed earthenware is often distinguished by the quality of its modelling. It differs from Astbury and Astbury-Whieldon wares in relying heavily on a wider spectrum of more vividly coloured glazes. The body is an improved creamware, having the same ingredients as white saltglaze stoneware, but fired at a lower temperature.

This Staffordshire saltglazed cat, c.1745 (4¾in/12cm), is an excellent example of agate ware – an earthenware made to resemble the semi-precious stone agate by building up layers of different-coloured clays. It differs from tortoiseshell ware in that the veined effect is in the mingled clays, rather than in the glaze. *P*

A Whieldon cornucopia (horn of plenty) wall-pocket, one of a pair, c.1760 (ht 9in/23cm). These objects, used as wall-mounted vases for flowers or ivy, were also made in creamware, agate ware, delftware and saltglaze. The quality of moulded decoration is a major factor in the value. *C*
* Whieldon also produced a waisted form of wall-pocket with the lower portion moulded as a satyr's head. Surviving examples are rare.

A rare Whieldon model of a dovecote, c.1755 (ht 7¾in/19.5cm), glazed in tones of mottled green, brown, cream and grey. *S*
* Whieldon wares in unusual shapes, such as this dovecote, are the ones that tend to fetch the highest prices. Candlestick figures and models of unusual animals are also very desirable.
* Other Whieldon wares include cottages (with figures) and cow-creamers – milkjugs modelled in the shape of cow, with the tail curved to form the handle, the mouth pierced for the spout, and a hole in the back for filling.

Late 18thC Sailor Tobies are a popular group. This creamware example is typical and of standard height, 11½in/29cm. The costume patterns can vary, and a straw hat sometimes replaces the wide-brimmed cap. The anchor at the feet is always present. *S*
* The Planter resembles the Sailor but lacks the anchor.

This rare and valuable Squire jug, late 18thC (ht 11¼in/28.5cm), is slimmer than the standard Toby. The figure is seated on a corner chair with an ale jug held to his belly (rather than on his knee). The pipe in his left hand is often missing, as in this example. *S*
* 18thC Squire jugs have been reproduced in large numbers in the 19th and 20thC.

The Toby jug first appeared during the second half of the 18thC, probably inspired by a 1761 print of Toby Fillpot, a legendary drinking character. The standard Toby, 9-10in/23-25cm high, is a corpulent seated figure in long coat, white stockings, buckled shoes and three-cornered hat. A jug of foaming ale is balanced on his left knee, gripped with the left hand and supported by the right. The crown of the hat (usually missing) is detachable for use as a cup. There are numerous variations on this form. One is the Shield Toby shown here, c.1780 (ht 9¾in/25cm): he holds an empty jug and has a boat-shaped shield to his left, inscribed "It is all out, then fill him agian", a misspelling found on all such jugs. *S*

CATEGORIES OF TOBY JUGS

Toby jugs fall into three groups:
* jugs with drab Whieldon-type coloured glazes in a limited palette. These are the most sought-after.
* jugs with underglaze decoration in the Prattware palette (see this page, right).
* jugs with enamels applied over a clear glaze (including jugs by Ralph and Enoch Wood).

DATING

Toby jugs were made throughout the 19thC right up to the present day, so the collector needs to exercise caution. In the 18thC the jug held by the Toby was always independently modelled. Patches of colour, warts, sores and black spots on the face are also 18thC characteristics; black-faced jugs are 19thC. Early jugs always have crisp definition.

This late 18thC Toby jug (ht 7in/17.5cm) is of the sought after Fiddler group. This is less rare than the Midshipmite, who holds a sword or a jug in his right hand, a glass in his left. *S*
* Variations include the ironing Taylor; and the Farrier, who wears an apron and holds a pair of pincers.

Pairs of pottery lions were produced in Staffordshire from c.1775. This example, c.1785 (lgth 12in/30cm), decorated in coloured glazes, is probably the work of John Wood. Lions after c.1800 are likely to be in overglaze enamels. *JH*

This plaque, c.1795 (dia. 8in/20.3cm), is an example of Prattware – a generic term for the creamware and pearlware, relief-decorated in bright underglaze colours, that was produced by the Pratt family and others. Decoration includes marine subjects, weddings and sporting scenes. *C*

CREAMWARE

Creamware could be neatly potted, accepted decoration well, glazed easily, and was light in weight. As it was also inexpensive to produce, its popularity was assured.

After Wedgwood was appointed Potter to Queen Charlotte in 1765, he renamed his product "Queen's Ware".

Creamware became highly fashionable in the later 1760s and 1770s, and Wedgwood even received orders from Catherine, Empress of Russia. His competitors flourished in Leeds, Bristol, Liverpool, Swansea, Derby and Staffordshire.

Typical forms of creamware include plate rims and baskets with openwork piercing – a Leeds speciality – and intertwined handles. Many pieces were left plain, although tasteful hand-painted decoration, often with honeysuckle or vine leaves, in a running border, is typical.

In 1779 Wedgwood made a white, more durable variant of creamware, known as "pearlware". This was copied by other manufacturers and decorated in underglaze blue (by hand painting or transfer printing) as well as polychrome. Pearlware often has a distinct blue tinge to the glaze.

A Wedgwood creamware trial dessert plate for the Catherine the Great service, made for the palace of La Grenouilliere in St Petersburg. The service, decorated with English views, was completed in 1774. *PC*

* Early Wedgwood creamware and Queen's Ware are marked with "WEDGWOOD", impressed. Creamware marked "WEDGWOOD & CO." is from the pottery of Ralph Wedgwood (from 1796), not to be confused with Josiah.

Early creamware (c.1760-8) was often painted in black and red enamels by Robinson & Rhodes, a company of decorators who had a workshop in Leeds. This teapot, c.1765 (ht 6in/15cm), painted with a huntsman and his dog by David Rhodes (who later worked for Wedgwood), exemplifies typical features of this group of wares – the pleasing contrast of black and red against the cream body, the simple vigour of the design. *JH*

* The "crabstock" style of spout and handle featured here, moulded to represent the gnarled branches of a crab-apple tree, is found on both saltglaze and creamware teapots.
* Relatively little creamware is marked. Shapes and patterns were copied freely, and hence are not reliable to collectors as a guide to attribution.

Creamware of a high quality, sometimes surpassing Wedgwood, was made in Leeds, where pierced work was favoured c.1780-1820. This Leeds creamware chestnut basket, c.1790 (ht 9½in/24cm), shows the intricacy that could be achieved. The twisted handles are a favourite Leeds feature, found also on teapots and coffee pots. *JH*

* Leeds also produced moulded pieces, including figure-moulded cruets and centrepieces in plain cream.
* The impressed mark, "Leeds Pottery", was used by the factory.
* Leeds creamware has been faked. Modern copies are too heavy and have a thick, white, glassy glaze, very different from the authentic Leeds glaze, which has a greenish tinge in the crevices.

A creamware teapot dipped in green glaze and gilded, c.1770 (ht 5¾in/12cm), from Swinton in Yorkshire. Pottery from this factory is unmarked, and identification often depends on archaeological evidence, as in this case: fragments showing an identical green glaze have been found on the site. *JH*

A Wedgwood Queen's Ware coffee pot, of the shell-edge shape with rope-twist handle, c.1770 (ht 8in/20.3cm). The piece is decorated with an iron-red transfer print of "Liverpool Birds". *WM*

* Creamware was transfer-printed from c.1760.

This creamware tea caddy is enamelled with the so-called "Miss Pitt" design, c.1765 (ht 4in/10cm). It was made at Cockpit Hill, Derby, which operated from c.1751 to 1779. It is typical of that pottery in its thick greeny-yellow glaze. This style of enamelling is more often found on saltglaze stoneware. *JH*

Later 18th-century Wedgwood

Wedgwood dominates the manufacture of the "dry-bodied" wares, which in composition fall between stoneware and earthenware. All the dry bodies are harder to find than creamware or pearlware.

After Wedgwood's factory at Burslem had become too small for his expanding operation, he opened a second factory in 1769, named "Etruria". The output consisted of ornamental wares in the fashionable Neo-classical style, based on pieces excavated at Pompeii and Herculaneum. Still in partnership with Thomas Bentley, he evolved his "black basaltes" (c.1767), a hard black unglazed dry body. Painted red or white in the Greek style, this was well suited for a range of "Etruscan" vases; it was also used for busts, plaques, tea wares and mugs.

Perhaps the most famous of all Wedgwood products is the jasper ware (1776), another fine hard-grained dry body. The white jasper body itself could be coloured to make "solid jasper", but after 1780 objects were usually dipped into a vessel of coloured jasper slip. Solid jasper came in blue, sage green, olive green and black, and very occasionally yellow, but "Wedgwood blue" is best-known. Jasper was imitated by many other potters.

Another important category of Wedgwood pottery is cane ware (from c.1775), a tan-coloured ware, which was sometimes used in a darker shade and shaped to imitate bamboo. "Rosso antico" was a form of redware, ranging in colour from light red to chocolate brown.

Bamboo tea wares on a tray, c.1775-80. The horizontal bands are an imitation of the binding on Chinese wares made in real bamboo. Wedgwood's aim in devising these innovations was to create new markets for dry-bodied pottery. *WM*

MARKS

As a rule of thumb, if a piece does not bear the factory mark it is not Wedgwood. (This does not apply to plaques designed to be installed in a room; and some items of creamware are also unmarked.)

* The simple name "WEDGWOOD" was impressed on wares from the beginning of the factory's history. It is the standard mark on useful wares even in the Wedgwood & Bentley period.
* "WEDGWOOD & BENTLEY" was impressed on ornamental wares c.1768-80. This was abbreviated to "W & B" on small cameos, plaques and the like. The firm's name in a circle, with "Etruria", is also found.
* The name "Wadgwood" found on a seal or other small item is indicative of a copy.

This pale blue and white jasper vase, mid-1780s, represents Wedgwood at its finest. The body is silky smooth, the applied reliefs crisp and undercut. *WM*

* Portrait medallions in jasperware are highly collectable. Other items include tablets, bell pulls, flower pots, and tea wares.
* 19thC blue jasper tended to be a darker shade.
* 18thC jasperware is hard to find in original condition.
* Contemporary copies by Adams, Neale and Turner are often of high quality.
* Later copies give themselves away by their inferior quality. Items were moulded in one piece and the background colour applied by brush around the raised motifs.

A blue jasperware *sucrier*, c.1790 (ht 4¾in/12cm), with applied decoration. The moulds were used into the 19thC. *C*

Basaltes was produced in greater numbers during the early period than jasperware. This bust, impressed "Wedgwood & Bentley", dates from c.1775-80. *WM*

* Because of its dense composition basaltes was ideal for busts, portrait medallions and intaglios (small portraits).
* Basaltes acquires a velvety smoothness with age.
* Wedgwood & Bentley basaltes wares are very valuable.

A "pebbleware" vase, raised on a black basaltes plinth, c.1770-80 (ht 15½in/39.5cm). Pebbleware, made by mixing coloured clays, is intended to imitate serpentine, agate, red porphyry and other stones, and is typically ornamented with festoons, wreaths and husks. *JH*

* The earlier creamwares that have been given a slight resemblance to porphyry, by applying a glaze of mixed colours, are less valuable.

Meissen Porcelain

The name Meissen is synonymous for many people with porcelain that is beautifully modelled, with a Rococo delicacy of touch, and exquisitely decorated, each piece a work of art. This reputation for quality is well deserved, especially in the period until c.1756.

When Augustus the Strong, Elector of Saxony, undertook his famous quest for the secret of making hard-paste porcelain, he enlisted – by force – the services of the alchemist Johann Friedrich Böttger. In the early 1700s Böttger succeeded in making fine-quality stonewares (see page 82) and in 1708 achieved an ivory-toned hybrid porcelain using alabaster. In 1710 the Royal Saxon Porcelain Factory was founded at Meissen, near Dresden, to exploit the fruits of Böttger's labours. The formula was improved in 1713 and perfected in 1719. The earliest products are based on silver forms, decorated in coloured enamels.

In 1720, when the kiln-master Stolzel returned to Meissen after being tempted away by a rival firm in Vienna, he brought with him J.G. Höroldt, a young but brilliant decorator. The combination of Höroldt's enamelling with Meissen's elegant Baroque shapes eclipsed all but the best Chinese porcelain. As well as chinoiseries, decoration includes some fine harbour scenes (1730s) as well as battles, Commedia dell'Arte scenes and stylized flowers. Many Meissen pieces were painted by outside decorators, or *Hausmaler* (literally, "house-painters").The colour of the paste itself progresses from a yellowish tinge (before 1720) to a brilliant white.

Meissen's range of products was extended following the arrival of a modeller, J. J. Kändler, in 1731. From c.1738 Kändler concentrated on figures used to decorate the banqueting tables of the Dresden court. The best Meissen figures date from the late 1730s and early 40s. Copies of 18th-century figures made in the 19th century lack the fine detailing of the originals.

During the mid-18th century the factory expanded. More than 600 workers were employed and large quantities of porcelain were produced for markets abroad. In the late 1750s Saxony became embroiled in the Seven Years' War and the factory was occupied by Prussian troops. Production was re-established after the war but without the former freshness and vigour. Old models were reproduced from original moulds – a practice continued today – and Sèvres Neo-classical styles were emulated.

Modern Meissen is identifiable by its grey-toned paste and the addition of "Germany" to the crossed swords mark.

The shape of this Böttger porcelain teapot of c.1710-19 (wdth 6¾in/17cm) is typical of the earliest porcelain teapots. Before c.1720 enamel colours were not always well-fired, and the slightly burned-out colours here suggest some problems with temperature control. *CG*

Chinese porcelain was directly copied at Meissen. This vase and cover (ht 12in/30cm) are decorated after a Wanli original with peonies, chrysanthemum and prunus motifs. The AR (Augustus Rex) monogram on the base indicates a date of 1725-30. *S*

* Blue and white Meissen is rare.

A Meissen octagonal dish of c.1742 (wdth 12in/30cm), painted with a harbour scene outside a Venetian palace. Elaborate scrollwork, as seen on this dish, was used to frame both European and chinoiserie subjects at this period. *CG*

* The first Meissen harbour scenes date from c.1724. They were very much in vogue in the 1730s and continued until the late 60s. Subjects were Oriental to begin with, then European. Both Venice and Genoa were represented. The most notable painter was the manager's relative, Christian Friedrich Höroldt. Designs were copied from engravings after J. W. Baur.

* Other octagonal wares from Meissen include attractive teabowls with saucers.

A Meissen coffee pot, c.1723, superbly decorated by J. G. Höroldt (ht 6½in/16.5cm). *CG*

* Höroldt's chinoiseries are usually framed in profuse scrolls in red, gold and lustre. He also adapted Chinese early *famille rose* and Japanese decorations.

A range of European birds in naturalistic colours was among Meissen's innovations. This bittern by Kändler made its appearance c.1755 (ht 15in/38cm). Augustus had a collection of live birds from which Kändler did some modelling. *CG*

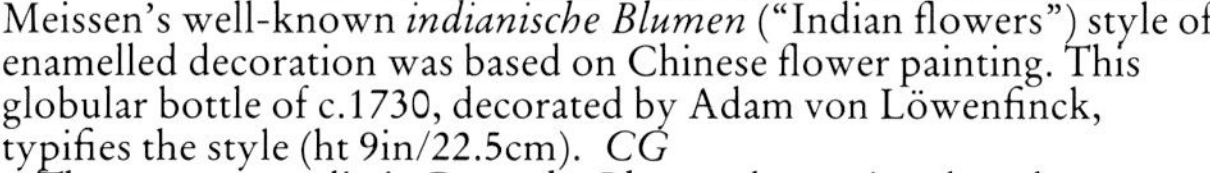

Meissen's well-known *indianische Blumen* ("Indian flowers") style of enamelled decoration was based on Chinese flower painting. This globular bottle of c.1730, decorated by Adam von Löwenfinck, typifies the style (ht 9in/22.5cm). *CG*

* The more naturalistic *Deutsche Blumen* decoration, based on botanical paintings, was popular after c.1735.
* There was also a naturalistic style of cut-flower (*Schnittblumen*) decoration associated particularly with the decorator J. G. Klinger in the 1740s.

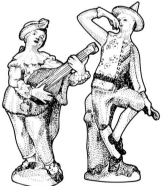

This group by J. J. Kändler, c.1740 (ht 7in/17.5cm), shows the spontaneity combined with technical accomplishment that characterizes Meissen figures at their best. Kändler's earliest figures were in a strong Baroque palette of yellow, red and black, and had a coarse vigour. By c.1750 both the modelling and the colours had become more delicate – mauve, green and pale yellow. Bases with Rococo scrolls replaced the earlier pedestals and mounds. *C*

* Kändler's assistants J. F. Eberlein and P. Reinicke also produced fine work in the master's style.
* Subjects include ladies in crinolines. The Commedia dell'Arte (Italian Comedy) figures include the following characters in a wide range of poses.

Scaramouche Harlequin

A plate of the Academic period, c.1765 (dia. 12¼in/28.5in), bearing the blue crossed swords and dot mark. The green chequered border surrounds a rustic vignette of a shepherd and his flock among the ruins of a temple. Ruined temples were part of the standard repertoire of Neo-classical themes, both in the fine arts and on porcelain decoration. *CG*

MARKS

The earliest factory mark was a pseudo-Chinese mark with caduceus (rod of Hermes, entwined with serpents). From c.1723 the factory used "KPM" (Königliche Porzellan Manufaktur). From 1724 the famous crossed-swords mark was used: it is still current. A dot between the hilts indicates the "Academic period", after 1763. A star between or below the hilts indicates the "Marcolini period", 1774-1814, but a star also appeared on blue-and-white wares of the 1720s. An incised line through the crossed swords mark indicates a piece not considered to be of the finest quality. Both the crossed-swords mark and the "AR" (Augustus Rex) monogram (mostly used 1725-30) have been much forged. Pressed model numbers also appear.

The crossed-swords mark was used in England in the 18thC by factories such as Worcester and Bow, and in the early 19th by Derby and Minton.

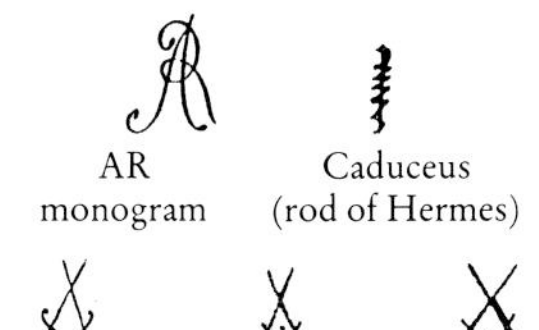

L'Avvocato (The Lawyer) Columbine

18th-century French Porcelain

Before hard-paste porcelain was successfully made in Germany, there had been various attempts in France to discover the secret. In 1693 the Chicaneau family began to produce soft-paste at St Cloud, near Paris. The heyday of St Cloud was c.1725-50, although the factory continued until the 1770s. Wares have a creamy body, with a thick, glossy glaze.

Soft-paste was also made at Chantilly, another factory near Paris, 1725-c.1780. The founder had a large collection of Japanese porcelain, which inspired most of Chantilly's output before c.1740. Early wares have an opaque tin glaze, giving a flatter look than St Cloud. After mid-century, Meissen and Vincennes were the main decorative influences. Chantilly wares have been much copied.

The third soft-paste manufactory in France, set up in Paris in 1734, transferred in 1748 to Mennecy, where production continued until a second move in 1773. Early pieces are similar to St Cloud wares, but with a soft, clear, glossy glaze which complements the bright enamels and creamy body.

When the Seven Years' War closed the Meissen factory, the buying public was left seeking a new arbiter of taste. This mantle fell upon the Sèvres factory in France, which under the influence of Madame de Pompadour caught the public imagination with light Rococo designs.

The origins of Sèvres are to be found in the French National soft-paste factory at Vincennes, founded in 1738. This was unsuccessful but a new company was set up there in 1745, with a 20-year monopoly to produce porcelain in the style of Meissen. In 1756 this factory, now a Royal Manufactory under Louis XV, moved to Sèvres.

The specialities of Sèvres were coloured grounds, gilding (there was a monopoly on this too) and ornate decoration. The predominant style was swirling Rococo gaiety initially, switching to the more serious Neo-classical manner in the 1770s. The range of domestic wares was vast, early pieces copying Meissen. After failures with polychrome figures in the Meissen tradition, figure production shifted its focus (c.1750-c.1775) to biscuit (white porcelain, unglazed, undecorated). Production of soft-paste ended in 1804.

From the early 1770s hard-paste porcelain was made at Sèvres. A technique used after the late 1770s was the fusion of translucent enamels over gilt or silver foil to create a jewelled effect.

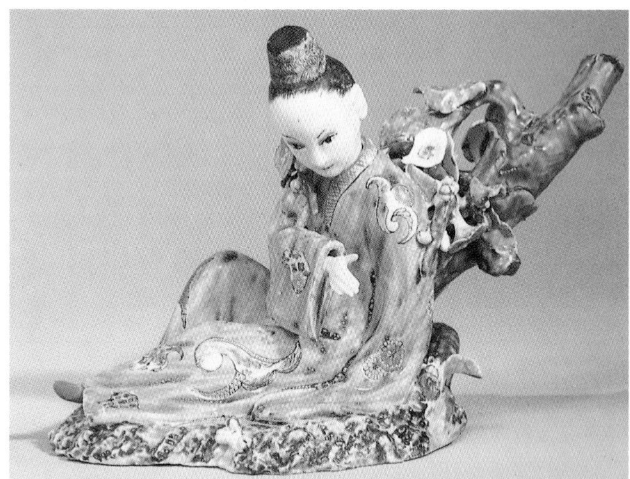

A charming Chantilly figure of a seated Oriental girl decorated in typically subtle colours, c.1730 (wdth 8in/20cm). The figure has a nodding head, pivoted on a metal pin connected to rods through the neck and shoulders. This feature was incorporated by several factories during the 1730s, including Meissen. On the girl's dress the Kakiemon style has been freely interpreted in a Rococo manner, with swirls. *C*

St Cloud cup and *trembleuse* stand, c.1735, shows a favourite St Cloud decoration – a border of blue lambequins, influenced by an earlier factory at Rouen. The moulded reeding is also typical. (A *trembleuse* is a cup and saucer, the saucer having a raised ring for the cup.) The St Cloud output also includes cache-pots, small boxes and sugar bowls. *CNY*

St C.
T

* St Cloud marks include a blue sun face, and "St C" over "T" (in blue or incised). The T indicates a date after 1722.

At Chantilly, Japanese Kakiemon motifs were imitated in a crisp style, as on this jug, c.1735 (ht 7½in/19.5cm). The decoration stands out brilliantly against the white glaze. *CNY*

* One-colour floral designs were introduced after 1755.

A Chantilly cache pot, c.1745 (ht 5½in/13.5cm). European-style decoration was prevalent at this period.

* A hunting horn mark in red (or sometimes blue) was used at Chantilly, although many wares were unmarked.

A Mennecy figure of a Chinaman, c.1735-40 (ht 6½in/16.5cm), with costume decorated in the Kakiemon palette. The beautiful ivory paste and the wet look of the glaze are typical. *S*

* The Mennecy mark was "DV" (Duke de Villeroy).

* Perhaps the finest Mennecy figures are groups of children at play, modelled after Boucher.

A Sèvres *rose Pompadour* milk jug, bearing the blue interlaced Ls mark and date letter E for 1757 (ht 5in/12.5cm). The gilding, coloured ribbon, swags of flowers and twig feet and handle show the combination of flamboyant sophistication and rusticity for which Sèvres, in its Rococo period, was famous. *C*

* The *rose Pompadour* ground colour was introduced c.1757 and discontinued after Madame Pompadour's death in 1764.
* There were various blue ground colours used by Vincennes-Sèvres: *bleu lapis*, a bright copper blue in vogue from the early 1750s (also known as *bleu de Vincennes*); *bleu céleste*, a cerulean blue introduced in 1753 (also known as *bleu nouveau*); the dark underglaze *gros bleu*; and the *bleu royal* (or *du roi*), a rich enamel blue.
* Other Sèvres ground colours include the very desirable *jaune jonquille* (jonquil yellow).
* Useful wares made at Sèvres include complete services, tea sets, ice-pails, potpourri vases, toilet wares – even clock cases.

A Sèvres cup and saucer painted inside a *bleu céleste* ground, covered with lacy scrolls. The marks include interlaced Ls and the date letters for 1781, as well as a decorator's mark. *S*

* By this period in the factory's history hard-paste was being made. New ground colours included brown, black and a dark blue.

This cup and saucer of c.1760 are similar in style to the example shown alongside, but note the different shape of the cup and the pattern of gilding: this is *caillouté* work, from the French word meaning "pebble". These meshed oval shapes were introduced by Sèvres c.1752. The style was copied at Worcester, Derby and Swansea. *S*

SÈVRES MARKS AND FORGERIES

Vincennes

Sèvres

Sèvres

The Royal cipher – interlaced Ls – was introduced in 1739. In 1753 a date coding mark was added – A for 1753, B for 1754, AA for 1779, BB for 1780, and so on, until 1793 when the Republic took control. Many Paris factories freely copied the Royal cipher; indeed, in more than 9 cases out of 10 the cipher is not genuine. Sèvres forgeries can often be detected by technical inadequacies or poor enamelling. The most easily detected sign is the use, on a hard-paste copy, of a mark found only on soft-paste.

This magnificent Vincennes cylindrical mug of 1753 is decorated in a *bleu lapis* ground with tooled gilding surrounding a reserved panel painted with birds amidst foliage. The cover with its angular finial is unusual: a floral finial would be more typical. *C*

* The painted decoration of a pair of birds is also found showing both birds flying, one with foliage in its beak. A version in gilt silhouette also occurs (above).

One of a pair of Sèvres *bleu céleste* ground potpourri vases, with pierced domed cover and contemporary ormolu mounts, c.1760 (ht 12in/31.5cm). The ram's heads and fruiting vine swags are part of a whole repertoire of popular Neo-classical motifs from which Sèvres drew – as did many other factories. *CNY*

The Meissen Influence

Continental factories at the time of Meissen's prevalence found that success could best be attained by producing Meissen-type wares in the Baroque style. Decoration was often derivative – chinoiseries, stylized flowers, harbour and military scenes, Kakiemon motifs. However, there is great pleasure for the collector in the multiplicity of styles that these factories, particularly the German ones, produced. Most makers used factory marks, but these are not always reliable, as many have been copied.

After Meissen, the dominant porcelain factory in central Europe was Vienna. In 1719 Charles du Paquier, who had been attempting to produce porcelain in Vienna since 1717, succeeded in tempting the Meissen kilnmaster Samuel Stolzel to join his operation. In 1719 Stolzel returned to Meissen after sabotaging du Paquier's raw materials, but the factory recovered from this blow and became a state enterprise in 1744, developing a semi-classical style.

Other important German and Italian porcelain factories are featured on these pages.

VIENNA, 1718-1864
The factory has three periods:
* the du Paquier period (1718-44) when wares were unmarked. Table wares followed Oriental and Meissen styles. There was a vogue for a black-painted decoration termed *Schwarzlot*.
* the "State" period 1744-84, dominated by Rococo styles. Decoration sometimes copied the paintings of Watteau and Boucher. Especially desirable are figures by J. J. Niedermayer.
* 1784-1864, embracing the Neo-classical period. Beautiful painted scenes of Vienna and landscapes date from the early 19thC. Sèvres was an influence.

Vienna marks

This Vienna (du Paquier) cream pot and cover, c.1725 (ht 4in/10cm), has chinoiserie decoration by J. P. Dannhöfer, who excelled at figure subjects. The touch of Rococo apparent in the handle hints at new influences which were to be more strongly felt in the 1750s and 60s. Du Paquier porcelain, now extremely rare, has a characteristically smoky body. *C*

A Vienna du Paquier hexagonal baluster vase and cover, c.1730 (ht 20in/51.5cm), – the centrepiece of a garniture. The trellis pattern background in iron red is a recurrent feature of du Paquier porcelain of the 1730s.
* Other Vienna motifs include naturalistic flowers (*Deutsche Blumen*), larger than those used at Meissen and spreading over the entire piece. *C*

HÖCHST, 1746-96
Hard-paste was made in Höchst from 1750 to 1796. Some superb chinoiserie groups were made, and in the period 1753-58 Höchst figures rivalled Meissen in quality. The finest were modelled by J. P. Melchior, 1767-79. After the factory was sold in 1796 some of the moulds were sent to the Damm factory, near Aschaffenburg, which used them to make figures and groups bearing the wheel mark.

Höchst marks

From c.1765, bases of Höchst figures were often formed as sections of rockwork topped by sparse grass, as in this example – a Sultana, modelled by J. P. Melchior, c.1770 (ht 8in/19.5cm). The strong, dark colours are characteristic of Melchior's work of this period. *C*

Höchst produced some attractive tableware, like this oval two-handled soup tureen and cover, c.1765 (wdth 12in/30cm). The handles are formed as leeks tied with a ribbon and the finial as parsnips, peas, a cauliflower floret and a garlic clove. The delicate landscape vignettes add greatly to the appeal of the piece, which bears the blue crowned wheel mark. *CG*

A Höchst dancing lady, c.1755 (ht 7in/18cm), probably modelled by J. F. V. Luck, shows the somewhat frothy style of figures made by the factory in its early Rococo period. Spotted and striped patterns in a light pink and blue palette were typical. Early figures, like this, tend to have bases edged with Rococo scrolling. Compare the grassy mound (left). *C*

BERLIN, 1752-present
* The first Berlin factory was started in 1752 by W. K. Wegely. A hard-paste porcelain was produced. Most surviving examples are white figures. The factory closed in 1757.
* In 1761 J. E. Gotzkowsky built a second factory, which was bought by Frederick the Great in 1763. Most of the styles derived from Meissen and Vincennes. A Berlin speciality was pieces with Mosaik borders, showing a repeat pattern of overlapping scales. Figures modelled by F. F. Meyer characteristically had disproportionately small heads and elongated bodies.
* The Royal Berlin Factory used various forms of sceptre mark.

Berlin is famous for its useful wares, especially its dinner services. This soup plate, c.1768 (dia. 9½in/24cm), is from a service made for Frederick the Great. The relief pattern was typical of dinner wares from a number of factories at this period. This particular design was peculiar to Berlin, but other relief patterns were borrowed from Meissen – for example, the "ozier" (moulded basketweave). *S*

LUDWIGSBURG, 1758-1824

This factory supplied porcelain to Karl Eugen, Duke of Württemberg. The body was greyish initially, with flaws in the glaze. However, some fine figures were made, as well as some largish groups. The best period was 1760-75. The chief modeller from 1762 to 1772 was Jean-Jacob Louis; bases of his figures sometimes bear an incised L. Also collectable are various items designed by G. F. Riedel and figures by J. C. W. Beyer. Apart from figures, typical wares include ornately decorated teapots, urns, vases and coffeepots on three legs. Painted motifs are characteristically large in proportion to the piece itself.

* Marks include a stag's antler.

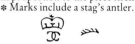

Ludwigsburg marks

Left A Ludwigsburg group of Rococo dancers, modelled by Joseph Nees, c.1765 (wdth 7in/18cm). Other figure subjects from this factory include mythological themes, Chinese figures, ordinary people from the streets, and "Venetian fair groups" by J. J. Louis. In the 1770s figures acquired a Neo-classical style. *CG*

VENICE FACTORIES

* The first Venice porcelain factory was founded by the Vezzi brothers in 1720, producing a hard paste like that of Böttger at Meissen. Shapes and patterns derive from Meissen and Vienna.
* A factory owned by G. Cozzi (1765-1812) made a greyish soft-paste, influenced by Meissen. An anchor mark was used.
* A factory at Le Nove made soft-paste from 1752, and later some hard-paste.

The Vezzi factory showed an independent spirit. This Vezzi teapot, c.1725 (wdth 5in/15cm), has the typical compressed globular body with steeply rising spout. Known Vezzi pieces number just a few hundred. *C*

* Vezzi enamel decoration often reflects Moghul Indian influence rather than Chinese.

CAPODIMONTE, 1743-59

Under the patronage of Charles Bourbon, this Naples factory produced some of the finest porcelain of the 18thC. G. Gricci modelled small-headed figures. The style of painting, with stippled-on colours, is distinctive. Early wares were often unmarked; many later pieces bear a fleur de lys (also used by Buen Retiro, Spain, where the factory was moved in 1759).

Cane handles and silver-mounted snuff boxes are a favourite Capodimonte collecting area. This snuff box, modelled by G. Gricci, c.1750-55 (dia. 3in/8cm), is typical in its use of applied shells and corals. *S*

NAPLES, 1771-1806

This factory was started by King Ferdinand IV. Early Naples resembles the wares of its predecessor, Capodimonte. Neo-classical pieces and figures in biscuit were produced. The mark was a crowned N – often copied.

Naples mark

A Naples écuelle, cover and stand, painted with vignettes showing dated eruptions of Vesuvius, c.1794 (stand dia. 9in/23.5cm) – a fine Neo-classical piece. Decoration in two tones of gold is typical of Naples. *C*

OTHER FACTORIES

Frankenthal (1755-99) produced a wide range of figures and domestic wares, in colours that tended to soak into the glaze and lacked brilliance.

Fürstenberg (which made porcelain from 1753) favoured high-relief Rococo scrolls to disguise technical problems with the body and glaze. Products included framed pictures, Commedia dell'Arte figures, and Neo-classical vases and tablewares.

Nymphenburg (1747-present), near Munich, is famous for superb Rococo figures made by Franz Bustelli from 1754 in a delicate, almost flawless porcelain: swivelled hips and thin, flat bases are characteristic.

Nymphenburg mark

Fulda (1764-89) produced some sought-after figures.

Doccia, (1735-present) This Italian factory, near Florence, made a hybrid greyish-white hard-paste. Wares are often confused with Capodimonte (soft-paste). The body was prone to firing flaws. Fine figures were made, sometimes in a palette that includes a unique iron red. Teawares with figures and garlands in low relief were much copied in the 19thC.

18thC English Coloured Porcelain

Porcelain decorated with coloured enamels was first produced in England in the late 1740s and 50s.

The factory at Chelsea (see pages 96-7) seems to have captured the market initially, although its competitors became successful in specific areas – Derby with figures, Bow with figures and dinner and display wares, the so-called "Girl in a Swing" factory (a Chelsea offshoot) with figures and scent bottles. By 1753 Worcester (see pages 98-9) was making inroads into the London market. Before long some more naively decorated wares, aimed at a less sophisticated clientele, were being made at Bow, Lowestoft, Liverpool and other factories. Occasionally, highly decorative wares from these makers rival the quality of Chelsea and Worcester.

Contemporary silverwares, and the products of Meissen and Sèvres, were three major influences in the mid-18th century. The shaping of footrims and plate edges and the flowing curves of handles and spouts often derive from silver prototypes. The Meissen influence shows, for example, in the excellent figures of Derby and Bow. Sèvres had an impact on Worcester in the 1760s, but was imitated earlier at Chelsea and Derby.

Although Meissen-inspired motifs had largely swept away chinoiseries in the fashionable London market by 1755, almost all the provincial factories continued to revel in chinoiserie for years to follow – Lowestoft until as late as 1790. Chelsea, Bow and Worcester imitated Japanese Kakiemon decoration. A lesser-known London factory founded by Nicholas Crisp at Vauxhall (his wares were formerly attributed to William Ball of Liverpool) captured the Kakiemon spirit with great success. The same factory also made wares with hand-coloured printed decoration.

Bow produced serviceable wares in the *famille rose* palette, dominated by a colour that varies from strong pink where thinly applied to a rich, fruity, reddish pink where applied more strongly. Other factories including Worcester and the Liverpool factories also decorated in *famille rose* during the mid-1750s and 1760s, although by c.1762 the style seems to have become unfashionable in London. *Famille verte* appears on Bow, Lowestoft and Liverpool wares, sometimes in rather "muddy" colours.

Floral designs remained popular throughout the 18th century, Chinese-style arrangements giving way to European bouquets by the late 1750s. Chelsea and Bow were the main producers of wares decorated with botanical specimens; Derby also produced fine plates in a similar style. The botanical vogue was revived in the late 18th and early 19th centuries.

From the late 1750s Worcester made some armorial services, as did Lowestoft in the late 1760s and 70s. Examples from these factories are rare; those from other English factories, rarer still.

BOW, LONDON, c.1746-76
Pre-1750 wares have a greyish paste against which colours stand out strongly. An ivory tone was often achieved by 1754. *Famille rose* colours were popular up to 1760. After 1760 quality deteriorates and colours become "muddy". Early pieces, if marked at all, bear devices such as:

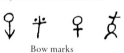

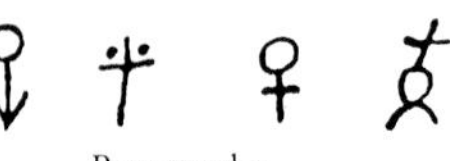

Bow marks

A Bow leaf dish, c.1760 (lgth 9½in/24cm), bearing the red anchor and dagger mark of the Giles decorating workshop, London. Leaf dishes, used to hold sauces, pickles, ginger and so on, were also made by other factories. *OSA*

* The most numerous Bow tablewares are those with Kakiemon designs (especially the quail or partridge pattern). The style is freer than at Worcester.

LONGTON HALL, Staffordshire, 1749-60
Enamels tend to "sit" on the surface of early polychrome wares, c.1753-4. The factory produced sophisticated shapes. Fine flower and bird painting was produced from 1756. Some pieces thought to be Longton Hall have been reattributed to a related factory at West Pans, Scotland, established in the 1760s. Few Longton Hall pieces are marked. All wares are now rare.

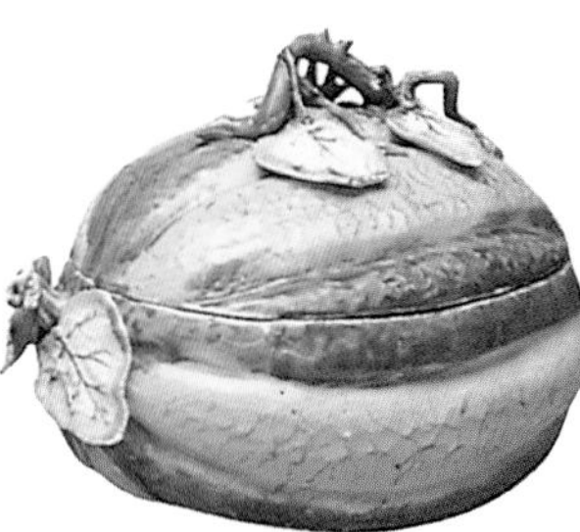

Longton Hall produced a range of naturalistic dinnerwares in rather harsh colours. Tureens such as this melon tureen of c.1755 (wdth 6in/15.5cm) and the cos lettuce tureen are extremely collectable. There have been many forgeries. *CNY*

* The rather ungainly appearance of Longton Hall vegetable tureens contrasts with the more sophisticated versions of Chelsea. The glaze is greyish and uneven.

CHAMPION'S BRISTOL, c.1773-81
Richard Champion took over the Bristol factory c.1773. Like Plymouth and New Hall, the factory made true hard-paste porcelain (see page 66). The body had a tendency to tears and firing cracks – defects that also appear on Plymouth wares, which are hard to distinguish from early Bristol.

A great deal of teaware was produced at Champion's Bristol, cups and saucers being the most common today. This chocolate cup and cover date from c.1775. The floral pattern and wet-looking colours are typical. *PC*

* This factory produced wares at both ends of the spectrum – elaborate armorial services, but also modest "cottage china".

PLYMOUTH, c.1768-70
The first English factory to produce hard-paste, founded by Wm Cookworthy. There were many technical problems, such as firing flaws and smokiness in the glaze. Enamelling includes floral and Chinese themes, and exotic birds in landscapes. Cookworthy moved the factory to Bristol c.1770. Usually there is no mark on Plymouth wares.

Straight or bell-shaped mugs were popular Plymouth products. This mug, c.1770 (ht 6in/15cm), is in *famille rose* colours. Bell-shaped mugs painted with exotic birds have been much copied. *C*

DERBY, c.1749-present
The moving spirit of this factory was William Duesbury, who later acquired Chelsea. The soft-paste body is lighter than that at Bow or Chelsea. Useful wares were few to begin with, but by the 1780s were made in greater numbers. Decoration includes fine landscapes and flower subjects (the best by Billingsley), seascapes and battles. Derby cabinet porcelain of 1780-1800 surpassed even Worcester. Marks seldom occur before c.1774.

Derby marks

Many Derby useful wares made before c.1790 bear an incised N. A painted D under a crown is found c.1770-82. Crossed batons between the D and the crown appeared thereafter – painted in puce, blue or black until 1800, and in red c.1800-25.

A Derby dish painted with a landscape, c.1795 (lgth 9½in/24cm). This rich blue, copied from Sèvres, was a popular colour in the useful wares of Derby's later period. There was a revival of pictorial painting in the last 15 years of the 18thC. *DDM*

A Derby candlestick shepherd group, c.1765 (ht 11in/28cm). Used on the dinner table, these pieces were made by Bow, Derby and Chelsea, c.1750-c.1800. Candlesticks produced by Derby were beautifully modelled (the drapery is always worth close examination), with less gilding than at Chelsea and less fragile bocages (floral or shrubby backgrounds) than Bow. *CNY*

This fine figure shows the quality of modelling consistently attained by Derby. Dating from c.1760, the figure – one of the "Ranelagh Figures" – commemorates a masked ball held in 1759 (ht 11½in/29cm). *PB*
* Size of porcelain figures in England seldom reaches more than 12 inches (30cm): Continental figures are taller. Scrolling Rococo bases appear c.1758, first at Bow, later at Chelsea and Derby.
* Early Derby figures are "dry-edged": that is, the glaze stops short of the bottom of the base (to make sure that the glaze did not stick to the kiln furniture during firing). A funnel-shaped cavity under the base is also common.
* Later figures, from c.1755, have three or more distinctive pad (or patch) marks on the base, where models rested in the kiln. These marks have darkened over time. Colouring tended to be pale.
* From c.1770 stronger-coloured enamels were used. From this time Derby also made figures in biscuit, inspired by Sèvres.

SOME OTHER FACTORIES
Lowestoft, 1757-c.1799
Coloured wares were made from c.1765. There was some fine flower painting, occasionally featuring a full-blown tulip. Most colour decoration is of modest quality, but Chinese figure decoration is sought after. Naive patterns of houses and birds in limited colours, mainly blue and red, are relatively common. Some shapes common in blue and white, such as pickle dishes, are rare and collectable in polychrome.

Liverpool
Most Liverpool factories concentrated on blue and white: polychrome wares are rare and very desirable. At Gilbody's (1754-61) coffee cans are most often found. Chinese and floral subjects were painted at Pennington's (c.1769-99).

Pinxton, 1796-1813
Before 1799 this factory, under William Billingsley, made some porcelain as fine as that he later made at Nantgarw-Swansea. Pinxton wares are rare. See page 108.

A Derby pair of figures of Autumn and Winter by William Coffee after originals by Pierre Stephan, c.1780 (ht 9in/23cm), with patch marks on the base. This piece dates from the Chelsea-Derby period – Duesbury had bought up Chelsea in 1770. However, it is likely that all the figures continued to be made at Derby, except for a few bearing the Chelsea gold anchor mark. *DDM*
* Chelsea-Derby period figures tend to be somewhat uniform and lacking in spirit. Incised model numbers are found after c.1770.

A Bow cherub, c.1765 (ht 6½in/16.5cm). The indifferent modelling and elaborately blossoming bocage are characteristic of this late period of Bow. The factory's best figures are the Meissen-inspired ones from the middle period, the mid and late 1750s: these include fine Commedia dell'Arte figures and some striking birds (especially cocks and hens). *SA*
* Elaborate bocages are not often found in perfect condition. Look for restoration.

Chelsea Porcelain

The Chelsea factory was established c.1745 by Nicholas Sprimont, a Flemish silversmith. Coloured tablewares predominated. The fine soft-paste body was initially very glassy, becoming cloudier in the Raised Anchor period (1749-52). Chelsea porcelain is highly esteemed and fetches high prices.

The influence of contemporary silver was most strongly felt from 1745 to 1754. A number of moulded shapes were copied directly from silver originals in the Triangle period (c.1745-9), including the much-copied goat and bee jug. By the late 1750s the silver influence had become more generalized.

In the early 1750s, during the Raised Anchor period, the factory produced some superb teawares and plates decorated with harbour scenes in the Meissen manner. Japanese Kakiemon decoration was popular. Figures were produced at this period for the first time.

The impact of Meissen continued into the Red Anchor period when fine floral painting and Meissen-style figures were fashionable. Other products include leaf-shaped dishes and vegetable-shaped tureens. Red anchor wares are generally of superb quality.

A particularly collectable Chelsea innovation is a form of decoration based on Aesop's fables, painted by J. H. O'Neale, c.1752 to c.1758. The style was occasionally copied by Worcester.

Sèvres influences appeared from c.1755 – for example, the use of blue ground colours with finely painted reserves. Rococo styles, with elaborate gilding, went on to dominate the Gold Anchor period. Figures and figurative candlesticks on scrolled Rococo bases are Derby-influenced but more ornate.

The Chelsea factory was bought by William Duesbury of Derby in 1770. Thereafter, until its closure in 1784, Derby styles were followed.

MARKS
Chelsea's wares are marked in a variety of ways corresponding to periods of production. Any anchor mark measuring a quarter of an inch or more should be questioned.

The triangle period, c.1745-9: an incised triangle. Another rare, early mark is the trident piercing a crown, in underglaze blue.

The raised anchor period, 1749-52: an applied anchor on a small oval pad. This can be picked out in red.

The red anchor period, 1752-6: a small anchor painted in red, or occasionally brown, enamel. The finer the ware, the smaller the anchor.

The gold anchor period, 1757-69: a small anchor painted in gold. The red and gold anchor marks were copied in the 19thC.

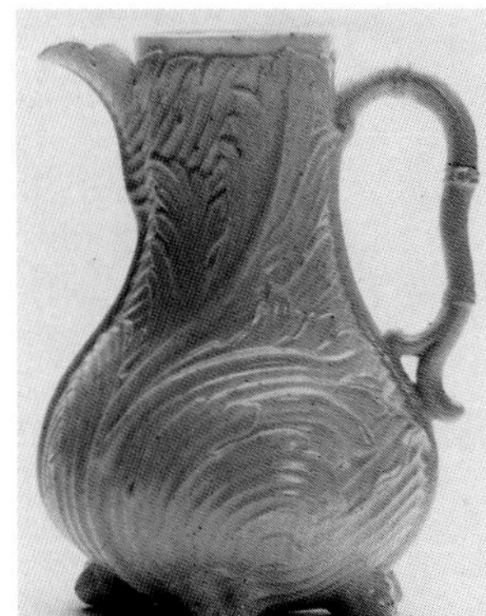

A very rare white pear-shaped coffee pot, c.1745-50 (ht 7in/18cm). One of the moulded acanthus leaves forms the spout, and the handle is fashioned as a stem. The piece bears the incised triangle mark. Moulded tea and coffee sets of this kind sometimes featured raised painted sprigs and insects, hiding defects. The waxy look is typical of this period. *S*

Kakiemon designs were a major influence in the Raised Anchor period. This sauceboat and dish date from c.1750. The superbly balanced asymmetry of the design, true to the Japanese spirit, is typical. *C*
* The usual Kakiemon palette of red, blue, green, yellow and turquoise is sometimes extended to include a delicate purple.
* A well-known Kakiemon pattern used at Chelsea is the Hob in the Well, illustrating the story of a boy who saved his friend's life by smashing the water jar into which he had fallen.
* The creamy, waxy glaze of the Raised Anchor period cannot easily be distinguished from the Red Anchor glaze.

The influence of silver wares is seen in the shape of this plate, c.1752 (dia. 9in/22.5cm). The harbour scene decoration, in a pale palette, is Meissen-inspired. *C*
* From the late 1740s Chelsea was managed by the silversmith Nicholas Sprimont, which helps to explain the frequency of pieces influenced by silverwares.
* Even on non-silver shapes, handle forms derived from silver wares are often seen.

This bowl, c.1752-6 (dia. 6in/15cm), is painted with an animal fable in the manner of J. H. O'Neale, who started his career at Chelsea and later worked for Worcester. The palette, with its warm brown, is characteristic, as is the extended lion's tail. *PC*
* Pieces decorated by O'Neale himself are among the most collectable of the Raised and Red Anchor periods.

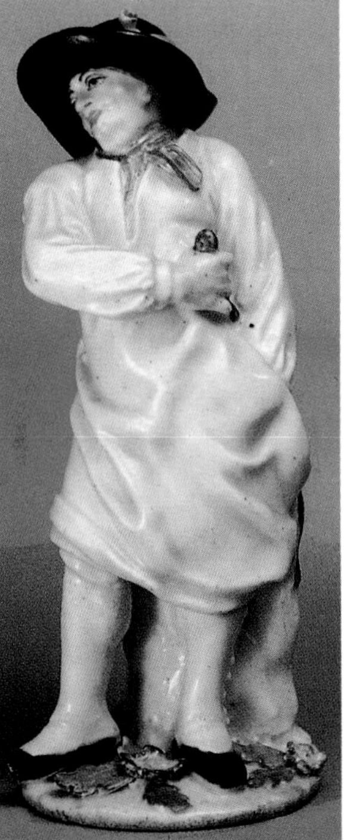

Red Anchor figures are unrivalled by any English factory. This ostler, standing next to a tree stump, dates from c.1755 and has the red anchor mark (ht 5½in/13cm). The modelling is typically subtle, not over-literal. The simple base is usual. *C*
* Thickly glazed, plain white figures were made c.1749-53.
* Meissen-like figures with scrolled bases appear c.1753-6.
* Gold Anchor figures were brilliantly coloured, with gilded Rococo bases and bocages (surrounding shrubs or foliage) densely dotted with flowers.

These Chelsea plates, marked with the gold anchor, c.1765, are decorated with exotic pheasant-like birds on rockwork, with lesser birds in the borders (dia. 8½in/21.5cm). *CNY*

* There is also a more naturalistic style of bird decoration, much rarer than these exotics. Both Chelsea and Worcester sometimes featured moths and insects as well.
* The Oriental Ho-Ho bird, with a red crest shaped like a paint brush, and blue and yellow on the body, appears on wares of the Triangle, Raised Anchor and Red Anchor periods.
* Exotic birds of "dishevelled" appearance were painted by the James Giles studio.
* Gold Anchor pieces have a light, open body, due to bone ash in the paste – this is distinct from the glassy appearance of the earlier porcelain. The glaze is often crazed.

This coffee cup (c.1750) and beaker (c.1745-9) (ht 3in/7.5cm) show two contrasting types of decoration, both typical. The coffee cup, flared and fluted, is painted with a loose bouquet. More desirable is the lobed beaker with its relief tea plant decoration. Good beakers are invariably expensive. *C*

* Relief prunus (plum) blossom decoration (above right) occurs at Chelsea in the Raised Anchor

Prunus decoration.

period on *blanc de chine* plates, cups, beakers, saucers, teapots, milkjugs and vases. The prunus also appears in a painted form in Kakiemon designs.

TOYS

Chelsea "toys" are a separate collecting area in themselves. Dating from the Red and Gold Anchor periods, they consist of various small items, an inch (2.5cm) or so high – seals (in the form of figures, Cupids, birds or animals), scent bottles, toothpick cases, needle cases. Often mounted in gold, they were sold by jewellers and widely exported to the Continent. They are sometimes inscribed in French.

The Red Anchor painting is often in a delicate purple monochrome, as in this octagonal saucer (sold with a matching octagonal tea bowl) painted in the O'Neale style with a military scene, c.1752 (red anchor mark). The octagonal form is very desirable. *C*

* Only about fifty per cent of pieces made in the Red Anchor period bear the red anchor mark.

TECHNICALITIES

* Chelsea wares of the Raised Anchor and Red Anchor periods, when held up to the light, tend to show "moons" (bright areas) and pinpricks caused by air holes in the body.

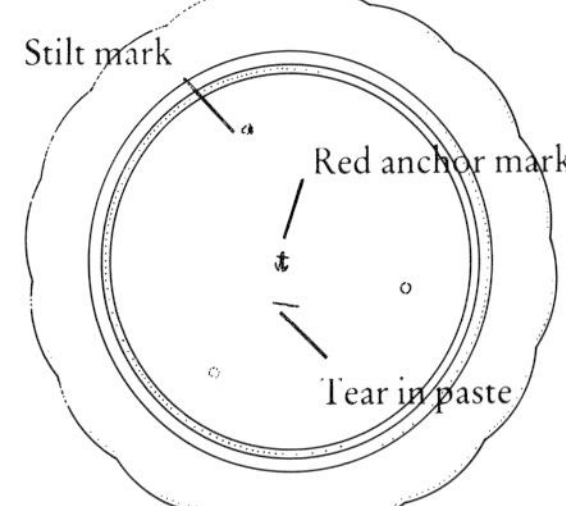

* Plates, dishes and saucers of the Red Anchor period were fired on small spurs or stilts, leaving marks (usually three) on the base. This method is used by no other English porcelain factory. Tears or other faults are also usual. The underside of the bowl illustrated above shows these features, as well as the small size of the red anchor mark.

A Chelsea artichoke tureen, with a finch finial on the cover, c.1755, red anchor mark (ht 6½in/16cm). Vegetable- and animal-shaped tureens are one of the highlights of the Red Anchor tablewares. Melons, cauliflowers and figs were also made. *C*

An asparagus tureen and cover, 1752 (lgth 7in/18cm), red anchor marks. This is more often found than the artichoke tureen above, but examples are still very pricey. *S*

* Chelsea also made a series of leaf dishes from c.1757, with moths and insects and often a caterpillar on the central leaf vein.

18th-century Worcester Porcelain

The Worcester Porcelain Company was founded in 1751 under the direction of Dr John Wall. From the outset the company's name was associated with quality – of design, manufacture and material. The soapstone porcelain body used at the factory, made to a formula bought from Lund's Bristol factory, shows green against electric light and is smooth and pleasant to the touch. The glaze never crazes.

Both blue and white (see page 102) and coloured porcelain was made. Production concentrated on useful wares, including tea and coffee sets, moulded tureens, sauceboats, bowls and jugs, openwork chestnut baskets, leaf-shaped pickle dishes and the like. Early pieces show the influence of either Chinese or silver forms, in equal measure. Complete dinner services are uncommon, as the soapstone body was unsuitable for large plates. Only a small number of figures was made.

Onglaze transfer printing was introduced c.1755 – before underglaze blue printing. Transfer-printed designs in black by the master engraver Robert Hancock, dating from c.1756 to 1774, are highly collectable. On some transfer-printed pieces the outlines were filled in with enamels.

Worcester is notable for its fine coloured grounds in the style developed by Sèvres. They were used as settings for superb painting of flowers or birds – or occasionally figures – and counterpointed by gilding in leafy scrolls and patterns.

Dr Wall died in 1776 and the new owner, William Davis, decided to concentrate on blue and white printed wares. This emphasis was continued by the Flight family who became owners in 1783. They were joined by Martin Barr in 1793. There was a spectacular revival of coloured wares at Worcester from around 1800 (see page 109).

A "Lord Henry Thynne" mug, c.1770, painted in bright enamels with a riverscape and castle inside a circular panel (ht 6¼in/15.5cm). Many Worcester designs took their name from a special commission by a wealthy patron. The Lord Henry Thynne pattern is characterized by a landscape enclosed by a gilt and turquoise husk border and surrounded by fruit, birds or insects. *S*

* Another famous pattern named after a rich patron is the "Joshua Reynolds" – a Kakiemon pattern featuring a ho-ho bird seated on a rock among a scattering of peonies. It was sometimes used with a deep blue border.

"Japan" patterns were a favourite form of decoration at Worcester from c.1767. This baluster vase of c.1770 (ht 12¼in/31cm) has panels painted with stylized flowering plants. Typical features include the chrysanthemum motif, the iron red ground, and the complex gilding. *S*

* Both the asymmetric Kakiemon style and the later Imari style, based on busy brocade patterns, were absorbed by Worcester.
* Rival English factories such as Chelsea and Derby also produced Japanese patterns, but Worcester had the widest range.

A rare early Worcester bowl of lobed form, c.1753 (8in/20cm), painted in the Chinese *famille verte* style with flowering wild cherry, peony and prunus plants issuing from pierced rocks. The piece bears an incised barbed "T" mark. Its boldly lobed form, vigorous decoration and bright, clean colours indicate an early date. *S*

* On Worcester and other soft-paste copies of Chinese *famille rose* and *famille verte* palettes, the enamels sank further into the glaze than on Chinese originals, giving a softer look.
* Worcester chinoiseries include Chinese figures crisply painted in enamels (including red and black), c.1760; and more elaborate designs in black or purple monochrome.

"Apple green" is a highly sought-after Worcester ground colour. This apple green écuelle and stand, c.1770 (lgth of stand 9in/23cm), has beautiful flower painting and gilt Rococo scroll borders. The presence of the original ladle greatly adds to the value. *S*

* Other coloured grounds used by this period include turquoise (*bleu céleste*), "wet blue", claret (borrowed from Chelsea) and a rare yellow. These grounds have sometimes been added to authentic Worcester by fakers.
* Blue, pink and yellow grounds appear in the very desirable "scale" versions: the colour was put on, as the name implies, in a pattern of scales resembling those on a fish. Scale blue is the earliest and most common of these patterns. Any form of damage to the ground or decoration, including rubbing, severely reduces the value.
* Gilding could not be applied directly onto the 18thC apple green ground: it always had to be used as a separate surround.

The cabbage leaf jug, decorated with overlapping leaves in low relief, was a Worcester innovation (c.1757), later copied at Lowestoft, Liverpool and Caughley. Often there is a mask below the spout, as in this example with the rare yellow ground, c.1760-65 (ht 9in/23cm). Some cabbage leaf mugs are painted in enamels, but this one has been transfer-printed in puce and the outline filled in with hand colouring. *S*

* This shape appeared in printed blue and white from c.1758.
* Worcester also made dishes of overlapping cabbage leaves.

This Worcester cabbage leaf mask jug transfer-printed in black, c.1760 (ht 11¾in/29.7cm), shows a rare fox hunting scene.

* Other subjects include the Tea Party, L'Amour (a beau kissing the hand of a lady) and The Fortune Teller. The earliest prints, in a dull brown, include battleships and squirrels. *S*

A sucrier (sugar bowl), cover and stand, c.1770 (ht 5½in/14cm), with exotic bird paintings within panels reserved on a "wet blue" ground. Decoration did not reach this standard until after the closure of the Chelsea factory (c.1768), when a number of Chelsea artists moved to Worcester. *S*

Worcester periods (18thC)
1751-83 First Period
1751-74 "Dr Wall" Period
1776-93 Davis/Flight Period
1793-1807 Flight & Barr Period

Many coloured wares from Worcester are unmarked. The fretted square, or seal mark, appears on many of the scale-blue wares (above).

C

Sometimes the crescent mark appears, but not as frequently as on Worcester blue and white.

COPIES

Worcester wares with Sèvres-type ground colours have been widely copied – especially by Samson of Paris, in a hard-paste porcelain easily distinguishable from the Worcester soft-paste. The enamels of hard-paste copies sit on the surface, and the gilding is always harshly metallic.

Earthenware copies have also been made: these, of course, are opaque, and therefore easy to differentiate.

The Royal Worcester Porcelain Co. itself made many reproductions in the late 19thC: these are in bone china and have the later factory marks.

A rare pink-scale deep plate, c.1770 (dia. 9in/25.8cm), painted in the London studio of James Giles (c.1760-78). Worcester was Giles' main client, but he served most other porcelain factories as well. *S*

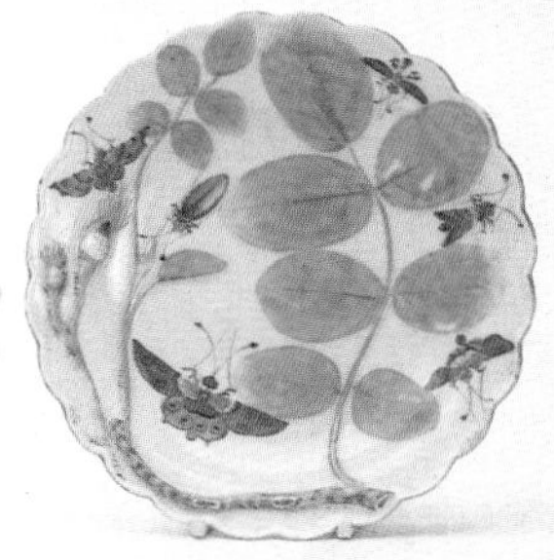

A Worcester "Blind Earl" (or "Earl of Coventry") plate, c.1765-70, painted in the Giles studio (dia. 7½in/19cm). This pattern, with large sprays of low-relief leaves, was first used at Chelsea, c.1755. *S*

18th-century English Blue and White

The strategy behind English blue and white porcelain was to break into the market created by the import of Chinese porcelain. Pieces were durable, inexpensive, for everyday use. Most are decorated with simple scenes in imitation of the Chinese, although the treatment is often naive. The finest work was done between the early 1750s and c.1770.

Only Worcester, Caughley, Plymouth and Bristol used a factory mark on their blue and white with any frequency, and much of the interest in this period stems from the challenge of attribution. Pieces from the Liverpool factories pose particular problems in this respect.

Three soft-paste formulas were developed concurrently at porcelain factories c.1745-47. Chelsea's porcelain, made with a proportion of glass, was intended mostly for ornament – only a small quantity of blue and white was produced. Bow (east London) manufactured a heavy robust bone-ash porcelain. The third formula was a soapstone porcelain, which allowed slightly finer potting; it was used in early experiments at Limehouse (also east London) and developed at Lund's factory in Bristol and at the Pomona Pot Works, Newcastle-under-Lyme. This was the staple product of Worcester (see pages 98-9). Shapes were often moulded with relief decoration derived from silver prototypes – swags, festoons, cartouches, fluting and so on.

The first transfer printing on porcelain was done by Robert Hancock on Bow (1756), although it was little used here. All the commercially successful factories went on to adopt printed patterns – especially Worcester (c.1760) and Caughley (see pages 98-9), and Lowestoft. Some factories, such as Samuel Gilbody's in Liverpool, enamelled some of their blurred designs with red outlines to make them more saleable.

The factories of Plymouth, Bristol (Cookworthy's and Champion's) and New Hall are linked by their manufacture of hard-paste porcelain, the rights to which were transferred from one to the other over a period of 24 years from 1768.

PLYMOUTH, 1768-70 and COOKWORTHY'S BRISTOL, 1770-74 (hard-paste)
Plymouth was the earliest English hard-paste factory. William Cookworthy's wares made here are often indistinguishable from those he made at Bristol, 1770 to 1774.
* The underglaze blue is often almost black in tone, although it can be a pale, bright blue.
* The surface of turned pieces usually exhibits "spiral wreathing" – spiralling lines twisting upwards.
* The Plymouth glaze is sometimes brown in tone due to smoke staining from the kiln.
* Plymouth wares are sometimes marked with a conjoined 2 and 4 – the alchemical sign for tin.
* Bristol wares are often marked with a blue cross.

A Plymouth saucer, c.1770, decorated in dark blue with a chinoiserie pattern imitating Worcester of the same period. Many blue and white factories failed to mark their wares, probably in the hope of passing them off as Oriental or Worcester. *V&A*

BOW, c.1746-76
Bow used its bone-ash formula for vast quantities of blue and white. After the death of Thomas Frye, the original patent-holder, in 1761 quality declined dramatically. Later pieces can resemble earthenware.
* Early wares were painted in a bright royal blue. The glaze can be thick and "lardy", often forming pools of thicker, blue-tinged glaze. Much of the potting was heavy.

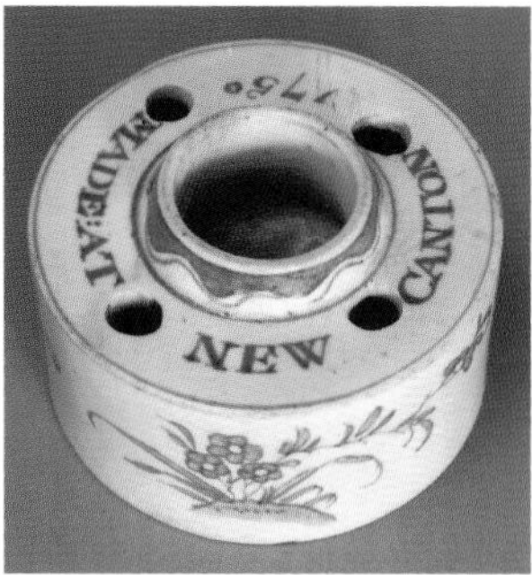

A Bow inkpot dated 1750 painted in the vivid underglaze royal blue that typifies the early products of the factory (dia. 3½in/9cm). "New Canton" was an alternative factory name. Only a handful of these dated inkwells are known. The brown staining along the margins of cracks is a Bow characteristic. *C*
* Some early wares are marked with a capital R incised beneath the glaze. Some of these pieces are more thinly potted, and painted in an inky blue.
* This darker blue becomes predominant after 1755, when wares are again quite thinly potted. Painters' numerals occur, 1753-6.

A Bow saucer, late 1750s (dia. 5in/12.7cm). The strong cobalt colours make this an unusual piece. Although the tree pattern is typical of Bow, it was also used by other factories. *MB*
* Bow concentrated on tablewares initially. Fine vases with birds in the reserves were made in the second half of the 1750s.
* Powder decoration (dusted or blown on rather than painted) was a speciality.

LOWESTOFT, 1757-99
This factory made a bone-ash porcelain similar to that of Bow.
* Early wares had a limited range of chinoiserie motifs (riverscapes, gardens, flowers). They were delicately drawn and shaded in at least two tones of pale grey-blue.
* Early themes were soon developed into standard patterns.
* The body of the earliest wares is off-white, sometimes with a pink or brown tone, and the glaze often clouded by bubbles.

A Lowestoft bottle, c.1764 (ht 10in/24.5cm). Wares of this period have a clear glossy glaze, and the blue is inky in tone. This blue continued in use, although many wares after 1775 have a brighter blue. *CNY*
* Painters' numbers were used at Lowestoft from 1759 to c.1774.
* Lowestoft made a speciality of inscribed and dated pieces.

DERBY
Blue and white was produced in small quantities, 1756-86.
* The Derby body is very white where unglazed, otherwise creamy. Derby blue and white is seldom marked.

A Derby basket (lgth 9¼in/23.5cm), c.1765. Other Derby products include asparagus servers, leaf-shaped pickle trays and small cream boats (easily confused with Lowestoft). Few teawares were made. *MB*

LONGTON HALL, 1749-60
This factory used a glassy paste formula. Early wares (including large vases with relief fruiting vines and squirrels) had flaws in the paste. Many pieces featured a streaky underglaze dark blue.
* Various underglaze blue marks were used – e, k, B, P and crossed Ls – but most wares are unmarked.

LUND'S BRISTOL, c.1749-51
Benjamin Lund was the first English porcelain manufacturer to use soapstone in his formula. His stock, and his licence to mine soapstone, were pruchased by the Worcester factory in 1752.
* Wares are decorated with Chinese designs in either a pale or an indigo-tinged blue. Sauceboats are plentiful.

This Liverpool tureen and cover, date 1764 (dia. 12in/30cm), with rope handles and a rabbit finial, was made at around the time the Chaffer's factory was taken over by Philip Christian. The masses of dots in the decoration, apparent on this piece, is characteristic of these factories. Early Chaffer's is grey in tone. *V&A*

LIVERPOOL AND VAUXHALL
Wares by the various factories operating at Liverpool, 1754-1800, are eagerly collected. The factories of Chaffer's, Christian and Seth Pennington occupied the same premises in an unbroken sequence from 1754 to 1799. The wares of Nicholas Crisp of Vauxhall, London, were until recently ascribed to William Reid & Partners, Liverpool (and before that to William Ball).
Nicholas Crisp, Vauxhall, 1755-64
Unusual items such as mortars, cornucopiae, trinket boxes and flowerpots were made, as well as the full range of teawares.
* The bright blue appears almost wet beneath the clear, soft glaze.
* Bow shapes and decoration were often imitated.
Samuel Gilbody's, c.1754-61
The rarest of all Liverpool porcelains. Difficult to distinguish from Chaffer's.
* The blue is sometimes blurred, with greyish tone. The glaze tends to be smooth and silky.
Richard Chaffer's & Partners, c.1754-65
Produced some bone-ash porcelain c.1755, and later turned to a soapstone formula (shows a green translucency when viewed by transmitted light).
* Occasionally bases are marked with painters' numerals.
Philip Christian & Son, 1765-76
After Christian took over Chaffer's, shapes, patterns and porcelain formula continued unchanged, but gradually the fluidity of decoration was lost.
Seth Pennington's, c.1769-99
In 1776 Seth Pennington added Christian's factory to his existing interests. The porcelain produced was now bone-ash, as Christian had sold his soapstone interests to the Worcester factory.
* Some highly collectable bowls painted with ships were produced in the 1770s and 80s.

A Longton Hall spoon tray, c.1755 (lgth 6in/15cm), damaged. The printed obelisk design is a desirable feature. *V&A*
* By 1755 the Longton Hall body had become more refined, and the control over the blue had improved, but there was still a tendency for it to "bleed" into the soft glaze.

A Lund's Bristol sauceboat, c.1750 (lgth 9in/22.8cm), with moulded decoration. The three blue dots, representing rocks, are a common feature of Lund's blue and white. They are taken from Chinese porcelain.
* Mountains on Lund's Bristol are typically represented by a series of blobs arranged as pairs of inverted Vs, and shaded with a paler tone of blue.
* Designs on Lund's Bristol are usually blurred.
* The grey-toned glaze is close-fitting but less clean in appearance and slightly thicker than early Worcester.

A Pennington's beaker, c.1785 (ht 4½in/11.4cm). Notice the poor join in the printed border. *V&A*
* Pennington's wares are often grey in tone, and the transfer printing smudgy. The glaze is often grey-blue.

Worcester and Caughley

In 1751 a partnership to manufacture porcelain at Worcester was established under the control of Dr John Wall. The partnership purchased from Benjamin Lund of Bristol a licence to mine soaprock, together with Lund's stock. The soapstone body of the 1750s has a lovely green translucency – apparent when pieces are held up to electric light. Worcester's earliest wares can be difficult to distinguish from later Lund's, but the Lund's patterns are often blurred by the pronounced thickness of the glaze.

Many collectors believe that over the next decade Worcester was making the finest blue and white porcelain ever produced in Europe. As contemporary advertisements put it, the body did not "fly", as many contemporary soft-pastes did – that is, scatter into pieces when boiling water was added. The quality of the potting was equalled by the refinement of moulded and painted decoration. Early designs are closely related to Chinese porcelain of the Kangxi period. By the 60s the factory was producing standard patterns and shapes in vast quantities. Transfer printing in underglaze blue was introduced c.1760; most Worcester blue and white wares were printed by c.1775.

Worcester's early moulded teawares, cream boats and sauce boats are among the factory's best achievements. Typically they have Rococo panels painted with Chinese fishing scenes.

The more commonplace pieces in blue and white were made in such quantities that they can still be obtained at reasonable prices.

The Caughley factory (pronounced "calf-ly") was situated near Bridgnorth, Shropshire, about forty miles upstream of the River Severn from Worcester. It started porcelain production in 1772 under Thomas Turner, using a soaprock formula in imitation of Worcester. Indeed, the whole enterprise seems to have been geared initially to exploit and undercut the Worcester market. Worcester printed patterns were copied, although Turner also produced exclusive designs. After 1776 the factory was pursuing a less derivative course. Gilding was often used to complement the blue and white decoration. Caughley wares are sometimes termed (and marked) "Salopian". The miniature or toy teawares, made for children, are now highly collectable.

Similarities of paste, shape and decoration can make Worcester and Caughley blue and white hard to tell apart. In printed patterns produced by both factories, there are sometimes differences of detail. Recently there have been some important re-attributions.

It is a fallacy that Caughley produced inferior Worcester, and any collector using quality as the basis of attribution is likely to go astray. In some cases, the standard of potting and decoration of Caughley wares is better than that of Worcester wares of the same period.

The Caughley factory was taken over by the Coalport management in 1799.

A Worcester printed teapot, c.1765 (ht 5½in/14cm), with a matching Lowestoft lid. This is one of the commonest Worcester patterns, dating from the period when designs had become more simplified. *MB*

* A lid from another factory is acceptable if the patterns and styles match. More desirable, however, would be a Worcester lid of the same pattern but from a different piece. Most desirable of all would be the original lid.
* The collectability of blue and white printed wares depends to a large extent on the clarity of the printing. This piece is of good but not excellent quality: sharper prints are often found.
* Worcester teapots never have cracks caused by contact with hot water – that is, cracks that do not lead to an edge.
* Well-formed flower and bud knobs are characteristic of Worcester teawares.

A Worcester gugglet bottle, c.1760 (ht 10½in/27cm), showing the naive style of chinoiserie typical of the factory's early period: patterns tended to be spindly, somewhat loose, and the colour more restricted in area than it became later. The piece has a good-quality workman's mark on the base – a desirable feature. *MB*

* Painters at this period worked freely, often mixing elements from different designs. Typical motifs are fences, birds, Chinese figures, willow trees and boats.
* By c.1765 painted patterns became more standardized, almost to the point of mass production.

This Worcester painted Dragon pattern bowl, c.1760-65 (dia. 7in/18cm), is a direct copy of a Chinese original. The blue is of good quality, showing the "heaped and piled" effect (that is, variations in density) that occurs on Ming blue and white decoration. The expression on the dragon's face is well caught – an aspect that collectors regard as important. *MB*

WORCESTER PERIODS
(18thC)
1751-83 First Period
1751-74 "Dr Wall" Period
1776-93 Davis/Flight Period
1793-1807 Barr and Flight & Barr Period

A Worcester coffee pot and cover painted in blue with the "Long Eliza" design, c.1760-65 (ht 9in/ 23cm). The underglaze blue is of good colour, but the painting lacks the spontaneity of the 1750s. *MB*

* Painted coffee pots are worth about half as much again as printed. A rare pattern can raise the value by a further 50 percent.
* "Long Elizas" are the tall, elegant ladies who often featured on the 18thC Chinese (Kangxi) blue and white porcelain imported to Europe and America, and were copied by Worcester and by manufacturers of delftware. The name comes from the Dutch, *Lange Lijzen*.

A Caughley printed blue and white saucer dish of the popular Cormorant and Fisherman pattern, c.1785 (dia. 8in/20.5cm). The short, fat fish being held by the fisherman is a sign of Caughley manufacture: the Worcester version of the same pattern shows a longer, slimmer fish (right). In the Worcester version the line of the fisherman behind is wriggly rather than taut. Moreover, the Worcester pattern tends to be in a lighter tone of blue. *MB*

Worcester: details

A Worcester moulded shell-shaped dish, c.1758, with workman's mark (lgth 4½in/ 11cm). Worcester moulding is renowned for its quality. The moulded chrysanthemum pattern is especially attractive. *MB*

WORCESTER MARKS (blue and white)

* A crescent mark in underglaze blue is found c.1755-90 – the commonest mark. The painted open crescent appears on painted wares. On printed pieces a printed cross-hatched or filled-in crescent is found.
* A version of the Meissen crossed swords, with a 9 below, is also not uncommon. Disguised numeral marks occur on blue printed wares, c.1775-90. In addition, imitation Chinese and alchemists' symbols are found.

A Caughley kidney-shaped blue-printed dish, c.1780 (lgth 9½in/ 24cm), with typically tight decoration. *OSA*

* Caughley printed wares were often gilded: this tends to detract from their value. Gilded rims on plates are particularly common. Iron red was also often added to improve a mediocre piece of printing.

WORCESTER OR CAUGHLEY?

* Common to both is the use of a soapstone body showing an orange translucency when held to electric light (although early Worcester shows a green translucency).
* Both used the open crescent mark.
* On pieces by both factories, the inside of foot rims may have a small glaze-free band (not on Worcester of the 1750s).
* Caughley never copied the violet-indigo tone of some late Worcester pieces.
* Worcester prints tend to have more cross-hatching.

CAUGHLEY MARKS

Many Caughley pieces are unmarked. However, these marks were used until c.1790:

* "Salopian" (sometimes in capital letters), impressed
* "S", "So" or "Sx", painted or printed in blue
* a blue printed C or open crescent.

19th-century English Pottery

The ceramic bodies pioneered by Wedgwood and pirated by rival firms continued to be produced, often in a debased form, throughout the 19th century. In this period we see the decline of pottery as a craft: it now became an industrial process.

This was the era of blue and white transfer-printed earthenware from the Staffordshire potteries, produced, notably, by Josiah Spode's factory at Stoke. For the collector, the loss of individuality, inevitable with any form of mass-production, is offset by the huge variety of patterns.

For many collectors, the appeal of Staffordshire earthenwares stems not only from their intrinsic charm but also from their evocation of the social and political context of the era. Figures and commemorative decoration present a lively pageant of contemporary figures in politics, entertainment, religion and even crime!

One popular technique of the period was lustre decoration, which created a metallic effect using pigments containing tiny quantities of gold ("copper" lustre) or platinum ("silver"). The potteries at Sunderland, in north-east England, are famous for their "splashed pink" lustres, used especially for commemorative wares.

"Etruscan wares", in imitation of red-figure Greek pottery, were made by F. & R. Pratt and by Dillwyn & Co. of Swansea. Wedgwood continued to make Neo-classical jasperware with white decoration; signed work by Émile Lessore is sought-after. Majolica (earthenware with coloured glazes) was made by Minton, Wedgwood and others.

From the mid-19th century there was a resurgence of artistic development in the pottery industry, centred around the marketing opportunities provided by exhibitions. The most ambitious and forward-looking companies appointed art directors to supervise the development of new products.

The term "Wemyss ware" (pronounced "weemz") refers to a style of pottery made at the Fife Pottery near Kircaldy in Scotland from 1880 to 1930. This large Wemyss model of a pig, painted with green shamrocks, is an early example (ht 17¼in/44cm). As well as these popular pigs, Wemyss wares include vases, flower holders, mugs and so on. *P*

A printed mug, c.1820, decorated with a scene of a farmer and his family in a dark-copper (gold) lustre ground (ht 3¾in/9.6cm). *S*
* Copper lustre was rare until c.1820, when it began to be widely used for mugs and jugs.
* Lustre was mostly used as partial decoration – often as a band or frame. Wedgwood made all-over silver lustres from c.1815.

A Queen's Ware (creamware) plate by Wedgwood, shaped in the "Spanish" style, late 1860s (dia. 9½in/24cm). The painting is by Émile Lessore, who trained at Sèvres and decorated various Wedgwood Queen's Wares, including plates, plaques and vases, from c.1860 until his death in 1876. *WM*

Blue and white transfer-printing could be applied to pearlware, creamware or ironstone (as well as bone china). This Wedgwood pearlware plate, with a combined ship and landscape pattern, dates from the first quarter of the 19thC (dia. 10in/25cm). Landscapes and botanical patterns were the most popular subjects, often enhanced by an elaborate border pattern. *WM*

Spatterwares are a colourful group of Staffordshire pottery, c.1825-40, made inexpensively in large quantities, mainly for export to America. The background decoration was applied with a sponge. The peacock on the left-hand plate here (dia. 6in/15cm) is the most popular central motif. *SNY*
* Red and blue are the most common spatterware colours; green is scarce, yellow even scarcer. Rare forms such as pitchers and sugar bowls fetch high prices. Some collectors prefer pieces on which the spatter is the sole decoration.

TRANSFER PRINTING

Staffordshire blue and white transfer-printed earthenware enjoyed its heyday c.1810-40. Smudged outlines were no longer the problem they had been in the 18thC. An improved transfer paper was introduced, allowing stipple to be added to line engraving.

Other colours were used as an alternative to blue after c.1820. Dark green, sepia and puce enjoyed successive vogues.

Multi-colour transfer printing (pink, brown and green) was used from c.1828, and in the 1840s it became possible to print the three colours simultaneously. However, blue and white continued to predominate. Sometimes overglaze colours were added to a blue outline.

F. & R. Pratt of Fenton (c.1847-88) used colour transfer printing for small pot lids and for tablewares with borders in green, red, pink, blue or maroon.

A Mason's ironstone jug, c.1825 (ht 9in/23cm), with a characteristically ornate all-over Japan pattern, bright colours and octagonal form. A snake or dragon handle was a popular Mason's feature. *BC*
* A wide variety of decorative jugs were made in the 19thC – among them ironstone, moulded stoneware, lustreware, pearlware and various "dry" bodies. Attractive collections can be formed at a reasonable cost.

A Mason's ironstone part dinner service, c.1820, printed in blue and enamelled with chinoiseries. *S.*
* Ten years ago, the realization that 19thC dinner services could be bought at less than the cost of new services stimulated this area of the market. For extensive services, prices are now high.

MASON'S IRONSTONE
Within the past twenty years some of the more interesting 19thC ceramic bodies have become popular collecting areas. Mason's ironstone, in particular, has a dedicated following. Patented in 1813, it was the most successful of the "stone chinas" – heavy earthenwares made with feldspar, similar to porcelain in appearance and with a similar "ring" when tapped with the fingernail.
* Mason's products include jugs, massive vases, dinner services and fireplace surrounds.
* Decoration was often transfer-printed with enamels applied on top. Strong blues, reds and greens are typical, sometimes with gilding. Blue and white wares were also made in quantity.
* Mason's wares are nearly always marked. The word "Improved" appears in the factory mark from c.1840.

A blue-printed Staffordshire part dinner service, c.1850. *P*
* Staffordshire blue and white is more desirable if marked. Unmarked pieces are virtually impossible to ascribe to a particular factory.
* Collections are often formed within specific areas, by factory or pattern – chinoiseries, topographic, botanical, birds and animals, historical, literary, rural scenes, American subjects.
* Early Staffordshire blue and white is light in weight, with a bluish glaze. Viewed at an angle, the surface should look slightly rippled. Flatware should normally have three stilt marks on the base near the rim, where the piece stood in the kiln.

This Minton majolica plant trough shows the vivid glazes that typify these wares (ht 14in/35.8cm). The term "majolica", coined by Minton (1850), was borrowed by Wedgwood and others. *C*
* Minton's products in majolica range from large jardinières and conservatory seats to small cheese stands and bread trays.
* Related to Minton's majolica is the firm's "Palissy" ware, which copied the work of Bernard Palissy, the 16thC French potter. These wares feature lizards and other animals or plants in high relief.
* Minton (1793-present) also made blue-printed earthenwares and stone china, as well as porcelain (see page 111).

FIGURES AND ANIMALS

Staffordshire figures and animals, with lively, naive modelling that often borders on folk art, are keenly collected. Originally intended as inexpensive ornaments for a mass market, they now command high prices, and fakes abound. Brightly coloured pearlware figures, groups and animals made by Yorkshire potters are also very collectable. Collectors often specialize in a particular theme – for example, sporting figures (or, even more specifically, cricket), royalty, or political subjects.

A Leeds pearlware stallion with black mane and tail and yellow bridle on a sponged green base with leaf border, c.1820 (ht 15in/38cm). Animals are among the most collectable of pearlwares. *C*

* Early pearlware can be recognized by the white appearance of undecorated areas; and by a bluish cast where the glaze is at its thickest.
* Wedgwood made pearlware tablewares. From 1840 the mark "Pearl" appears; from 1868 the mark is a "P".

This Yorkshire moneybox in bright underglaze colours, made by Emery, Mexborough, c.1838 (ht 10in/25cm), would have been used as a mantelpiece ornament. Some moneyboxes were in cottage form. *LR*

* Another useful object in elaborate ornamental form was the watch stand, with a hole for the watch.

Obadiah Sherratt, who operated c.1815-40, is a Burslem (Staffordshire) potter notable for vigorous figure groups. This is one of the most sought-after themes: Polito's Menagerie, c.1810 (ht 11½in/29.2cm). There are several versions of this subject, which may well have been sold as a souvenir by Polito, a travelling showman. The piece is modelled as a fairground booth, with four musicians and a lady visitor. The brightly coloured enamels are typical. *S*

* Sherratt's groups often have semi-literate inscriptions, with misspellings: in this example, note that "birds" is spelled "burds".
* Other subjects include a bull being baited by a dog under the control of its owner (c.1830; often copied); and the killing of a Lt Monroe, in soldier's uniform, by a Bengal tiger.

COPIES AND FAKES

Honest reproductions of Staffordshire portrait and flat-back figures have been made right up to the present day. Many of these have been passed off as authentic. Most reproductions are slip-cast rather than press-moulded, and therefore lighter in weight than the originals; there will also be a large vent hole (dia. about ⅜in/1cm) in the base. Because the moulds are taken from the figures themselves, which are glazed, there is also a give-away loss of detail. Pieces press-moulded from the original moulds are more difficult to detect. The deception may be indicated by a fine, even crackle on the glaze: on the genuine item the crackle would be uneven and widely spaced.

An Obadiah Sherratt cow, c.1820 (ht 7in/18cm), with the typical rainbow base and bocage (shrubby background). *LR*

* From c.1840 Staffordshire animals show a loss of detail.
* Staffordshire cow creamers (cow-shaped milk jugs) tend to have an oval green base, with an added milkmaid. Those from Swansea tend to have a rectangular base.

STAFFORDSHIRE FIGURES

Early 19thC figures are well-moulded, and decorated to resemble porcelain. Later, "flat-back" figures (with flat, undecorated backs) are more naive. Bright enamelled colours were used c.1840-60: these can flake if heavily applied. After c.1860 sparser colours were used – sometimes just black and white, with gilding. Criteria of value include: crispness of moulding; brightness of colours; the presence of an impressed or painted title on the base. Equestrian figures are popular.

This boxer, one of a pair of combatants, c.1811 (ht 10in/25cm), is not attributed to a particular factory but shows the quality of Staffordshire figures c.1810-20. As well as sport, popular themes include royalty, theatre, crime and politics. *PC*

The British lion and Napoleon III – a Victorian flatback figure, with the typical gilding on the base. The piece reflects British anxieties about a French invasion. Other military themes include the Crimean War and the Indian Mutiny. *RBE*

American Pottery

Functional redwares, made from alluvial clay, were first made in America from c.1625, continuing well into the 19th century. New England pieces tend to be relatively plain (although often with richly coloured glazes, or slip trailing). In Pennsylvania redwares were more imaginatively decorated, often with lively sgraffito designs cut through slip.

Stonewares made before 1790 are very rare. Ovoid jars and jugs were produced until c.1840-50, when straight-sided vessels supplanted them. Decoration could be incised, impressed, or coggled (impressed with a wheel). Saltglaze wares could be slip-trailed in blue, painted with a brush, or stencilled.

After 1860, most stoneware made in the south-eastern states was glazed with an olive or brown alkaline glaze both inside and out.

Yellow wares may be earthenware or stoneware. The "Rockingham"-glazed (that is, brown-mottled) yellow wares include the famous Rebeccah at the Well moulded teapot design and pitchers (jugs) with moulded hunting scenes and hound-shaped handles.

Creamware was copied, especially in Philadelphia from c.1790. Majolica was made, notably by Griffen, Smith & Hill of Phoenixville, Pennsylvania (c.1879-c.1890). Also popular was ironstone, often white moulded, sometimes hand-painted; main potteries include those in Trenton, New Jersey (notably Ott & Brewer and the Greenwood Pottery Co.). Transfer printing was not widely used until the 1840s: printed tablewares were made in East Liverpool, Ohio, and Trenton, New Jersey.

"Rockingham" wares such as this coffee pot, 1849-58, from Bennington, Vermont (ht 12¾in/32cm), are very much sought after – especially if the moulding is sharp. As well as pitchers, teapots and bowls, the range includes pie plates, door knobs, picture frames, and figures of dogs and lions. The name derives from the Marquis of Rockingham, who had made similar pottery at Swinton, Yorkshire, England. In America output continued from c.1835 to the end of the century. *BM*

Saltglazed jars and crocks could be either painted or trailed with blue (cobalt) slip: the method favoured varied according to the region. This two-gallon painted jar was produced by the New York Stoneware Co., Fort Edward, 1861-85; the maker's name is impressed on the shoulder (ht 11½in/29cm). Bird motifs were highly popular. *CNY*

* Some particularly attractive painted slip decoration, often with tulip designs or leaves, came from the Philadelphia area.
* Stonewares are more often marked than redwares.

One method of decorating redwares was to brush on, or splash on, metallic oxides – copper (green), manganese (black) or iron (brown) – to contrast with the red clay. This jar, made by John W. Bell and Co., Waynesboro, Pennsylvania, c.1880-95, is ornamented with manganese flowers and a band of coggled decoration around the shoulder (just visible in this picture) (ht 12½in/31cm). The interior of the jar is manganese-glazed, the exterior left unglazed. *CNY*

* Green glazes are especially sought after.

Moravian religious settlers in North Carolina made slip-decorated pottery in the 18th and 19thC. This 19thC Moravian bowl, decorated in brown with a central flower-head within concentric rings and a wavy border on a mustard yellow ground, is of the "Jacob Christ" type (13½in/34cm). *CNY*

* Also appealing is the brightly coloured slip decoration of the Shenandoah Valley (Virginia, Maryland and Pennsylvania), where the Bell family produced flowing designs, somewhat like Oriental characters, throughout the 19th century.

Blue and white transfer printing in the USA is not well documented before 1840. This early example – an earthenware plate – is from the American Pottery Co., Jersey City, NJ. By the second half of the century the technique was being widely used on inexpensive tablewares. After c.1880 printing was often combined with painting.

* Complete 19thC dinner services are very rare: most sets were built up piecemeal. *BM*
* Among the Trenton factories producing transfer-printed wares were Ott & Brewer, Cook & Hancock's Crescent Pottery Co. and Burroughs & Mountford Co. East Liverpool factories included the Dresden Pottery Co., Laughlin Bros. and Knowles, Taylor & Knowles Co.

Early 19th-century Porcelain

Bone china – very white and translucent, durable and inexpensive to manufacture – was adopted by Worcester (Flight and Barr) from c.1800 and shortly afterwards by Derby, Rockingham, Coalport and others. From the 1820s it became the staple body of the English porcelain industry. This and other porcelain bodies of the period will for many collectors never acquire the *cachet* of English soft-paste, but they form a fascinating collecting area, in which quality of decoration is a prime factor.

During the first twenty years of the 19th century Neo-classical forms prevailed in urns, vases and other imposing objects made for display. The forms and decorative motifs of the French Empire were a major influence, but there was also a revival of the light, delicate Rococo manner. Patterns of Japanese inspiration, with rich gilding, were followed by Derby and Worcester (Chamberlain's), especially c.1810-15. Fine naturalistic and topographical painting was produced at a number of factories c.1800-30.

An important figure was William Billingsley, known for both his fine soft-paste bodies (beset by a high proportion of kiln failures) and for his superb flower painting. He was employed at Derby, established a factory at Pinxton, then moved to Worcester before setting up a factory at Nantgarw, Wales, in 1813. The Nantgarw business was transferred to Swansea in 1814 and back to Nantgarw in 1817 before Billingsley moved to Coalport in 1819. Such complicated movements, reflected by the transfer of workers, methods and styles from one factory to another, emphasize the difficulties faced by the collector in identifying unmarked wares.

Painted pattern numbers appear on a large proportion of British porcelain from c.1790. More likely to be found on useful wares than ornamental, they can help with attribution and dating. Pattern names such as "Rose" or "Pekin", however, refer to standard designs made by many firms.

NANTGARW-SWANSEA, 1813-20
Pieces from these factories are scarce and much sought-after.
* Wares include some with Billingsley's superb flower painting. Wildflower designs were a Swansea speciality.
* The impressed mark, "Nant garw" (sometimes with "C.W." for China Works) is often virtually hidden by the glaze. Swansea marks include crossed tridents (often faked).
* Identification of Nantgarw and Swansea is complicated by the use of different pastes at different times; by close imitations by Coalport; and by many fakes.

A Swansea ice pail, c.1814-22 (dia. 8in/20cm). Nantgarw or Swansea porcelain in such ambitious shapes is rare: the main output was flatware and simple hollow ware. *C*

A rare Nantgarw butter tub and stand from the Duke of Gloucester Service, c.1813-22 (dia. of stand 7½in/19cm), with flower decoration and gilding and a rich *oeil de perdrix* ("partridge eye") pattern. As well as such ornately embellished pieces, Nantgarw made some delicate wares sparsely painted with floral sprays or other simple motifs. *C*

COALPORT, SHROPSHIRE, from c.1796
The best period began in 1820 with the use of a brilliant white feldspar china. Rococo wares, often confused with Rockingham, include flower-encrusted "Coalbrookdale" pieces (marked "C Dale" or "C.D."). Most wares were unmarked.

Coalport produced many pieces in the "Japan" style, such as this vase of c.1810 (ht 22in/56cm). Japan wares were also made by Derby and Spode. *SNY*

PINXTON, 1796-1813
A small Derbyshire factory near Mansfield, whose products were often inspired by Derby initially. Pinxton porcelain is very rare. Decoration includes simple sprigs and small-scale landscapes, sometimes identified local views. Some of the flower painting may be by Billingsley, who was a partner in the factory until c.1799.
* Pinxton is rarely marked, although some pieces bear the painted mark of the factory name. A script P is sometimes found, usually with a pattern number. A crescent and star mark, with various arrow symbols, may indicate Pinxton manufacture after 1799.

A Pinxton yellow ground trio of two cups and a saucer, decorated in the manner of William Billingsley, c.1800 (dia. of saucer 5¼in/13.4cm), bearing the pattern mark P113. Many Pinxton wares are decorated with small-scale landscapes of this kind – often named, local views. Yellow-ground Pinxton is especially sought. *C*

WORCESTER, from 1793
Following changes of ownership, this period is divided into the following phases of production:

B

* Flight & Barr, 1793-1807
The incised B mark is usually found on teawares.

BFB FBB

* Barr, Flight and Barr, 1807-13
* Flight, Barr and Barr, 1813-40
* Products include teawares with spiral fluting and sprig designs, and dinner services with tasteful decoration. Vases, cabinet cups, spill vases and the like typically feature excellent gilding, lovely ground colours – and often meticulous shell or feather painting. The body changed from a waxy, heavy soapstone to bone china in the mid-late 1830s.

CHAMBERLAIN'S WORCESTER, c.1786-1852
This breakaway factory initially decorated wares from Caughley. A greyish hard-paste was made from c.1791. A fine "Regent China" was used for expensive wares, 1811-20.

Left This Barr, Flight and Barr bough pot and cover, c.1810 (ht 7¾in/19.7cm), has superb feather painting that makes its origin instantly identifiable. *S*

ROCKINGHAM, c.1826-42
Ornately decorated porcelain was produced on the Marquess of Rockingham's estate at Swinton, Yorkshire, c.1826-42. In potting and decoration Rockingham was unsurpassed. Characteristic are: superb landscape and flower painting; fine coloured grounds (blue, green, red, grey); a fine, almost imperceptible crazing of the glaze. Much so-called "Rockingham" is actually Coalport. Most authentic wares have the griffin mark (red initially, puce after 1830).

Rockingham specialized in expensive wares such as this Rockingham dessert plate, made to royal order, 1832 (dia. 9¼in/23.5cm). Other pieces include superb vases and baskets. *CNY*

DERBY, c.1749
* 1800-11. Highlights include flower painting. The crown mark was used, in red.
* Bloor Derby, 1811-48. Fine painting includes fruit by Thomas Steel, flowers by Moses Webster, birds by Richard Dodson.

A Derby campana (inverted-bell-shape) vase, c.1815 (ht 13in/33cm). Landscape painting remained a factory speciality after 1800. This was a favourite early 19thC shape. *CNY*

A New Hall part tea set, c.1800, brightly decorated in mazarine-blue, orange and gilding with fruiting palm motifs (dia. of teapot 10¼in/26cm). *S*

* New Hall (1781-1835), in Staffordshire, made a durable hard-paste and bone china from c.1812. Tea sets and coffee sets, in distinctive moulded shapes, were the factory's mainstays.

* "New Hall" printed inside a double-lined circle first appears as a mark c.1812.

DERBY MARKS

To 1825 (red)

Bloor period (printed)

Later English Porcelain

The rise of Victorian porcelain as a collecting area coincides with the increasing difficulty of acquiring the best 18th-century wares. Later 19th-century porcelain is well-marked, and there is plenty of documentary evidence to provide a background to individual acquisitions. Although technical virtuosity sometimes outweighs artistic merit, outstanding pieces were made by Minton, Coalport, Copeland and others.

An interest in classical design prompted experiments to reproduce the appearance of marble in a porcelain body suitable for moulding into statuary. The need was met by "parian" – a waxy, unglazed body used by various firms for statues shown at the Great Exhibition of 1851. Useful wares were also made in the medium. Quality of parian varies widely.

Leading porcelain factories built upon the achievements of the past. Copeland, notably, concentrated on versions of the Sèvres style, with lovely ground colours and fine painting in reserve panels. Among the most important developments of the 19th century was the *pâte-sur-pâte* style of decoration introduced to Minton by a French employee, Marc Louis Solon. This involved the application of successive coats of translucent white slip on a dark body. Each coat was hand-carved to build up a three-dimensional design of great delicacy. The technique could take weeks to complete, and pieces were therefore expensive.

Japanese influence is seen in Worcester and Copeland during the 1870s and 80s. The Derby factory produced colourful "Japan" patterns, as well as fine dessert services and specimen plates hand-painted with delicate flowers, birds and local landscapes.

Some collectable work was produced by smaller factories such as Ridgway (dessert services), James Duke & Nephews (1860s) and Davenport (dessert services with landscapes). The Belleek factory in Northern Ireland is famous for its iridescent glaze.

Wares encrusted with porcelain shells or flowers became the vogue in the 1830s. This Chamberlain's Worcester two-handled oval tray, c.1840 (wdth 13in/33cm), is better painted than most. The subject – the "New Suspension Bridge at Clifton" – is identified on the reverse of the tray. *CNY*

* Chamberlain's Worcester operated from c.1786 to 1852.

COPELAND

The Stoke-on-Trent firm of Spode traded as Copeland & Garrett from 1833 to 1847, when Copeland became sole proprietor. Parian was made from 1846. The most desirable Copeland products include flower painting by C. F. Hürten (signed) and figure painting in gilt or jewelled borders by Samuel Alcock. A variety of marks was used, sometimes incorporating "Late Spode".

A large Copeland parian group of "The Sleep of Sorrow and The Dream of Joy", c.1875, made for the Ceramic and Crystal Palace Art Union (ht 18½in/47cm). *S*

* The most common colour for parian is white, but some later examples were tinted. Often there is a slight glaze. Minton and Copeland were the principal makers.

A Copeland vase, painted by L. Besche and signed, c.1880 (ht 15in/37cm). The cover is pierced and gilt, as is the base. *S*

* Besche was a French painter employed by the factory from 1872 to 1885.

LATER WORCESTER FACTORIES

* *Kerr & Binns, 1852-62*

Products included "Limoges enamels" – Renaissance-style pictures painted in white enamel on a blue ground. A shield-shaped mark was used on the finest pieces.

* *Royal Worcester Porcelain Co., 1862-present*

Notable for Japanese pieces from c.1870. Biscuit figures had painted details.

Royal Worcester's output includes pieces delicately hand-pierced or "reticulated" by George Owen (usually signed). This vase, attributed to Owen, dates from c.1890 (ht 12in/30cm). *S*

Artists employed by Royal Worcester to decorate tableware in the early 20thC include John Stinton (landscapes, cattle, sheep), Harry Davis (landscapes, sheep) and C. H. C. Baldwin (birds). This vase, c.1910 (ht 9in/23cm), is typical of John Stinton and his brother Harry. *S*

A rare Ridgway & Robey porcelain figure of a character from *Nicholas Nickleby* by Dickens, 1839 (ht 9in/23cm). *S*
* Ridgway & Robey operated only from 1837 to 1840. Dickens characters are the only known marked pieces made by the partnership.
* Dickens portrait figures were also made by W. Ridgway, Son & Co.

A porcelain fox-head stirrup cup, c.1825-50 (lgth 4½in/11cm). Stirrup cups form a distinct collecting area. They were used outdoors at hunt meets, and thus did not need a flat base to stand on. They were also made in earthenware. *S*
* Other shapes include deer, hares, fishes and many dogs.

A superb Minton *pâte-sur-pâte* vase by M. L. Solon, c.1890 (ht 21½in/54.5cm). Solon's pieces are all originals. He signed his work. *S*
* One of Solon's apprentices at Minton was Alboine Birks, who produced some fine white plates with *pâte-sur-pâte* central panels.
* *Pâte-sur-pâte* was also produced by the Worcester factories, who concentrated on flowers rather than figures. The initials "EL" on bases of vases refer to Edward Locke, who worked for Grainger's.
* Some relatively lumpish *pâte-sur-pâte* plaques and narrow vases were made by George Jones's Trent Pottery, 1876-86. These usually bear the indistinct initials G.J., impressed.

COALPORT
A Shropshire factory, founded c.1796. The best work was done after 1820, when excellent tablewares were made with Sèvres-type ground colours (the richest being *bleu du roi*, a brilliant dark blue). Ornamental wares included flower-encrusted "Coalbrookdale" pieces, parian figures and copies of Chelsea, Meissen and Sèvres. Later wares are sometimes "jewelled" with blobs of enamel.
* Various marks were used, including an "ampersand" mark, with initials C, S and N in the loops (Caughley, Swansea, Nantgarw).

Coalport employed some accomplished artists to paint in the Sèvres style. This vase, c.1870-75 (ht 17in/43cm), is decorated by John Randall, who was famous for his bird paintings (c.1835-81). After painting exotic birds in the Sèvres style (1850s and 60s), he turned to the more naturalistic approach evidenced here. *S*
* Coalport artists were not allowed to sign their work until the last years of the 19thC.

MINTON, 1793-present
The factory was known for its wide range of high-quality pottery (see page 105) and porcelain. Painting was often enhanced by a special soft glaze (from c.1851): such pieces bear a small "ermine" mark. Ground colours included a distinctive turquoise. Jesse Smith painted excellent roses in the 1850s. Especially rare and desirable are pieces decorated by the well-known Derby painters, Joseph Bancroft, George Hancock and Thomas Steele. Parian figures were made on a large scale from the late 1840s. Most of the best flower-encrusted "Coalbrookdale" wares are now attributed to Minton. Solon produced *pâte-sur-pâte* at Minton until 1904 (other factories had ceased to produce this ware by 1890).
* Pattern numbers were introduced early and reached 9000 by c.1850. Year symbols have appeared since 1842. Some of the finest pieces do not bear pattern numbers, as they are unique. All pieces bearing an "H" pattern number are 20thC.
* The impressed mark used from c.1860 changed from Minton to Mintons in 1873.

Later Continental Porcelain

The second half of the 19th century saw an expansion of the European porcelain industry, boosted by the discovery of new deposits of kaolin. Bohemia alone had almost 40 factories, employing over 6,500 people.

The period was dominated by historicism – that is, the nostalgic revival of earlier styles. In particular, Neo-Rococo and a corrupt version of the Napoleonic Empire style flourished. With the Franco-Prussian War of 1870-71 supremacy in porcelain design passed once and for all to central Europe.

Genuine hard-paste Sèvres of the 19th century is rare. More common are old soft-paste reject blanks sold off by the factory (up to 1840) and decorated (up to c.1880) by various Paris and Staffordshire factories, often with fake marks added.

Meissen figures by mid-century were finer in paste, painting and gilding than they had been in the late 18th century.

Coloured biscuit figures were made in their millions, and exported to Britain and America. Many are enhanced by 18th-century period costume, but the spirit has departed them: colouring tends to be less vivid than in the 18th century (except for some figures made in Italy and Thüringia), and the modelling is less meticulous.

Porcelain plaques, produced by Meissen, Vienna and Berlin and decorated by independent artists, are a distinct collecting area. Those from Berlin tend to fetch higher prices than comparable examples from other factories.

This French biscuit porcelain figure (ht 27in/68cm) is gigantic compared with the well-known figures of the 18thC. However, smaller examples were also made. *S*

* Biscuit porcelain is matt: it has been fired once, painted and fired again, without a glaze. This gives a natural look to the flesh.

This late 19thC vase (ht 25in/63.5cm) in the Japanese style is by Edmé Samson, the French maker who reproduced Chinese, Japanese, French and English porcelain of earlier periods. *SM*

* Most Samson pieces bore both his mark – the letter S – and the mark that would have appeared on the original piece. On imitations of Chinese porcelain, the S is incorporated into an imitation seal mark. Often the Samson mark has been unscrupulously removed.

* Samson used hard-paste (or sometimes earthenware) even to copy soft-paste originals.

Empire-inspired oviform vases on waisted plinths were widely produced in the late 19thC, notably by Sèvres and the Imperial Manufactory in Vienna. These Vienna vases, c.1800 (ht 45in/113cm), have the dark blue ground and abundant gilding typical of the factory. Claret was also favoured as a ground colour. *C*

* Vienna produced many vases with transfer-printed decoration in place of hand painting (often with spurious signatures).

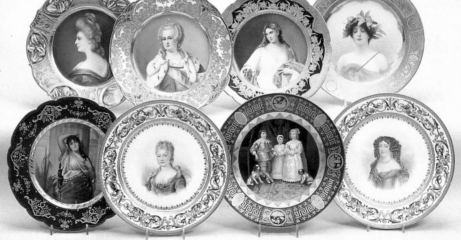

Many factories produced cabinet plates, for display, in the late 19thC. This selection (all dia. 9½in/24cm) includes two Sèvres plates with acanthus leaf borders (bottom row, right and second left), c.1864. The rest are German, c.1900. On the German plates, the well-rounded figures on shadowed grounds and the liberal border gilding borrow from the typical Vienna style. *S*

SÈVRES

The quality of Sèvres wares began to decline in the 1860s, but the sculptor Albert Carrier-Belleuse, who became director in 1876, attempted to restore the factory's prestige by innovation. He brought in other sculptors to design wares, including Auguste Rodin, and introduced new decoration, such as imitations of Chinese celadon, *flambé* and *sang-de-boeuf* glazes (1880s). However, the preponderance of Sèvres wares from the late 19thC remained traditional and ornate. Most vases were decorated with narrative panels – classical scenes, courting lovers, idyllic country pursuits and Napoleon I on campaign. Designs included exuberant gilding – for example, the eagle motif and the monogram, N, for Napoleon.

American Porcelain

The first successful manufacture of soft-paste porcelain in the United States was carried out by Bonnin & Morris, following a bone-ash formula, c.1770-1772. Output appears to have been confined to blue and white, in styles similar to those of Worcester in England. Surviving pieces are few.

The creation of a national porcelain industry after the Revolution was slow to follow. The level of Chinese imports remained high until the mid-1820s. Meanwhile, English and, to a lesser extent, French porcelain were also widely imported.

Only in 1826 was manufacture established on a commercial scale, by William Ellis Tucker in Philadelphia. Other manufacturers followed, and by 1875 the US porcelain industry was secure.

Major factories included Charles Cartlidge & Co. (c.1848-56) and William Boch & Bros. (c.1850-61), both of Greenpoint, New York. Pitchers (jugs) with low-relief decoration are a typical product. The Union Porcelain Works in Greenpoint, active from 1861, pioneered the use of underglaze colours.

However, the principal porcelain centres were East Liverpool, Ohio, and Trenton, New Jersey. Knowles, Taylor & Knowles in East Liverpool produced a Lotus ware – a version of Irish Belleek, thinly potted with a soft glaze – from 1889. The best-known Trenton firm was Ott & Brewer, which started porcelain production in 1876 and closed in 1892.

Parian was produced in America, initially by the United States Pottery Company in Bennington, Vermont. English designs were borrowed – for pitchers, figures, vases, ewers. Some pieces, with white relief motifs against a stippled vivid blue ground, imitated Wedgwood jasper ware.

This vase is a famous product of the Union Porcelain Works, Greenpoint, NY. Made in 1876 (ht 21¾in/55cm), it was designed by Karl Müller for the Philadelphia Centennial. Historical scenes are pictured in the biscuit panels around the base, lozenge panels show machinery, and animal heads, like trophies, appear at two levels. Well-documented pieces such as this command a high premium. *BM*

Parian was often fashioned into English shapes, but distinctive American forms were also produced. Some pieces featured historic subjects. This bamboo-handled parian pitcher has reliefs of George Washington holding a scroll, American flags, shield and liberty cap (and, on the reverse, George and Martha Washington), 19thC (ht 10½in/27cm). *CNY*

The oak-leaf motif was characteristic of the hand-painted wares produced by Charles Cartlidge & Co. of Greenpoint, New York. This oak-leaf pitcher dates from c.1850. Some pitchers of this design incorporate the American eagle in the spout with a shield below and an inscription in a cartouche in the side. *BM*

* Cartlidge & Co. operated from c.1848 to 1856. They are well-known for their Rococo Revival wares, of which this is an example. As well as tablewares, the factory produced doorknobs, candlesticks, plaques and portrait busts.

A Tucker porcelain pitcher, Philadelphia, 1826-38 (ht 8½in/22cm), with painted flower decoration. The bulbous body, outflaring neck, scalloped rim, scroll handle and standardized gilt pattern on the shoulder are typical of this factory. However, pieces in a similar style were made by Smith, Fife & Co., also in Philadelphia, c.1830. *CNY*

TUCKER PORCELAIN

William Ellis Tucker's Philadelphia porcelain company (founded 1826) operated as Tucker & Hulme from 1828. After William Ellis Tucker died in 1832, the factory was continued by Joseph Hemphill and Thomas Tucker (William's brother). The name was changed to the American Porcelain Company in 1835. It lasted until 1838.

Tucker porcelain closely followed French prototypes, and unmarked examples are often difficult to distinguish from French originals – a problem exacerbated by the fact that Tucker sometimes decorated French blanks.

Surviving Tucker porcelain is rare. Wares include vases, tea sets, coffee pots, pitchers and plates. Decoration on the hard white body includes delicate floral motifs with gilt trim, as well as American landscapes, historical portraits and emblems, sometimes executed in sepia.

Reference I

GLOSSARY

Agate ware Pottery that resembles agate (a variegated quartz).

Albarello A waisted drug jar.

Applied Attached separately, rather than being part of the **body**.

Arita porcelain Wares from the Arita kilns in Japan, including **Kakiemon** and **Imari** wares.

Armorial wares Pieces decorated with heraldry.

Artificial porcelain Another term for **soft-paste** porcelain.

Bail-handle An arched handle, fixed or hinged, over the lid of a vessel.

Baldachin A raised canopy, a popular motif on 18thC French ***faïence.***

Baluster vase A vase in a curving shape that resembles a balustrade support.

Barber's bowl A shaving bowl with a curved indent in the rim for a close fit under the chin.

Basalt/Basaltes Black **stoneware**, particularly that made by Wedgwood.

Bellarmine A bulbous **stoneware** bottle with a bearded mask, supposedly representing a cardinal of that name.

Bennington ware See **Rockingham ware**.

Bianco sopra bianco White decoration on a greyish or bluish ground, found on 16thC ***maiolica*** and 18thC English **delftware.**

Biscuit Unglazed porcelain or earthenware that has been fired only once. The term also refers to white porcelain (especially figures) left undecorated and unglazed.

Bisque Another, less correct term for **biscuit.**

Blue and white White Chinese or Western porcelain or Western earthenware (especially tin-glazed) with **cobalt blue** decoration, painted or printed.

Blue-dash charger A type of English **delft** charger with a pattern of blue dabs around the rim.

Blanc de Chine A highly translucent type of Chinese porcelain made from the late Ming period to the present day. It is left unpainted, and has a thick, rich **glaze**. Various European factories made copies.

Bocage A thicket or tight group of flowers that supports or surrounds a figure.

Body The material from which **pottery** or **porcelain** is made (although the term "paste" is more often used for porcelain). Also, the main part of an object, as distinct from lid, handles and so on.

Bonbonnière A small receptacle for sweetmeats, often in the form of a novelty.

Bone-ash An ingredient in a **soft-paste** formula used at Bow and other 18thC English porcelain factories.

Bone china (or just "china") A porcelain formula (combining **petuntse, kaolin** and dried bone) supposedly introduced by Josiah Spode II, c.1794. It became the mainstay of the English porcelain industry from c.1820.

Botanical wares Wares decorated with painted flowers copied from botanical plates. They were produced by most major 18thC porcelain factories.

Bourdalou A small female urinary receptacle, sometimes confused with a sauce boat.

Brocade pattern A pattern used on **Arita porcelain** of the **Imari** type, based on textile patterns. Imitations were made at Meissen, Worcester and elsewhere.

Brownware Salt-glazed brown **stoneware**, especially that made in England in Nottingham, Derby and elsewhere.

Brush pot A small pot used for holding calligraphy brushes.

Cabinet wares Cups, saucers and plates with high-quality decoration, made for display rather than use.

Cachepôt An ornamental container for a flower pot.

Cadogan teapot A type of novelty teapot that is closed at the top and filled through the base.

Caillouté Literally, "pebbled". An irregular pattern of meshed ovals, usually gilded.

Cameo A design in contrasting low relief, as found in **jasperwares** and the like.

Cancellation mark One or more strokes across a factory mark to indicate a flawed or discontinued piece.

Canton porcelain Export porcelain enamelled in Canton (China) and exported to the West in the 18thC and early 19thC.

Cartouche A decorative panel, moulded, painted or printed – usually an oval frame formed of scrollwork.

Castleford ware White stoneware (mainly jugs and teapots) with relief decoration and usually blue enamel borders. Made near Leeds, England, c. 1800-20.

Celadon A semi-translucent, usually green glaze used on Chinese **stoneware.**

Chantilly sprays Decorative stylized sprigs, usually in blue. First used at Chantilly, the pattern was adapted by some English porcelain factories.

China Originally, an alternative term for Chinese porcelain. Since the early 19thC the term has been used to refer to **bone china**.

China clay See **Kaolin.**

Chinese export porcelain Porcelain made for European tastes, for export, rather than to strictly traditional designs.

Chinoiseries European interpretations of Chinese decoration, often featuring Chinese landscapes, birds, figures, fences, dragons and so on.

Chocolate cup A large cup with two handles, a cover and a saucer.

Clobbering The application of fake decoration to a genuine piece of pottery or porcelain, for deceptive purposes.

Coalbrookdale ware Bone-china wares profusely encrusted with modelled flowers, made at Coalport, Rockingham and elsewhere in the 19thC.

Cobalt blue The colouring agent for blue and white porcelain.

Coffee can A straight-sided cylindrical cup, made at Sèvres and elsewhere.

Combed decoration A wavy pattern produced by dragging a comb through applied wet **slip**.

Commedia dell'Arte The Italian Comedy tradition, characters from which were modelled by Meissen, Nymphenburg and other porcelain factories.

Commemorative wares Wares that commemorate an event, such as a battle, coronation, disaster or the opening of a bridge.

Corn pitcher A jug with moulded corn (maize) decoration.

Cow creamer A cream jug in the form of a cow, especially the earthenware examples made in Staffordshire in the later 18th and 19thC.

Crabstock A type of handle or spout moulded as a gnarled crab-apple branch.

Crackle A network of cracks in the glaze of some Chinese porcelain, deliberately introduced as decoration.

Crazing Tiny surface cracks in the glaze of porcelain, caused by technical defects.

Creamware Cream-coloured earthenware with a transparent lead glaze, developed by Josiah Wedgwood c.1760.

Crinoline figures Meissen porcelain figures with wide hoop-skirts.

Delftware Tin-glazed earthenware made in the Netherlands or, with a small d, England.

Dessert service A set of wares decorated *en suite* for serving dessert, including plates, compôtiers, bowls and tureens.

Deutsche Blumen Painted naturalistic flowers, single or in bunches, used as porcelain decoration in the mid-18thC.

Dinner service A set of wares decorated *en suite* used at dinner. A full set may include plates, bowls, dishes, chargers, tureens, sauce boats, salt cellars and sugar casters, and sometimes custard cups and ornamental pieces.

Dry body A non-porous **stoneware** that required no glaze, made by Wedgwood and others.

Dry edge An unglazed edge around the base of some figures.

Earthenware Pottery that is not vitrified – hence, all pottery except **stoneware.**

Écuelle A covered shallow bowl, usually with two flat handles at the rim, and a stand.

Enamels Colours derived from metallic oxides and applied as **overglaze** decoration.

Faïence Tin-glazed earthenware made in France, Germany and Scandinavia.

Famille rose A much-imitated form of Chinese decoration, including a dominant opaque pink **enamel.**

Famille verte Chinese decoration that features a brilliant green **enamel**. The palette was much copied on European porcelain.

Feldspar porcelain A variation on the **bone china** formula, made from c.1820.

Feldspathic glaze The **glaze** on **hard-paste** porcelain, which fuses to a natural glass at very high temperatures.

Finial An ornamental apex, particularly on the cover of a tureen or similar, where it serves as a handle.

Fire-crack A crack in the body which appears during firing.

Flambé A type of Chinese glaze, usually of deep crimson splashed with blue.

Flatback A **Staffordshire** figure with a plain, flat back, intended for the mantelpiece.

Flatware Flat or shallow tableware, such as plates.

Flower-brick A **delftware** container for flower cuttings, similar to a brick in shape and size.

Foot-ring A projecting circular base on the underside of a plate or vessel.

Frit porcelain A **soft-paste** formula that includes fine white clay and powdered glass.

Garniture de cheminée A set of ornamental vases for the mantelpiece.

Gilding The application of gold, especially to porcelain.

Glaze A glassy coating that gives a smooth, shiny surface to **soft-paste** porcelain and **stoneware** and, additionally, seals porous bodies. **Hard-paste** porcelain has a **feldspathic glaze.**

Grisaille Painting on porcelain in shades of grey.

Ground A monochrome area of surface colour, to which painted and gilded decoration can be added.

Hard-paste The technical term for porcelain made in the Chinese fashion, with **kaolin** and **petuntse** in the formula.

Hausmaler Independent decorators (especially in Germany).

Hispano-Moresque ware Spanish tin-glazed **earthenwares**, decorated with **lustres**. Made from the 12thC.

Hybrid pastes Formulas that combine the ingredients of **hard-paste** and **soft-paste porcelain**, in an attempt to produce a more malleable body.

Imari Japanese porcelain with dense decoration, based on brocade patterns. A Chinese variant is termed "Chinese Imari".

Impressed Indented, as opposed to **incised**. Usually applied to factory marks.

Incised Scratched into the surface. Applied to marks, inscriptions and decoration.

Indianische Blumen The German term for floral decoration based on **Kakiemon** styles.

Ironstone china A type of English **stoneware**, made notably by Mason's.

Isnik A type of brilliantly decorated Turkish pottery.
Istoriato A type of narrative decoration on Italian ***maiolica*** plates.
Jackfield ware A type of black glazed pottery, made in England in the later 18thC (especially at Jackfield, Shropshire).
Japan patterns Japanese-inspired designs on English pottery and porcelain (for example, Worcester).
Japonaiserie European decoration based on Japanese motifs.
Jardinière A plant or flower container.
Jasper A hard, fine-grained **stoneware** introduced by Wedgwood.
Jaune jonquille A shade of yellow used as a **ground** colour by Sèvres.
Jewelled decoration An imitation of precious stones using drops of translucent **enamel** over gold and silver foil.
Kakiemon A style of decoration based on Japanese porcelain of the late 17thC – sparse, vividly coloured and usually assymetrical.
Kaolin (china clay) A fine white granite clay used in **hard-paste** porcelain.
Lambrequin A Baroque border pattern of scalloped drapery.
Lead glaze A transparent **glaze** incorporating lead oxide.
Leaf dish A small moulded porcelain tray in the form of a leaf.
Long Elizas An informal term for the tall ladies featured on 18thC Chinese blue and white, and copied on **Delftware** and English porcelain.
Loving cup A two-handled cup, generally urn-shaped. Made in various types of pottery.
Lustre A metallic, sometimes iridescent, form of decoration.
Maiolica Italian tin-glazed **earthenware.**
Majolica A 19thC type of earthenware using coloured **lead glazes.**
Mocha ware Inexpensive colour-banded pottery (mainly jugs and mugs), decorated with fern-like designs. Particularly associated with **Staffordshire**, but also made elsewhere.
Mount An ornamental attachment of ormolu (a brass-like alloy) or gilt-bronze used on high-quality porcelain.
Oeil de perdrixLiterally, "partridge eye". A pattern of dotted circles in enamel or gilding; used at Vincennes-Sèvres, copied at Meissen.
Openwork The use of decorative openings made by manipulating the clay into patterns.
Overglaze (on-glaze) Decoration (painted or printed) applied to a piece of pottery or porcelain after glazing.
Palette The group of colours used in a particular style or by a particular factory or decorator.
Parian An unglazed **biscuit** porcelain, resembling Parian marble. Favoured in 19thC England and America for figures.
Paste The composite material from which **porcelain** is made.
Patch marks Patches bare of glaze on the base of a figure, where the figure has stood on clay pads during firing.
Pâte-sur-pâte A type of 19thC porcelain featuring low-relief designs carved in **slip** and applied to a contrasting body.
Pearlware A white, hard, very durable form of **Queen's Ware,** also made by Wedgwood.
***Petit feu* enamels** Colours applied at low temperature (as opposed to *grand feu*, or high-temperature, colours).
Petuntse (china stone) A fusible, bonding mineral used in **hard-paste** porcelain.
Polychrome Decoration in more than two colours.
Porcelain A translucent white ceramic **body** made from **kaolin** and **pentuntse** (**hard-paste**) or another ingredient that induces translucency (**soft-paste**), and fired at a high temperature.
Porcellanous Having some of the ingredients or characteristics of **porcelain** but not its translucency.
Possett pot A vessel, sometimes multi-handled, for drinking posset, a hot beverage.
Pottery The generic term for all ceramic wares excluding **porcelain.**
Prattware Earthenware decorated in vivid **underglaze** colours, named after a **Staffordshire** potting family.
Press-moulded The term used for objects or applied ornament formed by pressing clay into an absorbent mould.
Puzzle-jug A jug with a globular body, **openwork** neck and three to seven spouts in the rim.
Queen's Ware Creamware made by Wedgwood, from 1765.
Redware Red **stoneware,** generally unglazed; often decorated with **applied** motifs in relief.
Reign-marks Four- or six-character marks on some Chinese porcelain denoting the name of the emperor and, on six-character, the dynasty. They do not necessarily indicate the period of manufacture.
Reserve A space within the **ground** colour, left blank for decoration.
Rockingham ware (USA) Pottery with a brown glaze, often mottled with yellow, made at Bennington (Vermont) and elsewhere.
Rococo A style of mid-18thC decoration, with asymmetric ornament and generous use of scrolls.
Rose Pompadour A rose-pink ground colour introduced at Sèvres.
Saltglaze A glazed **stoneware**: salt is added to the kiln during firing. White saltglaze can resemble porcelain. Buff, red and brown types were used for utilitarian objects.
Schnittblumen An early form of ***Deutsche blumen*** depicting individual cut flowers.
Scratch blue Incised decoration on **saltglaze** stoneware, filled with **cobalt** oxide to produce a blue pattern.
Sgraffito A design incised through **slip** to reveal the contrasting body beneath.
Slip A creamy mixture of clay and water, used to decorate pottery and for **slip casting** and **sprigging.**
Slip casting The manufacture of thin-bodied vessels using **slip** in a mould which absorbs the water.
Slip trailing The application of **slip** onto pottery as a form of surface decoration.
Slipware A type of English **earthenware** decorated largely with **slip.**
Soapstone (steatite) A **soft-paste** porcelain formula that substitutes soapstone for **petuntse.**
Soft-paste Porcelain made from **kaolin** and powdered glass (frit), soapstone or calcined bone (bone-ash). See also **hard-paste.**
Sprigged ware Pottery with low-relief decoration, attached to the body with **slip.**
Staffordshire English pottery region in the Midlands, based around Stoke-on-Trent.
Stamped Impressed with a stamp (used of marks).
Steatite See **Soapstone.**
Stilt marks Marks on the base of some plates and dishes left by the supports used during firing.
Stone china A type of heavy **earthenware** made with feldspar, with a resemblance to porcelain.
Stoneware A hybrid of **earthenware** and **porcelain**, made of clay and a fusible substance, such as sand or flint. It is not porous after firing.
Studio pottery Pottery that has been individually designed and crafted.
Tazza A large shallow bowl on a stemmed foot.
Tea bowl A small Oriental cup without a handle, also made widely in Europe (with a saucer) in the 18thC.
Tea service A set decorated *en suite* for serving tea, comprising cups, saucers, a teapot and stand, cream jug, sugar bowl, spoon tray, slop bowl and, initially, two large plates for food (small plates were introduced mid-19thC).
Terracotta A lightly fired red earthenware, usually unglazed.
Thrown wares Vessel shaped by hand on a rotating wheel.
Tin glaze An opaque white glaze containing tin oxide, used on ***faïence,*** **delftwares** and ***maiolica.***
Toby jug An 18th or 19thC jug representing a seated Englishman with three-cornered hat and mug of ale.
Tomb figures Pottery figures made in China and Japan for burial in a tomb.
Tomb guardian A fierce mythological animal or warrior figure made to protect the dead in Chinese tombs.
Tooled The term applied to gilding that has been worked with a tool into a pattern.
Tortoishell ware Creamware decorated with mingled **glazes** to produce a variegated effect.
Toys Small porcelain objects, such as scent-bottles and snuff boxes.
Transfer printing A type of printed decoration, whereby the design of an inked engraving is transferred to paper and from there to the ceramic object.
Translucency The light-transmitting quality of **porcelain,** which highlights the colour of the **body.**
Trembleuse A cup and saucer set with a projecting ring in the saucer into which the cup fits.
Tyg A large mug with two, four or more handles and sometimes several spouts.
Underglaze Decoration, usually painted or printed, applied before glazing. **Cobalt** blue is the most common underglaze colour.
Wall-pocket A vase for the wall.
Waster A deformed pot, discarded by the factory.
Watch stand A Victorian **flatback** piece with a hole in which to place a watch, used as a mantelpiece ornament.
Willow pattern Mock-Chinese decorative pattern, used on blue and white **transfer-printed** wares. The pattern showns two figures crossing a bridge, with a third in pursuit.
Wreathing Spiralling indented rings inside **thrown** pottery, left by the potter's fingers.

Reference II

SELECTED MAKERS
Page references in brackets refer to factory profiles given elsewhere.

GREAT BRITAIN AND IRELAND

Astbury, John (active c.1720-50) Staffordshire potter. Made redware teapots and jugs, as well as lead-glazed figures.
Ball, William (18thC) Liverpool porcelain maker, manager of **Pennington & Co.** Was once thought to have owned his own factory: however, wares attributed to Ball's have recently been re-ascribed to Nicholas Crisp of Vauxhall.
Barr, Flight & Barr See **Flight & Barr.**
Baxter Family of decorators, working from Coalport, Caughley and Worcester. Thomas, active 1814-21, worked for Worcester and Swansea.
Belleek (1863-present) Co. Fermanagh, Northern Ireland. Made thin porcelain with an iridescent glaze. Marks include crowned harp.
Billingsley, William (18thC-early 19thC). Decorator of porcelain for Derby, Worcester and Pinxton. Founded Nantgarw.
Booth, Enoch (19thC) Yorkshire potter. Well-known for work on bodies and glazes.
Bow (c.1746-76) London porcelain factory, also known as New Canton. Bone-ash formula. Painted anchor and dagger mark, attributed to decorator James Giles, on figures. (pages 94 and 100)
Brameld & Co (c.1806). Pottery at Swinton, Yorkshire.
Bristol (1770-81). Hard-paste porcelain factory; formerly at Plymouth. Richard Champion took over from William Cookworthy, 1773. See also page 100 and **Lund's Bristol.**
Castleford (c.1790-1821) Yorkshire pottery, best known for stoneware teapots.
Caughley (1772-99) Shropshire porcelain factory. Blue and white wares easily confused with Worcester. Marks include "C" and "Salopian". (pages 102-103)
Chaffer's & Partners (c.1754-65) Liverpool, porcelain. (page 101)
Chamberlain's (c.1786-1852) Worcester porcelain factory. A breakaway firm from the main Worcester factory. Flower and shell-encrusted painted wares, 1830s. Taken over by Kerr & Binns, 1852-62. (page 109)
Champion's (c.1773-81) Bristol hard-paste porcelain factory. (page 94)
Chelsea (established c.1745) London porcelain factory. Taken over by Derby, 1770. Closed 1784. Marks: include triangle, raised anchor, red anchor and gold anchor. (pages 96-7)
Christian & Son, Philip (1765-76) Liverpool porcelain (page 101).
Coalport (c.1796-present) Porcelain factory. (pages 108, 111)
Cockpit Hill Derbyshire pottery making creamware, 18thC.
Cookworthy, William Maker of first hard-paste porcelain in England. Opened factory at Plymouth (c.1768-70), later moved to Bristol, 1770. (page 100)
Copeland Stoke-on-Trent porcelain factory, formerly Spode. Traded as Copeland & Garrett, 1833-47. (page 110)
Crisp, Nicholas (1755-64) Vauxhall, London, porcelain factory, making blue and white. (page 101)
Davenport (1793-1887) Staffordshire factory. Porcelain first made c.1805. Japan patterns. Rare mark: "Longport".
De Morgan, William Potter based in London, 1872-1907. Best known for tiles.
Derby (c.1749-present) Porcelain factory. Made more coloured wares than blue and white. Marks include crossed swords with crown above, D beneath. (pages 95, 100 and 109)
Doulton (1815-present) Lambeth, London, factory, best-known for brown saltglaze stoneware.
Duesbury & Kean (late 18thC-early 19thC) Derby hard-paste factory.
Dwight, John (17thC) Fulham, London, potter, famous for red stonewares.
Elers, David and John (active c.1688-c.1700) Staffordshire potters. Red stoneware mugs, coffee pots and teapots.
Ferrybridge (founded 1792) Yorkshire pottery. Imitated Wedgwood.
Flight & Barr (1793-1840) Worcester porcelain factory. Took form of Flight & Barr, 1793-1807; Barr, Flight & Barr, 1807-13; Flight, Barr & Barr, 1813-40. Absorbed into Chamberlain's Worcester. (page 109)
Gilbody's, Samuel (active c.1754-61) Liverpool porcelain. (pages 95 and 101)
Giles, James (active c.1760-78) English decorator of Chelsea, Bow and Worcester; also glass. Mark: anchor and dagger.
Girl-in-a-Swing (c.1751-55) London, porcelain. Offshoot of Chelsea. Figures and "toys". Rare.
Goss (1858-1929) Stoke-on-Trent porcelain factory, famous for crested china.
Jackfield (c.1750-75) Shropshire pottery, famous for black glaze.
Kerr & Binns (1852-62) (page 110)
Lambeth (c.1601) London potteries making delftware.
Leeds Pottery (c.1760-1878) Yorkshire pottery, making creamware.
Limehouse (1747-49) London porcelain factory. Wares previously ascribed to Reid's, Liverpool.
Littler, William (active c.1749-60) Partner in Longton Hall; later established factory at West Pans, Scotland.
Longton Hall (1749-60) First successful Staffordshire porcelain factory. (pages 94 and 101)
Lowestoft (1757-c.1799) Suffolk porcelain factory. Most pieces unmarked except for painters' marks on pre-1770 wares. (pages 95 and 100)
Lund's Bristol (c.1749-51) Bristol Predecessor of Worcester in making soapstone porcelain. Little has survived; very few pieces are marked. (page 101)
Mason & Co., C.J. (established c.1802 as G.M. & C.J. Mason) Staffordshire factory, famous for ironstone china (1813). (page 105)
Minton (c.1793-present) Factory at Stoke-on-Trent, Staffordshire. Bone china; pâte-sur-pâte; majolica; tiles. (page 111)
Nantgarw-Swansea (1813-20) Welsh porcelain factory. (page 108)
New Hall (1781-1835) Hanley, Staffordshire, factory. Made hard-paste and, from c.1814, bone china.
O'Neale, J.H. (active c.1750) Decorator, famous for Aesop's Fable designs and landscapes. Worked for Chelsea, Worcester and Wedgwood. Sometimes his work is signed.
Pennington & Co., James (c.1769-99) Liverpool porcelain factory. (page 101)
Pennington, Seth (1769-99) Liverpool porcelain factory. (page 101)
Pinxton (1796-1813) Derbyshire porcelain factory. Rare. (pages 95 and 108)
Plymouth (c.1768-70) Earliest English hard-paste porcelain. Moved to Bristol, 1770 (Cookworthy's to 1774; Champion's to 1781). (pages 94 and 100)
Pomona Pot Works (c.1746-54) Early porcelain factory, Newcastle-under-Lyme. Wares presently unidentified but site wasters are similar to Limehouse.
Portobello (c.1786) Near Edinburgh, several potteries trading under various names.
Pratt family (c.1775-19thC) Staffordshire potters. F. & R. Pratt of Fenton (c.1847-88) developed multi-coloured printing, on pot lids and tablewares.
Rathbone, Thomas (active c.1808-37) Portobello potter.
Reid & Partners, William(1755-61) Liverpool porcelain factory. Some of the wares presently attributed to Reids factory were probably made at Limehouse or Pomona.
Rhodes, David (active c.1765-68) Decorator of Wedgwood and Leeds creamware.
Ridgway (active c.1792) Staffordshire potting family. Well-known for tea and dessert services. John & William Ridgway traded 1814-30.
Rockingham (c.1826-42) Porcelain made at Swinton, Yorkshire. Pottery made there from c.1745. (page 109)
Royal Worcester Porcelain Co. (1862-present) (page 110)
Sadler & Green (1756-99) Liverpool transfer-printing firm, worked for Liverpool, Longton Hall porcelain, and Wedgwood and other potteries.
Sherratt, Obadiah (active c.1815-40) Burslem, Staffordshire, potter.
Southwark London delftware centre.
Spode (founded 1770) Stoke-on-Trent porcelain factory. Traded as Copeland & Garrett, 1833-47.
Swansea See **Nantgarw-Swansea** (and page 108)
"Tebo, Mr" Mysterious "repairer" (assembler) whose mark (T or To) appears on some Bow, Plymouth, Bristol and Worcester porcelain.
Toft family (17thC) Slipware potters. Thomas is best known. (page 79)
Turner family (1756-1803) Staffordshire potters, based at Lane End. John I made stoneware, from 1756.
Walton, John (active c.1759) Burslem, Staffordshire, potter, renowned for figures in porcelain style.
Wedgwood Best-known Staffordshire pottery, founded by Josiah Wedgwood, who had partnered Whieldon from 1754. (pages 84 and 87)
Whieldon, Thomas (active 1740-80) Staffordshire potter, based at Little Fenton. Used coloured glazes. (page 84)
Wood family (active c.1754-1846) (Ralph I, John, Ralph II, Enoch) Burslem, Staffordshire, potters. Ralph I associated with coloured glazes. Lions, Toby jugs.
Worcester (1751-present) Soft-paste porcelain factory. Founded by Dr John Wall. (Wall period lasts until 1776.) Used soapstone formula. Marks include open and hatched crescent, pseudo-Chinese seal mark. See also **Flight & Barr, Chamberlain's Worcester** (and pages 98-9, 102-103 and 109)

FRANCE

Bonnefoy (late 18thC) Faïence, Marseilles.
Chantilly (1725-c.1800) Soft-paste factory, near Paris. Hunting horn mark in blue or red.
Limoges (1771) Hard-paste. Paris- and Sèvres-style decoration. Mark: "CD".
Lunéville (1731-19thC) Faïence. Also: hard-paste from c.1755.
Marseilles (late 17th-late 19thC) Faïence. At least 7 factories in 18thC. Fine painting in enamels: see **Veuve Perrin.**
Mennecy (1734-1806) Soft-paste factory, Ile de France. Mark: "D.V." in blue, red or black.
Moustiers (late 17th-late 19thC) Faïence. Factories include that of Joseph Olerys (1739-93), famous for enamelling.
Nast (c.1820) Near Paris. Porcelain.
Nevers (from 16thC) Faïence. Italian styles initially.
Niderviller (1765-19thC) Moselle. Hard-paste.
Rouen (16th-18thC) Early porcelain; faïence.

Samson, Edmé (established 1845) Paris copier. "S" mark has been dishonestly removed from many pieces.
St Cloud (c.1690-1766) Near Paris. Soft-paste. Sun mark and "St C" over "T".
Sceaux (c.1750-93) Faïence, similar to porcelain in style and decoration.
Sèvres (1756-c.1804) Near Paris. France's major porcelain factory. Formerly Vincennes. Mark: interlaced Ls, much copied. (pages 91 and 112)
Strasbourg (1721-81) Faïence. "H" mark stands for Hannong (proprietor).
Veuve Perrin (c.1748-c.1795) Marseilles. Faïence. Brilliant flower, fish and fruit decoration."VP" monogram has been much faked.
Vincennes (1738). Royal porcelain manufactory of Louis XV, soft-paste. Mark: famous interlaced Ls. Moved to Sèvres 1756. (page 91)

GERMANY
Berlin (1752-present). Hard-paste. (page 92)
Franz Anton Bustelli (1754) Nymphenburg modeller of Rococo figures.
Frankenthal (1755-99). Hard-paste. (page 93)
Fulda (1764-89) Faïence. Also porcelain.
Fürstenberg (c.1753-present). Hard-paste. (page 93)
Höchst (1746-96) Faïence. (page 92)
Höroldt, J. G. Meissen decorator.
Kändler, J. Meissen decorator.
Ludwigsburg (1758-1824) Hard-paste. (page 93)
Meissen (1710-present) Dresden. First and most influential German porcelain factory. (pages 88-9) Stoneware made from c.1709. Famous crossed swords mark often copied.
Nymphenburg (1747-present) Near Munich. Hard-paste. Mark: cross-hatched shield, impressed. (page 93)

AUSTRIA
Vienna (1718-1864). Hard-paste. State factory from 1744. (page 92)

ITALY
Cantagalli (19thC). Factory reproducing Renaissance wares, Hispano-Moresque lustre wares and Isnik pottery. Mark: singing cockerel.
Capodimonte (1743-59) Near Naples. High-quality soft-paste. Moved to Buen Retiro, Spain, 1759. Later mark: fleur de lys. (page 93)
Cozzi (1765-1812) Venice. Soft-paste. Mark: red or gilt anchor. (page 93)
Doccia (1735-present) Near Florence. Hard-paste. (page 93)
Este (c.1782) Near Padua. Creamware.
Gricci, G. Capodimonte figure modeller.
Naples (1771-1806) Soft-paste. Mark: crowned "N". Also creamware. (page 93)
Nove, Le (1728-1825) Near Bassano, Venice. Faïence and, from 1752, soft-paste. (page 93)
Treviso (late 18thC) Near Venice. Creamware.
Vezzi (1720-27) Venice. Hard-paste. Rare. (page 93)

SPAIN
Buen Retiro (1759-1812) Near Madrid. High-quality soft-paste (transferred from Capodimonte). Mark: fleur de lys.

BELGIUM
Brussels Two factories, producing hard-paste: Vaume (1786-90) and Kuhne (1787-1803).
Tournai (1750) Soft-paste. Made mostly earthenware in 19thC.

THE NETHERLANDS
Delft factories:
Die Dobbelde Schenkkan (1661-1713) (The Double Jug).
Die Drie Klokken (The Three Bells) (1725-64).
Die Grieksche A (c.1674-c.1722) (The Greek A). Pieces marked "SVE" (Samuel von Eenhorn) date from 1674-86. Best-known manager was Adriaen Kocks ("AK" mark).
Het Jonge Moriaenshooft (1660-92) (The Young Moor's Head).
Die Metalen Pot (1670-1721) (The Metal Pot).
De Paeuw (c.1651-c.1705) (The Peacock).
De Roos (1662-1712) (The Rose). Favoured religious subjects.

DENMARK
Copenhagen Soft-paste, 1759-65; hard-paste, 1771-present. Factory taken over by Frederick V, 1779; became Royal Copenhagen Manufactory.

SWEDEN
Marieberg (near Stockholm) Faïence, from 1760. Mennecy-style soft-paste, from 1766; hard-paste from c.1777.

RUSSIA
Moscow Hard-paste, 1765-present.
St Petersburg (now Leningrad) Imperial Porcelain Factory, 1744-present.

UNITED STATES
American Porcelain Co. See **Tucker**.
American Pottery Co. (1833-57) Jersey City, NJ. Stoneware with relief decoration. Daniel Greatbach produced the first American hound-handled jug moulds. Also, white earthware with blue transfer-printed decoration.
Anna Pottery (1859-94) Anna, Illinois. Stonewares. See also **Kirkpatrick, C. & W.**
Bell family (19thC) Redware potters in Shenandoah Valley (Pennsylvania, Maryland, Virginia). Famous for slip decoration.
Bennett Pottery (c.1850-1938) Baltimore, Ohio. Rockingham wares.
Bennington, Vermont (late 18th-mid-19thC). Major centre of pottery manufacture, specializing in Rockingham-type brownware; also redware, creamware and parian. The Fenton and Norton families were the main producers of Bennington wares.
Bloor, William (active c.1860) Maker of Rockingham wares and parian. Moved from East Liverpool, Ohio, to Trenton, New Jersey, 1862.
Boch, William, & Brothers (c.1850-61) Greenpoint, Long Island, NY. Porcelain. Became Union Porcelain Works.
Bonnin & Morris (1769-72) Philadelphia. First US porcelain factory. Used bone-ash formula, blue and white only. Extremely rare. Marks: "Z", "P", "S".
Cartlidge, Charles, & Co. (c.1848-56) Greenpoint, Long Island, NY. Soft-paste. Tableware, door furniture, candlesticks, busts, plaques, hand-painted Rococo-Revivial wares. Also, parian.
Ceramic Art Company (1889-1906) Trenton, New Jersey. Belleek-type porcelain. Later became Lenox Inc.
Christ, Rudolf (1750-1833) Moravian redware potter, Salem, North Carolina.
Edwards Pottery (1812-27) Charlestown, Mass. Stoneware with impressed decoration.
Greenwood Pottery Co. (1868-1933) Ironstone white wares, printed and painted wares, porcelain.
Griffen, Smith & Hill (1879-90) Phoenixville, Pennsylvania. Best-known American manufacturer of majolica, under trade name "Etruscan Majolica". Some forms based on Belleek porcelain. Many tea services.
Kirkpatrick, C. & W. Potters based at the Anna Pottery (1859-94), Anna, Illinois. Stonewares (such as bizarre-looking jugs covered with reptiles and spiders) and pig-shaped flasks.
Knowles, Taylor & Knowles (1870-1928) Main porcelain manufacturer in East Liverpool, Ohio. Initially made yellow- and brown-glazes wares, then ironstone. Famous for Belleek-type "Lotus Ware".
Lyman, Fenton & Co. (1849-52) Bennington, Vermont. Tablewares, Toby jugs, figures, doorknobs, ornaments. Made "flint enamel" wares, characterized by brilliant metallic tortoiseshell glaze. Parian from 1847; sometimes with blue ground in imitation of jasperware. Succeeded by United States Pottery Co. (1852-58).
Norton & Fenton (1845-47) Bennington, Vermont. Rockingham wares.
Ott & Brewer (1871-92) Trenton, New Jersey. Made ironstone initially (Etruria Pottery). Porcelain from 1876. "Belleek" from 1882, with gilded decoration. Also, parian.
Radford Pottery (1893-1910) Tiffin (later Zanesville), Ohio. Jasperware. Used Wedgwood and Turner moulds.
Remmey family (c.1735-20thC) New York and Philadelphia. Wares included saltglazed stoneware, particularly ovoid jars with loop handles.
Rookwood Pottery (1880-1959) Cincinati, Ohio. (See Art Nouveau, page 199)
Salamander Works (1836-42) Woodbridge, New Jersey. Rockingham stoneware.
Trenton Potteries, New Jersey. A number of prolific factories from c.1852. Output included white tablewares with printed or moulded decoration.
Tucker (1826-35) Philadelphia. Empire-style porcelain. Manufacture started by William Ellis Tucker. Partnered by Thomas Hulme from 1828. Renamed American Porcelain Co. (1835), closed 1838.
Union Porcelain Works (1861-1900) Greenpoint, Long Island, NY. Formerly William Boch & Bro. Employed Karl Müller as modeller from 1874. Mark: "UPW" with an eagle's head.
United States Pottery Co. (1847-58) Bennington, Vermont. Rockingham wares.
Willets Manufacturing Co. (1879-1908) Trenton, New Jersey. Ironstone, "belleek".

BIBLIOGRAPHY

Bly, John (ed.), *Is it Genuine?* (published in the USA as *The Confident Collector*) (1986)
Denker, Ellen and Bert, *The Main Street Pocket Guide to North American Pottery and Porcelain* (1985)
Divis, Jan, *European Porcelain* (1983)
Feild, Rachel, *Buying Antique Pottery and Porcelain* (1987)
Fisher, S.W., *English Pottery and Porcelain Marks* 1970
Godden, Geoffrey A., *Godden's Guide to English Porcelain* (1978)
Victorian Porcelain (1961)
Horne, Jonathan, *A Collection of Early English Pottery* (series of illustrated booklets)
Morley-Fletcher, Hugo, and Roger McIlroy, *Christie's Pictorial History of European Pottery* (1984)
Savage, George, and Harold Newman (eds.), *An Illustrated Dictionary of Ceramics* (2nd edn 1976)
Spero, Simon, *A Taste Entirely New: Chelsea Porcelain 1744-54* (exhibition catalogue 1988)
Watney, Bernard, *English Blue and White Porcelain of the 18th Century* (2nd edn 1973)

GLASS

Perhaps because of its fragility, and the decorative understatement of many of the best pieces, glass has been undervalued as a collecting area until comparatively recently. Other factors in this neglect may be the difficulties of authentication and attribution: forgeries abound in some areas, and only in the 19th century are marks commonly found. However, these problems are outweighed by the sheer variety of glass, the elegant shapes into which it has been fashioned, and the artistic and technical skills that have flourished within the medium.

Interest in 18th-century British glass is focused on drinking glasses, which evolved characteristic stem shapes after c.1690, the changes of style providing a dating guide. From c.1720 the common wine bottle was increasingly supplanted by clear glass decanters, again datable by style. Services of glass, although not unknown in the 18th century, really belong to the 19th century.

A viable Irish glass industry was started c.1780 when British glassmakers were recruited from Stourbridge and Bristol. They were first employed at Waterford, but the industry soon spread to Cork, Belfast and Dublin. Irish glass makers benefited from the absence of the excise tax which hampered their English competitors. The imposition of an excise tax in Ireland in 1825 (repealed in 1845) sounded the death knell for the Irish glass industry. Much cut glass described as "Irish" should really be termed "Anglo-Irish", as attribution is problematic.

Continental glass is an enormous field. Early products range from medieval German glass to early Venetian wares. More scope is offered by 18th- and 19th-century wares. Highly collectable is the beautiful engraved work done in Bohemia, Silesia, Saxony, Potsdam and elsewhere. Bohemia, in the 19th century, became synonymous with coloured glass: the best pieces can fetch staggering prices, but there are still bargains to be found.

French glass is disappointing until, in the second half of the 18th century, the establishment of factories such as St Louis and Baccarat.

For most collectors of American glass, the 18th century is an unattainable dream. In the 19th century, there is scope for acquiring mould-blown bottles and flat flasks with a variety of moulded decorative motifs. Pressed glass (popular from c.1840), coloured glass (1850s-70s), paperweights and later cut glass (1880-1905) all have their passionate adherents.

This chart concentrates on the main methods of decoration. Within each period, distinctive techniques are mentioned, as well as selected makers or decorators.

- Pre-17thC glass
- Façon de Venise
- Enamelling
- Engraving
- Coloured and decorative glass
- Cut glass
- Pressed glass
- Paperweights

	VENICE	LOW COUNTRI

1500-1600	ENAMELLING GILDING CRISTALLO LATTIMO (MILK GLASS) "FILIGREE" (LATTICINIO)	FOREST GLASS
		16th-late 17th century
1600-1700		
		DIAMOND-POINT *(c.1575-1690)* WHEEL *(from c.1690)*
1700-1800		English-style shapes were copi the Low Countries from the fi quarter of the 18thC.
	Venetian glass suffered loss of trade from the first quarter of the 18thC, because of competition from German potash and English lead glass.	WHEEL *(c.1690-1760) (Jacob S* STIPPLE *(c.1750)* *(F. Greenwood, A. Schoumar* VERRE EGLOMISÉ
1800-1900		

FRANCE	GERMANY/AUSTRIA	ENGLAND/IRELAND	UNITED STATES	
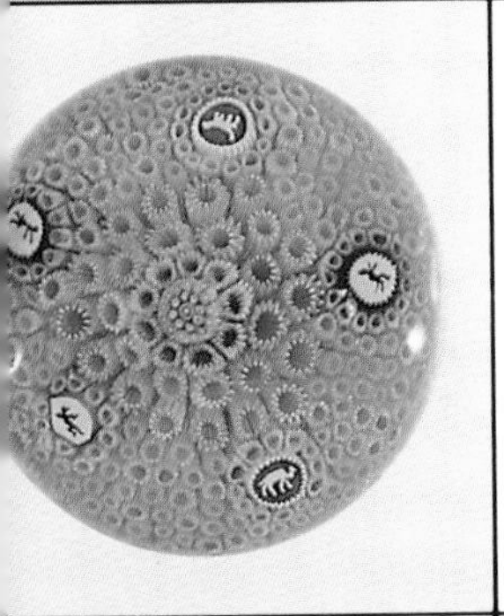				
VERRE DE FOUGÈRE (FOREST GLASS)	WALDGLAS (FOREST GLASS) ENAMELLING	FOREST GLASS (S.E. ENGLAND)		*1500-1600*
17th-18th century (NEVERS AND ORLEANS)		*From mid-16th century*		
	From mid-17th century (ARMORIAL) SCHWARZLOT *(Daniel and Ignaz Preissler)*			*1600-1700*
	WHEEL HOCHSCHNITT (HIGH RELIEF) TIEFSCHNITT (INTAGLIO)			
	GOLD RUBY GLASS *(Johann Kunckel)*			
		ON CLEAR GLASS *(Beilby family)* ON OPAQUE WHITE GLASS	*Stiegel, Pennsylvania*	*1700-1800*
	WHEEL ZWISCHENGOLDGLAS	WHEEL	*Stiegel, Pennsylvania*	
	MILCHGLAS (ENAMELLING)	"BRISTOL" (COLOURED) GLASS *(from c.1760)* "NAILSEA" *(from c.1790)*	*New Bremen Glass Factory, Maryland*	
Late 18th-early 19th century		*18th-19th centuries* *(England and Ireland)*	*Bakewell Glasshouse* *Libbey Glass Company*	
CAMEO OPALINE *(Baccarat)*	BIEDERMEIER GLASS (1815-45) TRANSPARENT ENAMELLING HYALITH AND LITHYALIN *(F. Egermann)* CAMEO OVERLAY (CASED)	"BRISTOL" *(to c.1825)* "NAILSEA" *(to c.1890)* CAMEO *(Thomas Webb)* OPALINE VASELINE SLAGWARE	"NAILSEA" OPALINE VASELINE	*1800-1900*
		Sowerby, Gateshead *Greener & Co., Sunderland* *G. Davidson, Gateshead*	*New England Glass Company* LACY GLASS *(c.1830-40)* *Boston & Sandwich Glass Company*	
Baccarat *St Louis* *Clichy*			*New England Glass Company*	

Basics

These are the most important considerations in the assessment of any item of glass:
* metal (body type)
* manufacturing method
* colour
* decoration
* marks (if any)
* authenticity
* repairs and reconstruction

METAL

The technical term for the substance of a piece of glass, particularly in its molten state, is "metal". Different metals result from the use of different ingredients. Identification of the metal provides clues to the age and authenticity of a piece.

Ingredients

Glass is a supercooled liquid formed from a fusion under high temperature of a silica (usually flint, quartz or sand) with an alkaline substance (usually soda or potash). Lime was often added to make the glass more stable, or lead to make it more durable and reflective. Different glassmaking centres used different combinations of these ingredients (depending on the raw materials available), and this has led to the diversity in the types of glass produced:

* *Soda glass* was made in Venice from the 13thC. The use of soda (from burnt seaweed) as the alkali gave the molten glass a plastic quality, enabling it to be twisted into elaborate shapes.
* *Potash glass* was produced from the 10thC in northern Europe, most notably in Bohemia (the region east of Bavaria). The potash content was derived from burning wood and bracken. As this type of glass was made in heavily wooded regions where these ingredients were found in abundance, it is referred to as *Waldglas* ("forest glass"). Potash glass quickly hardens as it cools, leaving little time for manipulation. It is thus well suited to cutting and engraving.
* *Lead glass*, made from potash with the addition of lead oxide (instead of lime), was developed in England by George Ravenscroft in the 1670s. It was adopted first in Ireland and then in the late 18thC in Continental Europe. This type of glass is characterized by its weight and clarity, which made it ideal for cutting (introduced c.1720).

MANUFACTURING PROCESSES

Free blowing

This is a process by which the glass is fashioned on a blowing iron and then transferred to a *pontil rod* for further shaping. It has been practised since the 1st century BC. The pontil rod left a pontil mark on the base (which could be ground and polished to remove it). From c.1830 a spring-clip (gadget) gradually superseded the pontil rod: this left no mark.

Blown moulding

During the 18th and 19thC some glasswares were produced by blowing liquid glass into moulds. The finished glass piece assumed the shape and pattern of the mould on both the inside and outside surfaces.

Press moulding

Pressed glass differs from blown-mould glass in dispensing with the blowing process. Instead, the glass was poured into a mould and pressed by a plunger. The technique was introduced c.1820. Press-moulded glass can be distinguished from blown-moulded by the smoothness of the inside surface.

* At the end of the 19thC, machine-operated methods evolved, by which the molten glass was blown into moulds from a source of mechanically controlled compressed air. Mass-produced items, such as medicine bottles, were manufactured in this way.

COLOUR

Tints

An aspect of glass manufacture up to the 15thC was the range of tints that occurred in the glass. Glassmakers' attempts to produce a glass that imitated the clarity of rock crystal found expression in *cristallo*. This was a clear glass produced in Venice from the 15thC. It evolved from the discovery that manganese dioxide helped to remove the tint from glass. Red lead was used with the same aim by English glassmakers from c.1710, and helped eliminate many of the darker tints.

Despite these discoveries, impurities were not satisfactorily controlled until the middle of the 18thC. The tint, which may be dark grey, green, blue or yellow, helps to identify the age and type of glass, although in many cases the hues are difficult to discern because they are so faint. Lead glass of the 17th and early 18thC often has a dark grey, yellow or green tint. Glass became increasingly clear during the 18th and 19thC as the production process became more controlled.

Coloured glass

The ancient Egyptians produced coloured glass, including blue, green, violet, black and red, to imitate semi-precious stones. This practice was also followed in Bohemian glass in the 17thC (see pages 124-5), when the range of metal oxides used in the colouring process increased. An important example is Johann Kunckel's "gold ruby" glass, in which gold chloride was added to the metal to produce a rich ruby colour.

In the first half of the 19thC, new colouring techniques were evolved in the Bohemian workshops, including fluorescent colours.

English coloured glass

Examples of 17th and early 18thC English coloured glass are rare. However, coloured glass was much in demand in the early 19thC. Notable types include:

* *"Bristol" glass* Despite its name, this was produced throughout Britain between c.1760 and c.1825. Products ranged from luxury items, such as scent bottles, to tablewares, including jugs, fingerbowls and decanters. These were manufactured in a variety of colours, most popularly in blue, but also in deep green and amethyst. Dark red "Bristol" glassware appeared later in the 19thC.
* *Nailsea* This is a generic term given to a range of 19thC glass objects, including jugs and bottles, that appeared in different shades of green and often incorporated flecks of white glass. Nailsea was made all over England but the name derives from the Nailsea factory, near Bristol, which produced these items as an offshoot of its window glass production. Nailsea was also produced in America during the 19thC.

Nailsea: a flagon with applied loop handle, English, c.1800. Som

* Most of the English coloured glassware found today dates from the 19thC when blue, green and amethyst were the most popular colours. However, "Bristol" blue decanters were made in abundance c.1770-1800, and companies such as Stourbridge continued to mass-produce inexpensive coloured glass to c.1920.

American coloured glass

This was made from the end of the 18thC, and constitutes a very important collecting area.

* Mould-blown tableware was produced in aquamarine, olive green and amethyst in the second half of the 18thC.
* By the mid-19thC ruby glass was being produced using the same methods that Johann Kunckel had used in the 17thC.
* The prestigious Boston & Sandwich Company produced glass in the 1860s decorated with dolphin motifs and coloured deep electric blue and opal white, as well as a press-moulded blue-yellow glass, which is often referred to as Vaseline glass.
* A broad category of glass known as "art glass" evolved from the mid-19thC, incorporating a range of new colouring techniques (see pages 184-5).

Glass in imitation of other materials

In Continental Europe in the middle of the 18thC, glassmakers realized the potential of coloured glass to imitate more expensive materials, such as porcelain. Various new types of decoration became fashionable:

* *Milchglas* This is a dense opaque white glass that resembles porcelain, produced in Bohemia c.1750. Its similarity to porcelain was emphasized by the use of painted floral motifs and chinoiserie scenes. A version was produced in England from c.1760. Before this, a milk white glass known as *lattimo* had been produced by the Venetians; in the 18thC fine enamelling on *lattimo* was practised by the Miotti family.
* *Hyalith* This is an opaque black or red glass which resembles agate, popular in Germany from c.1820.
* *Lithyalin* This is a polished opaque glass, similar to hyalith. It was made in Germany for a relatively short period between c.1829 and 1850 in a variety of strong colours, most often in brick or sealing-wax red.
* *Opaline* This type of glass derives its name from its opalescent surface. It was produced in France from c.1825 by Baccarat and other factories. Initially, wares (including urns, jugs and vases) were made in a milky-white glass; later examples are coloured pink, turquoise or apple green. Quality varied a great deal; the best pieces were made in lead glass and are therefore heavy. English opaline glass was produced from c.1840.

Opaline: a goblet, English, c.1850. Som

* *Slagware* This is a press-moulded glass produced in England between 1840 and 1900. It is streaked with brown, blue and purple to suggest the appearance of marble.
* *Jade glass* Glass bottles and bowls made to imitate jade were produced by the Chinese in the 18thC; such wares were often heavily carved. The Steuben Glassworks in America and Stevens & Williams in Stourbridge, England, were among the companies that produced jade-coloured glass from the 1860s. The best examples have a soft, radiant appearance. Rosaline, a pink-toned jade glass, was one of the most popular types in the second half of the 19thC.

CUT GLASS

Cutting facets into glassware exploits the refractive (light-transmitting) property of glass to the full. Cuts occur in a variety of patterns which catch scintillating highlights.

Most cut glass originates from Britain, Ireland and Northern Europe. During the 17th and 18thC a high standard was reached in Germany.

The types of incision in cut glass were limited to square-ended, hollow and V-shaped, depending on the shape of wheel edge – flat, round or mitre-shaped. The elaborate patterns on 18th and 19thC cut glass (see page 134) were achieved by combining these three basic cuts.

* Press-moulded imitations of cut glass can be identified by their rounded edges.

OTHER FORMS OF DECORATION

In addition to colouring and cutting, a variety of decorative techniques could be applied to glassware after it had been shaped. Applied decoration falls into the following categories:

* applying glass to glass
* decorating the surface
* engraving the surface

APPLIED SHAPES

One of the oldest methods of applied decoration was the addition of prunts – pieces of glass moulded into a variety of shapes – to the body of an object. The most common form of this decoration available today is on German beakers, made from the 16thC (see pages 124-5).

* The plasticity of the Venetian soda glass made it ideally suited to applied forms of decoration. Many 16th and 17thC Venetian vessels incorporate applied motifs of human masks.

SURFACE DECORATION

The principal techniques that fall into this category are enamelling and gilding.

Enamelling

Painting in coloured enamels was executed on Venetian glass from the end of the 15thC, but it was in Germany and the Low Countries from the mid-16thC that enamel decoration flowered most spectacularly (see pages 124-5).

Enamelling was not widely used in Britain until the middle of the 18thC. The Beilbys – William and Mary – are the most famous practitioners (see pages 128-9).

There are two forms of enamelling:

* *Fire enamelling* is the most permanent and most important form. The enamel was painted onto the surface and the glassware re-fired to fix the decoration.
* *Cold enamelling*, also known as "cold painting", involved simply painting the glass, without re-firing. This technique was used mainly on inexpensive items. Because the cold-enamelled decoration is easily rubbed off, few pieces have survived in good condition.

Special forms of enamelled decoration include:

* *Schwarzlot* A German technique using black enamel, especially practised by Johann Schaper from c.1665. Other exponents in the 17thC include Daniel Preissler and his son Ignaz. *Schwarzlot* was often outlined in red and gold. It continued through to the 19thC.
* *Transparent enamelling* A technique invented by Johann Schaper in the mid-17thC. The method was revived, especially by Samuel Mohn and his son Gottlob Samuel in Dresden, in the early 19thC.

Gilding

Gold has been applied both to the inside and to the surface of glasswares in a variety of forms, including paint, powder and foil. Most gilding that survives today has been fired onto the surface of plain glass. An alternative method was oil gilding, which involved applying a gold powder or leaf onto an oil base, and burnishing. Oil gilding was water-soluble, and therefore easily removed.

* Gilding was sometimes combined with enamelling, for example in 17thC Venetian glass.
* Gilding was also used with engraved decoration in 18thC German glass. *Zwischengoldglas*, literally "gold between glass", is a notable type that was particularly popular in Bohemia c.1730-55. Gold (or silver) foil, engraved with a fine needle, was inserted between a tight-fitting inner and outer sleeve of clear glass. The sleeves were then sealed by a disc in the base.
* Most gilded glassware was produced in Continental Europe, rather than in Britain, where it never attained the same popularity. However, some late 18th and 19thC English glass, including "Bristol blue", incorporated gilding as the only form of applied decoration.
* *Verre églomisé* is a decorative technique that employed gold or silver foil applied to the reverse of the glass. The foil was engraved and then backed by a layer of colour.

ENGRAVING

There are four main methods of engraving glass:

* diamond-point
* wheel engraving
* stipple engraving
* acid etching

Diamond-point

As the name suggests, this technique involves lightly scratching the surface of the glass with a hand tool, which incorporates a diamond "nib", used like a pencil to draw fine lines. This method was used in the 16thC by the Venetians and their imitators, and at the end of the 16thC in England. The most notable English examples are attributed to the London glass house of Jacob Verzelini. Examples of diamond-point engraving before the 17thC are rare.

Diamond-point: a mid-18thC Dutch example, on a wine glass. C

Wheel engraving

This technique is, in principle, similar to the methods of cutting glass. Copper wheels, varying in diameter from a pinhead to approximately 4 inches (10cm), were fed with a mixture of oil and emery, and rotated against the glass. This was done by a foot-operated treadle machine until c.1830, when powered machines were introduced. Areas of the engraving could be highlighted by polishing; and the depth of engraving could be varied, according to the shape and thickness of the wheel.

Wheel engraving: a Dutch goblet, c.1760. C

* Wheel engraving was applied to German glassware from the middle of the 17thC. The technique was introduced to England from Germany c.1720, and wheel-engraving became the most common form of engraving in England during the 18th and early 19thC.
* English wheel engraving can often be identified by its designs. Many early examples took the form of Baroque scrolls and meanders, which had been features of German glass. Floral sprays and borders were also popular in the early Georgian period. Fruiting vine and hop and barley motifs are common on wine and ale glasses in the first half of the 18thC. The quality of 18thC English engraving never equalled that of Continental work.
* Some of the most intricate Dutch wheel engraving was carried out by Jacob Sang (1750s). Very few examples of his work are signed. Authentic examples are much sought after.

Stipple engraving

This type of engraving used a diamond needle, which was lightly tapped and drawn against the surface of glass to create a series of dots or small lines. By varying the density of the dots and lines, areas of light and shade were produced. This is the most difficult engraving technique, and consequently good examples are rare. Most stipple engraving originates in the Netherlands, where, during the 18thC, some of the best work was executed by Aert Schouman, David Wolff and Frans Greenwood.

Stipple engraving: by David Wolff, c.1780-90. C

* Most English stippling is on facet-stem glasses.
* Stipple engravings by David Wolff are sometimes confused with those of an anonymous stippler, who may have been employed in Wolff's workshop. Both worked to a high standard. However, the stippled areas in Wolff's work are more delicately executed than in work done by his colleague, where the contrasts of light and shade are stronger.

Acid etching

This is the most recent form of engraving. The earliest example is dated c.1686 but the technique was not widely used until the 19thC.

The surface of the glass or vessel is covered with a varnish or resin, and the design scratched through with a needle or other sharp too. The surface of the glass is then exposed to hydrofluoric acid fumes, which etch through the scratched design.
* A semi-mechanical process for acid etching was introduced c.1860. This enabled intricate patterns to be produced faster, without any high level of skill. Such work can be identified by the shallowness of the design.
* Acid etching is often misidentified as wheel engraving. However, individual strokes left by the engraver's wheel can be clearly seen, whereas acid etching has an even finish; and the outline of acid-etched decoration is more sharply defined.

LATER TYPES OF DECORATION

As glass-making became more expert and controlled, several new (and revived) types of glass were produced, each incorporating a combination of techniques. Examples include:

Cameo glass
In this type of glass a figure or motif was usually set in white against a coloured background. The technique involved fusing together two or more layers of different-coloured glass. The outer layer, which was usually opaque white, was then carved on a wheel to create a raised design. Some of the best examples were made in Stourbridge, England, in the second half of the 19thC, especially by Thomas Webb. Imitations of cameo glass were made using moulds or acid treatment. Inferior reproductions may even be painted in white enamels. Most American cameo glass is acid-etched.

Cased and flashed glass
Cased (or overlay) glass is similar to cameo glass in that it consists of two or more layers of coloured glass moulded together. The outer layer is then cut away in patterns to reveal the coloured glass layer underneath. Cased glass was popular in Bohemia and England during the mid-19thC, and later became fashionable in the United States as well.

Flashed glass is similar to cased glass but the applied layer of colour is much thinner.

MARKS

A variety of marks can appear on glass, including:
* makers' marks
* engravers' marks
* registration marks.

These are usually engraved or acid-etched onto the item, or press-moulded, and constitute a useful dating device. However, marks appear much less frequently on glass than they do on pottery and porcelain because in many cases they detract from an object's aesthetic appeal.

Makers' and engravers' marks
Generally speaking, very little glass of the 18th and early 19thC is marked and, to a large extent, the particular factories where glass was made are not known. Usually all that can be surmised is the area of manufacture. However, there are exceptions:
* Some Irish decanters and bowls have the factory name embossed on the underside.
* Certain enamelled, painted and engraved wares have been signed by the decorator – for example, Dutch engraved glasses, German transparent-enamelled beakers and Beilby enamelled glasses.

In the second half of the 19thC marks became more widely used, referring to the manufacturer or the decorator, or both.

Registration marks
Glass made in Britain between 1842 and 1883 may be marked with a registration mark in the shape of a diamond. This includes a series of letters and numbers denoting year, month, day and parcel number. The parcel number identifies the batch number of a particular pattern.
* After 1883 the "diamond" mark was superseded by a registered number.
* It is important to remember that the mark refers to the date that the patent was registered, and not the date of manufacture.
* The diamond mark is not always reliable as a precise dating guide as the numbers on some pieces do not correspond with the Patent Office lists, possibly because of clerical errors.

AUTHENTICITY

19thC reproductions
Reproductions of Roman, Venetian and medieval German glass were made by several German glassworks in the second half of the 19thC. At the same period Venetian makers copied Venetian styles from the 14th and 16thC.

In Victorian England imitations of the 18thC tableware, especially drinking glasses, were made: these can often be detected because they do not always faithfully reproduce the proportions or the colours of the original wares.

Modern reproductions and fakes
The collector should also be aware of copies made to deceive. Glasses purporting to be 18thC should be approached with particular caution as 20thC fakes abound.

Several factors may help in detecting a fake:
* colour and texture of the "metal"
* manufacturing method
* proportions
* decoration
* signs of wear

Colour and texture of metal
Because of the difficulties of controlling impurities in the production process, much glassware made before the mid-18thC has a dark grey, yellow, green or blue tint, which appears in varying degrees of strength. It can be most clearly seen when compared directly with the clarity of modern glass: it is only just discernible on its own.
* An ultraviolet lamp is a useful dating aid, as it can help to distinguish between modern soda glass, which gives off a green-yellow light, and old lead glass, which shines with a blue-purple light.
* Small particles, either impurities from the furnace or undissolved silica, can be seen in some 18thC glass.

Manufacturing method
Free-blown glass shaped by hand has several characteristics that differentiate it from glass made by modern methods:
* A pontil mark – a circular rough mark – is often left on the base of a piece of glass at the point where it is broken from the pontil rod. Most 18thC glass has a pontil mark. However the presence of the pontil mark alone is no guarantee of age, as most 20thC handmade glass is made in exactly the same way. Neither is its absence indicative of a modern piece: at the beginning of the 19thC the feet of drinking glasses became flatter and the pontil mark was often ground out so that the piece remained stable on a table top. From c.1760 the pontil mark on many high-quality facet-stem glasses was ground out and polished.
* Striations, or fine ripples, can be seen running in random directions in glass that has been shaped by hand, whereas moulded glass is smooth. The foot of a drinking glass is the obvious place to look out for these signs.
* The rims and the edges of feet on antique glasses fashioned with hand tools are not always of even thickness, and there is often a small raised section, indentation or crease where the glassmaker removed the tool when the material was still plastic.
* The method of applying handles to jugs constitutes another useful dating guide. After c.1860 the handle became more securely attached to the jug, with the main join at the base of the handle and not, as before, at the top.

Proportions
The proportions of some categories of glass varied in different periods. In decanters, for example, the tapering shape of the mid-18thC gave way to more bulbous lines at the end of the 18thC. A knowledge of such changes may in some cases be the only way to detect a fake.

Decoration
The enamelling or gilding on a piece of glass should be examined carefully to see whether it is contemporary with the glass. Sometimes decoration has been added to a plain piece at a later date to enhance its value.
* The tones of 19thC coloured enamelling will appear harsher than enamelling from earlier periods.
* Gilding in the 16th and 17thC was applied to the glass surface in separate stages and has a layered appearance, which distinguishes it from the flat quality of later gilding.
* It is difficult to date the engraving on an antique glass with any certainty. However, new engraving has a rough, chalky appearance. Age and wear tone down this harshness, so that any glass that has been engraved for a century or more will appear grey if a white cloth is placed behind it. More importantly, wear will cause a smooth satin sheen on any flat, exposed part of the engraving.
* Many old drinking glasses have been engraved at a later date; this is particularly true of Jacobite, Williamite and Sunderland Bridge glasses (see pages 128 and 129).

Signs of wear
Glass is sometimes artificially worn to create the impression of age. The foot of a piece of glass is one of the prime areas to look for signs of wear; fake scratches will look too even and may run in the same direction, whereas genuine scratches are fine and irregular.

Repairs and reconstruction
Common repairs to glasswares range from grinding out chips, usually on the rim and foot of a glass or the neck of a decanter, to the replacement of a damaged section, such as a foot or bowl, by taking the equivalent part from another glass. A repair, no matter how skilfully executed, detracts from the value of any piece of glassware.
* Unless the piece is very rare, a replacement part renders it almost worthless.
* A join may indicate that a clean break has been repaired.
* Grinding to remove chips often leaves marks that can be seen through a magnifying glass. If these have been polished out, a halo effect can be seen.

Care and cleaning
Glass, particularly enamelled glass, should never be scrubbed. Washing in warm soapy water is the best cleaning method. The glass should then be dried thoroughly with a soft cloth to avoid staining. Items such as decanters should be stored with their stoppers off. Liquid left for a long period in a vase or decanter will at best leave a deposit, and at worst will cause permanent damage to the surface. Bleaching the inside can sometimes remove a deposit but more seriously stained glass should be taken to an expert and repolished.

Venetian Glass

The Venetian glass industry was well established in the 13th century, and by the 15th century Venice was exporting glass in great quantity to northern Europe. Early Venetian glass was simple in design, but during the Renaissance and the 17th century the characteristic light, thin-walled soda glass was worked into more extravagant shapes.

Coloured glass (green, blue and purple), as well as opaque white glass (*lattimo*), was being produced by the end of the 15th century. Enamelling on Venetian glass first appeared in the mid-15th century and was most often fired onto coloured glassware. Colourless glass, or *cristallo*, was first produced in Venice c.1450 and by the mid-16th century had supplanted coloured glass in popularity. Gilding was sometimes applied to *cristallo*.

Opaque white threads, known as *latticinio*, were often embedded in drinking glasses, tazzas and other vessels from the early 16th century in a variety of patterns: *vetro a reticello*, crisscrossed to form a lattice; *vetro a retorti*, in which the threads were twisted together in simple or complex designs; and *vetro a fili*, where the threads ran in parallel lines, forming straight or spiral patterns.

By the 18th century the Venetian glass industry had declined in the face of competition from Bohemian glass. Collectors should beware of mid-19th century imitations of 16th- and 17th-century Venetian glass. Such pieces are heavier than the originals.

This small flask, c.1740 (ht 3½in/9cm), demonstrates how, after the advent of *cristallo*, enamelling was often used to offset the clear glass. *C*

* As the quality of *cristallo* improved, few clear glass pieces made from the end of the 16thC were enamelled in all-over designs.
* Enamelling was also applied to coloured glass and to the opaque white glass known as *lattimo*.

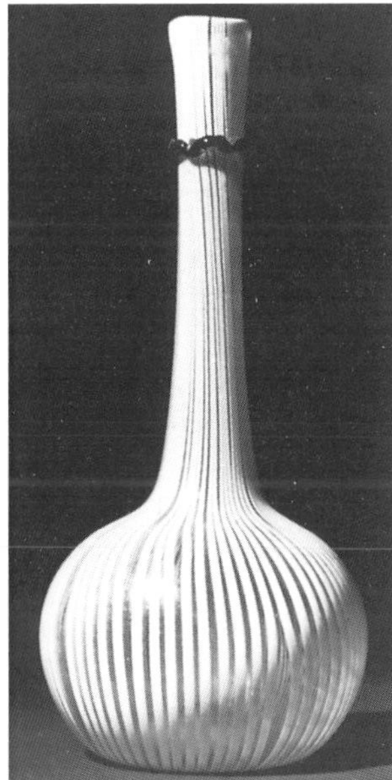

By the middle of the 16thC, glassmakers in the Netherlands, Germany, France and England were producing glass *à la façon de Venise* ("in the Venetian manner"). This *façon de Venise* bottle was made in the Low Countries in the 17thC (ht 12in/30.5cm) and incorporates *vetro a fili*. *C.*

Venetian glass goblets were rare until the 15thC. Early examples incorporating rich coloured glass and enamel gave way to clear glass goblets such as this early 17thC example (ht 6¾in/17cm), shaped in the traditional winged style. *C.*

* The emphasis in early 15thC drinking glasses was on simplicity of design. The wings on the stem, which usually took the form of a serpent, dragon, sea horse or lion, developed at the end of that century.

The tazza, a dish for cakes and fruit, was among the most popular items of luxury glass in the late 16th and early 17thC. This 17thC example (dia. 5¼in/13cm) is typical in its use of *cristallo*. Most tazzas were supported on a low, spreading foot and not on a stem, as in this example. *C*

* Some tazzas incorporated enamel emblems. In the late 16th and early 17thC, enamelling was often replaced by chain trailing – threads of glass applied to the surface of the tazza, forming a pattern of interlinked chains.

A rare Venetian armorial ewer, forming part of a set with a bowl, dating from the late 17thC (ht 8¾in/22.5cm). The elaborate decoration was diamond-point engraved. *S*

* Diamond-point engraving was introduced in Venice in the middle of the 16thC. However, engraving never became well established in Venice, because of the thinness of the soda glass.

German Glass

German glasswares form a broad collecting area, ranging from the early *Waldglas* ("forest glass") and beautiful early enamelling (very expensive) to the colourful innovations of the 18th and 19th centuries. Between these two poles are some spectacular decorative pieces. The term "Bohemian" refers strictly to the area east of Bavaria, but the label is often used loosely to describe glass from the Germanic region.

"Forest glass" was made in woodland regions, using the ashes of beechwood for potash – the key ingredient. A pale green tint is characteristic. The most enduring form of drinking glass was the *Römer*, with a distinctive egg-shaped bowl. Other types include the *Humpen*, a plain, straight-sided glass with a slightly flared foot; the slender, cylindrical, hollow-footed *Stangenglas*; and the *Pasglas* – a type of *Stangenglas* marked with divisions to indicate individual allowances in group drinking sessions.

Enamelled glass, based on Venetian models, began to appear c.1575 and became increasingly sophisticated from the late 17th century. Enamelled *Milchglas* (an opaque white glass) was produced in the 18th century as a substitute for porcelain. Special forms of enamelling include *Schwarzlot* (black) and transparent enameling (revived by the Mohn family c.1810).

Superb wheel engraving, deeply cut with strong contrasts of light and shade, was done from the late 17th until the last quarter of the 18th century. Bohemian engraving of the first half of the 19th century is often of unparalleled quality.

This 16thC beaker (ht 5½in/ 14.2cm) has the prunts characteristic of *Waldglas*. *S*

* In the 14th and 15thC prunts appeared in a variety of forms – some stamped with patterns, others spiked and curled downwards. In 16thC glass they can be found combined with enamelling. In the 17thC they became flatter, and a design known as the "raspberry" prunt evolved, each one formed of small blobs of glass, giving a texture like that of a raspberry.

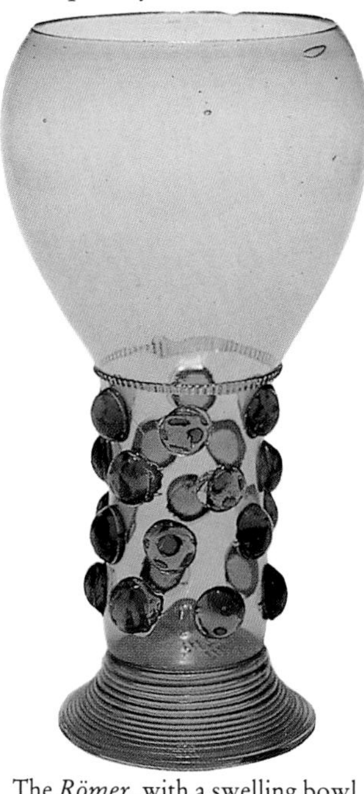

The *Römer*, with a swelling bowl incurving to the rim, was popular from the late 17thC to c.1825. This 17thC example (ht 9in/ 23cm) has the typical green tint. Also characteristic is the hollow, cylinder stem with applied prunts and the spun foot. *S*

This silver-mounted tankard, c.1680 (ht 5¾in/14.5cm), is a rare early example of ruby glass. The rich ruby-red colour was first produced in the 1680s by using gold chloride as a colouring agent. It was often used, as in this example, in conjunction with finely chased metal. Pieces in ruby glass were expensive, luxury items for a wealthy market. *S*

* At the end of the 17thC blue, purple and green glass appeared.
* In c.1830 the relatively inexpensive copper replaced gold in the process.

This Bohemian enamelled flask, c.1661 (ht 10¾in/27cm), shows how Venetian enamelling techniques were adapted to suit German taste. Designs included coats of arms, religious allegories, and hunting scenes. *S*

* The use of colour is restrained, bright colours generally being reserved for drinking glasses.

Zwischengoldglas – engraved gold foil "sandwiched" in glass – was used for beakers and tall covered goblets in the 18thC. This beaker dates from c.1793 (ht 4¼in/10.5cm). *S*

This *Stangenglas* ("pole glass"), dated 1717 (ht 10½in/26cm), with typical short spreading folded foot, carries the enamelled arms and initials of the high-ranking owner. The form was especially popular in the last quarter of the 16thC. The enamelled "hoops" are typical. *C*

* This form of glass, like the *Humpen* and *Passglas*, is also found with a domed cover topped by a finial.
* Much enamelling for the German market was done by the Venetians until after the mid-16thC, as well as by the Germans themselves. As Venetian styles influenced German work, the provenance of a piece is often difficult to determine.

In the Biedermeier period, c.1815-45, glassmakers in Vienna and other cities produced large numbers of enamelled beakers depicting topographic scenes. This rare example, c.1816 (ht 3½in/9.5cm), is by Gottlob Mohn: he and his father Samuel were the masters of the medium. *S*

* The enamels were thinly applied and translucent, often on straight-sided beakers such as this one. After 1814 a waisted beaker known as a *Ranftbecher* became more common.
* Subjects include allegorical figures, flowers and birds as well as scenes in and around Vienna.

This North Bohemian vase, c.1860 (ht 12in/30cm), is in blue overlay glass (see page 120) engraved with a scene of a stag, doe and hind by Franz Zach. *C*

This beaker, c.1665 (ht 11½in/29cm), is an important type of *Humpen* known as a *Reichsadlerhumpen* ("Imperial eagle beaker"), made after c.1570. The numerous coats of arms stretched out along the wings represent the various constituents of the political structure of the Empire. This design was produced until the 18thC – an example of the conservatism of German glassmaking. *S*

* Later examples have an Imperial orb, in place of the Crucifixion, on the breast of the bird.

REPRODUCTIONS

In the last half of the 19thC the Germans made many reproductions of antique German styles of glassware. The most important imitator was the Rheinesche Glashutten Aktien Gesellschaft, established in 1864. It concentrated on repro Roman, Venetian and Old German glass in the 1880s. Their pieces, which include an "antique green", give themselves away by their lack of imperfections. There was also a Bohemian factory (at Petersdorf) which produced some flatly enamelled wares in historic styles.

Note that 19thC glass is usually thicker and heavier than glass made in earlier periods. Biedermeier-style, cased and flashed glass beakers were made in the early 20thC: these are usually recognizable by the bright colours.

Glasswares in imitation of semi-precious stones were a Bohemian speciality. One type of the Biedermeier period was *Hyalith*, an agate-like glass in black or red, patented in 1820. It was often used with gilt chinoiserie motifs, as in this spill vase, c.1830 (4½in/12cm), made at the Buquoy Glasshouse. (Count Buquoy was its inventor.) *S*

* Black *Hyalith* was intended to imitate the popular Wedgwood black basalt pottery.

This scent bottle and stopper, by Egermann of Blottendorf, c.1830 (7¼in/18.5cm), is in *Lithyalin* – a polished opaque glass with swirling colours (more usually red) that simulated the appearance of agate and other semi-precious stones. *S*

* Egermann took out a patent on *Lithyalin* in 1828 but it was copied by other Bohemian factories, notably the Harrach glassworks.
* The technique had fallen into disuse by c.1850.
* Sometimes this type of glass is decorated with gilding.

English Drinking Glasses I

Early glasses were heavy and of large proportions. Bowl sizes varied considerably to begin with. As the 18th century progressed, glasses tended to become smaller and lighter, the metal became progressively clearer, and bowl sizes were standardized. The introduction of air, opaque white and then coloured threads into the stems reflected both changes in fashion and the increasing dexterity of the glass makers. After c.1830, changes in drinking glass styles became more gradual, leaving the 18th century as the period of maximum interest to collectors.

Ale was more potent than today, and was drunk from a smaller glass. The uninitiated might mistake this for a wine glass, although it had a distinctive bowl – slim and elongated. Another strong drink was cordial, drunk after tea in a small-bowled glass with a tall, thick stem. A special glass for the liqueur ratafia – like an ale glass but even more slender, the stem merging into the bowl – was developed after c.1740. Rummers, large bowled and short-stemmed, were used in taverns for various long drinks such as beer and cider; smaller versions were available for spirits.

DRINKING GLASS TYPES

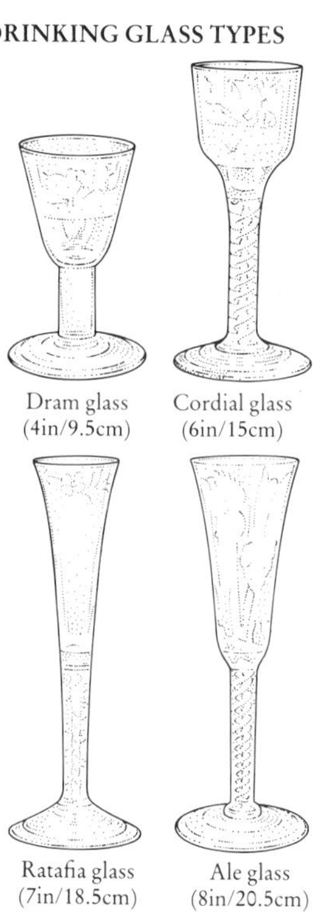

Dram glass (4in/9.5cm) | Cordial glass (6in/15cm)

Ratafia glass (7in/18.5cm) | Ale glass (8in/20.5cm)

Rummer (5in/13cm) | Dwarf ale glass (5in/13.5cm)

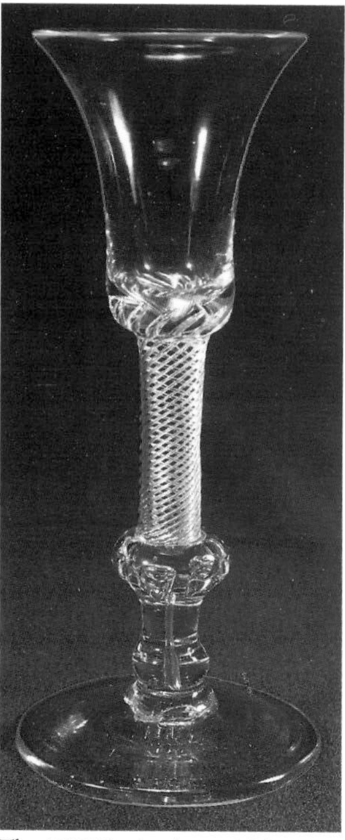

The 1745 Excise Act, which imposed a tax on the weight of material used for making lead glass, may have helped to shift the emphasis from shape to decoration. Twist stems, containing air filaments or threads of white or coloured glass, were a popular form of ornament between 1740 and 1775, developed from the tears incorporated in stems earlier in the century. The glass shown here has a composite stem (made of more than one piece), with multiple spiral air twist, c.1750 (ht 6½in/16cm). *Som*

Glasses of the late 17thC are rare. Although Venetian decoration shows an unmistakable influence, often in the form of a winged or pincered knop, or gadrooning around the base of a bowl, this is often quite subdued. The example above is a dwarf ale glass of c.1680 (5½in/14cm) with spiked gadrooning on the bowl. The folded foot is also typical. *Som*

This heavy baluster glass was the predominant style of the early 18thC – a conical, pointed or round funnel bowl on a baluster stem (named after the architectural term) consisting of one or more prominent knops. *Som*

Plain stems are found between c.1740 and c.1770 with every form of bowl (although the bucket bowl is seen only rarely before 1750). The earliest bowl was the trumpet. This example, c.1750 (5½in/14cm), has an ogee bowl. To relieve the austerity of a plain stem a tear-shaped air bubble was often included at the top. Hollow stems (c.1750-60) are rare. *Som*

"Balustroid" is the term for the slimmer baluster stem with less prominent knops – part of the general tendency between 1725 and 1760 for glasses to become lighter. Trumpet, round funnel and bell bowls are most prevalent; the ogee is also found. This balustroid wine glass, c.1730 (ht 6½in/16.5cm), has a true baluster knop, which is rarer than the inverted knop. *Som*

BOWLS

Old glasses should have striations or tooling marks on both bowl and foot. The bowl should invariably show three or more faint creases running diagonally down from the rim. Engraving on bowls was introduced c.1735, and often indicates a purpose – a fruiting vine for wine, hops and barley for ales. A floral or other purely decorative border may be found on some glasses. Many genuinely old glasses have been engraved later, and this is difficult to detect. Enamelling (from c.1760) is rarer than engraving. Gilding is found very occasionally.

A sonorous ring when the rim of the bowl is tapped with a fingernail should indicate lead glass. However, constructional features can affect this test – for example, it might be difficult to obtain a god ring from a small, heavy baluster glass.

Bucket   Waisted bucket

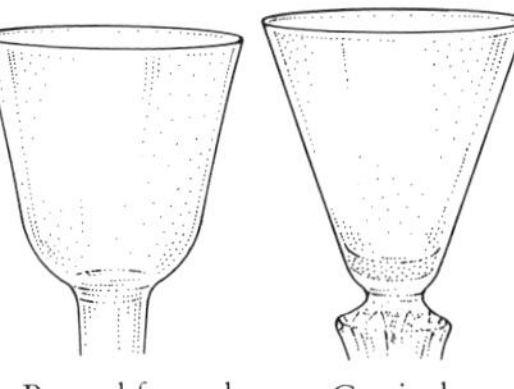

Round funnel   Conical

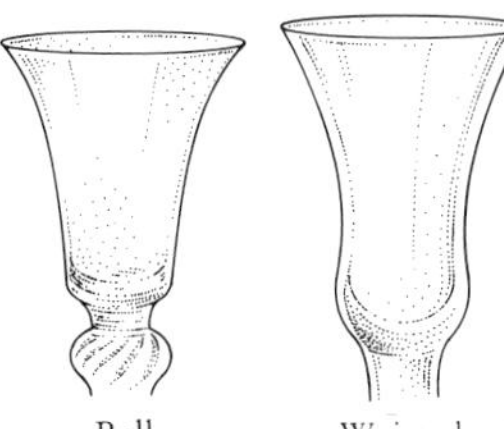

Bell   Waisted

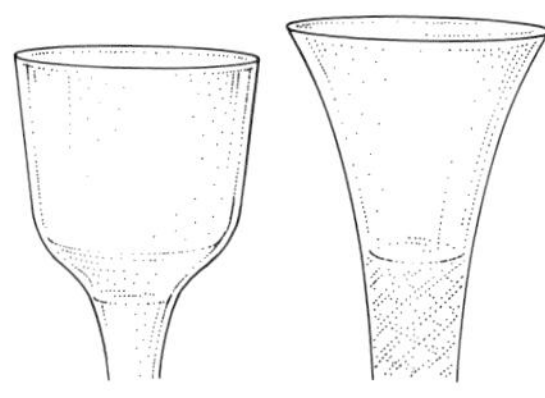

Ogee   Trumpet

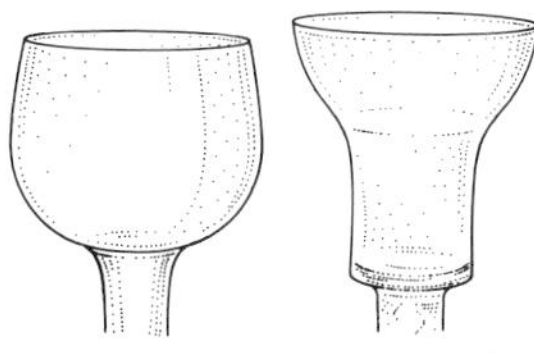

Cup   Pan-topped

Wine glasses are an immense and varied collecting area. At first influenced by Venetian exuberance, they developed their own characteristic forms after c.1680, moving from simple, sturdy styles to the lighter style represented above – a Newcastle light baluster wine glass of c.1750 (ht approx. 12in/30cm), engraved with a band of Baroque decoration. The stem has a collar and an air-beaded cushion knop. The plain conical foot is characteristic. The engraving on this glass is of very high quality and is almost certainly Dutch. *Som*

FEET

The diameter of the foot on a wine glass should generally be greater than that of the bowl. Feet were folded, or turned under, in early drinking glasses to produce a double thickness, a protection against chipping. This practice was largely discontinued from 1745, possibly because of the excise tax. However, folded feet were still used on many balustroid glasses.

All 18thC glasses (except a few facet-stem examples) should have a pontil mark (where the ponty rod was snapped off) under the foot. In the 19thC this mark was usually ground out. However, pontil marks were also left on some genuine early 19thC glasses; they are also to be found on some reproductions. A small, carefully made pontil on a very clear foot is usually indicative of a late date.

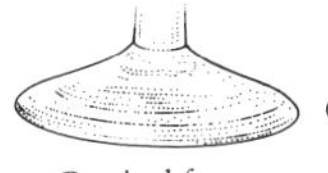

Conical foot   Domed foot

STEMS

Many glasses had formations known as knops – rounded projections or bulges in the stem. The most common form was the inverted baluster knop. Light baluster stems can have as many as five knops. Shouldered "Silesian" stems show German influence, which filtered through in the early 18thC.

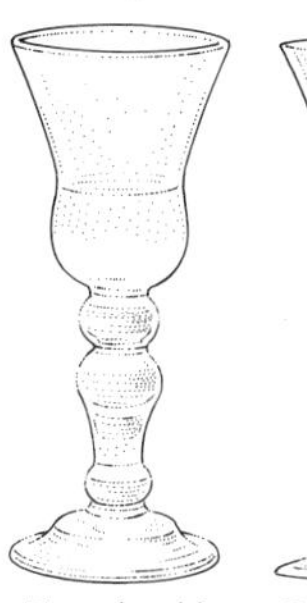

Two shoulder knops   Bobbin knop

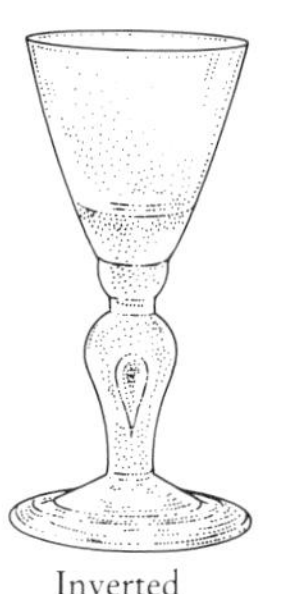

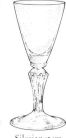

Inverted baluster   Silesian stem

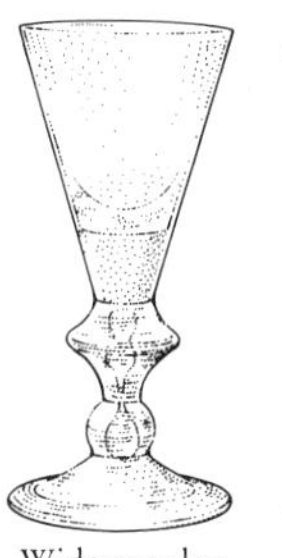

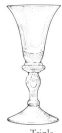

Wide angular knop and base knop   Triple annulated knop

TWISTS

Air-twist stems took many forms, ranging from 12 even filaments in a multiple spiral to a more complex arrangement of two series of twists, one inside the other. The incised twist was a less expensive method of producing a vaguely air-twist effect. Some twist stems incorporate opaque white glass. Colour twists, sometimes combined with air or opaque twists, are rare.

Multiple spiral

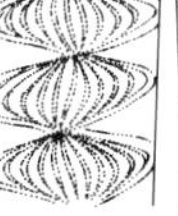

Single series

Double series

English Drinking Glasses II

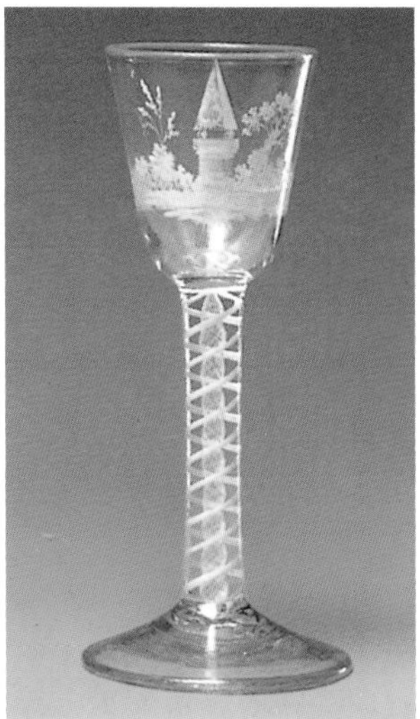

The brother and sister William and Mary Beilby produced some of the finest enamelling on English drinking glasses, 1762-78. William is considered the greater exponent; Mary's precise contribution is unknown. The motif on this wine glass, c.1770 (ht 5½in/14.5cm), shows the distinctive Beilby white enamel. The glass is not signed; the Beilbys reserved their mark for more elaborate pieces. *S*

* William also worked in coloured enamels; particularly notable are his coloured coats of arms on large goblets.

The colour-twist is a variation on the opaque-twist stem. Coloured threads were used instead of, or in addition to, white threads. The colours could be opaque or translucent. This wine glass dates from the heyday of the English twist stem, c.1770 (ht 5½in/14.5cm). It has a double-series opaque colour-twist stem. *S*

Jacob Sang wheel-engraved glass in Amsterdam, c.1737-62. This goblet, c.1760 (ht 8in/21cm), is of the so-called Newcastle type, a style of glass fashionable in the Netherlands, 1735-65, and possibly made there rather than in England, as is traditionally believed. *Som*

* Sang signed his glasses in a semicircle on the underside of the foot, "Jacob Sang, fecet, Amsterdam", with the date.

Rummers, which date from the late 18thC, hold 8-10 fluid ounces. The name is thought to derive from the *Roemer*, a large German wine glass. Rummers were traditionally used for rum toddies. Bowls took many shapes. This glass, c.1800 (ht 7in/17.5cm), shows a view of the Iron Bridge over the River Wear in Sunderland, England. *S*

The deep round funnel bowl was common on ale glasses after 1700. Engraved hops and barley, as on this glass, c.1750 (ht 8in/20.5cm), were typical bowl motifs during the first half of the 18thC. *Som*

* Twisted ribbing on the stem and body, known as the wrythen pattern, was used on Anglo-Venetian ale glasses from c.1680.
* Dwarf ales have very short, or rudimentary, stems.

Sweetmeat glasses, used for serving desserts, have tall stems and wide double-ogee bowls. This glass, c.1750 (ht 5½in/14.5cm), has a moulded Silesian stem. *Som*

Coloured drinking glasses were made in England from the 18thC. Green was the most common colour for single glasses, and occasionally sets from c.1760 – the date of this turquoise green wine glass (ht 5in/13.5cm). Amethyst and, very rarely, blue were also made. Amber glasses date from c.1830, red from c.1845. *Som*

* Modern fakes have clear feet and neat pontil marks and often have a cushion knop.

English gilt glasses are rare. They have a soft, lustrous finish, which is not durable, and most gilding found today shows considerable signs of wear. The coupling of a gilded floral design and an opaque twist stem, as on this unusually pristine wine glass, c.1760 (ht 6in/15cm), is typically British. *Som*

JACOBITE GLASSES
Jacobite glasses were used by secret societies who supported the claim to the throne of the descendants of the Roman Catholic Stuart king, James II of England, who abdicated in 1688 in favour of the Protestant William and Mary. The glasses were engraved with a variety of Stuart mottoes and emblems. The most frequently found Jacobite

symbol is the rose (*above*), representing the English crown. One or two buds beside the rose stand for the Pretenders: James II's son, James Francis Edward Stuart, known as the Old Pretender, and his son, Charles Edward Stuart (Bonnie Prince Charlie), the Young Pretender.

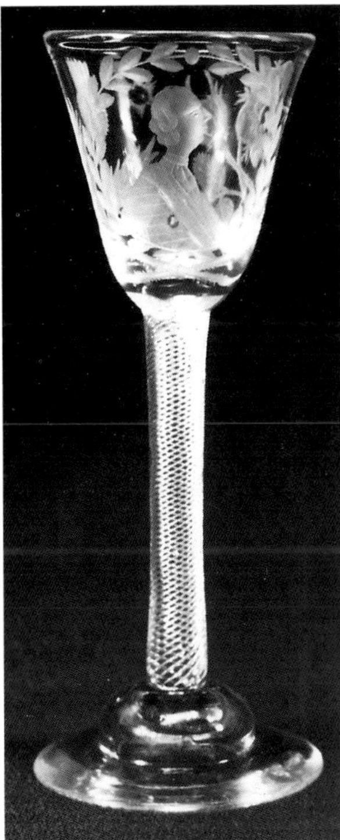

The Young Pretender's portrait often appeared on glasses, as in this fine example, c.1715 (ht 5½in/14cm), which also has a thistle and a rose. The Riband and Star of the Garter are shown on the wrong breast, probably copied from a copper plate engraving, which would show the design in reverse. *Som*

"Amen" glasses are a rare type of Jacobite glass. They incorporate verses of a Jacobite hymn ending with "Amen", hence the name. This example, 1745-50 (ht 8in/20cm), is of the highest quality with intricate diamond-point engraving on the bowl. In addition to the anthem, the bowl has emblems that represent the Old Pretender's claims to the Scottish throne: a crown, his royal cipher, the letters JR, and the figure 8, for the self-styled James VIII, worked into the monogram. *C*
*All "Amen" glasses and most other types of Jacobite glass are thought to date from after the decisive 1746 Battle of Culloden, in Scotland. In 1766 the Old Pretender died and the major Catholic powers repudiated Stuart claims to the English throne, which saw an end to the Jacobite cause, and therefore to Jacobite-engraved glasses. Jacobite copies from the 19thC were up to 13in/33cm tall, a size never made in the previous century.

DETECTING RESTORATION AND LATER ENGRAVING
The most common type of restoration is the grinding out of chips from rims and feet. This is more acceptable on feet than on rims. A knowledge of original proportions may expose such changes. Grinding marks usually show up under a strong magnifying glass, but they can be polished out, leaving a tell-tale halo. An uneven edge may suggest restoration, but could also indicate the use of hand tools in an authentic glass. Broken glass can be re-stuck if the break is a clean one. Alternatively, new parts can be used to replace damaged sections. Detection of new parts can be difficult, as some modern glass glues defeat ultraviolet light. However, re-cut stems often give the glass a heavy quality and recent cutting performed on an old glass may look obviously modern (see page 121). Later engraving can be difficult to identify if the engraving has some age to it. Genuine early engraving develops a sheen from wear.

Williamite glasses, dating from c.1750, commemorated the victory of King William III over James II at the Battle of the Boyne in Ireland in 1690. This example (ht 8in/20cm) has the typical features: an equestrian portrait of the King with an inscription to his memory and the date of the battle on the reverse. The applied vermicular collar on the glass is more unusual. *C*

Firing glasses were dram glasses made in England from c.1740. They were used at functions where toasts were performed, when they were rapped on tables, making a noise which resembled gunfire, hence the name. Ogee bowls are the most common but some of the glasses have ovoid or round funnel bowls. Some have Jacobite motifs or, as in this example, c.1760 (ht 3in/8.5cm), emblems of a masonic lodge. *Som*

Decanters

The first decanters, made in the late 17th century, were of heavy blown-moulded glass with high kicks, or indentations, in the base. The grain in the wooden mould was often impressed onto the surface of the glass. These early decanters were used to serve wine, but not to store it. They were broad-based and either had no stoppers at all, or had loose cork stoppers or plugs which were tied on with string.

The first true decanters appeared in the middle of the 18th century. These had an elegant tapering shape and were sometimes engraved. They were lighter in weight than their predecessors, possibly in response to the 1745 Excise Tax on glass. Glass stoppers were always used after this date. Neck rings became popular toward the end of the 18th century.

When the tax was repealed in 1845, English decanters became heavier in weight, with heavy cutting. By the end of the 18th century the bulbous or "Prussian" shape was introduced and prevailed, with little variation, throughout the 19th century. Ship's decanters had their own special form, broad-based for greater stability at sea.

In the second half of the 18th century, coloured decanters were made, usually in blue, green or amethyst.

Irish decanters are especially popular. Many of these were blown into a shallow mould which sometimes had the name of the glasshouse impressed into it. Copies exist of Cork decanters. These are usually well made and seldom engraved.

Decanters were made in numbers on the Continent, especially in larger sizes. They tend to be made from potash rather than lead glass and the resultant quality is markedly poorer. However, the French firm of Baccarat made good-quality lead glass decanters in the 1820s and 30s. These are slightly heavier than English ones. American decanters follow English styles. They are rare outside of America.

Decanters often have imitation labels bearing the name in gilt lettering of the wine or spirit for which they were intended. Some were made in sets of three with labels for brandy, rum and Hollands (gin). This "Bristol" blue club-shaped decanter, c.1790 (ht 7½in/19cm), has an oval simulated label. Engraved labels are rarer than gilded ones. Alternatively, silver labels were hung around the neck of the bottle (see the claret label above). *Som*

Two-bottle trolleys are not uncommon, but those with three bottles are extremely rare. The trolley shown here is made of black papier mâché with brass fittings and papier mâché coaster. It holds three ovoid decanters with flute-cut bodies, cut neck rings and mushroom stoppers, c.1810 (ht 9in/22.5cm). *Som*

* Sets of decanters were popular in the Victorian period.

Sizes and capacities vary. However, most decanters hold just over one bottle, while the rare magnum holds two. This barrel-shaped Irish decanter, c.1810 (ht 8in/20.5cm), is near-magnum-size. It is decorated with alternate panels of small diamonds and sunbursts with a similarly cut stopper, c.1810. *Som*

Many decanters have vertical flutes rising from the base, possibly to obscure the dregs that settled at the bottom. This flute-cut tapered decanter, c.1820 (ht 8½in/22cm) has a target, or bull's eye stopper. *Som*

NECK RINGS

On 18th and early 19thC decanters neck rings were applied separately and then moulded with a tool. The join in the neck ring was often carelessly made and, misleadingly, may appear as a crack.

In many middle to late-19thC decanters the neck rings are an integral part of the decanter. If a damaged neck has been replaced, it may be possible to feel a join inside the neck.

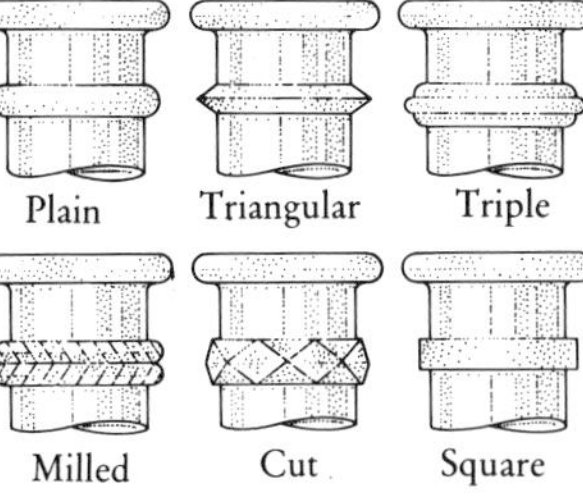

DECANTER SHAPES

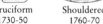

Cruciform 1730-50 — Shouldered 1760-70

Tapered c.1780 — Prussian 1790-1830

Ship's c.1820 — Fancy (Royal) 1830-50

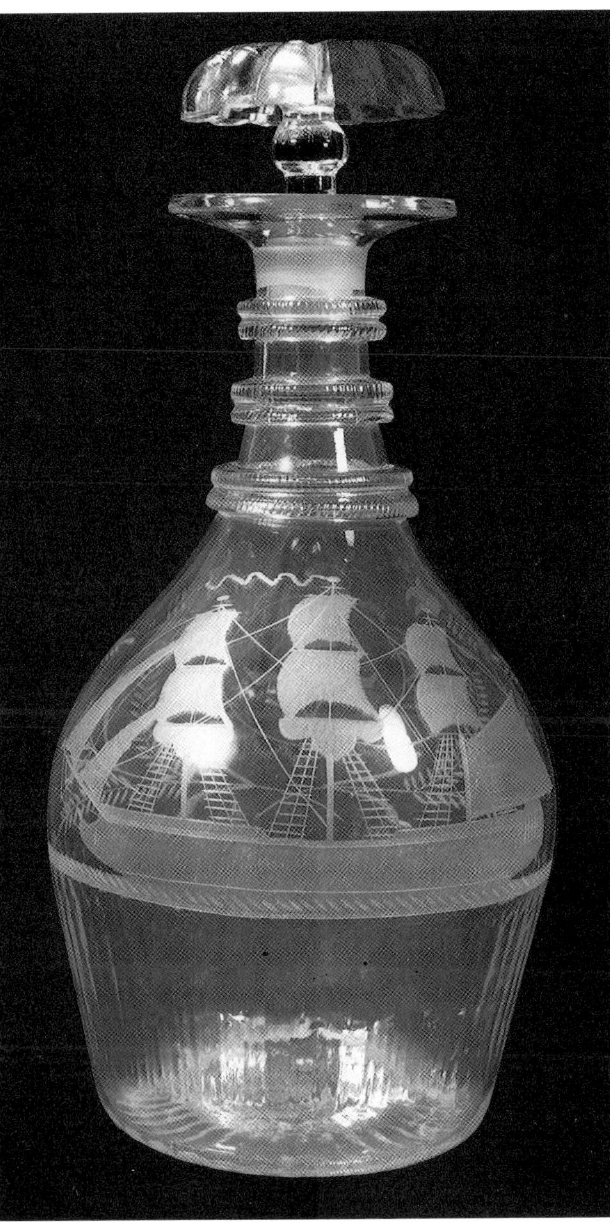

The moulded mushroom stopper and feathered neck rings suggest that this is an Irish decanter, although it is unmarked. It has an engraved ship on one side and floral decoration on the reverse, c.1810 (ht 8½in/22cm). *Som*

* Engraved scenes are unusual and very desirable. Monograms are more common. Ships and country scenes are very collectable.
* Some Irish decanters have only two neck rings instead of the usual three.
* Irish stoppers are often not ground, as English ones are, but are left loose and simply pushed well into the neck of the decanter. Some loose stoppers were ground at a later date, but this does not reduce their value.

PONTIL MARKS

Early 18thC decanters invariably show a pontil mark, or a ground-out area. From about the middle of the century shouldered and tapered decanters often show no pontil mark and no ground-out area, as a punty rod was not used. These bases are completely plain.

RESTORATIONS

On many old decanters a white deposit caused by corrosion has been buffed out using a mild abrasive. Such restoration does not spoil the decanter. Occasionally, hydrofluoric acid is used, which ruins the value, as it tends to reproduce any scratches, and give a patchy "orange peel" effect.

STOPPERS

It is difficult to guarantee that a stopper is original except on Victorian clear glass decanters, which often have matching numbers etched on the stopper and decanter neck and on coloured decanters, which often have the number painted on the stopper and underside of the decanter. Generally, a stopper is acceptable where it is the same cut and colour as the decanter and of the right style and period.

Broken stopper pegs can be replaced by gluing on a replacement and then grinding and polishing the whole peg. A very thin radial line will indicate where this has been done.

Decanters have often been damaged by the careless replacement of the stopper, or have been knocked over, the chipped surface or edge having been subsequently restored. This may alter the proportions of the lip but will not greatly affect the value.

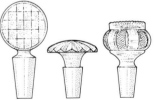

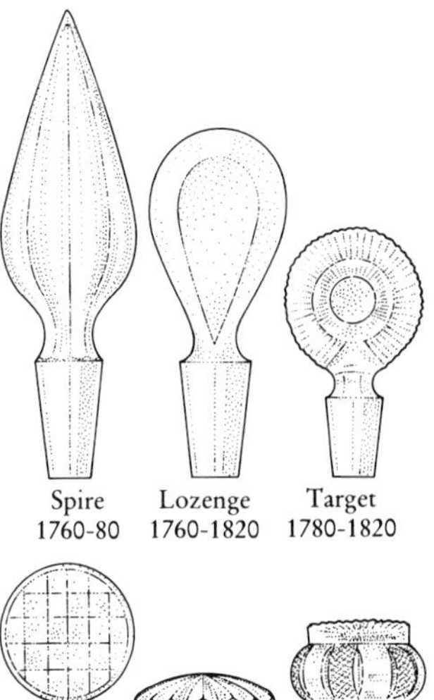

From the mid-19thC decanters often came in an oak tantalus, a lockable frame that prevented them from being opened without a key. The best have cut bottles, as in this example (ht of bottles 8½in/22cm). *Som*

Paperweights

Antique paperweights from the major French factories of Baccarat, Clichy and St Louis are the most widely collected. The finest can be dated to the 1840s. There are also good French examples attributed to the Pantin factory, although some authorities consider they originate from the as-yet-unidentified "Factory X". In the 1850s, as European glassworkers emigrated to America, important weights were produced there by the New England Glass Company, the Boston & Sandwich Glass Company and the Mount Washington Glass Company.

With the exception of some 19th-century Bohemian examples, and the rare English weights of George Bacchus & Sons of Birmingham, most others are considered inferior.

Paperweights are created by placing tiny sections cut from individually made coloured and patterned rods or "canes" in a mould, which are then set in clear molten glass. The canes themselves contain a multitude of motifs – stars, flowers, rolls, and even silhouettes of animals and humans. They may be closely packed, scattered or arranged in patterns. Flowers, fruit and occasionally insects, all pre-formed by lampwork (the sculpting of coloured glass over a small flame), may also be included. Ceramic portrait medallions or scenes, known as sulphides, were enclosed in glass to form plaques or paperweights. Overlay weights, so called because they include one or more opaque glass layers, have windows ("printies") cut into them, through which the inner pattern can be seen.

An examination of the canes and the way they are grouped (the "set-up") helps to identify a paperweight's origin. Baccarat and St Louis paperweights include signed and dated canes. Canes in Clichy weights occasionally contain the letter "C".

WEIGHT, QUALITY AND CONDITION
Genuine old weights tend to be heavier than later reproductions, because the glass, or "metal", contains a high proportion of lead oxide. This metal should be clear and unclouded, without any marked striations, although minute air bubbles and frit (tiny impurities) in the glass are not a serious fault, especially in rare specimens. The design should be accurately positioned and upright. Canes should not be distorted. Stems, leaves, fruits and petals must be unbroken and properly attached – occasionally they are found to have come adrift in the making.

Expert polishing of a slightly damaged weight can only improve it, as long as the magnifying effect of the dome is retained. Most weights on the market today have been wheel-polished when made, or at a later date. Original fire polishing is rare. Wheel polishing will often improve the appearance of an imperfectly fire-finished weight but the cutting must not go so deep as to expose the inner motif, or drastically alter proportions.

SHAPE AND SIZE
The dome, which acts as a magnifying lens, should be high enough to ensure an adequate enlargement of the small design elements within the weight. The profile of an antique weight should be tall, narrowing markedly toward the foot (a feature not found in later reproductions). Sometimes a star will be cut on the underside. Contrary to popular belief, this is not an indication of any particular factory – although it appears to have been more widely used at Baccarat than elsewhere. Paperweights vary considerably in size; this rarely gives any indication of origin, although Clichy produced the highest proportion of miniatures (weights under 2 inches/5cm in diameter). The standard size is from about 2 to 4 inches (5-10.2cm). Magnum weights, those of 4 inches (10.2cm) or more, are very rare and desirable.

The central "Clichy rose" signifies the origin of this weight (dia. 3⅛in/8cm). The pattern tends to "fall over the edge", which detracts from its value. *S*

Excessively large air bubbles around the animal is a fault to look out for in snake and other animal weights. This example (dia. 3in/7.6cm), with no such air bubbles, is from Baccarat. *CNY*

This St Louis miniature white pom-pom weight (dia. 2in/5cm) has a pink, rather than the usual white, *latticinio* ground. *S*

This swirl weight (dia. 2⅝in/6.7cm), with opaque threads and a central "pastry-mould" cane, is typical of Clichy. *S*

Many American companies used flowers. This upright bouquet (dia. 3¾in/9.4cm) was made by the New England Glass Company. *S*

The six-side facets of this rare Baccarat flat bouquet (3½in/8.9cm) are unusual and almost superfluous on such a decorative weight. *S*

Overlay paperweights, like this attractive Clichy example (dia. 2½ in/6.4cm), are rare, being costly and difficult to produce. *S*

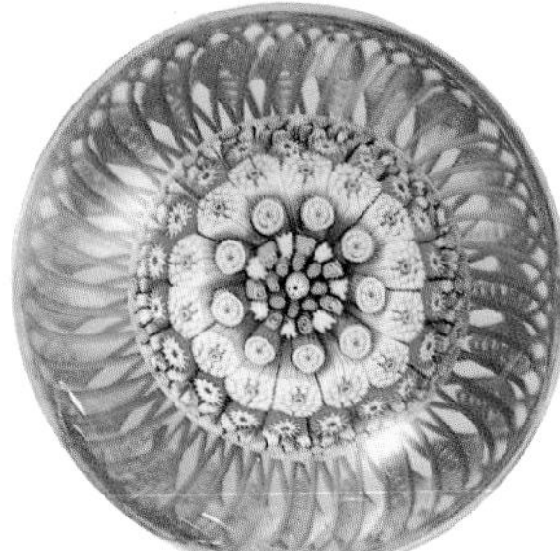
This St Louis weight (dia. 3in/7.6cm) is mushroom-shaped in profile. This type is often surrounded by a twisted cord. *S*

CLICHY, founded c.1837
Clichy weights are never dated and hardly ever signed in full, although the letter "C" may be incorporated into the pattern. Many weights contain the "Clichy rose" in white, combined with various colours. The factory also made extensive use of coloured grounds, moss green being one of the finest and rarest. Sulphides were produced, sometimes with *millefiori* garland borders. The finest and most exciting pieces are probably their ribbon-bound bouquets and splendid overlays. Generally regarded today as the finest weights, Clichy's products are among the most expensive.

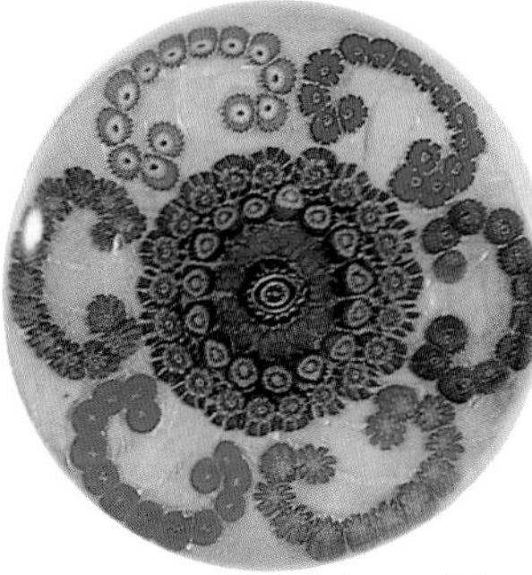

The "C" scroll *millefiori* weight is unique to Clichy. This example (dia. 3⅛in/7.9cm) shows the typical arrangement of scrolls, taken to be a Clichy signature. *S*

BACCARAT, founded 1764
Baccarat signed their weights more often than any other factory, using the initial B, mostly coupled with a date: 1846, 1847, 1848, or 1849 – other dates are virtually unknown. The factory specialized in strong, bright colours. Their flower weights are more naturalistic than those of other factories. They pioneered many techniques, including butterfly and snake weights, and a rock-like ground unique to Baccarat, which occasionally appears as the sole feature of decoration.

Baccarat sulphide weights, such as this example (dia. 3½in/8.9cm) which depicts a hunting scene, are comparatively rare. *S*

This fine Baccarat weight (dia. 2¾in/7cm) is an expensive type known as "carpet ground", because of the close-packed background of identical canes. There are a number of canes containing individual and amusing silhouettes – dog, monkey, stag, horse, cockerel and others. Some canes are inscribed "B 1848". Other types of paperweights with stylized floral patterns, known as *millefiori*, from the Italian for "thousand flowers", include:

* close-cane, in which randomly arranged upright canes cover the whole base
* weights in which the canes are arranged in formal patterns, sometimes on a coloured ground
* panelled or chequer designs in which single canes or groups are divided by horizontal bands. *S*

Among the variations on the standard paperweight form are weights such as this very rare Clichy pedestal weight (dia. 3in/7.6cm), which rests on a green and white striped foot and shows typical "Clichy roses" in its design. *S*

* Other items were produced with paperweight-style bases – including ink-bottles, vases, glasses and scent bottles.

ST LOUIS, founded 1767
The initials "SL" were occasionally used, sometimes with a date between 1845 and 1849; the rare date 1845 is the earliest shown by any French weight. The factory produced a more limited range of canes than its rivals, but quality was high. Carefully made fruit weights were a speciality, as were flowers – for example, dahlias and fuchsias. Jasper grounds (made with powdered glass of several colours) and *latticinio* in white and pink are characteristic of St Louis. Production almost certainly continued beyond 1849.

Crown weights were a St Louis speciality. Like this example (dia. 3in/7.6cm), they are hollow-blown, with canes in the form of twisted ribbons emanating from a central cane or cluster. *S*

UNITED STATES
The New England Glass Company made a diverse range of traditional weights, many reminiscent of St Louis, and some more unusual fruit-shaped weights on feet. The Boston & Sandwich Glass Company made floral weights and others; the date 1825 occurs, but this refers to the date of foundation of the factory. The Mount Washington Glass Company produced spectacular floral weights and plaques, frequently three-dimensional. The Whitall, Tatum Company invented an upright rose weight, on a pedestal.

This Boston & Sandwich weight (dia. 2½in/6.3cm) depicts the ponsettia with which the factory came to be identified. The jasper ground is also typical but can be confused with that of St Louis. *S*

Cut and Pressed Glass

Cutting of glass became popular in England c.1715 and initially was strongly influenced by German styles. Shallow cutting in simple designs characterized English cut glass throughout the 18th century. Hand cutting gave way to wheel cutting by steam power c.1830, when patterns became deeper and increasingly florid.

Early examples of Irish cut glass are heavily influenced by English techniques and forms. However, by the last decade of the 18th century these techniques were used to produce a variety of new pieces, peculiar to Ireland, such as oval butter-coolers.

Cutting was introduced to America c.1771 and followed English and Irish trends. Flute cutting was popular between 1830 and 1880. Brilliant-cut glass, cut with a deep mitre, became fashionable c.1880.

Moulded glass, formed by blowing glass into a decorated mould, was partially superseded in America c.1830 by the hugely popular machine-pressed glass: the glass was forced into a hinged mould with a plunger. "Lacy" glass, one of the most intricate, yet inexpensive forms of machine-pressed glass, also developed in America, in response to the huge demand for highly decorated affordable glass items.

The simple diamond cutting on the panels of this boat-shaped fruit bowl, c.1800 (ht 8in/21cm), is typical of Irish pieces c.1770-1800. The short knopped stem and moulded oval base are typical of late 18thC and early 19thC Irish fruit bowls. Simpler versions had a knopped stem on a square base. *Som*
* Bowls of this quality are hard to find.

The fan-cut staves, serrated rim and fan scallops on this butter dish, c.1825 (ht 5½in/13.5cm), are all standard features of Irish and English cut glass of the period. *Som*

This English plate, c.1825 (wdth 10in/25cm), with its radiating strawberry diamonds shows the more ambitious style of cutting in the early 19thC, compared with the late 18thC. *Som*

DATING AND AUTHENTICATION
There are no foolproof ways to authenticate cut glass. However, undulating lines suggest treadle-operated wheel cutting, in which the speed of the wheel was inconstant. Broad sweeps in the same plane indicate steam power cutting. Polishing in 18th and 19thC wheel-cut glass is uneven, and grain marks left by the stone wheels are often in evidence near the edges. Glass produced after 1900 by acid polishing has none of these marks, and the edges of cuts are smoother.

Many fakes of original Irish cut glass appeared after 1918. Some manufacturers, including the Cork Glass Co., and the Waterloo Glass House Co. (also Cork), marked their products on the base.

THE MAIN PATTERNS
Throughout the 18thC, cutting tended to be shallow and designs confined to simple geometric patterns. The variety of designs and the ingenuity with which they were combined became increasingly impressive in the first decades of the 19thC.

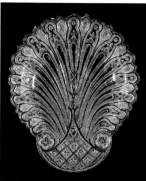

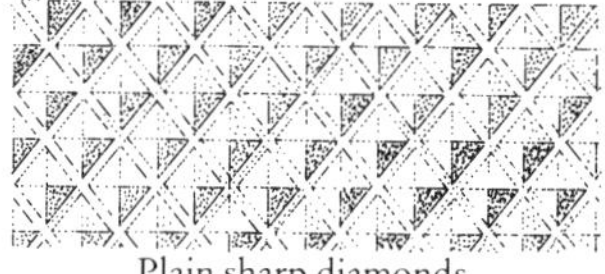

Plain sharp diamonds

Pillar flutes

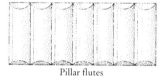

Star cutting

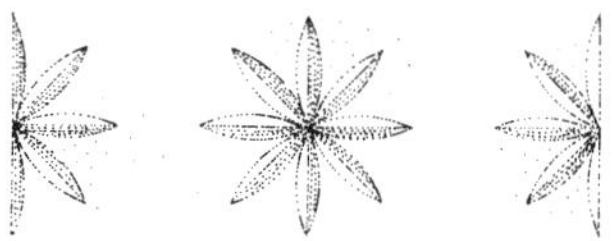

Strawberry diamonds

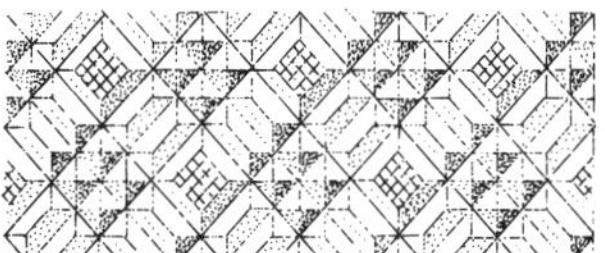

Cross-cut diamonds

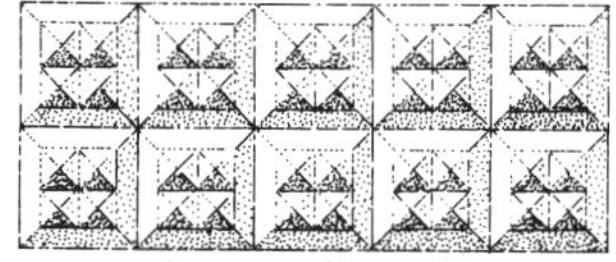

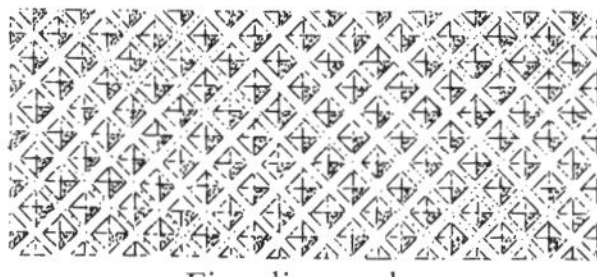

Fine diamonds

"Lacy" glass, one of the earliest and most popular forms of pressed glass, evolved as a method of incorporating as many facets as possible into one piece. There is great demand for pieces made before 1840, such as this New England tray, c.1830-45 (lgth 9½in/24cm), which is typical of the intricate designs achievable with "lacy" glass techniques. *Cor*

Many of the most interesting and sought-after pieces of pressed glass are commemorative, such as this American dish made at the end of the 19thC (dia 10½in/26.5cm). Other popular items include tumblers, jugs, and cup plates for drinking tea.
Decoration provides an approximate guide to dating:
* 1840s – heavy loops and ribbed effects
* 1860s – complex geometry and stylized flowers
* 1870s – elaborate naturalistic patterns
* 1880s – a revival of geometric patterns. *Cor*

In the late 19thC some companies, such as the Westmoreland Glass Co. in Pennsylvania, specialized in reproductions. It is difficult to differentiate between original pressed pieces and reproductions. However, genuine early pressed glass is heavy, and has bubbles and imperfections.
* The best method of discerning whether glass has been pressed or moulded is to touch the inside of the piece: pressed glass is smooth, whereas the inside of a blown-moulded piece bears the outline of the design.

Reference

GLOSSARY

Acid etching A technique for decorating glass which involves protecting the glass with an acid-resistant wax, scratching on the pattern and applying an acid treatment.
Acid polishing A process that gives cut glass a polished finish by briefly immersing it in a solution of hydrofluoric acid.
Art glass Highly decorated glass, late 19thC and 20thC.
Cameo glass Two or more layers of **cased glass** in different colours, the outer layer carved on a wheel to create a relief design.
Cased glass Glass of two or more layers of different colours, the outer layer(s) cut away.
Cristallo A clear fine soda glass produced in Venice from the 15thC.
Enamel A durable paint, consisting of metal oxides and oil, applied as decoration on glass. Often fired, to fix the decoration.
Engraving Decorating the surface of glass with wheels or diamond-pointed tools.
Flashed glass Clear glass coated with one or more thin layers of coloured glass. Often engraved.
Flint glass See **Lead glass**.
Frigger Any small glass object made by a craftsman after regular hours, using left-over glass.
Humpen A cylindrical German drinking glass made in varying sizes from the 16thC.
Knop A hollow or solid bulge in the stem of a drinking glass.
Lead glass A heavy brilliant glass introduced in England by George Ravenscroft c.1676, using lead oxide in place of lime. Also termed flint glass.
Merese A collar used between the bowl and stem of a drinking glass, or between the stem and foot.
Metal The basic material of glass, particularly in its molten state.
***Millefiori* glass** Glass embedded with short sections of multi-coloured glass canes; designed to resemble "a thousand flowers". Most often seen in paperweights.
Moulded glass Glass that has been either blown or pressed with a plunger into a mould to shape and decorate it.
Overlay glass A term sometimes used as a synonym for **cased glass.**
Pontil (or punty) rod The iron rod onto which blown glass is transferred from the blowpipe for final shaping. After the glass has cooled sufficiently it is removed from the pontil rod, leaving a pontil mark where it was joined.
Potash glass A hard glass in which potash, obtained from burnt wood, was the main flux. Made in Germany and Bohemia (as *Waldglas*) and in France (*verre de fougere*).
Prunt A blob of glass, shaped in a variety of forms, applied as decoration.
Romer (Roemer) A goblet made from the 15thC, in Germany and the Low Countries.
Rummer A short-stemmed goblet made in England in the late 18th and 19thC.
Soda glass A type of glass in which soda was the flux. Its malleable properties were exploited to the full by Venetian glassmakers in the 15th, 16th and 17thC.
Stippling An engraving technique which involved tapping and scratching a glass surface with a diamond point to create a pattern of minute dots and dashes.

SELECTED MAKERS

ENGLAND

Apsley Pellatt & Co. (1820-95) London. Best known for incorporation of sulphides (small cameos moulded in relief) in high-quality crystal cut glass.
Bacchus, George (1818-97) Birmingham. Coloured glass, including overlay. Printed opaline. Also, pressed glass.
Beilby, William and Mary (active c.1760-78) Brother and sister. Established an enamelling workshop in Newcastle-upon-Tyne c.1760. Worked mainly with white enamel, although William also worked in coloured enamels.
Davidson, George (founded 1867) Gateshead. Pressed (slag) glass. Mark: lion above a crown in a circle.
Greener & Co., H. (from 1869) Gateshead. Pressed (slag) glass. Mark: lion with star; after 1885 lion with axe.
Lloyd & Summerfield (from c.1780) Birmingham. Well-known for busts in cast glass.
Northwood, John Developed technique of cameo cutting. Worked for **Stevens & Williams.**
Powell, James (1835-1980) London. Acquired Whitefriars Glassworks (founded c.1680) in 1835. Produced many of the mid-19thC English paperweights. Closely associated with the Arts and Crafts Movement.
Ravenscroft, George (1618-81) Introduced lead glass c.1676. Mark: raven's head (very rare).
Richardson, W.H., B. & J. (1837-1937) Stourbridge. Products include ornate cut glass and coloured and overlay glass.
Rice Harris & Co. (c.1830-1937) Birmingham. Pressed glass, paperweights.
Sowerby's (from 1850) Gateshead. Pressed glass (slagware). Mark: peacock's head.
Stevens & Williams (from 1847) Stourbridge. Specialized in coloured wares, also known for "rock crystal" engraved glass.
Webb, Thomas (from 1856) Stourbridge. Cameo glass, satin glass, and other decorative wares.
Woodall, George Worked for **Webb's**, producing cameo glass.

IRELAND

Many of the products from the following main Irish glasshouses had the trade name impressed on the base.
Cork Glass Co., The (1783-1818) Cork. The Cork style of cutting was typified by: flat diamonds in ovals or circles, hollow facets, uneven quality of metal, "soft" appearance.
Edwards, Benjamin (active 1776-1812) Belfast. The company continued under his son Benjamin Jnr until 1827. Decanters are the only pieces bearing the trademark "B. Edwards Belfast".
Waterford Glass House (1783-1851) Waterford. Typical features are deep prismatic cutting, pillar-and-arch design, swags, and clear, even metal. Trademark: "Penrose, Waterford".
Waterloo Glass Company, The (1783-1835) Trademark: "Waterloo Co. Cork."

GERMANY AND BOHEMIA

Egermann, Friedrich (1777-1864) Patented Lithyalin (1828), an opaque glass with a marbled appearance that resembled agate. Also developed gold and ruby stains.
Gondelach, Franz (1663-1726) Engraver, using both high-relief and intaglio techniques.
Kunckel, Johann (1630-1703) Potsdam glass maker, best known for gold ruby glass.
Lehmann, Casper (1570-1622) A famous wheel engraver, in Prague.
Mohn, Gottlob Samuel (1789-1825) Son of **Samuel Mohn**, worked in same style.
Mohn, Samuel (1762-1815) Dresden. Transparent enameller, working on goblets and beakers. Many topographical scenes.
Preissler, Daniel (1636-1733) With his son Ignaz (b.1670), renowned for *Schwarzlot* (black) enamelled glass.
Schaper, Johann (1621-70) Nuremberg decorator, notable for *Schwarzlot* (black) enamelling.

FRANCE

Baccarat (founded 1764) Initially produced window glass and tablewares in soda glass. Lead crystal from 1813. Became Compagnie des Cristalleries de Baccarat, 1822. Opaline and agate glass. Coloured crystal from 1839, paperweights in the 1840s (see page 133).
Clichy (founded 1837) Near Paris. Paperweights from c.1845, including overlay weights (see page 133).
St Louis (founded 1760s) Produced English-inspired cut crystal from the 1780s and paperweights from 1845 (see page 133).

UNITED STATES

Bakewell Glasshouse (1808-82) Pittsburgh. Established by Benjamin Bakewell. Became the Pittsburgh Flint Glass Manufactory, 1813. Fine cut and engraved lead glass.
Boston & Sandwich Glass Company, The (1825-88) Sandwich, Mass. Produced mould-pressed, "lacy" (or "Sandwich") glass and lead glass. Dolphins in electric blue.
Libbey Glass Company (from 1888) Toledo, Ohio. Cut glass.
Mount Washington Glass Company, The (1837-94) Boston, Mass. Mould-blown, mould-pressed and cut glass. Produced art glass from 1880. Many wares silver-plated by Pairpoint Mfg Co.
New Bremen Glass Manufactory (c.1785-c.1795) Maryland. Goblets, bottles. Fine engraving.
New England Glass Company, The (1818-88) East Cambridge, Mass. Lead glass, mould-pressed and "lacy" glass, paperweights.
Stiegel, Henry William German-born maker, established American Flint Glass Works, Mannheim, Pennsylvania, 1763. Closed 1774. Fine-quality tableware, in English and European styles. Enamelling, engraving, pattern-moulding. Coloured glass, as well as clear.

BIBLIOGRAPHY

Buckley, William, *European Glass* (1926)
Hayes, E. Barrington, *Glass Through the Ages* (1959)
Honey, W.B., *A Handbook for the Study of Glass Vessels of All Periods and Countries and a Guide to the Museum Collections* (Victoria & Albert Museum) (1946)
Hughes, George Bernard, *English, Scottish and Irish Table Glass from the 16th Century to 1820* (1956)
Jokelson, Paul, *Antique French Paperweights* (1955)
McKearin, George S. and Helen, *American Glass* (1948)
Two Hundred Years of American Blown Glass (revised edn 1966)
Pellatt, Apsley, *Curiosities of Glassmaking* (1844)
Vose, Ruth Hurst, *Glass* (Connoisseur Guide) (1975)
Wakefield, Hugh, *Nineteenth Century British Glass* (1961)
Westropp, Michael, *Irish Glass* (1920)

CLOCKS

A clock is one of the most personal of antiques, and some have become very much part of the family. Indeed, for many years this was one of the few items besides the home and the bed to be mentioned in a will – which is fortunate for today's collector who wants to know the provenance of the clock he is buying. In addition, most English and some Continental clocks bear the name of the maker.

The only disadvantage of clocks as opposed to other collecting areas is that they are mechanical objects that require periodic attention; if neglected, they can be expensive to restore to good working order. It is worth bearing in mind that the cost of restoring a cheap clock can often be as great as that of restoring a valuable one. Thus, without a good knowledge of horology or expert advice, it is much better to buy a clock overhauled and in working order, and preferably guaranteed by an experienced clockmaker, than one that needs anything but the most rudimentary repair – for example, replacement glass panels. To put a badly neglected clock back into good condition can cost enormous sums, particularly if such features as pull-quarter repeat work, which causes the clock to strike, have been removed.

A further factor is that the clock must be assessed not just as a piece of furniture, although its aesthetic appeal is important, but also as a mechanical device. It is important to identify components that have been changed during the lifetime of the clock and to know which alterations are acceptable – for example, the renewal of a worn wheel or pinion is of no great consequence, but the replacement of a dial greatly reduces a clock's value.

It must be remembered that an auction catalogue description is just that and no more, and will not necessarily list all a clock's faults. However, it is possible to request a "condition report" on a particular clock, which should address itself to the three essential components: the case, the movement and the dial.

Like most antiques, clocks have increased dramatically in value over the last twenty years. Fashions change, but the most sought-after types today are fine mahogany longcase clocks with painted or brass faces, good English and French longcase regulators, complex skeleton clocks, 17th-century longcase and bracket clocks and complex or decorative carriage clocks.

	INNOVATIONS	LANTERN
1600-1650	*1650: First one-year clock*	*Verge escapement with bala wheel until c.1660*
1650-1700	*1656: First pendulum clock* *Anchor escapement from c.1675* *1675: Rack strike made repeat work possible*	*Verge escapement with bob pendulum c.1660-171* *30-hour clocks after c.168* *Winged lantern clocks*
1700-1750	*Break-arch dials on English longcase and bracket clocks from c.1710* *1720-30: First temperature-compensated pendulums* *1730: First cuckoo clock*	*Anchor escapement from c.* *Some clocks with break-arch dials by c.172*
1750-1800	*1780-1800: Birth of the marine chronometer, designed to find longitude at sea*	
1800-1850	*1802: Banjo clock patented in USA by Simon Willard*	
1850-1900	*Barometric compensation on clocks from 1870*	*Spring-driven versions (England and France)*

The chart shows the most popular types of clock in England, Continental Europe and the United States for the period between 1600 and 1900, together with major innovations and important stylistic developments

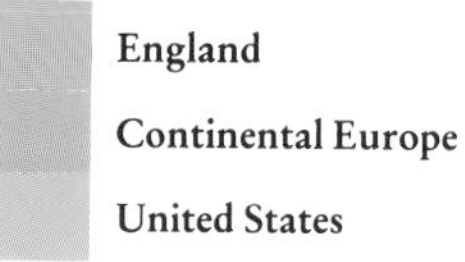

England

Continental Europe

United States

WALL 	TABLE & MANTEL 	LONGCASE 	CARRIAGE 	
	TABLE CLOCKS *(France and Germany)*			1600-1650
	BRACKET CLOCKS *(England, from 1660s)* *JOSEPH KNIBB (England)*	*Ebonized c.1670-85* *Walnut and olivewood c.1675-90* *Lavish marquetry 1690s (England and the Netherlands* *THOMAS TOMPION (England)*	*Forerunners of carriage clocks:* *Small weight-driven travelling clocks in wooden boxes*	1650-1700
OODED WALL CLOCKS *(England)* CARTEL CLOCKS *(France)*	BRACKET CLOCKS *(England)* *Verge escapement persisted on bracket clocks until c.1800* MANTEL CLOCKS *(France)* PORCELAIN CLOCKS *(France and Germany)*	*Lacquered chinoiseries decoration (especially c.1715-40)* *English movements and dials imported to USA*		1700-1750
TAVERN CLOCKS *(England)* CARTEL CLOCKS *(England)*	BRACKET CLOCKS *(England)* MANTEL CLOCKS *(France)* SKELETON CLOCKS *(France: evolved from French mantel clocks)* SHELF CLOCKS *(USA)*	*Pagoda tops c.1730-80 (England)* LONGCASE REGULATORS *(France and England)*	*Cappucines (early travelling clocks, French-Swiss border) c.1770-1800* *Pendules d'officier (France) c.1780-1800*	1750-1800
DIAL CLOCKS *(England)* VIENNA REGULATORS *(Austria)* BANJO, LYRE AND GIRANDOLE CLOCKS *(USA)*	BRACKET CLOCKS *(England)* MANTEL CLOCKS *(Vienna)* SKELETON CLOCKS *(England)* SHELF CLOCKS *(USA)*	*Painted dials* LONGCASE REGULATORS *(France and Vienna)*	*French carriage clocks from c.1810* *A.-L. BREGUET* *One-piece cases c.1840-50*	1800-1850
DIAL CLOCKS *with painted iron dials (England)* VIENNA REGULATORS *(Austria and, from c.1870, Germany: including spring-driven versions)*	SKELETON CLOCKS *(England)* SHELF CLOCKS *(USA)* NOVELTY CLOCKS	LONGCASE REGULATORS *in revival styles* TUBE-CHIMING LONGCASES	*Classic "gorge" case design from 1865* *Porcelain panels from c.1880*	1850-1900

Basics

Although the different categories of clock vary enormously in appearance and mechanism, there are certain key factors, common to all clocks, that should be carefully considered before a purchase is made.

THE MOVEMENT

All mechanical clocks have an *escapement*, a device that releases, at set intervals, a train of wheels and pinions to which the clock hands are attached, thus enabling the clock to keep time. There are two main types of escapement:

* the *verge* or *balance wheel*, used in clocks until c.1670

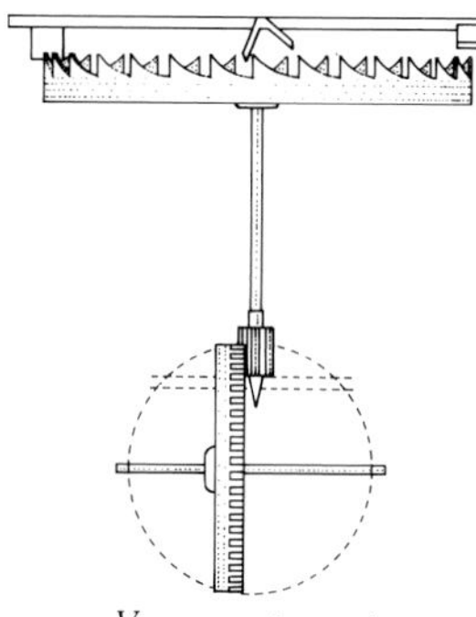

Verge escapement

* the *anchor*, which replaced the verge and was used in longcase clocks from c.1670 and in bracket and wall clocks from c.1800.

Anchor escapement

The frequency with which the train of wheels and pinions is released, and the hands allowed to move, is governed in early verge escapements by a rotating bar, or *foliot*. Later versions had a balance wheel instead of the foliot. The balance wheel was in turn replaced by the pendulum in 1660.

In clocks with an anchor escapement, the movement is controlled by an anchor-shaped device and pendulum.

Wheels

These are sometimes replaced. However, replacements are usually very obvious: most modern brass has a high copper content and lacks the yellow finish of older brass.

Fusees

The fusee was a conical-shaped spool used to even out the pull of the spring that provided the motive force in some clocks. The use of a spring instead of a weight made clocks far more portable than they had been.

Pendulums and **racks and snails**

In addition to the introduction of the anchor escapement, there were two other major developments that affected clocks in the 17thC:

* The *pendulum*, which was introduced in 1657, dramatically improved accuracy.
* The "*rack and snail*", introduced c.1675, enabled the striking of the hour to be synchronized with the movement of the hands.

It is very unusual to find clocks complete with their original foliot or balance wheel: most early clocks were converted to accommodate a pendulum.

* Many clocks have been converted from a verge to an anchor escapement. It is possible to distinguish between the verge and the anchor escapement, as the arc of the pendulum's swing in an anchor escapement is far less than in the verge pendulum, and instead of a small pendulum bob a large lenticular bob will have been used on the anchor escapement. The backplate of a bracket clock fitted with a verge escapement was often ornately engraved. If such engraving is concealed by a large pendulum bob, then it is likely that a conversion from verge to anchor escapement has taken place.

Weights and pendulum bobs

All good London-made clocks should have brass cased driving weights, although the brass on these is quite frequently damaged. Early provincial clocks usually have lead weights; the later ones employ iron.

Until c.1790 London-made clocks and most provincial ones have a brass-faced lead pendulum bob (the weight at the end of the pendulum). A small number of bobs were attractively painted and decorated; these were often made in Scotland.

American clocks usually have brass or tin pendulums.

Strikes

Most English clocks until c.1840 and carriage clocks between 1830 and 1870 strike or chime on bells. After this date gongs are more common.

CASES

An examination of the materials and fittings used in the clock case provides a useful indication of age, value and condition.

Wooden cases

Wood began to be widely used in cases with the establishment of the longcase clock, c.1660. Walnut and oak were the most popular woods until the advent of mahogany cases c.1730. Expensive clock cases used a dark, richly coloured mahogany from Cuba. More modest pieces were of a paler mahogany with a less interesting grain.

* Solid oak was most commonly used for clock cases made in the main English provincial towns.

Cases were often veneered in the first instance; or veneered or re-veneered at a later date, either to keep up with fashion or to improve the value of the clock. Later veneering was particularly prevalent in the Victorian and Edwardian periods, by which time the veneers would have been machine- rather than hand-made and are therefore likely to be thinner and more even than original veneer.

Lacquer

Lacquer appeared on cases between c.1680 and c.1780, usually on longcase clocks but was most popular 1710-60. The most popular motifs include Oriental figures, birds, plants and animals.

* Many lacquered cases are in poor condition as the carcass beneath has expanded and contracted with changes in temperature.

Brass cases

Carriage and lantern clocks have brass cases, and many cases, whether brass or wood, have brass fittings. Old brass is sand-cast, annealed and beaten out on a forge to spread and condense it. This process leaves hammering and casting marks. Modern brass is rolled out on a strip mill, a process that results in brass of even thickness. Modern brass can be artificially tarnished with chemicals to make it look old.

Hinges and locks

Early locks were of iron, later ones (from c.1700) of brass. Vienna regulators (see page 141) nearly always have brass fittings. Hinges and locks inevitably wear out and many are replaced from time to time; this type of restoration is acceptable.

DIALS

The dial is the "face" of the clock and is attached to the movement by a number of brass "feet". Four feet are usual in eight-day clocks and three in 30-hour clocks. Dial feet should always fit into their original fixing holes.

The dial plate

Dial plates, which form the basis of the dial, fall into four categories:

* Engraved brass dials. These were used on most early clocks, including lantern and early longcase clocks.
* Painted metal dials, which are found on most types of clock after c.1775.
* Painted wooden dials, which appear only on Continental clocks, especially 18thC German clocks, and on a few English wall clocks between c.1780 and 1800. They are also a feature of 18thC American clocks.
* Enamelled metal dials; these were used on all carriage clocks, on most French clocks, occasionally on fine English bracket clocks and very rarely, on English longcase clocks.

Brass dials

These were made from cast, hand-finished brass plate until c.1850, when mass-produced brass plate took over. The hours are engraved directly onto the plate or onto a detachable *chapter ring*.

There are several features that help to date a brass dial:

* ring winding holes, used c.1680-1720
* half-hour divisions, used until 1730-35
* quarter-hour divisions, used on London clocks until 1725 and up to several years later on provincial clocks
* decorative engraving on the spandrels and around the date aperture, used on London clocks until 1720 and on provincial clocks until 1770-80.

The all-over silvered brass dial was introduced c.1760 and was often fitted to wall, bracket and longcase clocks.

Painted dials have often been replaced by brass ones. This change can be detected by the faultless, even surface characteristic of modern rolled brass, and the lack of any signs of beating or ageing on the back of the dial. In addition, the engraving on the chapter ring may be acid-etched; more skilful fakes are hand-engraved. Chemically tarnished dials are hard to detect as they will have the uneven finish associated with old brass dials.

* The front of the dial needs constant repolishing, but the back should be left alone, as polish removes the signs of age that help to authenticate a clock.

Painted metal dials

Painted faces (also known as white-dials) were popular because they were clear to read and the white surface provided a good background for decoration. Designs became increasingly elaborate throughout the first half of the 19thC.

* *Crazing* on the dial surface – a small network of fine cracks – helps to authenticate an original painted dial. It also helps to distinguish between painted dials and the more expensive enamelled faces.
* Some painted dials have been removed and replaced with new brass dials. This reduces a clock's value by anything up to 50 percent.

Painted wooden dials

The wood of an authentic dial should have cracks caused by contraction brought about by extreme or sudden changes in temperature. If cracks are evident only on the back of the dial, it has probably been restored.

Enamelled metal dials

Enamelled dials on copper bases were fashionable in the late Georgian period in England and are usually found only on high-quality clocks. They were perennially popular in France, but never in America. The surface is harder than that of painted dials, which are often described as enamelled.

* The signature and the numerals are usually applied over the top of the glaze and will often be badly rubbed and may be in need of repair. This is not usually a serious problem.

Chapter rings

A chapter ring is the part of the dial on which the hours are engraved or painted. It is either an integral part of a flat all-over engraved and silvered brass dial, or a separate detachable ring which, together with the spandrels, appears as the raised part of a brass dial.

Flat dial with integral chapter ring and engraved spandrels. DR

Dial with detachable chapter ring and raised spandrels. DR

* Clocks with raised chapter rings have always been more popular than clocks with flat brass dials. Consequently, chapter rings were sometimes added to a flat dial to increase a clock's value. The best way to detect this is to remove the detachable chapter ring and see whether there is an integral one engraved beneath.
* From early times chapter rings were silvered to give them a good white finish. Most will have been re-silvered several times. This will not affect a clock's value. However, re-silvering can disguise additional or blocked holes, which indicate that a chapter ring has been added or replaced. The best way to check for holes is to examine the back of the ring or the front plate of the movement.
*Original dial surfaces in perfect condition are rare, owing to the effects of cleaning and age.

Hands

Early domestic clocks were relatively inaccurate and were thus fitted with only one hand. The chapter rings were divided into quarter-hours; only a few were marked with minute divisions. It was not until c.1660 that two hands were introduced in response to the increased accuracy brought about by the pendulum. The combination of a decorative hour hand and a longer, simpler minute hand lasted from about this date until c.1740, when matching steel hands became popular.
* Steel hands are usually blued by heating rather than painted. The process protects them from damage and made them easier to see: they will be a dark grey-blue colour.
* Replaced hands do not always reduce a clock's value but it is important that they match the age, style and quality of the clock.
* Brass, usually gilded, hands came into use c.1790 and became increasingly ornate during the 19thC.

SIGNATURES

English longcase and bracket clocks

These clocks were generally signed by the maker, and the signature may help to date and place a clock. However, it does not necessarily guarantee that the clock was made in the stated period, nor by the man whose name it bears. Moreover, grandfather, father and son may all have had the same name.

Genuine signatures are usually found in the following places:
* until 1690: along the bottom of the dial plate
* between 1690 and 1720: on the chapter ring
* after 1720: often on the chapter ring; sometimes on the boss in the arch or on an applied plaque

Bracket clocks are sometimes also signed on the backplate of the movement. From 1830 the name that appeared on the dial was increasingly that of the retailer rather than the maker.

French carriage clocks

Many French carriage clocks bear an English name on the dial and sometimes on the backplate as well, but these always refer to the retailer rather than to the maker. Some may also bear the stamp of the maker on the backplate or concealed within the movement.

Wall clocks

Some wall clocks bear the name of the shop for which they were made.

Skeleton clocks

These are seldom signed, apart from a few of the finest. Some skeleton clocks bear the signature of the retailer.

Fake signatures

Signatures are sometimes added to a previously unsigned clock at a later date. One way to detect this is to feel the engraving: old engraving is smooth, whereas new work feels sharper.

AUTHENTICITY

As well as clocks that are copies of earlier styles, there are two other categories of inauthentic clocks: *marriages* and *upgraded clocks*. Marriages occur when parts that don't belong together have been "married" at a later date. Upgrading occurs when improvements are made to a clock to make it more saleable, or to keep it in fashion.

Marriage of dial to movement

A popular type of marriage was that between a well-made eight-day movement with the decorative case and brass dial of an early 30-hour clock. This is usually easy to detect, as the early single-handed 30-day clocks have no outer minute ring for the minute hand.

Indications that a "marriage" between components from separate clocks has taken place include:
* signs on the back of the dial where the original feet have been cut off and replaced
* marks where the position of the winding holes in the dial has been changed to suit the present movement; alternatively, the winding holes may not match the winding squares accurately. See Dials, above

Marriage of dial to longcase case

Strips of wood glued inside the mask which surrounds the dial are a sign that the existing dial has been transferred from another, smaller clock, the wood helping to reduce the aperture. However, the dial will then look too small for the glazed aperture of the hood door.

Upgrading

In the Victorian period, clocks were often upgraded from simple hour-strike to quarter-chiming. This was sometimes done by adding a further train of wheels to the existing movement, but in other cases the whole movement was replaced. In these instances a circular join will be visible behind the chapter ring where the original centre of the dial has been cut out.

CONDITION

A clock's mechanism consists of a complex and fragile series of components and it is inevitable that these will show signs of wear over the years. Repair is often necessary, and the degree to which it detracts from a clock's value obviously depends on the amount and quality of the work.

Repairs to the movement

The wheels within the movement rotate on pivots, and it is usual to find wear in the holes in which the pivots run. If the pivot hole is surrounded by a series of smaller holes, the repairer has tried to spread the brass to close the worn pivot holes. It is difficult to remove evidence of this bad repair, even though the clock may have subsequently had the worn holes correctly filled, or "bushed" – this involves the inserting of a new brass disc with the correct size hole and is the only acceptable way to effect such a repair.

The steel of a pinion, or toothed gear, often shows signs of wear as a result of dust and oil. Some wear is a good sign of age, but should not be allowed to continue unchecked.

The steel pallets, which check the revolution of an anchor escape wheel, wear relatively quickly and have often been re-faced or replaced. Older collets, or (collars to which the anchor is fixed) are domed, whereas later ones, after c.1800, tend to be rectangular.

Replacement bells

Some clocks have had their bells replaced where the original ones have cracked. Such replacements can be difficult to detect but knowledge of the original type may help.

CARE AND ATTENTION

Most maintenance should be left to a specialist. However, there is no harm in carefully dusting and waxing a wooden case. Brass and silvered dials are protected with lacquer and should under no circumstances be placed in contact with water or detergent.

Cleaning and oiling the movement

Cleaning and oiling a clock's mechanism should be carried out with great care and usually by a specialist. Pivots and some levers, and other parts that move against each other, can be oiled by an expert, using a good clock oil. Wheels and pinions should never be oiled as this will encourage dust and dirt to stick and increase wear in the pinions..

Transporting clocks

The springs from which pendulums are suspended are fragile and easily broken in transit. Clocks with spring-drive and short pendulums, such as most 19thC French clocks, can be carried from one room to another, but should be held upright. For long-distance journeys the pendulum must be secured or removed. A clamp will usually be provided to secure the pendulum of a bracket clock. Longcase clocks should be dismantled before being moved – the weights and pendulum should be taken off the movement, and the movement removed from the case.

Lantern Clocks

The lantern was the first of the domestic clocks; it appeared on the Continent of Europe in the late 15th century and in England a hundred or so years later. Lantern clocks were never made in America.

Until 1660, lanterns were controlled by a balance wheel or, sometimes on the Continent, a foliot, and had two weights giving a duration of approximately 12 hours. Most had an alarm. Many of these clocks were subsequently converted from balance wheel or verge to anchor escapement with long pendulum.

Nearly all the clocks made after 1680 were of 30-hour duration. Some were designed to rest on a wooden wall bracket and others made use of a hoop and spikes to fix them to the wall. The later clocks tend to have larger and wider chapter rings and by c.1720 some incorporated break-arch dials.

In the second half of the 19th century there was a strong revival of interest in the lantern clock. However, because a weight-driven wall clock is untidy and difficult to house, most were made as spring clocks so they could be placed on a table. Also the weight-driven movements of some of the early clocks were replaced by spring-driven ones.

Lantern clocks are more difficult to assess than any other clock and should be approached with great caution. This is partly because of their age and the inevitable ills and alterations that have befallen them, and also because they are the easiest clocks to fake.

The most common type of lantern clock after 1680, this 30-hour example with original anchor escapement was made c.1720 (ht 15½in/39.5cm). It rests on an oak bracket. *DR*

An interesting and rare variation on these clocks is the winged lantern, in which the pendulum is situated in the centre and at the front rather than behind the movement. A long arc terminates at either end in an arrow, replacing the conventional pendulum bob, and this appears and disappears alternately in the glazed wings on either side of the clock. This example, c.1680 (ht 16in/40.5cm), is signed "John Ebsworth, London Fecit". *DR*

This verge escapement lantern clock was made c.1690, by Thomas Palmer of Shefford. There is a "hoop and spikes" at the back of the clock, used to fix it to the wall. *DR*.

* The earlier lantern clocks that have lived through at least two major advances in timekeeping have often been legitimately upgraded. However, escapements are sometimes changed to make clocks appear earlier than they really are. In such a case the style of dial and engraving might provide a clue to the clock's real date.
* Clocks that have been converted to a spring-driven mechanism have two hands but no minute scale.

HANDS

Early domestic clocks had only a single hand. This was usually simple and sturdily constructed, with a tail to increase the leverage and to reduce the chance of damage. The arrow shape of the tip, used until the 1660s, gave way to slightly more decorative, sometimes looped, styles as the 17thC progressed.

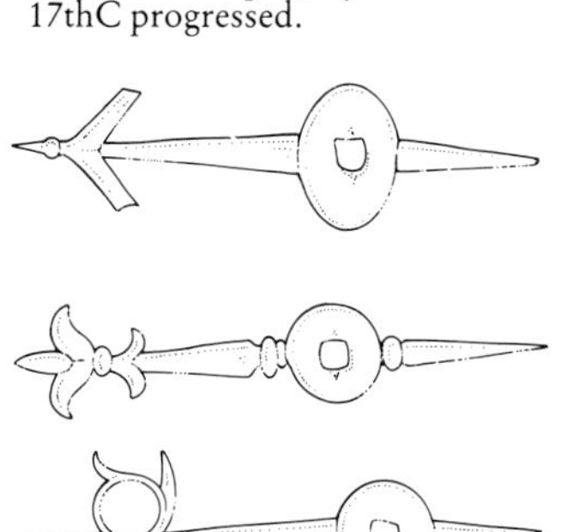

FRETS

Wall Clocks

The lantern clock was the earliest type of wall clock, but many other types appeared steadily in Europe and America from the 16th century and continued to be made well into the 19th century. Of these, the Vienna regulators are most prized, both in Europe and America. Other types include simple dial clocks, common in England in the 18th and 19th centuries, and the more decorative cartel clocks that originated in France.

This is not a category that is plagued by fakery. However, light restoration is not uncommon.

DIAL CLOCKS

Dial clocks came into general use in England between 1850 and 1940. They are usually spring-driven with circular dials. This example with a painted iron dial, c. 1880 (dia. 12in/30.5cm), is the most usual type. *DR*

TAVERN OR ACT OF PARLIAMENT CLOCKS

These large clocks are weight-driven and seldom strike. This is the commonest style, c.1780 (ht 5ft/150cm). The name derives from a tax imposed in England in 1797 on all privately owned timepieces, causing a greatly increased demand for clocks in public places. *DR*

AMERICAN WALL CLOCKS

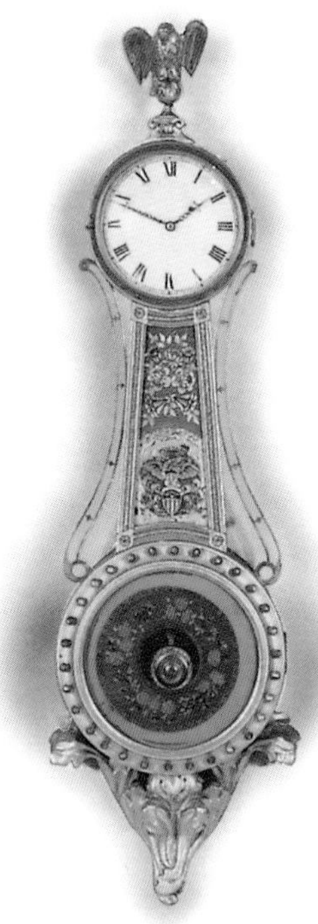

The most beautiful of the highly sought-after clocks produced in America in the 19thC is perhaps the banjo clock, patented by Simon Willard in 1802, and its variants, the Girandole and the Lyre. This Federal gilt and *églomisé* Girandole clock, by Lemuel Curtis of Massachusetts, c.1816 (ht 46in/117cm), has a circular box at the base; the banjo would usually have a square base. *CNY*

* All three types are comparatively rare, especially the Girandole. The banjo has often been reproduced.

VIENNA REGULATORS

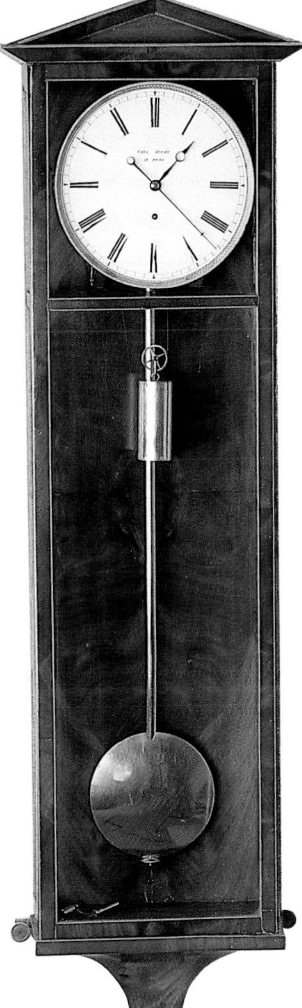

These are among the most attractive and sought-after type of clock, especially those made before c.1840. Good ones achieve a high degree of accuracy. Despite the name, the earlier ones were made throughout most of the Austro-Hungarian Empire. From 1870 they were mass-produced in large numbers in southern Germany. The quality of casework and hands deteriorated during the 19thC.

The clock shown above is a type known as the *Dachluhr* (roof top). It was made by Carl Suchy in Prague, c.1820 (lgth 38in/95cm), and is typical of the best Vienna regulators in its classic simplicity of design and high-quality movement. *PC*

* Precision regulators have seconds-beating pendulums that ensure accuracy. However, the seconds hand of many smaller Vienna regulators take only between 46 and 54 seconds to complete a revolution; this happens where the case is not long enough to accommodate a full-length pendulum.

There were three basic case types of Vienna regulator. The first to evolve was the *Laterndluhr* (lantern) (above right), in which the case is enlarged at top and bottom. This was followed by the *Dachluhr* (roof top) (shown left). The final style (above left) was more elaborate, with turnings and carving becoming more and more a feature of the cases. All types usually had a glass door and side panels.

CARTEL CLOCKS

Cartels are decorative spring-driven gilt clocks, usually with verge escapements. They were introduced in the 18thC. This French Louis XV example in a cartouche-shaped case is typical (ht 30in/76cm). *C*

Bracket, Mantel or Table Clocks

The term "bracket clock" can be confusing as it is unlikely that more than a few so-called bracket clocks ever rested on a bracket. The same is true of the term "mantel clock". To add to the confusion, the French version of the English bracket clock is usually referred to as a mantel clock.

To avoid inaccuracy the general term "table clock" is sometimes used to cover this range of clocks, although this has been more narrowly applied to just the earlier, usually all-metal, spring-driven clocks made in Continental Europe in the 16th and early 17th centuries. A further term sometimes employed for this group is "spring clocks", although this could also apply to many wall clocks.

The English bracket clock appeared in the 1660s. Whereas by the 1670s the longcase clock was being produced with anchor escapement and long pendulum, the verge escapement persisted on bracket clocks until c.1800. However, as with longcase clocks, the break-arch dial was adopted from 1715 and many other stylistic changes affected both types equally.

Silvered brass dials were used from c.1760, and painted dials from c.1780. An attractive alternative to these, usually found on high-quality clocks, was the hard enamelled dial.

Shelf clocks are peculiar to America. They were produced in large numbers in the 19th century, both in spring- and weight-driven versions. Often they took the form of simple rectangles, usually with glazed doors, and were shallow from front to back to make them suitable for standing on a shelf. In many ways they may be considered successors to longcase clocks.

DATING

The style and finish of the case provide a guide to dating, as does the shape of the dial. Ebony veneer was used c.1660-1850; walnut c.1670-1870; marquetry c.1680-1740; lacquer c.1700-c.1760; mahogany from c.1730; and rosewood from c.1790. Dials were square until c.1770; of broken arch form from c.1720; and round from c.1760.

CONDITION

It is quite common for the components of bracket clocks, especially early ones, to be missing, usually because these parts have given trouble in the past and are not essential to the running of the clock. The commonest of these missing features are the alarm mechanism, and the pull-quarter-repeat work, operated by a cord (when the cord is pulled the clock repeats the last hour and the quarter). Both of these features are expensive to replace. The indications that one or both of these mechanisms were originally present is a series of unaccounted-for holes in the backplate.

VERGE CONVERSIONS

Most bracket clocks made prior to 1800 originally had verge escapements, but many were converted in the 19thC to anchor escapements employing a large lenticular bob for the pendulum. This mars the appearance of the backplate, and thus most collectors would prefer the clock to be reconverted to its original verge escapement with small bob – again, a relatively expensive undertaking.

A rare form of American shelf clock made by Birge & Fuller, c.1850 (ht 26in/66cm), in which the clock is driven by a laminated spring rather like a cart spring. *DR*

* Initially shelf clocks had 30-hour weight-driven movements, but by 1816 some were made with 8-day movements.

Approximately 90 percent of bracket clocks produced before 1730 were ebonized, like this ebony-veneered bracket clock by Joseph Windmills, London, c.1690 (ht 13½in/34.5cm incl. handle). The beautifully engraved backplate is shown alongside (*right*). *DR*

BACKPLATES AND SIGNATURES

Before c.1670 backplates were plain. From that date restrained decoration began to appear. By 1680 the engraving was more profuse, the tulip being a motif commonly employed. By 1700 decoration was more elaborate still and remained so until c.1780. By 1800-05 the engraving was often confined to the border of the plates and the pendulum bob, and by 1820 had been largely discontinued. Before 1700 most clocks were signed in full on the backplate, as in the example above (c.1690), but after this date there is no clear pattern, some makers signing the backplate and others the dial.

Carriage Clocks

The spring was first used as an alternative to the weight for providing the motive power for clocks in the second half of the 15th century. This made possible the manufacture of watches and travelling clocks. However, it was only c.1780 that the French began to produce in quantity the travelling clock from which the carriage clock was shortly to evolve.

The first true carriage clock was produced by Breguet in Paris from 1810. In c.1830 Paul Garnier began to make carriage clocks in appreciable numbers, followed within 20 years by such firms as LeRoy and Raingo Frères. Between 1875 and 1910 the carriage clock was in the heyday of its production. Thereafter the number of clocks produced, and their quality, fell away dramatically.

Approximately 99 percent of all carriage clocks were made in France, but they were also produced in limited numbers in England by fine makers such as McCabe, Dent and Frodsham. These clocks are usually larger and more substantial than their French counterparts. American carriage clocks are comparatively rare. Styles usually follow French models.

Carriage clocks come in various degrees of complexity, from simple non-striking timepieces to striking, repeating and full, or *grande sonnerie*, clocks, which strike the quarter and hour at each quarter. (Those that strike the quarters only are known as *petite sonnerie*.) Other refinements are alarms, calendarwork and complex escapements. These added features increase the interest and value of the clock, but are liable to go wrong and are expensive to repair. Because of their relatively delicate nature, most carriage clocks require regular overhauling.

Decorative panels to the sides, back, occasionally the top, and also the dial, began to appear on carriage clocks from c.1870. Principally, these panels were pieces of Sèvres porcelain or enamelled panels from Limoges. This porcelain-panel carriage clock (ht incl. handle 7in/18cm) dates from 1890. Other forms of decoration included multi-coloured *champlevé* enamels. It is important that any panels or enamelwork are in good order; they are expensive to restore. *DR*

The moulded "gorge" case is the most classic of carriage clock case designs. This strike/repeat gorge-case carriage clock, c.1885 (ht incl. handle 7in/18cm), still has its original travelling case. *DR*

* Early case styles were squatter – for example, the rare "one-piece", popular from c.1835, in which the whole of the case other than the base and handle is made in one. The more flexible "multi-piece" appeared c.1840.

* Spare holes in the platform carrying the escapement, mounted at the top of the movement, may be an indication that the escapement has been replaced.

Miniature carriage clocks are more sought after and more expensive than standard sizes. This miniature oval clock (ht incl. handle 4in/10cm) has the typical white enamelled dial and Roman numerals. *DR*

* Giant carriage clocks are also relatively rare and will fetch between two and four times the price of a standard clock.

A fine *grande sonnerie* striking carriage clock by the eminent maker Henri Jacot (ht incl. handle 7½in/19cm). *DR*

* *Grande sonneries* can be silenced, made to strike the quarters only, or strike in full, by means of a lever beneath the clock or on the backplate.

Finely engraved decoration on cases first appeared in 1845. This large, beautifully engraved carriage clock, signed and numbered by Paul Garnier, with an attractive handle, dates from c.1860 (ht 7½in/19cm). *DR*

Longcase (or Tallcase) Clocks

The longcase was evolved, at least in part, to protect the weights and pendulum and make the clock look attractive. The verge escapement was used initially in conjunction with the short bob pendulum and a simple, classical design was employed for the cases. Early longcases were usually ebonized. Very few clocks survive from the period before 1670, and of those that do, many have been recased.

In 1670 the invention of the anchor escapement made possible the use of the long seconds-beating pendulum which simplified the fitting of a seconds hand. By this time the basic design of the longcase clock had been established and was to remain unaltered for at least two centuries.

During the 18th century America often imported English-made movements and dials; the cases were usually manufactured in America, frequently of cherrywood and, in the 19th century, mahogany. Comparatively few complete longcase clocks were made in the United States and thus they are more sought after than their English equivalents.

SIZE AND PROPORTIONS
Usually, the smaller the clock, the more keenly it is sought after; clocks made prior to 1690 were usually under 6 feet 9 inches (2.05m) and are highly prized. A slim, well-proportioned clock may be worth 2-3 times as much as a clock that is of similar age and quality but ill-proportioned.

ENGLISH PROVINCIAL CLOCKS
While fashion largely dictated clocks styles in London, there was more individuality in the provinces. There was also a time lag, with London styles being adopted more slowly in the country. The clock produced in greatest numbers outside London between 1690 and 1760 was probably the oak 30-hour longcase clock usually with a 10- or 11-inch (25.5-28cm) square brass dial. By the 1770s an increasing number of provincial 8-day longcase clocks were being made, some with oak or mahogany cases.

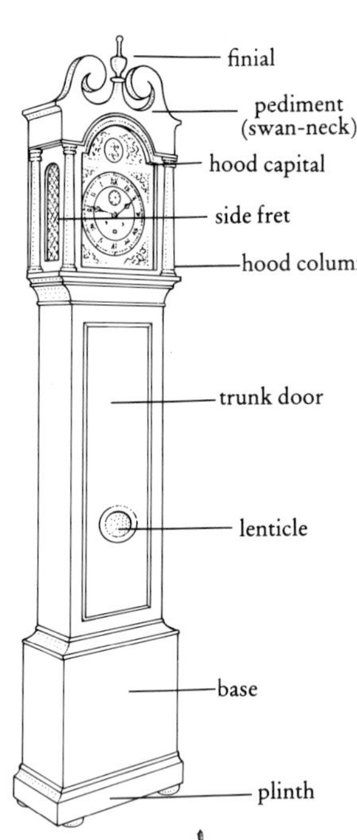

Features such as moon phases and complex calendarwork are much sought after by collectors and make this fine walnut longcase clock, c.1725 (ht 8ft/2.4m), very desirable. *DR*

A simple oak country longcase clock, c.1780 (ht 7ft 6in/2.3m) of 8-day duration. *DR*

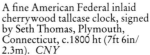

A fine American Federal inlaid cherrywood tallcase clock, signed by Seth Thomas, Plymouth, Connecticut, c.1800 ht (7ft 6in/2.3m). *CNY*

A mid-18thC green lacquer longcase clock (ht 7ft 7in/2.3m). *DR*
* Lacquer and chinoiserie decoration was at its height in the period 1715-40.

A walnut quarter-repeating month longcase clock, c.1690 (ht 6ft 11in/210cm), by Thomas Tompion (1639–1713), one of the foremost English makers of longcase clocks. *S*
* Tompion started to number his clocks in c.1685; this example is numbered 64.

DIALS
Initially most dials were brass. The painted dial began to be used c.1775. At first these were plain white all over, but fairly early on spandrels, either flat or raised gilt, appeared in the corners and these rapidly evolved into sprays of flowers. Moon phases were often depicted in the arch, sometimes accompanied by local buildings, scenes or ships. The amount of painted decoration on the dial continued to increase until by c.1840 the entire dial, except for the chapter ring, might be covered in decoration.

The value of a clock will be drastically reduced if its original dial has been replaced. This is not always easy to detect, although sometimes 4 spare holes may be seen in the frontplate.

CASE RESTORATION
The earlier the clock the more likely it is to have undergone extensive restoration: it would be rare to find the base rebuilt on a mid-19thC mahogany longcase regulator, but very common on a 17th or early 18thC walnut longcase clock – walnut is a wood particularly favoured by worms. Restorations are inevitable and to a degree acceptable, but they do affect the value. Reveneering is common, especially of walnut.

DURATION
If a clock has only a single driving weight suspended from a chain or rope, then it will almost invariably have a duration of only 30 hours (1 day). This type usually has less than half the value of an 8-day clock, which has two driving weights.

MARRIAGE OF MOVEMENT TO CASE
The case and movement were made by different craftsmen; the clockmaker "married" the movement into the case, often with indifferent results. It is sometimes possible to prove that the movement and case have always been together if the history of the clock has been recorded, or where there is a label in the door such as an equation table referring to the maker. If there is no such proof, the important factor is that the case and the movement are compatible and of the same age. It is only with the finer makers that it is important that the movement and case belong together.

MECHANICAL CONDITION
A clock that is going and fulfilling all its functions may need an overhaul, but this is not usually a serious problem. A cautious approach should be adopted toward a clock that is not working: new parts are costly.

MAKERS
With most longcase clocks the maker is usually not very significant although London names are preferred.

Skeleton and Novelty Clocks

The skeleton clock (in which the movement is left exposed) gradually evolved from the French mantel clock during the second half of the 18th century and probably first made its appearance in Austria c.1800. The earliest English skeleton clocks appeared c.1820, but from c.1840 English makers probably made at least ten times more than all the other countries combined.

Skeleton clocks were produced with a wide variety of brass frames – scroll, arabesque, Gothic, architectural and floral. Some showed a particular building or monument. The dials and escapements also showed considerable ingenuity. Movements were protected by glass domes, or shades.

Very few skeleton clocks were produced in America, apart from a few specialized pieces such as Aaron Crane's astronomical one-year-duration skeleton clocks.

During the 19th century in particular quite large numbers of clocks were made, primarily in America and France, that not only told the time but also intrigued in some way. Some of these take the form of an animal or person whose eyes move to and fro as the pendulum beats. In some clocks the moving feature operates only while the clock is striking.

Typical examples of novelty clocks are the glass-dialled clocks in which there is no apparent connection between the hands and the movement, and the statue clock. Skeleton and novelty clocks are both keenly sought after by many collectors.

An elaborate Swiss novelty clock, c.1880 (ht 24in/61cm), in which the movement is contained in the church tower. When a tune plays to mark the hour a man comes out of the church gates, the water and windmills turn and the ship rocks up and down on the waves. *DR*

This English skeleton clock, c.1850 (ht 21in/53.5cm), dates from the heyday of their production – 1840-90. Typically, it has a two-train fusee movement (one train for timekeeping and the other for striking). It is of fine quality, with well-executed hands and dial, and five-spoke wheelwork. The frame, which is in the form of a cathedral, is substantial, despite being delicately fretted-out. English skeleton clocks do not usually bear any maker's mark, but this one is signed by W. Powlton of Lancaster, England. *DR*

QUALITY

Quality is of paramount importance in skeleton clocks, where everything is on display. The wheelwork should be finely executed and the better clocks may have five or six spokes to each wheel instead of the four usually found on a bracket clock. Other signs of quality are well-executed pendulums, finely turned pillars, decorative colleting and clickwork and well-laid-out dials.

PROTECTIVE DOMES

It is not easy to find replacements for lost or damaged glass domes. A few standard sizes and shapes are available but usually it will be a matter of hunting around for an old one that approximately fits. However, even then, it is unlikely to be a good fit for the base and a new matching base may have to be made specially.

TARNISHING OF BRASSWORK

The brass frame of a skeleton clock is likely to tarnish gradually if it is not protected by a dome. If the brass is touched, unsightly finger marks that cannot be polished out will become apparent after a few months as the acid on the skin gradually attacks the metal.

The French made a series of clocks based on the Industrial Revolution, such as this "steam hammer", c.1885 (ht 20in/50cm), in which the hammer, acting as the pendulum, moves up and down. *DR*

* A popular model in this series is a ship's stern; the helmsman is part of the pendulum and rocks to and fro. Among the machinery and buildings copied were: beam engines, aeroplanes, lighthouses, railway locomotives and even gramophones.
* Nearly all these clocks, which are now highly collectable, were made to a high standard. However, their complexity makes them difficult to regulate and to overhaul.

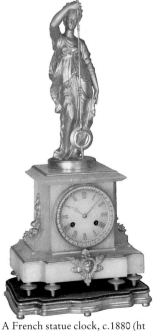

A French statue clock, c.1880 (ht 23in/58.5cm), whose pendulum, which swings to and fro as it is held by the outstretched hand of the girl, is apparently not connected with the movement in any way. *DR*

Reference

GLOSSARY

Anchor escapement An **escapement** shaped like an anchor. Introduced c.1670.
Arbor The shaft on which a wheel is mounted.
Automaton A clock with figures that move or strike.
Backplate The plate at the back of the movement.
Balance wheel The wheel that controls the going of a watch or clock.
Bezel The ring, usually brass, that secures the glass cover to the dial.
Bob The weight at the end of the **pendulum**.
Break arch An arch at the top of the dial on longcase and bracket clocks, first introduced c.1710.
Calendar aperture The window in some dials that displays the day of the month, and sometimes the month of the year.
Capital The cast brass or wood decoration at the top and bottom of columns, such as those on either side of the **hood.**
Chapter ring The part of the dial on which the hour numbers are engraved, attached or painted.
Collet A metal collar used to attach a wheel to its **arbor.**
Dial plate The plate to which the **chapter ring** and **spandrels** are attached.
Escapement The part of the clock that regulates it and transmits the impulse of the **train** to the pendulum or balance.
Escape wheel The wheel by which the pendulum or balance wheel, via the pallets, controls the timekeeping of the clock.
Finials Brass or wooden ornaments applied to the top of a clock.
Foliot A bar with adjustable weights attached, which acts as a balance in a **verge escapement.**
Fusee A conical spool that evens out the uneven pull of a **mainspring.**
Grande sonnerie A system of striking that repeats the last hour after each quarter has been chimed.
Hood The top part of a longcase clock, detachable to provide access to the movement.
Lenticle The glazed section of the trunk door of a longcase clock through which the **pendulum** may be seen. Used prior to 1715.
Lever escapement The **escapement** generally used on travelling clocks and watches, invented 1757; it employs two pivoted levers to connect the **pallets** and **balance wheel.**
Mainspring The spring that provides the power for the clock and drives its **train** of wheels.
Motion work The wheels and pinions that interconnect and drive the hands of a clock.
Pallet An arm or lever in the **escapement** that checks the movement of the **escape wheel** by intermittently engaging with the wheel's teeth.
Pendulum The device that swings at a fixed rate and controls the timekeeping.
Petite sonnerie A clock that strikes the hours and the quarters only, but usually **repeats** ***Grande sonnerie.***
Pinion A small, solid toothed wheel that engages with the larger clock wheels.
Plinth The base of a longcase clock.
Quarter chiming A clock that chimes each quarter-hour on two or more bells or gongs.
Repeat work A device that enables the clock to repeat the last hour or quarter when a cord is pulled or a button depressed.
Spandrels The decoration in the corners or arch of the dial.
Train An interconnected series of wheels and pinions used to transmit power – for example, from the spring to the striking mechanism.
Verge A rod with two **pallets.**
Verge escapement A mechanism used from c.1300 to regulate the movement (see page 138).

A SELECTION OF MAIN MAKERS

Not all clocks are marked; some carry the name of the retailer. Those makers who did sign their clocks usually used their full name, or, in the case of later French clocks, an abbreviation of it, or a stamp.

FRENCH CARRIAGE CLOCK MAKERS

Auguste, François (active from 1840) Paris.
Berolla (or **Berola**) (active 1820-80) Paris and London.
Bolviller (active from 1830) Paris.
Bourdin (active from 1820) Paris. Maker of exceptionally fine clocks.
Breguet, Abraham-Louis (1747-1823) Probably the finest of all French clockmakers. Designed the first carriage clocks but probably most bearing his name were made after his death. The firm continued into the 1950s.
Brocot, Louis-Gabriel and **Achille** (active 19thC) Introduced new forms of escapement.
Drocourt (active 1860-1900) Paris. Made large numbers of fine carriage clocks. Mark: "D & C" in a circle on either side of clock.
Garnier (active from 1825) Paris family of clockmakers, including Paul Jean.
Jacot, Henri (active c.1860) Le Locle. Mark: initials "HJ" and a parrot.
Japy Frères, Frédéric (1749-1813) and **Adolphe** (1813-97).
Maurice (active from c.1860) Paris company. Specialized in decorative carriage clocks.
Raingo Frères Paris. Family of 18th-19thC clockmakers.

FAMOUS ENGLISH MAKERS

Clay Family of London clock and watchmakers. Included Charles (active c.1730-50).
Clement (also **Clements**), **William** (active 1677-99) London. First to use anchor escapement in clocks, c.1676.
Dent, Edward John (1790-1853) London. Famous maker of all types of clocks. Made Big Ben 1850.
Duchesne, Claude (active 1689-1730) London and Paris.
East, Edward (c.1610-93) London. Watchmaker to the King.
Ebsworth, John (active 1657-1703) London. Made longcase, bracket and lantern clocks.
Ellicott, John (1706-72) London. Clockmaker to the King, Fellow of the Royal Society.
Frodsham London family of clockmakers, including William James (1778-1850), and Charles (active c.1850).
Fromanteel, Ahasuerus (1654-85) London. Member of family of watch and clock makers. First maker of pendulum clocks in England.
Gould, Christopher (active 1682-1718) London.
Jones, Henry (active 1654-95) London. Prolific maker. Mark: "Henry Jones in ye Temple".
Knibb, Joseph and **John** (active 1650-1711) London and Oxford. Made lantern, longcase and bracket clocks.
Loundes (also **Lowndes**), **Jonathan** (active 1680-1710) London. Watch and clockmaker.
McCabe, James (1780-1811). Firm continued by family until 1883. Fine carriage clocks and chronometers.
Massey (sometimes **Massy**), **Henry** (1692-1745) London.
Norton, Eardley (active 1762-94) London. Made watches and complex clocks.
Quare, Daniel (1649-1724) London. Eminent watch and clockmaker. Longcase clocks included several one-year models.
Stanton (also **Staunton**), **Edward** (active 1655-1707) London. Clocks include longcase and bracket.
Tompion, Thomas (1639-1713) London. The father of English clock and watch making. Marks: "Thomas Tompion"; "Thos. Tompion" (c.1680-1701, 1709-13); "Tho. Tompion Edw. Banger" (1701-1708); "T. Tompion G. Graham" (1711-13); clocks numbered from c.1680.
Williamson, Joseph (active 1686-1725) London. Watch and clockmaker.
Windmills, Joseph (active 1671-1723) Maker of watches and lantern, bracket and novelty clocks. Mark: "Joseph Windmills"; "Windmills" from c.1710 when in partnership with his son, Thomas.
Wise, John (active 1638-94) London. Member of family of watch and clockmakers.

AMERICAN MAKERS

Ansonia Clock Co. (1851-c.1930) Ansonia, Connecticut. Clocks included the Bobbing Doll and Swinging Doll timepieces.
Bagnall, Benjamin (1689-1773) Earliest known clockmaker in Boston. Sons Benjamin and Samuel were also clockmakers.
Birge & Fuller (partnership, 1844-48) Made shelf clocks, including steeple-cased models. Mark: "Puffin' Betsy".
Chandlee Clockmaker family in Philadelphia and Maryland from early 18thC. Included Benjamin, Goldsmith and Isaac.
Cottey, Abel (1655-1711) Philadelphia. Made longcase clocks with 8-day movements.
Crane, Aaron (active 1840-70) Made one-year clocks and others.
Curtis, Lemuel (1790-1857) Concord and Burlington. Made banjo, girandole, lyre and shelf clocks.
Terry Family of clockmakers (1792-c.1870), three members called Eli. In partnership with **Seth Thomas** and Silas Hoadley as Terry, Thomas & Hoadley, c.1808-10.
Thomas, Seth (1785-1859) Plymouth, Connecticut. Made a variety of clocks, some designed by **Eli Terry I**. Mark: signature; labels with company name.
Willard, Simon (1753-1848) Grafton and Roxbury. Invented the 8-day banjo clock in 1801.

GERMAN MAKERS OF MASS-PRODUCED CLOCKS

Becker, Gustav (1819-85) Freiburg. Mass-produced clocks and regulators.
Lenzkirsch company Mass-produced Vienna Regulators from 1870.

BIBLIOGRAPHY

Allix and Bonnert, *Carriage Clocks, Their History and Development* (1974)
Edwards, E. C., *The Grandfather Clock* (1971)
Ortenburger, Rick, *The Vienna and German Regulator* (4 vols 1979-87)
Palmer, Brooks, *The Book of American Clocks* (1979)
A Treasury of American Clocks (1967)
Roberts, Derek, *The English Longcase Clock* (1989)
British Skeleton Clocks (1987)
Robinson, T., *The Longcase Clock* (1981)
Rose, Ronald E., *English Dial Clocks* (1978)
Symonds, R. W., *Thomas Tompion: His Life and Work* (1951)
van Weijdom, F. H., *Viennese Clockmakers and What They Left Us* (1979)

RUGS AND CARPETS

Carpets and rugs have a long history. Excavations at the palace of the Assyrian king Assurbanipal, built over two and a half thousand years ago, revealed an alabaster floor carved with a design startlingly similar to the oldest surviving pile-knotted rug, known as the "Pazyryk", a highly developed and sophisticated carpet made at about the same time as the palace, and discovered in a frozen tomb in Siberia.

The Roman invention of the dome allowed architects to create vast spaces whose floors were given human scale by terrazzo panels decorated with squares, diamonds and circles – a bold repertoire shared with carpets of many kinds and all periods.

Giving the floor its due aesthetic consideration parallelled a significant growth in the production of handmade carpets in workshops established by rulers and wealthy patrons. By the time of the Dark Ages in Europe, a flourishing rug weaving industry existed in Egypt, while such cities as Baghdad, Damascus and Aleppo were carpet producers and exporters of equal distinction. Carpets may well have been woven in China for an even longer period.

In later centuries, miniature paintings from the Islamic courts of Persia, Turkey and India show the regal profusion of floor coverings, wall hangings and canopies. The great Classical carpets from the Safavid, Mughal, Ottoman and Mamluk realms are the survivors of this romantic age.

Oriental carpets have been collected by Europeans for many centuries and by the end of the 17th century they had entered the mainstream of domestic life. Interest waned in the 18th century but returned in the 19th as the fascination with exotic themes and a passion for all things Oriental swept through Europe and America.

There was a fall-off in demand between the 1920s and 50s, but in the 1960s there arose a new generation of collectors, able to travel widely and exposed to a wide diversity of cultural influences. Their knowledge, combined with heightened public awareness of creative interior design, has once again created a place for Oriental carpets.

There are probably more fallacies, misconceptions, half-truths and apocryphal tales surrounding "Oriental Carpets" than any other collecting area. There are very few consistent and reliable guidelines, and very little factual data with which beginners can equip themselves. Successful collecting depends on a good eye, and knowledge and experience acquired by observation and frequent handling. However, carpets are not as expensive as popular wisdom suggests. For the serious and informed collector there is still the opportunity to create a wonderful collection of woven masterpieces with a budget that would not stretch to even one fine item in some collecting areas.

This map shows the major rug-producing countries that are of most interest to the collector of antique rugs.

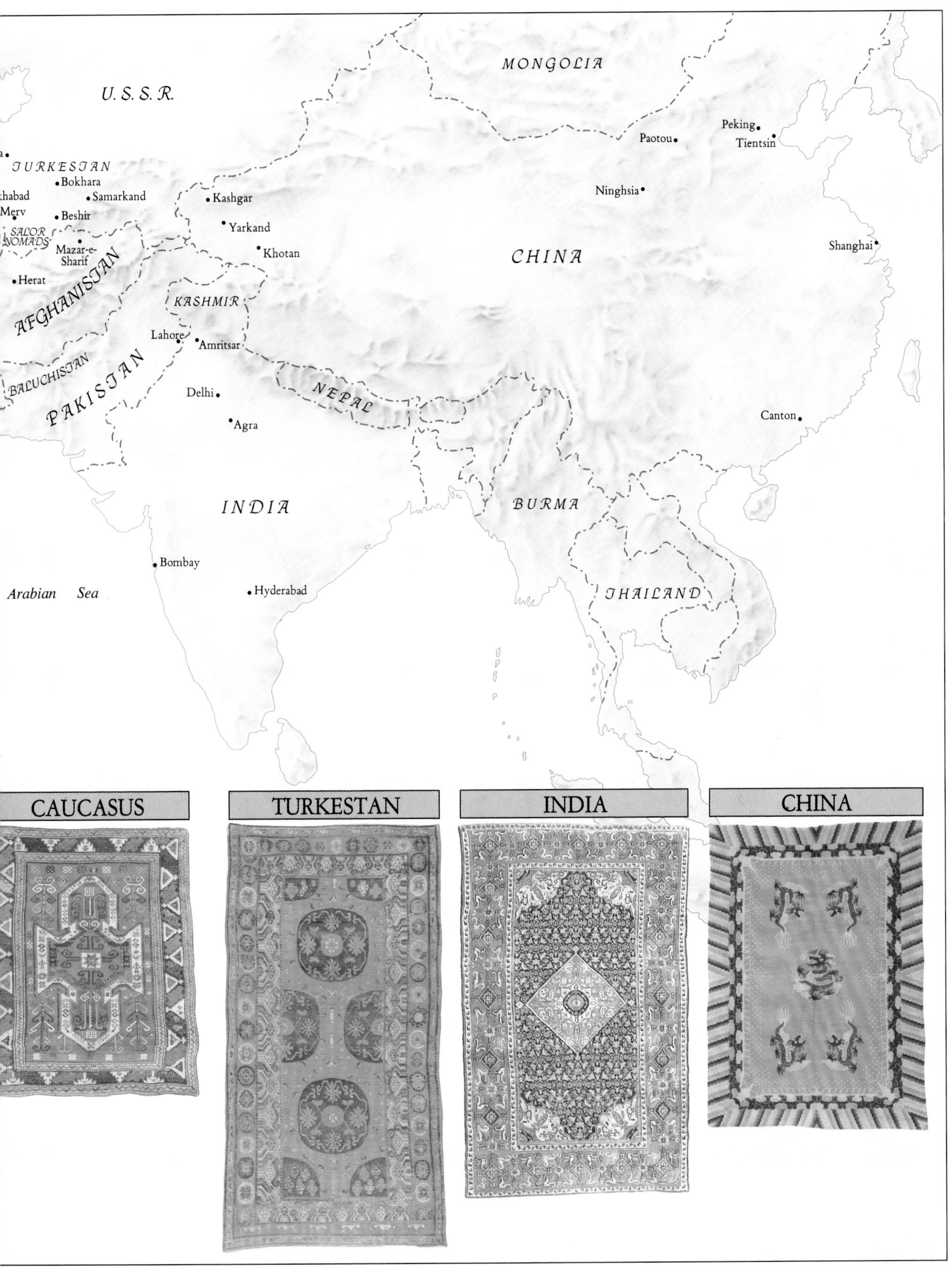
U. S. S. R.
MONGOLIA
TURKESTAN
Bokhara
Samarkand
Merv
Beshir
SALOR NOMADS
Mazar-e-Sharif
Herat
AFGHANISTAN
BALUCHISTAN
PAKISTAN
Kashgar
Yarkand
Khotan
KASHMIR
Lahore
Amritsar
Delhi
Agra
NEPAL
INDIA
Bombay
Hyderabad
Arabian Sea
Paotou
Peking
Tientsin
Ninghsia
CHINA
Shanghai
Canton
BURMA
THAILAND
CAUCASUS
TURKESTAN
INDIA
CHINA

Basics

RUG OR CARPET?

In Britain and Continental Europe the distinction between rugs and carpets is based on size. A piece small enough to hang on a wall, or up to approximately 6 feet (2m) long, is usually referred to as a rug. Anything larger is a carpet. However, in practice the terms are more or less interchangeable. In the United States all rugs and carpets are known as rugs.

COLLECTABLE OR DECORATIVE?

A confusing aspect of the field is the difference between collectors' pieces and decorative furnishings. More than 90 percent of the rugs and carpets the collector is likely to encounter belong to the latter category. However, the division is by no means clear-cut. Generally speaking, *decorative carpets* are large (the trade calls them "room-sized") and rarely more than 100 years old, if that. They are, for the most part, the products of town- and city-based commercial workshops established in the late 19thC, mainly in Persia, but also in all other weaving areas, to meet the demands of the affluent European and American market. Apart from the best decorative carpets, which are very highly priced and can be technical and aesthetic *tours de force*, these carpets remain primarily high-class furnishings.

Collector's pieces, on the other hand, were mainly made by nomadic tribal people or the inhabitants of countless remote villages. These fine collectable rugs and trappings are not necessarily any more or less proficiently made than their often much more expensive decorative counterparts, but as they were made essentially for domestic, ritual, ceremonial and functional use they retain the spirit of an ancient and sophisticated ethnic art.

* Rugs made by nomads in a tribal context tend to be made on narrow, horizontal looms that could be set up easily by tribes on the move.

COLOURS AND DYES

Colour is the most important factor in the assessment of any rug. The best colours are those achieved using natural vegetable and insect dyes, which were largely replaced after the last quarter of the 19thC by harsh commercially made dyes.

Natural dyes

Warm red colours are usually derived from the plant, madder. Occasionally, crimson comes from insect dyes such as cochineal, lac or kermes. Blue comes from indigo.

* The presence of cochineal indicates that the rug dates from after c.1850, when cochineal was first imported to the East.

Chemical (aniline) dyes

These were introduced toward the end of the 19thC. They are not colour-fast; colours tend to run or fade.

Chrome dyes

These are modern, first appearing in the early 20thC. They can be difficult to distinguish from natural dyes as they are colour-fast and don't fade. However, they lack the subtlety and sparkle of natural dyes, and are reproduced in a range of colours not available naturally, such as bright orange and yellow, electric blue and green, and some vivid pinks and purples. Chrome dyes are sometimes used in very small quantities as highlights in rugs that are otherwise naturally dyed.

HAND-MADE OR MACHINE-MADE?

The most desirable rugs are those hand-made by villagers or tribes. Also collectable, although slightly less so, are the rugs hand-woven in factories, which may have stiffer designs. Machine-made rugs, using loops instead of tied knots, are of no interest to the collector.

MATERIALS

The foundation material of a rug is usually wool, cotton or, much more rarely, silk. Wool is universal; silk is confined to certain areas. High-quality wool is fine and shiny. Poor-quality wool is harsh and coarse and lacks lustre. Although silk can be woven using the finest knots, it does not take dye well. With age, silk rugs become rotten or brittle, a condition known in the trade as *churuk*.

KNOTS

Rugs can usually be placed according to the type of knot used. The quality of the rug is determined by the fineness of the knots – the finer the knot, the more realistic the design that can be achieved. Knots are measured according to their number per square decimetre (15 sq. in): coarse Turkish rugs may have as few as 400 knots per sq. dm., whereas fine Persian or Indian rugs may have many thousands. A very finely woven rug will have only one weft shoot (crosswise packing thread) between each row of knots. Coarser rugs will have more wefts, thus saving on the amount of wool needed for making the knots.

The two main knot types are:

* Turkish, symmetric or Ghiordes, used in Turkey and by most of the Turkic tribal groups in Persia and Central Asia.
* Persian, assymetric or Senneh, used primarily in Iran and by some Central Asian groups.

The threads can be open to the left or right.

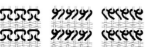

Turkish knot

Persian knot open to the left

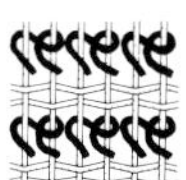

Persian knot open to the right

* The more finely knotted a carpet, the more hardwearing it is likely to be. Persian and Turkoman rugs are generally more finely knotted than Turkish rugs, which tend to be chunky, with large knots.

PILE

This is the upper surface of the rug. It can be either closely shorn or long and shaggy, depending on the local style. Both types of pile are equally acceptable.

* Many Oriental rugs have an uneven pile where corrosive metallic dyes have eaten away the wool. A few Turkish rugs produced since the end of the 19thC have reproduced this effect by sculpting the pile, to create areas that have different levels of relief. Such rugs should be avoided.
* Flatweaves are an important category of pileless rugs, which are not knotted but woven like a tapestry. Kilim is the most widely used flatweave technique (see page 157).

FRINGES

The presence of unworn or undamaged fringes usually means that the carpet is not very old, but otherwise fringes have no bearing on value. Fringes can be a continuation of the warps and may be braided, knotted or freely hung; or they may be attached, which is common in Persian rugs.

TYPES OF WEAVINGS

In addition to the familiar rugs and carpets there is also a range of other collectable weavings, such as tent bands, saddle bags, door rugs and weavings that depict important events such as weddings, woven specially for the occasion. A special type of rug is the prayer rug, on which Muslims kneel for prayer. They are usually small and finely worked, and often incorporate a *mihrab*, or prayer arch. Many prayer rugs come from Turkey, where they are widely used, whereas most Persian and Central Asian prayer rugs are made for the commercial market.

DESIGNS

There are thousands of rug designs and motifs: only experience will enable the collector to distinguish between them. The two basic background, or field, designs are the medallion (see page 151) and the all-over design, part of a larger repeat pattern (see page 156).

Borders

Almost all rugs have at least one main border. The narrow, minor borders are known as "guard stripes". The earlier the rug, the fewer the borders: early rugs usually have one main border and a tiny guard stripe. A proliferation of borders is not uncommon on rugs specifically intended for the Western market.

Symbols and motifs

Among the many thousands of symbols that appear on rugs from every region, the most universal is the tree-of-life. Floral motifs are common and animals sometimes appear, especially dragons. Many motifs have become progressively stylized since the 19thC and some designs have degenerated to the point where they can be very difficult to discern. The Moslem prohibition against the depiction of human figures is observed by Turks generally and also in Central Asia but is not widely observed elsewhere. Tribal rugs have a rich vocabulary of motifs, including goats, birds, wedding processions and other scenes associated with their way of life.

DATES

Some rugs have inwoven Islamic dates, which are generally reliable, except on Caucasian rugs (see page 154). However, the characters for 2 and 3 are very similar and the 3 may be changed to a 2 to suggest an earlier date. Sometimes only three characters are given: the 1 at the beginning of the date is implicit. Roman numerals sometimes appear on Armenian carpets after c.1900.

The first year of the Islamic calendar is AD 622, the date of the Pilgrimage of Mohammed from Mecca to Medina. The Islamic year is shorter than the Christian year by approximately one day every 34 years. For a quick conversion from an Islamic to a Christian date, add 583.

١	٢	٣	٤	٥	٦	٧	٨	٩
1	2	3	4	5	6	7	8	9

CONDITION

Condition is a factor in assessing value but even damaged rugs are collectable unless they are actually brittle or fall apart when touched.

All colours fade, especially in sunlight. Artificial colours are particularly susceptible to fading. However, a small amount of fading is desirable, as it can mellow the colours in an attractive way. The collector should beware of carpets that have been washed or bleached to give an appearance of ageing.

Fragments and damaged carpets can be stabilized, backed and mounted to be displayed as one would show paintings. Less seriously damaged pieces can be restored, often at considerable expense.

CARE AND ATTENTION

Carpets should not be dry-cleaned but may be cleaned by a professional carpet cleaner. Alternatively, they can be washed with plain warm or cold water and a mild detergent. Snow is effective for removing dust: the dust can be brushed off with the snow! Alternatively, dust should be beaten out regularly unless the carpet is very frail.

China and East Turkestan

Most surviving Chinese carpets have been woven since the late 19th century, specifically for the Western market, but behind them lies a long and varied history of urban production for the Imperial court and for Buddhist monasteries in both China and Tibet, as well as by nomads and oasis dwellers in the huge desert expanse of East Turkestan.

The attribution and dating of Chinese rugs is controversial, and the proper study of the Chinese tradition is still in its infancy. Some scholars say that carpet weaving was introduced to China by the Mongols in the 13th century, and that the production of carpets in an identifiably "Chinese style" did not begin until the end of the Ming Dynasty (1368-1644). However, recent archaeological evidence shows that knotted carpets have been made and used in China for several thousand years.

There are two main independent strands to traditional Chinese design. One encompasses a vocabulary of restrained small-scale pattern and refined floral forms, while the other is replete with graphic depictions of real and imaginary beasts and symbols of power, wealth and good luck. The influence of the nomadic Mongol and Turkic peoples in China's western provinces and along the Silk Roads to India and the West added a range of geometric designs to the repertoire, which were carried, along with ancient Chinese influences, to other cultures in westward migrations and conquests.

This mid-19thC Ninghsia pillar rug (8ft 11in × 4ft/2.72 × 1.22m) would have been used wrapped around a narrow wooden pillar in a Buddhist temple. Many Chinese rugs were borderless; the design should be read as continuous from edge to edge. The wide variety of symbols and motifs, without a strong central focus, is characteristic. *SNY*

* Other typical Chinese rugs include huge Peking carpets made for the Imperial court, monks' seat cushions and meditation rugs.

* An attractive 19thC Khotan carpet (12ft 3in × 6ft/37.3 × 18.4m) which shows a typical quincunxial (5 elements) medallion arrangement surrounded by floral sprays. *S*

* The fine carpets and prayer rugs made by the Islamic inhabitants of the East Turkestan oases of Kashgar, Yarkand and Khotan, in both wool and silk, have yet to realize their full potential as extremely desirable collector pieces and can still be acquired for relatively small sums.

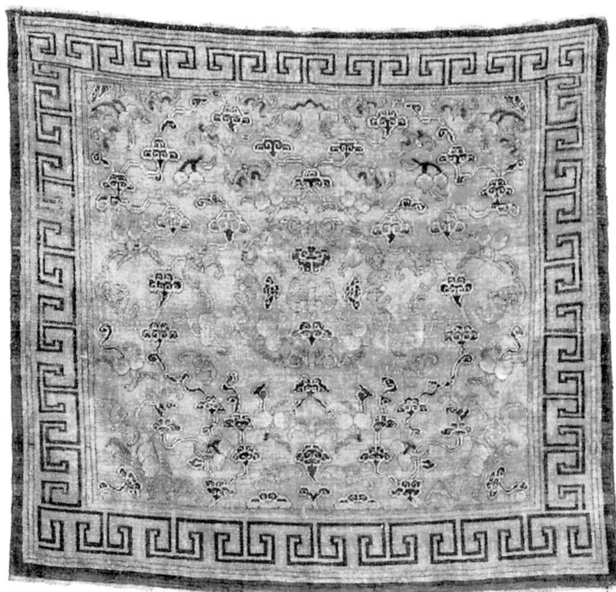

A wonderful rare late 18thC Kashgar silk mat (3 ft 5in × 3ft 1in/1.04 × 0.94m), woven on a silk foundation and in excellent condition. The design, while obviously of Chinese inspiration, is drawn with the graphic freedom typical of the best weavings from the oases of East Turkestan. *SNY*

* Some experts believe that small luxurious Chinese silk weavings with this format were made to be used as Imperial throne covers, which places them within an intriguing art-historical context, giving them an added cachet for the serious collector. Genuine early examples are also extremely rare; the one illustrated above is additionally remarkable for its excellent condition.

Kashgar silk carpets are especially rare. This lovely small carpet (4ft 8in × 3ft 3in/1.42 × 0.99m) was made around the turn of the 19thC. It is in fine condition and has excellent vegetable colours which have run slightly – a common occurrence in silk carpets. *SNY*

* The lily-patterned field is derived from 17thC Chinese textiles.

This early 19thC Chinese carpet (6ft × 3ft 11in/1.83 × 1.19m), although not in perfect condition, has the characteristic features of many good-quality Chinese weavings – a restrained and limited blue and ivory palette, an uncluttered field decorated with cloudbands and other motifs, and a chunky pile. *SNY*

Central Asia

The vast region between the Caspian Sea and the western borders of China is central to the history of Oriental carpets. It was home to the Scythian nomads in whose tombs the earliest known knotted carpet, made some 400 years before Christ, was discovered. Since the 8th century, warlike Turkish-speaking tribes have dominated Central Asia and successive waves of Turkic migrants have carried their culture and language as far west as the Mediterranean.

The carpets of their descendants who remained in Central Asia are among the most easily recognizable of all Eastern rugs. They are predominantly the work of tent-dwelling Turkoman tribes – Tekke, Salor, Yomut, Saryk, Ersari and others – and are distinguished by a rich and sombre palette with many different shades of red, blue and brown, wonderful glossy wool and complex geometric designs, laden with totemic symbolism. Typical Turkoman rugs have multiple rows of small medallions known as *guls* – a Persian word for flower. These are archaic insignia recording tribal origins. The Turkoman lands became part of the Russian Empire in the 19th century. Many nomads were settled around the oasis towns of West Turkestan, where they responded energetically to the same Western demand for fine commercial carpets that promoted the "Persian Revival" (see page 158).

A large proportion of the finest Turkoman weavings are in the form of various tent and animal trappings – tent door rugs (*ensis*), door surrounds (*kapunuks*), long bands used to tension the framework of the nomadic tent (*yolami*), storage bags (*chuvals* and *torbas*), as well as dowry and wedding camel decorations (*asmalyks* and *khalyks*), to name just the most common formats. Prayer rugs are rare, as are flatwoven items, and seldom high-quality.

In the past, the trade misleadingly called these Turkoman carpets "Bokharas", after the ancient Uzbek oasis town which has long been a principal trading centre for the region. Antique Uzbek carpets are quite different, and quite rare, being very loosely woven with long, chunky pile, unlike most Turkoman rugs, which generally have a short-cropped, even pile. They are sometimes known as *julkhyrs*, meaning "bearskins".

Rare antique Turkoman weavings are much sought after by specialist collectors and make some of the highest prices paid for 19th- and early 20th-century tribal rugs of all provenances. Their somewhat limited palette and restricted design repertoire are more than compensated for by their sophisticated nuances of detail and colour, serene layout and superior technical qualities, which rank them among the best of all Oriental carpets. Their rich tribal context, and the endless permutations of arcane variations of design, technique and attribution, have made Turkoman carpets largely the domain of a few specialist collectors (sometimes known as Turkomaniacs). The rarest types, irrespective of condition, attract fierce competition when they appear on the market.

This rare, 46-foot long (140m), Yomut mixed-technique (knotted pile and flatweave) tentband or *yolami* would have been used to hold together the wooden framework within the nomads' felt tent (*yurt*). The very best examples, such as this piece with its unusual piled white ground, are supremely collectable. Predominantly pile-woven tentbands, like this one, are the rarest type. *S*

The large main carpets of the various Turkoman tribes are identifiable by their consistent use of a restricted range of well-known tribal totemic symbols, or *guls*. This excellent mid-19thC Yomut example (10ft 4in × 5ft 11in/3.2 × 1.8m) has the design known as the *kepse gul*. *CNY*.

This rare Uzbek pile rug (5ft 11in × 3ft 4in/1.8m × 1m) from the late 19th or early 20thC, though not of outstanding quality, is eminently collectable because the stylized floral design is one usually seen, not on carpets, but on the famous *suzanis* – embroidered dowry textiles from the oasis towns of Central Asia such as Bukhara, Shakhrisyabz, Tashkent and Samarkand. *S*

GULS

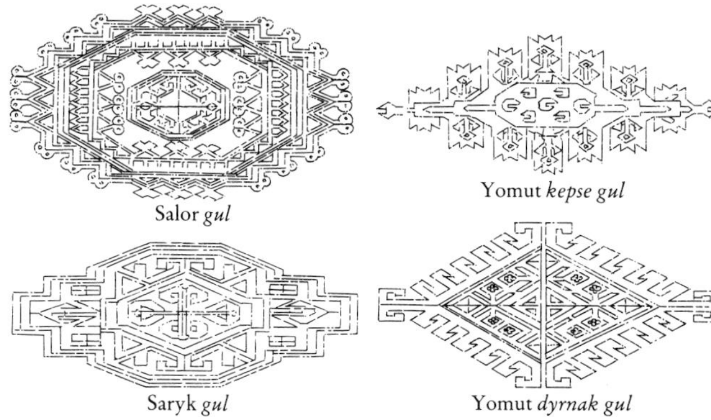

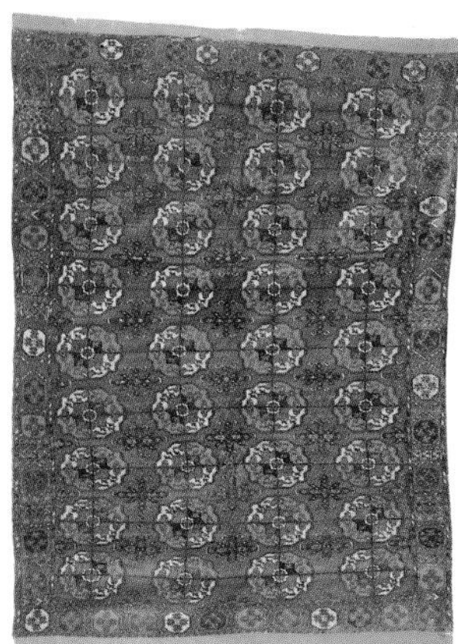

This large Turkoman carpet (8ft 1in × 6ft 1in/2.46 × 1.85m), one of a widely collected type, was made by the Tekke tribe. The relatively uncrowded field pattern with typical major and minor *guls*, the narrow, single, main border and the characteristic flatwoven ends are all indicative of a date before c.1880, when the introduction of synthetic dyes and a rapid escalation of commercial demand resulted in a dramatic loss of quality and artistry. *S*

* Later pieces tend to have a multiplicity of narrow borders, crowded fields with no "breathing space" between the design elements, flatter, more elongated medallions and coarser, harder wool.

Tent door rugs, or *ensi*, such as this 19thC Arabachi Turkoman example (5ft 6in × 4ft 7in/1.6 × 1.4m), are popular with collectors for their depiction of scenes of ceremonial life: the lower part of this rug shows a wedding caravan with camels bearing the bridal litter. They are also of a smaller and more manageable size than most Turkoman rugs. *CNY*

* Many dealers call these rugs "Hatchli", after the cross design dividing the field.

* It has been suggested that these rugs were intended as prayer rugs, or *namazlyks*, because of the niche at the top of the field; however, this seems unlikely.

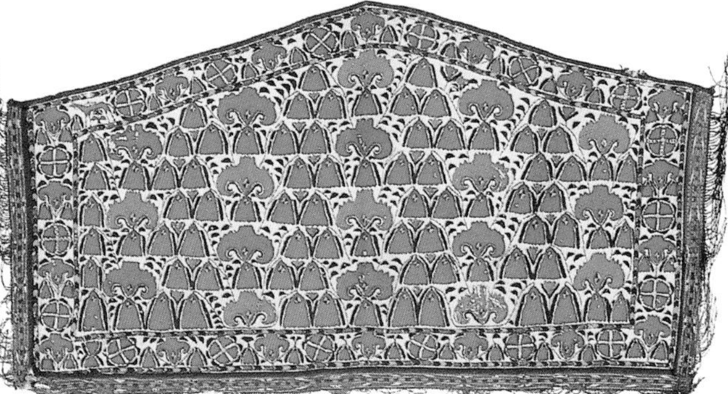

Not a rug at all, but a late 19thC unusual embroidered Tekke Turkoman five-sided *asmalyk* (4ft 6in × 2ft 4in/1.37 × 0.71m), which would have been used, like the more common knotted-pile examples, to adorn the bridal camel. Many serious specialist Turkoman collectors have recently opened their eyes to the great variety of artefacts, including animal trappings, tent decorations, storage bags and so on, made by these prolific Central Asian weavers. *SNY*

This 19thC Tekke *kapunuk*, or tent door hanging, for festive occasions such as wedding ceremonies (3ft 3in × 3ft/0.99 × 0.91m), although rather battered, is nevertheless a rare and extremely collectable item. *SNY*

* This design is more usually found on a type of tent bag known as a *mafrash*.

The carpets and trappings of the subgroups of the Ersari who live along the Amu Darya river in the southern USSR and Afghanistan are easily distinguished from those of other Turkoman tribes by their more varied, less busily geometric designs and wider range of colours. The design of this Beshir carpet from the second half of the 19thC (13ft 1in × 7ft 9in/3.99 × 2.36m) may derive from the ancient Chinese cloudband – the basis of many Oriental designs. *C*

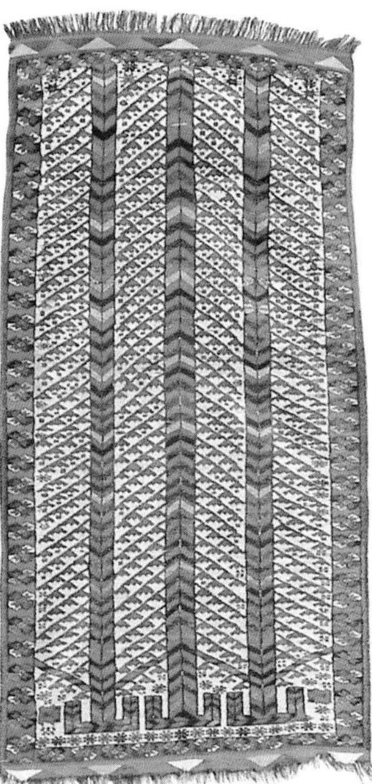

Lighter and more colourful than the weavings of other Turkoman tribes, this early 19thC Beshir tree-of-life rug from southwest Turkestan (6ft 9in × 3ft 5in/2.06 × 1.04m) has a wide appeal to the non-specialist collector. *PC*

* Many white-ground Beshir rugs have a prayer niche. Although this example does not, the three highly stylized directional trees would encourage some auctioneers to classify it as a prayer rug (which would be more expensive).

* Indian and Persian trees-of-life are more realistic than tribal ones.

Salor main carpets, sometimes called "S" group, are among the rarest and most imposing of all large Turkoman weavings. This handsome early part-silk example (9ft 8in × 7ft 8in/2.95 × 2.34m) is particularly rare and among the most expensive. *S*

* Salor trappings, like the tribe's main carpets, are rare, with extremely lustrous wool, a rich palette and superb drawing.

The Caucasus

The mountainous bridge between the Black and Caspian Seas is inhabited by many ethnic groups whose weavings include some of the most colourful of all Oriental rugs, many using powerful designs originating in the archaic Anatolian tradition. Few really early Classical Caucasian carpets survive. Many of the 17th- and 18th-century examples, such as the so-called "Dragon", "Blossom" and "Shield" carpets, were found in Turkish mosques. They appear to be largely the work of Armenians and Kurds whose traditional homelands straddle the border areas of Turkey, Syria, Persia and the Caucasus.

Most 19th-century Caucasian weavers were settled villagers using small looms, so their rugs are seldom large, and include a good proportion of prayer rugs and narrow runners. Rugs from the southern Caucasus (Karabagh and Kazak) are loosely woven with a long, lustrous pile dyed in strong, clear colours. Designs are simple and more dramatic than in the finely woven carpets from the north and east (Daghestan and Shirvan) which are more richly ornamented, using complex smaller-scaled geometric designs and a broader palette.

The flatweave tradition is strong in the Caucasus; and many distinctive kilims and *sumakh* (brocaded) carpets, bags and trappings were made in the 19th and early 20th centuries.

The best Caucasian rugs have a quality of direct warmth, colour and texture unmatched in most rugs from other regions, and are avidly collected. Examples in good condition formed one of the staples of the collector market, especially in Germany, for many years. They still command very high prices.

AGE AND AUTHENTICITY
Nearly all the Caucasian rugs and carpets on the market were commercially made between 1850 and 1920. Those dated to the 19thC by dealers are more likely to be from the first quarter of the 20thC or later. Those that do pre-date 1850 are much sought after. There is a perceptible loss of quality after c.1850-60, when a large volume of rugs began to be woven for export. The last five years have seen the emergence of a few convincing fakes of some of the most desirable types – good enough to deceive even experienced dealers.

COLOUR AND DESIGN
Caucasian rugs come in literally hundreds of designs and dozens of types which share a vocabulary of bold geometric forms. Good examples are known for their bright, vibrant colours.

CONDITION
Condition is particularly important to the value of this group. Collectors can benefit from the opportunity to buy somewhat worn, old and beautiful examples at prices that would be considerably higher if they were in good condition.

RESTORATION
It is not unusual to find Caucasian carpets which, apart from areas of damage, are in good pile. Generally, Caucasian carpets can be restored successfully, and many that appear to be in good condition will have had work done to them.

A Shirvan "Akstafa"-design rug, last quarter of the 19thC (9ft 7in × 3ft 8in/2.9 × 1.12m). Akstafa is in the Kazak district, but the style of the rug is typically Shirvan, with its "runner" format, medallions, fan-tailed birds and human and animal figures. *CNY*

This Shirvan prayer rug (5ft × 3ft 8in/1.5 × 1.12m) has the white field associated with rugs from the region. The Arabic date AH 1323 (1906) is repeated on either side of the prayer arch. *SZ*

* Superficially, Shirvan prayer rugs share many characteristics with other Caucasian prayer rugs and attribution can be difficult.
* Dates on Caucasian rugs should not be regarded as accurate: they were often woven into the rug by illiterate weavers who faithfully copied the design of another rug – date and all.

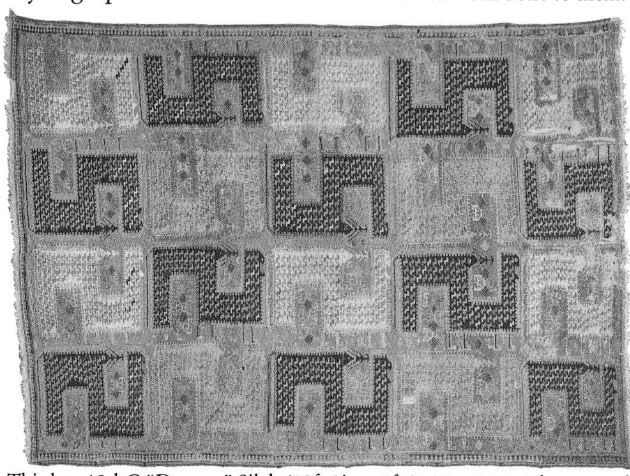

This late 19thC "Dragon" Sileh (10ft 3in × 7ft/3.12 × 2.13m) has one of the most striking and memorable designs of all carpets made with a brocaded, flatwoven technique. Some controversy exists as to how to read the large, zoomorphic "S"-like motifs, but this one justifies reading the design horizontally rather than vertically as is usually the case – 4 "legs" can be seen at the bottom of each dragon, or "S". Dragon Silehs have always been in great demand and in good condition sell for relatively high prices. This archaic and explicitly drawn example would offer an excellent opportunity to the discerning collector who would not be disturbed by its considerable wear. *C*

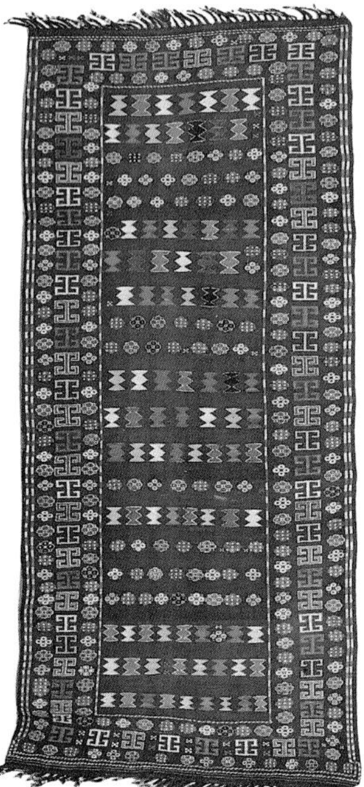

This well-drawn, brocaded mid-late 19thC flatweave (11ft 8in × 5ft/3.55 × 1.52m) is known either as a *Verneh* or a *Sileh*. It was probably woven in Azerbaijan, a region that straddles the modern border between northwest Iran and the USSR. *SNY*

This large 18thC Kuba carpet (18ft 1in × 8ft 7in/5.5 × 2.6m) belongs to the end of the great Classical tradition. Although it has a degenerate Dragon design, is worn and has some restoration, the carpet is still attractive. *C*

* Caucasian dragons are always heavily stylized. Toward the end of the 19thC the few beast-like details were abandoned, leaving the basic S-shape.

This carpet, second half of the 19thC (8ft 11in × 3ft 11in/2.7 × 1.2m), is typical of those from the Talish area, in its long narrow format, open dark blue field, inner frame of continuous zig-zag meander, or *medachyl*, and white ground border with squares and rosettes. *CNY*

This early Chelaberd rug, c.1850 (8ft 6in × 4ft 4in/2.6 ×1.3m), from the Karabagh area, has a well-drawn sunburst and good spacing. Such rugs are often fancifully called "Eagle" Kazaks (the eagle was thought to be a stylized version of the Imperial Russian eagle). Karabagh was once part of the northwest Safavid province of Azerbaijan with a large Armenian population; this explains the cross-fertilization of designs and traditions so prevalent in this rich weaving area. *C*

* Kazaks were once thought to be very rare, but this has proven not to be the case. Some are being faked in Anatolia and sold in Europe. However, these are usually obvious copies of widely publicized pieces.

KAZAK MOTIFS

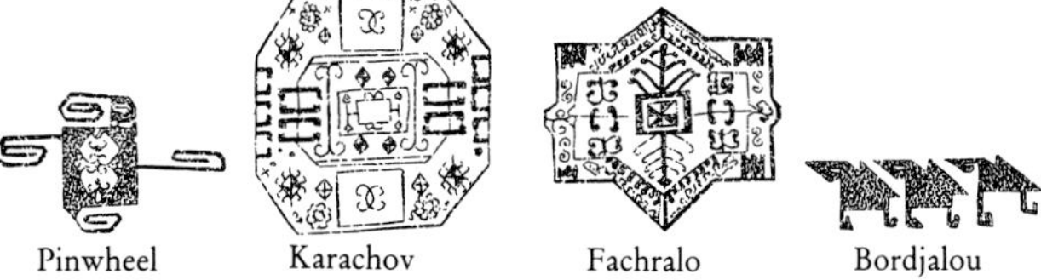

Kazak rugs are often named according to the distinctive motif that dominates them, but this attribution is somewhat arbitrary. The motifs above are each characteristic of a particular type of carpet. Some Kazaks have a combination of different motifs.

White ground "Star" Kazaks, like this example (7ft 9in × 5ft 2in/ 2.36 × 1.65m), are among the rarest of all Caucasian rug types and usually belong to the first half of the 19thC or perhaps even earlier. The design is quite unlike that of other Kazak rugs, except for the so-called "Pinwheel" or "Swastika" Kazaks (see below centre), which can be interpreted as a design variant of the Star. The ivory field is scattered with stylized floral motifs, birds and animals, typical of rugs from this area. *C*

* Genuine examples are rare but fakes abound. These are not as soft or resilient as the originals.

This 19thC Sewan Kazak, from the southwest Caucasus (7ft 10in × 5ft 3in/2.4 × 1.6m), displays the most dramatic and rare version of the "Shield" design. As with many other Kazak rugs, its design is an interpretation of much earlier Turkish village rugs. This rug is not only in excellent condition, but also an early member of the group, and sets a benchmark for comparison with others of similar design. *CNY*

* Some Classical carpets of the area, also referred to as having a "shield" design, are a different type of carpet altogether.

Turkey

Turkish carpets fall into two distinct and easily distinguished traditions. Tribal and nomadic weavers, drawing both on their Turkic heritage in Central Asia and on indigenous Anatolian iconography, produced boldly coloured carpets and kilims with timeless geometric designs (opposite page). The second type, woven in urban workshops or Imperial ateliers, is more formal and curvilinear, borrowing freely from the sophisticated style created in the Persian and Indian courts (this page).

Perhaps the most ancient type of village and nomadic weavings is flatwoven kilims. Woven throughout Anatolia, they are generally larger than pile rugs and, as domestic weavings, have preserved traditional designs longer than the knotted carpets, which were more influenced by commercial interests.

The more sophisticated urban workshop tradition flourished in the 16th and 17th centuries, mainly under the patronage of the Ottoman court. Ottoman carpet design was more naturalistic than the village and nomadic products.

In addition to the commercially produced workshop carpets associated with the Ushak area, exported to Europe in large numbers in the 16th and 17th centuries, there are many smaller rugs, often prayer rugs, which are directly connected with the court in Istanbul, although some of these may have been made in Cairo, then part of the Ottoman domain.

Production of collectable rugs in the prayer format in West and Central Anatolian centres such as Gördes, Kula and Ladik continued through the 18th and 19th centuries, and regained momentum in the early 20th with the fine silk prayer rugs from the Hereke workshops and from the masterweavers of Kum Kapi. These rugs are very pricey.

The particular aesthetic of some Turkish weaving can be elusive and less immediate than that of, say, Caucasian or Persian rugs. However, the rapidly increasing number of collectors who appreciate Turkish weaving is one of the most significant developments in rug collecting in the past decade.

This large, early 16thC fragment (6ft 7in × 12ft 2in/2 × 3.7m) is taken from what must have been a magnificent Ushak Medallion carpet. The intricate design of the main medallion, the presence of complex subsidiary medallions and the intricate floral infill indicate a carpet belonging to a highly sophisticated design tradition – a piece made for the Ottoman Court itself rather than for export. *S*

This splendid 16thC west Anatolian "Small Medallion" carpet from the Ushak region (7ft 2in × 4ft 7in/2.19 × 1.4m) is rare in being an early village workshop carpet in excellent condition. Its plain red field adds greatly to its serene elegance. *S*

* Early Turkish village rugs are today at the forefront of serious collecting. However, most examples are either heavily restored or damaged and fragmentary.

This 17thC "Bird" Ushak (5ft 4in × 3ft 4in/1.6 × 1m) is representative of the many Turkish rugs of its period woven in response to commercial demand in Europe and exported there in large numbers, particularly to the Balkans where many have been found in the Protestant churches of Transylvania. The so-called "bird" design is in fact a stylized floral pattern. *S*

Arabesque carpets, like this one from the Ushak region, c.1600 (4ft 11in × 3ft 9in/1.5 × 1.15m), were depicted by the Italian Renaissance artist Lorenzo Lotto (and others) in several paintings, and for this reason are popularly known as "Lottos". They were exported to Europe in great numbers in the 16th and 17thC, but very few have been found in Turkey itself. No serious collection of Turkish Classical rugs can be without one or more examples, whole or fragmentary, of this well-known group. *S*

* The field pattern depicted here is just a section of an infinite repeat design that draws on a much more complete pattern. Various sections of this complete design appear on many Lottos, although no two are alike.

An 18thC prayer rug (5ft 8in × 3ft 7in/1.73 × 1.09m) that draws on both traditional Anatolian village designs and workshop conventions from the previous century. *S*

* The prayer rugs from the Central Anatolian village of Ladik were highly sought after for most of this century, but demand has declined of late as collectors turn to the more obscure and challenging village weavings of lesser-known areas. The rather stiff and unfortunately coloured prayer rugs from Kula and Gördes (Ghiordes) have similarly fallen from favour.

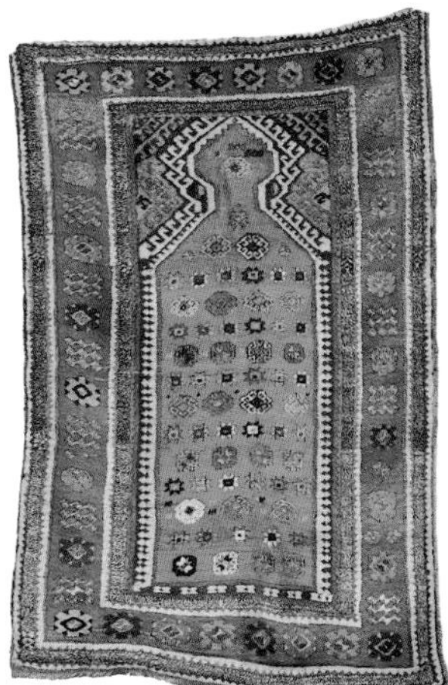

Yürük is the Turkish term for the myriad nomadic tribes of Central and Eastern Anatolia. Their rugs are distinctive for their long lustrous pile, bright colours, coarse weave and the profusion of abstract decorative infill. This mid-19thC prayer rug (5ft 4in × 3ft 5in/1.63 × 1.04m) is a very attractive and desirable example. As the rug is in good condition, the power of its design and its authentic tribal symbolism more than compensate for its relative coarseness. It is rugs such as this, as well as Anatolian kilims, that really typify the genuine Anatolian weaving tradition, and not the rather effete products of Turkey's urban workshops. *CNY*
* Very few such rugs pre-date 1800.

This rug, made in the west Anatolian village of Bergama in the third quarter of the 19thC (6ft 9in × 5ft 8in/2.06 × 1.73m), demonstrates the enduring strength of the formalized rug designs made in the workshops of the Ottoman Empire. Its so-called "Small-pattern Holbein" field design and serrated leaf border derive from the Ushak carpets of the 15th and 16thC. *CNY*
* Court workshop designs were often adopted and simplified by weavers from other villages. Such rugs may be placed by their colouring and shape.

Milas in southwest Anatolia has produced some of the most attractive of all Turkish village rugs, among them many prayer rugs, such as this example from the 19thC (4ft 11in × 3ft 8in/1.5 × 1.12m). *C*
* Southwest Anatolian prayer rugs are never very large, and have a delicate palette and a comparatively finer structure than rugs from most other Turkish villages.

CONDITION, RESTORATION AND MOUNTING
Many of the finest and oldest Turkish rugs and kilims survive only in a damaged state or as fragments. Until recently there was considerable market resistance to poor condition, but this attitude is changing rapidly as collectors begin to appreciate their qualities.

FAKES
The most competently produced fakes came, until quite recently, from the workshop of the Romanian masterweaver Theodor Tuduc. While it is rare to find reproductions of village rugs, quite a few convincing "very late" Classical carpets appear at auction. Auctioneers tend to indicate known fakes.

Yellow-ground Konya rugs with the Memling *gul* (6ft 5in x 5ft/1.95 × 1.53cm) are a very distinctive rug type from one of the richest weaving areas in Turkey – Central Anatolia. They generally have an archaic quality which recalls the famous 13th and 14thC carpets found in the Ala-eddin Mosque in Konya, but very few appear to predate the 18thC. *RB*

Anatolian kilims, like this 19thC example (12ft 11in × 3ft 6in/3.94 × 1.07m), seem to provide an authentic link with the earliest weaving traditions, in Asia Minor. Designs have retained elements of the clearly recognizable iconography of the Anatolian Neolithic culture. *C*
* After a period of obscurity, there is now enormous and growing interest in Anatolian kilims.

WEST ANATOLIAN PRAYER RUGS
The distinctive, stiffly drawn and rather formal 18th and 19thC prayer rugs made in the workshops of the West Anatolian towns of Gördes (Ghiordes) and Kula were once considered to be essential components of any serious collection of Oriental carpets. However, in recent years they have fallen out of fashion as connoisseurs have become more conscious of the merits of colourful and vital Anatolian village and nomadic weavings.

Persia

Nowhere in the rug weaving world is there a greater diversity of type, design, colour and technique than in Persia. Persian carpets have traditionally been woven in commercial workshops, in remote villages and in nomadic camps where rugs, trappings and kilims are not just items of trade but also essential articles of domestic use.

Carpet weaving reached its zenith in Persia during the 16th and 17th centuries. The Safavid court *ateliers* created exquisite Classical carpets and textiles, some of which found their way to Europe and, for the most part, now reside in museums and private collections. Their designs were mostly naturalistic, often alluding to the Muslim concept of Paradise as a garden. The court artists who drew cartoons for weavers were also manuscript illuminators. Their painterly style was dominated by curvilinear forms, fluid composition and the realistic representation of flora and fauna.

The quality and quantity of urban workshop weaving declined greatly in the 18th and early 19th centuries, until there was renewed impetus c.1860 in response to growing commercial demand from the West. Many of the large, high-quality, decorative Persian carpets, as well as a multitude of fine silk rugs and prayer rugs, were made during this "Revival Period". The best of these pieces show an artistic and technical virtuosity which makes them highly desirable.

Alongside urban production, tribal villagers and nomads, some of them Iranian but many of Turkic and Kurdish origin, wove the beautiful, small, brightly coloured rugs, tent and animal trappings and kilims, usually with totemic, geometric designs, that are so deservedly popular among today's collectors. Imposing larger carpets were made for tribal Khans. Today's nomads still weave, but their handsome traditional rugs and kilims are a thing of the past. Most modern weavings lack the spontaneity of genuine domestic work, and the quality of wool (often imported) and dyes (usually synthetic) rarely matches that of earlier pieces.

This early 17thC carpet (6ft 9in × 4ft 7in/2 × 1.4m) is one of the most interesting small Esfahan floral rugs known, not least for its extraordinarily fine state of preservation and bright unfaded colours – its condition was so good that it was thought to be a late copy. *C*

The design of this late 19thC fine Tabriz silk prayer rug (5ft 5in × 3ft 11in/1.65 × 1.2m) shows a strong Turkish influence. *C*
* The rust-red and yellow palette is characteristic.

The Qashqa'i of Fars Province are one of the major Turkic weaving tribes of Persia; their piled carpets and kilims have been collected avidly for many years and are testament to their often excellent quality and aesthetic attributes. This large carpet, almost 11 feet long (33.5m), has an indigo field overlaid with what is known as the Herati pattern, made up of a symmetrical arrangement of palmettes, floral rosettes and lancet leaves. The rug was most probably made by settled village Qashqa'i rather than a nomadic tribeswoman. *C*
* The Herati pattern is a Classical floral design found on many Persian rugs, consisting of leaves, palmettes and a central rosette.

COLLECTING AREAS
Most Western collectors in this area are concerned with the tribal weavings described above. There are also those specialists who collect carpets and weavings (very often in fragments) of the Safavid period. To do so successfully requires a great deal of detailed knowledge. The usually large carpets from urban workshops are for the most part used as grand furnishings. These two pages therefore concentrate on those types that are the staple of the modern Western collector.

This enormous carpet (27ft 10in × 8ft 6in/8.5 × 2.6m) has a design representing the Chahar Bagh or "Four Gardens", described in detail in the Koran as one of the features of Paradise. It would seem, however, that garden carpets pre-date Islam. When, in the 17thC, the Arabs sacked Ctesiphon, the Sasanian capital, they found the so-called "Spring Carpet of Chosroes", a huge weaving representing a garden, embellished with gold and silver thread and studded with jewels. It was cut up as booty and no part of it survives. *S*
* Garden designs appear on a huge range of Persian rugs and carpets, and, like prayer rugs, have a mystique that enhances their value. The "garden" consists of architectural-style floral motifs, laid out in compartments.

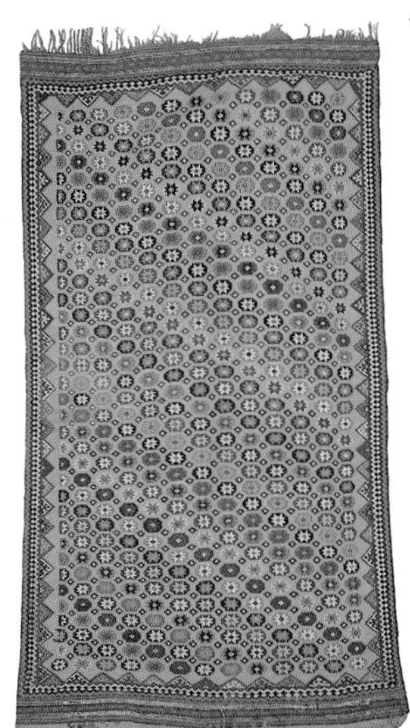

This splendid finely woven Qashqa'i kilim (9ft 10in × 5ft 4in/30 x 16.2m), with its rare yellow ground and the diagonal colour arrangement of the octagonal motifs, represents the upper end of the quality range in which these flatweaves are found. They have always been very popular with collectors, but vary widely in quality, from some of the most sumptuous Persian flatweaves, to weavings that are crude, dull and lifeless. Many pieces in the middle ground of these two extremes can have a combination of vegetable and synthetic colours (see page 150). *S*

Small Baluch carpets and trappings have, until recently, been avidly collected by those whose taste inclined towards the stark and sombre weavings of the Turkoman, but whose pockets were not deep enough. However, the very best Baluch rugs have a quality of wool and a range of genuinely archaic tribal design that equals any other group. Baluch rugs, such as this 19thC tree-of-life prayer rug (4ft 1½in × 2ft 10in/1.26 × 0.86m). *S*

Kurdish rugs from the Sehna (Sanandaj) region of western Iran (Persian Kurdistan) are characterized by all-over floral patterns which are derived from the 18thC brocaded textiles used to make shirts and waistcoats (*gilet persane*) in the Qajar court. This particular *boteh* design (4ft × 3ft 7in/1.47 × 1.09m) is more usually seen on the extremely finely woven flatwoven kilims from the area. *C*

A small saddle cover (3ft 6in × 3ft 2in/1.07 × 0.97m) made by the Kurds of northwest Iran, who are too often neglected in the history of carpet weaving, but who made many of the grand carpets of the Revival Period in the 19thC in such centres as Bijar, Sehna, Feraghan, Hammadan and Heriz. *CNY*

BOTEHS

Botehs are essentially floral or shrub designs that may have originated in India. Caucasian *botehs* tend to be more stylized than the fluid Persian ones.

Collectors have always been fascinated by woven trappings, perhaps because they are redolent of the life of the nomadic peoples of Asia. Their weavings were not merely utilitarian but were intended to bring colour and joy into an otherwise bleak existence. Many of the most elaborate were almost certainly woven specially for festive occasions. This wonderful brocaded saddle cover (6ft × 4ft 4in/1.83 × 1.32m) was made by the Shahsavan, a nomadic Turkic tribe from northwest Persia, whose name means "those who love the Shah". *CNY*

India

Carpet weaving is known to have begun in India at least as early as the 16th century, when the Mughal Emperor Akbar established workshops in Agra, Lahore and other cities, probably using skilled immigrant weavers from Persia. By the early 17th century, their reputation for quality was such that wealthy officials of the English East India Company began to commission carpets for export to Europe.

The best early Mughal carpets are among the most finely knotted ever made, using exceedingly fine, soft, shiny *pashmina* wool from the undercoat of the Kashmir goat. They are majestic, astonishingly beautiful and very rare; even the tiniest fragments, showing perhaps a single plant or a solitary blossom, are highly collectable and can be very expensive. The largest known collection of Mughal carpets comprises those made for the Palace at Amber, completed in 1630. These vary in size and shape: as well as rectangular and circular carpets, there are some irregularly shaped carpets, which may have been used as tent surrounds, or around fountains in the palace.

The style of early Indian weaving was clearly influenced by that of Safavid Persia, with which the Islamic Mughal Empire had close religious and cultural links, and also by the painting style of European illustrated books, such as Dutch herbals, which had reached the subcontinent by the 16th century. However, Indian weavers very quickly developed their own very distinctive designs which, during the 17th and 18th centuries, were typified by the highly naturalistic depiction of animals and flowers, often in lattice format, or *millefleurs* (thousand flowers) rugs and prayer rugs.

It appears that the craft was never firmly established and had almost ceased until, under colonial rule in the late 19th century, a substantial weaving industry was established consisting of cottage production, privately owned factories, and government workshops in the country's jails. Many of the most impressive large Indian decorative carpets, usually in derivative Persian-style designs but with a distinctive Indian palette, were the products of large looms in a number of prominent Indian jails.

Dhurrie making is almost certainly a native Indian craft and may well pre-date the manufacture of piled carpets by many centuries. As a major cotton producing country and one where, for obvious climatic reasons, heavy woollen carpets would not have been a natural domestic product, it is not surprising that these strong, flatwoven, cotton floor coverings were made in very large quantities. Using pleasing pastel colours, they were originally introduced to the European and American markets at very low prices.

Today, good old *dhurries* are highly desirable and can be very expensive. Neither 19th-century Indian pile carpets nor flatwoven cotton *dhurries* are collector carpets in the strictest sense, but the best examples are beginning to be collected by those with space to house them.

This extraordinary, grand 17thC Mughal carpet (6ft 9in × 4ft 4in/2.06 × 1.23m) has a most unusual geometricized field design in combination with more typical floral rosette and palmette borders. *S*

* The geometric repertoire is not typically Indian. Fairly naturalistic floral designs are far more characteristic.
* The weaving industry in India died out in the early 19thC but was revived at the end of the century. From this period on designs become markedly more degenerate.

When it was sold at auction this beautifully preserved Mughal silk carpet (7ft 3in × 4ft 10in/2.21 × 1.47m) was catalogued as 17thC, but the relative angularity of the drawing of the floral motifs suggests that it is 18thC – the motifs on earlier carpets are more realistically drawn, in a manner derived from Dutch herbal albums which reached India in the late 16thC. Whatever their date, complete Mughal carpets in good condition are exceedingly rare and most collectors have to be satisfied with badly damaged carpets or fragments. *S*

This incredibly finely woven (about 2,000 knots per square inch) *pashmina* wool mini-carpet (4ft × 2ft 8in/1.21 × 0.81m) was made in Kashmir in the early 20thC. Although not beautiful, it is a genuine curiosity, being a scaled-down copy of the very famous 16th or 17thC Safavid Persian cartouche carpet, pictures of which arrived at the Indian weaving centres at the beginning of this century. The weaving is so fine that the knots can barely be seen on the back. *S*

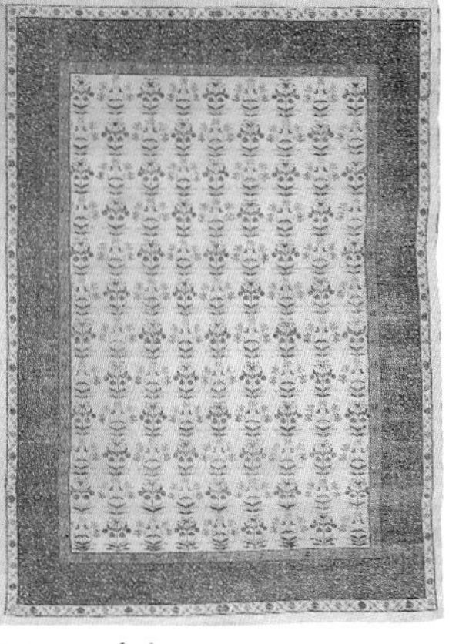

A turn-of-the-century carpet (13ft 5in × 9ft 8in/4.09 × 2.95m) from Amritsar in the Punjab, almost certainly made on one of the large looms installed in workshops in Indian jails. While not strictly speaking a collector's rug, as it is too large to display on a wall, it is nevertheless of interest as it replicates the freestanding realistically drawn floral designs found on the superb carpets of the Mughal Empire in earlier centuries, but in a palette adapted to Western tastes, rather than the more florid Indian colours. *C*

Reference

GLOSSARY

Abrash The variation of colour shades caused by the use of yarns from different dye batches.
Agra A type of large Indian decorative carpet.
Akstafa A popular type of carpet from the Eastern Caucasus, characterized by heavily stylized bird motifs.
Aksu ("white water") A stepped lattice Turkoman design.
Aniline dyes Synthetic, industrial dyes, often harsh, not always colour-fast, and inferior in tone to natural plant dyes. Widely used in all weaving areas after the last quarter of the 19thC.
Asmalyk or ***osmulduk*** A five- or seven-sided Turkoman camel flank decoration used at weddings.
Bakhshaish Large decorative northwest Persian village carpets.
Baluch The rugs of several different nomadic tribes.
Beshir The rugs of the tribe who live in the Beshir area close to the border between Afghanistan and Turkmenia.
Bijar Large decorative northwest Persian carpets.
Bokhara Old-fashioned "dealerese" for many types of Turkoman and Afghan rugs.
Boteh A leaf or shrub motif, with a curled tip, widely used in Persian, Caucasian and Indian weavings. The ancestor of the paisley pattern.
Brocade A richly woven rug with a raised design.
Cartoon The artist's drawing, usually on squared paper, from which the weaver works.
DOBAG (acronym) A type of modern Turkish rug made by a pioneering weaving project in Western Anatolia, using traditional designs and natural dyes.
Chajli An East Caucasian Shirvan rug type.
Chuval A large Turkoman tent bag.
Cicim A type of embroidered Turkish flatweave.
Cochineal, lac and **kermes** Brilliant red dyestuff derived from the crushed bodies of a particular family of insects.
Dhurrie A flatwoven cotton carpet from India, usually large.
Elem A skirt or panel in a different design above and/or below the main field, usually in Turkoman rugs and trappings.
Ensi A small rug, usually with a quartered **field**, used as a tent door by the Turkoman tribes. In outmoded "dealerese", a *hatchli*.
Field The background of a rug or carpet.
Flatweaves Pileless rugs, carpets and trappings in a variety of techniques.
Gabbeh A much sought-after south Persian domestic rug type, coarsely woven, with thick chunky wool, bright colours and bold abstract and pictorial designs.
Garden carpets Persian carpets of the 16th and 17thC, probably made in Tabriz, and depicting a conventionalized rendition of the
Gordes (Ghiordes) knot Also known as Turkish or symmetric knot. Used in Turkish, Caucasian, Kurdish, some Persian tribal and some Turkoman carpets.
Guls (Gols) The characteristic stylized geometric floral medallions found on Turkoman rugs, usually within some kind of lattice framework. Each tribe has its own style of medallion, supposed to represent the tribal totem.
Hajji Jalili An apocryphal Tabrizi masterweaver, the name sometimes used by dealers to describe a style and quality of Tabriz carpet.
Hejira The year of the Prophet Muhammed's pilgrimage from Mecca to Medina, and the first year of the Islamic calendar (AD 622).
Herati A widely used Persian floral repeat pattern with many variations.
Heriz Also known as Serapis, perhaps the best-known and most sought after type of large northwest Persian decorative carpets of the 19thC.
"Holbein" carpets Named after the painter Hans Holbein who depicted both "Large"- and "Small"-pattern Turkish Classical carpets of this type in his paintings.
Indigo The most widely used blue dyestuff. Synthetic indigo is one of the very few dyes that is identical to the naturally derived product.
Jufti knot A distinctive type of carpet knot, tied over several warp threads, characteristic of Classical carpets from Khorasan.
Kapunuk A Turkoman trapping used as a tent door surround.
Karaja Large, decorative carpets made by Kurdish tribes in northwest Persia.
Kazak The most desirable of Caucasian rug types.
Kejebe A widely used motif in Turkoman weavings.
Khalyk A decorative Turkoman trapping for the breast of the wedding procession camel.
Khila A type of Shirvan (Caucasian) carpet, usually decorated with ***botehs.***
Khorjin Saddle bags, usually for mules or donkeys.
Kilim *(gelim)* Rugs made with the most widely used flatweave technique, basically a weft-faced tapestry weave with some minor variations.
Kum Kapi ("Sand Gate") The Armenian quarter of Istanbul, which has given its name to a distinctive group of fine 20thC silk rugs and prayer rugs.
Lenkoran A type of south Caucasian rug with a distinctive crab-like medallion design.
Lesghi A type of northeast Caucasian rug whose main ornament is a highly stylized star.
Lori Pambak A type of carpet from the Southern Caucasus.
"Lotto" Distinctive type of Ushak arabesque carpet of the Ottoman period.
Lurs Tribal and nomadic weavers from Fars in southwest Iran.
Mafrash A large rectangular bedding bag (or a detached panel thereof) made by the Shahsavan and other nomadic groups.
Makri Type of West Anatolian village rug with an unusual design of two vertical panels with various designs in the field.
Malatya Tribal **kilims** from East Anatolia.
Mamluk Classical carpets with distinctive architectural medallion designs and a unique palette, made in Mamluk Egypt.
Marasali A distinctive type of northeast Caucasian prayer rug.
Memling gul A medallion design surrounded by hooks, first seen in carpets depicted by the painter Hans Memling, but widely used in Turkey and the Caucasus.
Mihrab The directional arch depicted on **prayer rugs.**
Millefleurs The all-over floral pattern seen on Indian Mughal carpets and **prayer rugs** and copied on some 19thC Persian prayer rugs.
Mina Khani A well-known floral design, used on many Persian, Turkoman and Baluch rugs.
Mohtashem The name of a semi-legendary masterweaver in Kashan in the late 19thC, now used to describe Kashan carpets of a certain quality.
Namazlyk A Turkoman prayer rug.
Okbash A Turkoman trapping, used to cover the ends of tent poles.
Palas A large, flatwoven, rug.
Perepedil A Caucasian rug design with ram's horn motifs.
Polonaise A rare type of fine silk and metal-thread Persian carpet, woven in Isfahan in the 17thC. Several were found in Poland.
Prayer rug A type of usually small rug on which the Muslims kneel to pray. Many incorporate a *mihrab*, or arch.
Rukorssi A small, squarish rug, often in mixed techniques, used to cover the eating surface in Persian village homes.
Runner A long narrow rug.
Saf A **prayer rug** or **kilim** with multiple **mihrabs.**
Sarouk A type of large west Persian decorative carpet.
Sehna knot One of the two main knot types (see page 150), also known as the Persian or asymmetric knot.
Selvedge Side-finished edging, formed by wrapping **wefts,** or inweaving supplementary yarns, around the outer **warp** threads.
Shoot In pile rugs, the passage of a **weft** across a fabric. One or more weft shoots follow each horizontal row of knots.
Sileh A type of flatwoven Caucasian **weft**-wrapped brocade with a characteristic S-shaped dragon design in rectangular divisions. Confusingly, called ***verneh*** in the Caucasus.
Sumakh A term that describes both a specific type of large flatwoven carpet and a wide variety of bags and trappings, made using a distinctive **weft**-wrapped brocaded technique. Many are made by the Shahsavan nomads of Moghan and Northwest Persia.
Talish Distinctive southeast Caucasian rug type, almost invariably in the **runner** format and often with a sparsely ornamented blue **field.**
Tekke The largest, best-known and most prolific of the Turkoman tribes.
Torba A Turkoman tent bag, somewhat smaller than a ***chuval.***
Transylvanian A variety of small, commercially produced Turkish carpets, made (probably in Ushak) in large numbers for export in the 17thC.
Vase carpets A distinct group of Classical Persian carpets with vase-type designs at the lower end of the **field,** which is covered by flowering plants.
Verneh see *Sileh.*
Wagireh A design sampler in the form of a small rug with full-size elements of all major parts of the design.
Warp The vertical threads in the foundation of a rug which run from one loom beam to the other. When a rug is completed, they are cut from the loom and may be made into fringes. The knots in pile rugs are tied to the warps.
Weft The horizontal threads in the foundation of a rug which are interwoven with the **warps**. In most **flatweaves**, the visible surface of the rug is composed of weft threads.
Yuncu A type of Anatolian **kilim.**
Yuruk Anatolian nomads and their carpets.
Zeikhur A type of Caucasian rug.

BIBLIOGRAPHY

General Books

Bennett, Ian, *Rugs and Carpets of the World* (1977)
Black, David (ed.), *World Rugs & Carpets* (1985)
Black, David and Clive Loveless, *The Undiscovered Kilim* (1977)
Brüggemann, Werner, and Harald Böhmer, *Rugs of the Peasants & Nomads of Anatolia* (1983)
Edwards, A. Cecil, *The Persian Carpet* (1953/63/88)
Eiland, Murray, *Oriental Rugs: A Comprehensive Guide* (1976)
McMullan, Joseph V., *Islamic Carpets* (1965)
Pinner, Robert and Walter B. Denny, *Oriental Carpet & Textile Studies, Vols. I-III* (1985/86/87)
Petsopoulos, Yanni, *Kilims* (1979)
Reinisch, Helmut, *Saddle-Bags* (1985)
Sylvester, David, and Donald King, *The Eastern Carpet in the Western World* (1983)
Stanzer, Wilfried, *Antique Oriental Carpets from Austrian Collections* (1986)
Thompson, Jon, *Carpets from the Tents, Cottages and Workshops of Asia* (1988)
Volkmann, Martin, *Old Eastern Carpets* (1985)

ARMS AND ARMOUR

Since the dawn of time man has been involved with weapons of war and other paraphernalia of conflict. Those who collect these relics today enjoy the past as one may enjoy history, reflecting on the bravery of leaders and heroes. This response is particularly appropriate to medals, which come under the umbrella category, militaria. Collectors of orders, decorations and medals will usually go to great lengths to discover the past service activities of the recipients.

Likewise, the collecting of uniform can be a fascinating pursuit. Although 18th-century uniform is hard to come by, the scope for the collector of 19th-century uniform is immense. Headdress is another major theme, and its popularity today is creating a highly priced market for the rarer specimens of the 18th and early 19th century. Other accoutrements, such as badges are more plentiful.

There are many more facets to militaria collecting – pictures, prints, postcards and even cigarette cards. And with diligent searching, a fine library of regimental histories can be acquired.

For the arms enthusiast an important factor to remember is that while you can collect all types of firearms without breaking the law, in most countries it is necessary to obtain a licence before firing any of them. In any case, all antique weapons should be examined by a qualified gunsmith before being used on a recognized shooting range.

Edged weapons is a large collecting area. The potential collector should avoid most 20th century items that do not fit into a clear line of historic development. A fine collection can still be assembled without going to great expense. In addition to bayonets, which are among the lower-priced edged weapons, European hunting hangers (bandsman's sidearms), made from c.1675 until the end of the 19th century, are still being sold at reasonable prices. Likewise, smallswords of the same period (if they are not silver-hilted) are still fairly inexpensive.

Another attractively priced area of edged weapons collecting is Eastern items. Many Indian, Persian and Arabic pieces are very well made and are now being appreciated for their quality. This will eventually lead to a noticeable rise in prices within a few years. Already the finer quality Eastern pieces are rivalling good European weapons in the figures they fetch at auction.

Armour is for most people prohibitively expensive: complete suits of armour are hard to find and rarely appear on the market. However, it is still possible to form an interesting collection, formed of various parts of different suits.

Spain

Britain

Italy

United States

With such a vast collecting area, and with so many stylistic variations between countries, it would be impossible to chart all the styles and developments. This chart therefore concentrates on the main British patterns and the periods when they were current. The most significant European and American developments are also shown.

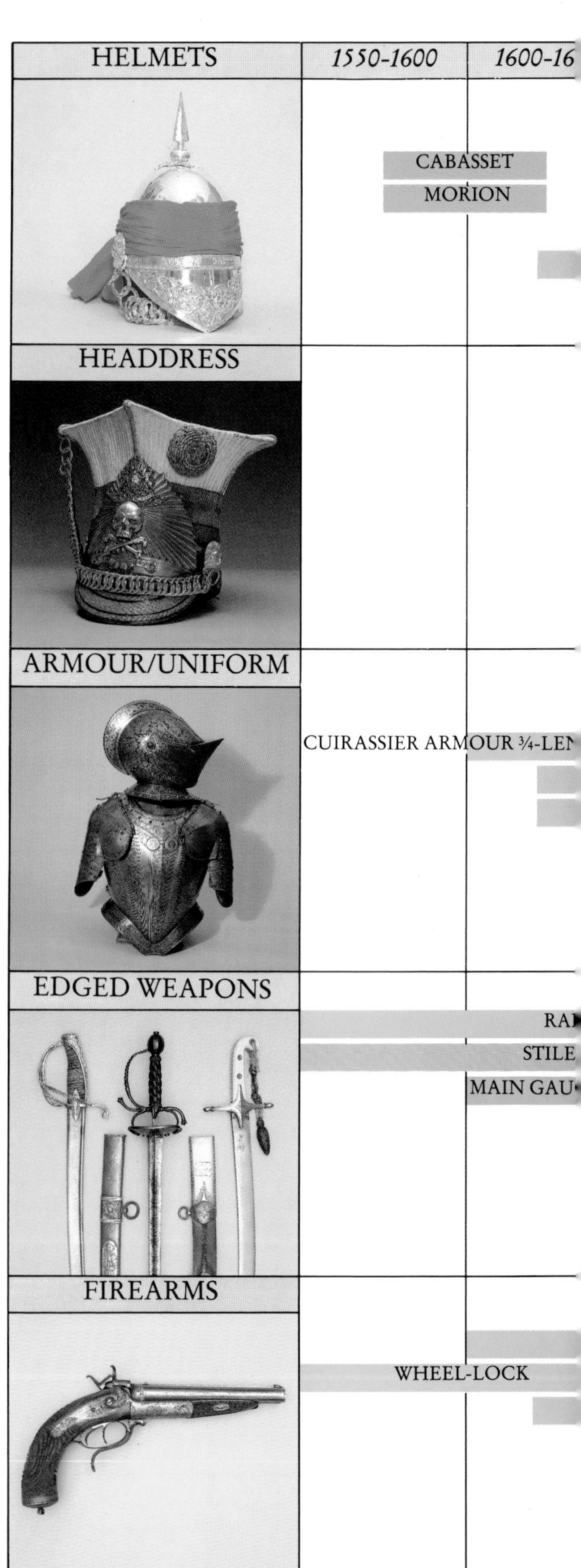

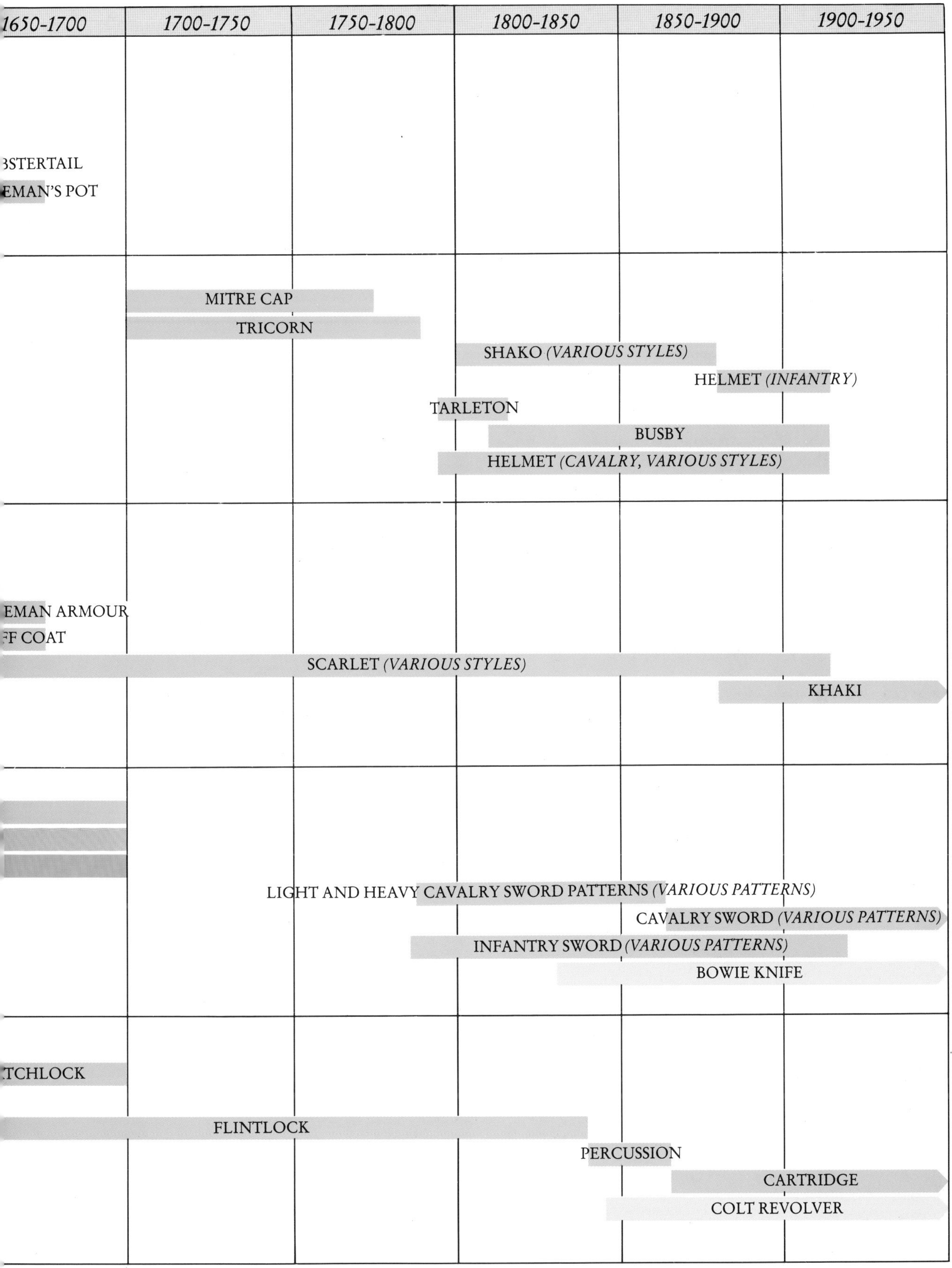

1650-1700	*1700-1750*	*1750-1800*	*1800-1850*	*1850-1900*	*1900-1950*

3STERTAIL

EMAN'S POT

MITRE CAP

TRICORN

SHAKO *(VARIOUS STYLES)*

HELMET *(INFANTRY)*

TARLETON

BUSBY

HELMET *(CAVALRY, VARIOUS STYLES)*

EMAN ARMOUR

FF COAT

SCARLET *(VARIOUS STYLES)*

KHAKI

LIGHT AND HEAVY CAVALRY SWORD PATTERNS *(VARIOUS PATTERNS)*

CAVALRY SWORD *(VARIOUS PATTERNS)*

INFANTRY SWORD *(VARIOUS PATTERNS)*

BOWIE KNIFE

TCHLOCK

FLINTLOCK

PERCUSSION

CARTRIDGE

COLT REVOLVER

Firearms I

The earliest forms of firearm, in use until the end of the 17th century, are the matchlock (a simple lever to hold a glowing slow-match) and the wheel-lock (which uses a mechanism). Both types are rare and are usually considered museum pieces. Survivors tend to be the higher-quality pieces, many of which were made for the nobility and are exquisitely decorated.

The two main types of antique firearms that collectors will encounter today are the flintlock and the percussion. Flintlocks, which first appeared in the mid-17th century, use a flint to strike sparks from a steel plate in order to ignite the powder charge. Percussion firearms, invented in the early 19th century, use a disposable metal cap containing a minute amount of solid explosive. The percussion method, although relatively unsophisticated, dominated firearms development until the widespread adoption of the modern metallic cartridge.

Many 17th-century firearms were made in Continental Europe. By the 18th century, gunmaking was firmly established in Britain, the most prestigious manufacturers being in London. This was the century of the sporting gentleman, and also of the famous Brown Bess musket that gave more than 100 years of faithful service to the British Army.

Duelling pistols were a fashionable affectation in Britain from the late Georgian to the mid-Victorian periods. Although seldom used for duelling, they were popular for target shooting, and by the mid-19th century specialized target pistols were available.

In the United States, Colonel Samuel Colt pioneered mass-production methods and interchangeable parts. Previously each individual firearm had been made as a separate item. Colt opened a workshop in London in 1852, and his pistols were frequently bought by British and Indian Army officers. However, Colt's monopoly did not last long, as a great number of imitations and improved weapons soon appeared on the market.

The change from ball and cap weapons to solid cartridge in the early 1870s marks a definitive break between antique and modern firearms.

English and Irish duelling pistols were generally made to a high standard. This pair of 20-bore flintlocks (lgth 17in/43cm) by Langson of Dublin, c.1780, is fitted in a mahogany case bearing the trade label "McDermott's of Dublin", probably the name of the retailer. *WAL*
* Duelling pistols are usually fairly light in weight for their size and should fit the hand well.
* Pairs of duelling pistols are much sought after, especially those that appear perfectly balanced when one is held in each hand.

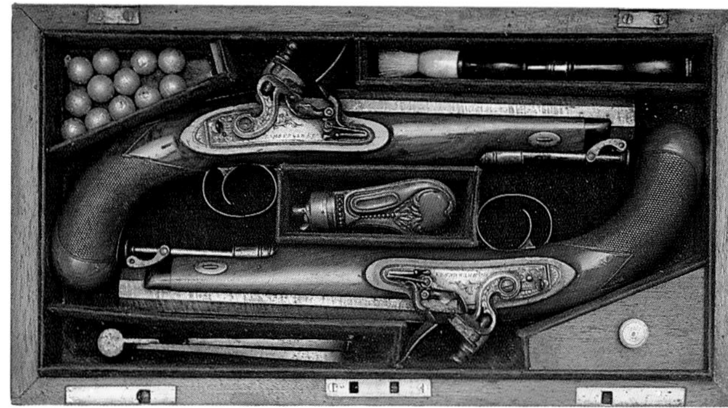

Army officers, who had to buy their own pistols, had priorities different from those of duellists. If their ramrod was dropped in battle, reloading was impossible and the weapon was rendered useless. This accounts for the popularity of the captive ramrod, held by an attachment below the muzzle. This pair of officer's 16-bore flintlock holster pistols, c.1810 (lgth 15½in/39cm), by the English firm Hamburger & Co., also features French-style cocks. The accessories – ball mould, flask, brush and turnscrew – fit snugly into the case and are probably original. *WAL*

Queen-Anne style pistols were popular throughout the 18thC. Today they are rare and very highly sought after, especially those made during her reign. English makers produced a variety of types. This holster pistol (lgth 11in/28cm) was made in England by Turvey, c.1730. It has many features peculiar to this type of gun:
* grotesque mask butts
* open-work side plates
* no wood, or stocking, forward of the trigger
* cannon barrel. *WAL*

This pair of small double-barrelled French boxlocks, (so-called because the locks were boxed in), c.1765 (lgth 5in/12.5cm), with highly decorated butts, has no maker's marks. They are typical of the anonymous "self-defence" pistols widely manufactured in France and Belgium during the 18thC. *WAL*

CONDITION

Breakage frequently occurs on the necks of the hammer or cock: check for cracks or signs of repair or even replacement. Pairs of pistols should always be looked at with one in each hand so that any restoration will be more readily apparent.

REPRODUCTIONS

Reproductions range from obvious decorative pieces to official commemorative issues of famous American guns. Examination of the marks on the barrel or stock, or in the case of a revolver, the frame or cylinder, may help to reveal whether or not the weapon is antique.

TYPES OF FIREARMS

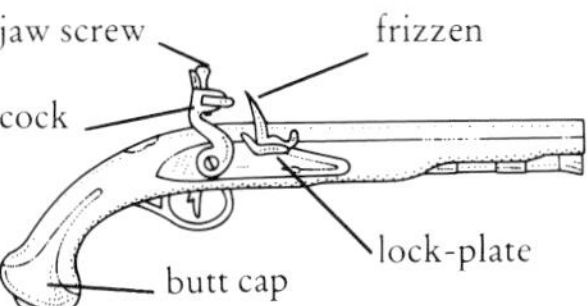

Flintlock pistol, late 18thC

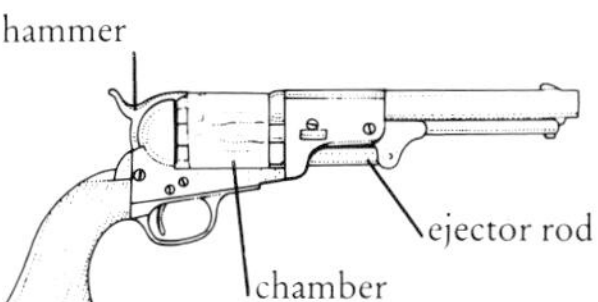

Colt solid-frame revolver, late 19thC

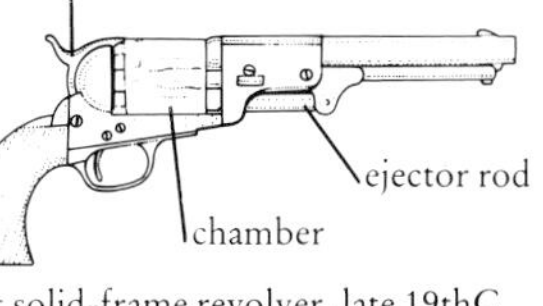

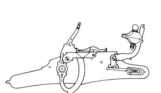

American Maynard lock, mid-19thC

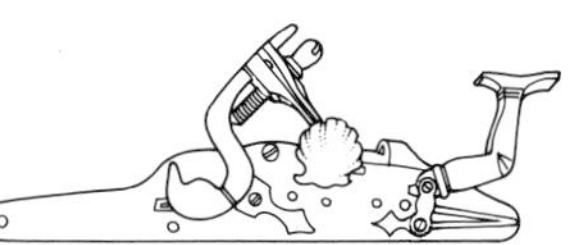

Forsyth "scent bottle" lock, early 19thC

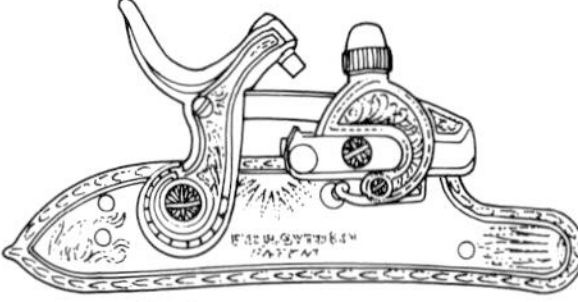

Segment lock

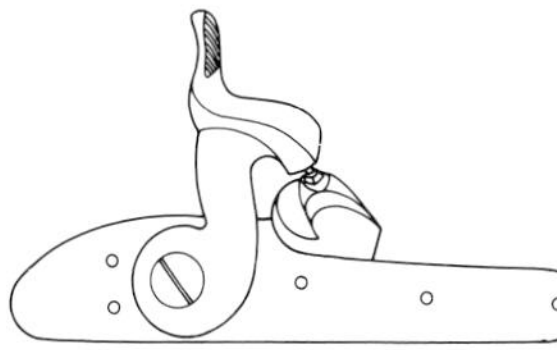

Percussion lock

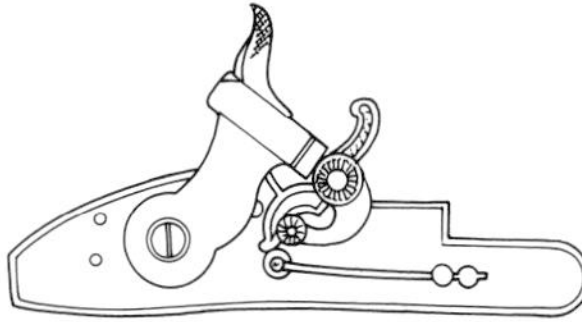

Netherlands lock

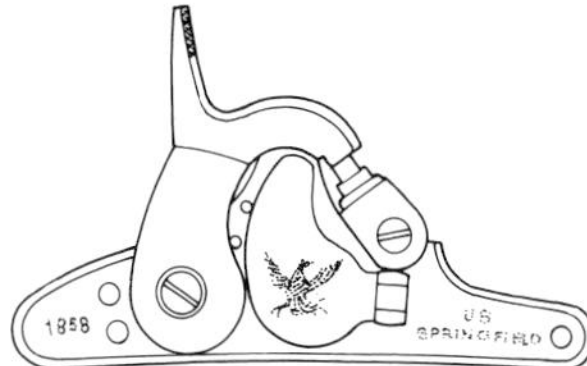

Tube lock

Some early air weapons have a strong resemblance to firearms. The octagonal barrel of this 1813 Austrian repeater (lgth 26in/66cm) looks substantial enough to take a full charge of powder, but the leather-covered iron air-reservoir simply unscrews for re-charging with a pump. *WAL*

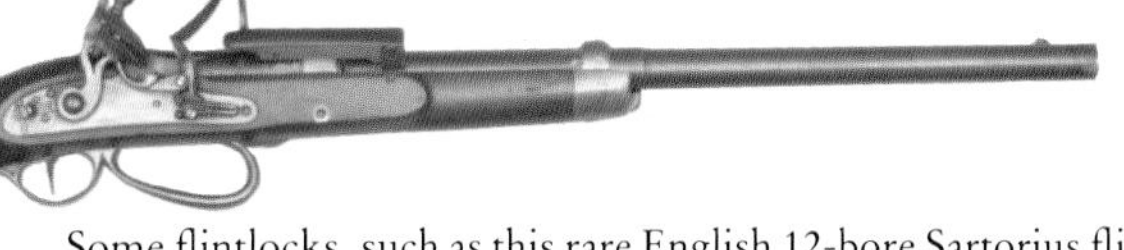

Some flintlocks, such as this rare English 12-bore Sartorius flintlock cavalry carbine, c.1820 (lgth 37in/94cm), have no ramrod and are loaded through an opening in the breech rather than down the barrel. Although quite rare, both sporting and military examples can be found *WAL*

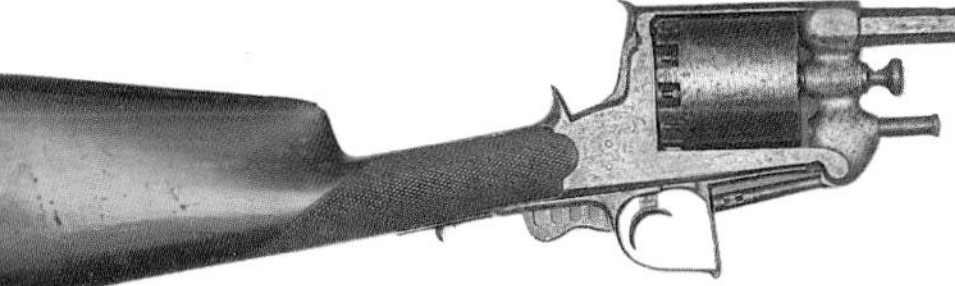

Although six chambers in the cylinder became the norm for handguns, the larger dimensions of a shoulder-arm permitted greater capacity. Hanson's patent 28-bore revolving percussion rifle, English (lgth 32in/81cm) has 10 chambers and a two trigger double-action. *WAL*

Blunderbusses have a flared barrel to enable different sizes of shot to be loaded. Although some have a bayonet or bayonet fitting they were not necessarily intended for army use. This example, c.1800 (lgth 30in/76cm), is fitted with a folding, spring-loaded bayonet and was intended to be used by naval boarding parties. *WAL*

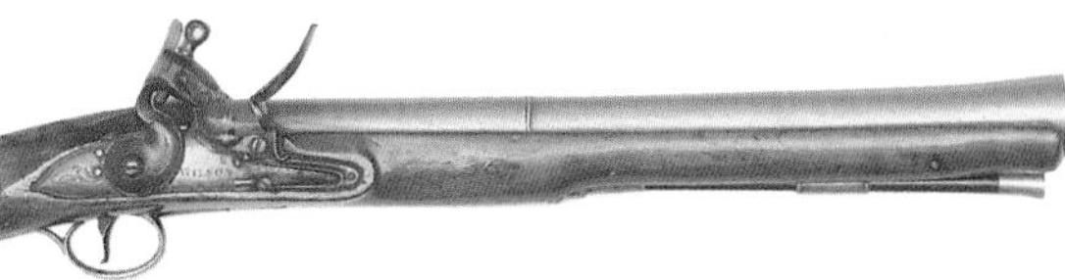

Gamekeepers and mail-coach drivers often carried a blunderbuss during the 18thC. This example (lgth 33in/84cm) is by the English maker, Wilson c.1765. *WAL*
* Brass was commonly used for blunderbuss barrels as it weathers the elements far better than steel.

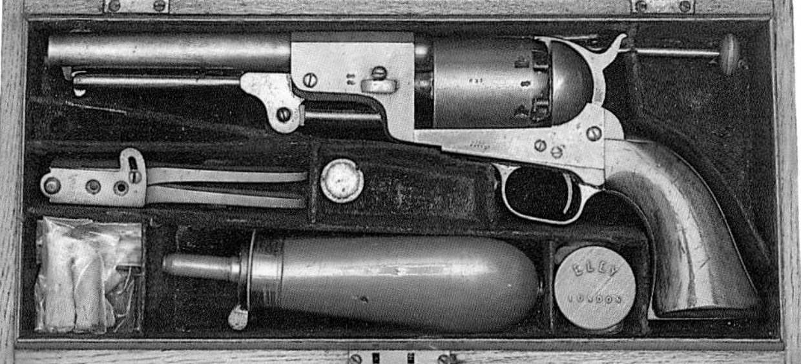

Although large and heavy, the six-shot 44-calibre Colt Dragoon Model 1848 percussion pistol was very effective. Colt Dragoons have Indian attack scenes engraved on the cylinder. This example (lgth 8in/20cm) was made at Colt's London factory, c.1855. *WAL*
* Mass-production methods meant that the components of a Colt pistol were interchangeable, but guns with matching numbers on all parts are very highly prized, especially if still in their original case, complete with accessories.
* The most collectable gun of the Colt range is the Navy Model.

BARREL SIZE

Guns are measured by bore size (imperial) or calibre size (decimal). Other weapons, usually flintlocks and percussion, are commonly referred to by their bore size; later ones by calibre.

PROOF MARKS

Most English firearms from the 18thC on bear the viewing mark (of the checker) and the proof mark on the barrel, guaranteeing that it was safe to fire at the time of examination.

Most European countries followed a similar system. Many pistols imported into England during the 19thC bear the Belgian Liège proof mark. Some Continental guns can be found with English proof marks.

Firearms II

CARE AND ATTENTION

Although the corrosive effect of gunpowder ignition is responsible for most of the pitting on antique firearms, many fine pieces have been spoilt by finger rust. Hastily put away after inspection, steel quickly acquires a reddish hue. Firearms should be wiped carefully after handling. Some collectors wear cotton gloves when picking up a gun. For long term storage, a good-quality furniture wax is preferred to heavy oiling, which can stain woodwork. Never leave an antique weapon with any mechanical part under strain, such as the hammer cocked.

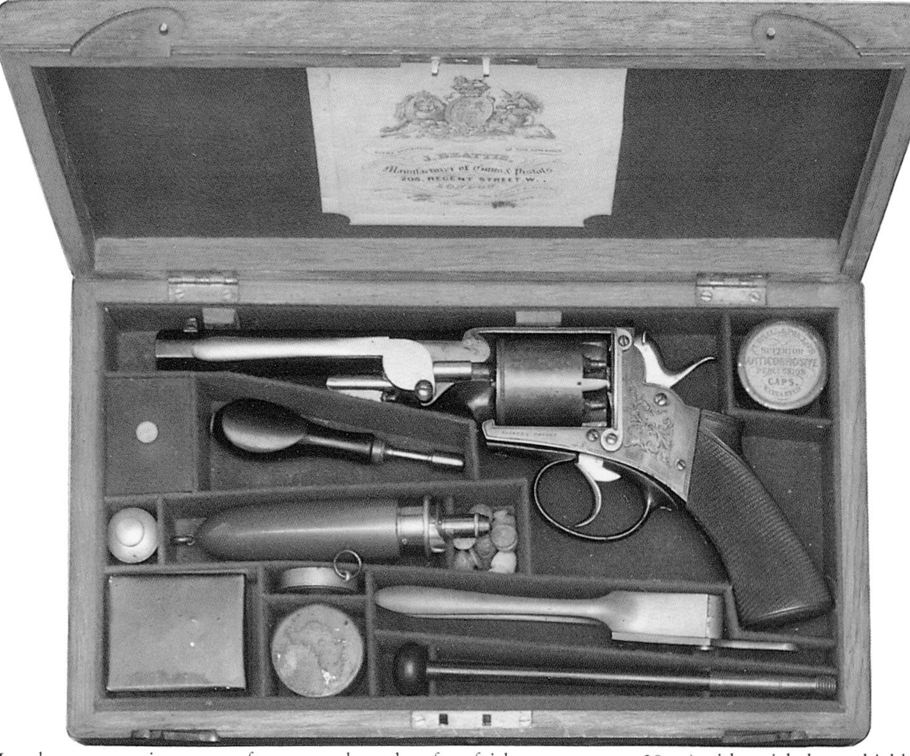

London was a major centre of firearms development during the latter half of the 19thC and many attractive and ingenious designs were produced. Some of these competed fiercely with Colt in markets throughout the world, and are therefore fairly widespread. Still with the maker's label, "J. Beattie, London", this original oak case contains a five-shot 54-bore Reeves' patent double-action percussion revolver (lgth 11in/ 28cm) with a nickel cap-shield behind the cylinder. Also included are the powder flask, oil bottle, cap dispenser, twin-cavity bullet mould, cleaning rod and ebony-handled nipple key with pricker. *WAL*

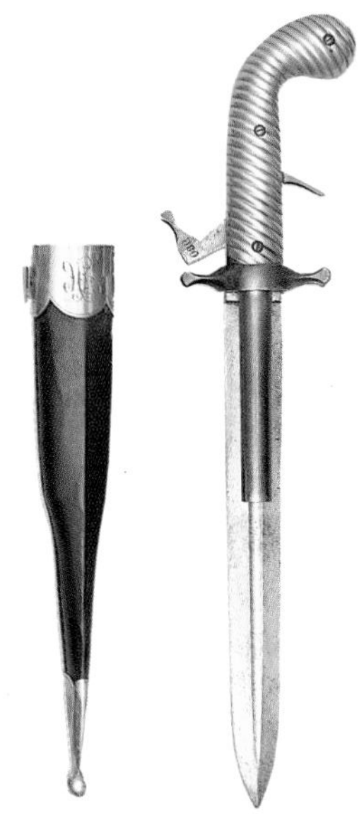

Combination pistols and daggers are seldom as graceful as this French 9mm double-barrelled percussion pistol dagger, c.1860 (lgth 12in/30.5cm). *WAL*

SINGLE- AND DOUBLE-ACTION AND SELF-COCKING REVOLVERS

With single-action, when the firer cocks the revolver with his thumb the hammer is drawn back and the weapon is cocked. With double-action, when the trigger is pressed the hammer lifts and returns in one movement. Self-cocking revolvers are fitted with double triggers, which allow the revolver to be cocked on the first pull of a trigger and fired on the second. Although these are the main actions, several variations were introduced.

PERCUSSION PEPPERBOX REVOLVERS

These date from the 1840s and are scarce today. They have several revolving barrels that turn each time the trigger is pressed so that the hammer strikes a fresh barrel each time. The weapon was probably designed more for self-defense than for attack. Many pepperbox pistols are unmarked, possibly because some makers did not want to be associated with a weapon that some people considered unethical.

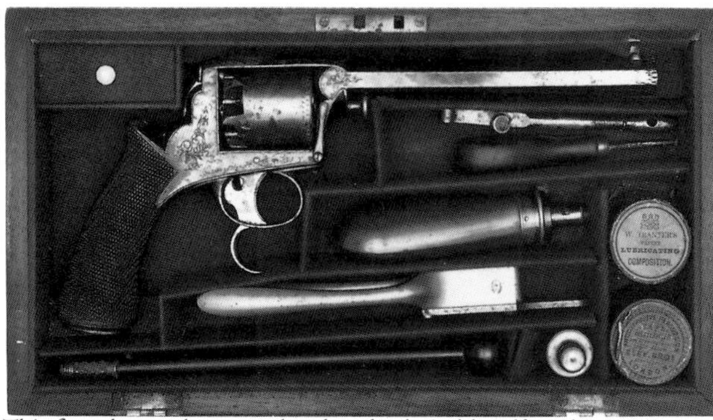

This five-shot 50-bore revolver has the desirable self-cocking action, patented by William Tranter (lgth 11½in/29cm).The frame is engraved "Adams" (a London gunmaker and relative of Tranter) and has a patent detachable rammer. The chequered grip, case-hardened cylinder and decorative scroll-work on the frame are typical of 19thC revolvers. The mahogany case has the original accessories, including bullet mould, powder flask, cleaning rod and lubricant. *WAL*

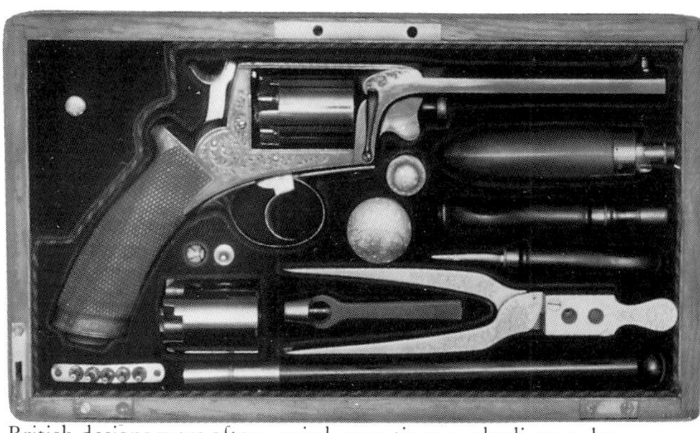

British designs were often copied, sometimes under licence, by Continental factories during the 19thC. This copy of the five-shot 54-bore Beaumont Adams revolver (lgth 11½in/29cm) has a typical Continental-style close-fitted oak case. The extra cylinder in the case is not a spare part, but was meant to be carried fully charged for rapid reloading. Such cased pistols were often purchased by colonial administrators as well as military officers. *WAL*

"Grapeshot" pistols were used by the Confederate States during the American Civil War. This 10-shot .42 calibre Le Mat "Grapeshot" revolver (lgth 12in/ 30.5cm) has a 16-bore shot barrel below the main barrel. *WAL*

This 26-bore holster pistol, c.1790 (lgth 16in/40.5cm), is by Wogdon of London, one of the ten most famous makers of duelling pistols. All his pistols command a premium. Cased pairs are especially valuable. *WAL*

Colt by no means had a monopoly over American manufacture. Produced by the Massachusetts Arms Company, this six-shot Wesson & Leavit revolver of c.1855 (lgth 11in/ 28cm) was single-action. Initially, the cylinder was rotated by hand; Wesson added the mechanical action. *WAL*

This six-shot .40-calibre double-action revolver, c.1860 (lgth 10in/ 25.5cm), superseded the pepperbox pistol. It has a fixed barrel and rotating cylinder, but retains the pepperbox-style flat hammer. It in turn was replaced by the solid-frame revolver. *WAL*

Remington is another name that evokes the Wild West. This six-shot .44-calibre single-action Army revolver, 1858 (lgth 12in/ 30.5cm) was used throughout the American Civil War. *WAL*

Spanish pistols are often extravagantly decorated. This double-barrelled 12-bore percussion pistol (lgth 10in/ 25.5cm) has the date 1856 in silver inlay on one barrel. The hammers have a chiselled serpent's head design and there are engraved external lock springs. *WAL*

George IV's visit to Scotland generated enthusiasm for national costume, and "traditional" all-metal designs of firearm were produced throughout the Victorian period. This example by Brown & Rhodds, c.1855 (lgth 9in/23cm), has a spring belt clip on the other side, and is highly decorated with a dolphin hammer and ram's horn-style butt. *WAL*

Pistols sometimes had a detachable shoulder stock to provide steadier aim at long distances. This 1856 pattern cavalry trooper's percussion pistol (lgth 15in/38cm) is the only such type adopted by the British Army. The stock is marked "N.S.Y. 5 troop 23" (North Somerset Yeomanry). *WAL*

HANDLING FIREARMS

Never point agun at anyone. Never assume a gun is unloaded. Looking down the barrel while holding a lighted cigarette, you can ignite a dormant, 100-year old powder charge. To confirm that a gun is unloaded, take the ramrod and measure the length of the barrel from the outside. Then insert the rod in the barrel to see if the length compares: if it does, the gun is probably unloaded. If in doubt treat the gun as loaded and seek expert advice.

Never cock an unloaded gun and pull the trigger; always ease down the hammer or cock with your thumb. Flintlocks are especially likely to suffer from invisible fatigue. Firing a percussion pistol without the cushioning effect of the metal cap (which contained the explosive) may break the hammer, and at the very least will damage the nipple, on which the cap was placed.

Militaria I

As well as weapons and armour, there is a wide variety of antiques associated with the militia, known collectively as militaria. They include uniforms (particularly headdress), badges, fastenings (such as shoulder belt plates and waist belt clasps), medals and various other items such as trophies, documents, postcards and paintings and prints of military subjects. Some collectors specialize in a particular category. Some limit their interest to items that relate to a specific regiment. Others concentrate on a particular period of military history.

UNIFORMS

Relatively few early 19thC uniforms survive, for as well as receiving an exceptional amount of hard wear, they are particularly susceptible to moths. Old uniforms should be carefully checked for holes and thinness, but a certain amount of wear is inevitable. Buttons are usually original, but contemporary replacements are acceptable. Short-tailed coatees were the dress of the day for regiments throughout the Napoleonic Wars, after which the British army became very foppish: coatee tails were lengthened almost to the back of the knees and headdress became larger and more ornate.

Drummers

During the Napoleonic period the drummers wore tunics made of the facing colour of their regiment's uniform – for example, the Gordon Highlanders had a scarlet coatee with yellow collar and cuffs; the main colour of the drummers' uniform would thus be yellow with scarlet facings.

THE CAVALRY HORSE

Cavalry horse accoutrements constitute a significant collecting area. The brass martingale (horse breastplate) is designed with regimental devices, often within a crown garter. Horse throat plumes, worn on full-dress parades, are made of horse-hair hanging in a brass mount and dyed to the regimental colours. Shabraques (horse cloths) are sometimes very elaborate. On the hind quarters bullion-woven regimental titles and devices may be found. In the early 19thC they were worn in battle, but since then have been used only on full-dress parade.

This post-1902-style dress uniform of an English officer has a white swan's feather plume on the headdress: the "undress" uniform would have a white horsehair plume. *WAL*

MILITARY HEADDRESS

Most collections begin with headdress from the end of the 18thC; earlier specimens (such as tricorn hats, mitre caps and grenadier fur caps) are rare. All British infantry headdress carries a badge bearing the regimental number. This system lasted until 1881, when the county regiment (the Cardwell system) was introduced. The first standard pattern for clothing appeared in 1768. By 1800 shakos were worn by most British regiments. The blue cloth helmet was issued from 1879 and worn until 1914 and thereafter only on ceremonial occasions and by bandsmen.

Cavalry regiments and other arms of the service (such as Dragoon Guards, Dragoons, Light Dragoons, Hussars and Lancers) also went through several changes of style.

Distinctively coloured plumes were used by regiments to identify each other quickly on the field. The colours of all regiments are well-documented. The colours for the last pattern of the Lancers' headdress were as follows:

5th Lancers – green
9th Lancers – black and white
12th Lancers – scarlet
16th Lancers – black
17th Lancers – white
21st Lancers – white

A shako is a type of headdress which is usually cylindrical and has a plume. In England there were eight different styles between 1800 and 1869. The "stove-pipe" design of this example, c.1800 (ht 7in/18cm), was first used at the beginning of the 19thC. *WAL*

Because it was worn in the famous battle, this headdress, the second of the eight designs, introduced in 1812, is referred to as the Waterloo shako. It has a false front to give an impression of height (with false front 8in/20cm). In 1816 it was replaced by the slightly bell-topped Regency shako. *WAL*

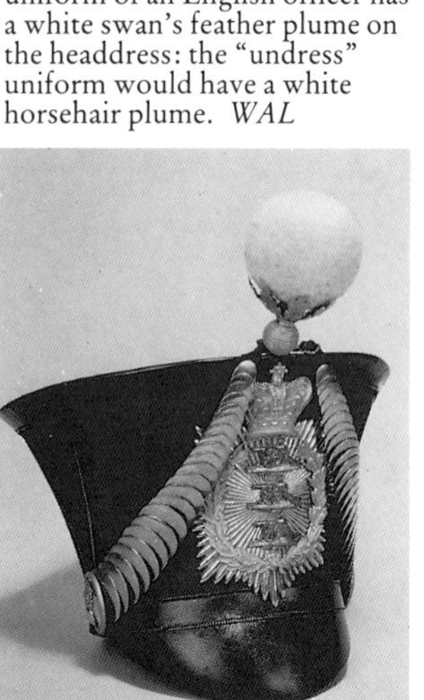

The "bell-top" shako, the fourth design, introduced in 1829, remained in service with the British army for 16 years. This Royal Artillery officer's shako (ht 7in/18cm) dates from 1831/2, a date confirmed by the style of device on the badge. *WAL*

* The woollen ball plume of this shako is shorter and of a different style from its predecessors. It never returned to the height of the earlier patterns.

* Like British shakos, Continental shakos went through several changes of shape. Many countries adopted and adapted each others' styles, or patterns.

The cylindrical "Albert" shako (ht 8½in/21.5cm) was the fifth British army design, issued in 1845. It was superseded in 1854 by the French-style shako, which was smaller, with a forward slope. *WAL*

* The penultimate design was the quilted shako, 1861-8. From this date shakos were not as deep. However, the quilted padding soaked up rainwater and the style was superseded in 1869 by the last pattern shako, which was unquilted.

Continuing a style that originated in the First Empire, this French dragoon officer's gilded helmet, with its brush-like horsehair plume, dates from 1858 (ht 15in/38cm). The turban surrounding the helmet at the ear bosses is also made of horsehair. *WAL*

The ball top is characteristic of both British and German artillery helmets. This helmet, or *Pickelhaube* (ht 8in/20cm), belonged to an officer of the Imperial German Garde Artillery. *WAL*

This magnificent helmet, c.1900 (ht 10in/25.5cm), was worn by a dragoon officer in the Imperial Austrian army – the cypher "F.J.I.", stands for Franz Joseph I. The large metal comb is embossed with a design depicting a lion slaying a serpent. *WAL*

* Collectors need not worry unduly about the authenticity of headdress. The wrong badge, plume or chin-chain may be fitted, but the complexity involved in making helmets and headdress means that they are very unlikely to be faked. A few copies of headdress from the Napoleonic period have been made, but these too are rare. However, collectors should beware of reproductions of the Imperial German Garde du Corps eagles: these are numerous and of very high quality.

European officer's helmets can usually be distinguished from those of other ranks by their:

* high-quality construction
* gilt metal badges, rather than brass
* trefoil fastenings at the ear bosses (German cuirassiers only).

This Imperial German Cuirassier officer's helmet, c.1900 (ht 12in/30.5cm), has all three of these quality features. *WAL*

The fur busby originated with the Hungarian Hussars, whose style and dash captured the imagination of other regiments. This Prussian officer's busby (ht 7½in/19cm), from the 2nd *Leib* Hussars, dates from c.1900. *WAL*

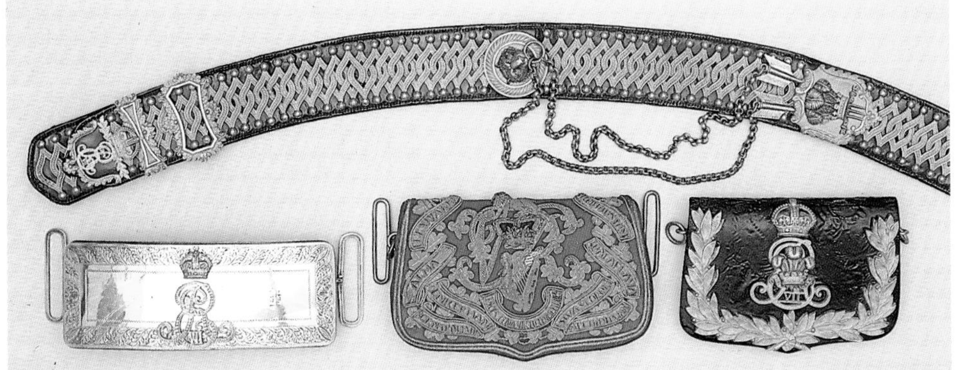

Cavalry pouches are made in metal, cloth-covered leather or leather and are usually 6-7in (15-18cm) long. The left-hand pouch, above, is an Edward VII universal silver pattern worn by several regiments; the larger central pouch is an embroidered example from the 8th Royal Irish Hussars. The shoulder pouch belt *centre*, and the right-hand pouch are from the 10th (Prince of Wales' Royal) Hussars – the only British Hussar regiment to have an overlaid gilt chain ornament on the shoulder pouch belt. Ordinarily the belts were of leather or lace-covered cloth. *WAL*

* The arrow prickers attached to the chains of the shoulder belt were for clearing the touch holes of pistols and carbines (in later years they became purely ornamental).

BLUE CLOTH HELMETS

A typical starting piece for a headdress collection is the widely available British officer's blue cloth spiked helmet. Be wary if the badge has been replaced (revealed by extra fixing holes inside), but do not condemn the helmet out of hand: officers transferred regiments, and it was less expensive to change the badge than the whole helmet. There were three similar styles of blue cloth helmet, introduced in 1879, 1881 and 1902. The 1878 pattern has a round peak with a regimentary numbered badge; the 1881 and 1902 patterns have a pointed one with a county badge. Before 1902 the buckle on the garter of the helmet badge is ornamental; from that date it is plain. The pre-1902 helmet also has the so-called Queen's Crown on the badge; from 1902 the badge bears the King's Crown.

Militaria II

The history of many military trophies is often revealed by an engraved inscription, as is the case with this George III silver presentation goblet of 1819 (ht 7½in/19cm) and William IV silver presentation snuff box of 1834 (3 × 2 × 1in/7.6 × 5 × 2.5cm). *WAL*

* Other popular military trophies with collectors are figurines and equestrian figures.

Tight-fitting cavalry uniforms did not allow for pockets, so officers carried a sabretache, a sort of leather wallet for holding maps and messages. Like many early 19thC examples, this William IV 3rd Dragoon Guards officer's full-dress sabretache (approx. 13 × 8in/33 × 20cm) does not bear the name of the regiment but is identifiable by the lace pattern on the edge. *WAL*

Paintings of troops, particularly cavalry, were popular subjects with 19thC European artists, and original paintings or engravings are highly collectable. This oil painting on a wooden panel, c.1900 (7 × 11in/18 × 28cm), by J. Matthews shows an officer of the 16th Lancers in full review order. *WAL*

* Richard Simkin (1851-1926) was a popular British watercolourist of military uniform. His best works are his slightly stylized, almost caricatured figures, produced between the end of the 19thC and the outbreak of the First World War. However, his uniforms cannot be regarded as accurate in every detail. His work is usually signed.
* Orlando Norie (1832-1901) is a collectable watercolourist who portrayed Crimea war scenes and some single figures and cavalry units.

Silver was often used to embellish items of officers' attire. It is malleable and can be woven into decorative "lace" or braids, as in this late Victorian embroidered cloth-covered leather pouch (wdth approx. 6in/15cm), with silver lace trim. The shoulder belt is also silver braid. *WAL*

SHOULDER BELTS

Shoulder belt plates, used to fasten the belt on which the sword was supported, were worn by the British army from the late 18thC. Between 1812 and 1855 they were worn by officers only. Shoulder belts were no longer used in the British army after 1855, but they were retained by Scottish regiments for wear with Highland full dress uniform.

WAIST BELT CLASPS

Waist belt clasps replaced shoulder belt plates and were used to fasten a sword belt with the carrying slings attached. Officers' clasps were of copper-gilt, often overlaid with silver designs; other clasps were brass.

British army shoulder belts generally had a metal plate bearing the title of the regiment. Many of these are highly decorative and very collectable. They need not be with their original shoulder belt. Those illustrated here are all early-mid-19thC. *WAL*

* Earlier plates, from the time of the Napoleonic Wars, are the most rare and desirable. They are generally oval.
* Officer's belt plates are silver or copper-gilt. Non-officer plates are made of brass.

FAKE BRITISH PLATES

There are a few fakes known of the die-struck NCO's shoulder belt plates. One of the regiments whose shoulder plates are faked is the 72nd Regiment. The officers' patterns are complex, and reproduction would be too expensive and time-consuming to be worthwhile. The reverse of a genuine plate will be copper, possibly with splashes of gilt at the edges. If it is gilt on both sides, it has almost certainly been regilded, which is usually detrimental to value.

Badges are probably the most popular collecting area of all militaria, and include pouch and pouch belt badges, cap and collar badges, and shako and helmet plates. The scope is enormous, with badges from cavalry, yeomanry and infantry regiments, also various volunteer regiments and battalions, and the different royal crowns. The top two rows of the cap badges shown here represent so-called Colonial regiments from Northern Province (Sudan), Canada, Australia and India; all four badges in the bottom row are hallmarked silver officer's badges. *WAL*

* The badges of other ranks are made of brass or white metal.

FAKE BADGES

Some cap badges can fetch high prices, and fakes do appear on the market. A fake brass badge tends to bend more readily than a genuine one. Reproductions, or re-strikes, may be made from original dies and, as long as they are priced as such, make useful "gap fillers". It can be difficult to identify a re-strike, especially if it has been distressed.

DECORATIONS AND MEDALS

The Napoleonic Wars are a popular period for collectors, as are the Crimean War, Indian Mutiny and other Victorian wars. Medals from the Boer War are plentiful. The two main types of medals are campaign medals, and those awarded to bravery in action, such as the Distinguished Conduct Medal, first issued after the Crimean War, the Distinguished Service order, for senior officers, and the Military Cross, instituted in the First World War for officers up to captain. Other ranks had the Military Medal for bravery. Most cherished of all is the Victoria Cross, always highly priced, although the value depends on the action and the deed. Convincing fakes exist. However, Victoria Crosses can be authenticated with the firm authorized to make them.

* Each branch of the service had its own awards for gallantry. The Royal Air Force has a Distinguished Flying Cross and medal.

Officer's headdress badges are larger and more elaborate than cap badges and are often made in gilt metal or silvered. All of these examples are from the period 1812-38; two of them (*top right* and *bottom centre*) are from the Royal Regiment of Artillery. *WAL*

Military medals, *left to right*: Military General Service (M.G.S.) Medal, Waterloo Medal, Crimea Medal, Indian Mutiny Medal and Turkish Crimea Medal. M.G.S. medals were issued with a bar for battles fought by regiments during the Napoleonic period. They are rare, as they were not issued until 1849 (they bear Queen Victoria's head) and recipients had to be alive to claim them. The Waterloo Medal (shown here with unofficial suspender – it should be an iron ring) was issued soon after the battle. *WAL*

* Most British medals of the 19th and 20thC are inscribed on the edge with the recipient's name and regiment. Some were issued unnamed but could be later impressed at the recipient's request.
* Bars increase a medal's desirability. It is important to check the soldier's and regiment's history with the regimental roll before buying a medal, to confirm that the recipient named was entitled to the decoration.
* Continental medals are often uninscribed.
* Replacement campaign ribbons are available from most reputable dealers.

Armour

As firearms became more powerful, armour became increasingly redundant. In fact, wearing it could actually cause injury, as metal from the armour, as well as the musket ball itself, could be forced into the flesh. At the beginning of England's Civil War, 1642, the three-quarter length cuirassiers' armour was still in evidence. However, within a few years metal gave way to leather. The buff leather coat could withstand a spent musket ball and when worn with a musket-proof breast plate (many of these bore a musket ball indented test mark), it gave better protection and allowed greater movement.

Except in certain regiments in Continental Europe, armour was virtually extinct by the 18th century. Body armour survives today, but is used mostly for ceremonial purposes; the breast and back plates of the English Household Cavalry regiments, whose Life Guards were nicknamed the "Tin Bellies", are a notable example. The bullet-proof vests and flak jackets worn by modern armies can also be categorized as armour.

Complete suits of armour are seldom seen on the open market today. Most genuine suits are either in museums or are part of private collections in the great country houses. Most of the best collections were amassed during the Victorian Gothic revival. However, collectors today should not be discouraged from pursuing this important collecting interest. Many part suits and pieces of armour, including helmets, gorgets (protective armour for the throat and shoulders), and breast and back plates are regularly sold by dealers and auction houses. Many suits, even those in prestigious collections, are "marriages", made up of parts that did not start life together. These have come about as a result of demand outweighing supply. Compromises will be necessary to acquire an armour collection, but individual parts should be genuine.

Funerary helmets, made to be worn at the funeral of the head of the family, are very collectable. The gauge of metal is sometimes thin in parts, probably as a result of being repaired, or of being made from poor-quality metal or even from parts taken from other pieces. Such helmets are sometimes taken to be tinny Victorian or Edwardian reproductions. Invariably they are surmounted with a tall spike to take the carved and painted wood crest of the family.

Parts of tilting armour sometimes appear on the market. These overlaid a field suit to protect the vulnerable left side of the wearer. They were invariably plain in order to prevent a lance from being caught in any crevices. Horse armour is also very collectable, especially the chanfron, the headpiece that protected a horse's ears, forehead and face. Today chanfrons are often used as central pieces in wall displays.

Eastern armour is very different from Western armour, probably because the climates are so different, although some Indo-Persian armour is reminiscent of Western styles.

CROMWELLIAN ARMOUR
17thC Cromwellian armour, including "lobster-tailed" helmets, pikeman's pots (simple helmets), breast and back plates, tassets (overlapping plates below the waists of suits) for pikemans' armour, and gauntlets, constitutes an important and accessible collecting area.

The ear flaps on a helmet and the shoulder straps on a backplate are vulnerable. Repairs are acceptable, provided that they are of a high standard. The articulated "lobster tail" at the back of some helmets should also be carefully examined as the rivets that connect the separate plates have sometimes been replaced. The original three-bar visor and "lobster tail" on a Cromwellian helmet have sometimes been replaced by a visor or tail from another helmet.

Cromwellian backplates sometimes bear armourers' marks on the neck area, which adds to their value.

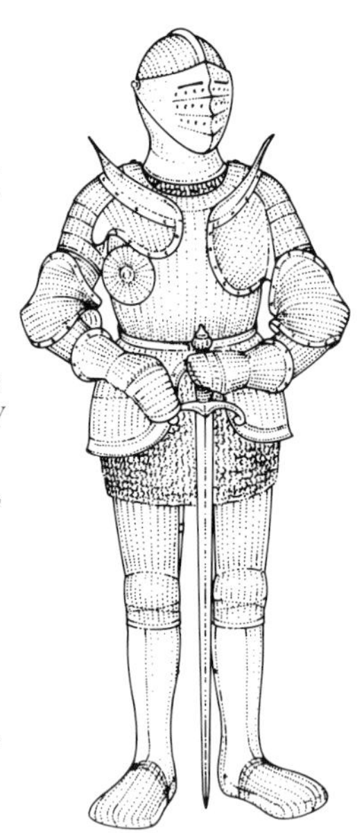

This mid-16thC Italian half-armour has pauldrons – plates for shoulder protection, made up of six overlapping plates, or lames.
* Some fine-quality Georgian copies of 16thC Italian-style armour exist, complete with etched decoration. *WAL*

This French Cuirassier officer's helmet and companion breast and backplate or cuirass, c.1870 (lgth 25in/63.5cm), is the last type of traditional armour. *WAL*

The steel of this 18thC southern Indian armguard or "bazu-band" (lgth 13in/33cm) has been chiselled with bands of foliage and scaled decoration on the end which fits over the elbow. The forearm is further protected by a hinged plate. *WAL*

This early 17thC gorget (wdth 12in/30.5cm) is made of two pieces. The front plate and rim of the neck pieces, which are articulated, have roped edges. *WAL*

* Gorgets are among the pieces of armour most regularly sold by dealers.

The ball-shaped indentation and the two studs helps to identify this trooper's breast plate, c.1640 (lgth 15in/38cm), as Cromwellian. The studs were a regular feature of Cromwellian armour and were used to attach the shoulder straps which joined front and back plates. *WAL*

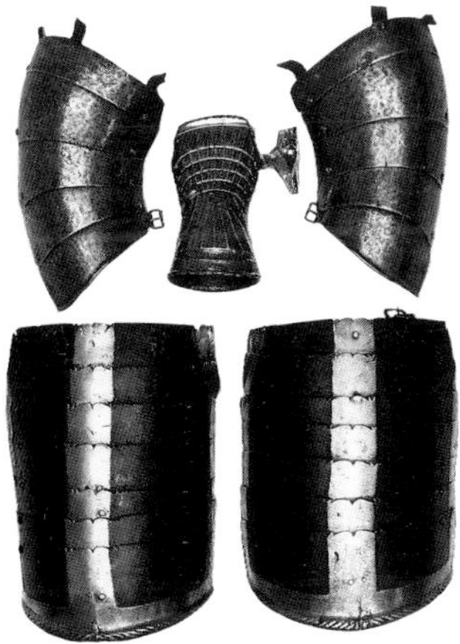

The separate hinged thumbpiece on this Maximilian gauntlet, c.1520 (lgth 9in/23cm), allowed the wearer a stronger grip. The pair of spaulders to protect the shoulders (lgth 12in/30.5cm) and the pair of black and white tassets (lgth 14in/35.5cm) are both from late 16thC German armours. *WAL*

Many fine-quality copies of suits of armour were made in the late 18th and early 19thC. The fluted designs of 16thC Maximilian armours make them one of the most attractive styles, and thus one of the most often reproduced, especially by armour enthusiasts in the Georgian period. Good reproductions, such as this one from c.1820, are well articulated and properly proportioned, and are heavy: such suits should weigh 58-60lb (26-27kg).

* Early 20thC reproductions are inferior: the metal is thin, the anatomy is inaccurate and the articulation often faulty.

MAINTENANCE AND CARE

An equal mixture of turpentine and paraffin, combined with a small amount of methylated spirits, is an effective treatment for rust on armour. After the solution has been well worked in with fine wire wool, it should be left to cake on for a day. The armour should then be polished with balls of newspaper, and waxed.

HELMETS

A helmet consists of a "skull", to protect the top of the head, usually made from one piece of metal. "Close" helmets have a variety of additional parts which are hinged or riveted to the "skull", including: a visor to protect the face, with breathing holes or "breaths"; ear flaps; and a nose guard, often adjustable. Helmets with articulated neck guards, known as "lobster tails", appeared in the early 17thC in several European countries. They were made famous in England by Cromwell's cavalry.

The very small mouth on this cuirassier's close helmet, c.1630, (ht 10½ in/26.5cm) is of "Todenkopf" (death head) form and helps to identify it as German. The visor incorporates radial breaths. *WAL*

The use of chain mail as a neckguard, known as a camail, on this 19thC Indo-Persian Kula Khud (ht 11in/28cm), together with the ornate plume sockets and sliding nose bar, are typical of Oriental helmets. *WAL*

* Some Persian helmets are surmounted by spikes. Steel crescent-shaped finials are most often found on Turkish helmets.

Edged Weapons

Edged weapons fall into various collecting categories, such as British military swords, European swords and daggers, and Eastern and Native weapons.

There are three basic types of military sword: heavy cavalry (with a straight blade), light cavalry (with a curved blade) and infantry. Light infantry, bandsmen, pioneer and corps troops also had their own patterns.

The first official patterns of British military swords were introduced in 1786 (infantry) and 1788 (cavalry). The 1796 pattern for cavalry and infantry lasted throughout the Napoleonic Wars with a few regimental variations. In 1803 Grenadier and Light Company officers were given a different pattern, with a curved blade, similar to that carried by light cavalry. In 1821 and 1822 new patterns were issued for officers of the cavalry and infantry. In 1864 a new pattern was issued for other ranks of heavy and light cavalry. Officers of heavy and light cavalry continued to carry their two different 1821 patterns until 1896, when all adopted the heavy cavalry pattern. A universal pattern was introduced in 1908 for other ranks and in 1912 for officers. Further infantry patterns were issued in 1845, 1854, 1892, 1895 and 1897. The final 1897 pattern is still used today with full-dress.

Rapiers in the 16th century were originally used for both cut and thrust. Unlike sabres, which have a curved blade, rapiers have a slender, pointed blade. Changes in duelling practice turned them into thrusting-only weapons during the 17th century, evolving into the smallsword during the 18th century. Originally the smallsword had a steel or brass hilt and was used by military officers; as the 18th century progressed it developed into a fashionable silver-hilted weapon worn by gentlemen, until being phased out during the early 19th century.

During the 17th and 18th centuries, Spain and Italy were notorious for their "daggers". In Spain the dagger used was the *main gauche* ("left hand") which had an elaborate hilt, and was held in the left-hand and used in conjunction with the rapier held in the right. In Italy, the stiletto was favoured – a small all-steel stabbing dagger with a triangular-shaped blade. Daggers used by gunners have a scale of horizontal numbered gradients marked on the blade to measure the size of bore.

IDENTIFYING SWORDS AND BAYONETS

Letters and numbers on edged weapons may provide a clue to the regiment or unit to which they were issued – for example, "A 16L" stands for "A squadron 16th Lancers".

If a military sword bears the British Royal Arms, look in the second quarter of the shield for a fleur-de-lys; if this is present, it is pre-1801. In 1801 Britain relinquished her ancient claim to France, and the arms of Scotland replaced the fleur-de-lys. Many British military swords of the latter half of the 18thC have German blades, indicated by "Solingen" on the back of the blade. Military swords of the 19thC sometimes have officer's initials and/or the name of the regiment engraved on them. Be wary of swords engraved with famous names, especially if offered without provenance.

Reproductions abound. Look for signs of honest wear on the blade and hilt. A genuine military sword will have a firm blade: fakers usually use untempered steel, which is easily bent.

CARE AND ATTENTION

Blades should be wiped after handling. Rust spots can be cleaned by rubbing the edge of a copper coin over the affected area, although this will not remove the stain. Blades should be waxed after cleaning: oil attracts dust and fluff. Treat leather scabbards and sheaths with leather oil. Never grasp a leather scabbard too tightly when drawing: weakened scabbards can mean cut fingers.

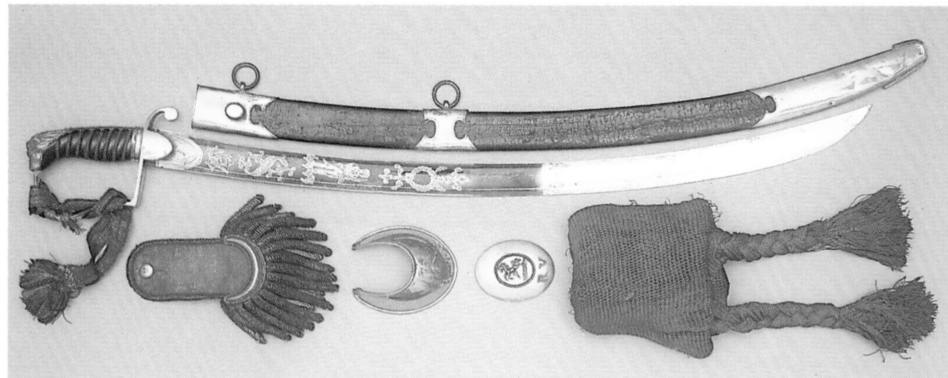

Officer's swords are often found accompanied by symbols of rank, as with this officer's sabre, or cavalry sword (blade 29½in/75cm), of 1800, complete with an epaulette, a gorget (or metal badge) and a crimson waist sash made of woven netting, which could be stretched out and used to carry the wounded from the field. The oval plate was worn across the chest on the cross belt from which the scabbard hung. *WAL*

* Although this sabre bears the name of the gunmaker, Palmer, from c.1850, the name would often be that of the retailer.

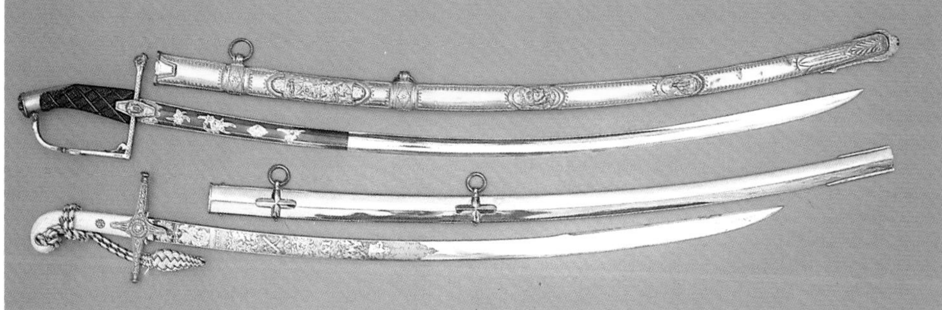

The amount of decoration on a military sword betokens the status of the owner. The richly blued and inlaid French dress sabre (*top*, blade 33½in/85cm) of the Napoleonic era belonged to a high-ranking officer in the light cavalry. Although less elaborate, the English 1831 pattern William IV general officer's sword with clipped-back blade (*above*, lgth 37in/94cm), has an ornate engraving, which greatly adds to its desirability. *WAL*

* The hilts of American swords are similar to those of European swords. The eagle head motif sometimes appears on pommels and quillons.

* Officers' swords invariably have wire-bound fish-skin grips; other ranks' have wire-bound leather.

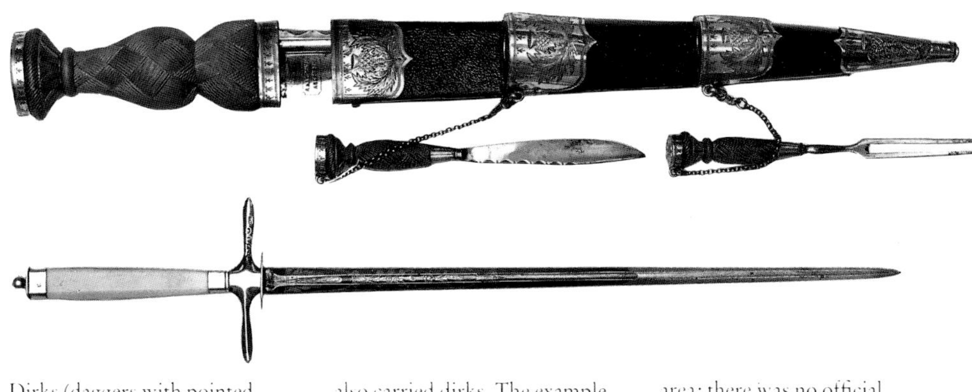

Dirks (daggers with pointed blades) were often carried by junior naval officers, as was this example (*top*, blade 12in/30.5cm). Scottish Highlanders also carried dirks. The example above is Victorian (blade 12in/30.5cm). *WAL*

❊ Georgian naval dirks are an interesting and varied collecting area: there was no official pattern, so the cutler could exercise his artistic licence to a far greater degree than was possible with some other weapons.

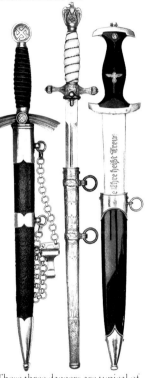

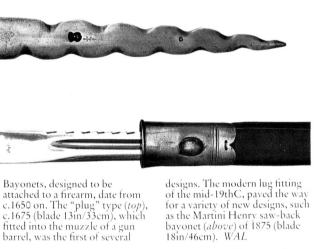

Bayonets, designed to be attached to a firearm, date from c.1650 on. The "plug" type (*top*), c.1675 (blade 13in/33cm), which fitted into the muzzle of a gun barrel, was the first of several designs. The modern lug fitting of the mid-19thC, paved the way for a variety of new designs, such as the Martini Henry saw-back bayonet (*above*) of 1875 (blade 18in/46cm). *WAL*

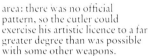

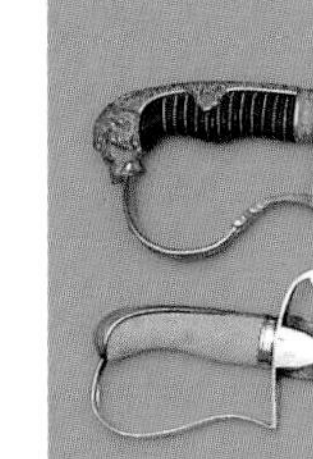

Many swept-hilt rapiers are German, like this example, c.1630 (blade 14in/35.5cm). *WAL*

❊ Rapiers with a cup-shaped hilt are usually Spanish or Italian.

Rapier hilt

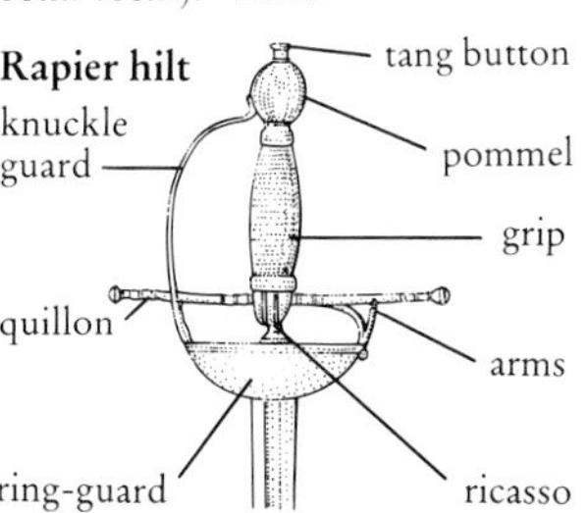

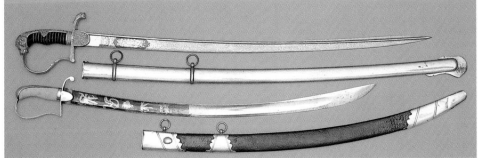

German swords were very highly regarded in the 19thC for the quality of both the steel and the finish. The Imperial German Cavalry officer's sword (*top*, blade 32in/81cm) has a piped-back blade with a watered steel pattern. The grip is of bound fishskin and has a lion's-head pommel. The back quillon is chiselled into a leopard's head. The heavy-bladed Georgian light cavalry dress sword, *above*, c.1806 (blade 31in/79cm), bears the address of a London cutler on the locket of the leather dress scabbard (a metal scabbard would probably be used in battle). The blade is marked "J. J. Runkel, Solingen" along the back edge. *WAL*

GERMAN DAGGERS

The Nazis introduced dagger fetishism into 1930s Germany. The most common daggers of the period are those of the German army, navy and airforce, but there were many more patterns such as those of the Nazi Red Cross, Diplomatic Service, Hitler Youth, Railway Protection, Land Customs and so on.

These three daggers are typical of 1930s German styles. The 1934 pattern Luftwaffe Dress dagger (*above left*, lgth 17in/43cm) retains the original chain hanger. The more conventional Naval Officer's dirk, or dagger (*above centre*, lgth 16½in/42cm) has an eagle and swastika pommel. The 1933 SS dagger (*above right*, lgth 14¾in/37.5cm) has a black scabbard and grip. *WAL*

❊ SA daggers are identical to SS daggers but have brown fittings and a different inscription on the blade.

❊ Copies of German Third Reich daggers are prolific. They are not always easy to detect, as the originals are only 40 or 50 years old. The rarer the type of dagger the more wary the collector should be. If possible, compare any German dagger with a known genuine specimen, as discrepancies in details such as engraving or makers' marks can usually expose a fake.

EASTERN AND NATIVE WEAPONS

During the 19thC, Britain's huge empire made the country probably the largest repository of edged weapons in the world. Countless thousands of souvenirs were brought home by returning troops and these are still to be found in fair numbers. Types vary from Chinese swords of the Boxer rebellion, through tulwars and kukris from India, and spears taken from Zulus and Ashantis, to bizarre axe-swords captured in the Sudan. Eastern and Native weapons are often extremely attractive, and have price-tags to match. The novice should be aware that many traditional designs are still being made, not with any intention to deceive, but for everday use. Japanese swords were made in quantity during the Second World War and have been reproduced ever since. The post-war tourism boom has also put a considerable number of very recently made items into circulation. By and large, a genuine native weapon should be suitable (in terms of finish and strength) for its intended purpose. However, few have anything like the robustness of European blades, and this fragility often reflects local standards of manufacture and available materials. These weapons are seldom in mint condition: signs of wear and tear are usual. Decoration especially might seem crude and commercial, with bright leather colours and utilitarian metals, such as brass and aluminium; however, the best examples display considerable artistry and craftsmanship.

Left to right The Japanese carved bone sword (blade 15½in/39cm) has a carved grip and scabbard. The scabbard of the Burmese silver-mounted sword, or Dha (blade 18in/45.5cm), has the characteristic square end, with Western-style scroll-work on the silver. The wavy-bladed kris (13in/33cm) is from Bali. These weapons are often designed with a cheap replacable blade: the blade was broken off inside the victim. The semi-precious stone pommel of the beautifully decorated dirk set, early 20thC (blade 12in/30.5cm) is a traditional Scottish design. The axe, c.1650 (lgth 23in/58.5cm), is a ceremonial German *Steigerhacke*, carried only in parades. *WAL*

BOWIE KNIVES

Tradition has it that the distinctive, clipped-back blade of the Bowie knife resulted from the American Colonel, Jim Bowie, grinding down a broken sword into a fighting knife in the early 19thC. His knife became part of the mythology of the American West, and was considered an essential item of "frontier" equipment during the later 19thC.

Sheffield cutlers were quick to catch on to this valuable export opportunity, and Sheffield-made Bowies captured a large proportion of the market, many of them exported through the Hudson Bay Company. They ranged from the starkly utilitarian to those covered with elaborate decoration and patriotic (American) slogans.

Today, original 19thC Bowie knives are very highly sought after, especially by American collectors.

England produced some of the finest Bowie knives, both decorative and utilitarian. Although there was considerable variation of design, they all have a distinctive "clipped-back" blade. The "classic" Bowie has a coffin-shaped handle of wood, bone, horn or mother-of-pearl, as in the folding example (*above left*, lgth 8in/20cm) (note the catch low down on the handle). This knife also has a blank escutcheon for an engraved name or initials. The back blade sometimes carries an edge for skinning. Beardshaw's bowie (*above centre*, lgth 12in/30.5cm) has a horn handle; the blade bears the American eagle and V.R. Some bowies have a retaining spring clip to prevent the knife from falling out of the sheath, as in the example by Wilkinson & Son of London (*far right*, lgth 12in/30.5cm). *WAL*

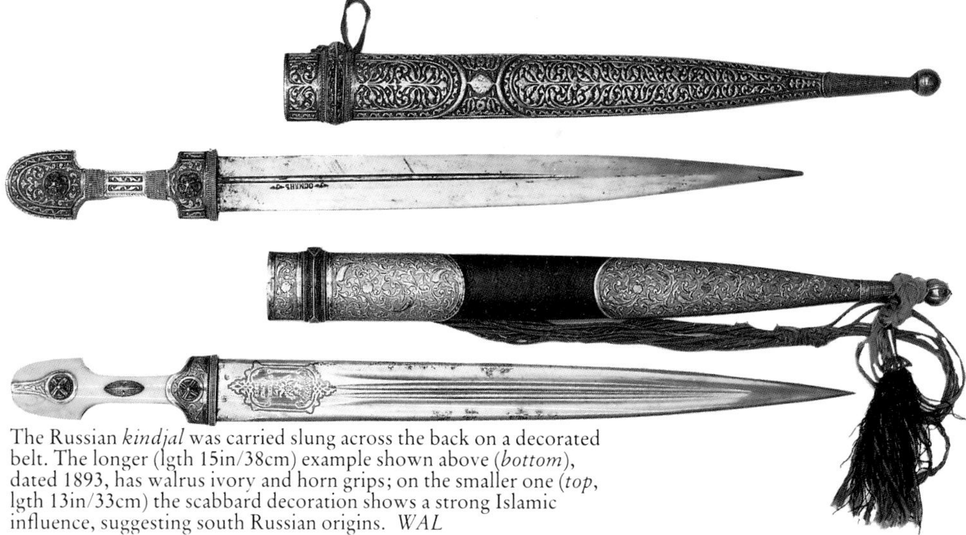

The Russian *kindjal* was carried slung across the back on a decorated belt. The longer (lgth 15in/38cm) example shown above (*bottom*), dated 1893, has walrus ivory and horn grips; on the smaller one (*top*, lgth 13in/33cm) the scabbard decoration shows a strong Islamic influence, suggesting south Russian origins. *WAL*

Reference

GLOSSARY

Armet A type of closed helmet.
Armour A protective outfit, all or partly of metal.
Arquebus A heavy gun.
Baldric A shoulder belt for a sword.
Bandolier A shoulder belt to support cartridge holders.
Barrel The part of a firearm through which a projectile is discharged.
Basket hilt A **hilt** that completely encloses the hand.
Basinet A 14thC helmet, often with a point.
Bayonet A blade attached to the **muzzle** of a firearm.
Bazu-band An Indian armguard.
Blunderbuss A gun or **pistol** with a bell-mouthed **barrel.**
Bore The inside of a **barrel**; also the diameter of a **barrel.**
Bowie knife A hunting knife with a cutting blade and a pointed end.
Breechloader A firearm loaded from the rear of the **barrel.**
Burgonet An open helmet.
Busby A fur helmet.
Butt The rear end of a gun.
Cabasset A helmet worn by foot soldiers.
Calibre The diameter of a **barrel**, shell or bullet.
Camail Protective **chain mail** for the neck and shoulders.
Carbine A gun similar to, but shorter and lighter than, a **musket.**
Carronade A form of cannon made in Carron, Scotland.
Cartridge An encased charge of gunpowder.
Chain mail Flexible armour made of metal rings riveted together.
Chamber The part of the **barrel** where the charge is ignited.
Claymore A Scottish longsword that requires a two-handed grip.
Coatee A short coat.
Cock The arm of a gun that holds the igniting agent, activated by a spring.
Crossbow A bow which requires pre-setting before firing.
Cuirass A breastplate.
Daisho A pair of Japanese swords, one large, one small.
Dirk A type of dagger.
Double-action A gun that can be fired without setting the **cock.**
Dress (or diplomatic) sword A sword worn for show, not for use.
Elbow gauntlet A 17thC protective sleeve and hand protector.
Epaulette Decoration usually found on the shoulders of military uniforms.
Flintlock A firing mechanism, whereby a flint strikes metal to create a spark.
Forte The thickest part of a sword-blade, near the **hilt.**
Fusil A small **flintlock musket.**
Gauntlet A leather glove, sometimes armoured.
Gorget A piece of armour that protects the neck.
Grapeshot A number of cast-iron balls fitted within a case for firing from a cannon.
Greaves Armour for the part of the leg below the knee.
Guidon A flag carried by cavalry.
Halberd A spear fitted with a double axe.
Hilt The handle of a bladed weapon.
Jambiya A curved knife, used in the Muslim world.
Jezail An Afghan gun.
Katana The long sword of a **daisho.**
Katar An Indian thrusting dagger.
Kepie A soft cap with a round top and a peak.
Kindjal A Caucasian short sword with a broad, double-edged blade.
Klewang A Malaysian sword.
Kris A Malaysian dagger with a wavy blade and an angled **hilt.**
Kukri A heavy curved sword used by the Gurkas of Nepal.
Kulah khud A Persian helmet.
Lames Strips of overlapping metal on armour.
Lance A horseman's spear.
Linstock A polearm used to ignite cannons.
Lock The firing mechanism of a gun.
Long arm A firearm with a long barrel.
Mace An all-metal club, often with a flanged head.
Main gauche A dagger for the left hand.
Mandau A Dyak head-hunter's sword.
Matchlock The earliest form of mechanical gun ignition.
Morion A round helmet with a rim and a crest.
Mortar A type of cannon for high-angle fire.
Mortuary sword A sword with a **basket hilt.**
Musket A heavy **long arm**.
Muzzle The front end of the **barrel.**
Nimcha A North African **sabre.**
Nipple The hollow cone on which the cap containing the powder is placed.
Pan The hollow that holds the igniting material in a gun.
Partizan A broad-bladed polearm.
Patchbox A storage compartment in the **butt** of a gun.
Pepperbox A firearm with a revolving cylinder of 5 or 6 **barrels** and usually a **percussion** action.
Percussion lock Method of igniting the charge in a gun using a cap.
Pike A long-shafted polearm.
Pistol A handgun with a short **barrel.**
Pommel A knob on the end of a **hilt.**
Poniard A small, slim dagger.
Proof mark The mark certifying the efficiency of a **barrel.**
Quillon The crossguard between the **hilt** and the blade of a sword.
Rapier A thrusting sword, usually with an elaborate guard.
Revolver A **pistol** with a revolving cylinder containing a number of **chambers.**
Ricasso The squared part of a sword blade above the guard.
Rifle A gun with spiral grooves in the **barrel**. These enhance the accuracy of a shot.
Sabatons Foot armour with broad toes.
Sabre A Slightly curved, single-edged sword.
Sashqua A curved Cossack sword, without **quillons.**
Scabbard or **sheath** A holder for a bladed weapon.
Scimitar A Curved Eastern sword.
Shabraque A saddle cloth.
Shako A peaked headdress, of conical or cylindrical shape.
Shamshir A curved Persian sword.
Shashqa A Circassian sword.
Shell or **shellguard** A protective plate beneath the **quillons.**
Shotel An Abyssinian sword.
Single-action or **self-cocking** A gun that requires cocking before being fired.
Skean-dhu A small **dirk** worn by Scottish Highlanders.
Smallsword A thrusting sword.
Spadroon A cut-and-thrust sword.
Spaulders Shoulder armour.
Spontoon A half **pike.**
Stiletto A small Italian thrusting dagger.
Stock The support for the **barrel** of a gun, usually of wood, that provides a grip.
Tabard A garment bearing a coat of arms.
Tachi A single-edged, slightly curved Japanese Samurai sword.
Tang The part of the sword blade that is inserted into the **hilt.**
Tanto A Japanese Samurai dagger, used with the **Tachi.**
Targe A round Scottish shield.
Tassets Overlapping plates in **armour** for the groin and thighs.
Tomahawk A fighting axe of the North American Indian.
Tschinke An East German **wheellock** gun.
Tsuba A Japanese sword guard.
Vambrace Armour to fit the forearm.
Visor A movable face protector on a helmet.
Wakizashi The short sword of a **daisho.**
Wheel-lock An ignition system whereby a revolving wheel sparks a flint that ignites the charge.
Yari A Japanese spear.

SELECTED GUNSMITHS

Britain
Adams, Robert and John 1851-92
Baker, Ezekiel 1775-1832
Brander, William 1690-1750. Became Brander & Pots 1825-32
Colts Patent Repeating Arms Ltd 1852-57. (English branch of Amerian firm.)
Egg, Durs 1770-1834
Enfield Royal Manufactory 1855-present day
Ferguson, Patrick 1774-80
Forsyth, Alexander John 1805-19
Greener, W. 1829-69
Kerr & Co. 1855-94
Ketland, William 1740-1804
Mortimer, H.W. 1780-1835
Nock, Henry 1769-1810
Parker, William 1790-1840
Purdey, James 1816-68
Richards, Westley 1812-72
Rigby, Williams 1827-67
Tatham & Egg 1760-1800
Tranter, William 1853-85
Twigg, T. 1760-80
Wilkinson & Sons 1806-70
Wogdon 1760-97

United States
Allen, Ethan 1834-71
Collier, Elisha Haydon 1807-63
Colt, Samuel 1836-62
Deringer, Henry Jnr 1806-68
Hall, John Harris 1811-41
Manhattan Firearms Mfg Co 1840-70
Maynard Arms Co. 1851-65
North, Simeon 1794-1852
Remington, Eliphalet 1816-61
Sharps, Christian 1848-74
Spencer, Christopher 1860-9
Starr Arms Co. 1860-68
Winchester Repeating Arms Co. 1867-present day.

BIBLIOGRAPHY

Firearms
Blackmore, H., *Guns and Rifles of the World* (1965)
Blair, C., *Pistols of the World* (1968)
George, J.N., *English Guns and Rifles* (1947)
English Pistols and Revolvers (1938)
Hayward, J.F., *The Arts of the Gunmakers* two volumes (1962 & 1963)

Arms and Armour
Blair, C., *European Armour* (1958)
European and American Arms (1962)
Laking, Sir Guy, *A Record of European Arms and Armour through Seven Centuries* (1920-1922)
Norman, A.V.B., *Arms and Armour* (1964)
Stone, G.C., *A Glossary of the Construction, Decoration and Use of Arms and Armour in All Countries and All Times* (1961)
Journals of the Arms and Armour Society London.
The Wallace Collection catalogues (1962)

Edged Weapons
Abels, Robert, *Classic Bowie Knives* (1967)
Annis, Cmdr. May R.N. & P., *Swords for Sea Service* two volumes (1970)
Aylward, J.D., *The Smallsword in England* (1960)
Kiesling, Paul, *Bayonets of the World* four volumes (1974)
Peterson, Harold L., *American Knives* (1958)
Robson, Brian, *Swords of the British Army* (1975)
Washer, Richard, *The Sheffield Bowie and Pocket Knife Makers 1825-1925* (1974)

Militaria
Carman, W.Y., *Headdress of the British Army: Cavalry* (1968)
Headdress of the British Army: Yeomanry (1970)
Kipling & King, *Headdress Badges of the British Army* two volumes (1973 & 1979)
Parkyn, *Shoulder Belt Plates and Buttons* (1956)
Short, Chichester & Burgess, *Records and Badges of the British Army* (1900)

ART NOUVEAU

These maps show the key British, European and American craftsmen, retail outlets and schools of design. The medium or media in which the craftsmen worked are indicated by letters after their name.

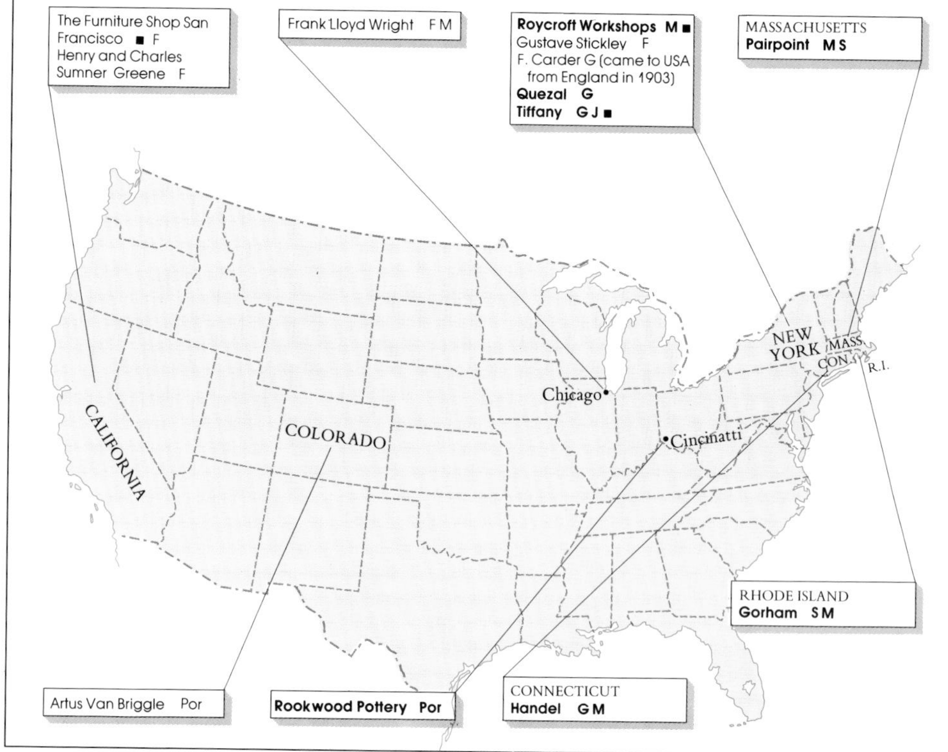

F Furniture
G Glass
J Jewelry
M Metalwork
P Pottery
Pe Pewter
Por Porcelain
Pos Posters
S Sculpture
T Textiles
■ Retail outlet

Baillie Scott — Major Designer
Roycroft Workshops — Factory

"Art Nouveau" is the name given to a cluster of decorative styles that evolved in Europe and America toward the end of the 19th century and continued until c.1914. The initial inspiration came from two movements that had flourished in England not long before: the Aesthetic Movement, which sought to elevate design to the level of fine arts; and the Arts and Crafts Movement, which emulated medieval ideals of craftsmanship.

The term "Art Nouveau" derives from the Paris shop of the German entrepreneur Samuel Bing, "La Maison de l'Art Nouveau", which opened at the end of 1895 and became the major outlet for the glass of Emile Gallé, the lamps of Louis C. Tiffany, the jewelry of René Lalique and the furniture of Eugene Vallin – all landmarks in Art Nouveau design. However, the most famous Art Nouveau landmarks defy collection because they are fixtures – for example, the wrought-iron Métro station entrances by Hector Guimard (also known for his small-scale metalwares). Their highly sculptural forms taken from nature – the organic slender stalks terminating in bud-like lamp fitments – epitomize a style that spread infectiously, injecting new life into all kinds of functional objects. Woodland and water nymphs, sinuous whiplash lines or peacock feathers appeared on furniture, table lamps, mirror frames, posters, jewelry, door handles, crumb scoops – nothing was considered too trivial to merit embellishment.

A chief exponent of this curvilinear version of Art Nouveau is Alphonse Mucha, the Czech artist and posterist working in Paris. Like many other artefacts of the period, especially bronzes and small-scale sculptures, Mucha's posters celebrate the female form, often in fantastical settings, attired in exotic costume and imbued with erotic or ethereal suggestion. Eroticism was a theme of the period, and tends to have a stimulating effect on prices.

Two other major centres of the "new art" were Scotland and Austria. The Scottish architect and designer Charles Rennie Mackintosh joined forces with Herbert MacNair and the MacDonald sisters, Frances and Margaret, to form "The Glasgow Four". Tending to disregard the curvilinear exuberance of the French, this group instead created a controlled, straight-lined style, with a vertical emphasis that was highly influential – particularly in furniture.

In Vienna, spectacular Art Nouveau pieces were designed by the Secessionists – a group of artists and designers who had become disillusioned with the Viennese arts establishment. The leading figures were Josef Hoffmann and Kolomon Moser who in 1903 founded the Wiener Werkstätte ("Vienna Workshops"). These produced a wide range of objects, many in a style indebted to Mackintosh.

There are three distinct tiers of collecting in Art Nouveau: highly expensive handcrafted works by top names such as Carlo Bugatti or Christopher Dresser; fine but more affordable pieces that embody the key virtues of the style; and mass-produced items (including many made for Liberty's) that can still be acquired at relatively modest prices.

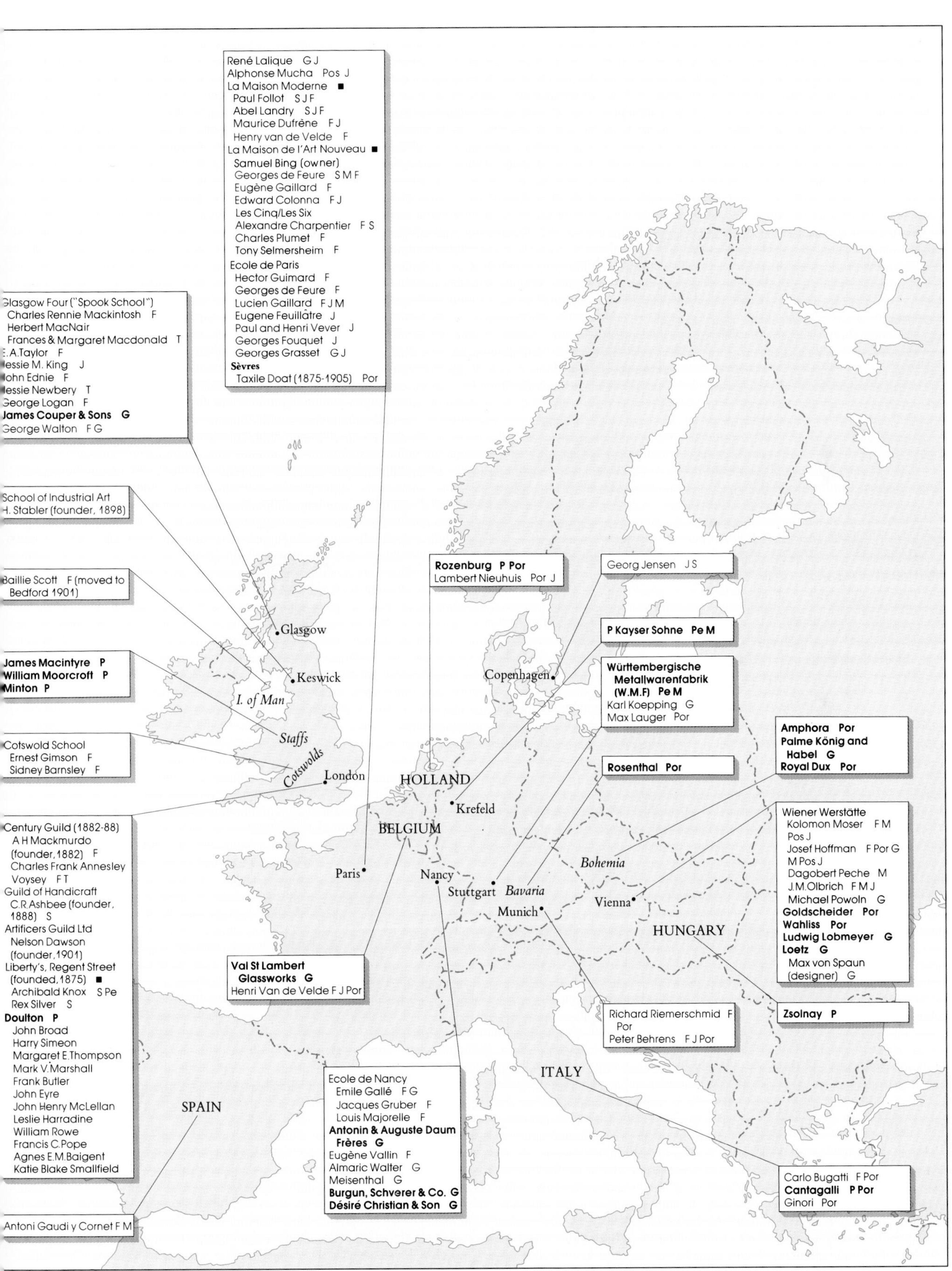
René Lalique G J
Alphonse Mucha Pos J
La Maison Moderne ■
Paul Follot S J F
Abel Landry S J F
Maurice Dufrêne F J
Henry van de Velde F
La Maison de l'Art Nouveau ■
Samuel Bing (owner)
Georges de Feure S M F
Eugène Gaillard F
Edward Colonna F J
Les Cinq/Les Six
Alexandre Charpentier F S
Charles Plumet F
Tony Selmersheim F
Ecole de Paris
Hector Guimard F
Georges de Feure F
Lucien Gaillard F J M
Eugene Feuillâtre J
Paul and Henri Vever J
Georges Fouquet J
Georges Grasset G J
Sèvres
Taxile Doat (1875-1905) Por
Glasgow Four ("Spook School")
Charles Rennie Mackintosh F
Herbert MacNair
Frances & Margaret Macdonald T
E.A.Taylor F
Jessie M. King J
John Ednie F
Jessie Newbery T
George Logan F
James Couper & Sons G
George Walton F G
School of Industrial Art
H. Stabler (founder, 1898)
Baillie Scott F (moved to Bedford 1901)
James Macintyre P
William Moorcroft P
Minton P
Cotswold School
Ernest Gimson F
Sidney Barnsley F
Century Guild (1882-88)
A H Mackmurdo (founder, 1882) F
Charles Frank Annesley Voysey F T
Guild of Handicraft
C.R.Ashbee (founder, 1888) S
Artificers Guild Ltd
Nelson Dawson (founder, 1901)
Liberty's, Regent Street (founded, 1875) ■
Archibald Knox S Pe
Rex Silver S
Doulton P
John Broad
Harry Simeon
Margaret E.Thompson
Mark V. Marshall
Frank Butler
John Eyre
John Henry McLellan
Leslie Harradine
William Rowe
Francis C.Pope
Agnes E.M.Baigent
Katie Blake Smallfield
Antoni Gaudi y Cornet F M
Rozenburg P Por
Lambert Nieuhuis Por J
Georg Jensen J S
P Kayser Sohne Pe M
Württembergische Metallwarenfabrik (W.M.F) Pe M
Karl Koepping G
Max Lauger Por
Rosenthal Por
Amphora Por
Palme König and Habel G
Royal Dux Por
Wiener Werstätte
Kolomon Moser F M Pos J
Josef Hoffman F Por G M Pos J
Dagobert Peche M
J.M.Olbrich F M J
Michael Powoln G
Goldscheider Por
Wahliss Por
Ludwig Lobmeyer G
Loetz G
Max von Spaun (designer) G
Zsolnay P
Richard Riemerschmid F Por
Peter Behrens F J Por
Val St Lambert Glassworks G
Henri Van de Velde F J Por
Ecole de Nancy
Emile Gallé F G
Jacques Gruber F
Louis Majorelle F
Antonin & Auguste Daum Frères G
Eugène Vallin F
Almaric Walter G
Meisenthal G
Burgun, Schverer & Co. G
Désiré Christian & Son G
Carlo Bugatti F Por
Cantagalli P Por
Ginori Por
Glasgow
Keswick
I. of Man
Staffs
Cotswolds
London
Paris
HOLLAND
BELGIUM
Krefeld
Copenhagen
Nancy
Stuttgart
Bavaria
Munich
Bohemia
Vienna
HUNGARY
ITALY
SPAIN

Furniture

Of all the applied arts, furniture probably offers the best illustration of the many styles that collectively fit into the category Art Nouveau.

British furniture described – and sometimes miscatalogued – as "Art Nouveau" is often more accurately labelled Arts and Crafts, as it lacks the sinuous forms associated with the new style. In fact, much of this furniture is an interplay of old and new. Even true Art Nouveau furniture in Britain tends to use traditional cabinet-making methods – the style is applied *to* the structure rather than being reflected *in* the structure.

Art Nouveau furniture from Britain is characterized by pierced effects, Celtic motifs, brass and copper appliqués and a use of traditional native woods such as oak. Liberty's hand-finished furniture maintained a high quality, but was mass-produced and widely affordable. Liberty furniture survives in quantity and is highly collectable. Contemporary catalogues give a good idea of the range of styles and motifs. Much of the Liberty output was influenced by, and thus often confused with, that of the highly influential Charles Rennie Mackintosh and other Glaswegians, such as E.A. Taylor and George Walton. Any piece that still bears the Liberty label commands a premium. Major English designers include: Ernest Gimson, C.F.A. Voysey (the architect-turned craftsman, whose work exhibited a strong Arts and Crafts influence, with austere lines and selective ornament) and the founders of the Cotswold school, Ernest and Sidney Barnsley.

The French took the organic motifs of the Arts and Crafts movement and developed the style from there, following sculptural forms rather than the rigid rules of carpentry adhered to by the British. They preferred more elaborate materials such as fruitwoods, and for their decorative finishes looked to the local flora and insects of the surrounding countryside for inspiration. Florid curvilinear furniture will nearly always be French. Of the French designers, only Émile Gallé and Louis Majorelle – whose work is often remarkably similar – signed their pieces.

The development of the Art Nouveau style in Europe did not have a strong impact on America, where furniture remained simple, and uncorrupted by naturalistic motifs. However, the Greene brothers, Henry and Charles, produced furniture in designs reminiscent of the Japanese styles that had influenced so much European Art Nouveau. Gustav Stickley made simple furniture, of similar form and construction.

Large, commissioned pieces are rare and for most people prohibitively expensive. The smaller, more functional pieces – such as writing desks – have tended to survive 20th-century purges better than – for example, beds, which come up more rarely. Tables are also hard to find. Chairs are numerous; although they are often in need of reupholstery, this does not seriously reduce their desirability.

This mahogany cabinet with fruitwood inlay (ht 6ft/183cm) is of a type often referred to as "Liberty style", although it was probably manufactured and retailed through other outlets. Like much English furniture of the period, it is a compromise of the French Art Nouveau style with Arts and Crafts. Mass-produced and hand-finished, these cabinets were made and survive in quantity. *S*

The basic shape of this mahogany dining room chair (ht 3ft/91.5cm), designed by A. H. Mackmurdo in the 1880s, is traditional, but the whiplash motifs are pure Art Nouveau. *B*
* Tapering legs and spread feet were a tendency of the period.

A mother-of-pearl inlaid beech armchair designed by Baillie Scott in 1900/01 (ht approx. 3ft/90cm). The simple perpendicular effect, and the combination of avant garde shapes with Arts and Crafts-style decoration, is characteristic of Scott's work. *B*

A Macassar ebony veneered stationery cabinet by Ernest Gimson, which illustrates his expertise in intricate inlay. (Macassar is a rare form of ebony.) The central peacock motif – a very popular device – is composed of lapis lazuli, abalone and mother of pearl. The cabinet has a hinged door enclosing an alcove, and side panel doors, and dates from c.1910 (ht 25in/63cm). Gimson made few cabinets. *P*

* A master of geometric inlay, Gimson combined traditional techniques with innovative designs. The diagonal grain was to become a feature in Art Deco work, especially that of Ruhlmann.

* Gimson was a member of the English Cotswold School. His pieces were individually commissioned, so it is unusual to find any two the same.

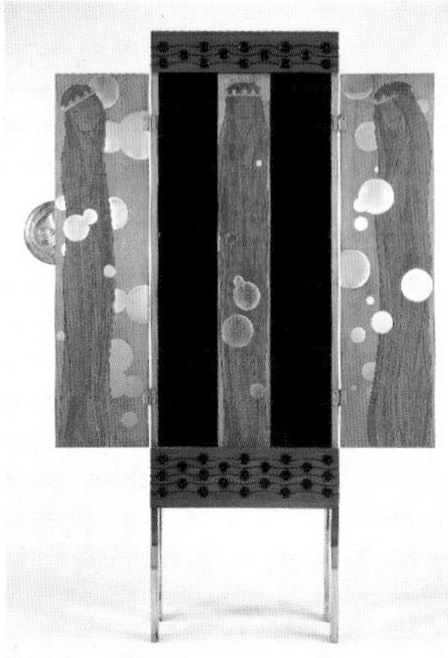

A rare cabinet designed by the Wiener Werkstätte artist Kolomon Moser, c.1900 (ht approx. 5ft/150cm). The interior opens to reveal three mysterious maidens in marquetry among bubbles of silvered metal.The figural decoration employed by Moser is similar to that used by the Glasgow Four, which earned them the title of the "Spook School". Moser's maidens are ethereal but have faces, unlike those of Mackintosh. *SM*

A Majorelle marquetry cabinet with a back mirror, inlaid with flowers and butterflies, c.1900 (ht approx. 4ft/120cm). In its sculptural qualities and delicate inlay work, this piece typifies the Nancy School of design. *CNY*

THE NANCY SCHOOL

Furniture was one of the many interests of this school of design, formed by Emile Gallé and Louis Majorelle, natives of Nancy in the Alsace region of France, with such craftsmen as Eugene Vallin and Jacques Gruber. Their furniture embodies strong sculptural qualities with marquetry panel decoration incorporating native and exotic woods. Frogs' heads, organic pads and so on, often appear on furniture feet. Anonymous pieces from the Nancy School are almost as much in demand as attributed works by individual craftsmen.

THE PARIS SCHOOL

Some fine furniture was made in Paris by a group that included Eugene Gaillard, Edward Colona, the Dutch-Belgian George de Feure and the multi-talented Hector Guimard. They differed from their contemporaries in Nancy in advocating stylized organic forms and slender lines that incorporated whiplash motifs and similar sinuous abstract forms. Panel decoration emphasized the use of natural grains and figuring. A high degree of sophisticated elegance is evident in the giltwood furniture of George de Feure.

A marquetry umbrella stand with inlaid decorative panels, c.1900 (ht approx. 3ft/90cm), designed by Emile Gallé and signed on the left-hand side at the bottom. *CNY*

* It can be difficult to tell Majorelle's and Gallé's work apart stylistically, but their pieces are always signed. Majorelle's inlay tends to be on a smaller scale than Gallé's. Both men used the grain of wood as a decorative element. Gallé regularly included marquetry inlay in his furniture; with Majorelle it was occasional.

Carlo Bugatti often made furniture for complete interiors. His work shows a strong Moorish influence, often embellished with novel decorative elements that include metal appliqués and inlay, fringed tassels and vellum-covered timber. This ladies' writing desk, 1897 (ht approx. 4ft/120cm), is made of ebonized wood and rosewood with pewter and ivory inlay. *C*

* Delicate, intricate furniture is susceptible to damage. The tassels and inlay work on Bugatti pieces are particularly vulnerable. Nevertheless, because of the relative rarity of larger pieces of furniture, even those with defects are still collectable.

Ceramics

The influence of Japanese wares is as evident in Art Nouveau ceramics as in other media.

In England some Doulton wares bore only a token gesture of Art Nouveau decoration applied to a conventional or uninteresting form. An exception is the sylph-like fairy-tale maidens with their entourage of sprites, designed by Margaret E. Thompson. Also highly collectable is the work of Frank Butler, Mark V. Marshall and Eliza Simmance.

Meanwhile, the English firm of Minton was producing its "Secessionist" wares, designed by Léon Solon and John Wadsworth; their unconventional forms are decorated with formalized flower designs and colourful glazes.

The "Florian-ware" pottery produced by James Macintyre and Co. and designed by William Moorcroft was, and still is, enormously popular. The German artist potter Max Läuger produced vases with strikingly similar slip-trailed decoration.

In France the Sèvres factory produced tablewares designed by Edward Colona and George de Feure and a series of white biscuit porcelain figures by Agathon Leonard. The Massier family operating from the south of France concentrated on developing lustre-decorated pottery. Their products bear a close resemblance to those produced in Hungary by the Zsolnay (pronounced "Jerni") Pottery. A number of Massier pieces were decorated by the celebrated artist Lucien Levy-Dhurmer, whose signature or initials can be found on the base.

In Bohemia the Royal Dux factory produced a vast range of Art Nouveau wares, often in the form of water nymphs clambering or seated upon large conch or nautilus shells, and decorated with green and ivory colours heightened with gilt.

The Dutch contribution to Art Nouveau ceramics came from the Rozenburg manufactory in The Hague. Decoration by such artists as Samuel Schellink and W. P. Hartgring incorporated exotic flowers and birds against complicated reserves of Japanese influence. The factory's earthenware products lack the finesse of their dainty eggshell porcelain wares and tend to look rather sombre.

In the United States many "Art Potteries" flourished at the turn of the last century. The most eminent was the Rookwood pottery of Cincinatti, Ohio, founded in 1880. A large proportion of the Rookwood output was matt-glazed wares, but it was the underglazed artist-decorated pieces that ensured the pottery's international reputation. Flower subjects may have been the staple decoration but the American Indian portraits painted by William P. McDonald or Matthew A. Daly are more keenly sought after.

It is often difficult to distinguish between some of the iridescent pottery and glass produced in this period. However, the base of a piece of glass tends to have a smoothed-out pontil mark, while the outer rim of pottery is often ground to reveal the coarse grain.

MOORCROFT

Florian ware (*right*) was one of the Macintyre factory's most popular ranges; the slender pieces were especially coveted. It was produced c.1904-c.1913 and signed with Moorcroft's facsimile signature. The factory made Aurelian ware in the 1880s with designs reminiscent of William Morris. In 1913 Moorcroft established his own pottery. The early pieces are impress-marked "Moorcroft Burslem" and have an impressed or transfer-printed facsimile signature. Later pieces are marked "Corbridge".

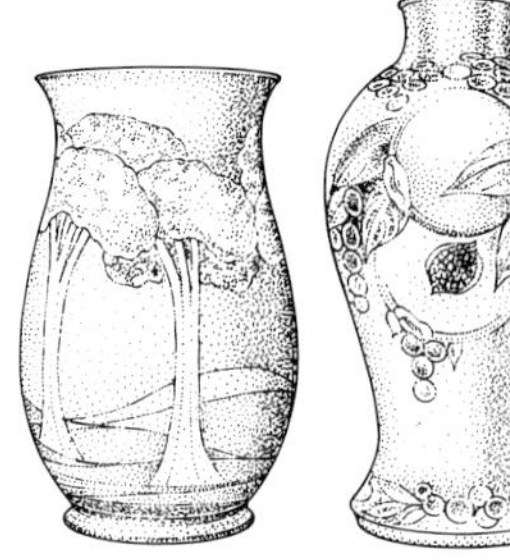

His most popular patterns were: Hazeldene Moonlit Blue (*above left*), the pomegranate design (*above right*) and the tall trees design.The pottery was carried on c.1945 by his son Walter Moorcroft, who signed his initials WM.

A Florian-ware pottery vase designed by William Moorcroft, c.1900 (ht 11in/28cm) for the firm of Macintyre. The slip-trail style of decoration is known as "tubeline", a term also applied to some Minton wares. *B*

Porcelain from the Rosenthal factory in Germany has yet to be fully appreciated and may well be poised for reassessment. This vase, made in 1917 (ht 8in/20cm), is typical of the firm's Rosario range. Green enamel was occasionally used along with blue. All their wares – they also made figures, often of satyrs or fauns – are of fine quality. *B*

A moulded lustre vase, c.1920 (ht 14in/35cm) from the Hungarian pottery of Zsolnay. The thick iridescent glaze – called eosin – was applied to many of the pottery's other wares. The bases carry the Zsolnay mark of the five towers of Pécs. *B*

The style and colours of this Royal Dux figural group of c.1910 (ht 12in/30cm) are typical of the factory's Art Nouveau (and Classical) figures. Pieces signed "Royal Dux Bohemia" are pre–1918. A "Czechoslovakia" mark indicates a later date. *B*
* Two Austrian firms, Riessner, Stellmacher & Kessel and Ernst Wahliss, were making similar wares at the time.

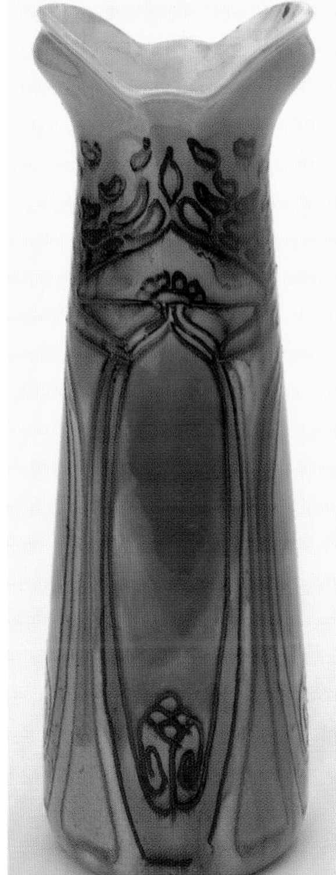

A vase typical of Minton's Secessionist wares in its form, colouring and use of organic motifs (ht approx. 10in/25cm). Although not highly valued today, they represent an important contribution to Art Nouveau ceramic design by the British pottery industry and may therefore be reassessed in the future. These vases survive in great numbers. *B*

A distinctively British, Royal Doulton stoneware figure of a Lily Maid (ht 24in/61.5cm) modelled by Gilbert Bayes in 1924. The figure is typical of Bayes in its innocent and anatomically correct form. *C*
* All Bayes' pieces are signed on the base with his name and the Doulton Lambeth mark. Most of them were intended to be outdoors: his range of crow-like birds were used as ornaments for gateposts and washing lines! However, the figures are resilient and have survived surprisingly well. Bayes is just beginning to attract the attention of collectors after a long period of relative obscurity.

A lustre-decorated charger designed by William De Morgan and painted by Charles Passenger in 1900 (dia. 14in/35.5cm). *B*
* Lustre ware, which grew in popularity between the late 19th and early 20thC, is very much associated with the Pilkington factory in Lancashire, England. They eventually retailed their wares under the name Royal Lancastrian Pottery.

A Rozenburg eggshell porcelain vase (ht 10½in/26.5cm) decorated by Samuel Schellinck, c.1902. The failure rate of designs such as this was very high. *CAm*

ROOKWOOD
Rookwood was the leading American "Art Pottery". It employed the novel technique of encasing pottery in silver deposits by an electrolytic process that allows silver to be attracted to the pottery surface.

Until 1910 the wares were usually signed by the artist and carried a date and shape number. Anything marked on the base as a "second" or "give-away" has a fault or imperfection which should be reflected in the price. Beware of similar wares by the Lonhuda Pottery of W.A. Long, S.A. Weller, J.B. Owens or the Roseville Pottery.

From 1886 the monogram R-P was used. A flame was added for each year from 1887 until 1900, after which roman numerals were added for the years of the 20thC.

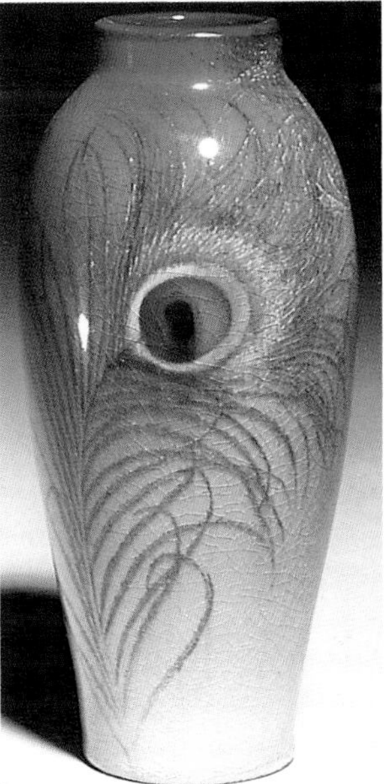

A Rookwood pottery vase with the peacock feather motif that was used by artists on both sides of the Atlantic. It was decorated in 1900 by Carl Schmidt (ht 8½in/21.5cm). *CNY*

Rookwood wares that depicted Indians were very popular.

Glass

Victorian taste for most of the 19th century favoured glassware heavily decorated with cut or engraved motifs. However, changing tastes and an interest in more sophisticated production techniques at the end of the century led to the development of the softer, more restrained cameo and iridescent glass that is so closely identified with Art Nouveau.

In 1878 the French designer and craftsman Emile Gallé, who was to become the undisputed master of cameo glass, exhibited his first glass creations: enamelled wares with historical subjects (the Islamic and Japanese-decorated pieces came later). His strongest competitor was the St Denis glassworks of Auguste Legras. Antonin and Auguste Daum's Nancy glassworks produced cameo and enamelled wares which closely resemble the work of Gallé.

In Austria some cameo glass was produced at the Loetz glassworks but the output was small compared with their iridescent glassware, first exhibited in 1898. The driving force at Loetz was Max von Spaun who was responsible for introducing various techniques including the simulation of hardstones such as onyx and cornelian. Kolomon Moser and other members of the Wiener Werkstätte designed iridescent glassware for Loetz.

In the United States Louis Comfort Tiffany shared von Spaun's fascination with iridescence. He acquired his own glassworks in 1892 and within three years launched his table lamps. With their colourful and varied glass panel shades and cast bronze bases, these are the dazzling highlight of Art Nouveau glassware design.

Other types of experimental glass were produced in this period. The Glasgow glassworks of James Couper & Sons made a heavily bubbled glassware of green, amber and sometimes pink hue with Roman and Isnik shapes after designs by Dr Christopher Dresser and George Walton among others. The name "Clutha", stencilled onto each piece, derives from the Scottish word for "cloudy".

The London glassworks of James Powell & Sons popularized Venetian-inspired glassware, often in green or "vaseline" colour (that is, green toning to opaque pale yellow).

Not all glass of the period was signed and the output of many factories was similar enough to lead to confusion of attribution. The best way to become familiar with the particular characteristics of each factory is to browse among contemporary periodicals. If a seller attributes a piece to an artist or factory, he should be able to provide proof of authenticity. A designer's monogram and maker's stamp on pieces where you would expect to find one, could more than quadruple the value of an object.

A signed Gallé blowout, or mould-blown, lamp with a bronze mount, base and shade, c.1900 (ht 18in/45cm). *C*
* Gallé is best known for his cameo glass. His personal creations are scarce and very expensive. They are often inscribed with contemporary French verse and referred to as *vases parlants*. He experimented with metal oxides, which gave a translucent colour to the glass. Etching, air bubbles and metallic strips were all used for decorative effect. From 1900 he made glass lampshades. All the objects made at his factory are marked, but it is impossible to attribute relief signatures to Gallé himself. After Gallé's death in 1904 a star was added after the mark.

A German "Orivit" gilt, bronze and clear glass vase, 1905, with typical Art Nouveau maskheads (ht 10in/25cm). Similar vases were mass-produced in Germany, either by Olbrich or Gustav Gurschner, and by Kayserzinn and WMF. Though already popular, there is still scope for the collector. *B*

A pewter-mounted glass vase (ht 10in/25cm) designed in 1905 by Josef Maria Olbrich, a member of the Wiener Werkstätte. The vase is a hybrid of the French and German treatment of Art Nouveau. More purist members of the Wiener Werkstätte were working in modern geometric forms. *C*

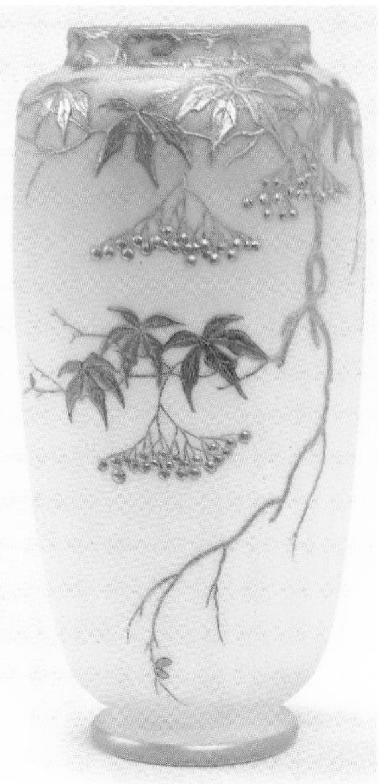

The toned effect of this Queen's Burmese vase by Webb, c.1890 (ht 12in/30cm), was developed by the American Mount Washington glassworks as Peachblow. The effect was achieved with gold and uranium oxides – which rendered all Burmese ware radioactive for 100 years. Fakes and copies abound. The circular signature of Mount Washington is not easily copied. American Peachblow has a polished surface; that of Webb's Burmese ware is matt. *B*

A Tiffany domed shade on a bronze stand

A Tiffany conical shade on a bronze twisted vine base

A Tiffany Favrile paperweight glass vase (ht 8½in/22cm) produced in 1909. (Favrile is the trade name for the company's hand-made iridescent glass.) The underside of the vase is engraved "8156 TIFFANY FAVRILE". The paperweight effect is distributed throughout the body of the vase. *S*

* Other common Tiffany marks are "L.C.T." (Tiffany's initials) and "T.G.C." (Tiffany Glass, Decorating Co.), both with or without the word FAVRILE. Not all Tiffany glassware was iridescent. Some pieces were given a gold sheen by the use of gold chloride; blue, green and white lustre wares were also made, while blue and gold were combined in lava ware. Cypriote ware, of brown or opaque glass, was given a corroded appearance by the application of powdered glass.

This Tiffany grape leaded glass and bronze lamp (ht 26in/65cm) is an elaborate variation on his standard grape table lamp. As in most of his lamps, the organic shade is made from opaque pieces of Favrile glass set in bronze, on a bronze tree-like stand. Tiffany lamps are usually marked on the inner rim of the shade and on the base underside. The base of this example is impressed "TIFFANY STUDIOS NEW YORK 28276". *CNY*

Above left: Palme-König vase, c.1900 (ht 4in/10cm). *B above right:* Loetz vase, c.1900 (ht 10½in/27cm). *CG* Palme-König vases are often misattributed to Loetz because of their iridescence but they lack the quality of Loetz: the glass is thinner and the iridescent trailing decoration seems less controlled than Loetz's ornately feathered effect. Palme-König and Loetz wares are usually unsigned, although some Loetz pieces bear etched crossed arrows. Palme-König bases are often moulded. Loetz pieces, unless specifically intended to be mounted, have a polished pontil mark. The collector should be wary of Palme-König pieces bearing spurious Loetz marks. Loetz glass made for export to America and England was marked "Loetz, Austria".

A clear and blue flash wine glass, 1905 (ht 8in/20cm), part of a suite designed by the Secessionist artisan Otto Prutscher, and considered avant garde in its day. Variations exist in other colours, including red, black, green and yellow. Pieces are collected for their individual appeal. Complete sets are unlikely to turn up. They were unmarked and were not copied or faked. *B*

A typical overlaid and etched glass vase made in 1900, with the etched signature "Daum, Nancy" and the snail handles that were popular in this period (ht 8in/20 cm). Daum wares bear the cross of Lorraine that was also occasionally used by Gallé. *CNY*

* Daum glass was sometimes sold in wrought mounts made by Louis Majorelle. The glass would have the Daum mark. Daum also produced glass shades for the serpent lamps of Edgar Brandt.

Sculpture and Metalwork

The symbolism and sensuality of Art Nouveau had a catalyst effect on sculpture, transforming the stale reworking of Baroque and Neo-classical themes. At the same time, the introduction of smaller-scale bronzes made decorative sculpture more affordable than hitherto. The American actress Loïe Fuller – the living embodiment of Art Nouveau – was a popular subject for the statuettes produced in such quantity in Europe at this time. The interest in sculptural forms was also expressed in highly figurative treatments of functional objects. Paper knives, for example, were given handles in the shape of nymphs – a particular speciality of the Germans.

Most Art Nouveau decorative sculpture came from France. The dream maidens of Maurice Bouval, their flowing tresses adorned by large flowerheads, are sensual in the manner of Mucha. Other important sculptors of the period include Jean Dampt and Emmanuel Villanis.

Commemorative plaques and medallions enjoyed renewed attention from many leading designers, including Pierre Roche, René Lalique and Edmond Becker. Alexandre Charpentier is especially interesting for his distinctive technique of depicting figures partially enveloped by swirling mists.

In England the style that emerged in the last quarter of the 19th century came to be described as "New Sculpture". To qualify, an artist had to embody natural forms with human feeling. The giants in this field were Alfred Gilbert and George Frampton, but fine pieces were also made by Alfred Drury, Albert Toft, Edgar Bertram Mackennal and others.

The use of spelter was widely promoted as a less expensive alternative to bronze. This silver-coloured metal is an alloy of zinc combined with aluminium or lead. It can be patinated to resemble bronze, but is lighter in weight.

Art Nouveau also signalled a revival in the English pewter industry, stimulated by European precedent. The German manufacturer J.P. Kayser introduced a highly individual range of pewterware using organic forms, retailed under the name "Kayserzinn". Kayser's success inspired Liberty to introduce his own range of pewterware, called "Tudric": these wares had design similarities with the firm's "Cymric" silver, but were more affordable and reached a much wider market.

The integration of form and function is best illustrated in table lamps. The newly available electric lights lent themselves especially well to this treatment. Plants and maidens concealed light fittings in their trailing leafage or garments. The Frenchmen Raoul Larche and Leo Laporte-Blairsy were particularly adept at such disguises.

Sculptural metalwork in America often tended toward the conservative. For example, the copperwares of the Roycroft workshops displayed an influence more readily recognizable as Arts and Crafts than Art Nouveau.

Many figures of the period were first displayed in plaster or clay, then cast in bronze if popular. This gilt bronze dancing figure, *La Cothurne* (ht 21in/53cm), was cast from a model by the Frenchman Agathon Leonard. It is one in a series that was also made in white biscuit porcelain by the Sèvres factory. *C*

The Sluggard by Frederic Lord Leighton exemplifies the work of the English New Sculpture movement. It was first issued in bronze in 1886 (ht 20in/51.5cm) and was subsequently cast in two sizes. Leighton's sculptures embody a real feeling of movement and a break from traditional themes. *S*

The German firm WMF (Württembergische Metallwaren-fabrik) popularized electroplated wares. This ice bucket featuring a nymph in high relief has the typically German whiplash handle. *ST*

* The WMF mark – a stork within a triangle, and the company's initials – is so tiny that it is often missed. There is no standard place for it, although the footrim is likely. Sometimes it was worked discreetly into the decoration.

This bronze fisherman and mermaid, c.1898 (ht 24in/60cm), by Edouard Lanteri is another example of the "New Sculpture" movement. The mermaid emerges from a mass of bronze, like a half-finished sculpture – or a being in the process of incarnation. Such transformations are a typical theme of Art Nouveau bronzes. *P*

Several popular figures by Théodore Rivière commemorate the role of leading ladies of the stage: this mildly erotic bronze group, entitled *Carthage*, 1901 (ht 27in/68.5cm), depicts a scene from the play *Salammbo* in which the title role was played by the actress Sarah Bernhardt. *C*

Water nymphs were popular subjects among Art Nouveau sculptors. This maiden (ht 22in/57cm) was modelled by Louis Chalon in 1901 from the unusual combination of carved marble and gilt bronze. *C*
* The hair style, known as *en chignon*, is typical of the period, and the most usual alternative to the ubiquitous windswept tresses.

A copper urn by the American designer and architect Frank Lloyd Wright (ht 18in/46cm). Although made in 1903, its simplified form looks forward to the Art Deco period. *CNY*
* Wright was the foremost exponent of the Prairie School. His early work reveals a sympathy with American Arts and Crafts, which was in turn influenced by Voysey and other British designers. Though available in the United States, his work is hard to come by in England.

This rare bronze oil lamp was designed by Leo Laporte-Blairsy in 1900 (ht 20in/50cm). The birds nestling elegantly against the stem are typical of this artist's concern for detail. *CAm*

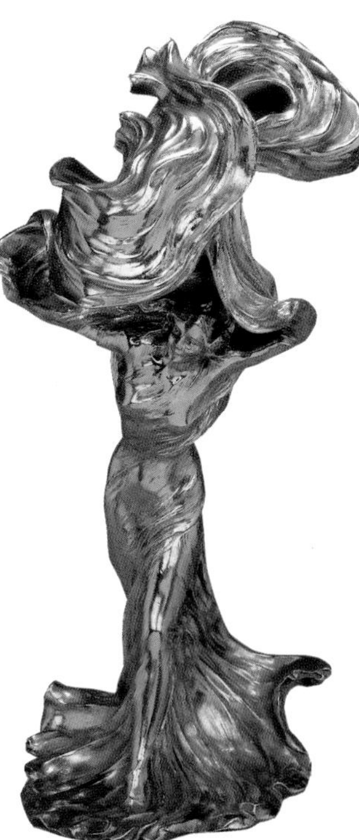

This gilt bronze table lamp in the form of Loïe Fuller (ht approx. 25in/63.5cm) was designed by Raoul Larche. Such lamps were mass-produced but have not survived in large numbers. The electrical fitting is concealed within the billowing drape above the head and shoulders. *B*
* This lamp has been much copied, and forgeries are difficult to detect. French copies made in the 1970s are convincing, and even have the foundry mark, and sometimes contemporary wires and fittings.

TABLE LAMPS

Sculptural table lamps are much more readily available, and generally more affordable, than statuettes. Lighting was a particular preoccupation between 1895 and 1905, coinciding with the excitement at the spread of electricity. The most frequently found form is the flower, which has an obvious affinity with the function. Female forms were also popular – especially wood nymphs and water nymphs, which were mostly naked. There was also a hybrid flower-woman, known as a *femme-fleur*.

MARKS

Bronze sculptures sometimes bear not only the designer's signature but also a foundry mark. These are often hard to decipher. Some bronzes were produced in limited editions, in which case they would also bear a number. Utility objects in bronze are often unsigned.

Silver and Jewelry

The Arts and Crafts Movement helped to reprieve a British silver industry entrenched in the Victorian concept of smothering form with decoration.

The revival in silver manufacture was led by C.R. Ashbee who founded the Guild of Handicraft in 1888. His distinctive style, which included the use of accentuated wirework handles, came to typify the Guild's work. The designs of Dr Christopher Dresser were mass-produced by such established manufacturers as Elkington & Co., Hukin & Heath and James Dixon & Co. Dresser's forms are mostly devoid of decoration and rely upon the principle of "fitness for purpose", the object satisfying both aesthetic and functional requirements.

The influence of Celtic art is evident in the pieces designed by Archibald Knox, the leading light of Liberty's successful silverware range launched in 1899 under the trade name of Cymric.

The influence of British design, and especially of Dresser, Ashbee and Mackintosh, extended to the work produced in Austria by the Wiener Werkstätte (Vienna Workshops), which gained mature expression in the work emanating from Germany's Bauhaus.

French jewellers who adopted the Art Nouveau style were far more successful than silversmiths in the same country. They included the multi-talented René Lalique, Georges Fouquet, Lucien Gaillard and Paul and Henri Vever. British jewelry in this period was developed on a mass-production basis that went against the ethics advocated by the various guilds. It was Liberty who turned the tables on the guilds by mass-producing jewelry that emulated the hand finish of the craftsman.

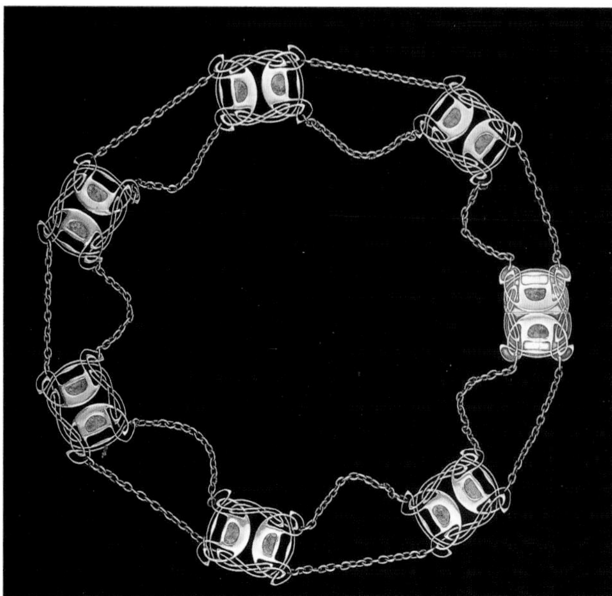

A silver belt designed by Archibald Knox for the Cymric range of Liberty & Co. It comprises seven Celtic panel motifs embellished with mottled orange and green enamel; hallmarked Birmingham 1903. *S*

* None of Liberty's designers were allowed to sign their pieces and Knox is the only one whose work can be identified with any certainty. Along with Celtic motifs, he favoured entrelac (interlacing) designs, often enhanced by blue and green enamel.

This rare gold and enamel pendant by René Lalique, c.1900, stamped "Lalique" (lgth 4in/9.5cm), shows the artist's preference for ornate enamelwork and baroque pearls, reminiscent of the designs and materials of Renaissance jewelry. *S*

* If a chain is original to a piece it will be of comparable quality and may be similarly decorated.

LIBERTY

Celtic motifs characterize Liberty's Cymic range, produced c.1901-c.1926. Cymric jewelry, candlesticks, vases and silver caskets were made in large numbers; many of them were manufactured by W.H. Haseler of Birmingham. Popular colours were peacock and kingfisher. Baroque pearls and turquoise were much favoured. The word "CYMRIC" usually appears on pieces, together with the usual silver hallmarks. Some silver objects have had enamels added to give them the Cymric look.

* Liberty's Tudric range of domestic ware in pewter shared many Cymric motifs. Items often carry the mark "TUDRIC PEWTER" followed by the stock number, or "English Pewter".

* The commemorative spoons and buckles produced by Liberty in 1902 for Edward VII's coronation are collectable and relatively expensive, especially in their original presentation cases.

A rare silver table clock designed by Josef Hoffmann and executed by Alfred Meyer for the Wiener Werkstätte, c.1906 (ht 11in/28cm). The chequerboard design is typical of Viennese Art Nouveau. The clock bears the Austrian silver mark and the maker's mark (many members of the Wiener Werkstätte had their own monogram). *CNY*

* Hoffmann designed a series of silver and painted metalwares using geometric piercing. He also produced items in white lacquered metal; these have not survived in good condition.

* The movement fitted in Art Nouveau (and Art Deco) clocks is not an important collecting factor, although it is preferable to have the original. In this example, Hoffmann would have designed the dial and chapter ring.

* Clocks were also made in the Cymric range, but these are not as rare as the Wiener Werkstätte examples.

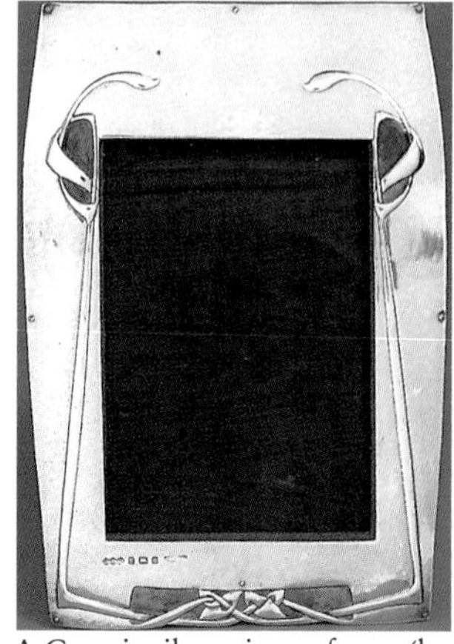

A Cymric silver picture frame (ht 8½in/21cm) designed for Liberty by Archibald Knox with typical stylized Celtic strapwork and motifs, heightened by turquoise and green enamelling to give a jewel-like quality. Hallmarked Birmingham 1904. *C*

* "Silver-coloured metal", a term that often appears in auction catalogues, has a lower silver content than the minimun legal level for items described as "silver" in England, and such pieces are likely to be Continental.

Right This snake bracelet designed for Sarah Bernhardt by Alphonse Mucha and executed by Georges Fouquet in 1899 is arguably one of the most important pieces of Art Nouveau jewelry. It is composed of gold, enamel and diamonds in the form of a bangle which is joined to a ring by a fine gold chain. *CG*

* Although unique, the bracelet is typical of its period in its use of opal, much admired for its translucence and changeable colours; while the serpent is an age-old symbol of sensuality and femininity which appealed to the new image of the liberated female, and in its form reflects the new interest in subtle, sinuous curves.

* Mucha is best known for his distinctive posters (see page 190-1). Fouquet, as well as designing jewelry and carrying out Mucha's designs, created a style known as *mille-neuf-cent*, which incorporated coloured and precious stones and enamel.

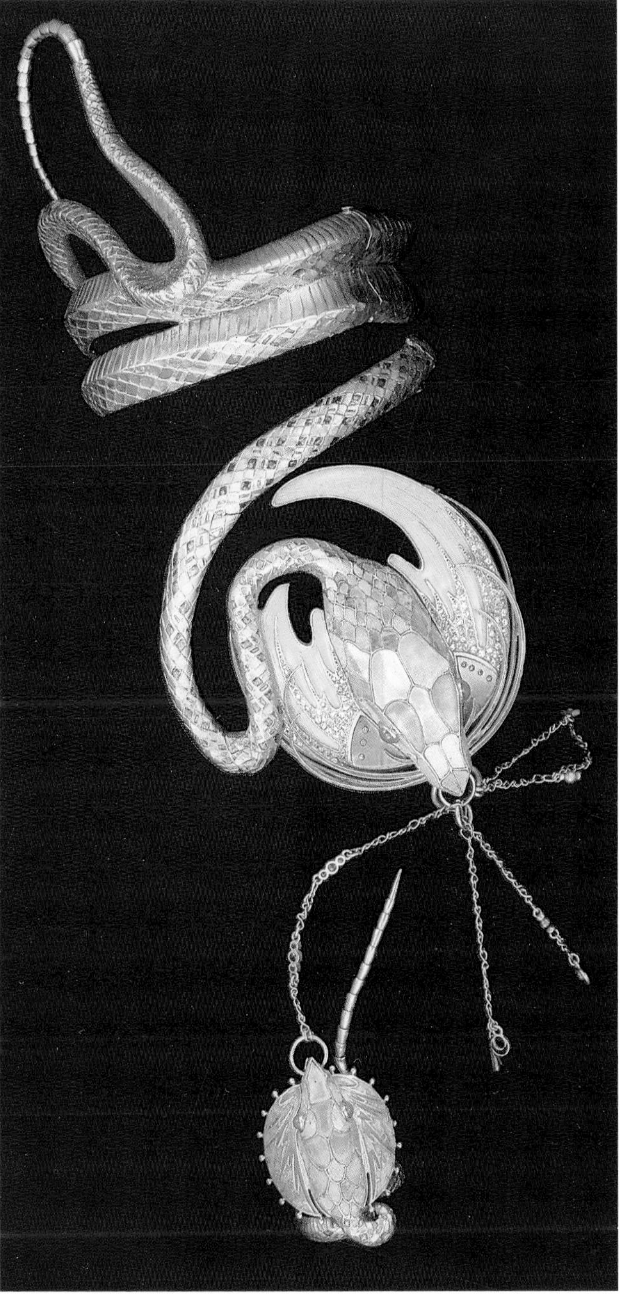

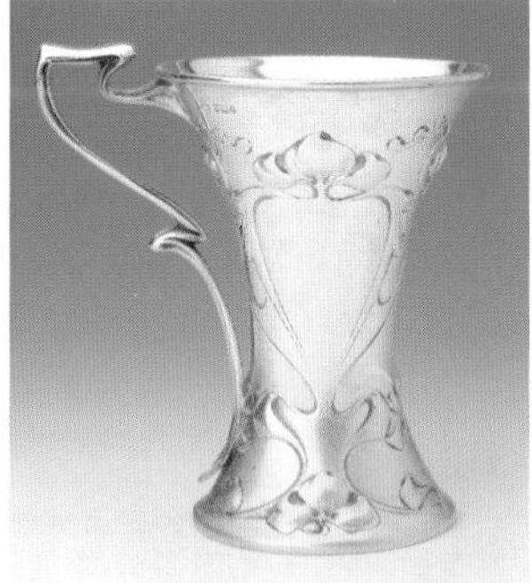

An unusually shaped English silver tankard, c.1905 (ht 6in/15cm), retailed through Mappin & Webb and decorated with stylized irises. The style is "international" Art Nouveau: the form reveals a strong Belgian influence, while the whiplash handle is commonly found in both France and Germany. The plain panel would lend itself well to engraving, but this would seriously reduce the value of the article. *B*

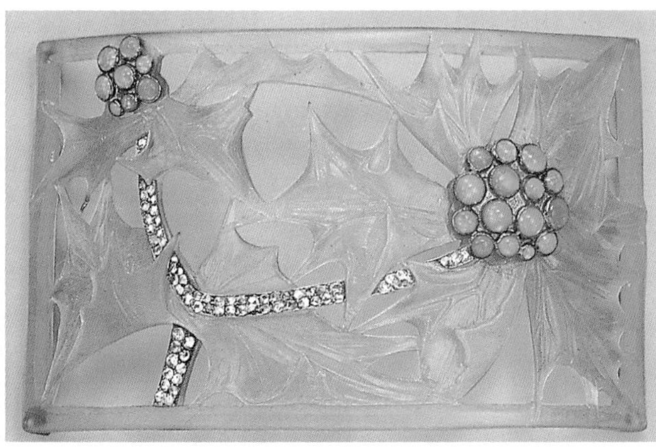

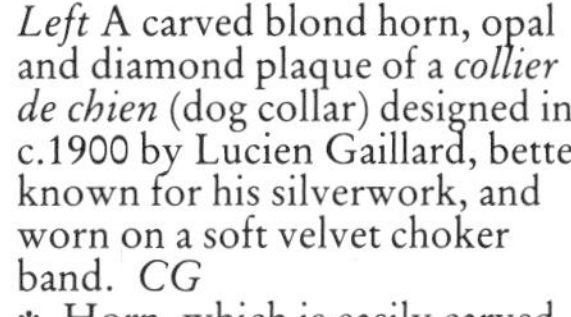

Left A carved blond horn, opal and diamond plaque of a *collier de chien* (dog collar) designed in c.1900 by Lucien Gaillard, better known for his silverwork, and worn on a soft velvet choker band. *CG*

* Horn, which is easily carved, was also used by Lalique and Fouquet. Although horn had no intrinsic value, these popular pieces would have commanded a high price because of their elaborate design.

* Lalique's influence on Gaillard was so strong that it is often difficult to tell their work apart. However, their pieces would always have been signed.

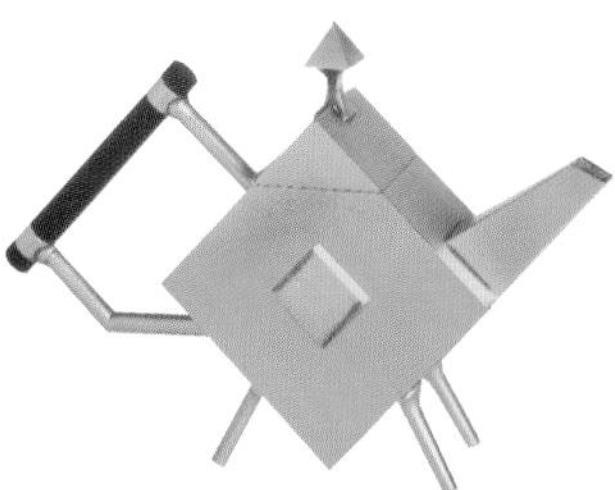

A unique silver-plated teapot (ht 7in/18cm) designed by Dr Christopher Dresser, c.1885, which exemplifies his principle of "fitness for purpose". Its geometrical construction is akin to Bauhaus design of the 1920s and thus almost 40 years ahead of its time. *P*

* The Japanese influence, with its emphasis on simplified form, is clearly discernible in the lozenge motifs and geometry of Dresser's designs. He also made tureens, claret jugs and folding toast racks; many of these items bear the rod handle he favoured (see below).

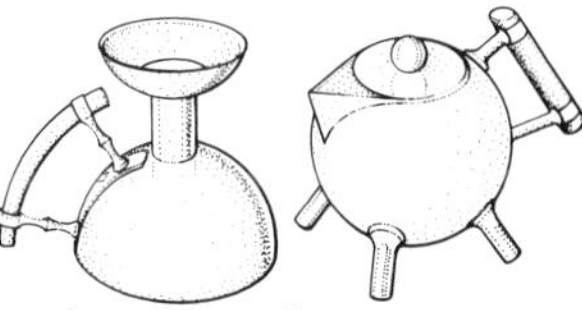

Other Dresser shapes: a candlestick and a cream jug.

A silver and opalescent blown glass decorative chalice designed by René Lalique in 1904 and numbered 32 on the footrim (ht 8in/20cm). It is not known how many chalices were made, but this is thought to be one of the last of its series. Pine cones were a decorative motif employed by Lalique in several media – for example, in his furniture and leatherwork. He commonly depicted flowers, insects and women. Opalescent glass, especially that designed by Lalique, was very popular throughout the period. *B*

Posters

The development of Art Nouveau design, together with improvements in lithographic techniques, helped to establish the poster as an art form in its own right. Before this most posters were printed in letterpress, which was much less versatile.

The pioneer of French poster advertising was Jules Chéret. In the 1890s his bold two-dimensional designs, like those of Henri de Toulouse-Lautrec, transformed the Parisian boulevards into an enormous art gallery. Poster enthusiasts would emerge under cover of darkness to sponge new creations off the hoardings. The Czech artist Alphonse Mucha was also working in Paris. His original use of pastel colours and sinuous lines appealed to Sarah Bernhardt, who employed him to design many of the posters advertising her roles.

In England the poster was not so much a feature of the street scene: instead it was employed indoors to promote theatrical productions and art gallery exhibitions. English posterists included Aubrey Beardsley, Dudley Hardy and the "Beggarstaff Brothers", William Nicholson and James Pryde. As in other media, Mackintosh's designs inspired Viennese Secessionist artists such as Kolomon Moser and Gustav Klimt. Secessionist posters are especially collectable now.

Poster art in the United States had been developing steadily throughout the 19th century, advertising such diverse events as art exhibitions, Wild West shows and circuses. Edward Penfield became America's leading poster artist, with his interpretation of "All-American" characters of the time. Maxfield Parrish, the English-born Louis Rhead and the book illustrator Will Bradley were all popular posterists.

The popularity of poster art declined after 1900, although the First World War saw the effective use of the medium for propaganda purposes.

One of a series of posters designed by Alphonse Mucha in 1898 to advertise Job cigarette papers. The harmonious colour scheme, the dreamy woman with her abundance of hair and her quintessentially modern pose – languorously smoking – are typical of Mucha. Other Mucha posters promote champagne, beer and biscuits. Signed (20 × 15½in/50 × 39cm). *CNY*

* Mucha often elongated his posters, filling the spaces with Celtic, Japanese and Byzantine motifs. His detractors called this the "noodle" or "macaroni" style, because of the swirling forms. He frequently used gold and silver to set off his restrained palette.

CONDITION

Many posters that survive today never found their way onto walls, and it is these examples in their virgin state that are most desirable. Often, posters have been linen-backed for display: this is acceptable, although less desirable. You may also come across a framed poster. Don't try to detach it unless you are sure you will not damage it in the process. Most posters will have suffered some wear and tear and are likely to have fold marks and tears and the inevitable degree of fading where the poster has not been protected from direct light. Strength of colour adds to the value, as do areas of gilding that give some posters a jewel-like quality. Sets are desirable. Modern reproductions are plentiful but easy to distinguish from originals by the obviously modern paper.

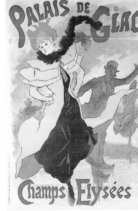

These two posters designed by Jules Chéret in 1893 advertise the appearance of Loïe Fuller at the Folies-Bergère and the delights of ice skating at the Palais de Glace. The vivid red and yellow central figures within a strong outline, coupled with a minimum of text, epitomize Chéret's style. The typography of the Palais de Glace poster is typically French in its amoeba-like forms. Both posters were printed by Chaix of Paris. (Folies-Bergère: 48½ × 34¾in/123 × 88cm; Palais de Glace: 48¾ × 37½ in/124 × 95cm) *CSK*

An early Maxfield Parrish poster, 1896, with flat colours and a Japanese woodblock influence that later gave way to the more sophisticated subjects and techniques for which he is better known. Signed (24 × 34in/61 × 86.5cm). *CNY*

Above A poster designed by Charles Rennie Mackintosh in 1896 with a perpendicular neo-Gothic influence. The eerie, somewhat menacing style earned the Glasgow School the title of "The Spook School". Signed (97½ × 40in/248 × 101cm). *B*

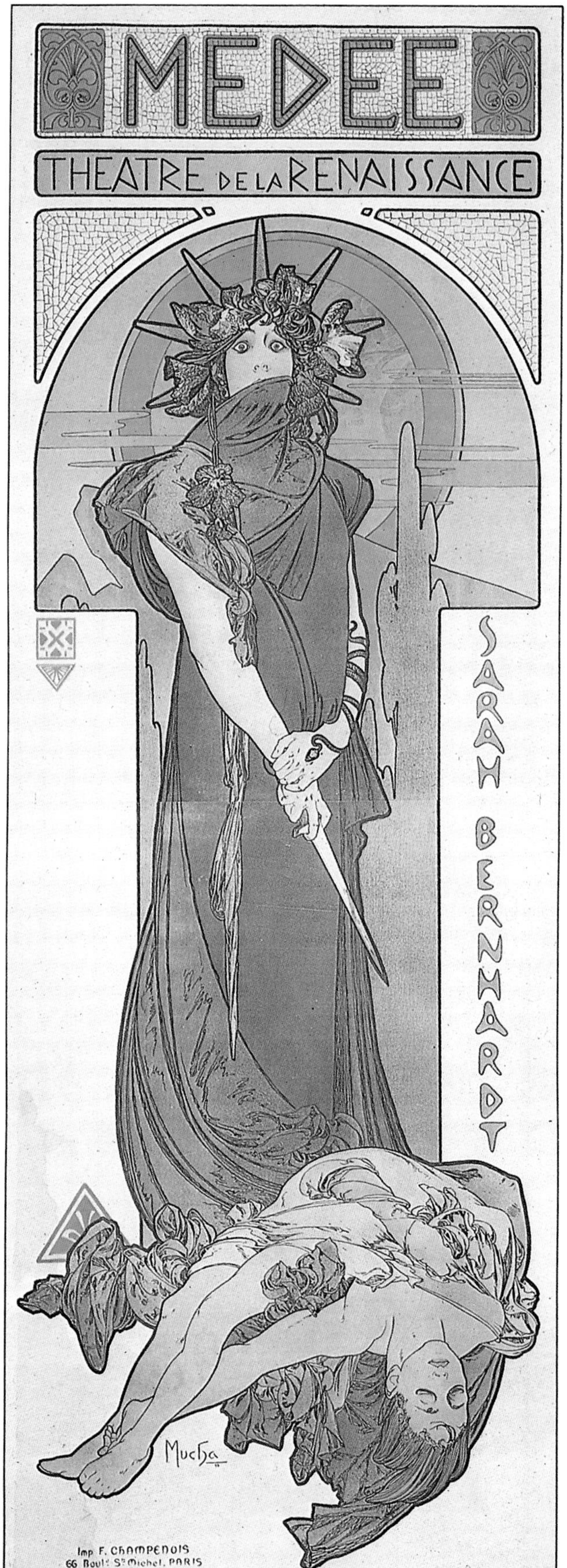

Right One of Mucha's most striking designs, this poster of 1898 (29¼ × 82½in/74.5 × 209.5cm), advertises the appearance of Sarah Bernhardt at the Théâtre de la Renaissance. The image is sharp and the colours very vivid. *P*

Reference

GLOSSARY

Abalone shell An ear-shaped shell lined with mother-of-pearl.
Baroque pearl An irregularly shaped pearl.
Blister pearl A knobby pearl.
Blond horn Pale horn, sometimes bleached; an inexpensive, easily carved material used in jewelry.
Blowout (mould-blown) Term used to describe glass objects formed by blowing molten glass into a mould.
Cameo glass Glass composed of two or more layers of different colours, carved or etched away to create a design in relief.
Cloisonné Enamel work, the colours divided by wire; the effect is similar to stained glass.
Conch shell A coloured, spiral mollusc shell, often large.
Entrelac Interlacing designs.
Eosin An iridescent glaze used on pottery from the Zsolnay factory.
Facsimile signature An exact copy of a signature.
Hardstone A generic term given to non-precious stones.
Impressed Describes a stamped design or mark.
Incised Describes a design or mark cut into the surface of the object.
Iridescent glass Glass with a lustrous appearance, shot through with a range of colours.
Jardinière A decorative container for house plants.
Leaded glass Glass sections held together by lead, used in stained glass windows and Tiffany lamps.
Letterpress A method of printing an image on paper from a raised, inked surface.
Lithography A printing process using a flat stone or metal sheet treated so that some areas will not take ink.
Losses A catalogue term for wear and tear of paper and other delicate materials.
Lustreware A type of pottery characterized by its sheen.
Macassar A rare form of ebony.
Maskhead A decorative female half-head.
Mille-neuf-cent A decorative form combining coloured and precious stones, pearls and enamelwork.
Onglaze (overglaze) Decorative treatment whereby decoration is applied over a glaze.
Opalescence A milky iridescence suggesting the qualities of opal.
Overlay The layer of glass applied to a glass body and carved away – for example, to create **cameo glass**.
Pâte-de-verre Glassware made from translucent powdered glass suspended in a paste which has fused in a mould.
Saltglaze Brown or off-white glassy stoneware produced by adding salt to the kiln at firing.
Slip Clay mixed with water and paint for decorating pottery.
Slip-trail A network of fine lines of **slip** applied to pottery, sometimes called "tubeline".
Spelter A zinc alloy, a less expensive alternative to bronze.
Stone glass Densely coloured glass that resembles stone.
Transfer printing The transfer of an inked image from an engraved surface to paper and from there to ceramics or enamels.
Underglaze In ceramics, a colour or design painted before the application of the glaze.
Vaseline A colour effect in glass which tones from green to opaque pale yellow.
Whiplash style (eel style) S-shaped ornamentation.
Wirework The decorative use of interwoven wire.

SELECTED DESIGNERS, MANUFACTURERS, RETAILERS AND MOVEMENTS

Arts and Crafts Movement (c.1870-90) English movement, spearheaded by William Morris, which attempted to emulate the styles and craftsmanship of the Middle Ages.
Ashbee, Charles Robert (1863-1942) British architect, designer. Founded the Guild of Handicraft in 1888. He influenced the **Vienna Secessionists**. By 1911 Ashbee wrote in favour of the machine, a reversal of his earlier antipathy. Mark on silver: "CRA".
Baillie Scott, Mackay Hugh (1865-1945) British architect and designer; his simple furniture and interiors made a united design.
Bauhaus German design school, 1919-1933, founded by **Walter Gropius**. Pure, geometrical forms are at the heart of much Bauhaus design.
Bing, Samuel (1838-1905) German connoisseur, opened "La Maison de l'Art Nouveau" in Paris, 1895, selling decorative arts.
Bradley, William (1868-1962) Self-taught American graphic artist, influenced by the work of William Morris and **Aubrey Beardsley.**
Bugatti, Carlo (1855-1940) Italian furniture designer, known for his exotic creations.
Century Guild Group of British artist-craftsmen, founded 1882 by

A.H. Mackmurdo and others.
Charpentier, Alexandre (1856-1909) French metalworker and furniture designer, member of **Nancy School**. Made bas-reliefs, bronze medals and door furniture incorporating nude figures.
Chéret, Jules (1836-1932) French graphic artist, best known for his vibrant poster designs.

Colonna, Edward (1862-1948) German designer, lived in Paris, 1890s, member of **Paris School**. Some wares sold by **Bing.**
Cotswold School Group formed in Gloucestershire, England by the furniture designers **Ernest Gimson** and Sidney Barnsley (1865-1926).
Couper & Sons, James (1890s) Scottish glass manufacturers, best known for their "Clutha" ware designed by **Dresser** and **Walton.**

Daly, Matthew (active c.1900) One of the artists who decorated **Rookwood** pottery with American Indian portraits.
Daum, Auguste and **Antonin** (1853-1909, 1864-1930) French brother glassmakers, members of the **Nancy School**. Followers of **Gallé**, they produced cameo and enamelled glassware inspired by his designs but less adventurous.
de Feure, George (1868-1943) French artist and designer, member of the **Paris School**.
De Morgan, William Frend (1839-1917) English ceramic designer, specialized in tile designs. In partnership with **C.** and **F. Passenger**, 1898-1907.
Doulton & Co. (established c.1815) **(Royal Doulton** 1901) English pottery firm. Marks: company name, artist's mark, name of ware, lion over coronet (from 1902), lion on stoneware from 1922.
Dresser, Christopher (1834-1904) Scottish designer. His pieces combine utility with aesthetics and reflect a Japanese influence. Artistic director of **Hukin & Heath** from c.1878.
Elkington & Co. (founded c.1835). English cutlery firm, one of the first companies to produce austere Art Nouveau designs, rather than florid forms. **Dresser** designed pieces, 1875-88.
Fouquet, Georges (1862-1957) French designer and jewelry manufacturer. He created the *mille-neuf-cent* style. Mark: "Gges. Fouquet".
Gaillard, Lucien (1862-1933) French silversmith and jeweler, member of **Paris School**. Influenced by **Lalique**.
Gallé, Émile (1846-1904) French. The most influential Art Nouveau glassmaker, he created or revived many techniques such as cameo glass, initially hand-made but, from 1899, factory-produced. His 300-strong team also made glass electric lighting from c.1900. Co-founder of **Nancy School**. Furniture designed from mid-1880s.

Gimson, Ernest (1864-1919) English designer, particularly of furniture which combined traditional and innovative forms.
Glasgow School Design movement at the turn of the century led by "The Glasgow Four", **Charles Rennie Mackintosh**, Herbert MacNair and Margaret and Frances MacDonald. Restrained design and craftsmanship were central principles. Influential in Austria and Germany.
Greene & Greene Partnership formed 1893 between Henry and Charles Sumner Greene (1870-1954, 1868-1957), American cabinet-makers. Influenced by traditional Japanese design.
Gropius, Walter (1883-1969) German architect, founder of the **Bauhaus**. Exponent of modernist principles: simple lines in machine-made goods of modern materials.
Gruber, Jacques (1870-1936) French furniture maker and member of the **Nancy School**, he worked for the **Daum** brothers and for **Majorelle.**
Guimard, Hector (1867-1942) French pioneer of Art Nouveau; architect and designer and exponent of unified design. Member of the **Paris School**.
Handicraft, Guild of (founded 1888) Led by **Ashbee**, this British group upheld the importance of craftsmanship in the applied arts.
Hoffmann, Josef (1870-1956) Austrian architect and designer, co-founder of the **Vienna Secession** and the **Wiener Werkstätte**. Geometrical jewelry, metalwork and furniture designs foreshadow Art Deco.

Hukin & Heath English silver and metalware manufacturers, 1879-1953. Specialized in tea and coffee sets.
Knox, Archibald (1864-1933) English designer and craftsman. Emphasized Celtic motifs in his work. Designed Cymric silverware and Tudric pewterware for **Liberty & Co.**, unsigned.
Lalique, René (1860-1945) Innovative French designer, especially of jewelry and glass. The dragonfly was a favourite motif. Turned to glass at the end of the 19thC, abandoned jewelry altogether in 1914.
Laporte-Blairsy, Leo (1865-1923) French sculptor and designer of silverware and jewelry, he often used marine motifs.
Larche, Raoul-François (1860-1912) French sculptor who made designs for mass-produced series in bronze and porcelain. His most famous designs were his Loïe Fuller statuettes and lamps.
Läuger, Max (1864-1952) German architect and sculptor, artist potter from late 19thC.
Legras, Auguste (active 1864-1909) French glass designer and manufacturer. Used techniques developed by **Daum** and combined cameo-cutting with enamel work.

Léonard, Agathon (b. 1841) Pseudonym of van Weydeveldt. French sculptor who worked in bronze and porcelain and made designs for **Sèvres**, c.1900.
Liberty & Co. (1875-present) English retail firm, established by Arthur Lasenby Liberty. Advanced the cause of Arts and Crafts on a commercial scale. A Paris branch existed 1889-1931. Inspired *stile liberte*, the Italian term for Art Nouveau. Mark: company name on some wares.
Loetz (Lötz) Witwe (established 1836) Bohemian glassware company under direction of **Max von Spaun**. Their iridescent glass very like that of **Tiffany**.

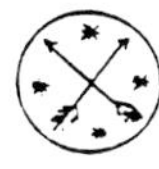

Macintyre & Co., James (established c.1847) English pottery firm. Art Pottery section under direction of **Moorcroft**, 1897-1913. Marks: transfer-printed name or initials of the company, sometimes with the title of the ware.
Mackennal, Edgar Bertram (1863-1931) Australian sculptor, emigrated to England, 1882. Exponent of "New Sculpture". Mark: signature.
Mackintosh, Charles Rennie (1868-1928) Scottish architect and designer, leading figure of the **Glasgow School**. Influenced German and Austrian design.
Mackmurdo, Arthur Heygate (1851-1942) British pioneer of Art Nouveau; with others, founded the **Century Guild**, a British group of artist-craftsmen, formed 1882. Used many flower and stalk motifs from 1884.
Majorelle, Louis (1859-1926) French artist and designer of metalwork and furniture. Co-founder with **Gallé** of the **Nancy School**. Workshop produced hand- and machine-made goods.
Mappin & Webb (founded 1774 by Jonathan Mappin) English silversmiths, engravers, cutlers and jewelers. Until the First World War there were branches throughout the world.
Marshall, Mark Villars (1879-1912) English potter and designer. Often worked on saltglazed stoneware. Used low- and high-relief and open-work. Reptiles and figures were recurrent motifs. Mark: incised "MVM".
Martin Brothers (1873-1914) London pottery firm, pioneers of unique art pottery. Best known for their grotesque birds. Marks: "R.W. Martin & Brothers"; "Martin Brothers".
Massier (active from 1872) French family of potters who specialized in lustre-decorated wares. The symbolist painter Lucien Lévy-Dhurmer was artistic director in the 1880s.
Minton (1793-present) English pottery. Art Nouveau earthenware vases made under **Léon Solon** using slip-trail decoration and coloured glazes.
Moorcroft, William (1872-1945) English potter. 1889-1913, head of Art Pottery department of **Macintyre & Co.** Decorative elements taken from nature. Established own pottery with Macintyre staff, 1913.
Moser, Kolomon (1868-1918) Austrian designer, painter and architect; member of the **Vienna Secession** and founder member of the **Wiener Werkstätte.**

Mount Washington (established 1837) American glass manufacturers, New Bedford, Mass. "Peachblow" was their most famous range. The factory also made cut glass.
Mucha, Alphonse (1860-1939) Czechoslovakian designer, best known for his poster designs of beautiful women. He also designed jewelry, seen in the influential *Documents Décoratifs.*

Nancy School (École de Nancy) A group of artists and designers which formed around **Gallé** and **Majorelle** in the 1890s. Native and exotic woods were used in furniture, the local flora and fauna providing decorative motifs.
Olbrich, Josef Maria (1867-1908) Austrian architect, artist and designer, co-founder of the **Vienna Secession** (1897).
Palme-König (established 1786) Bohemian glass manufacturers. Produced iridescent glass in the late 19thC.

Paris School (École de Paris) French design group which favoured stylized and abstract organic forms in furniture.
Passenger, Charles and **Frederick** English potters, partners of **De Morgan**, 1898-1907. Charles used lustre finish with tall-ship and nature motifs; he initialled his work. Frederick continued to produce Isnik-type tiles in the 1920s and 30s.
Penfield, Edward (1866-1925) American graphic artist, best known for his "All-American" characters.

Prairie School American modernist movement in domestic architecture initiated by **Frank Lloyd Wright**, c.1895.
Prutscher, Otto (1880-1949) Austrian designer, particularly of jewelry and furniture. Member of the **Vienna Secession** and the **Wiener Werkstätte**.

Rhead, Louis (1857-1926) British graphic artist who emigrated to America in 1883. He made lithographic posters from 1890.
Rookwood (1880-1941) American art pottery. Japanese and natural motifs were favoured, as well as the popular Indian head motif.
Rosenthal (established 1879) German pottery known for porcelain figurines and lightly decorated tableware.
Royal Dux (Duxer Porzellanmanufaktur A.G.) Ceramics factory, established 1860 in Bohemia. Water nymphs on shells, portrait busts and highly decorated vases were popular products. Large proportion of output exported to America. Marks: "E" (proprietor E. Eichler) in an oval, surrounded by "Royal Dux Bohemia".
Rozenburg (established 1885) Dutch ceramics factory. From 1900 made very thin earthenware with translucent bodies. Also used rich enamel colours on a white ground.
Sèvres French ceramics factory, established mid-18thC. Art Nouveau porcelain vases and figures produced in 1890s.
Solon, Léon (1872-1957) English ceramics designer. Art director and chief designer for **Minton**, 1900-1909. Co-designed Seccessionist wares with John Wadsworth.
Stickley, Gustav (1857-1942) American furniture designer and publisher of *The Craftsman* magazine. Greatly influenced by the **Arts and Crafts Movement.**
Tiffany, Louis Comfort (1848-1933). Highly influential American designer. Traded as Tiffany Glass & Decorating Co.; renamed Tiffany Studios in 1900. Patented iridescent favrile glass in 1880. Produced pottery from 1905. Tiffany became art director of Tiffany & Co., the family firm, in 1902. Made exclusive art jewelry.

L.C.T.

Toulouse-Lautrec, Henri de (1864-1901) French artist and posterist, famous for his representations of Parisian café life.
van de Velde, Henry (1863-1957) Belgian architect, illustrator and furniture designer. He was very influential in advancing the Art Nouveau style.

Vienna Secession (founded 1897) A breakaway group of architects, designers and artists from the conservative, official artistic institutions. Berlin and Munich also had Secession groups.
von Spaun, Max Ritter (d. 1909) Bohemian glass designer, grandson of Johann Loetz. Director of **Loetz Witwe**, 1879-1908. Encouraged the development and production of iridescent glass (1890).
Wahliss, Ernst (1836-1900) Bohemian ceramics manufacturer, established Alexandra Porcelain Works c.1880. Took over the Amphora factory (1897), known for its elaborate wares which are often mistaken for **Royal Dux.**
Walton, George (1867-1933) Scottish architect and designer. Member of the **Glasgow School**. Established George Walton & Co., Ecclesiastical & House Decorators, 1888. He designed for **Liberty & Co.** (1897) and "Clutha" glassware for **James Couper & Sons**.
Wiener Werkstätte (Viennese Workshops) (1903-32) An off-shoot of the **Vienna Secession**, inspired by the **Arts and Crafts Movement.** Aimed to combine utility with aesthetic qualities in a broad range of designs.

WMF (Württembergische Metallwarenfabrik) (established 1880) German metalware manufacturers. Produced extravagant pieces in pewter, German silver (a nickel-silver alloy), and glass.
Wright, Frank Lloyd (1867-1959) American architect and designer who emphasized the purity of form and the unity of design. Founder of the **Prairie School.**
Zsolnay (established 1862) Hungarian pottery factory. Used rich colour glazes and lustre decoration, 1893-1910.

BIBLIOGRAPHY

Amaya, Mario, *Art Nouveau* (1966)
Anscombe, Isabelle and Charlotte Gere, *Arts and Crafts in Britain and America* (1978)
Battersby, Martin, *The World of Art Nouveau* (1968)
Dawes, Nicholas, *Lalique Glass* (1986)
Garner, Philippe, *Émile Gallé* (1976)
Koch, Robert, *Louis C. Tiffany's Glass Bronzes Lamps* (1971)
Larner, Gerald and Celia, *The Glasgow Style* (1979)
Neuwirth, Waltraud, *Wiener Werkstätte* (1984)
Page, Marion, *Furniture Designed by Architects* (1980)
Rheims, M., *The Age of Art Nouveau* (1966).

ART DECO

These maps show the key British, European and American craftsmen, retail outlets and schools of design. The medium or media in which the craftsmen worked are indicated by letters after their name.

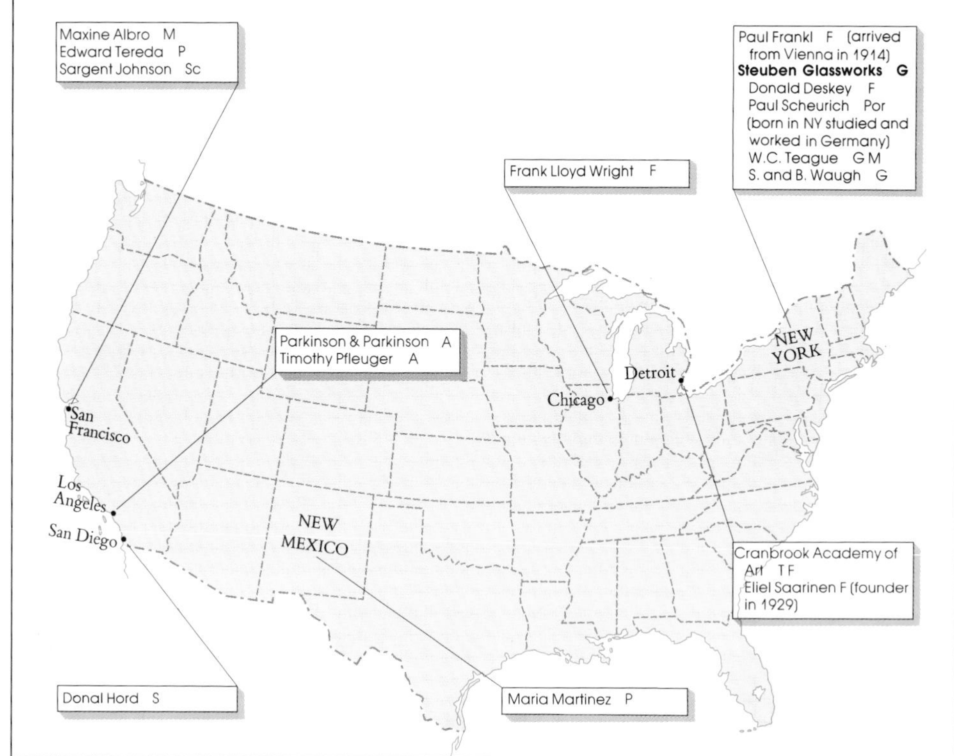

Br Bronze
F Furniture
G Glass
J Jewelry
M Metalwork
P Pottery
Pe Pewter
Por Porcelain
Pos Posters
S Sculpture
T Textiles
▪ Retail outlet

Clarice Cliff — Major Designer
Wedgwood — Factory

"Art Deco" is the term given to decorative styles of the 1920s and 30s that evolved out of certain aspects of Art Nouveau (see pages 178-193). For a long time ignored by collectors as of minor consequence, Art Deco is now very much in vogue, and prices are rising. Among the most recognizable artefacts in the style are extrovert, innovative pottery (notably by the English maker Clarice Cliff) and mantelpiece ornaments in bronze and ivory, often featuring athletic-looking women, who tended to look modern even when portrayed in archaic dress – a dramatic contrast to the languorous maidens of Art Nouveau.

Craftsman-made pieces, such as the Oriental-inspired pottery of the Frenchmen Emile Decoeur and Emile Lenoble, fetch high prices that will be beyond the reach of most collectors. More accessible are the mass-produced hand-finished items. Apart from the most fragile wares, such as cocktail glasses, which have not tended to survive in quantity, there is still plenty of scope in all media.

Art Deco reflected both changes in the way that fashionable people lived and influences from abroad that were perceived as intriguingly exotic. The famous glass car mascots of René Lalique typify the style's preoccupation with speed. Other motifs that regularly recur are Egyptian elements and designs from tribal Africa and Aztec Central America. To appreciate Art Deco pieces, we need to see them in the contecxt of the Roaring Twenties – the era which ushered in new dance crazes such as the Charleston, the explosion of jazz and Hollywood films.

Two very different approaches co-existed beneath the Art Deco umbrella: the Traditionalist and the Modernist. The Traditionalists mainly adapted forms from the golden years of French 18th- and early 19th-century furniture design. The chief advocates of this style were the French – for example, the cabinetmaker Jacques Emile Ruhlmann. Emphasis was placed on a balance of fine craftsmanship, tasteful design and the use of exotic woods and materials – such as amboyna wood and sharkskin.

The Modernists, including Marcel Breuer and the British furniture manufacturers, Isokon, reacted against the exclusivity of the Traditionalists by favouring mass production and the use of machine-made materials.

The style reached its zenith in the 1925 Paris "Exposition Internationale des Arts Décoratifs et Industriels Modernes", from which the term "Art Deco" was later extracted. German designers – many of whom advocated the Modernist approach – were not invited to attend. After the exhibition Traditionalism and Modernism continued to develop side by side for the next 15 years.

Pieces of the 1920s were once greatly preferred to those of the 30s, and French design was thought superior to British. However, over the last 10-15 years a more even-handed assessment has developed. The ceramics of Clarice Cliff and, increasingly, Keith Murray are fetching very high prices. One area that has perhaps not yet realized its full potential is British glassware.

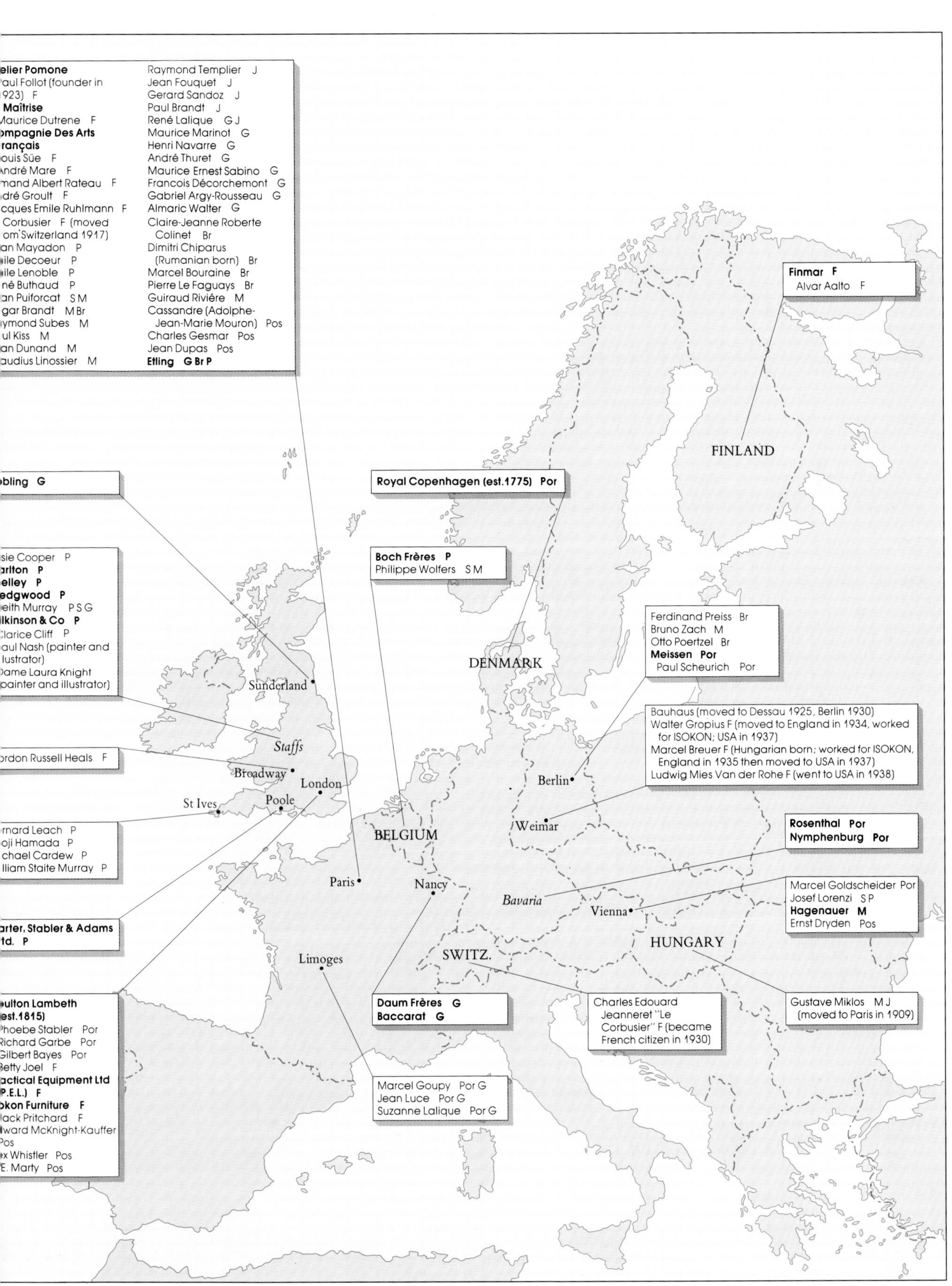
elier Pomone
'aul Follot (founder in
923) F
Maîtrise
/laurice Dutrene F
ompagnie Des Arts
rançais
ouis Süe F
ndré Mare F
mand Albert Rateau F
dré Groult F
cques Emile Ruhlmann F
Corbusier F (moved
om Switzerland 1917)
an Mayadon P
ile Decoeur P
ile Lenoble P
né Buthaud P
an Puiforcat S M
gar Brandt M Br
ymond Subes M
ul Kiss M
an Dunand M
audius Linossier M
Raymond Templier J
Jean Fouquet J
Gerard Sandoz J
Paul Brandt J
René Lalique G J
Maurice Marinot G
Henri Navarre G
André Thuret G
Maurice Ernest Sabino G
Francois Décorchemont G
Gabriel Argy-Rousseau G
Almaric Walter G
Claire-Jeanne Roberte Colinet Br
Dimitri Chiparus (Rumanian born) Br
Marcel Bouraine Br
Pierre Le Faguays Br
Guiraud Riviére M
Cassandre (Adolphe-Jean-Marie Mouron) Pos
Charles Gesmar Pos
Jean Dupas Pos
Etling G Br P
Finmar F
Alvar Aalto F
FINLAND
bling G
Royal Copenhagen (est.1775) Por
Boch Frères P
Philippe Wolfers S M
sie Cooper P
arlton P
elley P
edgwood P
eith Murray P S G
ilkinson & Co P
Clarice Cliff P
aul Nash (painter and
lustrator)
Dame Laura Knight
painter and illustrator)
Ferdinand Preiss Br
Bruno Zach M
Otto Poertzel Br
Meissen Por
Paul Scheurich Por
DENMARK
Sunderland
Staffs
ordon Russell Heals F
Broadway
London
St Ives
Poole
Bauhaus (moved to Dessau 1925, Berlin 1930)
Walter Gropius F (moved to England in 1934, worked for ISOKON; USA in 1937)
Marcel Breuer F (Hungarian born; worked for ISOKON, England in 1935 then moved to USA in 1937)
Ludwig Mies Van der Rohe F (went to USA in 1938)
Berlin
Weimar
BELGIUM
rnard Leach P
oji Hamada P
chael Cardew P
lliam Staite Murray P
Rosenthal Por
Nymphenburg Por
Paris
Nancy
Bavaria
Vienna
Marcel Goldscheider Por
Josef Lorenzi S P
Hagenauer M
Ernst Dryden Pos
arter, Stabler & Adams
td. P
HUNGARY
Limoges
SWITZ.
oulton Lambeth
est.1815)
Phoebe Stabler Por
Richard Garbe Por
Gilbert Bayes Por
Betty Joel F
actical Equipment Ltd
P.E.L.) F
okon Furniture F
ack Pritchard F
ward McKnight-Kauffer
Pos
x Whistler Pos
E. Marty Pos
Daum Frères G
Baccarat G
Charles Edouard Jeanneret "Le Corbusier" F (became French citizen in 1930)
Gustave Miklos M J
(moved to Paris in 1909)
Marcel Goupy Por G
Jean Luce Por G
Suzanne Lalique Por G

Furniture

Some craftsmen, though by no means all, responded to the changes in people's lifestyles after the First World War and the consequent demand for new types of furniture, such as cocktail cabinets and elaborate dressing tables, that were as much decorative as functional. Technological developments made mass production possible, and designers experimented with unusual woods such as amboyna and Macassar ebony, and new materials such as steel, concrete and plate glass. However, many manufacturers continued to produce conventional furniture, with the occasional concession to the new style. Furniture of the period is so diverse that it is difficult to classify, but clean lines and a challenging virtuosity of design entitle a piece to be called Art Deco.

The French were the most willing to make the transition from curvilinear extravagance to the more sober and controlled demands of Art Deco. In Paris the buying public could find good design in Paul Follot's "Pomone" workshops and The Galeries Lafayette, which housed the "La Maîtrise" workshop of Maurice Dufrêne. Louis Süe and André Mare established their "Compagnie des Arts Français" in 1919. Other eminent makers are André Groult, Armand-Albert Rateau and Jacques Emile Ruhlmann. However, their products were for most people prohibitively expensive: the cost of a double bed by Ruhlmann was comparable with that of an average Parisian apartment. Partly as a reaction to this exclusiveness, the Modernists set out to create machine-made furnishings that were more affordable and less pretentious, such as the tubular steel furniture designed by Le Corbusier.

In Germany the most avant garde designs emanated from the Bauhaus, the best-known names being Walter Gropius, Marcel Breuer and Ludwig Mies van der Rohe.

The British did not embrace Art Deco with open arms, although by the 1930s a large amount of mass-produced furniture appeared that was often an odd compromise of earlier forms blended with Art Deco motifs, perhaps sunrays and stylized roses or chevrons. There were several good Art Deco designers, such as Gordon Russel Heals and Betty Joel. These two worked with pale veneers, which made the large furniture (fashionable at the time) seem less overpowering. Such articles are relatively less expensive today than when first made. The English firm Practical Equipment Limited (P.E.L.) produced tubular steel frame chairs and steel and glass furnishings which catered for those living in smaller spaces. The laminated wood furniture of Jack Pritchard's Isokon also provided for the more modest home.

Craftsman-made pieces are rare and expensive. Modern reproductions, which abound, are not likely to be confused with the fine quality and detail of the originals. Original mass-produced furniture, though still somewhat expensive, is more affordable and survives in greater quantity.

This rare, utilitarian table (ht approx. 23in/58cm) was designed by Mies van der Rohe in 1929, when Modernism was still considered avant garde. His ottoman of similar form, with a padded leather seat, was more popular and therefore easier to find today. *CM*

* Mies van der Rohe is best known for his "Barcelona chair", also made in 1929.
* Scratches and signs of wear are hard to fake well and help to authenticate an original piece.

Successful Art Deco furniture often combined simple form with exotic materials and subtle decoration. This Macassar ebony table (ht 25½in/65cm), made by Ruhlmann in 1933, uses the radiating wood grain as a decorative element. Elegant, slender feet such as these ones on gilt bronze terminals were popular, even on heavy pieces, to which they lent a degree of elegance. *CNY*

A rare Macassar ebony marquetry giltwood and marble commode by Süe et Mare, c.1925 (33 × 68in/84.5 × 173cm). The exotic door panels are inlaid with turtles and a sea bed design by the artist Mathurin Meheut. This enormous sculptural piece of furniture is typical of the Parisian High Deco style. Many of Süe et Mare's pieces were massive, with intricate decoration such as floral inlays incorporating ivory and mother-of-pearl. This piece (unmarked but too characteristic to be misattributed) is highly original; however, much of the work of the period borrowed from 18th and 19thC forms. *CNY*

* Süe et Mare pieces were commissioned and made to the highest standards. None were marked; the style was their trademark.

The pillar and column supports of this innovative dining table and chairs, 1932 (ht 31in/79.5cm), are fitted for illumination. The glass top is inset with three moulded glass panels by René Lalique, who also made the supports.

* Art Deco furniture that incorporates vulnerable mirrors or glass has not survived in quantity.

More than any other craftsman of the period, Ruhlmann achieved the balance between luxury and simplicity. This armoire, executed in exotic amboyna inlaid with ivory, has a light feel despite its massive form and minimal decoration, c.1925 (56 × 69in/142.5 × 176cm). *CM*
* Ruhlmann also made lamp stands, desks and chairs and in 1933 began to incorporate tubular steel into his furniture. All of his work carries a branded signature.

A chaise longue in laminated wood by the ex-Bauhaus designer Marcel Breuer, c.1930 (ht 30in/76cm). He made some designs for Isokon before moving to the United States, where he produced inexpensive but attractive furniture that now fetches high prices. *P*
* Laminated wood was first employed in furniture in the Art Deco period. The Finnish company Finmar under Alvar Aalto also used it, in designs that were very similar to those of Isokon. Laminated wood tends to chip and flake and the furniture has not survived in quantity. Finmar's products are not marked but the *Decorative Arts Journal* shows the full range of their products.

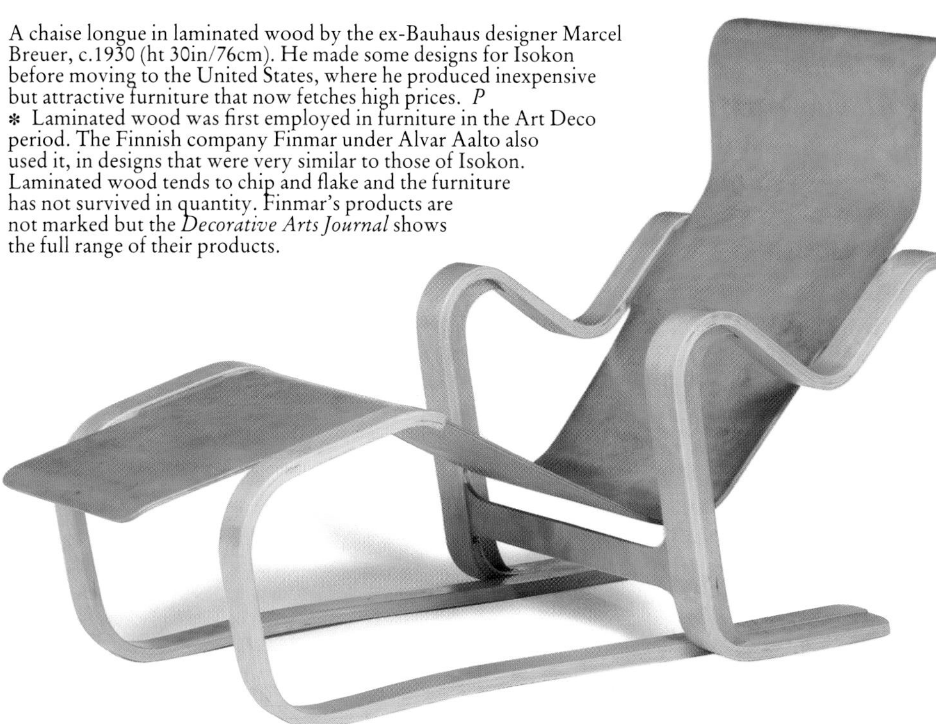

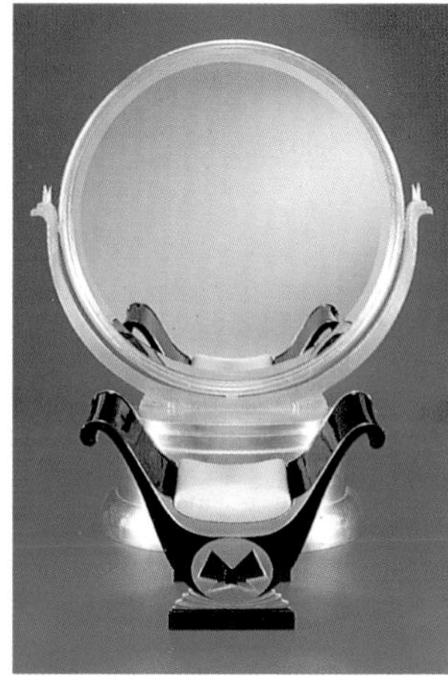

Above This 1930 lacquered and silvered wod dressing table and stool (65 × 56in/165 × 142cm) from the "Skyscraper" range by American designer Paul Frankl, relies on a combination of complicated form and scant decoration. *CNY*
* Frankl's "Skyscraper" pieces show an awareness of the needs of smaller, urban spaces. All his pieces bear a named metal tag.

Right In complete contrast with Frankl's table, this rare bronze, marble and ivory dressing table by Rateau, c.1920-22 (35½ × 60½in/90 × 154cm), has a simple form, with the decorative elements dominant. Nevertheless, both pieces are recognizably Art Deco by virtue of their innovative, uncluttered look. *CNY*

A 3-leaf lacquered screen made in 1930 by the American architect Donald Deskey (78 × 59in/198 × 149cm). The strong geometric motifs are typical of the American interpretation of Art Deco in many media. The screen is signed "Deskey-Vollmer". *CNY*
* America was not slow to respond to changes taking place in design on the Continent. The first ventures into Art Deco were architectural – for example, the Chrysler building, which introduced the concept of coordinated interiors and exteriors. Frank Lloyd Wright, Frankl and Deskey captured something of the spirit of the new age in their furniture, and their pieces are highly collectable.

Ceramics

Bright colours and attractive white and cream glazes are the keynotes of Art Deco ceramics. Pottery and tableware took on bold geometric shapes with attractive hand-finished decoration. Brightly coloured glazes were popular in America. China figures were produced in great numbers: favourite subjects were modern women, naked or scantily dressed, sporting figures and animals.

In England the Doulton Lambeth potteries made small bone china figures that maintained a cautious balance between the traditional crinolined lady and the modern woman. Figures by Phoebe Stabler, Richard Garbe and Gilbert Bayes are especially collectable. The Wedgwood range of vases, bowls, covered boxes and inkstands, many designed by the New Zealander Keith Murray, epitomize machine age geometry, enhanced by monochrome matt glazes of subdued green, grey-blue and ivory.

The greatest exponent of geometric wares was Clarice Cliff of the Newport pottery which belonged to Wilkinson & Co. of Staffordshire. She created a range of brightly enamelled straw-glazed pottery retailed under names such as "Bizarre" and "Fantasque". In Cliff's hands, coffee pots became tapering cylinders with pierced triangular bracket handles and sugar bowls were often upturned cone sections, supported by flange feet, that gave the appearance of a rocket base. Susie Cooper's designs, more subdued, are very popular. Her most collectable wares are those made in the 1930s.

The Shelley potteries produced elegant porcelain tea and coffee wares using geometric shapes and primary-coloured enamel decoration with silver lustre trim. Poole potteries introduced their highly distinctive painted wares in near pastel colours against ivory reserves. Their stylish portrait plates are highly prized by collectors.

Artist potters came into their own in this period. Bernard Leach, Michael Cardew, Shoji Hamada and William Staite Murray offered a finely crafted alternative to the mass-produced wares from Staffordshire. Most of their work is signed.

In Germany Art Deco ceramic wares found expression through large and established factories such as Meissen (especially the figures of Paul Scheurich), Rosenthal and Nymphenburg.

In Belgium the Boch Frères factory produced a range of wares with crackled white grounds overlaid with floral or bird designs in vivid enamel colours with incised outlines.

The French centre for mass-produced porcelain was Limoges, which employed several top designers including Marcel Goupy, Jean Luce and Suzanne Lalique. French artist potters catered for the discerning few. The most eminent were Jean Mayadon, Emile Decoeur and Emile Lenoble. Decoeur and Lenoble made sandstone pots covered with thick glazes, Lenoble often incising geometric designs. Incised decoration also featured in the work of René Buthaud.

A vase designed by Clarice Cliff for the Staffordshire Newport pottery of A.J. Wilkinson, 1935 (ht 14in/35cm). Cliff's designs (painted either by herself or by various decorators) used a highly distinctive palette – bold designs appeared in bright colours. *CSK*
* Most single Cliff pieces are affordable, unless they are of rare designs. Sets, and pieces with more elaborate decoration, command higher prices.
* The Wilkinson pottery issued wares decorated by Paul Nash and Dame Laura Knight. The latter's circus series is eagerly sought after.

Clarice Cliff reproductions abound but these are clearly marked as such. However, at the end of 1985 and throughout 1986 fakes appeared in the south of England, especially Kent. The colours give away the fake Cliff vase shown above: they are darker than in the genuine piece, and more patchy. The glaze on the handle is especially uneven. The footrim, which is neat and clean on the original, is here untidy and irregular. *B/TW*

All Cliff wares carry the black printed mark of the pottery, the name of the design and the designer's facsimile signature. Fakes are hard to detect on the basis of the signature alone. A crackle effect like the one on the faked "Bizarre" signature (*top*), may be cause for suspicion, but some genuine pieces *have* appeared with such crazing. Most, however, are smooth like the genuine "Fantasque" signature (*above*). On flatware, three circles, or stilt marks, around the signature where the pot stood in the kiln are a sign of authenticity. *B/TW*

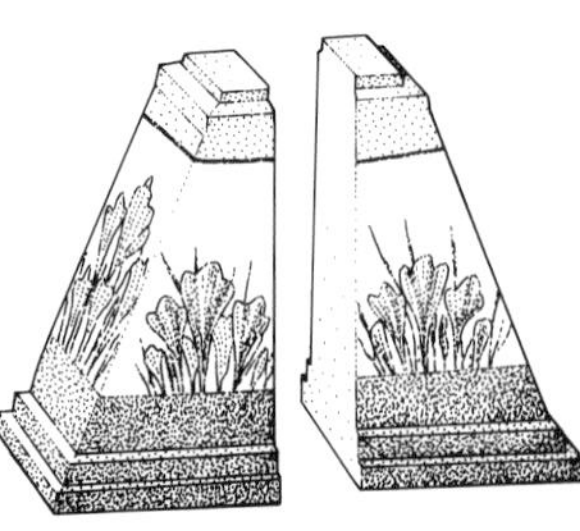

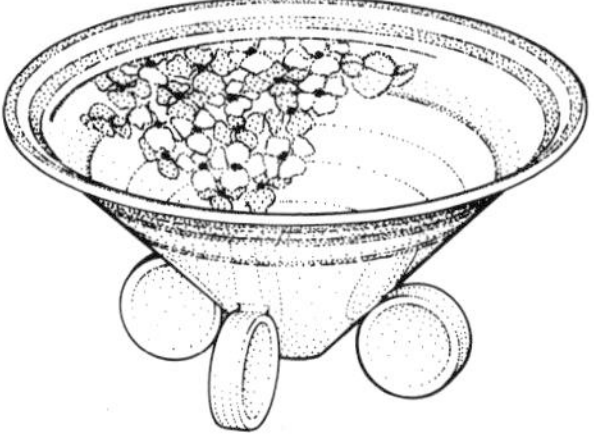

Examples of Clarice Cliff's adventurous designs: book-ends, a teapot and a sugar bowl.

Keith Murray's matt white glaze wares, retailed under the title "Moonstone", were among the most successful Art Deco pieces produced by Wedgwood. The severe geometry of this vase, c.1935 (ht 10in/25cm), almost gives it the appearance of a machine component. *B*

* Murray has only recently begun to be regarded as one of the most important Art Deco designers. His work, although still affordable today, is likely to become more expensive. In addition to his pale-coloured geometric wares, Murray also made a range of vases in darker colours, which are more eagerly hunted. A genuine piece will be marked with his facsimile signature.

The ready availability of quantities of cheap mass-produced earthenware figures has given the medium a bad name, but many of the more finely produced ranges, often by artists working in expensive materials such as bronze and ivory, are underrated. This Goldscheider figure of a dancing girl, 1930 (ht 14in/35cm), was designed by Lorenzl (see page 202). Hollywood-style figures in exotic costumes are usually of fairly high quality, although the same designs were also mass-produced in chalk plaster. Figures usually have both the pottery's and the artist's marks. *B*

During the 1920s and 30s there was a growing appreciation of the subtlety and sophistication of African art, which was further popularized by the success of the *Revue Negre.* René Buthaud was one of the most successful of the artists who incorporated African figures and motifs into his work. This incised and enamelled painted earthenware vase, c.1931 (ht 14in/35cm), with carved-away (*sgraffito*) decoration is a fine example. *CNY*

* Buthaud made a number of painted vases, all with this type of stylized face, and all highly desirable. He also produced faïence vases with similar painted figural decoration.

* Some ceramics of the period combine geometric and figurative elements – for example, mask-like faces, in silhouette, emerging from a background of overlapping geometric shapes.

Buthaud was not exclusively preoccupied with figurative work. This almost spherical vase, made c.1925 (ht 9½in/24cm), with interlocked curves that accentuate its form, shows a belated influence of Cubism in Art Deco ceramics. The crackled glaze was also used by other potters, such as Boch Frères and Royal Copenhagen. *B*

* In the same monochrome palette, Buthaud also produced some near-spherical vases decorated with quasi-mythical figures.

The Negro form was often modelled in a stylized way, as in this terracotta figure of an African dancer, c.1930 (ht 21in/54cm), by Paul Scheurich which represents a departure from the more traditional figures that he produced for Meissen. *C*

* Elaborate figures tended to be made in smaller quantities than simpler ones as the life of the moulds was usually shorter.

* Tribal influences also appeared in wall plaques and ceramic masks of the period.

The large size and dramatic colours of this jar and cover, c.1930 (ht 12in/31.5cm), make it one of the most desirable Carlton products. The Chinese form and vivid semi-abstract design add to its value. Similar examples with stunning geometric designs are rarer and more desirable still. However, there are also many Carlton products of the 1930s that emulate Wedgwood fairyland lustre ware or leaf-shaped dishes and cruets: these are of lesser commercial value. *C*

Glass

The imaginative glasswares of the Art Deco period reflect a new awareness of the potential of glass generally. Old techniques such as enamelling or acid etching were adapted to create new styles.

A changing lifestyle led to new products, in particular the scent bottle: examples commissioned by perfume manufacturers became more elaborate in response to increasing competition. Cocktail glasses, which were more prone to breakage, survive in smaller quantities.

French designers led the field, in particular René Lalique, whose output in the period was probably greater than that of all the other manufacturers combined: more than eight million pieces emanated from his workshop. He is best known for his opalescent glass, but the items produced in solid colours, especially blue, tend to be more expensive.

Lalique revived the *cire perdue* or "lost wax" process to produce vases and figures that today are the ultimate prize for the collector. Each is a "one-off" item cast in clear or frosted glass from a mould which, in order to retrieve the glass, was broken beyond repair. Perhaps Lalique's most novel creations are the 27 types of car mascots, which include animals and birds, a comet and the *Victoire,* better known as *The Spirit of the Wind,* modelled as an Amazon head with swept-back hair.

In contrast to Lalique's policy of glass for the masses, another Frenchman, Maurice Marinot, designed and made individual vases, bowls and bottles with stoppers for a limited market. The work of Henri Navarre and André Thuret is in an equally experimental style but more affordable.

Maurice Ernest Sabino was for many years thought of, unfairly, as a second-rate Lalique because of his penchant for opalescent glass. His work, an odd mixture of blandness and brilliance, includes some interesting figures. Other makers in opalescent glass included Verlys, Hunebelle and Etling in France and the Jobling glassworks in England.

Francoise Décorchement, Gabriel Argy-Rousseau and Alméric Walter made *pâte-de-verre* glass – a glass paste heated to a critical temperature which allows it to fuse within a mould. *Pâte-de-cristal* follows the same procedure, but with a greater proportion of lead added to achieve a near transparent appearance. The Daum glassworks at Nancy embraced Art Deco with enthusiasm. They produced heavy vases with deep acid-cut geometric decoration that incorporated contrasting smooth and granular surfaces.

English production was less innovative. The market suffered strong competition from Czechoslovakian imports of inexpensive table glass, some of which aped the geometric and enamelled forms of the French company Baccarat. In the United States the Steuben Glass Works were the premier producers during the 1920s and 30s. The company's art glass included Modernist wares by W.D. Teague and Sidney B. Waugh.

LALIQUE

The comprehensive 1932 Lalique catalogue (since reprinted) is essential for any serious collector. Some early designs are still in production today: originals of these are not especially collectable. Those examples made in Lalique's lifetime bear the initial "R".

Mythical figures such as this nymph and faun often feature in Lalique's glass. This scent bottle and stopper (ht 6in/15cm) entitled *Le Baiser du Faune* was designed in 1930 for the perfume company Molinard. *B*

* The scent bottles in greatest demand are those with the more inventive forms like those above. Sealed bottles with original contents and cartons are always at a premium. More than one stopper was designed for some bottles.

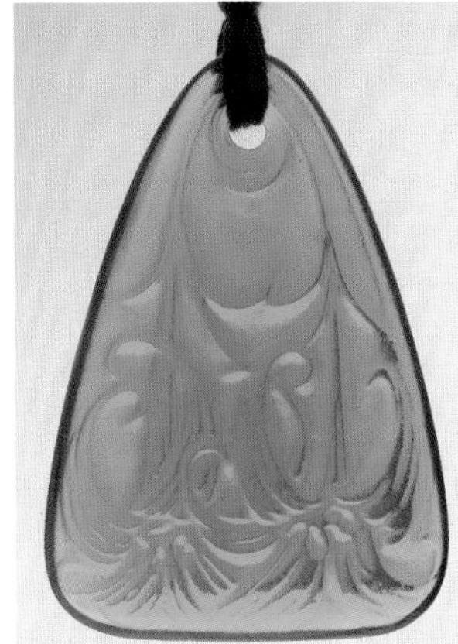

Lalique's finest jewelry belongs to the Art Nouveau period. However, he designed some remarkable Art Deco jewelry that incorporated the results of his early experiments with glass – for example, bracelets and brooches with coloured foil backing to create the effect of gemstones. The electric blue colour of this 1931 pendant (lgth 2¼in/5.5cm) increases its desirability. *B*

SIGNATURES
Early pieces are marked "R. Lalique, France" in script, and often give the model number. The "L" was sometimes elongated. Another mark is "R. LALIQUE", stencilled or wheelcut. After Lalique's death in 1945 pieces were marked "Lalique, France", without the R.

An enamelled glass vase decorated by Maurice Marinot, c.1918-20 (ht 8in/20cm). Although better known for his sculptural, internally decorated glassware, Marinot was equally proficient with enamel decoration. His earliest pieces are enamelled, and decorated in a brilliantly colourful, vivacious style that owes much to Matisse and the Fauve painters. Recently, Marinot's enamelled work has begun to outstrip his sculptural pieces in value. *CM*

* The work of this craftsman is seldom offered for sale. He produced only about 2,500 pieces, all designed and fashioned by himself. The range consists mostly of vases, with some perfume bottles and jars with covers. Pieces tend to be heavy in form, and very much an acquired taste.
* Other glass designers working in enamel included Marcel Goupy (mythological scenes, flowers, stylized landscapes), Jean Luce (flowers or geometrical shapes) and many of the Wiener Werkstätte artists.

A *pâte-de-verre* table lamp (ht 16in/41cm) by Gabriel Argy-Rousseau, c.1925. The glass base and shade are supported by wrought-iron mounts: the use of wrought iron for this purpose would have been unthinkable 20 years earlier. *CNY*

* Argy-Rousseau was a prolific glassmaker who specialized in *pâte-de-verre* and also worked in *pâte-de-cristal.* He made vases, lamps, ashtrays and jewelry, all incise-moulded with his initials.

Lalique's vases were designed as pieces of sculpture rather than as receptacles for flowers. Form and decoration were often integral, as in this amber vase, 1930 (ht 10in/25cm), retailed under the name "Serpent", also made in clear, bronze, black and red. *CNY*

* Some fakes have appeared, often those with budgerigar or archer motifs. These are of lighter weight than the originals and the colours are weaker, often in a pale lime green not used by Lalique. They have a block capital signature moulded in low relief with angular letters that are unlike any known Lalique mark.

Marinot was concerned with technical possibilities and the control of glass as a sculptural medium. His glassware was thick-walled and incorporated carefully controlled air bubbles, together with chemical and metallic inclusions, like the copper and russet inserts in this bottle and stopper, 1932 (ht 6½in/16.5cm). Other Marinot techniques included: the juxtaposition of coloured and clear glass in a sandwich effect; acid etching; and crackle glass. *CG*

A frosted deep acid-etched 1920s glass table lamp by Daum of Nancy (ht 16in/40.5cm), whose signature it bears. The fittings, which are usually original, are considered important by collectors. *S*

* Deep acid-etching was a technique popular during the 1920s and 30s. Daum used it on a range of vases and lamps, all with heavy forms, often executed in frosted or coloured glass. The most popular colours were electric blue, green-tinted and smoky grey.
* Collectors should beware of lamp bases offered for sale as vases.

Bronzes

The demand for sculptures that had been growing since the second half of the 19th century continued in the 1920s and 30s, with an emphasis on smaller figures, either carved in ivory, cast in bronze or made of a novel and expensive combination of bronze and ivory known as chryselephantine.

Women were the most popular subjects, not the pre-First World War seductress, but the newly independent, self-possessed female, often depicted as an Amazon. Naked or scantily clad dancing maidens in athletic positions, and sporting figures were made in quantity. Mass production popularized bronzes for domestic interiors but the best figures were hand-made, or at least hand-finished.

The French and Germans led the field. The most popular French sculptors are Jeanne Robert Colinet, the Rumanian-born Dimitri Chiparus; Marcel Bouraine; and Pierre La Faguay.

The women portrayed by the German Bruno Zach belong to the Berlin nightclubs and cabaret bars. Often dressed in revealing camisoles or leather suits, and occasionally brandishing whips, his subjects display an air of eroticism that hints at the perverse. The figures of his countryman Ferdinand Preiss are more mainstream. Otto Poertzel and the Viennese Josef Lorenzl are also popular.

The Viennese foundry of Hagenauer catered for a new enthusiasm for Negro and Savage art by producing a variety of figures and face masks. An obvious African tribal influence is also evident in the primitive style of the all-bronze creations of Gustave Miklos, made for a connoisseur market.

Chryselephantine is still very expensive, even when unsigned. All-bronze or all-ivory figures are more affordable.

Decadent overtones are strong in the work of Bruno Zach. This bronze group of an amorous couple dates from c.1925. Zach's figures ranged from 6in to 3ft (15-90cm); this example is 10in/25.5cm. The figure is marked "Zach". *CNY*

* Erotic subjects are collectable and appear occasionally at auction. A number of novel erotic bronzes are the work of Franz Bergman and are signed "Namgreb" (an anagram of his name).

The figures of Ferdinand Preiss show an acute understanding of the female form. At 14½in/37cm, this bronze and ivory *Cabaret Girl* from c.1930 is among the tallest of his figures. *S*

* Preiss had his own foundry from 1906. All the pieces that emanate from it bear the foundry mark "PK". Preiss' personal creations are usually signed "F. Preiss". His more affordable figures include those carved from a single piece of ivory – for example, his nude studies, usually mounted on green onyx pedestals. He also made mass-produced, hand-finished, aryan-type figures in which all the parts were carved separately and screwed to the bronze.

The streamlined, futuristic costume of this 1930 bronze and ivory figure *Kora* (ht 14in/35.5cm) is typical of Chiparus. Several of his females are depicted in tight bodices and ankle length skirts with razor sharp pleats; others wear suits with scale and stud designs and space-age helmets or skull caps. *B*

* Many Art Deco bronze figures stand on marble or onyx pyramids or ziggurats, sometimes with carved Egyptian scenes (see right); these were inspired by the discovery in 1923 of Tutankhamen's tomb.

This bronze and ivory figure titled *Danseuse de Thèbes* (ht 10in/25.5cm) is one in a series of dancers of the world sculpted by Colinet during the 1920s. It is inscribed "Cl. J.R. Colinet". It is not known for certain how many dancers were in the series. *C*

* Colinet made an almost identical figure in patinated bronze which, though twice the size, would fetch only about a quarter of the price of its bronze and ivory counterpart.

Penthesilia, a patinated bronze figure of an Amazon archer by Marcel Bouraine, 1920s (ht 17in/43cm), marked "M.A. Bouraine". The exaggerated pose is typically dramatic. Bouraine made other Amazon archers and javelin throwers in silvered and patinated bronze. *S*

* Much of Bouraine's work was commissioned and distributed by the Parisian firm Etling, an atelier which, like Liberty in London, commissioned work from a number of designers.

FAKES, CONDITION AND SIGNATURES

Bronzes and ivories are a minefield for the unsuspecting, as they are regularly faked or reproduced. However, anyone familiar with the feel of the originals is unlikely to be fooled. Many bronzes have been artificially aged by the application of salt to the nuts holding the piece onto the base, giving them a rusty appearance. Faked ivory faces and hands may be crudely carved. Where you suspect that a bronze and ivory figure has been faked, check the join between the two materials: it should feel smooth. The ivory of some ivory and bronze pieces has been copied in white plastic, which will not have the same veined appearance as the original. The bases of these copies would still be made of some form of marble, so that there would not be a noticeable disparity of weights. Many figures have been reproduced in cheaper materials such as spelter.

Condition is paramount: the extremities of figures are especially vulnerable. Ivory is delicate and cracks easily. This is particularly undesirable where the cracks extend down the face, giving a disfiguring veined look.

When not signed on the bronze, a signature can usually be found on the marble or agate base.

Snakes were a recurring decorative element in the work of Edgar Brandt. These ones, made c.1925 (ht 17 ½in/44cm), were also made in alabaster. All of Brandt's work was stamped. His floor lamps with snake motifs have shades by Daum. He is better known for the fine quality of his wrought work. *P*

A silvered bronze figure cast from a model by Guiraud Rivière, entitled *The Comet,* c.1925 (ht 25in/63cm). The stylized hair is a departure from the exotic coiffure of the Art Nouveau period, and the striking streamlined effect is similarly innovative. The figure is inscribed "GUIRAUD-RIVIERE" and "ETLING. PARIS". *CNY*

* Sculptors of the period were caught up in the general fascination with speed and movement and set out to encapsulate it in their work.

Silver, Jewelry and Metalwork

Art Deco jewelry and metalwork are characterized by their innovative use of materials and by experimentation with decorative techniques that resulted in bold new forms for traditional items such as tea services, cigarette boxes and clocks.

The French once again took the lead. Jean Puiforcat and the firm of Orfèvrerie Christofle produced some highly original silver tea services. Puiforcat's Modernist designs took simple forms with polished surfaces that sometimes incorporated mahogany, ivory and semi-precious stones.

The Art Deco period saw a revival of decorative iron work. The leading craftsmen included Edgar Brandt, Raymond Subes and Paul Kiss. Jean Dunand and Claudius Linossier adapted brassware as a decorative medium.

During the 1920s and 30s French jewellers continued to produce their staple creations but now with the emphasis on large gemstones: composition was a secondary consideration. Jewelry changed with fashion, resulting in longer earrings to complement shorter hair, and longer necklaces to suit low necklines.

The most exciting jewelry designs were made by Raymond Templier, Jean Fouquet, Gerard Sandoz and Paul Brandt. American jewelry was influenced by French design but tended to be more showy. In America and Europe the period witnessed the huge success of inexpensive dress jewelry which is often misrepresented as typical Art Deco jewelry.

Good-quality English Art Deco silver is conspicuous only by its absence, with the possible exception of Keith Murray's designs. Several silversmiths misunderstood the style and embellished standard forms with Art Deco ornament.

Experimentation with novel combinations of materials is typical of the period. This stunning Belgian onyx-mounted lacquered silver and ivory vase made in 1930 (ht 11½in/29cm) by Marcel Wolfers combines geometric form with fine-quality craftsmanship. *CNY*

* Wolfers was not a prolific maker, and any article by him is likely to be of superb quality and very costly. All his work is stamped and signed.

The few English pieces that were made in the Art Deco style reveal a strong French influence, as shown by this 1938 Wakeley & Wheeler silver and mother-of-pearl "Mermaid" cup and cover (ht 14½in/37cm) designed by R. Gleadowe and engraved by G.T. Friend. *S*

* Mermaids were a popular motif in the period, and often appear on the creations of Lalique.

Albert Cheuret was one of a handful of French designers who succeeded in making the transition from Art Nouveau to Art Deco. The pod shape of this rare silvered-bronze vase, c.1925 (7¾in/19.5cm), bears some resemblance to his earlier, more organic work, but the overlapping ribbons are pure Art Deco. Cheuret also made silver candlesticks and lamps, using alabaster in his later lamps. Much of his work represents naturalistic as well as organic forms. Cheuret usually inscribed his work with his full name. *CNY*

A teapot (ht 7in/18cm) from an English electroplated silver tea and coffee set, 1935. The innovative geometric forms are compromised by the safe, more traditional finial and loop handles. Compared with the Puiforcat service, right, the British design appears tame, and this will inevitably be reflected in the price. These sets were mass-produced in the 1930s, and bear the stamp "EPNS" for electroplated nickel silver.The same set in solid silver would still be more affordable than the more avant garde French version. *B*

Tea sets acquired bold new shapes in the hands of the more daring designers such as Jean Puiforcat. Highly original in design, this set from 1925 (ht of coffeepot: 5in/13cm) includes clear glass strap handles and arched finials. As with the products of the Bauhaus, function and decoration are perfectly fused. Sets by Puiforcat and Christofle were made and survive in great numbers. *SNY*

* Tea sets usually consist of a teapot, coffeepot, milk jug and sugar bowl. There is sometimes a jug for hot water. Incomplete sets are not worth collecting.

Novelty items flourished in the 1920s and 30s, but attention to detail remained high. Although this French silver and enamel box, made in 1925, is only 5in/12cm long, it contains compartments, mirror, notebook and a pencil. The caricature is of the singer Enrico Caruso, who may have designed it himself. *P*

❋ Enamel boxes were usually executed in strongly coloured bold geometric designs, sometimes with a broken eggshell effect. The chain should have a finger loop.

The fascination with speed that prevailed throughout the 1920s is epitomized in this Austrian silver and enamel novelty cigarette case, c.1920 (wdth 5in/13cm), decorated with a Bugatti-type racing car and signed by the artist, F. Zwichl. This design shows the car at speed and about to leap from the lid. Other versions exist with different models. *C*

A brass bust by the Austrian foundry Hagenauer, c.1925. All their figures have a stylized look, often with elongated, pointed features. Chromed metal, often with a textured surface, was used, sometimes combined with carved wood. The company also made metal table mirrors. This bust is a fairly typical height – 17in/43cm – although sizes ranged from as small as 1-2in/2.5-5cm to as large as 2 feet/60cm. *C*

Left A chinoiserie silver and inlaid enamelled ladies' compact made in 1925 in the manner of Van Cleef and Arpels of Paris, but not signed. It is of very high quality. Its small surface (ht 4in/10cm), enlarged here to show the excellent detailing, is decorated with a liberal quantity of the precious and semi-precious stones popular in the period: diamonds, mother-of-pearl, lapis lazuli, and, in the clasp at each end, sapphires. *B*

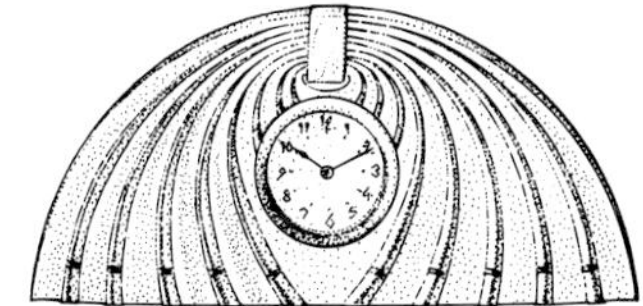

Clocks gave Art Deco designers scope for ingenuity. The motif of the clock *above*, designed by Albert Cheuret c.1930, is integral to the form, while the silver table clock, *left* (ht approx. 10in/26cm), designed c.1930 by Jean E. Puiforcat, dispenses with a solid dial and has distinctive numerals: note the 10. Other clocks of the period, which had conventional round or square dials surrounded by imaginative designs, were often mounted on a solid plinth of onyx or marble. Clocks by Preiss incorporate his characteristic slender modern women. *CNY*

Posters

The fascination with speed and technology extended to poster design as to other media in the period. The most common subjects were ships, cars and trains: indeed, a thematic approach to collecting is a valid alternative to concentrating on the work of particular artists.

The curvilinear extravagances evident in Art Nouveau poster design had vanished entirely by 1920. In their place came the use of cubistic and geometric symbols. The French artist Adolphe-Jean-Marie Mouron (better known as Cassandre) was the leading exponent. Another Frenchman, Charles Gesmar (1900-28), made posters for the *Folies-Bergère* and the music hall singer Mistinguett – the subject of many posters of the period.

The poster was often used to promote travel and tourism. A series for London Transport was produced by Edward McKnight-Kauffer, Rex Whistler and A.E. Marty, as well as the famous French painter and muralist Jean Dupas, whose distinctive females had accentuated high foreheads and soft, slightly elongated faces.

Ernst Dryden was the leading Austrian posterist. Originally signing his work "Deutsch", he began to call himself Dryden shortly after the First World War. He designed posters for such diverse products as Blaupunkt cigarettes, Bugatti racing cars, *Cinzano* and I.G. Farben, a paint manufacturer. He later became art director for the magazine *Die Dame* and was responsible for most of their front covers.

Posters of the period were not intended to last, and were therefore printed on very thin paper. While a certain degree of damage is almost unavoidable, the central image should be as unspoilt as possible, with the colours clear and strong. Small tears are acceptable around the edges, and some fading and folds (again, depending on position) may not be too detrimental to value. A poster more severely damaged, or very yellow with age, is probably not worth buying, unless it is a rarity.

Inventive wit is often a feature of Art Deco posters. This striking red and white design for *Cinzano* by Ernst Dryden is characteristically imaginative. Posters of the period increasingly depict a central image against a plain, uncluttered background. The poster is signed bottom right. This is the original poster design, measuring 14 × 10in (35 × 25cm); the poster itself would be three times bigger. *B*

* Dryden's male faces were slick, moustached, Hollywood types.
* Very little of Dryden's work had appeared on the open market until the discovery in 1976 of a huge number of his drawings, sketches and posters, which were on the point of being thrown away.

Abstract, stylized designs, suggesting an exhilarating new world, replaced the earlier more realistic image. The silver tracks, which give an effect of speed, space and distance, lead the traveller to a distant star in this 1927 poster by Cassandre (41 × 30in/105 × 75.5cm) advertising the Etoile du Nord railway service. *B*

* Many images of the period are shown from a bird's eye view, or make use of dramatic perspective effects.
* Stronger colours were more in evidence in the period than muted tones: red and black appear often in Cassandre's work.

Reference

GLOSSARY

Amboyna A mottled, highly grained Indonesian wood.
Chryselephantine An expensive combination of ivory and a metal, usually bronze.
Cire perdue The French term for "lost wax", a casting process that results in unique glass casts.
Modernism/Functionalism International movement in furniture design, 1930s. Clean lines and the cube shape were emphasized.
Pâte-de-cristal An almost transparent glass made of powdered glass paste which has fused in a mould.
Pâte-de-verre A translucent glass, similar to *pâte-de-cristal* but with a lower proportion of lead.
Raku A form of Japanese earthenware.
Sgraffito Carved-away decoration on pottery.
Ziggurat A stepped pyramid shape, used for the pedestals of small bronze figures.

SELECTED DESIGNERS, MANUFACTURERS AND RETAILERS

Aalto, Alvar (1898-1976) Finnish modernist architect and furniture designer.
Argy-Rousseau, Gabriel (1885-1953) French glass designer. Marks: "G. Argy-Rousseau"; initials.
Bauhaus (1919-1933) German design school whose members sought to relate form to function.
Bergman, Franz (dates unknown) Viennese sculptor. Mark: "Namgreb" (anagram of name).
Boch Frères (established 1841) Belgian ceramics firm which produced brightly decorated crackled white wares.
Bouraine, Marcel (dates unknown) French sculptor of figures in silvered and patinated bronze. Mark: "M. A. Bouraine".
Brandt, Edgar-William (1880-1960) French designer and metalworker.
Breuer, Marcel (1902-81) Hungarian-born architect and furniture designer.
Buthaud, René (b.1886) French painter and artist potter.
Cassandre (Adolphe-Jean-Marie Mouron) (1901-68) French artist and posterist in a geometrical manner.
Chiparus, Dimitri (Demètre) (dates unknown) Rumanian-born sculptor who worked in Paris in the 1920s.
Cliff, Clarice (1899-1972) English pottery designer and decorator.
Cooper, Susie (b.1902) English potter. Designed wares for A. E. Gray & Co. (1925) and established her own company in 1932, later taken over by Wedgwood.

Daum (established 1875) French glassworks. Mark: "Daum, Nancy" with the Cross of Lorraine.
Decoeur, Émile (1876-1953) French artist potter. Specialized in stoneware of simple shapes.
Décorchement, Françoise-Émile (1880-1971) French glass maker.
Deskey, Donald (b.1894) American architect and designer.
Dryden, Ernst (dates unknown) Leading Austrian graphic designer.
Dupas, Jean (1882-1964) French painter, muralist and poster artist.
Etling (early 20thC) Paris firm which commissioned and distributed work by many designers.
Follot, Paul (1877-1941) French interior decorator and designer.
Frankl, Paul (1886-1958) Austrian architect and furniture designer, settled in America, 1914. Worked in native woods. Mark: metal tag with the name of the manufactory – "Skyscraper".
Gesmar, Charles (1900-28) French artist and posterist.
Goldscheider, Marcel (1885-1953) Austrian ceramics manufacturer, founded factory in 1886. Mark: pottery and artist's mark.

Goupy, Marcel (1886-1954) (retd) French artist and designer of glass and pottery.
Gropius, Walter (1883-1969) German architect, founder of the **Bauhaus** and director until 1928.
Groult, André (1884-1967) French interior decorator and furniture designer.
Hagenauer (established 1898) Austrian foundry based in Vienna.

Heal, Sir Ambrose (1872-1959) English cabinet maker. Managing director of Heal & Son from 1907.
Heals, Gordon Russell (1892-1980) English furniture designer.
Hunebelle, André (dates unknown) French glass artist, inspired by Lalique.
Isokon Furniture Co. English furniture manufacturers, established 1931 by Jack Pritchard. Made mass-produced items.
Joel, Betty (b.1896) English furniture designer of functional pieces.
Lalique, René (1860-1945) French glass maker, prolific manufacturer of Daum crystal and opalescent glass.
Leach, Bernard (1887-1979) English artist potter. He made raku earthenware, using a Japanese technique of hand-modelling.

Le Corbusier (Charles Edouard Jeanneret) (1887-1965) Swiss modernist architect and designer, became French citizen in 1930.
Luce, Jean (1895-1964) French designer. Used enamel decoration on porcelain and glass. Mark: painted crossed "LL" in rectangle.
McKnight-Kauffer, Edward (1890-1954) American painter and graphic artist, worked in England.

Marinot, Maurice (1882-1960) French painter, sculptor and glass designer and technician. Interested in the sculptural qualities of glass.
Meissen German pottery manufacturers, established early 18thC. Mark: variations of crossed swords, 1924-34 dot between sword blades.
Mies van der Rohe, Ludwig (1886-1969) German modernist architect and furniture designer.
Murray, Keith (1892-1981) New Zealand-born architect and designer, settled in England, 1935.
Navarre, Henri (1885-1971) French glass artist, influenced by Marinot.
Poertzel, Otto (b.1876) German sculptor.
Poole Pottery (1921-present) (Originally Carter, Stabler & Adams.) Made hand-thrown and hand-decorated pottery.

Practical Equipment Limited (PEL) (established 1931) English manufacturers of tubular steel and glass furnishings.
Preiss, Ferdinand (b.1883) German sculptor. Opened foundry in 1906. Mark: "F. Preiss"; foundry mark "PK".
Rateau, Armand-Albert (1882-1938) French interior decorator and furniture designer.
Rietveld, Gerrit Thomas (1888-1964) Dutch architect and furniture designer, joined De Stijl, 1919.
Rivière, Guiraud (dates unknown) French sculptor and metalworker.
Rosenthal (established 1879) German porcelain factory.
Royal Copenhagen (established 1775) Danish pottery factory. Marks: crown and three waves motif with "Denmark", "Danmark" or "Royal Copenhagen".
Ruhlmann, Jacques-Émile (1879-1933) French painter and master-cabinetmaker.
Sabino, Maurice Ernest (1878-1961) French glass artist, inspired by **Lalique**. Mark: "Sabino, Paris".
Scheurich, Paul (1883-1945) American porcelain modeller who studied and worked in Germany.
Shelley potteries (1860-1925) (Originally Foley pottery) English pottery firm.
Stabler, Phoebe (d.1955) English. Designed and made ceramics, enamels and jewelry with her husband Harold. Mark: "STABLER, HAMMERSMITH LONDON" with date and mould number.
Staite Murray, William (1881-1962) English engineer, painter and potter, influenced by Japanese artist-potter Shoji Hamada.
Steuben Glass Works (established 1903) Prolific American glass manufacturers. Artists designed and decorated some art wares.

Süe, Louis (1875-1968) and **Mare, André** (1887-1932) Collaborating French furniture, carpet and textile designers.
Thonet Brothers (Gebrüder Thonet, Thonet Frères) (established 1853) Viennese manufacturers of bentwood furniture. Designers included **Le Corbusier** and **Mies van der Rohe**. Marks: variations on name, stamped or on label, and design number.
Thuret, André (1898-1965) French glass artist.
Wedgwood (established 1759) English pottery company. Used matt glazes and lustre decoration on Art Deco wares.
Wiener Werkstätte (Viennese Workshops) (1903-32) Association of artist-craftsmen.
Wilkinson Ltd, A. J. (from late 19thC) English pottery company, **Clarice Cliff** was art director.
Wright, Frank Lloyd (1867-1959) American architect and designer. His furniture was sometimes built-in.
Zach, Bruno (dates unknown) German sculptor.

BIBLIOGRAPHY

Arwas, Victor, *Art Deco Sculpture* (1975)
Glass: Art Nouveau to Art Deco (1977)
Battersby, Martin, *The Decorative Twenties* (1969)
Brunhammer, Yvonne, *The Nineteen-Twenties-Style* (1959)
Catley, Bryan, *Art Deco and Other Figures* (1978)
Editions Graphiques Gallery, *Chryselephantine Sculptures of the 20s and 30s* (1973)
Grover, Kay and Lee, *Carved and Decorated European Art Glass* (1970)
Hillier, Bevis, *Art Deco* (1968)
The World of Art Deco (1971)
Posters (1969)
Jones-North, Jacquelyne Y., *Commercial Perfume Bottles* (1987)
Klein, Dan, *All Colour Book of Art Deco* (1974)
McClinton, Katharine Morrison, *Art Deco: A Guide for Collectors* (1977)
Lalique for Collectors (1975)
Rickards, Maurice, *Posters of the Twenties* (1968)
Victoria and Albert Museum, *Art Deco* (1975)

DOLLS

Like any objects placed in the care of children, dolls have often been damaged by an excess of enthusiasm. Rag dolls have had an especially high loss rate, partly because their simple construction and cheap materials made them readily disposable. At the other end of the scale, many fine 19th- and early 20th-century dolls made for the wealthier classes still exist in good condition.

Wooden dolls from the time of George II (1727–1760), still in their original clothes, have come onto the market in recent years and have made record prices. These were all miniature adults rather than babies or children: child dolls were not made in any quantity until around 1900.

One area of doll collecting in particular is linked to an interest in fashion. The French bisque (unglazed china) dolls of the later 19th century are desirable not only for their finely modelled heads but also for their clothes – often intricate copies of the fashions of the time, with dress and hats, layers of underclothes, socks and shoes, all meticulously rendered.

Part of the appeal of dolls is their relation to the social and historical context. Collectors acquire a special understanding, which also affects the way they look at other objects – a porcelain figure, the costumes in a period play, or even the simple doll shape of a wooden skittle. The historical jigsaw is absorbing and endless. Individual elements of a doll – materials, eyes, hair, jointing, makers' marks – have a complex history of their own. For the technically minded, there is the fascinating story of mechanisms for walking, talking, crying, even swimming.

Fakes are usually restricted to dolls in the upper price bracket. The most common category of deception is the bisque head, found on a genuinely old body – add a mohair wig, cork pate and paperweight eyes and the deception is complete. In detecting fakes there is no substitute for experience.

Replacement parts are perfectly acceptable in such a high-casualty collecting field, but will have a detrimental effect on value.

The collector should always keep a record of purchases – where a doll was bought, the price and so on, with a photograph if possible. If the doll is altered in any way after purchase, perhaps by replacing the wig or a damaged hand, the old pieces should be kept, along with a note saying what has been done.

This chart looks at some of the most important categories of doll manufacture. The coloured bands show the main periods of production. Within these categories individual doll types and (in italics) selected makers are listed. The types of head indicated are found with various body materials.

Wood

Fabric

Papier mâche/composition

Poured wax

Wax-over-composition

Glazed china

Bisque (French)

Bisque (German)

Automata (French)

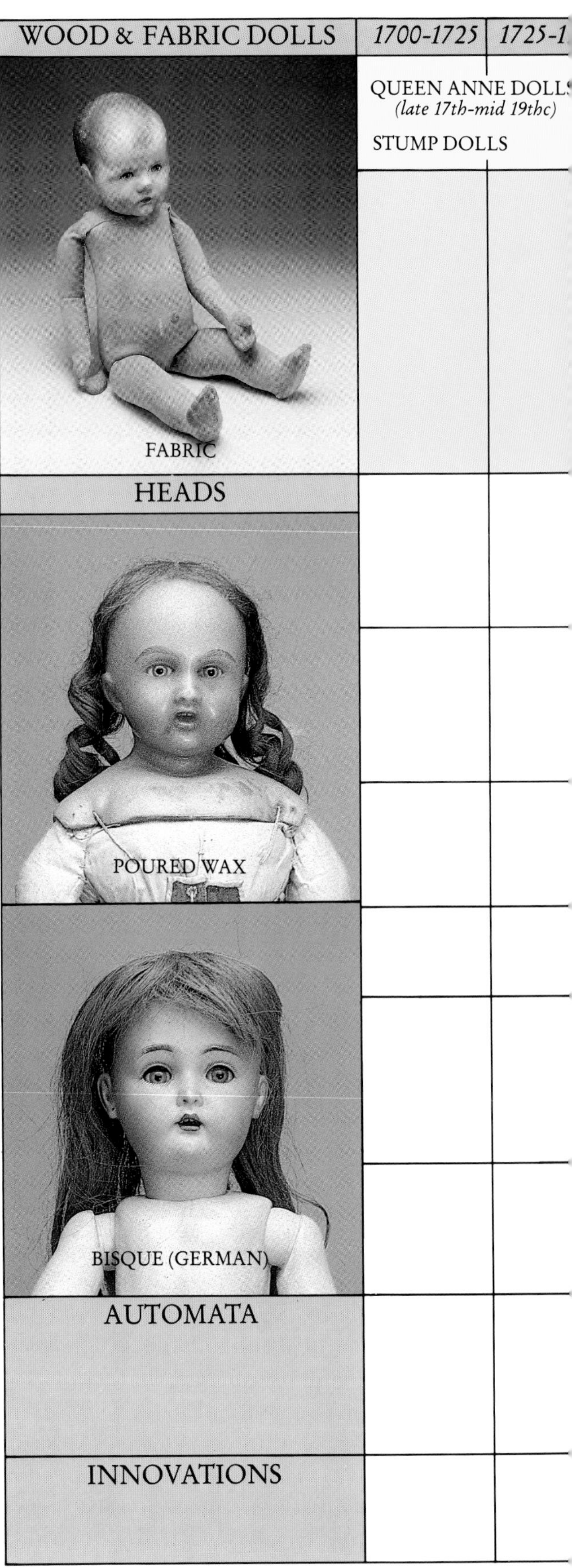

WOOD & FABRIC DOLLS
1700-1725
1725-1
QUEEN ANNE DOLLS
(late 17th-mid 19thc)
STUMP DOLLS
FABRIC
HEADS
POURED WAX
BISQUE (GERMAN)
AUTOMATA
INNOVATIONS

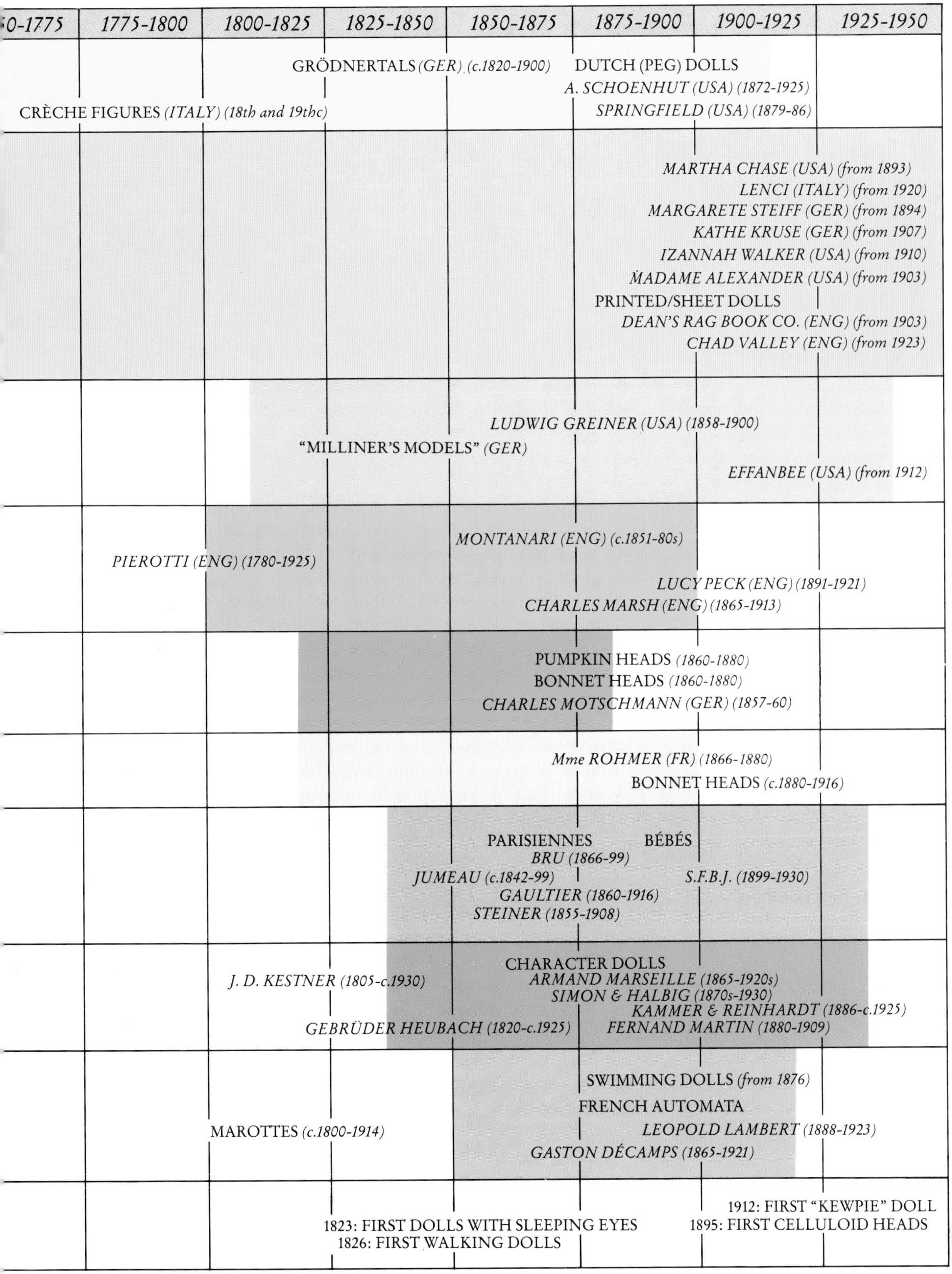

0-1775	1775-1800	1800-1825	1825-1850	1850-1875	1875-1900	1900-1925	1925-1950

GRÖDNERTALS *(GER) (c.1820-1900)*
DUTCH (PEG) DOLLS
A. SCHOENHUT (USA) (1872-1925)
CRÈCHE FIGURES *(ITALY) (18th and 19thc)*
SPRINGFIELD (USA) (1879-86)

MARTHA CHASE (USA) (from 1893)
LENCI (ITALY) (from 1920)
MARGARETE STEIFF (GER) (from 1894)
KATHE KRUSE (GER) (from 1907)
IZANNAH WALKER (USA) (from 1910)
MADAME ALEXANDER (USA) (from 1903)
PRINTED/SHEET DOLLS
DEAN'S RAG BOOK CO. (ENG) (from 1903)
CHAD VALLEY (ENG) (from 1923)

LUDWIG GREINER (USA) (1858-1900)
"MILLINER'S MODELS" *(GER)*
EFFANBEE (USA) (from 1912)

MONTANARI (ENG) (c.1851-80s)
PIEROTTI (ENG) (1780-1925)
LUCY PECK (ENG) (1891-1921)
CHARLES MARSH (ENG) (1865-1913)

PUMPKIN HEADS *(1860-1880)*
BONNET HEADS *(1860-1880)*
CHARLES MOTSCHMANN (GER) (1857-60)

Mme ROHMER (FR) (1866-1880)
BONNET HEADS *(c.1880-1916)*

PARISIENNES BÉBÉS
BRU (1866-99)
JUMEAU (c.1842-99)
S.F.B.J. (1899-1930)
GAULTIER (1860-1916)
STEINER (1855-1908)

CHARACTER DOLLS
ARMAND MARSEILLE (1865-1920s)
J. D. KESTNER (1805-c.1930)
SIMON & HALBIG (1870s-1930)
KAMMER & REINHARDT (1886-c.1925)
GEBRÜDER HEUBACH (1820-c.1925)
FERNAND MARTIN (1880-1909)

SWIMMING DOLLS *(from 1876)*
FRENCH AUTOMATA
MAROTTES *(c.1800-1914)*
LEOPOLD LAMBERT (1888-1923)
GASTON DÉCAMPS (1865-1921)

1912: FIRST "KEWPIE" DOLL
1823: FIRST DOLLS WITH SLEEPING EYES
1895: FIRST CELLULOID HEADS
1826: FIRST WALKING DOLLS

Wood

Durable and readily available, wood was the natural choice for early dolls. The simple skittle shape was the basis of English dolls from the 17th and 18th centuries, the head and torso carved from one piece, the hands characteristically fork-like. Those that have survived in good condition are rare and expensive, but rather worn examples may be found at a reasonable price. The craftsmen are unknown and the dolls not marked.

Wooden dolls were made in large numbers in Austria and Germany from the 17th to the 20th century. Early 19th-century Grödnertal dolls (named after the district in Austria, now Italy, where they were made) are much sought after. However, their high quality was not maintained, and later peg or "Dutch" (probably from "Deutsch") dolls of the region were more crudely constructed. These are, nonetheless, of interest to collectors.

By the end of the 19th century America had become active in the manufacture of wooden dolls. The first factory for mass production was set up in 1882. Leading producers included the Vermont Novelty Works. Particularly desirable are the "Springfield" dolls with moulded composition-over-wood heads, metal hands and feet and sophisticated jointing, patented by Joel Ellis in 1873 and subsequently made by several firms in Vermont. Also very desirable are spring-jointed dolls made in the early 1900s by the *emigré* Albert Schoenhut.

Old heads of wooden dolls have often been put on newer bodies, but this is usually easy to detect.

An early George III wooden doll c.1760–70, (ht 21in/53.5cm), of rare quality and condition. The head and torso are carved from one piece. A typical feature of the period is the pupil-less glass or enamel eyes with dotted outlines and eyebrows and red dots at the corners. The clothes are original. *S*

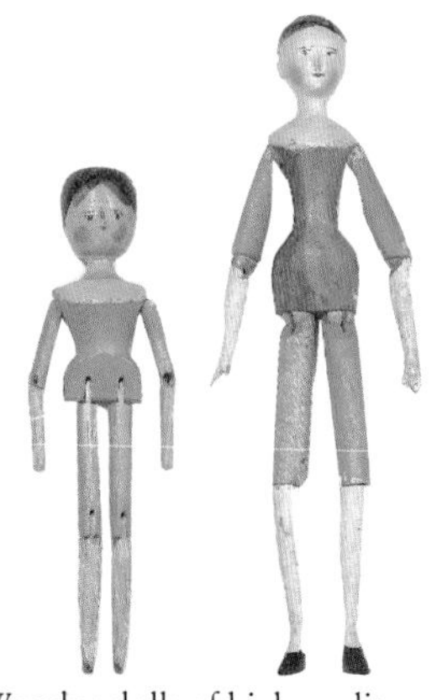

Wooden dolls of high quality were made in quantity until around the mid-19thC. The Dutch or peg doll on the right from the late 19thC (ht 12in/30cm) has painted hair and eyes, carved ears and is nicely proportioned. It is unusually fine for its date: by this time the average quality of imported dolls had deterioriated. The smaller doll on the left, of the same period (ht 9in/23cm), is more crudely constructed, without hands or feet: such dolls were made in vast quantities. *SS*

This doll, c.1830 (ht 12½in/32cm), though unmarked, has typical Grödnertal characteristics: small, rather pointed face, rouged cheeks and rosebud mouth, painted eyes, carved yellow comb on the crown of the head, black painted hair and curls at the side of the face. The limbs are delicate and the hands spoon/shaped. Also typical are the joints at shoulder, elbow, hip and knee. Grödernertals were widely exported to America and the rest of Europe by the end of the 19thC. Sizes ranged from 1in (2.5cm) to about 24in (60cm). *SS*

* Grödnertals of the early 19thC were painted over a base of gesso (plaster) and varnished: the gesso has often become rubbed on prominent parts of heads, but repair should not be attempted.
* A yellowish tinge is due to ageing of the varnish: the skin colour would originally have been off-white or pinkish.
* From the late 1840s heads usually consisted of a wood core overlaid with brotteig, or plaster, which is often cracked or broken off. Sometimes the only decoration was a spot of black painted hair. By the mid-19thC a small nose was usually fixed to the face.
* Grödnertal pedlar dolls, with baskets of wares, are desirable.
* Water should never be used for cleaning, as gesso and varnish are water-soluble.

SONNENBERG

Sonnenberg in Thüringia, Germany, was an important doll centre. The first dolls were made before 1700. Formed from a single piece of carved wood, they were more primitive than Grödnertals.

Papier Mâché and Composition

Hand-made papier mâché was used in France for dolls' heads as early as the 16th century. From c.1810 the German Toy Factories at Sonneberg began to mass-produce moulded dolls' heads in the material using a pressure process that eliminated hand kneading. Papier mâché dolls were popular until the 1870s and are now much-collected. Those with moulded heads were described as "milliners' models", for reasons that have not been established.

In America the most important producer was Ludwig Greiner of Philadelphia, whose dolls have papier mâché heads lined with muslin or linen.

Composition dolls were sometimes called "indestructible" – although the medium can in fact be delicate. They were made from various amalgams, incorporating paper or wood pulp, and makers developed their own secret recipes. Some collectors sensibly use the term "composition" to cover toughened forms of papier mâché.

Cast composition was used for shoulder-heads and socket heads (mainly from c.1820) before it became the most popular body material from the 1880s. Composition dolls of the early 20th century are not especially popular with collectors.

A composition-headed baby doll, early 20thC, marked "EFFanBEE" (ht 12½in/32m). It has a cloth body and is dressed in a silk gown and bonnet decorated with ribbons and lace. *C*

* EFFanBEE was the trademark of the American company Fleischaker & Baum, and was first used in 1913. They specialized in baby dolls and by 1915 had produced well over 100 varieties, including sullen-looking "Baby Grumpy", re-introduced in 1920. Some of the dolls had real hair.

This German doll of c.1830 is a typical papier mâché shoulder-head, with wood limbs and a kid body (ht 8½in/21cm). The green bands covering the elbow and knee joints are characteristic, as are the painted eyes and moulded hair and simply carved feet. *SS*

"French-type" papier mâché shoulder-headed dolls had heads by German firms such as Johann Müller and Andreas Voit. This example is mid–19thC (ht 23½in/60cm). The wig covers painted black hair. Typical features are the pink kid body, set-in glass eyes, open mouth with bamboo teeth, and pierced nostrils. The original costume, richly detailed, is a desirable feature. *CSK*

CONDITION

Both papier mâché and composition are prone to cracking and crumbling. Where the paintwork has been protected with varnish, this tends to wear on the prominent parts of the head, such as the nose and chin. Damage can also occur to composition bodies where the two halves join, and at the sockets. On sockets that have been reinforced with wood, the reinforcements often collapse, with the result that the limbs may slip into the body. Re-stringing with elastic should be carried out with care, as excess pressure will break the doll.

Particularly vulnerable to being crushed are the inferior "carton" composition bodies of the 1920s and 30s. Moreover, the components were fixed together by staples, which have often rusted and damaged the joins.

Cleaning should be carried out with a soft brush, avoiding water as the varnish is water-soluble.

c.1805 *c.1820*

ASPECTS OF PAPIER MÂCHÉ

Papier mâché heads of the mid–19thC were usually attached to hand-stitched bodies, small-waisted, with long slender wooden arms and wooden lower legs. Many such dolls were made in the great dollmaking centre of Sonneberg, Germany, where the first papier mâché heads were made c.1807.

* Hair may take the form of a wig (as shown, left), or alternatively it could be moulded. With moulded hair, more elaborate styles were possible, and these can provide a useful dating guide.
* Papier mâché dolls are unmarked, and are thus impossible to attribute to particular makers.

A composition Bye-Lo Baby doll, c.1923 (ht 17in/43cm), in christening clothes and bonnet. Bye-Lo dolls were spectacularly successful. Designed by Grace Storey Putnam for the American company Borgfeldt and first produced in 1923, they had heads of composition, wax or bisque, on a cloth body (which came in 7 sizes). The design was modelled from a three-day old baby. Celluloid hands are often found and some of the bodies contained squeakers. *SS*

* The features described in Storey's original patent for the Bye-Lo were "eyes slightly narrowed, mouth closed, fat rolls at back of neck, neck constructed to fit a socket." In practice, however, the first Bye-Los had a flange neck.

Felt and Cloth

Most early fabric (or rag) dolls have perished, survivors mostly dating from the early years of the century. The most famous are the durable, washable dolls with muslin heads and painted faces produced in Germany by Käthe Kruse from 1910, resembling her own children. Felt dolls include those made in Germany by Margarete Steiff and in Italy by Enrico Scavani (1910-50), whose trade name was Lenci, reputedly his pet name for his wife. Steiff's tall, thin soldiers, portly gentlemen and officious-looking policemen are almost caricatures. They have become collectors' items over the past few years, perhaps in the slipstream of the highly popular Steiff Teddy Bear.

In the USA, Izannah Walker made sturdy, plain dolls, c.1860-c.1880. Another key name was Martha Jenks Chase, who from the 1880s made dolls with heads in stockinet – an elastic fabric, knitted from silk or cotton. The features were hand-painted with rough brush strokes for hair and the bodies were sateen or, later, cloth filled with cotton wool. Madame Alexander's dolls in cloth and other materials, made from the 1920s, are immensely popular in the USA and are beginning to acquire a following in Britain. Her named dolls included Scarlett O'Hara, Alice in Wonderland and Princess Elizabeth.

Printed dolls for home sewing and filling, sold in sheet form throughout the 19th century and after, form a distinct collecting area of their own. In England, Dean's Rag Book Co. made "Tru to Life" character dolls such as Charlie Chaplin, George Robey and Lupino Lane (1920), while Chad Valley of Birmingham in 1923 introduced sheet dolls to their range of pressed felt-faced dolls. Norah Wellings, who was with Chad Valley for a short time, established a factory in Wellington, Shropshire; cloth dolls made here include black dolls with wide smiling mouths and cheeky sailors (sold as souvenirs on ocean liners). Wellings was one of the few doll-makers to use velvet.

Many makers of cloth or felt dolls used a stamp or label on the sole of the foot, but these are often lost or rubbed away.

Soft dolls are vulnerable to scuffing, moths and dirt, but it is surprising how many are found in good condition. Collectors should be on their guard against imitations, which can usually be detected by their inferior quality.

This Steiff character doll in painted felt, c. 1913 (ht 13in/33cm), with jointed neck, shoulders and hips, has the central face seam that typifies this maker. From 1905, the trademark of a metal "Steiff" ear button was used. Large feet are also characteristic. *CSK*

* Early Steiff dolls (1894-1908) are felt; from 1908 plush and velvet were added to the repertoire. The dolls measured up to 19in/48cm.
* As well as child dolls like this one, Steiff also produced soldiers, including some specially for the American market (for example, "Sgt Kelly" and "Privates Sharkey and Murphy", v. 1909).

Käthe Kruse's "Du Mein" baby, c. 1925 (ht 20in/51cm), is sand-filled stockinet, which gives it a realistic weight and floppy neck. There is a realistic knotted navel. All Kruse dolls were named and numbered on the sole of the left foot. It has been suggested that the lower the number the older the doll, but this has not been proven. A much rarer version of "Du Mein" called "Traumerchen" came with painted sleeping eyes. *SC*

* The first Käthe Kruse dolls were produced by established factories but she found their efforts unsatisfactory and set up her own workshop in 1918. Her early dolls, made of waterproof calico stuffed with hair, had waterproof seams and were exactly 17¼in/44cm high.

A Martha Chase cloth doll, c. 1904 (ht 21in/53cm), with typical applied ears, thick painted hair and a stockinet-covered head. Martha Chase dolls pre-1920 had stitch-jointing at shoulders, elbows, hips and knees; later ones were jointed only at hip and shoulder. Some dolls were fully painted, and washable. Some had applied thumbs. *S*

* All Chase dolls carried the company mark, on the thigh or under the arm, but often this has been rubbed off.
* Styles range from babies to characters such as Lewis Carroll's Alice in Wonderland.

This felt doll, c. 1927 (ht 22in/56cm), is typical of Lenci in its chubby face, side-glancing eyes and two stitched-together middle fingers on each hand. Lenci bodies were initially of moulded felt, but in time these were superseded by cotton bodies with felt shoulders and limbs (enabling skirts and low necklines to be worn). *CSK*

* The sideways glance was used by many makers of felt dolls from the 1920s. Lenci faces often have a petulant look.

Wax

The term "wax" usually refers to the head or shoulder-head of a doll: few all-wax dolls have survived. Poured wax dolls are made by repeatedly dipping the head into molten wax and pouring away the residue. Wax-over-composition heads, which were stronger, all have a wax skin over a composition base. Although some people find the lifelike sheen of wax dolls somewhat off-putting, there are many passionate collectors.

Many makers in England and Germany, and a few in France, made wax-over-composition dolls during the 19th century (mainly c.1820-c.1880), mostly with shoulder-head on a cloth body. Either the wax was coloured or the base material was tinted and covered with a layer of white wax. The dolls made in Germany by Charles Motschmann have a cloth torso and composition pelvis.

The finest poured wax dolls were made in England from the mid–19th to the early 20th century: Montanari, Pierotti, Charles Marsh and Lucy Peck are the best-known names. These child dolls have closed mouths, chubby features, glass eyes, inserted (often human) hair and eyebrows and, usually, a very slight turn to the head.

Wax is delicate, and should never be exposed to direct sunlight. Cleaning of wax dolls, or repairs, should be left to experts. All wax dolls are susceptible to cracking. Heads and limbs of wax-over-composition dolls are often crazed, where the two materials have expanded at different rates.

Superbly realistic, and made with great attention to detail, this poured wax doll, made for the wealthy, shows the incomparable level of artistry that was reached in the English wax doll industry in the 19thC. The dominant names were Montanari and Pierotti, but few poured wax dolls were marked, making attribution difficult. This example is from c.1880 (ht 20in/51cm). Typical features are the slightly turned head, fixed glass eyes (mostly blue) and individually inserted hair. Some Montanari dolls, called "rag babies", had a layer of muslin stretched over the wax to give a smooth finish. As with Pierottis, the wax shoulder-head and lower parts of the limbs are typically attached to the stuffed kid or cloth torso by robust threads. *S*

* Wax doll heads were modelled by hand until c.1850. From then on they were produced industrially in moulds – a process that made the features more resistant to wear.

A common type of wax-over-composition doll is the "pumpkin head", made 1850-90. This example of c.1860 (ht 12½in/32cm) has the typical over-large, globe-like head, and moulded hair-band and hair. *S*

* A variation on the pumpkin head is the "bonnet head", with moulded curls and hat, cloth body, spoon-shaped hands, and wooden lower limbs with painted boots. These dolls were made in Germany c.1860.

This wax-over-composition doll, c.1875 (ht 19½in/50cm), is probably by Cuno & Otto Dressel. The eyes are painted, the wig of blonde wool. *CSK*

* Dressel, based in Thüringia in Germany, made dolls in composition and bisque as well as wax, their wax dolls, like those of all the German manufacturers, are of poorer quality than the best English ones; being lightweight, they were particuarly suitable for export. Some of their dolls had red waxed booties.

* A common type of wax-over-composition dolls is a "slit-head", with hair inserted in a central slit along the crown.

A signature increases value, as most wax dolls are unmarked. Any maker's mark or shop stamp will be on the body or chest, on the back of the shoulder plate, or sometimes the neck (as with the Pierotti, in the detail above). Montanaris may have an "M" engraved on the inside of the shoulder-head. Faked signatures are not uncommon: it is easy to incise into the surface of the wax. However, recently added signatures inevitably have a fresher look than genuine ones. *MB*

A fine Pierotti poured wax doll, c.1890 (ht 17in/43cm), showing the typically delicate features on a chubby face. *S*

* Pierotti wax was often pale, as with other wax dolls, but some examples have a high colour, which is almost puce.

* Most Pierottis are unmarked but very occasionally "Pierotti" may be scratched across the shoulder plate. A shop stamp on the chest or body is found more frequently and is equally desirable.

Bisque and China I

"China" dolls are those with heads and limbs of glazed hard-paste porcelain, which is shiny and cool to the touch; bodies are of wood, cloth or kid. They were popular during the first half of the 19th century, especially after 1830: from c.1850 bisque began to be more widely used. The usual colour is white: a pink tint on the heads is comparatively rare. Most china dolls were made in Germany. Earlier examples are usually rougher on the inside than later ones, which were made by more sophisticated techniques.

Bisque dolls are by far the largest collecting area. They were popular from the mid–19th century until well into the 20th. Bisque is unglazed china, twice fired: but instead of a glaze being applied at the second firing, the features are tinted and re-fired at a lower temperature, to produce a matt, usually pinkish finish, more delicate and natural than that of china dolls.

French and German manufacturers dominated the bisque market. The most beautiful and collectable bisque dolls were made in France, by notable makers such as Jumeau, Bru, Gaultier and Steiner. The late 19th-century French fashion doll, or Parisienne, dressed in fine fashions of the day, is avidly sought after. Dolls described as "bébés" are not baby dolls but represent children between infancy and about 8 years old.

In 1899 the French doll makers, fearful of high-quality competition from Germany (see page 216), formed a consortium, the Société Française de Fabrication des Bébés et Jouets (SFBJ), which manufactured under this trade mark from 1905. Design and quality vary enormously among the different SFBJ ranges.

Both these German china dolls have cloth bodies with china lower limbs. The one on the left, c.1880 (ht 18in/46cm), has the dark moulded hair, elaborately piled on the head, that is typical of china dolls. The more unusual boy doll on the right, c.1860 (ht 16in/41cm), has dark brown brushstroke hair. Both dolls have painted eyes – the usual style in china dolls until the late 19thC. *SS*

* Dark hair is most common. Blonde hair is rarer until the 1870s, and adds to the value. Some hairstyles are very elaborate.

* In a similar style, but in unglazed china, are the dolls known as "parian".

A Jumeau bisque fashion doll, c.1870 (ht 16in/40.5cm), with jointed composition body and real hair wig. The expression is typical. Jumeau quality varied widely – this example is especially fine. *SB*

* The Jumeau factory was founded by Pierre Jumeau in 1842. In 1899 the company became a founder member of the SFBJ.

A bisque doll in silk and satin dress by Jules Steiner of Paris, c.1870 (ht 16½in/42cm), impressed "Sie. A 1". ("Sie." is an abbreviation of Société). The wig is lambswool, the body of jointed papier mâché. Typical features of Steiner include: fingers of equal length, big toe standing apart from the others, and a pate of pressed cardboard (sometimes purple) instead of the cork pate usually found on French dolls. An undercoat of purple paint can often be seen through the flesh colour. Steiner made dolls from 1855 to 1908. *S*

FACIAL FEATURES
The facial features here are typical of French and German bisque dolls of the late 19thC. The glass eyes have red dots in the corners for added realism. The eyebrows are feathered, and the eyelashes consist of diagonal strokes. The tight bow mouth is characteristic of some bisque and most glazed china dolls. This example has a wig of real hair. *SS*

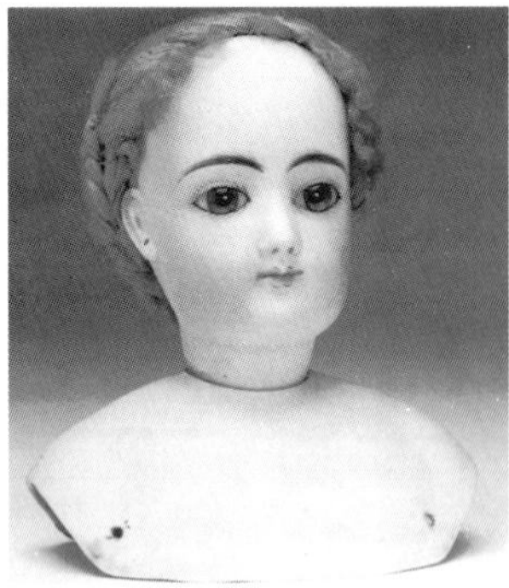

HEADS
Bisque shoulder heads were sewn onto a cloth or kid body through holes in the shoulder plate. This is a typical example, c.1870 (ht 5½in/13cm). China shoulder heads were of similar construction, but without the swivel neck. *SS*

* Another type of bisque head, used with composition bodies, was the socket head: the neck was held by a wooden cup that was fixed to the body by elastic.

EYES
The Bru doll (right) has fixed "paperweight eyes" – that is, they bulge, and the irises have white threads in them, making them more naturalistic. Such eyes are also found on Jumeau and other French dolls.

MOUTH
Most early bisque heads have mouths that are either "closed" (as in the Bru doll, right) or "open-closed": the latter term means that the lips appear to be parted, but without an incision in the bisque. Both types are more collectable than "open mouth" dolls.

HAIR
The wig fits over a cork, cardboard or plaster pate. Mohair is most commonly used: it is fine and soft and can be made into a variety of styles. Human hair is also often found, and tends to be in better condition. Replacement wigs have a nylon mesh base, which makes them easy to recognize.

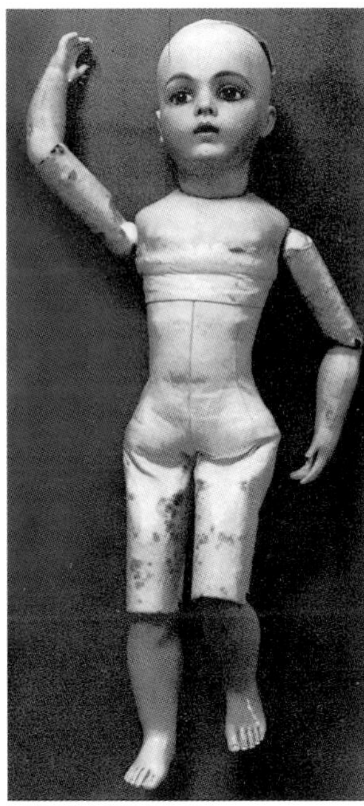

BODY AND LIMBS
Early bisque heads have cloth or kid bodies, or sometimes composition. The example above (from the Bru doll, right) is kid, with bisque forearms and wooden lower legs. The scalloped edge on the torso is typical. *SS*

After c.1875 the emphasis in bisque doll production began to shift from adult faces to child faces. The two major Parisian makers were Jumeau and Bru. This Bru Jeune bisque doll of c.1875 (ht 24in/61cm) has the most important features – excellent condition, original costume and smooth, fine-quality bisque. *SS*

CONDITION
Bisque dolls should be inspected gently. The most valuable part, and the most vulnerable to damage, is the head, which should be examined under a magnifying glass for any cracks or chips. If the wig can be removed, shining a strong light inside the head cavity will show up any hairline cracks, damage or restoration. Great care must be taken to avoid "wig pulls" – small flakes of bisque removed with the wig. If animal glue has been used, removing the wig will usually be quite easy; modern glue can make it impossible. There is no need to glue the wig back on once it has been taken off: it will sit quite firmly on the head without adhesive. Anyone buying a bisque or china doll for investment should wherever possible choose a head in perfect condition, as damage can reduce the value by at least a half. Silk costumes have withstood the ravages of time less well than cotton. Original or contemporary costumes are an added bonus.

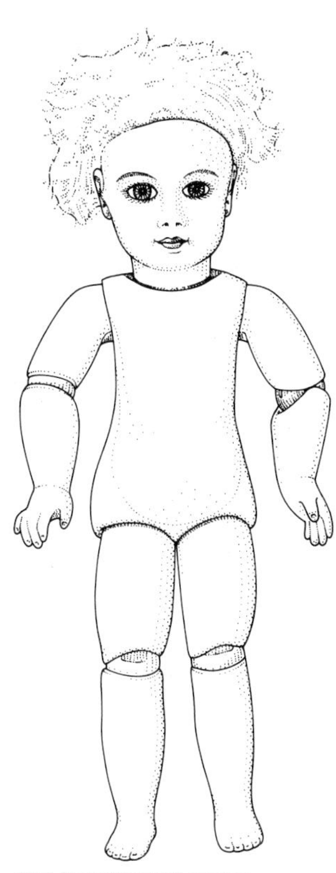

COMPOSITION BODIES
Later bisque heads, of the socket type, were commonly attached to composition bodies, as shown above. These are sometimes ball-jointed. Fingers are often missing. Some large French dolls had lightweight papier mâché bodies.

BRU· JNE

MARKS
Most makers of bisque dolls incised marks on the back of the head or shoulder plate – trade mark, mould number, name, initials and/or size numbers. Bodies are not usually marked. A small proportion of the heads came from factories that produced a whole range of porcelain products – in which case, books of general porcelain marks offer a useful guide to identification.

Bisque and China II

The Germans, meanwhile, had become formidable makers of quality dolls, most of which came from the Sonneberg area of Thüringia. The firm of J.D. Kestner, founded in 1805, concentrated on papier mâché and wax to begin with, but later became known for fine bisque-headed dolls. The superb heads made by Simon & Halbig appeared on bodies from many makers, including Kämmer & Reinhardt, with whom they eventually merged. The most prolific maker in Germany was Armand Marseille. These are just some of the best-known names: there were around 100 makers in Thüringia in the years leading up to 1914.

A landmark in bisque dollmaking was the exhibition of lifelike "art dolls" in Munich in 1908. This stimulated a deluge of baby character dolls, whose features were intended to be realistic rather than pretty. Carl Bergner made babies with two, or sometimes three, faces – happy, sad or sleeping – on one head which turned within a cardboard hood. Sleeping eyes, first fitted into these dolls in 1914, gave a great boost to sales when production continued after the War.

Celluloid, lightweight and robust, began to be a rival to bisque from c.1900. From 1905 celluloid jointed dolls appeared. However, bisque dolls continued to be made until the 1930s.

A pair of bisque-headed doll's house dolls, German, c.1890. Adult male dolls with moulded moustaches and beards are rare. Both dolls have cloth bodies and bisque lower limbs, with moulded boots and shoes. (ht 5½/6in-14/16cm). *S*

* Male dolls are more common in doll's house size than in standard sizes. Boys and servants are represented, as well as fathers.

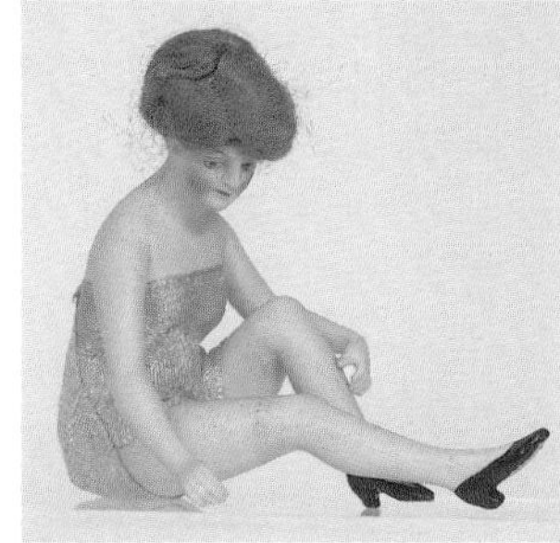

An all-bisque bathing belle, produced in Germany by an unknown maker, c.1920. These saucy little figures, either nude or dressed in brief net or ribbon costumes, are not strictly dolls but are a very popular collecting field. They are very fragile, and must be in perfect condition to be valuable. Sizes ranged between 3½ and 6in/9–15cm. *MB*

Oriental dolls are an important category of bisque character doll. This one, with a composition body, is by J.D. Kestner, c.1914 (ht 13in/33cm). Kestner made dolls and doll parts from 1816. Typically, they had plaster pates. *S*

* The Kestner mark is "JDK", but this is frequently lacking.

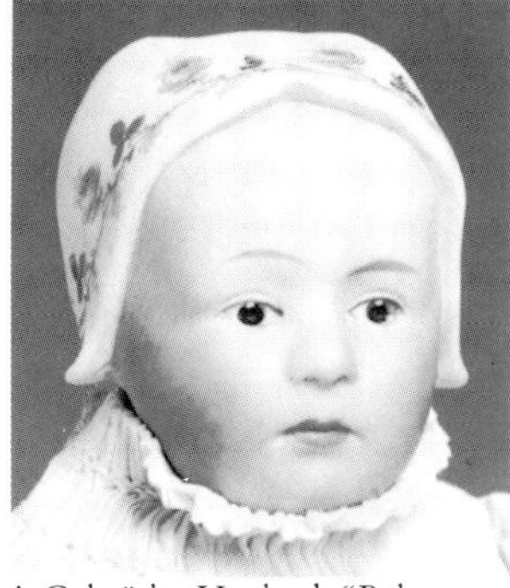

A Gebrüder Heubach "Baby Stuart" bisque character boy doll, c.1912 (ht 10in/25cm), with closed pouty mouth, intaglio blue eyes and moulded white bonnet decorated with flowers. *SS*

* A much rarer version of this doll has a removable bisque bonnet. Another has a fixed bonnet with holes for a ribbon.

* Gebrüder Heubach concentrated heavily on character dolls, including googly-eyed, winking, whistling (activated by pressing) and scowling. Bodies are often of poor quality, yet the fine heads make these dolls collectable.

* The factory mark is "Heubach" in a square or as a sunburst (above). Heads often have small stamped green figures.

* Gebrüder Heubach often used pink-tinted bisque rather than white bisque overpainted, as was favoured by other makers.

* Another firm of the same name is generally referred to as "Heubach Köppelsdorf", after the area where it was based.

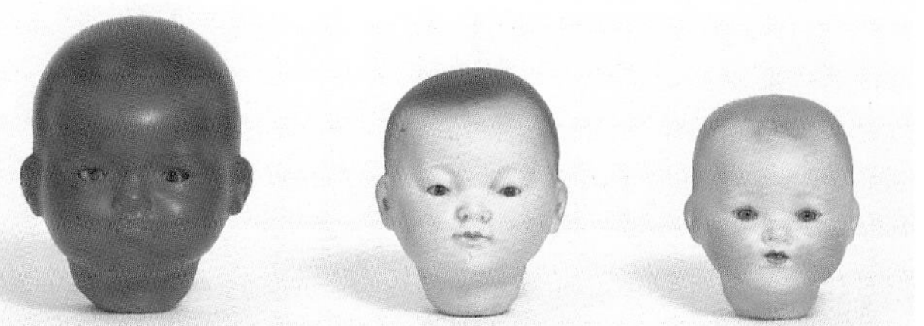

"My Dream Baby", a range of heads by Armand Marseille, was made in vast numbers, 1924-6. Both open mouth (mould no. 341) and closed mouth (351) forms were produced. The Oriental version is one of the rarest, and the most expensive. *MB*

* Armand Marseille's output of dolls was enormous. They are almost invariably marked "AM" or with the name in full.

The impish Kewpie, with its topknot, wings, webbed hands and sideways-glancing eyes, was based on a cartoon by the American, Rose O'Neil, and first made by Kestner in 1912. Bisque examples like these, made in Germany (ht 6½in/17cm), are much less common than the later versions in celluloid. Composition was also used.
✻ Sizes range from buttonhole figures to 17in/43cm bisque dolls, now rare. Within a year of first production, several American companies (notably Fulper) were making the doll under licence. Variations on the standard form included jointed legs, and hugging pairs and Negro Kewpies (from 1914). *CP*

CELLULOID

Celluloid was developed as a lightweight alternative to bisque. Early manufacture was beset by problems of inflammability. Most celluloid dolls were made by the Rheinische Gummi und Celluloid Fabrik of Mannheim, whose trademark is a turtle; later it was known as the "Schildkrot" works. Independent makers would bring their designs to this company for manufacture. Some celluloid heads were cast in the same moulds as bisque heads. A flesh tone was achieved by adding pigment to the surface and varnishing.

Kämmer & Reinhardt, founded 1885, made dolls that combined fine quality with a high level of innovation. In 1918 the firm merged with Simon & Halbig, who had produced all their bisque heads. This character doll (*above*), 1909 (ht 21½in/55cm), with jointed wood and composition body, is an example of their work. *S*
✻ At the base of S & H heads is a figure that denotes the finished height in cm: checking the measurement may sometimes reveal a replacement body.
✻ S & H bisque heads are also found on French automata, Edison phonograph dolls and on Jumeau bodies.

Left "Googly-eyed" dolls, with heads in bisque, were a popular German export. The bulging eyes are nearly always accompanied by a "watermelon" smile. These examples are by Kämmer & Reinhardt, c.1914 (ht 14¼in/36cm); the bodies are wood and composition and ball-jointed. *S*
✻ Googly-eyed dolls were also made by Kestner, Gebrüder Heubach and others.

Automata

The great age of automata was 1880-1920, the 19th-century French ones, mostly on music boxes, reigning supreme. Leopold Lambert, Gustave Vichy, Gaston Decamps, J. Phalibois and Fernand Martin were prominent makers, mostly of "parlour pieces" made for the amusement of adults – conjurers, musicians, acrobats, flower sellers, and mothers wheeling babies in prams.

Automata of a simpler kind can be equally innovative. Particularly popular were Marottes: these had bisque heads and conical bodies, were mounted on an ivory or wooden baton and played tunes as they were twirled around. Clockwork swimming dolls in bathing costumes concealing cork bodies were designed to propel themselves in water.

The first walking doll appeared in 1826. Talking and kiss-throwing were other desirable attributes. Talking was activated by moving the arms, exerting pressure or turning the body; pulling a string was a popular method from the 1880s to 1914. Jumeau in Paris made talking dolls from 1865. In 1890 a French patent was issued for moving lips. Early talkers merely squeaked, but by the 1890s (after Edison produced a miniaturized phonograph) there were more sophisticated phonograph dolls which played speeches and songs on wax cylinders inside the torso.

Important American patents included Madam Hendren's soft-bodied, walking, talking "Mama Doll" (1918), which was much-copied, by EFFanBEE and others. The automata made by Edward Riley Ives of Bridgeport are very collectable. Automata bodies marked with patents can help to date heads supplied by other makers.

"The Unexpected Return" by J. Phalibois, c.1860 (ht 25½in/65cm), represents the upper end of the market for French automata. A glass dome (removed here for clarity) protects the delicate model, which is typical in its mixture of materials. The woman has a bisque head with fixed glass eyes, a mohair wig over a cork pate, and wooden hands; the soldier has a papier mâché head, with moving glass eyes. The base beneath the bower contains a keywind and pull-string stop-start musical movement. *SS*

A Jules Steiner walking-talking bisque shoulder-head doll, c.1860 (ht 15in/38cm). Mechanical Steiners are marked on the mechanism, here exposed within the cardboard "skirt". *S*

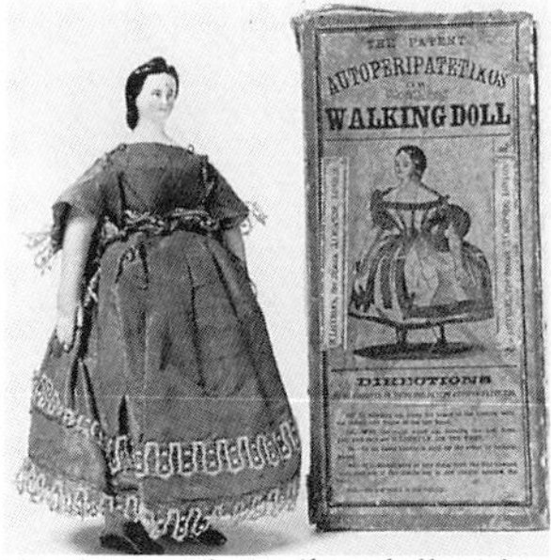

An Autoperipatetikos doll with china head and shoulders (ht 9½in/24cm). She has kid arms and a conical cardboard skirt containing the keywind walking mechanism. The underside is printed "Patented July 15th 1862; also in Europe 20th Dec. 1862. This Doll is only intended to walk on a smooth surface". The original box adds greatly to the value. The clockwork movement, operating rods inside the boots, gives the illusion of real walking. *S*

* The Autoperipatetikos ("self-propelling" doll) was patented by Enoch Rice Morrison in the USA in 1862.

* These dolls were given a variety of heads: papier-mâché, rag, china or untinted bisque.

A musical dunce by Gustave Vichy, c.1890, with composition face and bisque forearms (ht 20in/51cm). The table conceals the keywind mechanism. The "cap-ears", one leg and right arm lift while the head shakes and nods. The quality of workmanship is typically French. *S*

This "General Butler" is an example of the clockwork walking doll patented in the USA by Arthur E. Hotchkiss. Hotchkiss characters are easy to recognize by their large cast-iron feet, two wooden rollers under each, and distinctive large hands. *MWSM*

Reference

GLOSSARY

Automaton A mechanical toy, doll or group of dolls with concealed clockwork movement.
Autoperipatetikos The Greek word for "self-propelling", applied to Enoch Rice Morrison's walking doll (1862). The term is often used for other clockwork dolls.
Bald head A head with no crown opening. It can be covered by a wig.
Ball-jointed The term applied to a doll whose limbs are attached by a ball and socket, allowing the greatest possible movement.
Bébé A French doll representing a child from infancy to about 7 years old.
Bent-limb The term applied to a doll with five-piece body and curved arms and legs.
Bisque Unglazed porcelain.
***Brevité* (Bté)** Patent registered mark, found on French dolls.
Carton A cardboard **composition**, used for some dolls' bodies in the 1920s and 30s.
Character doll One with an individualistic expression rather than an idealized appearance.
Cloth dolls Dolls made of linen, muslin, cotton or calico. Felt and velvet are often included in this category. "Rag" is a generic term for all fabrics.
Composition The substance used for dolls' heads and bodies, made up of various inexpensive ingredients such as wood pulp, rags, sawdust and glue.
Crazing A network of small cracks on the surface of a doll's head, torso or limbs.
DEP The abbreviation (for *Deposé* or *Deponirt*) used on French and German dolls indicating a registered design or patent.
DRGM The mark used on German dolls indicating a registered design or patent. Abbreviation for *Deutsches Reichs Gebrauchs Muster.*
Dutch doll See **Peg doll**.
Excelsior Soft wood shavings used as stuffing.
Fashion doll One representing a woman or adolescent with well-finished, fashionable clothes. Such dolls usually had a **bisque** head and kid body. Some French examples are known as "Parisiennes".
Fixed eyes Eyes, other than painted eyes, that do not move.
Flange neck head A head with a ridge at the base of the neck.
Flirty eyes Eyes that move from side to side and also close.
Frozen Charlie or **Charlotte** An unjointed all-china doll of the late 19th/early 20thC.
Ges. Gesch. A design registration or patent mark on German dolls. An abbreviation for *Gesetzlich Geschutzt.*
Gesso Plaster of paris, used as a ground for painting.
Googly eyes Disproportionately large round eyes looking to one side.
Gutta percha A synthetic substance similar to rubber, used for dolls in the later 19thC.
Incised (or impressed) mark A mark impressed into the back of the head or shoulder plate.
Inserted hair Hair set into the scalp of wax dolls.
Intaglio eyes Eyes carved into a **bisque** head.
Lower limbs The arm from elbow to hand; the leg from knee to foot.
Marotte A legless doll on a baton with a musical movement in its conical body, activated when the doll is twirled. A type of **poupard**.
Moulded hair Hair formed as part of the head.
Open mouth Parted lips created by a small opening.
Open-closed mouth A mouth that appears to be open, but has no opening between the lips.
Painted bisque Bisque covered with a layer of flesh-coloured paint, but not fired; the paint can therefore wash or flake off.
Paperweight eyes Realistic blown glass eyes, usually in French dolls.
Papier mâché Moulded paper pulp.
Parian A fine white porcelain. The term is loosely applied to unpainted **bisque**.
Pate A crown piece, under the wig and over the crown opening, of cardboard, cork or plaster.
Peg doll A simple, jointed wooden doll.
Portrait doll A doll intended to represent a particular person, sometimes similar only in name. The term is used to describe early Jumeau dolls.
Poupard A legless doll on a stick.
Poured wax A head or shoulder head formed by repeatedly dipping into molten wax.
Printed doll Features and details of a doll printed on fabric, for home assembly.
Shoulder head A doll's head and shoulders moulded in one piece. Sometimes abbreviated – for example, to shoulder bisque, a shoulder head in **bisque**.
Sleeping eyes Eyes that can move from open to closed.
Socket head A swivelling head which fits snugly into a doll's body.
Stump doll A doll made from a single piece of wood.
Swivel head A turning head which fits into a shoulder plate.
Stockinet An elastic fabric, knitted from silk or cotton, used for doll heads and bodies.
Topsy-turvy dolls A rag doll that has two torsos, each with a different head, one hidden beneath the reversible skirt.
Two-faced doll A doll with a revolving head, showing different expressions or colours at the front and back. Three-faced dolls were also made.
Vinyl A non-inflammable, flexible plastic.
Voice box A mechanical device by which a doll talks, cries or sings.
Watermelon mouth A thin-lipped smiling mouth turned up at the sides, often found on **googly-eyed** dolls.
Wax-over-composition A head or **shoulder head** of **composition** covered with a layer of wax.
Weighted eyes Eyes that close by means of weights when the head is tilted.
Wig pulls Small flakes of **bisque**, accidentally removed at the same time as a wig.
Wired eyes Eyes that can be made to close by means of wires.

SELECTED MAKERS

Bergner, Carl (active Sonneberg, 1890-1909) Specialized in two- and three-faced dolls in bisque and wax-over-composition.
Borgfeldt (active New York from 1881) Manufactured, distributed and imported a variety of dolls.
Bru (Bru Jeune & Cie.) French, founded 1866, joined SFBJ 1899. Famous for bisque dolls.
Chad Valley English, active from 1923 (Johnson Brothers Ltd., 1860-1923). Made fabric dolls.
Chase, Martha Jenks (active USA from 1893) Made dolls with stockinet heads.
Dean's Rag Book Co. English. Made printed dolls from 1903.
Dressel (active Sonneberg from 1700) Produced dolls from many materials.

Ellis, Britton & Eaton (Springfield, Vermont, 1858-69) Made china and all-wood dolls. Succeeded by the Vermont Novelty Works.
Fleischaker & Baum (active New York from 1910) Specialized in composition baby dolls. "EFFanBEE" trademark from 1913.

Gaultier, François (active France from 1860) Made porcelain doll heads and parts. Perhaps the same company as Gautier. Mark: "F.G."
Gebrüder Heubach (active Thüringia from 1820) Made bisque and china child and character dolls and heads.
Greiner, Ludwig Philadelphia. Patented papier mâché doll's head in USA, 1858, rights extended 1872. Mark: name and patent date.
Hotchkiss, Arthur E. Patented walking doll with clockwork mechanism in USA, 1875.
Jumeau (French, c.1842-99) Member SFBJ 1899-1925. Specialized in bisque bébés and fashion dolls. Won gold medal at Paris Exhibition, 1878."Médaille d'Or" often stamped on bodies.

DÉPOSÉ
E.7 J.

Kämmer & Reinhardt (active Thüringia from 1886) Best known for character dolls, introduced 1909.

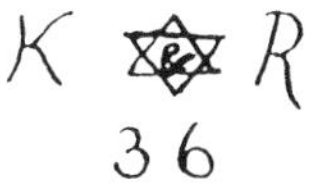

Kestner, J.D. (active Thüringia from 1805) Made complete dolls and parts in wood, bisque and china.

G 11
made in Germany
243
J. D.K.

Kruse, Käthe (active Germany early 20thC) Made lifelike cloth dolls from 1912.
Lenci (active Turin from 1920) Trademark of Enrico Scavini. Made pressed felt dolls. Mark: "Lenci" on sole of foot.
Marseille, Armand (active Thüringia, 1865-1920s) Porcelain factory. Prolific manufacturers of composition and bisque dolls.
Montanari (active London, 1851-80s) Poured wax dolls.
Pierotti (active London from 1780) Made poured wax dolls.

Pierotti

SFBJ (founded France 1899) *Société de Fabrication des Bébés et Jouets.* Consortium of doll makers. Most dolls had bisque heads on jointed composition bodies. Mark: "SFBJ Paris" + number.
Simon & Halbig (active Thüringia from 1870s) Porcelain factory. All-bisque dolls and bisque, composition and celluloid heads.
Steiff, Margarete (active Würtemberg from 1894) Made felt, plush and velvet dolls. Mark: metal "Steiff" ear-button, 1905.

Steiner, Jules (Société Steiner) (French, 1855-1908) Specialized in mechanical dolls and bébés with bisque heads.

J. STEINER
S^TE S.G.D.G.
PARIS
FI^RE A 11

BIBLIOGRAPHY

Bailly, Christian, *Automata, The Golden Age, 1848-1914* (1987)
Cieslik, Jürgen & Marianne, *Dolls: European Dolls 1800-1930* (1979)
Coleman, D.S., E.A. & E.J., *The Collector's Encyclopedia of Dolls* (1968)
Desmonde, Kay, *Dolls* (1974)
Earnshaw, Nora, *Collecting Dolls* (1987)
Foulke, Jan, *Blue Book: Dolls & Values* (regularly updated)
Goodfellow, Caroline G., *Understanding Dolls* (1983)
King, Constance Eileen, *The Collector's History of Dolls* (1977)

TOYS

There are two remarkable things about collectable toys: the first is that, compared with other antiques, they are not very old, and the second is that a large proportion of them were produced in Germany.

Many of the most valuable old toys are not antiques at all in the strict sense, as they were made in the half-century between 1890 and 1940. This was the period when the manufacture of consumer products became concentrated in factories; and, indeed, most collectable old toys were produced in a factory rather than in a workshop or studio.

There were many small manufacturers of toys in America, Great Britain, France, Italy and Spain who were content to produce toys for their home markets. These are collected today, but usually only in the countries for which they were made. Often these small manufacturers were not primarily toymakers, but had developed a range of toys as a profitable sideline. However, the German makers were different: many of them produced nothing but toys and they looked to export a large part of their output. They would even create special versions of a toy for the largest export markets. German toys had an international appeal, and it is this more than anything that makes them the most sought-after today.

The old toys considered here are divided into categories according to the materials of which they are made. Some materials were virtually exclusive to a particular country. For example, cast-iron toys were not widely produced outside America, nor were they exported in quantity, so they remain largely the preserve of American collectors.

Although many of the materials were intrinsically strong, the toys themselves were often delicately made and fragile. Therefore, the condition in which the toy has survived is crucial. Moreover, many toys include mass-produced parts that can be difficult to reproduce without special machinery. This means that restoration can be a difficult process. Ironically, it is the later, less expensive pieces, which include no hand-made parts and no hand finishing, that are often the most difficult to restore.

Because it is very rare to find toys in mint or near-mint condition, such toys always command a premium. The presence of the original box, especially if it has a colourful or interesting label, will greatly enhance a toy's value. The term "mint and boxed" is often misused but has become part of the toy collector's vocabulary representing the ultimate in condition.

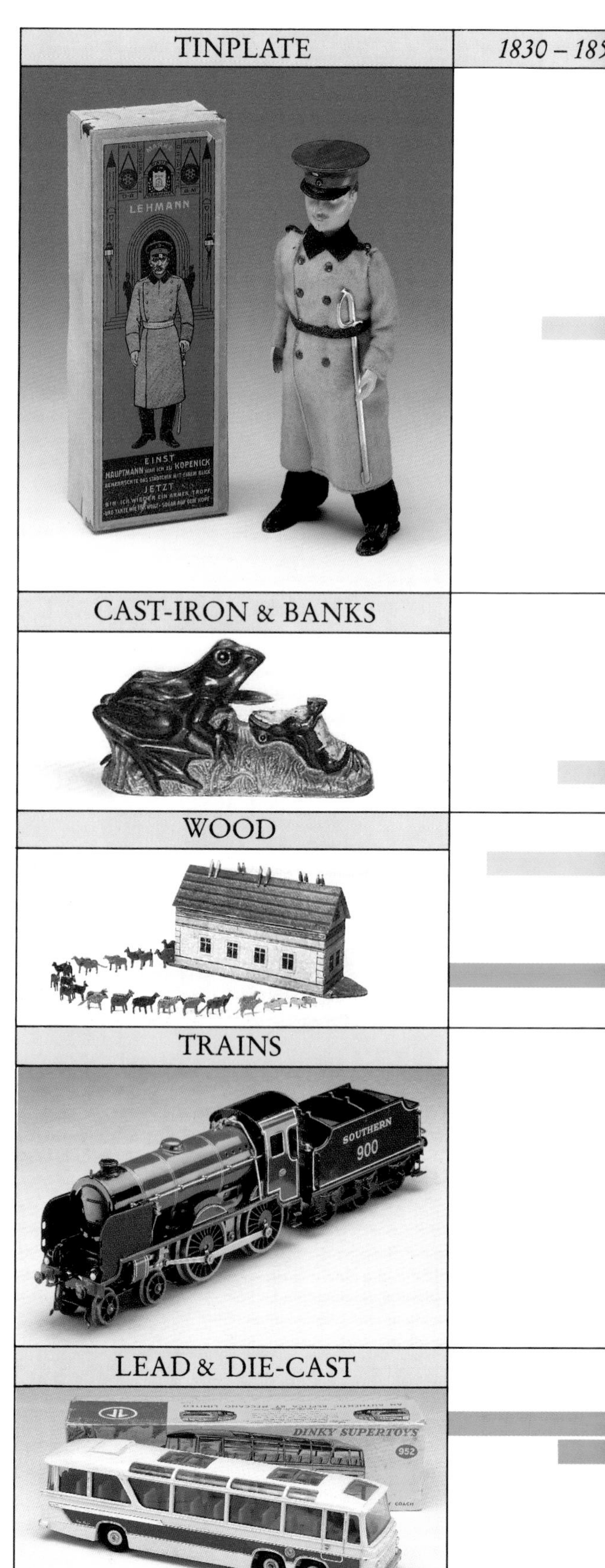

Germany
United States
Britain
France
Japan

The chart shows the major categories of collectable toys and the leading makers and factories and their periods of production. Where the precise date of foundation or closure of a company is unknown, the approximate date is indicated with a question mark. An arrow head is used for companies still in existence. A broken line indicates that the toys produced over that period are not likely to be collectable.

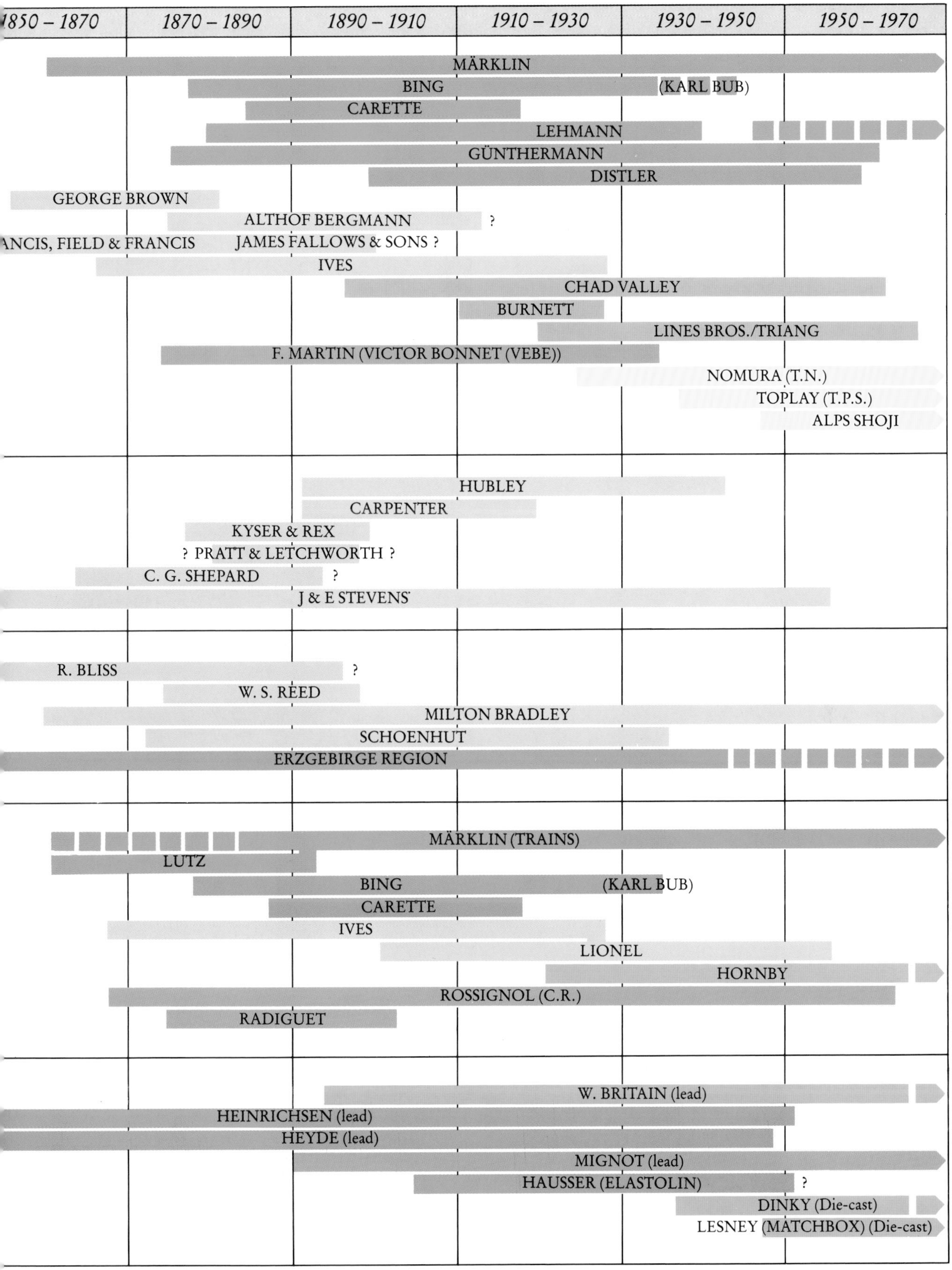

1850 – 1870	1870 – 1890	1890 – 1910	1910 – 1930	1930 – 1950	1950 – 1970

MÄRKLIN
BING (KARL BUB)
CARETTE
LEHMANN
GÜNTHERMANN
DISTLER
GEORGE BROWN
ALTHOF BERGMANN ?
ANCIS, FIELD & FRANCIS
JAMES FALLOWS & SONS ?
IVES
CHAD VALLEY
BURNETT
LINES BROS./TRIANG
F. MARTIN (VICTOR BONNET (VEBE))
NOMURA (T.N.)
TOPLAY (T.P.S.)
ALPS SHOJI

HUBLEY
CARPENTER
KYSER & REX
? PRATT & LETCHWORTH ?
C. G. SHEPARD ?
J & E STEVENS

R. BLISS ?
W. S. REED
MILTON BRADLEY
SCHOENHUT
ERZGEBIRGE REGION

MÄRKLIN (TRAINS)
LUTZ
BING (KARL BUB)
CARETTE
IVES
LIONEL
HORNBY
ROSSIGNOL (C.R.)
RADIGUET

W. BRITAIN (lead)
HEINRICHSEN (lead)
HEYDE (lead)
MIGNOT (lead)
HAUSSER (ELASTOLIN) ?
DINKY (Die-cast)
LESNEY (MATCHBOX) (Die-cast)

Wooden Toys

It is often difficult to distinguish between home-made and factory-produced wooden toys. Nevertheless, a number of important manufacturers made products that are generally distinctive and easily recognized. As in other branches of toy collecting, knowledge of the maker will greatly increase the toy's value. Germany was pre-eminent in the production of wooden toys, as of tin toys, and many were made specially for export.

An important distinction can be drawn between American wooden toys and European ones. American toys are characterized by the application of lithographed paper to flat surfaces cut to shape. European toys are usually fully carved, or turned, and any decoration is painted directly on to the wood. This means that American toys are much more difficult to restore successfully and, therefore, the condition in which a piece has survived is more important than it is for European wooden toys.

The 19th-century American toymakers Charles M. Crandall and his cousin Jesse A. Crandall patented in 1867 a unique tongue-and-groove system which allowed blocks to be interlocked. They went on to apply the principle to wooden figures, the heads and limbs of which were interchangeable, so that many permutations could be made. Some of the Crandalls' patents were taken up by H. Jewitt & Co. of London, which produced its own versions of the jointed figures.

These brightly painted papier mâché skittles on a solid wooden base (ht 8in/20cm) were made in Germany in the late 19thC. *PC*
* Similar papier mâché skittles were made in England and France.
* Papier mâché superseded wood for skittles as this medium enabled complicated forms to be produced in quantity much more easily and inexpensively than wood, without the need for hand carving. However, it is more vulnerable to damage and condition is therefore an important factor.

Arks were often just decorated storage boxes for the animals, which were the real focus of interest, although the ark of this Noah's Ark, made in Germany c.1850, is attractive in its own right. *S*
* Many Noah's Ark animals have survived in excellent condition, possibly because the toys were regarded as being suitable for Sunday play only.
* Arks with hulls are more desirable than flat-bottomed ones.

THE RING METHOD

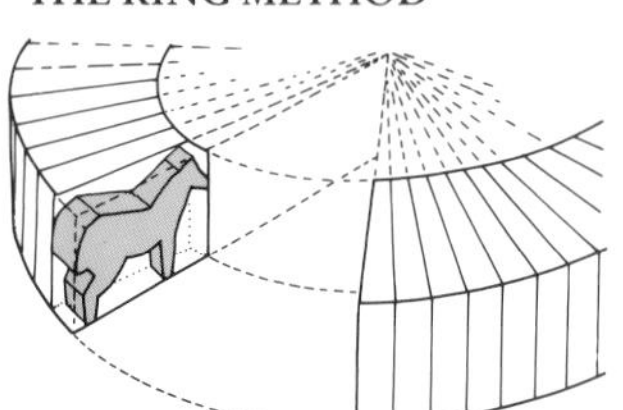

The hand carving of wooden animals for farmyards and arks was a laborious process which was superseded in the late 19thC by the ring method. A large circle of wood was turned so as to produce a large groove (representing the space under the belly of animal), and sometimes a second groove for the nape of the neck. The animals were then cut from the ring in slices. The legs were separated and then details such as ears and horns were carved in. This method produced an unrealistic uniformity; horses, dogs, sheep and antelopes often have the same basic shape. Whereas early hand-carved animals are fully rounded with fine detail, the ring method produced animals which tapered (usually to the front).

Playing "shop" has long been popular, and miniature shops have a long history. Butcher's shops like this one, c.1860 (ht 18in/46cm), were particularly common in England. Some may have stood in the empty window of a real butcher's shop when it was closed. The more sides of meat displayed, the more desirable the toy. *PC*
* Many elaborate toy shops, with drawers and shelves containing miniature items of food and other goods, were also made in France and Germany in the 19thC.

Albert Schoenhut, perhaps the best American manufacturer of wooden toys, was born in Germany of a great toy-making family and his toys are European in style. The most successful was the Humpty Dumpty Circus of 1902. The bandwagon above is a rare and unusually elaborate item. *PC*
* Many Schoenhut toys found today need the rubber cords in their joints re-strung, but this does not seriously reduce their value.
* Generally, Schoenhut animals with glass eyes are more collectable than those with painted eyes.

Cast-iron Toys

Toys and banks (novelty money boxes) made of cast iron are almost exclusively American, and the collecting of these toys is largely an American activity.

Cast-iron banks appeared after the American Civil War when America was swept by a craze for hoarding coins in response to paper money of very low denomination printed by both sides during the war. By the 1880s the banks had become quite sophisticated and increasingly popular. Cast-iron toys appeared at the same time and many were produced as a sideline by companies such as The Kenton Hardware Co.

From a collector's point of view the problem with cast-iron toys is the nature of the material itself. Although cast-iron is hard and very durable, it is extremely brittle and will break easily if dropped. Therefore, cast-iron toys are often found with damage (which is almost impossible to repair effectively), and the price of complete pieces with good original paint will usually reflect their scarcity.

REPRODUCTIONS
Many reproductions have come on to the market, and although these vary in quality some have been good enough to deceive even specialist dealers and collectors. Several checks can be made:

* Some pieces are labelled as reproductions or have "Made in Taiwan" or something similar cast into them. Be suspicious of any piece that looks as though it may have had lettering removed.
* The casting of originals is generally smooth and finely detailed, whereas the reproductions are rough and lack detail.
* Genuine examples are boldly painted with a depth of colour and patination that is hard to fake. Old paint usually shows evidence of fine crazing, or cracks. A piece should be regarded with suspicion if no such signs are visible under a magnifying glass. Some reproductions are artificially rusted and have hardly any paint. Originals are rarely found in this condition.
* Most reproductions of banks were made using an original bank as a pattern. These recasts are smaller than the originals. Collectors should familiarize themselves with the base sizes. A book of the base tracings of original banks is available so that collectors can make sure that a bank is as large as it should be. However, this method is not infallible as the base of the English version of some banks is not the same as the American version of the same bank.
* Many old banks have patent dates cast into their bases, but this does not alone guarantee that the bank is old. Be suspicious, as there are more reproduction cast-iron toys and banks than there are surviving originals.

REPAIR AND REPAINTING
A repair to a cast-iron toy or bank is acceptable to most collectors, provided that it is honestly and competently done. Repainting is not so acceptable, although when it has been well done it can be difficult to spot without the aid of ultraviolet light. Both repair and repainting will greatly affect value. Generally speaking, good restoration will devalue a rare piece less than it will devalue a common piece. Seek advice before attempting to restore or repaint an old toy or bank.

The survival of a large number of patent papers has helped to date and identify the designer (if not the manufacturer) of many banks. This Girl Skipping Rope (ht 10½in/26.5cm) is a very desirable and colourful bank produced by J. & E. Stevens of Cromwell, Connecticut; it was protected by a patent issued in May 1890. *PC*

This Ryan monoplane, made by Hubley in 1932, is modelled on the *Spirit of St Louis* which Charles A. Lindbergh flew solo across the Atlantic in 1927. Its bold, clean lines and sturdiness are typical of American cast-iron toys between the World Wars. *PC*

* Cast-iron toys were popular for only a short period. Many early ones are of vehicles. Among the major 19thC manufacturers were Francis W. Carpenter & Co. and J. & E. Stevens & Co. In the 1920s and 1930s these toys became increasingly uncompetitive against toys made of lithographed tinplate. The Hubley Manufacturing Co. of Pennsylvania was one of the great companies that went out of business when the use of cast iron for toys was prohibited during the Second World War.

This Mason Bank, c.1880 (ht 7¾in/19.5cm), produced by the Shepherd Hardware Co. of Buffalo, NY, is one of many desirable banks with moving parts: when the lever at the side is depressed the hod carrier throws one coin from his hod forward into the bank; and the Mason raises and lowers his trowel and puts a brick in place. *PC*

The "Tammany" Bank (ht 5½in/14cm) is a popular bank which turns up frequently. The fat man sitting in the chair is Boss Tweed, head of the notoriously corrupt Democratic party in New York in the 1870s which had its headquarters at Tammany Hall. When a coin is placed in his hand he gently slips it into his breast pocket and nods his appreciation. Many cast-iron banks have similar old-fashioned satirical or comical themes which greatly add to their charm and interest for the collector. *PC*

Die-cast Toys

Die-cast toys are made from metal or plastic formed under pressure in a mould. They originated in France with the small vehicles, approximately 1½in/4cm long, made in the first 20 years of this century. Many of these are marked "S.R.". At the same time Ernst Plank was producing similar toys in Germany. However, the most significant developments were taking place in America.

The Chicago publishing and printing company, Dowst, had developed the technology of casting lead alloys for typesetting. This eventually facilitated the production of small inexpensive castings of cars known as "cracker-jack toys". Refined and enlarged versions of these were later sold by Dowst under the trade name Tootsie Toys. In the early 1930s the Tootsie range included some of the best-ever diecast cars, with separate castings for the chassis, body and radiator, and realistic rubber tyres.

Despite these developments in America, it was the British company Meccano, already making Meccano building sets and Hornby trains, that made die-cast toys a commercial success. In response to Tootsie Toys, Meccano introduced its Modelled Miniatures range in 1933, which was extended the following year and renamed Dinky Toys. With their fine detail and attractive paintwork, these were soon very popular. Early Dinky models were not produced to any consistent scale, but after c.1936 1:43 became established as the standard scale, not only for Dinky Toys but also for toys by the other major manufacturers. In 1948 Dinky introduced Supertoys, and a range of accessories such as petrol pumps.

As with toy trains, smaller-scale models in time became more popular. Early in the 1950s the British company Lesney introduced the Matchbox series of attractively packaged toy vehicles.

This Dinky Weetabix van from the mid-1950s (ht 2½in/6cm) is typical of the fine commercial vehicles made by the company. The quality of the castings and, above all, of the paintwork helped these toys to become the major force in diecast vehicles. *MaB*

∗ In the 1950s each toy came with its own box, the presence of which is of crucial importance to its value today.

This Routemaster bus, c.1955 (ht 3in/8cm), was part of the Spot-On range made by the British company Triang in response to the success of Dinky Toys. Although many collectors agree that Spot-On models were superior, they never threatened Dinky's supremacy. The same is true of Corgi toys, although these benefited from innovative features such as perspex (plexiglas) windows. *MaB*

This pre-War set of Dinky aircraft, c.1937, is valuable not only because aircraft are perenially popular, but also because the relative fragility of the pieces makes complete sets scarce. *MaB*

∗ Early Dinky Toys were made of a zinc alloy known as Zamak, or Mazak, which can suffer from corrosion or fatigue. This problem, made worse by sudden temperature changes and by sunlight, can render a model worthless. Careful storage can arrest deterioration. Prospective buyers of both Dinky and Tootsie models should check for signs of cracking or warping.

In 1952 Lesney Toys produced a small gilded coronation coach on a scale of 1:75, based on OO Gauge railways (see page 229). This was such an enormous success that the company followed it up with their Matchbox range of models, exemplified by this horse-drawn London bus, c.1956 (ht 1¾in/4.5cm), which is roughly in scale with a OO Gauge railway. Although the box is rather larger than a matchbox, it is printed to resemble one. *MaB*

Lead Figures

Small, thin figures, known as "flats", have been produced, mostly in Germany, since the early 18th century. However, in the 19th century solid casting of fully-rounded figures became the most popular form in Europe. The major manufacturers of these figures were Heyde, in Germany, and Mignot in France.

In Britain and America the most popular method of manufacture from the late 19th century until the 1950s was hollow casting – a process invented by the Britain family in England. Hollow casting involves the pouring of a molten mixture of lead, tin and antimony into an engraved mould so that a skin is formed on the inside of the mould. As the antimony cools it expands and gives fine detail to the casting without the support of solid metal. The bulk of the alloy is poured out while still molten, and this is why hollow-cast figures have holes at their head or feet. These figures use less metal than solid figures, and are thus less expensive to make and to transport.

No company dominates any area of collectable toys in the way that William Britain & Sons dominates lead figures. The company began by making remarkable automata, which are today among the most expensive of English toys. They took out a patent on the hollow casting of lead figures in 1893. The range grew until 1941; as well as soldiers, there are civilian figures for toy railways, farms, circuses, and so on. Britain's ceased production of lead figures in 1966.

The other major manufacturers of hollow-cast figures were John Hill & Co. (Johillco) in England, and Barclay & Manoil in America.

The other important type of figure is that made by compression moulding of composition onto a wire skeleton. The figures produced in this way are usually larger than lead ones. The major manufacturers, both German, were Hausser (Elastolin) and Lineol. These toys are usually marked on the base with the company name.

This set of Indian Army Madras Lancers (ht 2¾in/7cm), produced by Britain's in 1937, is the largest known set of cavalry figures. *P*

* Lead figures of this type were not made to the same scale. The standard size of figures made by Britain's is 54mm/2⅛in, which is 1/32 life size and theoretically in scale with Gauge 1 railways. This size has remained the most popular in Britain and America. (00 gauge railways are usually equal to a figure height of 20mm/¾in or 1/72 life size.)

* Britain's sets made after c.1898 are numbered. However, this should not be used as the only way to determine date as numbers were repeated on sets made until the 1960s.

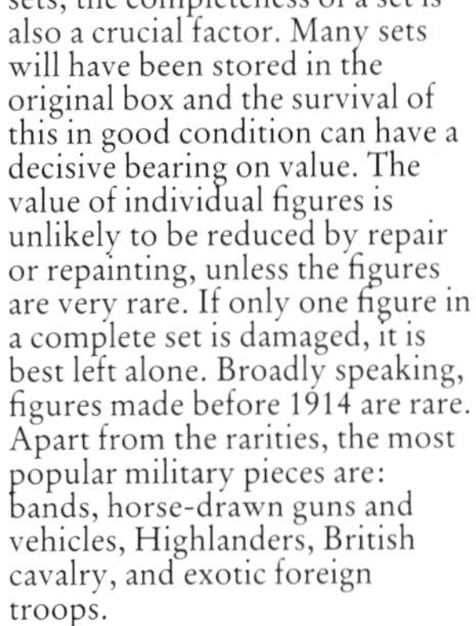

CONDITION AND RARITY

The condition of the paint on lead figures is very important and, since most were produced in sets, the completeness of a set is also a crucial factor. Many sets will have been stored in the original box and the survival of this in good condition can have a decisive bearing on value. The value of individual figures is unlikely to be reduced by repair or repainting, unless the figures are very rare. If only one figure in a complete set is damaged, it is best left alone. Broadly speaking, figures made before 1914 are rare. Apart from the rarities, the most popular military pieces are: bands, horse-drawn guns and vehicles, Highlanders, British cavalry, and exotic foreign troops.

This Royal Horse Artillery gun team made by Britain's in the 1920s (ht 2¾in/7cm) is in fine condition. The box label carries the set number 318. *P*

* Until 1900 most Britain's figures have fixed arms and oval bases with no marks. From 1900 until 1916 most have square bases, and many have a copyright date cast into the base or an applied label.

* Illustrated box labels by Fred Whisstock (from 1906) add value if the box is in good condition.

The German firm Heinrichsen was the major manufacturer of flats until 1945. This knight, c.1900, (ht 3½in/9cm), was made in Nuremberg by another important manufacturer, Besold.

* Flats with a deliberately old-fashioned look are still being produced in Germany. Although not intended to deceive, they do turn up in sales as "antique toys". They are almost impossible to distinguish from old figures except for their brighter finish. *P*

Tin Toys

Most adults above the age of 40 probably have some childhood memories of tin toys. They are hard (even sharp) to the touch and yet delicate and easily broken, with colours that are bright and bold.

The term "tin toy" (which is a misnomer, as they were made of tinplated steel) covers a wide variety, from superb German toys made by such manufacturers as Bing, Carette, Märklin and Lehmann to toy robots made in Japan in the 1950s and 60s. Nor were they exclusively tinplate, but at all periods they often included parts made of other materials – cloth, wood, die-cast alloys, glass and all kinds of plastic from celluloid to vinyl.

Tin toys were essentially products of the Industrial Revolution. Until the early 19th century most toys were wooden and home-made. When tinplate from South Wales became widely available, large-scale production in factories made it possible to produce quite complicated toys inexpensively, and at the same time there was an expanding and prosperous middle class to buy them.

It was in the 1830s that the first tin toy factories opened in America. These catered largely for the domestic market. The toys were produced for a short period compared with tin toys made in Europe. Large-scale production by the German industry for worldwide distribution was not achieved until the last years of the 19th century and, with only a few notable exceptions, the production of German tin toys did not survive the Second World War.

CONDITION

The most important factor in considering an old tinplate toy is condition. This is affected by three major points:
* rusting
* damaged finish – chipping or flaking if the toy is painted; scratching or rubbing if it has a printed finish
* bending, denting or loss of some parts.

Some defects can be repaired (see above right) but this can reduce the value of a toy by as much as half. Battery-operated toys are notoriously difficult to repair.

This pull toy of a lady leading a horse, made by James Fallows & Sons of Philadelphia in the early 1880s (ht 12in/30cm), is typical of American tin toys of the period in its simple lines and hand-painted decoration. *SNY*
* Few American toys have clockwork mechanisms.

ERNST PAUL LEHMANN

Ernst Paul Lehmann was a visionary toy maker who began producing a series of tinplate toys in Brandenburg, W. Germany, in 1881. Lehmann toys are recognizable by their rare combination of ingenious movement and light-hearted pastiche of real life.

Performing pigs were a popular circus act at the turn of the century. *Paddy's Dancing Pig* (ht 4½in/11cm), by Lehmann, was patented in 1903 and produced until 1935. *PC*
* Many Lehmann toys have patent dates printed on them, which are useful in giving the earliest possible date of manufacture.

RESTORATION

Until 1890 tin toys were hand-finished by painting. These early toys are thus often easier to restore than later, printed ones. The background colour was often put on with an airbrush and the detail was usually stencilled or applied by hand with a brush. After 1890 the use of printed parts became widespread, and after the First World War virtually universal. It is possible to find some toys where the early versions are painted and later versions have printed parts. It is extremely difficult to reproduce the effect of commercially-lithographed tinplate, especially the high quality of early lithography. The other difficulty for restorers of tin toys is that of replacing a factory-stamped part by hand, especially if the pressing is deep.

The tinplate body of this "Gordon Bennett racer", produced by the German maker, Carette, c.1904 (lgth 10½in/27cm), is lithographed; the figures are hand-painted. Such a combination is quite common in toys produced in the period 1900-14. *MaB*
* In the late 1880s and 1890s Carette supplied Bing with parts for toys. These parts carry Bing marks.

The Mikado Family, first produced in 1894 (ht 7in/18cm), is one of the early Lehmann toys. It is operated by a flywheel, unlike later tin toys, which had clockwork motors. Although Lehmann toys do not have the cleverest or most complicated movements, they include an element of fantasy or exoticism that makes them remarkable. They were widely exported and were surprisingly inexpensive. *MaB*
* The French toymaker Fernand Martin made automated tin toys, usually clothed, with pressed brass faces. A series started in 1889 consisted of 50 characters, modelled on real people.

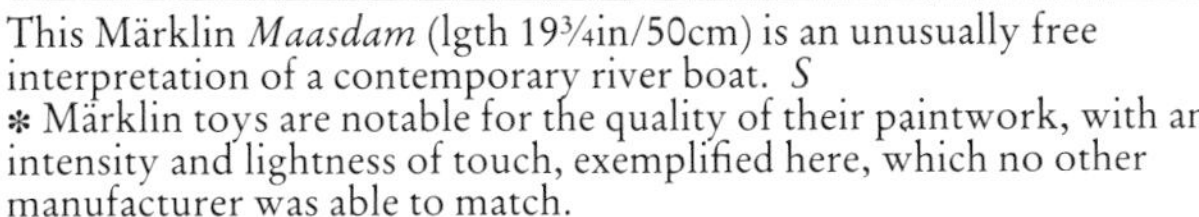

This Märklin *Maasdam* (lgth 19¾in/50cm) is an unusually free interpretation of a contemporary river boat. *S*

✻ Märklin toys are notable for the quality of their paintwork, with an intensity and lightness of touch, exemplified here, which no other manufacturer was able to match.

REPRODUCTIONS AND FAKES

Reproduction of lithographed toys is almost unknown. A number of tinplate toys have been re-issued in recent years, notably some of the pre-War products of Paya in Spain. However, these are intended as "collectors' editions" rather than as fakes. Some tin toys have appeared in Western Europe from Russia, Czechoslovakia, Hong Kong and China. These are distinguishable from earlier tin toys by the lack of detail and the high gloss finish.

The clockwork motor and adjustable steering add to the desirability of this beautifully lithographed tin tanker (ht 11in/28cm), produced by Johann Distler & Co. in Nuremberg in the early 1930s. *MaB*

✻ Road vehicles, some of which have doors that open, often come with drivers; these are not necessarily in scale with the vehicle.

✻ Most German toy vehicles are marked "Made in Germany", "DRGM", or "DRP" and many carry makers' marks as well.

MÄRKLIN

Widely regarded as the supreme toy makers 1880-1915, this German factory produced tin boats, cars, trains, steam engines and novelty toys as well as dolls' house furniture and spinning tops.

BING

Another high-quality German manufacturer. The period of finest quality was 1902-6. Many toys produced after 1920 have the look and feel of large-company mass production.

This Bing model of *Columbia* (lgth 26½in/67cm) of 1908 is notable for its realism – compare it with Märklin's more fanciful *Maasdam*, left. *S*

This toy robot, Robby (ht 13in/32.5cm), was produced in Japan in the late 1950s, following the popularity of the robot in the 1956 film *The Forbidden Planet*. *P*

✻ There were many different types of robot – nearly all of them made in Japan.

✻ To a lesser extent, space technology also provided inspiration for Japanese toys.

In addition to robots, the Japanese concentrated on beautifully detailed tin cars, particularly of American prototypes, which were produced in the 1950s and 60s. This Ford convertible by Haji (lgth 12in/31cm) dates from 1956 and features adjustable steering and a friction (push and go) motor. *MaB*

✻ Most collectors regard Japanese cars and robots of this period as the last great collectable tin toys.

Trains and Stations

Trains were made in lead and wood from the 1830s but most collectors are interested in toys from the 1890s and later.

In the 1870s and 80s a number of small German firms, such as Lutz, Rock & Graner and Büchner, produced beautifully made, expensive tin toys, but few have survived. In 1891 Märklin produced a complete railway system in three sizes, or gauges. Gradually, a full range of accessories was added. Throughout the 1890s, the German manufacturers, many based in Nuremberg, expanded rapidly.

The country's toy industry declined after the First World War, but by the mid-1930s Märklin was strong again, especially in Germany, with a range of O gauge products – the finest ever produced at this scale.

In Britain, model trains were regarded as serious scientific teaching aids rather than playthings. The locomotives, made of brass and steam-powered, are known as "dribblers", because water trickled from their cylinders as they moved along. They were still being produced in the 1890s, looking almost exactly as they had done in the 1840s. Until 1914 most of the trains intended for use as toys in Britain were imported from German firms such as Märklin, Bing and Carette.

In France, there was a parallel development of "dribblers", particularly by the firm of Radiguet & Massiot, but the French used tin for most of their early trains. A number of small companies made these simple floor trains, so-called because they did not run on rails. These trains can be identified by the makers' initials with which they were marked – for example, C.R. (Charles Rossignol), and E.V. (Emile Favre). Curiously, these tin floor trains, like the British model trains, also retained the look of the earliest prototypes at the turn of the century and were still being produced with the outlines of real locomotives from 50 years earlier.

The impact of the "iron road" was probably greater in America than anywhere else, and the toy trains that developed here were very different from those in Europe. The need was for a toy that could be assembled easily in a factory from a few basic shapes and that was sturdy enough to be shipped long-distance to customers spread over a large area. The American toy locomotives, made from a relatively heavy tinplate, were usually brightly coloured in red and gold and were often decorated with flowers and other patterns applied with stencils. The other major differences from European toys were that the American manufacturers generally produced only a locomotive and tender (coaches are very rare) and if they had any motive power it was clockwork (no live steam trains were produced). The locomotive also looked different: it was typically American with large bells and lamps, a cow catcher on the front, a large cab and a tall chimney.

In the 1880s and 90s trains made of wood or cast iron were produced in America. (See pages 222-3.)

This locomotive, "Giant", is 18 inches (45cm) long and was produced by Ives in the late 1870s. Apart from its unusually large size, it is typical of many 19thC American trains: it has a very distinctive outline and is brightly coloured with a wealth of decorative detail. *PC*

* In the USA after the First World War Lionel were producing solid but basic electric trains, and their "Standard Gauge" (2⅛in/5.4cm) came to dominate the market.

The British firm Hornby introduced this Gauge O Metropolitan Railway locomotive in 1925. In its general appearance it is similar to the contemporary American products of Ives and Lionel. *MaB*

* By the end of the 1920s Hornby's O Gauge products had overtaken the Germans and were dominating the market. In France JEP (Jouets de Paris) were similarly successful.

Throughout the 1930s there was a general trend toward realism and more realistic scale modelling. Trains also became smaller during the 30s. This famous Schools Class Gauge O engine "Eton" was produced by Hornby in 1937 and is typical of the high quality and attention to detail that characterized toys of the period, especially those made by Hornby. *MaB*

CLASSIFICATION

In the 1890s Märklin introduced a range of locomotives in Gauges I, II and III – 48mm, 54mm and 75mm (1⅞in, 2⅛in and 3in). These measurements relate to the distance between one rail centre and the other. This system was replaced by a more accurate system measuring the distance between the inside edge of each rail (coincidentally making American 2in Gauge compatible with the new European Gauge II). Between the Wars, O Gauge (35mm/1⅜in) was universally popular; and after 1945 smaller gauges (down to 16.5mm) with letter names such as OO, HO and N took over. However, widely different scales were adopted by different makers, and there were variations in the sizes of trains of the same gauge.

Locomotives are also described in terms of the arrangement of their wheels. Thus, one with four leading wheels, four driving wheels and two trailing wheels would be a 4-4-2.

This Gauge I summer car with a canopied promenade down one side, was produced by Märklin in 1902. The quality of the painting and the wealth of detail typify Märklin's production in the period from 1890 to 1914. *S*

* Märklin's toys are generally more imaginative and less prosaic than those of Bing and the other major German manufacturers.

This beautifully delicate trainset, complete with plaster figures, was probably made by the North German firm of Lutz about 1870, although recent research indicates that it may in fact have been made by Büchner, another eminent German manufacturer. The technical expertise of Lutz and its tradition of quality were added to Märklin's experience of volume production and its developing sales network when the two companies merged in 1891. *DA/S*

In addition to locomotives and carriages, there are also specialized coaches, such as this Gauge O Märklin ambulance coach, c.1910/12. *CSK*

* Märklin made a series of specialized vehicles with accurate logos for American breweries and other companies, such as Heinz. These are particularly collectable – and very expensive.

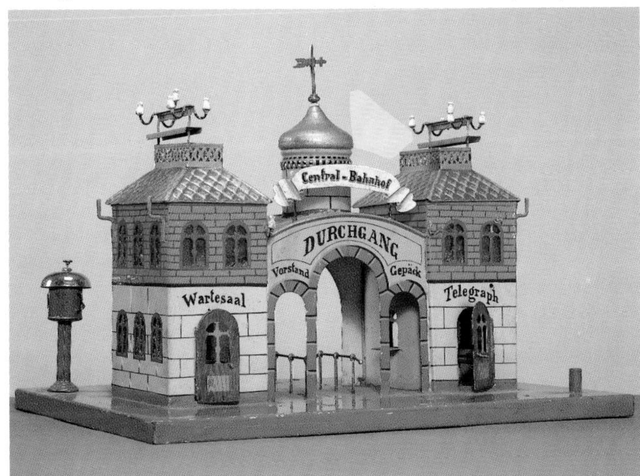

German companies were the first to realize the commercial potential of producing a complete range of accessories and trackside buildings for toy trains. This Gauge 1 Märklin station dates from c.1900 and is a magnificent toy in itself. Such stations were produced with signs in German, English and French. *S*

This 4-2-0 Gauge III locomotive was made by the German firm Carette c.1902. It is steampowered, but because it has never been fired the original paintwork is almost perfect – live steam locomotives usually show signs of burning, especially around the boiler. This locomotive has a "Continental" outline, which makes it saleable in most markets – most of the major German manufacturers produced toys that looked like the real trains of a particular country. *S*

* Boxed locomotives are rare. Some of the labels on the boxes that have survived are exquisitely designed and printed.

Comic Characters

Few areas of toy collecting have expanded as rapidly in recent years as comic character toys. They were produced in many materials, including tin, lead, wood, rubber, cast iron and even glass.

Cartoon favourites such as Walt Disney's Mickey and Minnie Mouse, Donald Duck and Pluto are very collectable, as are Popeye, Felix the Cat, Betty Boop and other fictional characters. Among real-life stars, Charlie Chaplin was the most influential, but toys of Harold Lloyd, Amos n' Andy and the ventriloquist's doll Charlie McCarthy were also popular.

Early comic character toys were an American phenomenon. The first such toy was "The Yellow Kid in a Goat Cart", created in 1896 by the artist R. F. Outcault and produced in cast iron as a three-dimensional representation of a newspaper character.

A popular comic strip boosted the circulation of a newspaper, and before long toy producers saw that this popularity could be turned into sales. Manufacturers competed energetically for licences to produce comic-character toys and by 1928 their production was well-established. The Lionel Corporation secured a contract with the Walt Disney Company in 1934 to produce a Mickey and Minnie toy that featured the pair with a railway handcar. This was such an overwhelming success that it rescued the company from the threat of financial ruin.

Also very successful between the Wars were the inexpensive but amusing toys of Louis Marx, notably his Merrymakers Mouse Orchestra and a range of stage and screen characters.

Until 1938 "Walt Disney Enterprises" or "Walter E. Disney" usually appeared on German and American Disney toys. British toys were marked "Walt Disney Mickey Mouse Ltd". In 1939 the name changed to Walt Disney Productions. The value of a toy is greater if the box confirms that it was made with the permission of the Walt Disney Company.

German manufacturers were the first to be licensed to produce Mickey Mouse toys. This hurdy-gurdy (ht 8in/20cm), made in 1931 by the Nuremberg company of Johann Distler, depicts an early version of Mickey turning the crank while the jointed tin figure of Minnie dances to the tune produced by a very simple musical box. © *1989 The Walt Disney Company*

* This thin, toothy rat-like Mickey is the earliest version and the most popular with collectors today. The typical "pie-cut" eyes – with one "slice" removed from the black eye are clearly visible.
* The golden age of Disney collectables was 1928-38. Important ones include Mickey and Minnie on a moter-cycle, by Tipp and Co., c.1932; Mickey the Musical Mouse; and Mickey the Drummer, by Nifty.

This toy (lgth 9in/22cm), depicting the characters Maggie and Jiggs, was almost certainly made by Gebrüder Einfalt in 1924 for Nifty – Einfalt was the only company to produce this type of steel band toy, but Maggie and Jiggs appears in the Nifty catalogue. George McManus created the henpecked husband and shrewish wife in 1913 as a popular strip cartoon. *PC*

Throughout the 1930s the Japanese made Disney character toys in celluloid such as this example (ht 9in/23cm). Despite the vulnerability of the material, a large number have survived. © *1989 The Walt Disney Company*

* In the 1950s Mickey became chubbier and lost his tail.

The most collectable Donald Ducks are the early ones with long bills. This Donald was made in Japan, 1930s (ht 7in/18cm). Early Japanese toys are sparsely marked; reproductions may say "Walt Disney Productions" or "W.D.P." © *1989 The Walt Disney Company*

Reference

GLOSSARY

Cow catcher A metal frame on the front of American **model** trains, to remove obstructions from the track.
Crazing A random pattern of fine cracks in the paint of a hand-enamelled toy – a sign that the paint is old.
Die-cast The term for a shape formed in a metal mould under pressure.
Embossed Pressed decoration on tinplate.
Fatigue A form of corrosion of the alloy of which some **die-cast** toys are made.
Flywheel The motive power of some toys before 1914, operating on the inertia principle.
Lead rot Similar to **fatigue**, but affecting the alloys of which lead figures are made.
Lithography/Litho The process by which sheets of tinplate are printed in the flat before being pressed into shapes.
Live steam A toy or model that is powered by steam.
Mechanical bank A savings money box in which the deposit of the coins depends on some mechanical action.
Mint A toy that is without the slightest blemish. In reality, near-mint is the best condition in which one is likely to find a toy.
Model A miniature representation of a vehicle or building, made exactly to scale. Sometimes a pejorative term suggesting that charm has been sacrificed for detail.
Novelty toy Any non-vehicular mechanical toy.
Rust A reddish-brown oxide, the main enemy of cast-iron and tin toys. The catalogue term "surface rusting" indicates a reddish bloom on the surface which is sometimes removable. "Rust spotting" is more serious as the paint or lithography will probably have been destroyed under the spots. "Rusted through" means that the metal has been completely eaten away.
Still bank A savings money box which has no mechanical movement involved in the deposit of coins.
Tender A vehicle which carries the fuel and water used in steam locomotives.
Tinplate Thin sheets of steel coated with a tin-based alloy.
Turned A term used of a wooden toy that has been rotated and carved into shape on a lathe.

SELECTED MAKERS

Bing, Gebrüder (1879-1932) Nuremberg, Germany. Tin toys, especially cars, boats and trains; stations and railway accessories.
Bliss Manufacturing Company (1832-90s) Pawtucket, Rhode Island, USA. Wooden toys with brightly lithographed designs on paper. Dolls' houses from c.1895 are highly prized.
Britain's Ltd, William (1860-1966) London. Made lead military figures from 1893. Mark: "Copyright Wm. Britain" with date on label; mark cast into horses from 1900; labels on foot soldiers replaced by lettering cast into base, 1905.
Brown, George (active 1856-80) Forestville, Connecticut, USA. Specialized in mechanical toys. Became the Stephens & Brown Manufacturing Company in 1868, producing tin and clockwork toys.
Carette & Cie., Georges (1886-1917) Frenchman based in Nuremberg. Among the first in Europe to introduce electric trains. In the early 20thC produced a large range of cars, boats and railways.

Carpenter & Co., Francis W. (1894-1925) Harrison, NY. Cast-iron toys, including many horse-drawn vehicles.
Chad Valley (1897-1955) Trade name of Johnson Brothers, based in Birmingham, England. Tin toys from the late 1890s and self-assembly toys.
Crandall, Charles M. and **Jessie A.** (1840s-1905) Brooklyn, New York. Patented a tongue-and-groove system of flat printed wooden blocks in 1867 (see page 222). Produced a series of wooden toys with interlocking and interchangeable parts.
Dinky see **Hornby**
Distler & Co., Johann (established late 19thC) Based in Nuremberg, Germany. Made tin vehicles, penny toys and comic characters.

Dowst Company Chicago publishing house which in the 1920s started to produce die-cast "crackerjack" toys, and later the more sophisticated Tootsie Toys.
Fallows & Son, J. M. (1874-1900) Philadelphia, USA. Made river boats and horse-drawn vehicles in tin.
Francis, Field & Francis (1838-70s) Also known as the Philadelphia Tin Toy Manufacturing Company. Tin toys and doll's-house furniture.
Günthermann (1887-1965) Nuremberg. Clockwork toys and many fine hand-enamelled novelty toys.

Haji Mansei Toy Co. (founded 1951) Japanese manufacturers of model tin cars.
Heyde (1840-1944) Dresden, Germany. Semi-solid and solid lead figures and boxed sets of armies. Work widely copied.
Hornby, Frank (1863-1936) England. Made **Meccano** from 1908, Hornby trains from 1920 and Dinky toys from 1933.
Hubley Manufacturing Co. (1894-1940s) Lancaster, Pennsylvania. Cast-iron toys, banks and gun caps.
Ives, Edward Riley (1868-1928) Established factory in Plymouth, and later Bridgeport, Connecticut. Became Ives & Blakeslee, 1872. Cast-iron and tin toys. Absorbed by **Lionel**, 1931.
Lehmann, Ernst Paul (1881-present) Established company in Brandenburg, Germany. Early tin toys had flywheel mechanisms, later versions had clockwork.

Lesney (1951-present) British company. Introduced the Matchbox series of miniature die-cast vehicles. Most clearly marked "Lesney", "Matchbox", or "Mako".
Lines, G. & J. (active 19th-20thC) London. Wooden rocking horses and hobby horses. Tri-Ang works acquired 1919. Wooden toys, pedal cars, and, from c.1930, metal cars. Trade marks: "Tri-ang", "Triangtois" and "Minic".
Lionel (1901-1950s) New York and New Jersey. As The Lionel Manufacturing Company, made toy trams and trains, and, from 1908, train sets. Disney toys from 1934. Products marked with name.
Lütz, Ludwig Established company in Ellwangen an der Jagst, Germany c.1846. Made tin carriages, train sets and doll's house furniture. **Märklin** took over the company, 1891.
Märklin (1859-present) Goppingen, Germany. Made tin vehicles, novelty toys and dolls' house furniture. Railway items always the most important of their products.
Martin, Fernand (active 1876-1912) Paris. Factory reputedly made approx. 800,000 tin toys a year. Taken over by Victor Bonnet et Cie. (VÉBÉ) early in 1920s.

Meccano see **Hornby**
Mettoy Co. Ltd. (1933-present) British company, founded by Henry Ullmann, former proprietor of German company **Tipp & Co.** Made tinplate Mettoy toys, 1930s-50s, and die-cast Corgi toys from the 1960s.
Mignot (1825-present) Paris. Most famous French manufacturer of solid, flat and some hollow figures.
Paya, (Established 1880s) Ibi, Spain. Tin toys, especially cars and O Gauge trains. Toys still produced as collector's items.

Plank, Ernst (active 1866-1930s) Nuremberg. Instrument making company, working in tin and brass. Produced 80,000 steam engines, ships and trains in 1899. Steam-driven cars from 1904.

Reed Toy Co., W. S. (1876-97) Leominster, Massachusetts, USA. Made wooden toys, such as ships, decorated with lithographed paper.
Rossignol, Charles (c.1868-1962) Paris. Produced floor trains, cars, boats and famous series of Paris buses. Mark "CR" appears on nearly all toys.

C.R.

Schoenhut, Albert (1872-c.1935) America. The "Humpty Dumpty Circus", registered 1902, was the company's most successful product. It could be bought in units or as a boxed set which came with a book.
Schreyer & Co. (Schuco) (1912-78) Clockwork figures with tinplate bodies covered in plush or felt and "one-piece" tin cars. Motorcycles with ingenious movements very much sought after.

Shepard Hardware Co. (1866-c.1892) Buffalo, N. Y. Sidney Shepard. Tin toys and cast-iron toys.
Stevens & Co., J. & E. (1843-c.1930) Based in Cromwell, Connecticut. Best known for cast-iron toys and banks.
Tipp & Co. (1912-71) Nuremberg. Produced fine tin cars in the 1930s, and comic character toys.

BIBLIOGRAPHY

Carlson, P., *Toy Trains – A History* (1986)
Cieslik, J. & M., *Lehmann Toys* (1982)
Gibson C., *History of Dinky Toys* (1962)
Hillier, M., *Automata and Mechanical Toys* (1976)
Kürtz, H., and Ehrlich, B., *The Art of the Toy Soldier* (1987)
Lesser, R., *A Celebration of Comic Art and Memorabilia* (1975)
Levy, A., *A Century of Model Trains* (1974)
Norman, Bill, *The Bank Book* (1984)
Pressland, D., *The Art of the Tin Toy* (1976)
Remise, J., and Fondin, J., *The Golden Age of Toys* (1967)

SILVER

The collector of silver has an advantage over collectors of other types of items as most wares have a set of marks, the hallmarks, that guarantee their quality and provide information on the date and place of manufacture, and the maker. Practicality has an enormous bearing on value: larger, important pieces of silver by famous makers are expensive because there is a worldwide market for the best examples of any art form, whereas the price of lesser items tends to be determined by how useful, as well as how attractive, they are.

Inexperienced collectors will probably look first for a set of marks, whereas this is the last factor a professional will consider: ideally, a piece of silver will be identifiable stylistically as well as through hallmarks, which can be faked (see page 234). Most late 17th-century silver tends to be rather light in weight as the metal was in fairly short supply. Early 18th-century items are heavier and the form and surface are generally fairly plain. Increasing prosperity in the reign of George II led to a greater degree of ornamentation, which prevailed until the Neo-classical designs of the late 18th century made an appearance. In the early 19th century weight became synonymous with quality and some very heavy pieces were produced. The Victorians were fond of fussy services and over-decoration and were generally content to cover familiar shapes with elaborate chasing.

Continental silver of all periods tends to be more elaborate than the English equivalent; whereas American silver, at least until the 19th century, is relatively plain. There was a strong Dutch influence, especially in New York, until the end of the 18th century, when English influences took over. These endured until the War of Independence when French styles became popular. In the 19th century an increasingly wealthy American society was able to indulge its fancy for Victorian elaboration, often taking it one stage further. However, American of this period is probably more imaginative than English and is often of higher quality.

Traditionally, most people start their collection with an 18th- or 19th-century coffee pot and a pair of candlesticks. These are now relatively expensive and there is a broad range of smaller, readily available items that are more affordable, such as cream jugs, sugar bowls, salt cellars and tea pots. Curiosities abound – for example, stirrup cups and pap boats (see page 256), and items that border on the verge of usefulness such as wine funnels. Silver can be collected according to maker, or according to function, or thematically – for example, tea wares. The novice should be particularly careful about buying single items that may originally have been part of a pair or set: such pieces suffer a disproportionate drop in value.

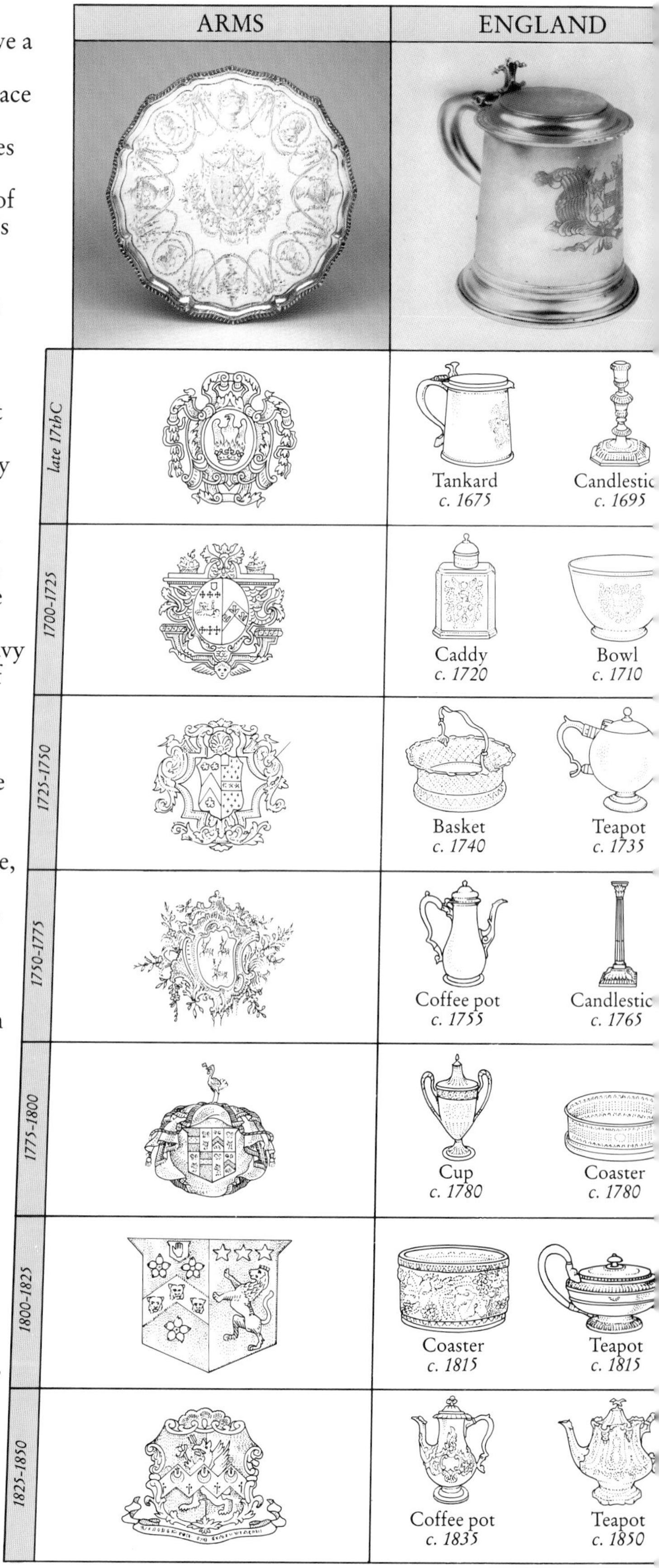

	ARMS	ENGLAND	
late 17thC		Tankard *c. 1675*	Candlestic *c. 1695*
1700-1725		Caddy *c. 1720*	Bowl *c. 1710*
1725-1750		Basket *c. 1740*	Teapot *c. 1735*
1750-1775		Coffee pot *c. 1755*	Candlestic *c. 1765*
1775-1800		Cup *c. 1780*	Coaster *c. 1780*
1800-1825		Coaster *c. 1815*	Teapot *c. 1815*
1825-1850		Coffee pot *c. 1835*	Teapot *c. 1850*

This chart shows the development of silver shapes and styles of decoration in Britain, the United States and Continental Europe between the end of the 17thC and the middle of the 19thC – the main collecting period. In the left-hand column typical arms are shown for each period; the right hand column lists the major makers.

B **The Baltic**
F **France**
G **Germany**
H **The Netherlands**
I **Italy**

UNITED STATES	EUROPE	IMPORTANT MAKERS	

 Bowl *c. 1695* — Tankard *c. 1690*	 Tankard (G) *c. 1675* — Beaker (H) *c. 1660*	*Anthony Nelme* *Benjamin Pyne*	*late 17thC*
 Dram cup *c. 1700* — Sugar bowl *c. 1720*	 Tankard (B) *c. 1700* — Beaker (F) *c. 1720*	*Pierre Harache II* *Simon Pantin* *Pierre Platel* *David Willaume*	*1700-1725*
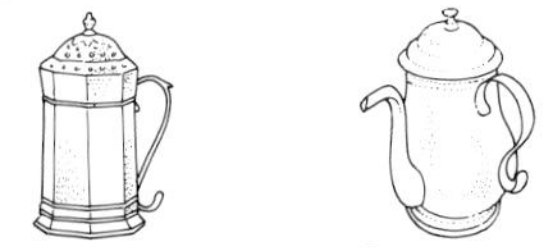 epper caster *c. 1740* — Spout cup *c. 1750*	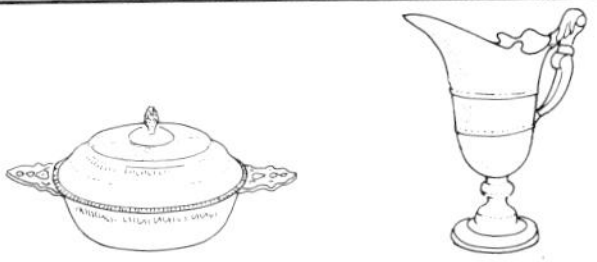 Ecuelle (F) *c. 1740* — Ewer (I) *c. 1740*	*Peter Archambo* *John Cafe* *Paul Crespin* *Eliza Godfrey* *Paul de Lamerie* *George Wickes*	*1725-1750*
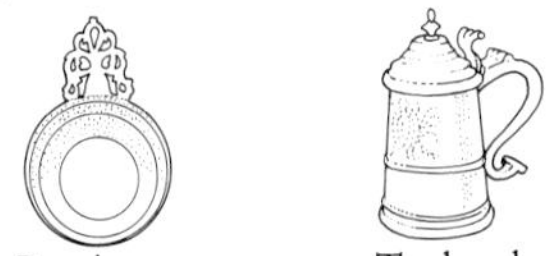 Porringer *c. 1760* — Tankard *c. 1775*	 Candlestick (I) *c. 1770* — Chocolate pot (F) *c. 1775*	*Thomas Gilpin* *Thomas Hemming* *David Hennell* *Edward Wakelin*	*1750-1775*
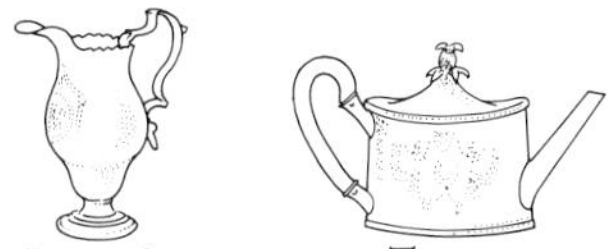 Cream jug *c. 1785* — Teapot *c. 1790*	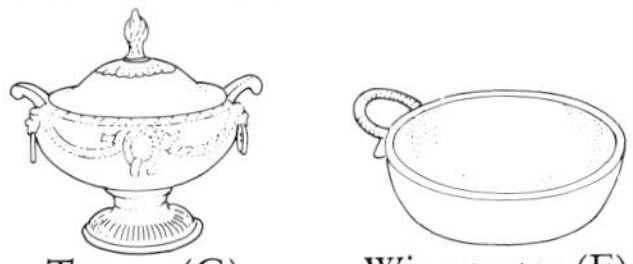 Tureen (G) *c. 1780* — Wine taster (F) *c. 1785*	*Hester Bateman* *Matthew Boulton* *Henry Chawner* *William Eley* *Andrew Fogelberg* *John Scofield*	*1775-1800*
 Cream jug *c. 1805* — Tureen *c. 1820*	 Coffee pot (F) *c.1800* — Vase (F) *c. 1800*	*Edward Barnard* *Rebecca Emes* *Edward Farrell* *Samuel Hennell* *Benjamin Smith* *Paul Storr*	*1800-1825*
 Jug *c. 1825* — Teapot *c. 1850*	 Salt cellar (F) *c. 1850* — Coffee pot (F) *c. 1850*	*George Adams* *C. T. Fox* *G. Fox* *Robert Garrard*	*1825-1850*

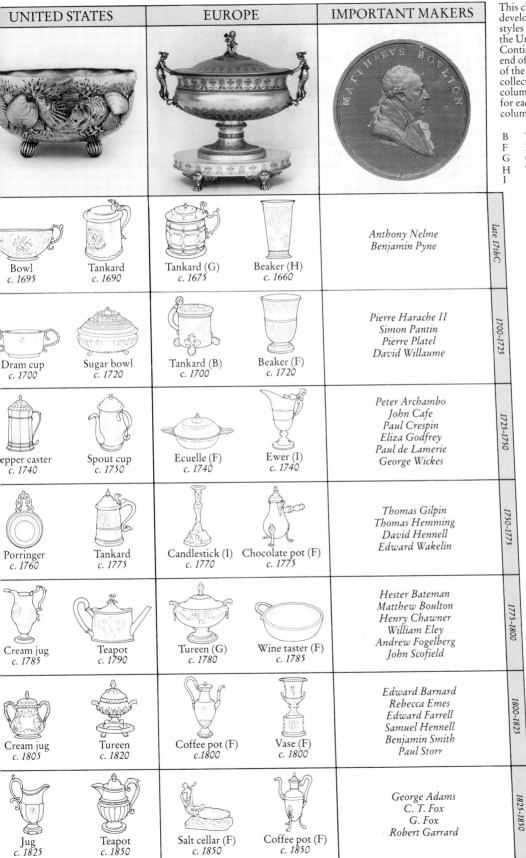

Basics I

An initial assessment of any piece of silver should take note of the following key points:
* hallmarks
* type of metal
* patina
* weight
* type and style of decoration
* coats of arms and inscriptions
* condition

HALLMARKS

British silver has been struck with hallmarks applied at the Goldsmiths Hall (hence the word hallmark) since 1478. Most English silver bears a minimum of four marks which, historically, guaranteed that a piece of silver was of the required legal standard. The use made today of the date letter and maker's mark in identifying antiques is an unintended by-product. Hallmarks are a good guide to age and authenticity, but should not be regarded as definitive, as they can be worn to the point of illegibility, faked, or even let-in from other pieces of silver.

Standard set of marks

The main marks are:

1. The sterling guarantee
Sterling is the British term for silver that is at least 92.5 percent pure. The mark that guaranteed this percentage was a leopard's head from 1300, which had acquired a crown by 1478. From 1544 a lion *passant* shown walking to the left was used to indicate sterling quality and the leopard's head became the London town mark. From 1820 it appears uncrowned.

   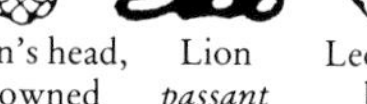

Lion's head, crowned | Lion *passant* | Leopard's head

Between 1697 and 1720 a higher standard of silver, known as the Britannia standard, was introduced in order to discourage the melting down of coinage to be turned into artefacts at a time when supplies of the metal were limited. During this period, on silver that reached the required standard, the town and sterling marks were replaced by Britannia and a Britannia lion's head in profile.

Britannia | lion's head

* The original sterling marks were revived in 1720, but the Britannia mark was sometimes used after that date as an alternative mark to indicate silver of the higher quality. Its use is optional today.
* The letter F was used from 1843 to indicate that imported foreign silver reached the required British standard.

2. The town mark
This varied according to the assay office of the individual town.

 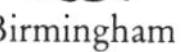 

Birmingham | Chester

Norwich | Sheffield

* The London mark of the leopard's head was sometimes used on provincial silver in addition to the town mark.
* The standard Scottish mark is the thistle and the lion *rampant* for Glasgow. The Edinburgh mark, used since 1485 until the present day, is a castle on a rock.

Scotland | Edinburgh from 1485 | Glasgow from 1819

* Ireland, whose only official assay office was in Dublin, had its own system using the crowned harp as a standard and town mark followed by a personification of Hibernia from 1730. Irish silver was also made in numerous provincial locations and marked locally. Town marks were not used. Instead, pieces were sometimes simply stamped "Sterling" with the maker's name or mark.

Dublin | Hibernia

3. The date letter
This appears in London from 1478, later in other parts of the country. It is unique from year to year and assay office to office, but usually follows an alphabetical sequence. The letter is always enclosed by a shield.

1721 | 1741 | 1781 | 1801

4. The maker's mark
Used on silver from 1363, the early marks were signs or symbols, as few people could read; this remained the case until the late 17thC when initials and symbols were combined, the symbols falling from use during the next 100 years. The initials are those of the Christian name and surname, except on Britannia standard wares (between 1697 and 1720), where the first two letters of the surname are used instead.

Ayme Videau c.1739-1747 | Paul Storr c.1792-1834

The sovereign's head
Used between 1784 and 1890 (and in Dublin from 1807), this mark indicated that duty had been paid on the item. The sovereign's head mark for George III after 1785 is hard to distinguish from those used for George IV and William IV.

George III 1784-85 | George III 1785-1820 | Victoria 1837-90

Continental silver marks
These were not as systematically applied as English marks were, although they were used in the same way as a sign of quality or during a period when duty was payable. However, town marks were used, and these provide a clue to the date and place of manufacture. The French had a strict system that included the use of date letters. Each component of a French piece bears a separate set of marks.

Amsterdam 18thC | Vienna mid-18thC | Paris early 19thC

US hallmarks
Despite 18thC attempts in Philadelphia and 19thC attempts in Baltimore, no enduring formal national system of hallmarking and assay was ever established and the silver is mostly stamped with either the maker's name or his initials. From the mid-19thC silver tends to be stamped "Sterling" and for a brief time the word "coin" also appears occasionally, indicating the origin of the metal.

TRANSPOSED MARKS AND FAKES

There are four main types of deception relating to hallmarks:
* forged marks
* transposed marks
* duty dodgers
* illegal alterations

Forged marks
Marks are struck with steel dies – a complicated and expensive process. However, most forged marks are struck with brass dies, known as "soft punches" because of the lack of clarity in the resultant image. Marks can also be cast from a genuine piece. If this has happened there will usually be small granulations visible in the outline of the stamping which would not be there if the marks had been struck.

Transposed marks
These are sets of marks taken from damaged or low-value objects and inserted into more saleable pieces. Apart from discrepancies between the style and the date indicated by the hallmark, this practice may also be detected by the presence of a faint outline around the marks where they have been soldered onto the piece, which shows up when it is tarnished or breathed on. However, this may be covered over by electroplating.

Duty dodgers
There are two types of duty dodging. The first occurred when the silversmith made a small piece of silver, such as a small dish, sent it for assay and then cut out the marks and transferred them to a larger piece. Although such items do not conform to the hallmarking Acts, they are at least made by the man whose mark appears on them. The second type occurred when the silversmith cut out the marks from another, usually older, small piece of silver that had been properly hallmarked, and set them into the base of a larger, heavier piece, adding his own maker's mark and sometimes striking it again over the date letter to disguise it. By not sending the piece for assay he avoided the duty, which was charged per ounce between 1719 and 1759, and again between 1784 and 1890. This type of duty dodger may be detected where the maker's mark is of a more recent date than the hallmark.

Illegal alterations
An Act of 1844 made it an offence to make unhallmarked additions to a piece or to alter its purpose. It is now illegal to sell many such items – for example, christening mugs converted to cream jugs, tankards made into wine or hot water jugs and salvers or plates with new borders. (See the sections that follow, on individual categories of silver, for guidance on how to spot these conversions.) Of all the categories of fakes, this is the best-intentioned as its purpose was simply to make more useful or more fashionable an otherwise unwanted item, rather than being done to deceive the buyer.
* The marks on detachable lids, and on stands, should correspond with those on the body. If their date is not contemporary with that of the piece, this is an indication that the part has been replaced or added.

TYPES OF SILVER AND SILVER-COLOURED METALS

The main categories are:
* sterling silver, identified by hallmarks
* Sheffield Plate
* electroplate

Pieces in sterling silver may be made by raising or casting, or individual pieces could be made using a combination of the two.

Raising
Silver is raised from a sheet, which is hammered perfectly flat, then cut to size and worked into the required shape with a series of hammer blows. This method requires the metal to be annealed, or strengthened, at intervals to prevent it from becoming brittle. Clumsy annealing may result in disfiguring marks, known as "fire staining". This can be especially serious on silver that is left plain, as the surface marks will not be covered by decoration.

Casting
Many handles, spouts and finials, and some feet, were cast separately in a mould and then soldered onto the piece. It is likely that many of these items, which often conform to a standard pattern, were supplied by specialist workshops who mass-produced these items for several silversmiths. A large number of candlesticks were also cast.

A two-handled raised cup and cover with cast handles. S

Sheffield Plate
The increasing prosperity of the merchant and trading classes led to a search for a silver substitute, which resulted in 1740 in the invention of Sheffield Plate. Sheffield Plate is a specialist collecting area in its own right. It is always less expensive than silver but can command high prices when in good condition.

Sheffield Plate was made by binding a sheet of sterling silver to an ingot of copper and fusing them together in a furnace. The resultant metal was rolled or hammered into sheet and made up into objects.

The so-called "double sandwich" dates from c.1770. Used for pieces that had a visible interior (mugs, bowls and so on), it consisted of a sheet of silver each side of a piece of copper; early makers applied a film of solder over the bare edge of copper; such pieces are very rare. Late in the 18thC, borders were applied with a U-shaped section of silver wire to conceal the copper (this can be felt as a lip on the underside). The silver border has often worn through to the dull lead beneath – a useful identification point.

From the end of the 18thC the borders of Sheffield Plate pieces became increasingly florid, more so than on sterling silver wares, probably because they could be produced far less expensively than solid silver borders.

Borders should be carefully examined for wear. A little copper showing is generally considered attractive, but more than that is not.

* Engraving, which requires the removal of metal, does not feature in Sheffield Plate (except for coats of arms), as it would have meant cutting through to the copper base.

A Sheffield Plate wine cooler, c.1830, with silver-covered lead borders and handles. S

* Decoration is always flat-chased, and the pattern should be visible on the underside. In early days the copper showed through where coats of arms were engraved, but from the end of the 18thC a more heavily plated disc, which could take the engraving, was neatly let into the piece. In Regency times this method was superseded by letting in a pure silver oblong; as the rest of the object has a surface of sterling standard, it oxidizes at a different rate from the pure silver part, which is therefore readily visible.

A Sheffield plate coffee pot, c.1830 with chased decoration. S

* A piece with "Sheffield plate" stamped on it is electroplate made in Sheffield in the 19thC, rather than genuine Sheffield Plate.
* Most pieces of Sheffield Plate hollow ware, such as candlesticks and coffeepots, have a visible seam. If no seam is visible, the article has either been replated and the seam covered up in the process, or it is not Sheffield Plate.
* Some articles have a liner – for example, urns. Once this is removed, a dull leadish colour, caused by tin, should be visible on the inside. A silver colour inside indicates replating.
* Most Sheffield Plate is unmarked. Some makers used a symbol. Some early 19thC Sheffield Plate bore marks that resembled those used on sterling silver.

British plate
Made chiefly between c.1830 and 1840, this replaced the silver element in Sheffield Plate with a silver-coloured alloy. It was less expensive than Sheffield Plate, as it contained no silver. It ceased to be made once electroplating became popular in the 1840s. Marks bear a superficial resemblance to those of sterling silver.

Electroplating
This method was used from c.1840 and gradually replaced Sheffield Plate, which after the Great Exhibition of 1851 became increasingly rare. Electroplating creates a film of pure silver which is white and harsher in appearance than the soft glow of Sheffield Plate. The process involves covering one metal with a thin layer of silver by electro-deposition. The base metal was initially copper, but later nickel, hence the term EPNS (electro-plated nickel silver). Styles followed those that were most popular in silver.

* The most popular electroplated items are candlesticks, entrée dishes and cake baskets. Tea sets are becoming increasingly popular. Being far less expensive even than Sheffield Plate, electroplated wares are not collected for their intrinsic worth but as inexpensive silver-style items. Electroplated flatware services provide the only alternative to silver, as it proved impossible to make flatware in Sheffield Plate without a large ugly seam.
* Unlike Sheffield Plate, most electroplate has makers' marks and indications of quality such as "A1" or "EPNS". Some silversmiths made both electroplate and Sterling silver – for example, James Dixon & Sons; Elkington; and Walker & Hall. Although they used similar marks on both their silver and their electroplate, the marks are applied in a noticeably different way.

Gold plating/gilding
Very few objects were made of gold, owing to the high cost of this metal, and of these few have survived the attractions of being melted down. Gilding is a method of giving a gold finish to a silver or electroplate article. This can be done in one of two ways:
* fire gilding
* electrogilding:

Fire gilding
This was a dangerous process that involved painting an amalgam of gold and mercury onto the surface of the silver. This was then heated to a temperature at which the mercury evaporated leaving the gold fused to the body of the object. Mercury and its fumes being highly poisonous, the gilders tended to have short lives, and this process is now illegal in many countries.

Electrogilding
This method was first used in the mid-19thC and gives a much brassier look than fire gilding. Gold applied in this way does not endure well. Such pieces bear the usual silver marks.
* The term "parcel gilding" refers to an article that has been partially gilt.

PATINA
Colour, or patina, is important to value. Over years of use, silver suffers small knocks and bruises due to handling, and scratching caused by grit in polishing cloths. This tempers the metal and gives it a highly prized soft, bluish glow quite unlike the chrome plate look of a new piece on whose bright surface every scratch can be clearly seen.

Sometimes a piece has been polished up on a buffing wheel, either after repair or to remove excess dirt. This destroys any patina or colour that has built up and damages both the appearance of the piece and its value.

WEIGHT
An item that is more than the average weight may not look correspondingly larger or heavier than its lighter counterpart. However, extra weight *is* synonymous with quality. From a practical point of view, heavier silver wears better and is less easily broken than flimsier wares. Many people find heavier silver more satisfying to use, as it feels better in the hand.

Scratch weights
Auction catalogues sometimes refer to the "scratch weight" of a piece, which is occasionally found engraved on the underside. This shows how many ounces and pennyweight the article weighed when made – silver always loses some weight in the polishing. If the current weight is much lower than the scratch weight, it may be an indication that the piece has been altered in some way, or that it has been worn by over-zealous polishing. Even greater suspicion should be aroused where the current weight is more than the scratch weight.

Melting price
This is the scrap value of any silver item that is melted down. The price is calculated per ounce of silver; the quality of the article is irrelevant to the melting price.

DECORATION
Silver styles changed according to the taste of the period and thus provide a good indication of date and, occasionally, of origin. The surface of the metal was generally decorated in one form or another (although much 18thC American silver and early 18thC English silver is plain). The main types of decoration are:
* engraving
* bright cutting
* chasing (embossing)
* flat chasing
* cut-card

Engraving
This is the cutting out of metal with a tool. Fine engraving was carried out in Continental Europe, particularly in the Netherlands and Germany, where prints provided much of the inspiration. The best

Basics II

A Dutch beaker, c.1660, elaborately engraved by Soon van Hendrich. S

English engraving is superb; the finest engravers were William Hogarth, Simon Gribelin and James Sympson. Good American engravers include Joseph Leddel and Nathaniel Hurd. American engravers more often signed their work than English ones.

Bright cutting
This type of decoration was popular at the end of the 18thC. It is identical in execution to engraving but the design stands out more sharply and reflects the light, as the metal has been cut with a burnished steel tool which polishes the silver as it cuts.

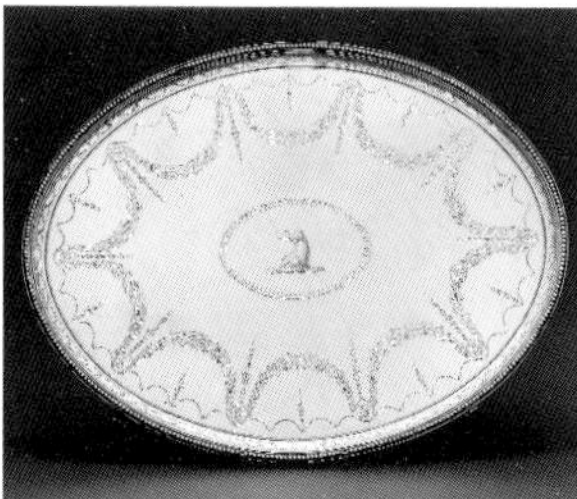

A salver with bright-cut decoration, c.1780. S

Chinoiserie
The late 17thC produced some pieces, particularly tankards and monteiths, that were engraved with chinoiserie scenes of Oriental figures, birds and exotic landscapes. As these charmingly naive subjects are generally very similar in execution, it has been suggested that a single specialist engraver was responsible for all these pieces, although this theory has not been proven.

* Chinoiserie-decorated pieces should not be overcleaned and should retain their original clarity. They will usually have been well looked-after: condition tends to be

Typical chinoiserie work from the late 17thC. S

paramount on chinoiserie pieces. The detail must be absolutely clear.

Chasing (embossing)
Chasing was popular at the end of the 17thC and again in the mid-18thC. It is a form of decoration in relief in which the metal is pushed into the required pattern with a hammer or punch. No silver is removed, as it is with engraving, although it may sometimes be mistaken for engraving. The pattern is raised above the surface and can be clearly seen on one side; its imprint can be seen on the reverse. Several 18thC silversmiths, such as Paul de Lamerie and Ayme Videau, are well known for the quality of their chasing. Common motifs are flowers, foliage and scrolls of various types. Chasing was also popular with the Victorians, who often decorated the plain surfaces of old silver.

An 18thC jug with high-quality chased decoration. S

It is sometimes hard to tell the difference between 18th and 19thC work, although genuine 18thC chasing has a more natural and lively appearance compared to the slightly mechanical feel of Victorian work. An 18thC piece will be chased and then marked. On a piece to which the chasing was added at a later date, the chasing will go through the marks; otherwise the marks will go through the chasing.

Flat chasing
This is executed in the same way as chasing, but the pattern appears in low relief. It can be confused with

A tankard from c.1705 with 19thC chasing. S

engraving, although the reverse of any chasing will reveal the imprint of the pattern, whereas engraving is visible on one side only.

Cut-card decoration
Good-quality late 17th and early 18thC pieces are sometimes overlaid with cut-card decoration – pieces of silver, usually in the form of foliage, which are made separately and then soldered to the body to provide attractive reinforcing for handle sockets or spouts of coffee pots. Occasionally it appears underneath, and therefore out of sight, around the sockets of salvers on single feet. Such decoration is an invariable sign of quality.

American decorative styles
The various decorative styles described above, and the borders that follow, are all features of American silver, although often at a later date than in England.

Silver was both made in America and imported from England. The Dutch influence was strong initially. By the end of the 17thC English styles predominated, except in New York, where Dutch styles lingered for another half-century. Much American-made silver before the early 18thC resembles English silver of an earlier period, as styles often took a while to find their way across the Atlantic. American silver of the 18thC tends to be plain as the more elaborate European styles never caught the American imagination.

The quality of production during the 17th and 18thC was often very high, especially as American silversmiths had to compete with European imports.

Following the War of Independence and the partial dissociation with all things English, there was a brief flirtation with French styles. During the 19thC native influences gradually took over, culminating in the immensely showy, often very large, productions at the end of that century. Chasing and cast work were especially popular, sometimes combined with Neo-classical designs. Neglected for a long period, these later pieces have recently received renewed attention.

BORDERS
The borders of silver can often provide a clue to the date of the article, although the collector should bear in mind that many 18thC styles were reproduced in the 19thC. Similar decoration also appears around some feet.

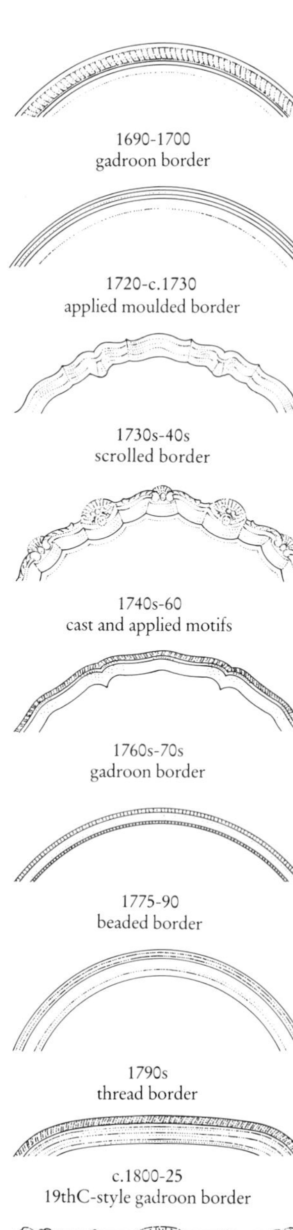

1690-1700
gadroon border

1720-c.1730
applied moulded border

1730s-40s
scrolled border

1740s-60
cast and applied motifs

1760s-70s
gadroon border

1775-90
beaded border

1790s
thread border

c.1800-25
19thC-style gadroon border

c.1810-25
gadroon and shell border

c.1850-c.1895
shell and scroll border

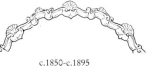

COATS OF ARMS

It has always been fashionable for families to engrave their coat of arms, crest or monogram within a decorative cartouche in a prominent place on a piece of silver, especially on larger items. The type of shield and the style of cartouche can provide help in dating a piece that lacks a full set of marks, and may even indicate the original owner.

A full coat of arms, c.1729 in a particularly fine Baroque Cartouche. S

A full set of armorials can appear on larger pieces: it comprises a coat or arms, surrounded by a cartouche, mantling, a motto and, for members of the peerage, a coronet and supporters.

The colours of heraldry are represented by specific patterns of lines.

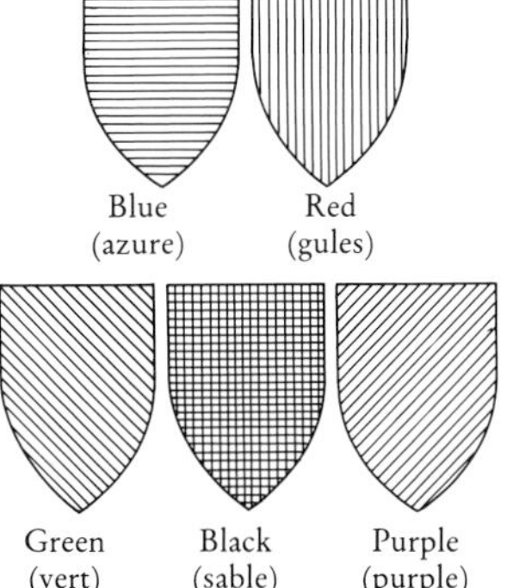

Green and purple are uncommon. Silver is represented by a blank shield, and gold by a shield filled with tiny dots.
On smaller pieces of silver the family crest was often used. There is an important distinction to be made between a crest and a coat of arms: a single crest may be shared by anything up to 20 families whereas a coat of arms is traceable to a particular family or even a particular man and wife, which adds to the interest of the piece.
* Crests are sometimes coupled with mottoes. English crests have the motto below them, whereas Scottish crests have the motto over the top.

Scottish crest with motto above. S

Arms are a good guide to dating. They are also used in Continental Europe, in styles that correspond with the English styles of each period. German arms often include helmets.

REPLACEMENTS AND ERASURES OF ARMS

When silver changed hands, the new owners sometimes erased the existing coat of arms and replaced it with their own. This usually leaves the metal thin where the work has been carried out and always reduces the value of the item, sometimes considerably. If the silver is too thin to be re-engraved, a new coat of arms is sometimes engraved onto the side opposite the original arms. Some coats of arms were removed but not replaced. Large plain surfaces are suspicious. They can be tested for the removal of arms by pushing with the thumbs on the suspected place to see if it dents. A more gentle test would be to rub the area from the back with a thumbnail while looking at the front closely to see if the surface moves.
* Sometimes a new coat of arms was added to an existing cartouche. In such a case, the engraving of the arms would feel sharper to the touch than the cartouche, which would inevitably be somewhat worn.

INSCRIPTIONS

Inscriptions that are contemporary with the piece add to its value. The most desirable are those that have a naval or military content, or are connected with institutions such as Lloyds or the East India Company. Those that bear the names of well-known people are also desirable. However, religious inscriptions (and items intended for religious, rather than for secular use), are not in great demand.
* Inscriptions to civil engineers were common in the Victorian period.

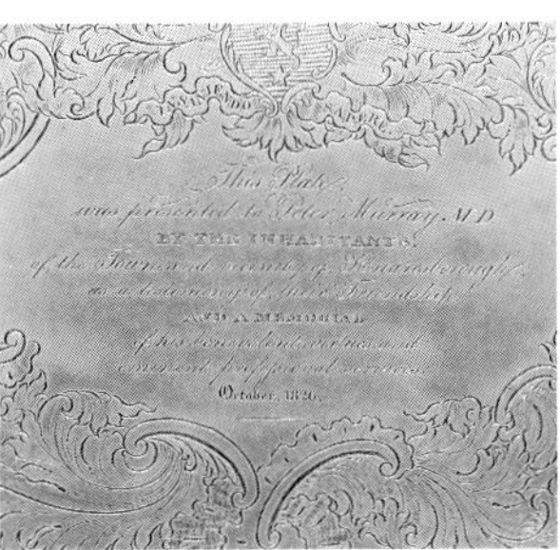

A typical inscription, c.1826. S

Initials

Some pieces, particularly earlier ones, are engraved with three initials in a triangle. The upper single initial usually represents that of the family surname, and the lower two are the initials of the forenames of the husband and wife. Pieces thus engraved were often given as wedding presents. Initials can be helpful in tracing a coat of arms or a crest to a particular family or person.

A beaker from 1665 showing the family initial "E" and the intials "R" and "M" for the forenames of husband and wife. S

CONDITION

Any repair is greatly detrimental to value, except on very rare pieces. Sometimes poor design, such as the feet being too small for the body, or the piece being too heavy for the base, leads to damage, and of course accidents or misuse take their toll. Damage properly repaired with silver solder can be hard to spot. More frequently, lead is used in repairs, which can be unsightly and is very detrimental to value.

Any item with feet is especially vulnerable, as the feet often get pushed up through the base over a period of time.

Articles with handles, such as teapots, cream jugs and sugar basins, are also vulnerable: the metal of the body is often pulled away by the handle. Although such tears can be repaired, a visible patch would be apparent on the inside of the article. A handle that has simply come unsoldered is not a problem, as it can simply be resoldered in the same place without leaving a repair mark.

Hinges are difficult to repair because of expansion and contraction of the metal.

Pierced decoration is very prone to damage. Casters, cake baskets and similarly decorated articles should always be carefully checked.

On teapots, coffee pots and other items that have an inside, recent repairs, effected using heat, will have rendered the inside surface a bright matt coloured.

Repairs made using lead solder are evident low down ot the right of the handle of this fake teapot, made up from the bottom of a mug with a spout, handle and lid added. In addition, the teapot incorporates other undesirable features, such as later Victorian chasing which has been worn through on the highlights. *S*
* The finial on a made-up piece may well retain its original marks. The lid is unlikely to be marked.

CLEANING AND CARE

Silver is not especially fragile but it does need looking after. Contrary to popular opinion, it doesn't tarnish that rapidly, unless kept in an unsuitably damp place. Any proprietory silver polish can be used for cleaning, and a toothbrush may be useful for removing polish from nooks and crannies.

Corrosion spots are usually caused by salt getting in under a glass liner, or may occur on a cellar without a lining, where the gilding has worn. Such spots can be professionally removed.

Silver should be washed in warm soapy water. It is not dishwasher-proof as the abrasive powder dulls the surface. Any stains should be professionally removed. Silver gilt does not need to be cleaned with silver polish – a warm wash and a thorough dry should be sufficient.

Teapots and Cream Jugs

Tea, coffee and chocolate all came to England during the second half of the 17th century. Although 17th-century coffee and chocolate pots exist, there are almost no teapots until the early 18th century.

As tea was expensive until the 1760s, early teapots are small. The earliest are pear-shaped, but in about 1730 the bullet teapot takes over until 1750. Silver teapots are rare between then and c.1770 when the drum-shaped teapot appears, followed by the oval shape that lasted until teapots became oblong in the early 19th century.

The difference between a coffee pot and a chocolate pot is that the latter has a hinged or detachable cap or finial in the lid through which a rod was inserted to stir up the chocolate sediment.

Coffee and chocolate pots are taller than teapots so as to keep the spout above the sediment. The 18th century starts with side handled tapering cylindrical examples with high domed covers until c.1730, after which date chocolate pots are seldom seen. Coffee pots take on a baluster-shape from 1730 until 1800, when they are vase shaped. Like the teapots, they then become oblong, before reverting in the 19th century to mainly baluster styles.

No milk or cream jug pre-dates the reign of Queen Anne and they are very rare until the 1720s. Early examples tend to be baluster-shaped, octagonal ones are much sought after. The smaller pitcher milk jug endures until c.1730 on a central foot and then on three feet until the 1760s when the central foot returns. Design then passes through the pear and helmet shapes until at the end of the century the cream jug matches the teapot or set.

TEAPOTS

Early American teapots are scarce, although they exist in fairly large numbers from the end of the 18thC. This rare American teapot by Peter van Dyck of New York was made c.1730 (ht 8in/20cm), rather later than it would have been in England; silversmiths in America were still drawing their inspiration from Europe. *CNY*

Drum, or cylindrical, teapots are usually made of good gauge silver and are thus one of the most desirable types. Dating from 1770, this is an unusual example, with stamped leafage below the border, an unusual faceted spout and detailed handle sockets (ht 5¼in/13cm). *S*
* Teapots are marked in a group on the base, apart from some early 19thC ones marked in a line near the handle. Lids bear the lion *passant*, maker's mark, and after 1784, the sovereign's head and date letter.
* All teapots should be checked at the hinges for signs of wear. Loose handles do not reduce the value as they can be tightened and repinned.
* All teapots should be checked at the hinges for signs of wear. Loose handles do not reduce the value as they can be tightened and repinned.

Bullet teapots are much sought after. However, some of them have lids which are either detachable or flush, with a concealed hinge. These are often unmarked and therefore avoided by collectors. The hinge in this example from c.1735 (ht 4¾in/12cm) was put on before the base was soldered in, making repairs virtually impossible. The hallmark was on a separate disc applied to the base. The handle is not original. *S*
* Georgian teapots usually had plain wood loop handles. These were often replaced by silver ones in the Victorian period but Scottish teapots originally had silver handles.
* Bullet teapots are usually the only type to be faked.

The bright-cutting, crest and oval cartouche add to the desirability of this typical c.1780 teapot (ht approx. 5½in/14cm). *S*
* The marks on any stand should match those of the pot.
* At the end of the 18thC spouts were made up from sheet, which is prone to splitting.

This typical early 19thC teapot (ht 5¾in/14.5cm) is one of the least desirable types, despite the bright-cutting. The angular handle and the four ball feet are not very delicate and the square section spout is considered unattractive. Even the best ones do not command high prices. *S*

COFFEE POTS

Irish coffee pots are often chased all over but English ones are likely to be chased only at top and bottom, as in this example, c.1750 (ht 9¼in/23.5cm). *S*

* A good plain pot will command a higher price than most chased examples as it can be difficult to confirm that the chasing is contemporary and because chasing is out of fashion.

This desirable bellied pot on a raised foot (ht 10½in/26.5m) dates from 1770. The other side is typically embellished with a crest or coat of arms. The pot has reinforcing discs on the handle and around the spout. *POU*

Vase-shaped bodies like this one from the end of the 18thC (ht 11¼ in/28.5cm) are desirable. The attractive bright-cut decoration is in good condition, being sharp and clear. *S*

This very fine coffee pot by Philip Rollos, c.1711 (ht 10½in/27 cm), has cut card decoration at the handle sockets, spout and finial which also acts as reinforcement: an invariable sign of quality that adds considerably to the price. It has the typical Queen Anne high domed cover. The thumbpiece and position of the handle at right angles to the spout are also characteristic. *CG*

MARKS
Coffee and chocolate pots are marked in a group below the handle or in a line to the right of it. The lids should also be marked with the lion *passant*, except on some pots from the 1740s, on tuck-in bases. After 1784 lids should also be struck with the sovereign's-head duty stamp.
CONDITION
Reinforcement discs at the handle sockets should be checked for signs of being later additions to cover torn metal. Signs of wear are most likely to show at the hinges and finials.
CONVERSIONS
Many coffee pots have been made from large mugs or tankards. These can be detected by looking at the marks: tankard lids are fully marked in the centre, whereas the lid of a coffee pot has a maximum of three marks on the bezel. The proportions of such a pot will look unlikely.

Coffee pots can usually be dated by their shape and the height of the lid.

CREAM JUGS

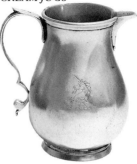

This popular pitcher cream jug, c.1725 (ht 3¼in/8cm), is the earliest, readily available type. *S*

* Cream jugs are one of the easiest types of silver to fake. Queen Anne casters with pierced tops are vulnerable to damage. When this occurs they are often turned into early 18thC pitcher cream jugs. Conversions are not always easy to spot. Many small christening mugs have been converted by the addition of a spout but these are usually easy to recognize.

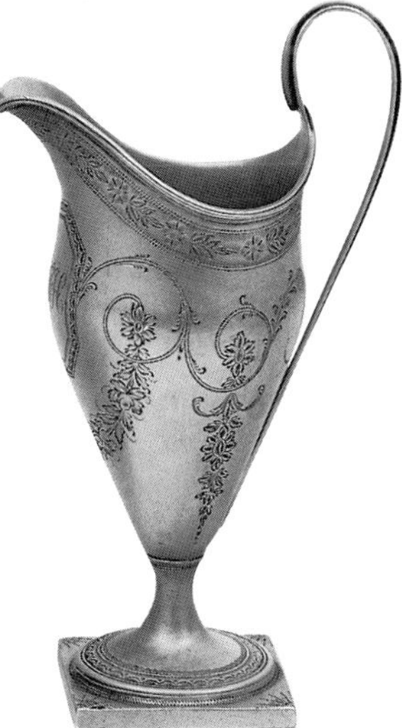

A late 18thC cream jug on a pedestal base (ht 4½in/11cm), which is more secure and less prone to damage than the separate feet prevalent in the middle of the century. *S*

* These cream jugs are often marked underneath in each corner; any marked in a line on the foot rim may have been made up from another item.
MARKS
Early cream jugs are marked in a group on the base. Later examples are marked in a line to the right of the handle or, particularly at the end of the 18thC, below the lip.
DAMAGE
Handles, lips and rims are prone to damage and splitting. The feet of mid-18thC cream jugs may be cracked or pushed up through the body. Crests or initials were often replaced.

Candlesticks

Despite their obvious necessity, candlesticks have not survived in numbers prior to 1660, and American candlesticks before 1760 can almost be counted on the fingers. Even after that date, American candlesticks are rare.

The typical late 17th-century candlestick is raised from sheet metal and has a cluster column stem. This style was superseded toward the end of the century by the cast candlestick, which continued until after the middle of the 18th century, when increasing mechanization brought about the introduction of loaded candlesticks stamped from sheet.

Candlesticks became taller as the 18th century progressed, starting at about 6 or 7 inches (15-18cm), rising to 10 inches (25cm) in the 1750s and going up to 12 inches (30.5cm) by the start of the 19th century; Victorian candlesticks returned to about 10 inches (25.5cm).

Nozzles, which are detachable and stop the wax pouring down the stem of the candlestick, became a regular feature in the 1740s. They usually conform in outline to the base of the candlestick and have the same decoration.

Tapersticks, made to hold a wax taper, exist from the reign of Queen Anne on and follow the style of candlesticks of the period. Unlike full-size candlesticks, they are acceptable singly; pairs are rare and can usually command almost the same price as full-size candlesticks.

Chamber candlesticks, used to light our ancestors to bed, have not, as a rule, survived in good condition. The earliest examples date from the early 18th century and have flat handles. From c.1720 the ring or scroll handle was standard and is frequently fitted with a slot to take the conical extinguisher found from the middle of the century on.

Chambersticks are usually sold singly, although they were made in large sets. The border decoration on the pan of this example from the 1780s (ht 5½in/14cm) is repeated on the nozzle and extinguisher. The slot in the centre is designed to take a pair of snuffers for trimming the wicks. Apart from the very earliest chambersticks with a flat handle and some more fanciful Regency designs, variations are few and borders are simple. *S*

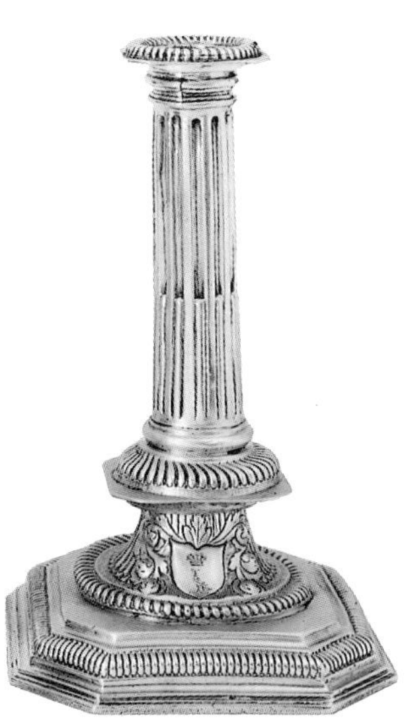

This candlestick (ht 10½in/26.5cm) from 1690 is typical of the end of the 17thC. Made from pieces of sheet silver and hollow throughout, this type is usually fairly lightweight and prone to denting, as has happened at the top of the fluting in this example. They can also split, or come apart at the seam. The gadrooning is similar to that used on other silver at the end of the 17thC. The crest and coronet are later additions. *S*

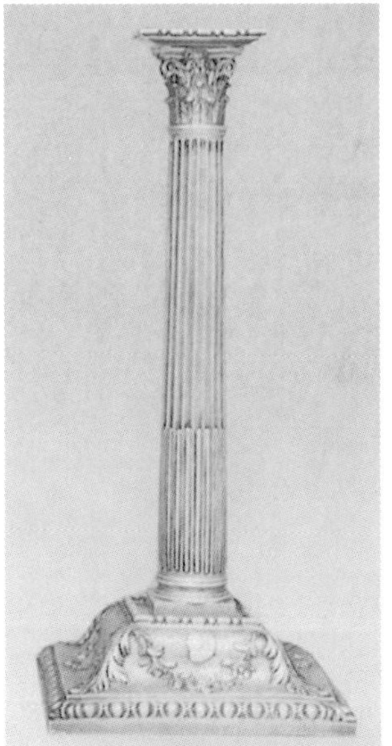

This Corinthian column candlestick made by William Cafe dates from the 1760s and is stamped out of sheet; it is loaded with pitch to give it substance, which can make repair difficult. At 13 inches high (33cm), it is very tall. *CNY*

* Occasionally, this type is marked on the inside of the stick, and the mark is then covered by the loading.

Cast candlesticks, more durable than sheet, were produced after c.1690; this example dates from 1730. From then on candlesticks generally became taller, although this is still relatively short, at 6in (15.5cm). This style of candlestick is popular among collectors who like plain good-quality pieces. *S*

* Many candlesticks after 1730 were produced in multiples of pairs.
* Candlesticks embellished with figures were popular from c.1740 but are now rare.

This very typical stamped and loaded candlestick is immediately recognizable as being made in Sheffield, a major centre of candlestick production of the period. The foliate decoration, although somewhat restrained here, is characteristic. *CNY*

* The highlights should be checked for holes made by polishing.

This elegant Neo-classical cast candlestick from 1782 (ht 11in/ 28cm) is typical of the maker John Scofield. Pairs are very desirable. Cast candlesticks were relatively uncomon in this period. *S*

* Scofield was one of the finest English silversmiths working at the end of the 18thC. His wares are always high-quality and command high prices. *C*

* Cast candlesticks are faked by simply taking another casting, marks and all! Any pair of candlesticks which has the marks in precisely the same place on each stick is very suspect.

This popular version of the Corinthian column, with removable drip tray and simple square stepped base, was made in large numbers as late as the beginning of the 20thC and is still in production today. This example is 7in (18cm) but they were made in a range of sizes; the smaller ones (approx. 4-5in/10-13cm) are very popular. *CDC*

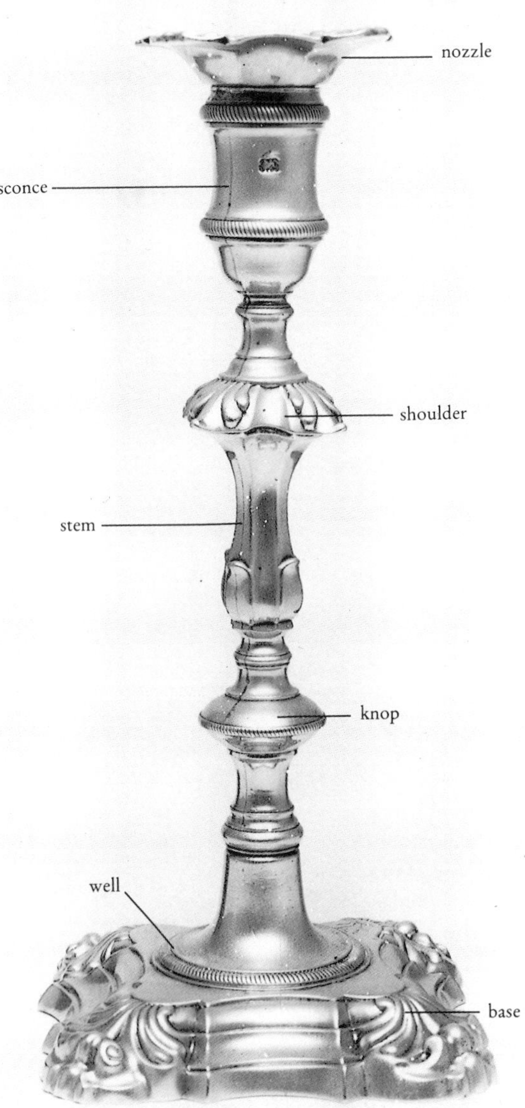

This is the standard mid-18thC candlestick (ht 10in/25cm) produced on a vast scale by specialist makers such as John and William Cafe. The sunk centre and the four corners with shell decoration are desirable features. *S*

* To constitute a pair, the candlesticks have to be made by the same man in the same year (or two or three years apart). Identical sticks by different makers are not regarded as a pair, even if they come from the same workshop. While single chambersticks and tapersticks are acceptable, single full-size candlesticks have little value.

MARKS

Sheet metal candlesticks are usually marked in a line on the stem just above the base. Cast candlesticks can be marked in the well, and if so the marks are likely to be worn. More often, they are marked underneath in each corner if the candlestick is square, or in a line if it is circular. Cast candlesticks can also be marked on the outside of the base, where again wear is likely, or on the inside rim, in which case they are sometimes hard to find.

The sconce on cast candlesticks is cast separately, so any made prior to 1784 should ideally have a lion *passant* struck on it, although this may have worn off. The nozzle should have the maker's mark and lion *passant*.

Chamber candlesticks are marked in a line, usually on the base; nozzles and extinguishers should have a maker's mark and lion *passant*.

Candelabra branches must be fully marked. Detachable drip pans, sconces and nozzles must bear at least a lion *passant*.

CHRONOLOGY OF STYLES

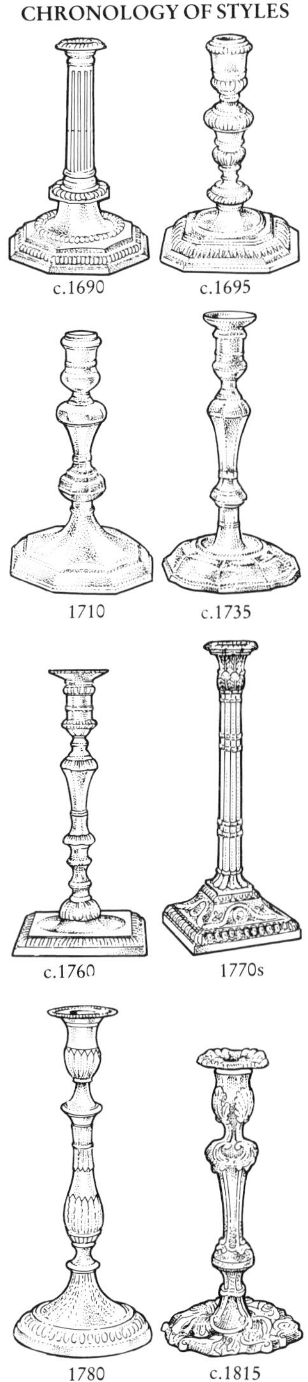

DAMAGE

Cast candlesticks are made in sections: the base, the stem and the sconce. If the seam on the stem and sconce is not in alignment, the candlestick has been heavily repaired. Any that show casting flaws in the metal should be avoided.

Stems of sheet candlesticks are prone to splitting. The highlights of loaded sticks should be checked for wear. Nozzles sometimes show signs of resoldering.

Drinking Vessels

The first beakers were made before English silver was hallmarked, and are relatively common in England and the Continent of Europe, but rarely found in America. The basic form varies very little: 16th and early 17th century examples are taller and have a slightly broader base than those of the 18th century. They were not made in the 19th century.

The diminutive of the beaker is the tumbler cup, found in England between 1660 and the end of the 18th century. These are hammered up from a single piece of silver. As most of the weight is at the base, they tumble upright if pushed on their side, hence the name. Examples from the 17th century tend to be broader than they are high and are usually plain.

The earliest domestic jugs appear in about 1660. Except the very first ones, they are almost invariably of baluster form and relatively plain throughout the 18th century. Until the end of the reign of George I they are sometimes found with covers. The grander examples were occasionally made in pairs. As the handles are silver and without insulation, they probably held only cold liquid.

Tankards, which differ from mugs in being lidded, were made in vast numbers during the 120 years from 1660, before losing popularity as taste turned from ale to wine and spirits. Early tankards are straight-sided and late 17th-century examples are sometimes chased with gadroons or acanthus leaves, applied with cut card work, or engraved with chinoiserie. The 18th-century tankard was plain, perhaps with a coat of arms. Most of those made in the 19th century are presentation pieces.

American tankards are relatively plentiful. Late 17th and early 18th-century examples from New York and Pennsylvania often have fairly elaborate handles and a band of leafage around the base. Tankards from Boston are plainer.

The earliest mugs date from the 1680s and are bulbous with a cylindrical reeded neck – a shape derived from contemporary pottery. Those made at the start of the 18th century have straight, slightly tapered sides on a moulded base; the baluster shape gradually predominates after 1730, although many of the mugs that were made in Newcastle retain their straight sides. While 17th-century mugs are found with chinoiserie engraving or chased with gadroons, those from the 18th century were usually plain, and any decoration is of a later date. With the onset of the 19th century, mugs lost their practical use, but became popular christening presents. The later mug is therefore smaller and anything but plain, the Victorian examples being particularly ornate.

Silver goblets were made in early times but seem to have fallen out of favour in the 17th century, only to reappear in the 1760s to replace the beaker. The form is standardized at the end of the 18th century as a plain bowl on a trumpet-shaped foot. This becomes more elaborate during Regency times and the Victorians took the decoration further still – in extreme examples hardly any plain surface remains.

BEAKERS AND TUMBLER CUPS

An English provincial beaker, c.1670 (ht 4in/10cm), with late 17thC plumed leafage and Elizabethan-style strapwork. *S*

* Beakers are usually marked in a group underneath.
* Beakers and tumbler cups should be examined for splits at the rim and for thin spots where engraving has been removed.

Large 18thC beakers were always plain, with only a crest for decoration. This beaker from 1780 (ht 4in/10cm) has the plain border and beaded footrim typical of the period. *S*

This mid-18thC tumbler cup (ht 3¾in/9.5cm), has the typical baluster sides of the period. *S*

* Tumbler cups are marked underneath or on the side.

JUGS

Most early or mid-18thC jugs are circular, baluster- or pear-shaped. This 1726 covered example (ht 7¼in/18cm) has a distinctive oval shape. Unusually, the hinge shuts back on itself, rather than being flat or at right angles to the handle socket. This more complicated design, typical of the 18thC, is indicative of quality, and therefore the type is more expensive. Special care has also been taken over the finely-engraved coat of arms. *S*

* Jugs have a full set of marks on the body or base and a maker's mark and lion *passant* on any cover.
* Jugs can be made up from tankards but the odd shape should give such conversions away. In addition, if the lid has a full set of marks it could only have come from a tankard.

English and Irish beer jugs are very similar, although the large spout of this pear-shaped jug on a domed spreading foot, c.1727 (ht 9in/23cm), is typically Irish. *S*

* Irish jugs often had chased blooms and scrolls, but the same decoration on an English jug of the period is unlikely and should be carefully examined.
* Many jugs, especially the oval, lidded sort, were probably used for shaving. Those that are accompanied by bowls were specifically made for that purpose.

TANKARDS
A late 17thC tankard (ht 7in/18cm) with highly desirable chinoiserie decoration. *S*
* Tankard hinges, always on top of the handle, are usually bold and fairly simple. The dent on the handle is pleasing, as it shows that the thumbpiece has always come down in the same place.

MARKS
Tankards have a full set on the side of the body or base and on the lid. On early tankards the lid marks are in a straight line across the top; on later examples they are in a group inside.

DAMAGE AND CONDITION
No longer of much practical use and often inelegant, tankards tend to be bought by specialist collectors – provided that they are in peak condition. However, tankards in their day were among the most used – and abused – pieces of silver. They can be heavy when full, which can strain the handles; these, being hollow and made up from sheet, are expensive to repair. Handle sockets should be undamaged and any reinforcing discs must be original. The rim, especially near the handle, is prone to splitting.

CONVERSIONS
Covers developed domes as the 18thC progressed and some earlier pieces were given domes to update them: stretch marks and thinness on the lid are a sign of this. In addition, the hallmarks may no longer be present and any that have survived will not be in the conventional straight line.

The Victorians often converted mugs and tankards to jugs by fitting them with spouts. Such conversions must be marked to be legally saleable. The handles will have been fitted with ivory heat-resistant fillets. Those that were later re-converted are hard to detect.

This late 17thC tankard (ht 6¾in/17cm), the earliest sort in circulation, has the straight sides typical of the period. The acanthus leafage or a broad band of gadrooning are the only readily accepted forms of chasing on a tankard: anything else is considered Victorian and far less desirable. The coat of arms here is original and is surrounded by a crest and foliate mantling rather than the usual crossed plumes. *S*

The plain baluster shape, used on tankards and mugs between 1735 and 1760, is the most popular tankard style – far more so than the tapered shape that prevailed toward the end of the century. This English example (ht 9in/21cm) was made in 1740 by Edward Vincent. The dome, already evident, becomes more pronounced as the century wears on, until c.1800. The girdle is a regular feature from now on. *S*
* 18thC tankards (like mugs) were invariably plain, enlivened only by a coat of arms.

This is the final shape of the tankard before it became a presentation piece. Although the good quality and solidity of this example, c.1800 (5½in/14cm), is typical, it is the least popular type today, and consequently the least expensive. The reeding appeared c.1780 and was current until c.1820. In form and decoration it resembles many small christening mugs of the period. *S*

This tankard (ht 9½in/24cm) was chased by the Victorians and given an unhallmarked, and therefore illegal, fox finial and spout to make it more decorative and more useful. This is an extreme example of a frequent alteration: the piece was made in 1729 and would have been plain. *S*

MUGS
Victorian christening mugs are very popular, especially those that incorporate figures of children, as on the side panel of this example (ht 4½in/11.5cm). Typically, the front panel opposite the handle bears an inscription. The mug is of good quality and heavy: the cast figures will have been made up separately and then applied. *S*
* Until the end of the 18thC mugs are usually marked in a group on the underside of the base; thereafter in a line by the handle.
* Like tankards, mugs should be checked at the handles and rims, and carefully examined for traces of erasing.

GOBLETS
One of a fine pair of goblets made in 1794 in the standard form for the period. These are well-proportioned, attractively bright-cut, and have a contemporary coat of arms. They are also silver-gilt which makes them considerably more expensive than silver (ht 6in/15cm).
* Goblets are marked below the rim, on a curve under the foot or in a straight line round the rim of the base. Those marked on the rim of the foot should be checked for seams at either side of the marks – signs that they have been transferred from a less expensive item.
* Stems are vulnerable, especially where they join the bowl, and they sometimes show signs of having been repaired.

The most common shape for mugs is the baluster. This large example (ht 4½in/11.5cm) dates from the 1740s. It has superb flat-chasing by Aymé Videau, a maker of French origins. The cast handle may appear on other pieces of his, such as sauce boats. *S*
* A very large mug may be a tankard without a cover. This conversion is not illegal but should be reflected in the price of even a good-quality piece. Mugs have scroll motifs at the tops of the handles; tankards do not.

Mugs became simpler during the later 19thC. This beaded example from the 1860s (ht 4in/10cm) has a basic handle and no foot, although the engraved decoration is charming. The maker's mark on the left is that of Martin Hall and Co., who made many christening mugs. *S*
* This type of mug, and the one above, is sometimes found in a case.
* Beaded decoration usually dates from the 1860s or the 1780s: the style will tell you which.

Like other Irish silver, goblets are similar to English examples. This is one of a pair of Irish George III bell-shaped goblets, c.1770 (ht 6in/15cm), with an engraved coat of arms in a Rococo cartouche. *S*

A Regency goblet with leafy scrolls in a band around the rim (ht 6½in/16.5cm). The surface decoration is still relatively modest: as the century progressed, goblets became covered in engraving. *S*

Cruets

Spices were used to enhance or disguise the taste of food in an age when keeping it fresh was a problem. They were usually held in casters, so-called because they cast their contents over the food.

Until about 1780 casters often came in sets of three: one with large piercing for sugar crushed from a loaf; one for pepper, and a third for other spices, or for dry mustard (in which case the caster would have a "blind" cover, without piercing). Framed cruets exist from c.1700: these usually comprise three casters and two bottles for oil and vinegar, all held by a silver, or Warwick, frame. Modern style mustard pots appear from c.1760. These usually have glass liners and are often pierced. After c.1780 casters came singly or in pairs.

The shape of the caster has scarcely altered since the early 18th century. The early cylindrical and baluster shapes come with bayonet-type covers. These have two flaps that fit through wire at the rim and are turned to hold the lid in place. The popular octagonal examples appear in the reign of George I and thereafter covers have bezels fitting inside the caster bodies.

From the early 18th century salt was kept in pairs of salt cellars. In the mid-18th century most are on three feet. The exceptions are trenchers, the common form at the start of the period, and some that were made at the end of the 18th and early 19th century. Some very grand salts were made in Regency and Victorian times.

This is a fine version, c.1760, of the typical pear-shaped caster set of the mid-late 18thC (ht of tallest 7¼in/18.5cm). The piercing is elaborate; on more modest examples it consists of alternating pierced panels, one plain and the other more fancy – for example, lozenge shapes alongside stylized leafy scrolls. *S*

* From the 1790s, the pear-shaped caster became gradually more elongated, with a narrower foot.
* Holes on 18thC casters are large, as early spices were coarsely ground. To render them suitable for today's finely-ground pepper, they are sometimes "sleeved"; that is, a silver caster-head or sleeve with smaller piercing is inserted into the original. This is an acceptable modification but may reduce the value of a piece by a well-known maker. Sleeves can sometimes be removed if they were inserted neatly.
* Many casters have a crest; the best may also have a coat of arms.

Most of the trencher salt cellars available today date from c.1690-c.1720. This is a typical example from c.1710 (wdth 2in/5cm). *S*

* Circular and triangular trenchers were also made.
* The marks on many early 18thC trencher salt cellars are in the bowl, and often worn.

MARKS

Casters of the 18thC are generally marked in a group under the base. Some early 18th and 19thC examples are marked in a line on the side of the body. By the mid-18thC salt cellars are marked in a group on the base or occasionally in a line on the body. Mustard pots are marked in a group on the base, in a line on the body or in a curve round the base. Covers should be marked.

FAKES

The marks and style should agree. Fake salt cellars can be detected by their irregular shape. The easiest way to fake a mustard pot is to add a lid and a handle to a salt cellar, although the absence of a cover mark should be a clue.

The basic design of this compressed circular salt cellar, one of a set by Paul de Lamerie, 1734 (wdth 4in/11cm), was ubiquitous in the middle of the 18thC. Untypically, this example has four rather than three feet; these take the form of paws instead of the traditional simple hoof feet. *CNY*

The inside of this salt cellar is gilded to resist corrosion. It was made by Henry Chawner, c.1790 (wdth 5½in/14cm), a reliable and prolific maker, and is typical of the good-quality pieces produced in the late 18thC. Those with cast bases, as in this example, are much sought after. *S*

This is a typical early cylindrical pierced mustard pot, c.1770 (ht 3½in/9cm). These were always made singly, with blue glass liners and are seldom found in perfect condition. *S*

This mustard pot, c.1820 (ht 3¾in/9.5cm), has the massive proportions typical of the Regency period. The range of ornament makes it highly desirable. *S*

Novelty sets were especially popular with the Victorians. This owl, c.1885 (ht 4½in/11.5cm), is part of a fairly standard set but is nonetheless desirable. The beak of the owl conceals the end of the mustard spoon, which is usually a mouse. *S*

DAMAGE

Piercing is often damaged. With mustard pots this can occur when the lining is removed for cleaning. Finials are easily torn: untidy solder on the inside is an indication that a torn finial has been mended. Feet should be intact. Salt readily corrodes. The resultant staining can be polished away; however, the base will be thin. Mustard pot hinges may be wobbly, and handles should be examined for signs of wear or repair. Thumbpieces and covers are easily bent or worn.

Bowls

Punch bowls and monteiths first appeared at the end of the 17th century. Early monteiths were smaller than punch bowls, with a waved border on the rim whose function was apparently to enable glasses to be hung on the scalloped notches of the rim by their stems, with their bowls cooling in iced water. The name is said to derive from a Scotsman called Monteith who is reputed to have had a cloak with a scalloped edge. The monteith rapidly expanded in size and by the 1690s had acquired handles, usually hung from lions' masks. As the monteith approached the size of the punch bowl the rim was often detachable so that the bowl could do duty as either; these rims have often been lost.

Early monteiths tend to have gadroon borders on at least the foot mount and there is almost invariably space on the body for a large and impressive coat of arms. The rims are often decorated with shells or cherubs' masks.

Bowls with an early 18th-century appearance are easily made up from tureen liners or dishes of a later date. It is often apparent that such bowls are not genuine as the style of decoration rarely accords with the date of the marks – usually late 18th-century.

There are various derivatives of the basic bowl. A shallow bowl with a pierced handle is known in England as a bleeding bowl and in America as a porringer, which seems more reasonable as these bowls were almost certainly used for porridge. In America porringers were largely an 18th-century item. Styles followed the form of English ones of an earlier period.

Bleeding bowls were made in England for about 100 years after the accession of Charles I in 1625. The earliest ones have straight sides and are indistinguishable from skillet covers. Later types have curved sides. As a rule the handles tended to become more elaborate over the years.

The English porringer, used for a variety of drinks and mixtures, is a two-handled, rather deeper bowl, with straight sides. Some have a spout. Those with baluster sides are sometimes known as caudle cups: caudle was a sweet, spicy, warm drink apparently given to invalids and women in childbirth. The earliest survivors date from the middle of the 17th century; the caudle cup continued for 50 years or so, but the porringer in its final form survived until the middle of the 18th century. Its successors are the cups and covers produced in an infinite variety of styles down to the present day.

The brandy saucepan is an 18th-century product. While some of the smaller ones may well have been used for heating brandy, the larger ones must surely have been used for something else. The earlier examples have baluster or slightly flared bodies, whereas those made at the end of the century sometimes have straight sides. Some have a cover.

An item peculiar to America is a small, shallow two-handled bowl from which whisky was drunk. It had the same basic shape as some 18th-century English bowls made in the Channel Islands.

A caudle cup and cover, c.1665 (ht 8in/21.5cm; wdth 10in/25cm), with typical caryatid handles, chased floral decoration, a lion and unicorn, and so-called "Stuart flowers" at the base. *P*
* This type of bold, fairly coarse decoration is the only type of chasing that is acceptable for the date.

American porringers were produced in quantity; this example from 1760 was made in Philadelphia (dia. 5in/12.5cm). The elaborate piercing of the handle is more or less standard throughout the 18thC. There was no formal hallmarking system in America and most pieces would have had the initial and surname of the maker. In England this sort of bowl was generally made only until the beginning of the 17thC. English examples as late as this would be considered very much out of period. *CNY*

An English porringer made in London in 1685 (ht 6¼in/16cm), engraved with chinoiserie figures and a contemporary coat of arms. The decoration is certainly contemporary: a porringer that was originally intended to be plain is likely to have had a more elaborate coat of arms. *S*
* Porringers were often made without covers: there is no easy way to tell which ones had covers and which did not.

This type of porringer was made throughout much of the 18thC until the 1760s in a variety of sizes, often embellished with lobes and flutes. It is one of the most usual sorts and is relatively inexpensive (ht 4½in/11.5cm). *S*

A typical late 17thC monteith (dia. 10¾in/27.5cm) with the most commonly found features: gadrooning, a detachable marked rim and drop handles. The chasing is characteristically loose and irregular. The detailed scallop work is typical of the end of the 17th and beginning of the 18thC, while the cherub masks in the border were a popular motif at the time and often appear on 19thC reproductions. The light patch on the inside of the rim was made by the solder when a new piece of silver was inserted to make a repair. *S*

* Detachable rims, which add considerably to the value, ceased to be made c.1720.

This is a typical late-Victorian lobed and fluted monteith (dia. 12½in/32cm) with a later coat of arms. Such examples are sometimes made to appear earlier by letting in marks from pieces of Georgian silver. However, the Victorian bowls have a neater base and a more mechanical appearance than Georgian ones. Also, Victorian chasing is more regular and elaborate than earlier decoration. If a liner has been reshaped, the marks would be at an awkward angle. *S*

* Lobed and fluted decoration features regularly on late 19th and early 20thC silver.

A particularly plain but solid mid-18thC bowl made in 1730 (dia. 9in/23cm). The shield-shaped coat of arms is about 50 years later; in such a case the sides of the bowl should be checked for signs that an earlier coat of arms has not been removed. *SNY*

MARKS

Early punch bowls or monteiths will be marked in a straight line on the side of the body; detachable rims must also be fully marked. Later examples are likely to be marked at the points of the compass underneath. English bleeding bowls can be marked in either of these ways and in addition there should be a lion *passant* on the handle signifying its silver content. Porringers and caudle cups are marked in the same way as other bowls, and in addition any covers must also be fully marked on examples earlier than the mid-18thC. Thereafter a maker's mark and lion *passant* are sufficient.

Brandy saucepans are usually marked in a group on the base; these marks can be badly worn due to heavy cleaning to remove stains made in heating the pan.

FAKES

Porringers and caudle cups, brandy saucepans and bleeding bowls are unlikely to be faked. Punch bowls and monteiths, however, have been extensively faked; they can either be made up from liners, in which case the leopard's head town mark may be absent or, more commonly, they have let-in marks taken from another piece.

An early 19thC punch bowl with simple bright-cut decoration (dia. 11¾in/46cm). This type of punch bowl is frequently Scottish; this one was made in Edinburgh. Typical of Scottish bowls is the band of trailing leafage. The military inscription adds interest to an otherwise simple, almost plain, piece of silver. *C*

* Being large, punch bowls were not made in great numbers and were likely candidates for being melted down. They have not therefore survived in quantity. They are always desirable, although they are usually fairly simple – even those from the mid-18thC, when elaborate decoration was the norm on most silver.

DAMAGE

The usual checks should be made to see if any original arms or crests have been removed, leaving the metal thin. Pieces with embossed decoration should be examined on the inside for evidence of solder having been used to repair holes made by over-polishing. Signs of repair are also common at the handle sockets. Rims are vulnerable to splitting, especially those of monteiths. On caudle cups the metal where the finial joins the cover is prone to tearing.

A baluster brandy saucepan and cover (ht 6¼in/16cm). This is an Irish piece dating from 1814. A slightly unusual feature is the hinged flap attached to the cover which goes over the spout – an indication of a relatively late date. *S*

* Very occasionally brandy saucepans are found with a stand and burner.

Sauce Boats and Tureens

The earliest English and American sauce boats date from the reign of George I. Frequently fairly shallow and thus with a small capacity, they nevertheless fetch high prices. At first they have simple waved borders, but soon acquire gadroon edges that predominate until the 1770s, when punched or beaded borders appear. With the turn of the century and the onset of Regency influence the sauce boat becomes more elaborate with massive borders and feet, and the handles can become a major feature, as they occasionally were in the mid–18th century. Design stagnated during the 19th century and later examples follow the style of their predecessors. Sauceboats always come in pairs. Only American examples are acceptable singly.

Soup tureens, expensive even in their own day, can be found from the reign of George II, but were not made in quantity before the 1760s. They are usually oval. Early examples stand on four feet until about 1780, when they rest on a central foot. In the early years of the 19th century they return to four feet. The best tureens are sometimes found on stands, which greatly increases the value. Borders generally follow the fashion of the period. The best pieces are decorated with vegetables, crustacea and other animals. Sometimes the more complicatedly shaped tureens were fitted with detachable liners made of plate.

Although soup tureens were made for the grander houses throughout the 19th century, sauce tureens, which nearly always have a lid, almost exactly span the reigns of George III and George IV. They largely follow the design of contemporary soup tureens and some were even made *en suite*. Sauce tureens on stands are rare, although there are a few mid–18th century examples. The designers seem to have reserved their decorative fancies for the larger soup tureen, although heraldic finials are more often seen on sauce tureens than on soup tureens.

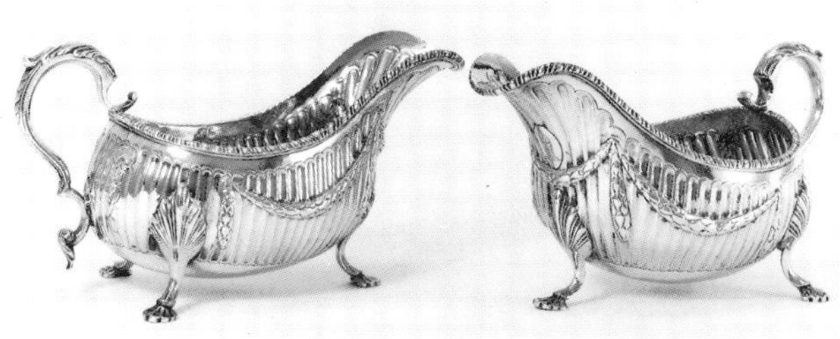

The rather low-slung, bellied appearance of this pair of sauce boats (wdth 8in/21cm) at once marks them out as Irish. Made by William Hughes in Dublin, 1772, they are unusually substantial, with gadroon borders and chased flutes and swags. *S*

* Plain examples are frequently found at this date in Dublin with punched beaded borders that are prone to splitting, as they tend to be more lightly made.

This is a fine-quality George IV sauceboat (ht 9in/22cm), one of a set of six made by Robert Garrard in 1826. At this period tureens were more common. The piece has several outstanding features: a heavy cast foot; applied shell and strapwork motifs; and leaf-capped scroll handles. *S*

* Throughout the first half of the 18thC handles became an increasingly important feature, often appearing in the form of birds, human figures and fantastic animals.

SAUCE BOATS

The design of sauceboats changed during the 18thC: from the two-handled, lipped type, to the single-handled boat on a central oval foot, then the three-footed type, and a solid single-foot version.

FAKES

Fake sauceboats are uncommon: a knowledge of the proportions of the genuine article should safeguard against deception.

American sauce boats are rare and consequently very expensive. Their development paralleled that of the English sauce boat. This example, made by John Coburn of Boston, c.1750 (wdth 8½in/21.5cm), appears superficially to resemble its English counterpart in every respect. However, it is shallower, and has a squatter appearance. Also, the handle socket is not mounted direct to the body as in English sauceboats. *CNY*

MARKS

Sauce boats are generally marked in a straight line underneath. Some from the 1770s are marked under the lip, where they often get rubbed. Those on a central foot can be marked either on the rim or on the inside of the foot.

DAMAGE

Early sauce boats on a central base are not prone to damage, although coats of arms are sometimes removed or replaced. Sauce boats with feet are much more vulnerable as the feet often get bent out, or are pushed up through the body; they can also crack. The handle sockets of more lightly made examples need careful examination. Sauce boats with simple waved borders and an applied wire mount are prone to splitting, as is the rim of the type of sauce boat made in the late 18thC with a punched border.

SOUP AND SAUCE TUREENS

Only relatively grand houses had soup tureens. This is a particularly fine example by Paul Storr, 1815 (wdth 18in/45cm), with several of the features identified with fine tureens of the period:

* lion-mask handles
* leafy feet
* a decorative coat of arms (the coronet and monogram are later additions). *S*

FAKES

This is not a category in which fakes abound. The most likely fake is one with a body made up from a liner, in which case the marks may be incomplete and the cover will either have a wrong mark or none at all. Attention should be paid to tureens with rim bases, as it is relatively easy to let in marks from something like a spoon.

MARKS

Soup tureens are fully marked on the base, except for those on a pedestal foot, which are found with marks on the rim or on the inside of the foot. Prior to 1784 the lids were also fully hallmarked and thereafter it is usual to have at least the maker's mark, lion *passant* and date letter and sovereign's head. Sauce tureens are fully marked on the body, but before 1784 are likely to have only the maker's mark and lion *passant* on the cover; after 1784 covers should be marked in the same way as soup tureen covers. Any liner or stand will generally bear a full set of hallmarks, with the exception of the town mark.

DAMAGE

For both soup and sauce tureens the most likely areas of damage are where a coat of arms has been removed or replaced. Although some soup tureens are massive enough to withstand this operation, later arms always make a difference to the value. Even with careful use the feet are often inadequate and can be pushed through the body. The finials on oval late 18thC tureens are often not detachable, and as the cover is usually rather light, the metal can get stretched or torn here.

Made c.1760, this is the earliest type of soup tureen available today (wdth 17¼in/44cm). Examples from 1780 and later are more common. Unusually, it has a horse finial rather than the more typical vegetables or fruit. The lion's paw feet are also unexpected, more often appearing on tureens of the early 19thC. Applied decoration is, as ever, a sign of quality. *S*

The melon pattern of this soup tureen (wdth 23in/58.5cm) was common during the 1830s and used for a wide variety of articles. The arms are those of a well-known family from northern England. *SNY*

* The presence of a stand greatly increases the value. These are usually attached to the tureen by nuts and bolts. Pairs of tureens also fetch a premium.

This relatively common boat-shaped sauce tureen with batswing fluting from the end of the 18thC (wdth 16¾in/42.5cm) was made by Paul Storr. It shows the strong influence of Andrew Fogelberg, under whom he was apprenticed. This would be an early Storr piece: he entered his mark in 1793. Its quality gives it value but, because it lacks the traditional Storr characteristics – gilding, massive size and lions' mask handles – it is not greatly appealing to Storr collectors. The same is true of late Storr. *S*

Oblong sauce tureens were popular for the first 20 years or so of the 19thC. This example (wdth 8½in/21.5cm) dates from 1810, and is characteristically simple, with only a crest and some plain gadrooning. Today they are not as sought after as oval and circular examples, which are considered more attractive. *SC*

Salvers, Trays, Plates and Dishes

The difference between salvers and trays is that trays have handles and salvers do not. Trays are not found before the late 18th century. Most early salvers perished in the English Civil War and there are few survivors before the reign of Queen Anne.

The Americans imported many salvers from England. Those they made themselves are similar to English ones at an earlier period, and because rare, are expensive. The most common pre-Revolution salver has a shell and scroll border and is more restrained than English salvers of the period.

Salvers under 6 inches (15cm), are occasionally called waiters. The early 18th-century salver is found with a central foot and is sometimes wrongly called a tazza. Borders generally follow those of the period; more expensive items may be more elaborate.

There are few oblong salvers, and square examples tend to date from c.1720-40, when a few rare octofoil examples were also made. Oval salvers, usually from the late 18th century, are much sought after. Trays are usually oblong or oval, and being larger than salvers, are more expensive. Trays from the 1750s are rare and command high prices. Very large round salvers, being awkward to use, are not as collectable as their size might indicate.

The earliest surviving plates and their attendant serving dishes are early 18th century. At this time borders are absent but a thread moulding appears by the 1720s. By about 1730 the gadroon border takes over and the outline becomes waved and remains so, although plain circular plates were produced again at the end of the 18th century. More expensive plates have shell-decorated borders and some Regency ones have tied reed borders; beaded borders appear c.1780.

Shaped oval meat dishes were made *en suite* with the plates and most popular are the very small and the very large. Some of the largest have tree-like wells for draining the juices and occasionally a mazarine, although these have frequently been separated from their dishes. A set would have comprised six dozen dinner plates, two dozen soup plates and 15 or 20 dishes. Such sets are very rare today.

This type of tray, c.1835 (wdth 29in/73cm), is a perenially good seller, with its leafy shell and gadroon border and elaborate handles. The coat of arms of a peer – in this case a baron – are easy to research. It is typical of the period, inspired by George IV's preference for heavy, high-quality silver. Articles in this style are not uncommon. *C*

Each section of a separate cast border, as on this large silver gilt salver by William Cripps, c.1750 (wdth 22½in/57cm), should bear a lion *passant* and preferably the maker's mark. The crest is untypical as it stands inside the cartouche without a coat of arms. It is so clearly defined that it may be a later addition. *C*

Armorials are usually the only type of surface decoration on pre-1730 salvers. This 1690 example (dia. 10¼in/26cm) has a gadrooned border. *S*

* Central feet were usually soldered onto the base. Only the finest salvers had screw-on feet.

Square salvers, popular during the reign of George I, were usually made by the finest silversmiths, like this engraved example by Paul de Lamerie, 1725 (6in/15cm sq.). *S*

* Engraving is the most usual type of decoration.

The beaded border on this 1780s salver (dia. 8in/20cm) was popular c.1775-90. It is centred here by a typical coat of arms in a shield-shaped cartouche. The commemorative inscription is unusual and clearly relates to a well known figure. *S*

The shell and scroll border of this Victorian salver, c.1840 (dia. 24½in/62cm), resembles that used 100 years earlier, but the decoration is more elaborate. The arms, a pastiche of an earlier style, have flowers that are too regular to be 18thC. *S*

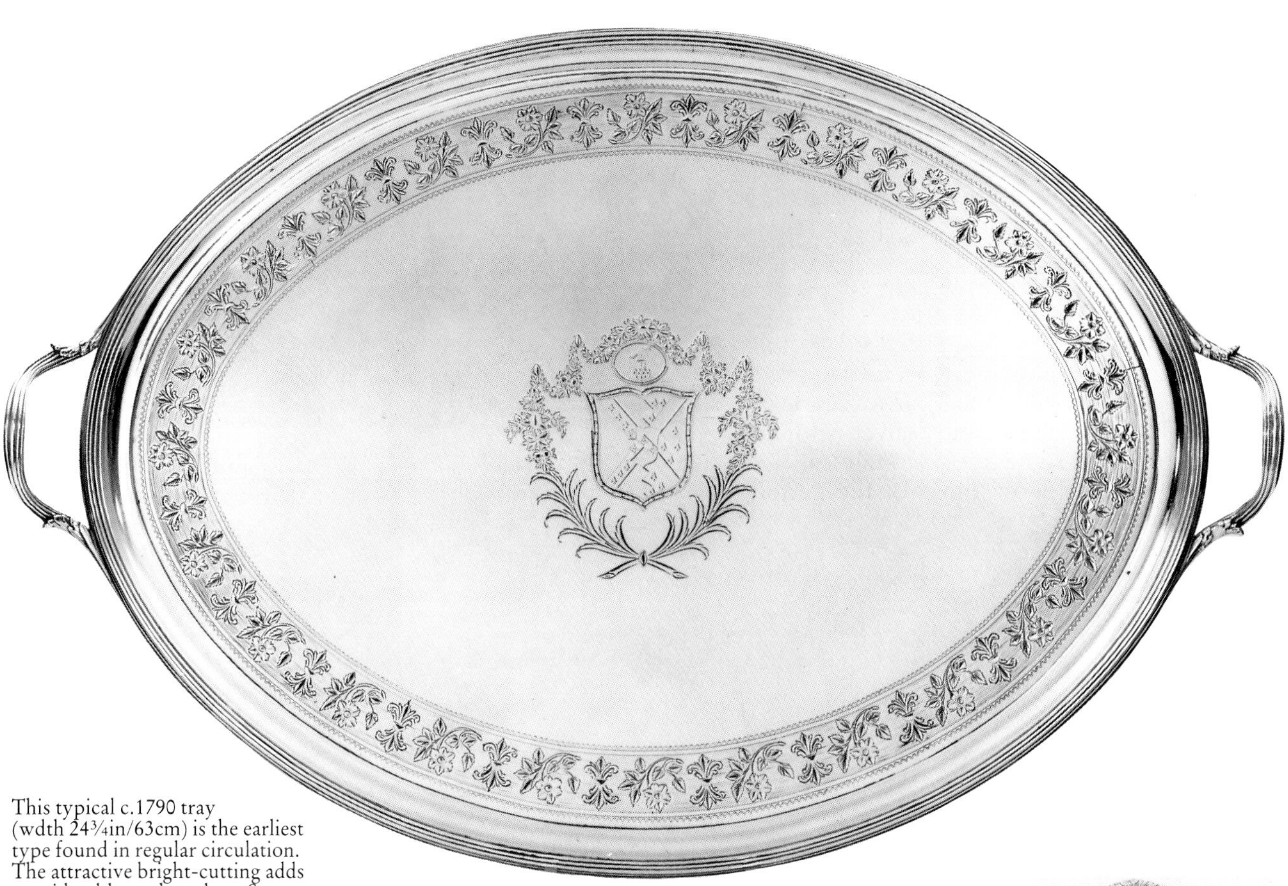

This typical c.1790 tray (wdth 24¾in/63cm) is the earliest type found in regular circulation. The attractive bright-cutting adds considerably to the value. *S*

FAKES
The most common type of faked salver is one with a border that has been "updated", usually for the sake of fashion; the old border and feet were cut off and new ones applied. However, the new border will not conform to the style prevalent when the hallmarks were applied. Sometimes, very rarely, new borders and feet were legally hallmarked but although this makes those pieces saleable, they are still very much less valuable than unaltered ones.

DAMAGE
Look carefully for:
* signs of solder around the feet where they may have pushed through the surface
* splitting, especially on lighter pieces around borders
* thinness in the centre or dips on the surface, either front or back: a sign that the original crest or arms has been removed and replaced with later versions.

MARKS
Central feet should be marked, as these were often replaced if damaged, or as tastes changed. Early 18thC salvers are marked on the surface and should have a lion *passant* or Britannia on the foot itself. Later salvers and trays have a full set of marks on the body. Handles and feet are not marked, but borders that have simply been clamped on must bear the lion *passant* and preferably the maker's mark as well. Salvers and trays are nearly always marked in a straight line.

This is by far the most usual sort of dinner plate (wdth 9¾in/23cm) and can be found from c.1730 until the 20thC. *S*
* Dinner plates have a secondary use as smart place mats. Many soup plates were later reshaped into meat plates, especially as few meals regularly included soup: the metal from the bowl is hammered flat, or cut out, leaving a seam. Borders are sometimes replaced, with the result that the marks may be moved nearer the edge of a piece than would be usual.
* Plates and dishes are marked underneath the rim in a straight line. Most meat plates have a coat of arms on the border.
* The shell and gadroon border is popular and easy to match. Plates with plain round gadroon borders are not so collectable and less expensive. Queen Anne sets of plain or no-border plates are very expensive, even singly.

This meat dish made by Paul Storr in 1811 has the typical Regency border. The set would have comprised single dishes of about 22in/56cm going down to pairs or sets of about 12in/30cm each. *S*
* Knife scratches are preferable to a shiny surface from which they have been polished out.
* Meat dishes are usually marked underneath the rim near the border.

Entrée dishes are usually sold in pairs; single ones are very hard to sell. This pair (lgth 13in/32cm) was made by Paul Storr in 1818. Matching stands add to the value, although they are usually silver plate. Until the 1830s most entrée dishes are oblong or cushion shaped – that is, with curved sides. Many early examples are dull, tinny and lightweight, and thus inexpensive. Round or oval dishes were more common after 1830. *CNY*
* The covers are detachable, but each will have a number or row of dots that aligns with the same numbers or dots on the tureen when the cover is in place, as the fit is individual. Handles are usually detachable except early ones, which were soldered.

Flatware

Although the Romans used spoons, the earliest period for collecting English spoons is the Middle Ages. Scottish spoons exist from the end of the 16th century. Until the introduction of the fork in 1660, food was eaten either with a spoon or from the blade of the knife.

Early spoons had curved, fig-shaped bowls and decorative finials. The most common types of finial are the apostle and the seal top; the "seal" was hexagonal at first, then oval and finally round by the time it dies out in the 1660s. There was a set size for a spoon until the 1670s, when differences developed between table spoons, dessert spoons and teaspoons, and longer-handled serving spoons were introduced.

Late 17th-century spoons initially keep the old fashioned type of bowl and have very plain tops. However, by the 1680s the form of the bowl had evolved into the shape it is today, and the spoon terminal had a so-called trefid end. This became less pronounced until it matured into the dog-nose pattern of the Queen Anne period. At this period spoons generally have a rat-tail, or reinforcing rib, down the back of the bowl. Thereafter, throughout the 18th century, there are really only two patterns: the Hanoverian and the Old English. During the 18th century the so-called rat-tail had disappeared and the bowl became less oval and more pointed.

The early 19th century saw the introduction of many patterns, of which the least popular is possibly the Fiddle. Some very elaborate patterns were produced by Paul Storr, and more new types appeared in the Victorian period.

Forks were introduced to England in the late 17th century in the styles of spoons of the period. Until the 1770s most were made with three prongs; thereafter four prongs became normal.

The 18th-century knife has a steel blade and a hollow silver handle with a resin core. The silver on the handle is frequently stamped from very thin sheet and is normally badly worn; it is also subject to damage if the resin expands. Knives are rarely included in sets of flatware, and in fact it is more sensible to use modern ones which stand up much better to hard usage.

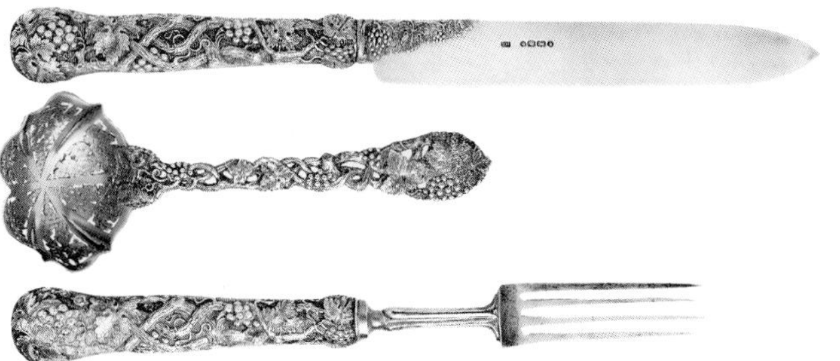

This and similar richly decorated patterns date from Regency times. They sometimes appear as large dessert services. A set comprising a knife, fork and spoon in this pattern was a popular christening present. The pieces shown above were made by Francis Higgins. *S*

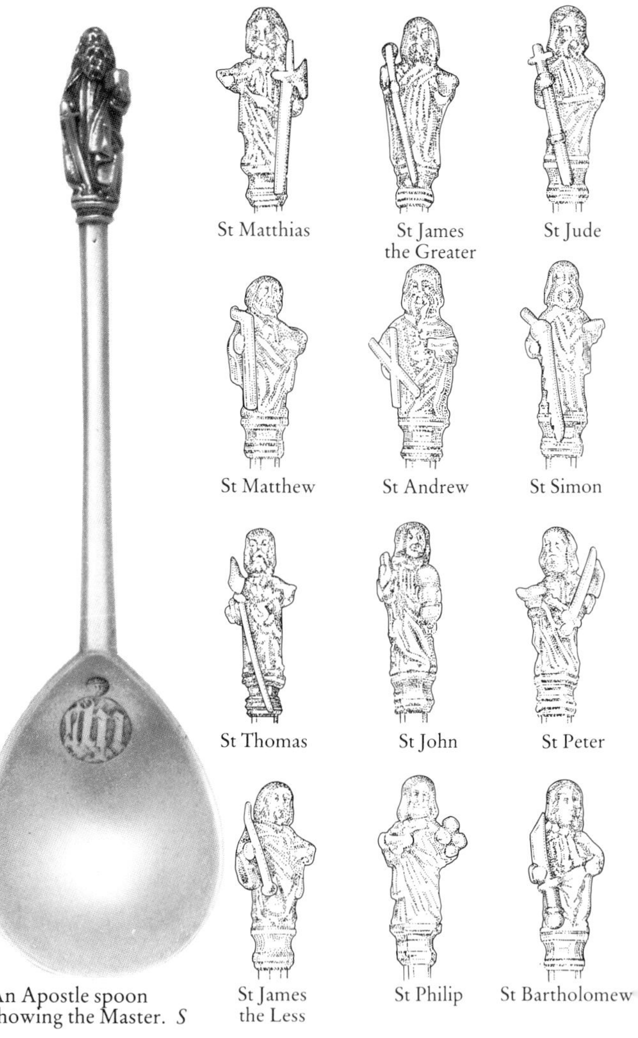

An Apostle spoon showing the Master. *S*

It is possible to recognize the individual Apostles by the emblems they hold in their right hand. Full sets, consisting of The Master and the twelve Apostles, are now virtually impossible to come by.

SPOON TYPES

Rat-tail
Trefid
Old English
King's
Onslow
King's husk
Old English thread
Queen's
Fiddle thread
Albert or Charlotte
Fiddle thread and shell
Beaded
Hour glass
Albany

MARKS
London Apostle and seal-top spoons are marked in the bowl at the base of the handle with a leopard's head; the remaining marks are on the reverse of the stem. Provincial spoons have the town mark in the bowl and the maker's mark struck once or twice on the back.

From c.1680 all spoon and fork marks are on the back of the stem at the end nearest the bowl. From c.1780 they were marked at the opposite end, where there was a broader expanse of metal. In the 18thC, knife handles often have just the maker's mark, and sometimes the lion *passant*; later examples are fully marked.

FAKES
Apostle spoons have always been valuable and at the beginning of the 20thC many copies were made by re-shaping the bowls of the 18thC spoons, trimming the stems and then applying a suitable finial. These will be in the wrong style for the period of the marks, and they will not be marked in the bowl. Genuine Apostle spoons have hexagonal stems.

Dessert forks are more expensive than dessert spoons, so many spoons have been converted into forks. This is done by cutting off the bowl and soldering on some new prongs; the spoon is then electroplated to cover up the solder joints. Three-pronged forks are very rare, and many have been made up from other pieces.

A selection from a Victorian Kings Husk pattern service. The ideal service comprises a dozen each of table spoons, dessert spoons, dessert forks and teaspoons. Serving pieces are a bonus. The most desirable services are "straight sets", made by the same maker in the same year. *S*

In the sequence above, the very plain Commonwealth Puritan spoon, c.1655 (*right*), is the last type to have a mark in the bowl. It was superseded by the trefid spoon of 1685 (*centre*); this has very clear marks and a rat-tail bowl. The initial "D" on the top line relates to the family name, and the initials on the second line to the first names of husband and wife. The spoon, *left*, is a dog-nose spoon, current from the last years of the 17thC until c.1715. *S*

WEAR
Worn flatware is one of the few categories of silver to be worth only its scrap value. Once a piece is very worn, satisfactory restoration is virtually impossible.

Above The spoon on the left is in fairly good condition; the central one is worn – note how the bowl shape has been eroded. The spoon on the right has also suffered in usage but has been reshaped to disguise wear. The bowl of this spoon, being thin from reworking, will be noticeably flexible; its unusual proportions should also arouse suspicion. *S*

Above The fork on the left is in fairly good condition. The central one is worn by years of scraping across plate. That on the right was similarly worn but the tines have been trimmed level to disguise signs of wear. That this has happened is apparent in such a comparison but can be difficult to spot in the absence of a genuine, unaltered fork. *S*

CADDY SPOONS

Caddy spoons date from the 1770s on, and some tea caddies of the period have interior fittings to hold them. They were made in a large variety of shapes, many of them with leafy bowls. Rare designs include the jockey cap, illustrated above, top. This is sometimes found as a fake, made up from a watch case, with a peak added. Most caddy spoons are stamped or raised by hand; they are rarely cast. *S*

Baskets

Baskets described in old invoices as being for bread or cake have for a long time been more often used for fruit.

Although baskets existed in England in the 17th century, examples earlier than 1740 are rare. After this date, they survive in very large numbers. American baskets are very rare. As most baskets have pierced decoration and were in daily use for a long time, it is important to check them carefully for damage, especially those with pierced decoration.

As with many different types of silver, baskets were made more lightly as the years passed, due probably to increasing demand from the less wealthy section of the population, and to the introduction of the rolling mill, which led to large-scale production. However, the Regency period produced some notably heavy examples. Weight at this time was considered synonymous with quality.

The oval shape and swing handle was standardized by 1740. A basket of this date rests on a rim base rather than on separate feet. This would always have been an expensive piece of silver, and should therefore have a fine coat of arms engraved in the base, sometimes framed by flat chasing as on salvers of the period.

Baskets had feet in the middle of the 18th century until mass production set in. Oblong and circular shapes appeared by the end of the century, and thereafter baskets were usually circular.

Pierced panels separated by beading were fairly common on baskets between c.1760 and c.1780. This example from c.1780 (wdth 13¼in/ 33.5cm) is lighter in weight and appearance than mid-18thC baskets, and is supported by a plainer handle. The beading and husk garlands are typical of the 1780s. *S*

* This style of basket is particularly prone to damage: the silver is likely to be thinner where the beads are punched in. Holes often appear with polishing. Similarly, the arms and the detail on the husks are often polished away.

* The marks on this type of basket are often on the inside by the handle, and have sometimes been partly or even wholly removed by the piercing, executed after the marks were struck.

This basket made in 1736 by Peter Archambo (wdth 12½in/ 32cm) is the earliest type in general circulation. The bold, free-flowing piercing and caryatid handles are typical, as is the construction: the base is made separately from the sides. There is no coat of arms but a cartouche has been prepared for one. *SNY*

* This is a popular type of basket, as it is solid and not vulnerable to damage.

* Archambo was one of the leading silversmiths in the early-mid 18thC, known for his good-quality dinner services and domestic wares.

By the time of this example from the 1750s (wdth 12½in/32cm), baskets were made in one piece. The bodies, which are shallower than on early examples, are hammered up from sheet, although the borders and feet are cast. This is a more vulnerable type of basket: it survives in great numbers but is seldom found in perfect condition. The four cast feet, typical of the mid-18thC, are liable to stress and are easily pushed through the base. The flange is also delicate. *SS*

* At this period leafage on the handles sometimes replaced caryatids although the form of the handle remained basically unchanged.

Baskets without handles are uncommon, and should always be examined to see whether a handle has been removed. The wirework of this example from c.1790 (wdth 10½in/26.5cm) is another unusual feature. *S*

* Where the hoops are mounted onto the body, they tend to spring apart. Untidy solder is a sign of this.

A standard Victorian cake basket, c.1872, on a foot (wdth 10in/ 25.5cm). The base has shrunk and the piercing has been replaced by flat chasing, visible on both sides of the body. The waved rim has the applied blooms, leaves and scrolls typical of the period. *S*

MARKS
Early baskets are usually marked underneath or in a line on the side; later ones on the side or the base. Ideally, handles will also be marked, although this is unlikely on early baskets.

DAMAGE
Baskets with damaged piercing cannot be repaired satisfactorily. Pierced handles should be checked for breaks. Hinges and the junction of base and feet are also vulnerable areas. There may be thin patches on the base where a crest or coat of arms has been removed. Dents on the border where it has been struck by the handle which is hinged and movable), do not affect value.

SWEET AND SUGAR BASKETS
Sweet baskets are miniature versions of the bread baskets made between c.1750-c.1770. They became increasingly scarce during the 1770s and had more or less died out by 1780. Pierced, and invariably lightweight, they are seldom in good condition.

Vase-shaped or oval baskets with pedestal bases were made for sugar at the end of the 18thC. They are either fitted with glass liners and pierced, or simply have gilded interiors. Like sweet baskets, they have swing handles. Goblet-shaped sugar vases with lift-off covers were made in America in fairly large numbers from the end of the 18thC.

Caddies

Tea was extremely expensive in the 18th century, and it was therefore natural that the containers to hold it should be made in silver. Early caddies are oblong or octagonal and have a detachable cap which doubles as a measure. The early ones in particular are sometimes lead-lined with sliding bases or covers for ease of filling.

At first caddies came singly, but in the 1720s pairs became common, one for green and one for black tea. At this date they can be found in a lockable case. In the smartest sets there is sometimes a set of teaspoons, sugar nips and a mote spoon, but not a caddy spoon as these do not appear until the 1780s. How people measured the tea between the demise of the detachable cap and the introduction of the caddy spoon is not known. Hinged lids on caddies are preferred to lids that lift off. The increasing availability of and fondness for sugar led to caddies being produced in sets of three; initially the sugar container looked like another caddy but soon evolved into a slightly different shape.

Caddies are found in a variety of shapes, but oval predominates at the end of the 18th century. The years from 1770 onward also see the introduction of the single tea caddy with an individual lock; fitted cases becoming increasingly rare as a result. As with other silverware, caddy decoration was at its most fanciful in the mid-18th century. Samuel Taylor was the main English maker at this time, specializing in circular richly chased caddies, which are particularly sought after today.

From the 19th century most caddies were made in wood, papier mâché or a variety of other materials. The few silver ones that *were* made at the end of the century are fairly ordinary.

A set of two flat-chased caddies and a sugar box, all with contemporary arms, 1740 (ht of sugar box 4½in/11.5cm), in a fitted box with silver mounts. These are good quality, though not the best. *C*

* Caddies in fitted wooden boxes are unusual. The boxes are often covered in shagreen with velvet lining and gilt thread borders. Although the mounts on the box are often silver, they are rarely marked.

MARKS

Bodies and lids should have a full set of hallmarks. Any detachable slides should also carry the maker's mark and lion *passant*. Early 18thC detachable caps are usually unmarked.

DAMAGE

Check for the removal of arms. Early caddies would have the arms on the side opposite the marks. If the marks and arms are now on the same side, this may be a sign that a set of arms has been erased from the other side. Hinges are difficult to repair. The finial will either be soldered, or fixed with a nut and thread. The chased caddies of the 1760s in particular are prone to wear on the highlights and should be checked for holes.

A typical caddy from 1715 (ht 5in/12.5cm), with a sliding cover, detachable cap and coat of arms. *S*

* The coat of arms is an important feature and a caddy of this date without one would be most unusual.

This type of caddy was in fairly standard production between c.1760 and c.1770. In this example (ht 5¼in/13.5cm), the separate feet, a typical feature, are rather weakly made and would be prone to cracking or even breaking. The chased decoration has lost some of its exuberance. *S*

Vase-shaped caddies, such as this example by Thomas Heming from 1775 (ht 4½in/11.5cm), are uncommon. Those that exist are often found in sets of three. *S*

Flat top caddies are highly desirable now, especially those with engraved Chinese characters, which were sometimes applied upside down. This English caddy, c.1780 (ht 5in/12.5cm), has its own lock and a crest of a sailing ship. *S*

This late 18thC caddy (ht 5¾in/14.5cm) is typical in its oval shape, bright-cut engraving and stained ivory pineapple finial. It is likely to have been made by Henry Chawner. *S*

* These caddies often have matching teapots.

Reference

GLOSSARY

Alloy A mixture of metals; in the context of silver, the base metals added to silver to strengthen it. Sterling silver is 92.5 percent pure and is usually mixed with copper. The Britannia standard of 95.8 percent pure was compulsory 1697-1720.

Annealing The process by which silver is made red-hot and then rapidly cooled in order to soften the metal sufficiently for it to be worked without splitting.

Argyll A kind of sauce boat, said to have been invented in the 18thC by the Duke of Argyll to keep sauces hot. Argylls look like miniature teapots and are most commonly found "double-skinned", the outer shell intended for hot water, the inner core for gravy. An alternative design has a cylindrical tube or a hot iron rod running down the centre to keep the water hot. The spouts are frequently very narrow, as gravy in the 18thC simply consisted of the juices of the meat.

Armorial An engraved crest or coat of arms. Early coats of arms can be difficult to identify, but by the reign of George II heraldic colours could be differentiated by improved engraving techniques.

Assay The testing of metal to establish its purity. Silver that passed the test was given a stamped date letter in Britain, and also in France until the Revolution (1789).

Bayonet fitting An effective method of fixing a cover to a body by means of two locking lugs that are slotted into a flange and rotated.

Beading A decorative border of tight beads, usually cast.

Bezel The inner locating (fixing) rim of a cover – for example, on coffee pots and teapots; often the site of cover marks.

Biggin The small cylindrical coffee or hot water jug with a short spout and domed cover made for a few years in the late 17th- early 18thC.

Blind caster A caster with an unpierced, engraved cover rather than a pierced pattern. Blind casters were probably used for dry mustard.

Bright-cut A form of engraving that causes the design to stand out sharply.

Britannia Standard A mark used on British silver between 1697 and 1720, indicative of high quality.

British plate A silver substitute c.1830-40; superseded by **electroplating.**

Canteen Technically, a box used to contain knives, forks and spoons, but widely used to indicate a full service, usually for twelve people.

Cartouche The decorative frame or panel surrounding a coat of arms.

Caster A vessel for sprinkling salt, pepper or sugar.

Chafing dish Originally a dish with a charcoal burner that kept plates hot, but now applied to a dish used for cooking at the table.

Chalice The goblet or wine cup used at Catholic mass and communion services. Recusant chalices, used secretly in England during periods of Catholic intolerance (16th-18thC), tend to be inadequately marked and were made in such a way that they could be taken apart and hidden.

Charger A large circular or oval dish or plate, usually richly decorated.

Chasing Also known as embossing. Decoration worked into the silver with a hammer or punch. The pattern is raised above the surface.

Chinoiserie The European fashion for decorating silver with naive Oriental figures and scenes, prevalent in the late 17th and again in the mid-18thC.

Cruet A frame for holding **casters** and bottles containing condiments.

Cut-card decoration Flat shapes of applied silver, used as decoration and reinforcement, especially around the rims of tea and coffee pots.

Die-stamping The production of patterned silver by the use of "male" and "female" dies – that is, solid moulds with complementary patterns that are pressed together, either side of **sheet silver**. Die-stamping was introduced toward the end of the 18thC. Long-lasting steel dies made mass production of elaborate silver relatively easy and inexpensive in the 19thC.

Dish ring Used to keep hot plates away from the table surface. Dish rings usually had concave sides, pierced with animal shapes. The type known as a potato ring is almost exclusively Irish and dates from the mid-18thC on. Today dish rings are given blue glass liners and used as dessert baskets.

Duty dodger Silver whose marks have been taken from another piece in order to avoid paying duty.

Electroplating (EPNS or EP on copper) Silver applied over a copper or nickel alloy in a process used from c.1840.

Embossing See **Chasing**

Épergne A large centrepiece for a table consisting of a central bowl and several smaller bowls that can usually be detached. They were used from the mid-18thC for displaying and serving fruit and sweetmeats.

Erasure The removal of an existing coat of arms, which is sometimes replaced by new arms.

Ewer A large jug with a lip that is often part of a set with a basin. Ewers originally held the water used by diners to wash their hands during meals, prior to the introduction of the fork.

Filigree Openwork wire panels decorated with little silver beads. Most filigrees found today come from India, Spain or North Africa, countries that have been producing filigrees in large quantities since the end of the 19thC.

Flagon A jug, usually tall and cylindrical in shape. Most flagons have religious associations, emphasized by inscriptions.

Flat chasing Similar to **chasing** but the pattern appears in low relief.

Flatware Technically, the term embraces all flat objects, such as plates and **salvers**, but more specifically it is applied to services of spoons and forks.

Gadrooning A border composed of a succession of alternating lobes and flutes, usually curved.

Gilding A method of applying a gold finish to a silver or electroplated item.

Hallmarks The marks on silver that indicate it has been passed at **assay**. The term derives from the Goldsmiths Hall, London, where the marks were struck.

Hollow ware Any hollow vessels, such as teapots and coffee pots.

Loading A system for strengthening and stabilizing candlesticks and sometimes candelabra, whereby an iron rod is secured inside the body using pitch or plaster of Paris. Loading facilitated the use of stamped **sheet silver** for candlesticks, a less expensive technique than moulding.

Mantling The background against which a coat of arms is displayed.

Pap boat A small, shallow oval bowl with a lip, used for feeding children or invalids. Most pap boats date from the second half of the 18thC.

Plate Originally applied to domestic wares made of silver and gold, this term now tends to refer to articles made of base metal covered with silver, either by fusion, as in **Sheffield Plate**, or by **electroplating.**

Raising The process by which a piece of **hollow ware** is hammered into shape, using **annealed** silver.

Salver A flat dish, similar to a tray but with no handles.

Sheet Sheet silver and sheet metal describe the panels of silver and **plate** used primarily in the manufacture of candlesticks.

Sheffield Plate A silver substitute used from c.1740, made by binding and fusing together sterling silver and copper.

Sterling silver British term for silver that contains at least 92.5 percent pure silver.

Tureen A large bowl on a foot for serving soup.

SELECTED MAKERS

All the makers listed below would have employed several staff in large workshops. Thus, the maker's mark does not denote that a piece was made by the individual whose mark it bears.

All the makers named were active in England, unless otherwise stated.

Adams, George Entered a mark in 1840 in London. **Henry Chawner's** son-in-law, he worked for Chawner & Co. One of the most frequently encountered marks of the Victorian period.

George Adams

Bateman family *Hester* (active 1761-90) ran a large workshop in London with a considerable output, much of it engraved. Her sons *Peter* and *Jonathan* entered a mark in 1790. The partnership was brief, as Jonathan died in 1791; the mark is thus very rare. Peter went into partnership with Jonathan's widow *Anne*; Anne's son *William* joined them in 1800. Anne retired in 1805 and Peter in 1815 when William entered his own mark. His son, also *William*, entered a mark in 1827.

Peter & Anne Bateman

Hester Bateman

William Bateman (senior)

Boulton, Matthew Took over father's Birmingham Soho Factory in 1759, making silver, Sheffield Plate and ormolu. Partnership with John Fothergill, 1762-82. Silver bears the Chester or London hallmark until 1773 when a Birmingham assay office was opened. Boulton died in 1809 but the mark of his company continued into the Victorian period.

Matthew Boulton

Cafe, John Entered a mark in 1740 in London. With his brother William as his apprentice and then partner, he produced a colossal number of cast candlesticks in the mid-18thC. John Cafe died in 1757; William's mark 1757-75.

John Cafe

William Cafe

Chawner, Henry The son of a silversmith, he entered a mark in 1786 in London. Partnership with John Emes, 1796-1808. Their mark is found on fine-quality domestic products, particularly tea sets.

Henry Chawner

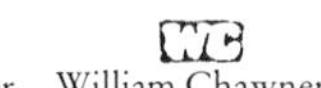

William Chawner

Coburn, John Worked in Boston, Mass., mid-18thC. Domestic wares in an English style.

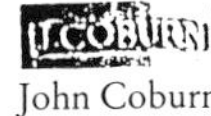

John Coburn

Coney, John (1656-1722). Trained by **Hull** and **Sanderson** in Boston, Mass. Made tablewares, combining earlier English forms with gadrooning and fluting.

John Coney

Dummer, Jeremiah Apprenticed to **John Hull** in Boston, Mass. Credited with introducing gadrooning to America, c.1680.

Jeremiah Dummer

Edwards, John Emigrated to Boston, Mass., from England; probably trained by **Jeremiah Dummer**, active late 17th-early 18thC. Partnership with John Allen. Designs, particularly porringers, display American innovations.

John Edwards

Eley, Fearn & Chawner The dominant English flatware producers of the first part of the 19thC, based in London. *William Fearn* entered a mark in 1769. Made flatware in partnership with George Smith, from 1786. Entered a mark with *William Eley* in 1797. Joined by Fearn's former apprentice *William Chawner* (not to be confused with his earlier namesake) in 1808. Chawner entered a mark on his own in 1814.

William Eley & William Fearn

Emes, Rebeccah, and **Edward Barnard** Partnership 1808-29, after the death of Rebeccah's husband John Emes who had been in partnership with **Henry Chawner;** Edward Barnard had been the workshop foreman. The firm, based in London, had a substantial production of well-made silver including numerous table centrepieces and race cups. Barnard later went into partnership with his sons.

Rebecca Emes & Edward Barnard

Farrell, Edward (active 1813-35) Mark found on some of the most remarkable productions of the time, such as ornamental tea services cast with Dutch drinking scenes and large elaborate pieces made for his patron the Duke of York.

Edward Farrell

Fox family *Charles Junior* entered a mark in 1822 in London; he worked initially with his father. The firm produced individual work of high quality. Joined in 1841 by his sons *C. T.* and *George Fox* who entered their mark. C. T. Fox retired in 1860; George's mark, 1861-1900.

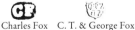

Charles Fox

C. T. & George Fox

Garrard, Robert Son of a silversmith of the same name, he entered a mark in 1818. Traded in London as Robert Garrard & Brothers and later as R. & S. Garrard. In 1843 they succeeded Rundell, Bridge & Co. as Crown Jewellers, an appointement their successors hold today. Among the best-known firms, the name Garrard is synonymous with fine design and quality of execution.

Robert Garrard

Godfrey, Eliza Widow of two early 18thC silversmiths, Abraham Buteux and Benjamin Godfrey. She entered her mark in 1741 in London, presumably on the latter's death. Her work survives in quantity and is more affordable than that of the other great female silversmith, **Hester Bateman.** She was a Pantin by birth, one of a family of Huguenot silversmiths with a fine reputation for design and quality.

Eliza Godfrey

Hennell family *Robert Hennell* entered a mark in 1763 in London when in partnership with his father *David* who was a specialist maker of salt cellars. Formed partnership with his own son, also *David*, in 1795; joined by another son, *Samuel*, in 1802. His nephew, also *Robert*, worked as a silversmith and engraver until his retirement in 1833 when his son, another *Robert*, carried on the business, entering a mark in 1834. This Robert died in 1868.

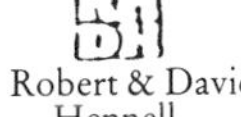

Robert Hennell — Robert & David Hennell

Hull, John Emigrated from England to Boston, Mass. c.1634; worked with his brother. Elected Mintmaster for Massachusetts, 1652. In partnership with **Robert Sanderson**: **Jeremiah Dummer** was one of his pupils.

John Hull

de Lamerie, Paul The most famous silversmith working in London, active 1712-51. Apprenticed to Pierre Platel, an outstanding Huguenot silversmith; entered his own mark in 1713. Worked exclusively in Britannia-standard silver until 1733. His reputation derives from his Rococo deigns and superb quality of castings. As with **Paul Storr,** de Lamerie's mark on a piece multiplies the value many times.

Paul de Lamerie

Rollos, Philip French Huguenot, active in London 1701-22. Ornate commissions included work for George I.

Philip Rollos

Rundell, Philip and **John Bridge** (active c.1780-1802) Highly successful London silver and goldsmiths' company to the aristocracy. Rundell, Bridge & Rundell, 1805-39. Crown Jewellers before **Garrard.**

Rundell, Bridge & Rundell

Sanderson, Robert Born London, 1608, emigrated to America c.1640. Settled in Boston, Mass. Mark: "RS" beneath a sun.

Robert Sanderson

Scofield, John Briefly in partnership with Robert Jones 1776; entered own mark 1778 in London. Prolific, particularly known for candlesticks. The elegance and quality of his work make Scofield one of the outstanding late 18thC makers.

John Scofield

Storr, Paul The most famous English silversmith of the 19thC. Worked in London, particularly well known for the massive Neo-classical silver-gilt supplied to the Prince Regent and his circle. Brief partnership with William Frisbee in 1792; entered a mark on his own, January 1793. Worked for **Rundell, Bridge & Rundell,** the Court jewellers, c.1807-19. His work is sometimes confused with that of fellow employees, Benjamin Smith and Digby Scott. Storr & Mortimer, 1822-38. Firm became Mortimer & Hunt in 1838, then Hunt & Roskell, 1843-end 19thC. Quality of production was high throughout.

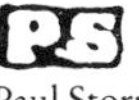

Paul Storr

Terry & Williams Irish silversmiths based in Cork, Ireland. Carden Terry began working c.1776. Brief partnership with son-in-law, Williams, from 1795; on latter's death, partnership with daughter Jane until c.1821. Mark: "C.T. & J.E."

Terry & Williams

van Dyck, Peter Active first half 18thC, New York. Particularly made teawares, in an earlier European style.

Peter van Dyck

Winslow, Edward Born 1669, Boston, Mass. Probably trained by **Dummer.** Worked in an English Baroque style.

Edward Winslow

Wood, Samuel Apprenticed to Thomas Bamford, a specialist caster maker in London; own mark 1733-46. Prolific – Wood is to casters in the mid-18thC what the **Cafe** family is to candlesticks.

Samuel Wood

BIBLIOGRAPHY

Bradbury, Frederick, *Bradbury's Book of Hallmarks* (1975)
History of Old Sheffield Plate (1968)
Buhler & Hood, *American Silver in Yale University Art Gallery* (1970)
Clayton, Michael, *The Collector's Dictionary of Gold and Silver* (1985)
Culme, John, *The Directory of Gold and Silversmiths* (1987)
Grimwade, Arthur, *London Goldsmiths 1697-1837* (1976)
Jackson, Charles, *English Goldsmiths and Their Marks* (1921)
Waldron, Peter, *Price Guide to Antique Silver* (1982)

Date Letter Cycles

The cycle of letters that represent the date is changed every 20 years. Six letters, (j, v, w, x, y, z) are not used. The initial letter for each London cycle between 1558 and 1956 is shown below.

1558	1578	1598
1618	1638	1658
1678	1697	1716
1736	1756	1776
1796	1816	1836
1856	1876	1896
1916	1936	1956

Selection of Town Marks

Antwerp — Augsburg

Bergen — Berlin

Hamburg — Lisbon

Rome — St Petersburg (Leningrad)

Turin — Vienna

BAROMETERS

This chart shows the technical and stylistic development of British barometers between 1650 and 1950.

	STICK	WHEEL or BANJO	ANEROID	BAROGRAPH
1650-1700	INDIVIDUAL BAROMETERS FOR RICH PATRONS BY QUARE AND TOMPION	INDIVIDUAL BAROMETERS FOR RICH PATRONS BY QUARE AND TOMPION		
1700-1750	CLOCK-CASE-TYPE DESIGNS ROYAL SOCIETY THERMOMETER SCALE *c.1710-c.1725* FAHRENHEIT SCALE FROM *c.1725*	CLOCK-CASE-TYPE DESIGNS FAHRENHEIT SCALE FROM *c.1750*		
1750-1800	VERNIER SCALE *c.1750* HYGROMETER *c.1760* BULB-CISTERN TUBES *c.1790*	HYGROMETER *c.1760* BANJO SHAPE *c.1780*		
1800-1850	SYMPIESOMETER *c.1818*	SPIRIT LEVEL *c.1800* SMALL CLOCKS *c.1830* MIRRORS *c.1845*		
1850-1900	HEAVILY CARVED OAK CASES *c.1860* ADMIRAL FITZROY BAROMETER *c.1870*	HEAVILY CARVED OAK CASES *c.1860*	POCKET BAROMETERS *c.1860* SURVEYORS BAROMETERS WITH MAGNIFIERS *c.1865* CARVED BANJO-SHAPED CASES *c.1865*	MERCURY *c.1865* ANEROID *c.1870*
1900-1950	REPRODUCTIONS OF EARLIER DESIGNS	REPRODUCTIONS OF BROKEN-AND SCROLL-PEDIMENT CASES	ART NOUVEAU DESIGNS MILLIBAR SCALE *c.1914*	MILLIBAR SCALE *c.1914* GATE SUSPENSION *c.1920*

Combining the appeal of historic technology with functional purpose – the measurement of atmospheric pressure – barometers make a highly attractive collecting area.

The mercurial barometer was invented in Italy c.1643 and a year later was introduced to England, where it was used by scientists for measuring heights. It was not until c.1675 that barometers were used in the home.

Barometers were made in quantity in the late 17th century in France, the Netherlands and Germany; a limited number were made in Italy and Switzerland. All these were generally more ornamental than the English versions. Barometers were not made in America until the 19th century: before that they were mostly imported from England.

When considering the purchase of a barometer, the collector should take into account the age, condition and degree of restoration, as well as the quality of the veneers, inlays, register plate engraving and brass-work. Well-figured veneers, stringing and crossbanding, coupled with finely engraved register plates and thermometer scales, all indicate a high-quality instrument.

Collectors should be wary of fakes. New instruments have been aged artificially using old timber, and brown varnish and wax have been used to make newish wood look older. Early instruments should show greeny-brown oxidation on the metal rather than the black of chemically-induced patination.

Tubes are often replaced, as the mercury becomes oxidized when it is dirty, causing air bubbles to form. A new tube does not affect a barometer's value. Any tube, whether original or a replacement, should be examined carefully for air bubbles or breaks in the mercury column, as this will render any readings inaccurate. A good test is to tilt the barometer slowly until the mercury rises to fill the vacuum at the top – a distinct "tick" should be heard; if not, it is likely that air has got into the tube.

A barometer can be placed anywhere in the home, although the best site is away from the sun, open fires and radiators. Care should be taken when moving a mercury barometer: it is important to ensure that the cistern containing the mercury at the bottom is always lower than the top of the tube, otherwise the mercury will spill. Before being transported, the tube should be plugged with a specially designed stopper, but if this is not possible the barometer should be carried at an angle greater than 45° from the vertical. Aneroid barometers can be moved without difficulty but they should always be handled with care.

Stick Barometers

Most early barometers are of the stick variety. They incorporate a straight sealed tube, the lower end of which is open and immersed in a cistern of mercury. The movement of the mercury column is read directly from the register plate. In the 17th century the cistern containing the mercury was left uncovered. In the 18th century sealed wooden cisterns and decorated covers were introduced: the finest examples greatly add to the value of a barometer. In the 19th century scales became more complex.

Stick barometers are usually more accurate than wheel barometers and are the most expensive type.

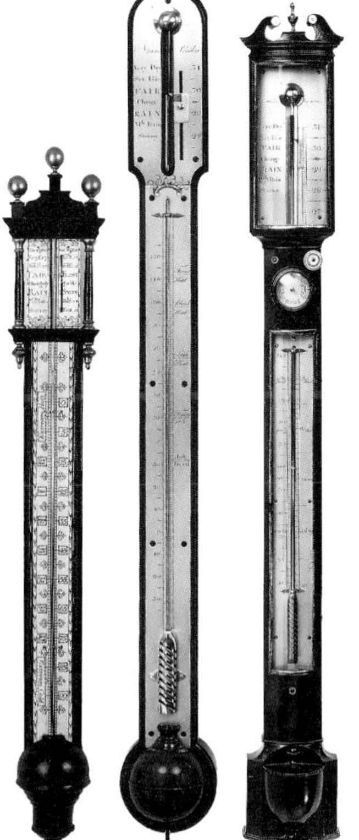

Above left This early 18thC walnut barometer (ht 39in/99cm) is typical of the period, with its clock-like moulded cresting, ball finials, and side pillars. Also characteristic is the Royal Society thermometer scale, calibrated from 0 to 90 degrees. This was the most widespread scale during the early 18thC until Fahrenheit was introduced c.1725. *EB*

* Walnut was popular in the early 18thC. Mahogany was introduced c.1740, and rosewood c.1850.

Above centre Round tops were common during the second half of the 18thC and again c.1850. This mahogany example, c.1770 (ht 37in/94cm), also has a hemispherical cistern cover, a regular feature 1755-1850. *EB*

Above right The bow-front on this mahogany barometer, c.1800 (ht 39in/99cm), was popular c.1780-c.1850, as it emphasized the highly grained wood. *EB*

Angle barometers, in which the upper part of the tube is turned nearly to the horizontal, were able to measure the movement of the mercury over a larger scale than their "straight tube" counterparts. However, they were never popular, being unsightly and unwieldy. This mahogany example by Whitehurst, Derby, c.1770 (ht 39in/99cm), has a 21-inch scale, providing a magnification of × 7. *EB*

* Angle barometers were often mounted on mirror frames to obscure the shortcomings in design.

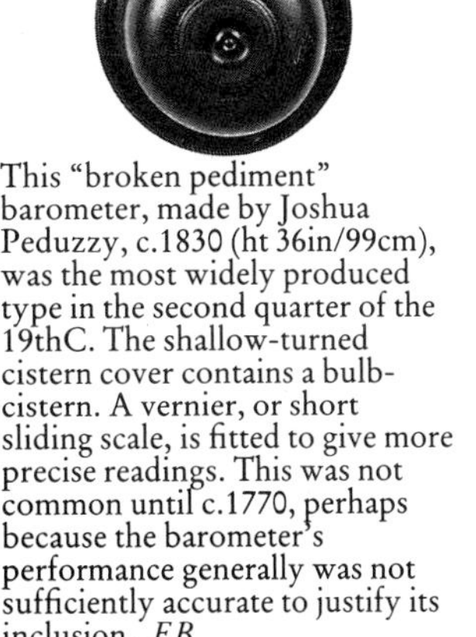

This "broken pediment" barometer, made by Joshua Peduzzy, c.1830 (ht 36in/99cm), was the most widely produced type in the second quarter of the 19thC. The shallow-turned cistern cover contains a bulb-cistern. A vernier, or short sliding scale, is fitted to give more precise readings. This was not common until c.1770, perhaps because the barometer's performance generally was not sufficiently accurate to justify its inclusion. *EB*

THE BULB-CISTERN TUBE

In early English barometers the tube and the cistern for storing the mercury were separate components. The bulb-cistern tube, introduced in the early 18thC, incorporated both elements, but was not an immediate success as it made the barometer less accurate and more difficult to move. With the increase of mass-production in the 19thC, the inexpensive bulb-cistern became better established.

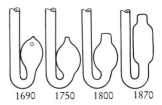

1690 1750 1800 1870

Above Bulb-cistern tubes with their approximate date of introduction.

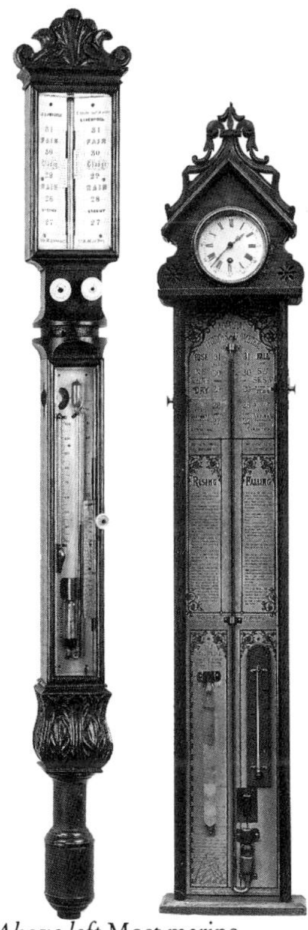

Above left Most marine barometers were fitted with thermometers, but this carved walnut example, c.1870 (ht 39½in/100cm), has a sympiesometer, which uses gas instead of mercury for recording air pressure. *EB*

Above right From c.1870 a series of inexpensive Fitzroy barometers was produced, named after the British Admiral Fitzroy. The carved oak frame and register plates of this example, c.1885 (ht 46in/117cm), are typical. *EB*

Wheel Barometers

The first wheel barometers were made only for richer patrons and are thus of fine quality, especially those made prior to 1720, of which very few remain. It is difficult to generalize about early designs as they tend to be characteristic of their makers. However, at the beginning of the 19th century Italian immigrants introduced the "banjo" shape to England. By c.1820 the "banjo" type of wheel barometer had become as popular as its bulb-cistern stick counterpart and remained so throughout the 19th century.

Diameters of wheel barometer dials range from 6 inches (15cm) to 14 inches (35.5cm); the most commonly found are the 8-inch (20cm) dials, while the rarest are the 6-inch (15cm) and 4-inch (10cm).

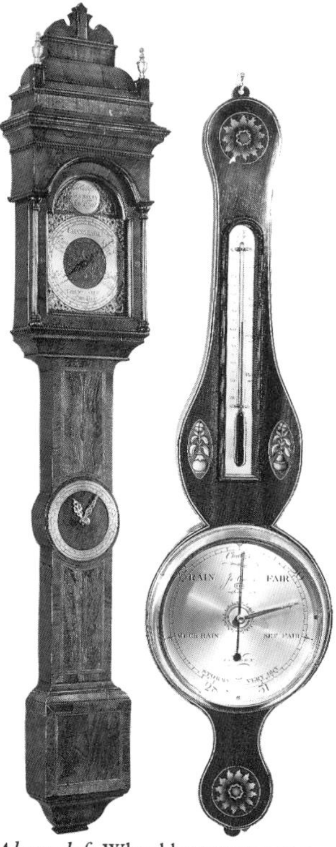

Above left Wheel barometer case designs of the mid-18thC were inspired by grandfather clock cases of the period, as in this example, by J. Hallifax of Barnsley, c.1740 (ht 48in/122cm). *EB*

Above right Until c.1780 cases were individually designed. This mahogany barometer, with its round top and floral marquetry by James Gatty, London, c.1780 (ht 36½in/93cm), is a typical early example of the mass-produced "banjo" design which became popular later. *EB*

* Mahogany was first used on wheel barometers in 1740 and remained the most commonly used wood until the middle of the 19thC. Satinwood and rosewood provided popular alternatives in the Regency and early Victorian periods respectively.

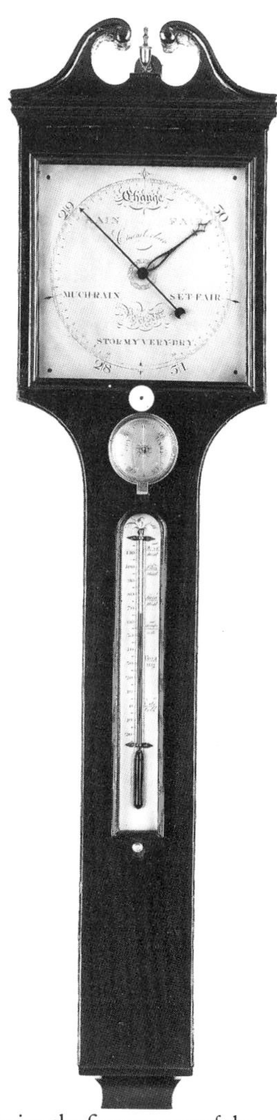

During the first quarter of the 19thC some wheel barometers were designed as companions to grandfather and other clocks. This fine example in mahogany made by Chamberlain, c.1810 (ht 42in/107cm), incorporates a hygrometer and scroll pediment – features often found together in this period. *EB*

PEDIMENTS

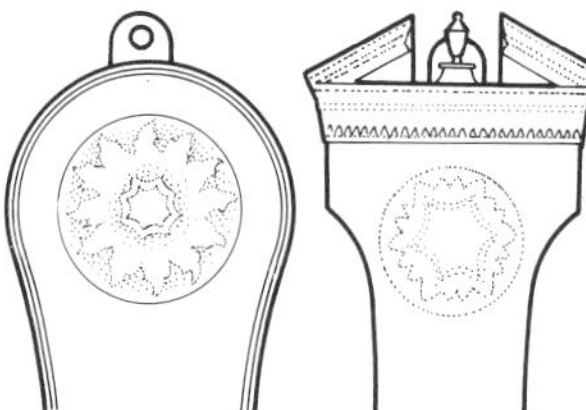

Round top 1780-1820 | Broken pediment 1800-1830

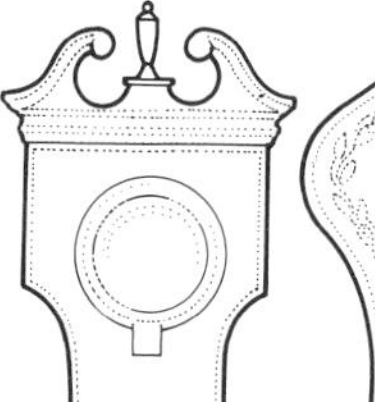

Scroll pediment 1800-1850 | Onion top 1850-1860

DIALS

The style of engraving varied in different periods: Roman capitals and lower case, Roman italics and joined copperplate script were all used in the 18thC. During the first quarter of the 19thC the word "Change" was engraved in Gothic style, while "Fair" and "Rain" appeared in broad Roman serif capitals. By the end of the 19thC, Roman sanserif was used for the principal weather indications.

Change RAIN FAIR

Gothic | Broad serif | Sanserif

THE MECHANISM

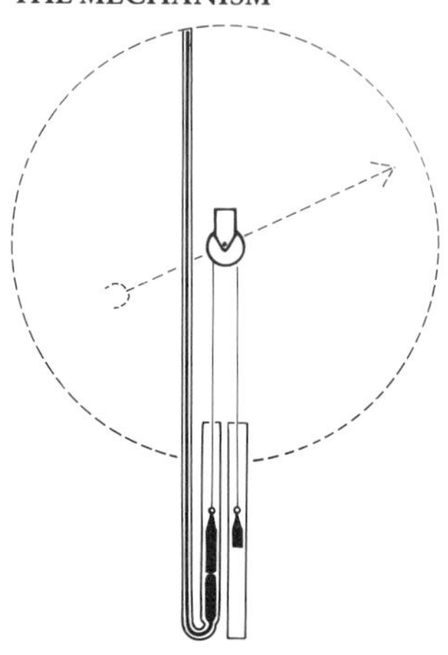

Wheel barometers incorporate a siphon-shaped tube containing mercury, the shorter arm of which is open to the air. A glass weight rests on the surface of the mercury and is suspended by a silk cord which is attached via a pulley to a counter weight. The rise and fall of the mercury moves a wheel, which in turn causes a pointer to move over the dial. The wheel design provided a bigger reading scale than that of the stick barometer.

This mahogany barometer with an engraved signature, Trombetta, c.1820 (ht 39in/99cm), has a flower head and shell inlay, a design known as the "Sheraton Shell"; along with the broken pediment, this was popular in the Regency period. *EB*

* A great number of barometers in this style were made by Italians in London between 1815 and 1825.

HYGROMETERS

Hygrometers, for measuring humidity, were first fitted to wheel barometers c.1760 and by the early 19thC had become a standard feature. They are occasionally found in stick barometers.

*Hygrometers are now largely of decorative value only, as the oatbeard (a head of oat used to measure moisture) soon disintegrates.

Aneroid Barometers

The aneroid barometer, invented in 1843, consists of a small chamber evacuated of air, which rises and falls with changes in atmospheric pressure. The compact size of this type facilitated the production of pocket-size barometers for travellers in the third quarter of the 19th century. In the 1860s and 70s the number of barometer accessories increased: wooden cases covered in leather for added protection against the elements, magnifying glasses to help read increasingly detailed scales, and stands, usually made from oak or mahogany, for domestic use, were all readily available. Stands were made to fit a number of different barometers. By 1900 aneroid barometers were the most popular type.

General trends in design are difficult to identify, apart from the imitation of wheel barometer cases from c.1865 and the preoccupation with reducing the barometer's size.

This barometer, c.1865 (dia. 4½in/11.5cm), with its glazed card dial and brass cylindrical case, is typical of a design popular between 1860 and 1875. Hanging rings were fitted; stands, usually made from carved oak, could be purchased separately. *EB*

Most pocket barometers were fitted with engraved, silvered dials. Marine barometers, such as this one by Dollond, London, c.1880 (dia. 5in/12.5cm), were made with enamelled or porcelain dials, as these were less likely to corrode from contact with salt. *EB*

* Early pocket barometers had a diameter of about 2 inches (5cm), becoming progressively smaller during the 19thC – the smallest ones measuring as little as ¾ inch (2cm) across.
* Barometers with larger dials, but incorporating marine-type carved oak cases, were made for hanging in rooms and halls in the second half of the 19thC.

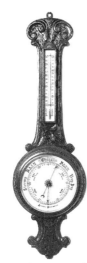

From c.1865 some aneroid barometers, such as this one in carved oak, c.1895 (ht 34in/86cm), were made to imitate wheel barometers, which were more expensive. A long door in the back of the case indicates a mercury wheel system, whereas an aneroid barometer will have a small hole through which the mechanism can be adjusted. *EB*

Pocket- and watch-sized barometers became increasingly common in the 1860s and 70s. They can often be found with the original wooden case, usually covered in silk or leather. This example of c.1870 (dia. 1¾in/4.5cm) has an inner altitude scale calibrated from 0 to 10,000 feet (3,260m), which enables it to measure heights. *EB*

* Very few open-dial barometers were made. This scarcity, combined with the additional attraction of a design that enables the working mechanism to be seen, makes them more expensive than other pocket aneroids.

Surveying instruments were made from c.1870 and were used by surveyors and mining engineers. Many are equipped with a magnifying glass to help read the small scale divisions. The rotating magnifier on this aneroid barometer made by Casella, London, c.1890 (dia. 4½in/11.5cm), ensures an accuracy to 4 feet (122cm) on an altitude scale which ranges from 4,000ft (1,300m) above sea level to 2,000ft (660m) below. *EB*

* Although these barometers were still being made during the first quarter of the 20thC, they are relatively rare.
* Cassella was a prolific maker of all types of barometer from 1838 until well into the 20thC.
* Surveying instruments are fairly robust and are usually found in good condition. Replacement parts can be obtained but are expensive.
* The lack of a case seriously reduces the value.

BAROGRAPHS

Barographs evolved in the 1860s. In addition to registering variations in air pressure, they also record these changes in a continuous graph. Early examples were regulated by a clock mechanism: a sharp pointer scratched a trace on a rotating drum coated with lampblack. The lampblack barograph was very short-lived and is therefore very rare. Later versions, such as those shown, above left, c.1885 (ht 9½in/24cm), and right, c.1920 (ht 8in/20.5cm), use a small pen on a roll printed with days of the week and air pressure in either inches or millimetres. Millibars were added early in the 20thC. *EB*

Reference

GLOSSARY

Aneroid barometer A barometer which uses an evacuated sealed chamber instead of mercury to measure air pressure. Invented c.1843.

Angle barometer A barometer in which the recording section of the tube is turned almost to the horizontal to extend the scale.

Banjo barometer A type of wheel barometer, so called because of its shape.

Barograph An **aneroid barometer** with a self-recording mechanism actuated by clockwork.

Bayonet tube A mercury tube that is crimped below the register plates to allow its lower part to be concealed in the case. Introduced c.1700.

Bulb or **Bottle cistern tube** A tube fitted to stick barometers, which is bent upward and fitted with a glass bulb cistern for containing the mercury.

Cistern tube A mercury tube fitted into stick barometers, the lower end of which is sealed into a boxwood cistern.

Double angle barometer A barometer in which the tube is bent in two directions below the recording section to extend the scale.

Gate suspension A two-point adjustable bearing fitted to the pen arm of a barograph to reduce friction on the chart.

Hygrometer An instrument for measuring humidity.

Marine barometer A stick barometer fitted with gimbals and a constricted tube to minimize oscillations in the mercury.

Portable barometer A **cistern tube** with a leather base and adjustable screw to contain and restrict the mercury in the tube.

Réaumur scale Thermometer with a freezing point of zero and a boiling point of 80°.

Register plates The scale of a barometer against which the mercury level is read.

Royal Society scale Thermometer calibrated from 0° "Extreme Hot" down to 90°, "Extreme Cold".

Siphon tube A U-shaped tube fitted in **wheel barometers** where the level of mercury in the short arm is used to record air pressure.

Stick barometer A **cistern tube** barometer housed in a slender case. It records air pressure by the height of the mercury column.

Storm glass A glass which contains a liquid solution, designed to help forecast changes in the weather by responding to electrification in the air. Never fully efficient.

Sympiesometer An instrument that uses a gas and coloured oil to record air pressure.

Vernier scale A short scale added to the traditional 3-inch (7.5cm) scale on stick barometers to give more precise readings than had previously been possible.

Wheel barometer A barometer with a round **register plate** and **siphon tube**, in which the mercury movement is measured by a weight attached to a pulley that turns the pointer on the dial.

IMPORTANT MAKERS

All the makers listed below worked in London, unless otherwise stated. Makers' signatures are engraved, often giving location of business. Stick barometers were always engraved with the makers' name on the register plate, but wheel barometers were engraved on the dial or on the spirit level plate. Toward the end of the 19thC some wheel barometers were engraved only with "Warranted Correct" on the spirit level plate. Aneroids were engraved on the dial.

STICK BAROMETERS

Ayscough, James active 1732-63. Better known as a retailer of barometers.

Berge, Matthew active 1800-19.

Bird, John 1709-76. Also made navigational instruments, especially noted for his scales.

Blunt, Thomas active from 1760. Apprenticed to **Edward Nairne**. Favoured round-topped mahogany cases.

Burton, George active 1772-1815.

Campbell, J. active c.1870. Liverpool.

Cole, Benjamin 1695-1766.

Delander, Daniel 1674-1733.

Gardner, John active 1765-1819, Glasgow.

Heath, Thomas active 1714-73.

Martin, Benjamin 1704-82.

Newman, John Frederick active 1816-60. One of the leading makers of the 19thC. Made the Royal Society's standard barometer in 1822.

Peduzzi & Co. active in Manchester c.1830. Sometimes spelt "Peduzzy". Italian immigrant family who also made wheel barometers.

Pyefinch, Henry active 1739-90.

Quare, Daniel 1649-1724. Renowned for his "pillar" barometers, which are often forged.

Ramsden, Jesse 1731-1800.

Roncheti, Bapt. active 1785-1815, Manchester.

Sisson, Jeremiah active 1747-88.

Tagliabue, Caesar active 1807-46. In partnership with Louis Casella from 1838.

Troughton & Simms active 1826-60.

ANGLE BAROMETERS

Lainton, Samuel active 1825-60, Halifax.

Orme, Charles 1688–1747, Ashby-de-la-Zouch, Leicestershire. Credited with originating the use of multiple tubes in angle barometers.

Robb, William active 1776–1816, Montrose, Scotland.

Scarlett, Edward active 1700-43.

WHEEL BAROMETERS

Amadio, Francis active 1820-44.

Betally, C. active 1787–1807, London & Paris.

Chamberlain, active c.1810, Portsea.

Ellicott, John 1706-72. Well-known clockmaker. Produced longcase clocks fitted with barometers.

Gatty, James 1780–1815. Best known for his "banjo" barometers.

Hallifax, John 1694–1750, Barnsley. Engraved signature: "J. Hallifax Barnsley Invt & Fect".

Lione, Dominick active 1805-36. In partnership with **Joseph Somalvico** until 1819.

Somalvico, Joseph active 1805–19. In partnership with **Dominick Lione.**

Tompion, Thomas 1638–1713. Master clockmaker and maker of wheel barometers for William III. Much copied.

Trombetta, Charles active Norwich c.1820.

Whitehurst family active 1713–1855, Derby. Included John, who founded the business in 1736. His brother, James, and nephew, John, succeeded him.

ANEROID BAROMETERS

Casella, Louis active 1838-60, "maker to the Admiralty". Traded under Casella and Tagliabue 1838-46 which became Louis Casella and Co. 1848.

Chadburn Bros. active 1837-60, Sheffield & Liverpool.

Dollond, active throughout the 19thC. Trades today as "Dollond & Aitchison" Opticians.

Hicks, James J. 1862-1952. Also made stick and wheel barometers.

Negretti & Zambra active from 1850. Produced marine and mountain barometers; also sympesiometers, watch-sized pocket barometers, stick and wheel barometers.

Short & Mason active from 1900.

GENERAL

Adams family of barometer makers active from c.1735. Produced stick, angle and wheel barometers.

Adie, Alexander 1774-1858, Edinburgh. Known chiefly as the inventor of the sympesiometer patented in 1818. Produced stick and marine barometers.

Aiano, Charles active 1826-41, Canterbury. Produced stick and wheel barometers.

Cuff, John 1708-72, best known as optical instrument-maker. Made stick and angle barometers.

Dollond family business active from c.1752. Under the aegis of its founder, Peter, the company produced mostly functional rather than decorative stick and marine barometers. His nephew, George, took over in 1821, making wheel barometers, and the company continued to make a wide range of barometers throughout the 19thC.

Dring & Fage active 1798-1860. Prestigious firm which produced stick, marine and wheel barometers. Some wheel barometers had square dials at the top of the case.

Howorth, Charles active 1823-52, Halifax. Produced stick and angle barometers.

Jones, Thomas 1775-1852. Made marine barometers and sold wheel barometers.

Jones, William & Samuel active 1794-1860. Produced wheel and stick barometers and marine barometers from 1799.

Knie, Balthazer active 1776-1817, Edinburgh. Born in Germany. Produced stick, angle and wheel barometers.

Manticha, Dominick active 1780-1800. Specialized in double tube barometers but also made stick and wheel barometers.

Molliner, Charles active 1784-1801, Edinburgh. Produced stick and angle barometers.

Molton, Francis active 1822-30, Norwich. Produced stick and wheel barometers.

Nairne, Edward 1726-1806. In partnership with **Thomas Blunt** from 1774. Invented new mercury tube for marine barometer. Also produced stick barometers.

Patrick, John active 1686-1720. Produced stick and angle barometers.

Ronketti, John Merry active 1790–1819. Italian immigrant, established in London by 1790. Produced stick and wheel barometers.

Russell, John active 1783–1800, Falkirk, Scotland. Made "royal" wheel barometers for George III and IV, also produced stick barometers.

Springer, Joshua active 1759–1808, Bristol. Produced stick, angle and wheel barometers.

Watkins, Francis active 1737-74. Produced stick and angle barometers.

Watkins & Hill active 1819-56. Produced stick and wheel barometers.

Watkins & Smith active 1763-74. Produced stick and angle barometers.

Wynne, Henry active 1680–1709. Sometimes spelt Wynn or Win. Produced stick and angle barometers.

BIBLIOGRAPHY

Banfield, Edwin, *Antique Barometers: An Illustrated Survey* (1989)
Barometers: Aneroid and Barographs (1985)
Barometers: Stick or Cistern Tube (1985)
Barometers: Wheel or Banjo (1985)
Bolle, Bert, *Barometers* (1982)
Goodison, Nicholas *English Barometers and their Makers, 1680 to 1860* (1977)

PLACES TO VISIT

The field of antiques is so vast that it would be impossible to make a comprehensive list of all the museums and houses open to the public where antiques can be seen. However, some of the places with major collections are listed below.

GREAT BRITAIN AND IRELAND

American Museum in Britain,
Claverton Manor,
Bath
Ceramics, Clocks, Furniture, Silver

Apsley House,
Wellington Museum,
149 Piccadilly, Hyde Park Corner,
London W1V 9FA
Ceramics

Ashmolean Museum,
Beaumont Street,
Oxford
Ceramics, Clocks, Glass, Silver

Bethnal Green Museum of Childhood,
Cambridge Heath Road,
London E2
Dolls, Toys

Birmingham Art Gallery,
Chamberlain Square,
Birmingham
Glass

Blenheim Palace,
Woodstock, Oxon.
Furniture

Bristol City Art Gallery,
Queen's Road,
Bristol
Glass

British Museum,
Great Russell Street,
London WC1
Ceramics, Clocks, Glass, Sheffield Plate, Silver

Burghley House,
Stamford, Northants.
Furniture

Castle Museum,
Nottingham NG1 6EL
Ceramics

Castle Museum,
Tower Street,
York
Ceramics, Sheffield Plate, Silver

Cecil Higgins Art Gallery and Museum,
Castle Close,
Bedford
Ceramics, Glass

Cutler's Company,
Hallamshire,
Cutler's Hall,
Church Street,
Sheffield S1 1HG
Sheffield Plate, Silver

Dyson Perrins Museum,
Seven Street,
Worcester
Ceramics

Fitzwilliam Museum,
Trumpington Street,
Cambridge
Ceramics, Clocks, Glass

Ham House,
Richmond, Surrey
Furniture

Hampton Court Palace,
Hampton, Middlesex
Ceramics, Furniture

Harewood House,
Leeds, West Yorkshire
Furniture

Imperial War Museum,
Lambeth Road,
London SE1 6HZ
Arms and Armour

Knole,
Sevenoaks, Kent
Furniture

Laing Art Gallery and Museum,
Higham Place,
Newcastle
Ceramics, Glass

Lady Lever Art Gallery,
Port Sunlight, Wirral,
Merseyside L62 5EQ
Furniture

London Toy and Model Museum,
21–23 Craven Hill,
London W2 3EM
Toys

Longleat House,
Warminster, Wiltshire
Ceramics

Manchester City Art Gallery,
Mosley Street,
Manchester
Glass

National Museum of Ireland,
Kildare Street and Marrion Street,
Dublin 2,
Ireland
Irish Glass

National Museum of Wales,
Cathays Road,
Cardiff
Ceramics

Pilkington Glass Museum,
Pilkington Brothers Ltd.,
Prescot Road,
St Helens,
Merseyside WA10 3TT
Glass

Royal Pavilion,
Brighton, Sussex
Furniture

The Science Museum,
Exhibition Road,
South Kensington,
London SW7 2DD
Barometers

Sheffield City Museum,
Weston Park,
Sheffield
Sheffield Plate

Stoke-on-Trent City Museum and Art Gallery,
Broad Street,
Hanley, Stoke-on-Trent
Ceramics

Syon House,
Brentford, Middlesex
Clocks

Victoria and Albert Museum,
Cromwell Road,
London SW1
Art Nouveau, Ceramics, Clocks, Furniture, Glass, Rugs and Carpets, Sheffield Plate, Silver

Waddesdon Manor,
Aylesbury, Bucks.
Ceramics, Furniture

Wallace Collection,
Hertford House,
Manchester Square,
London W1M 6BN
Ceramics, Furniture

Wedgwood Museum,
Josiah Wedgwood and Sons Limited
Barlaston,
Stoke-on-Trent,
Staffordshire ST12 9ES
Ceramics

Wilton House,
Salisbury, Wiltshire
Furniture

Windsor Castle,
Windsor, Berkshire
Furniture

UNITED STATES

The American Clock and Watch Museum,
100 Maple Street,
Bristol, Connecticut 06010
Clocks

Art Institute of Chicago,
Michigan Avenue at Adams Street,
Chicago, IL 60603
Ceramics, Silver

Birmingham Museum of Art,
Oscar Wells Memorial Building,
2000 8th Avenue North,
Birmingham, Alabama 35203
Ceramics

Boston Museum of Fine Arts,
479 Huntingdon Avenue,
Boston, Massachussets 02115
Ceramics, Silver

Brooklyn Museum,
200 Eastern Parkway,
Brooklyn, New York 11238
Ceramics

Buten Museum of Wedgwood,
246 N. Bowman Avenue,
Merion, Pennsylvania 19066
Ceramics

Cincinnati Art Museum,
Eden Park,
Cincinnati, Ohio 45202
Art Nouveau

Cleveland Museum of Art,
11150 East Boulevard,
Cleveland, Ohio 4410
Ceramics

Colonial Williamsburg,
Goodwin Building,
Williamsburg, Virginia 23185
Ceramics, Furniture

Corning Museum of Glass,
One Museum Way,
Corning, NY 14830
Glass

Fairfield Historical Society,
636 Old Post Road,
Fairfield, Connecticut 06430
Ceramics

Fogg Art Museum,
Harvard University,
32 Quincy Street,
Cambridge, Massachusetts 02138
Ceramics, Silver

Fort Morris,
Midway, Sunbury,
Georgia 31320
Arms and Armour

Henry Francis du Pont Winterthur Museum,
Winterthur, Delaware 19735
Ceramics, Furniture, Silver

John Paul Getty Museum,
17985 Pacific Coast Highway,
Malibu, California
Furniture

Grand Rapids Art Museum,
230 East Fulton Street,
Grand Rapids, Michigan 49502
Ceramics

Heritage Foundation Collection of Silver,
The Street,
Deerfield, Massachusetts 01342
Silver

Holyoke Museum-Wistariahurst,
238 Cabot Street,
Holyoke, Massachusetts 01040
Furniture

Kingsbridge Historical Society,
144 West 228th Street,
New York, NY 10463
Ceramics

Margaret Woodbury Strong Museum,
1 Manhattan Square,
Rochester
New York 14607
Dolls, Toys

Metropolitan Museum of Art,
Fifth Avenue at 82nd Street,
New York, NY 10028
Art Nouveau, Furniture, Glass, Rugs and Carpets, Silver

Minneapolis Institute of Arts,
201 East 24th Street,
Minneapolis, Minnesota 55404
Silver

National Gallery of Art,
Constitution Avenue,
NW Washington DC 20565
Furniture

Philadelphia Museum of Art,
26th Street and Benjamin Franklin Parkway,
Philadelphia, PA 19101
Ceramics, Rugs and Carpets, Silver

RW Norton Art Gallery,
4747 Creswell,
Shreveport, LA
Ceramics

Shelburne Museum,
Route 7,
Shelburne, Vermont 05482
Ceramics

Smithsonian Institute,
1000 Jefferson Drive,
SW Washington DC
Ceramics, Clocks, Glass

The Textile Museum,
2320 South Street,
NW Washington DC 20008
Rugs and Carpets

Toledo Museum of Art,
Monroe Street and Scottswood Avenue,
Toledo, Ohio 43601
Glass

Wadsworth Atheneum,
600 Main Street,
Hartford, Connecticut 06103
Ceramics

Walter Chrysler Museum,
Mowbray Arch and Olney Road,
Norfolk, Virginia 23510
Art Nouveau, Glass

Willard House and Clock Shop,
Willard Street,
Grafton, Massachusetts 01519
Clocks

William Trent House,
539 South Warren Street,
Trenton, New Jersey 08611
Furniture

Women's City Club of Boston,
40 Beacon Street,
Boston, Massachusetts 02108
Furniture

Yale University Art Gallery,
1111 Chapel Street,
New Haven, Connecticut 06510
Silver

INDEX

Major entries are in **bold**.

C

I

J

K

L

M

T

U

V

W

ACKNOWLEDGMENTS

Thanks are due to the following for their generous help in the preparation of this book:
Betsy Amster, Willington, Connecticut
Antique Toy World magazine, Chicago, Illinois
Ian Booth
Peter Bradshaw, Sheffield
Pauline Coakley, London
Collector's Showcase magazine, San Diego, California
Stuart Drysdale, Perthshire Paperweights Ltd.
Joy Greenway, Sotheby's, Chester
Roger Hearn
Jonathan Horne, London
Hunterian Art Gallery, University of Glasgow
Margaret Woodbury Strong Museum, Rochester, New York
Mint and Boxed, London
Rippon Boswell & Co., West Germany
Saloman Stodell, Amsterdam
The Walt Disney Company, London
Thomas Warde, London
The Trustees of the Wedgwood Museum, Stoke-on-Trent, Staffs.

Photographs from the collection of the Brooklyn Museum, New York: 107 (top) Museum Purchase fund, 107 (bottom, right) Museum Purchase fund, 113 (top) Gift of Carll and Franklin Chase in memory of Pastora Forest Smith Chase, 113 (bottom, centre) Gift of Arthur W. Clement.
The Lutz train set on page 229 is from the collection of His Grace the Duke of Atholl at Blair Castle, Perthshire.

CHART AND MAP PICTURES:
Furniture, pages 10–11: England *S*, France *S*, Low Countries *S*, Italy *S*, Germany & Austria *S*, United States *CNY*.
Pottery and Porcelain, pages 64–5: All pictures: *S*
Glass, pages 118–19: Venice *C*, Low Countries *C*, France *SNY*, Germany/Austria *S*, England/Ireland *S*, United States *Cor*
Clocks, pages 136–7: Innovations *C*, Lantern *S*, Wall *DR*, Table & Mantel *DR*, Longcase *C*, Carriage *CSK*.
Rugs and Carpets, 148–9: All pictures: *S*
Arms and Armour, 162–3: All pictures: *WAL*
Dolls, 208–9: All pictures: *SS*
Toys, 220–1: Tinplate *MaB*, Cast-iron & Banks *S*, Wood *S*, Trains *MaB*, Lead & Die-cast *MaB*
Silver, 232–3: All pictures: *S*

Special thanks are due to Ward Lloyd for his contribution to the section on paperweights.

PICTURE CREDITS

The publishers would like to thank the following auction houses, museums, dealers, collectors and other sources for kindly supplying pictures for use in this book.

B Bonham's, London
B/TW Thomas Warde for Bonham's
BC Belinda Coote Antiques, London
BM Brooklyn Museum, New York
C Christie's, London
CAm Christie's, Amsterdam
CG Christie's, Geneva
CHK Christie's, Hong Kong
CNY Christie's, New York
Cor Corning Museum of Glass, New York
CP Cieslik's Puppenmagazin, West Germany
CR Christie's, Rome
CS Connie Speight, London
CSc Christie's, Scotland
CSK Christie's, South Kensington
DA Duke of Atholl, Blair Castle, Perthshire
DDM Dickinson, Davy & Markham, Brigg, South Humberside
DR Derek Roberts Antiques, Tonbridge, Kent
EB Edwin Banfield, Trowbridge, Wiltshire
JH Jonathan Horne (Antiques) Ltd, London
LR Leonard Russell, Newhaven, Sussex
MaB Mint and Boxed, London
MB Mitchell Beazley, London
MWSM Margaret Woodbury Strong Museum, New York
OSA The Old School Antiques, Dorney, Windsor, Berks.
P Phillips, London
PB Peter Bradshaw, Sheffield
PC Private Collection
POU Sheila Poulton, London
RBE Ron Beech, Hove, Sussex
RD Richard Davidson, Petworth, West Sussex
S Sotheby's, London
SC Sotheby's, Chester
SM Sotheby's, Monaco
SNY Sotheby's, New York
SS Sotheby's, Sussex
SSA Saloman Stodell Antiquités, Amsterdam
ST "Style" (Pauline Coakley)
SZ Sotheby's, Zurich
V&A Victoria and Albert Museum, London
WAL Wallis & Wallis, Lewes, Sussex
WM Wedgwood Museum, Barlaston, Stoke-on-Trent
WW Woolley & Wallis, Salisbury, Wiltshire